VOLUME 1: TO 1500

TRADITIONS **FOURTH EDITION**
&ENCOUNTERS
A BRIEF GLOBAL HISTORY

Jerry H. Bentley

UNIVERSITY OF HAWAI'I

Herbert F. Ziegler

UNIVERSITY OF HAWAI'I

Heather E. Streets-Salter

NORTHEASTERN UNIVERSITY

McGraw Hill Education

Learn without Limits

Better-Prepared Students

SmartBook®, powered by the LearnSmart adaptive engine, makes study time as productive and efficient as possible. It identifies and closes knowledge gaps through a continually adapting reading experience. By highlighting content based on what a student knows and doesn't know at that moment in time, this capability ensures that every minute spent with SmartBook is returned to the student as the most value-added minute possible.

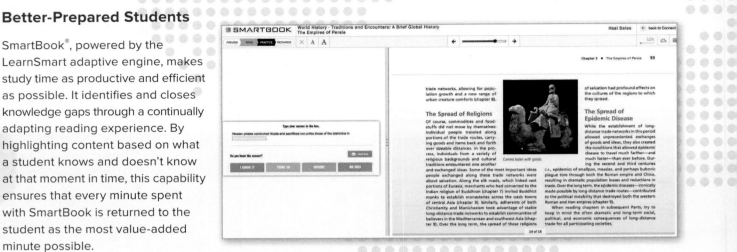

Students tell us:

- "I just wanted to let you know that **I love this Connect thing.** The LearnSmart modules are great and really help me to learn the material. I even downloaded their app for my phone." —Colorado State University

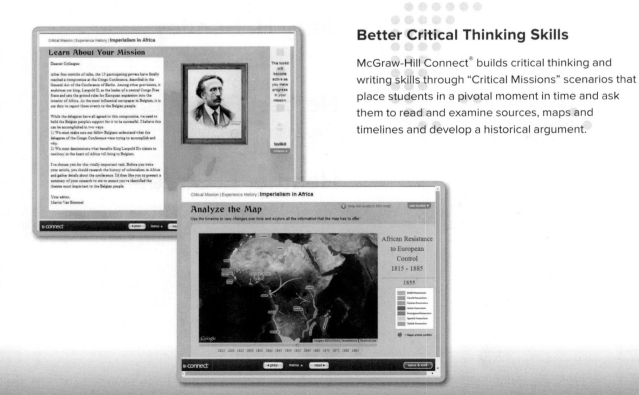

Better Critical Thinking Skills

McGraw-Hill Connect® builds critical thinking and writing skills through "Critical Missions" scenarios that place students in a pivotal moment in time and ask them to read and examine sources, maps and timelines and develop a historical argument.

Better Geography Skills

Interactive maps and map activities in Connect give students a hand-on understanding of geography. Students click on the boxes in the map legend to see changing boundaries, visualize migration routes or analyze war battles and election results. With some interactive maps, students manipulate a slider to help them better understand change over time.

Instructors say:

- "Five weeks into the semester, students in my three [course] sections have averages of 99.93, 99.97, and 100% respectively on the LearnSmart modules. **I would NEVER get that kind of learning and accuracy if I just assigned them to 'read the chapter and take notes'** or 'read the chapter and reflect' or some other reading-based assignment." —Florida State College at Jacksonville
- "LearnSmart has won my heart." —McLennan Community College

Better Grades

Connect offers a number of powerful reports and charts to give you the information you need to easily evaluate performance and keep students on a path to success. Connect Insight – now available for both students and instructors – is a series of visual data displays that provide at-a-glance information regarding student performance. Either quick review or in-depth, these reports remove the guesswork so you can focus on what matters most.

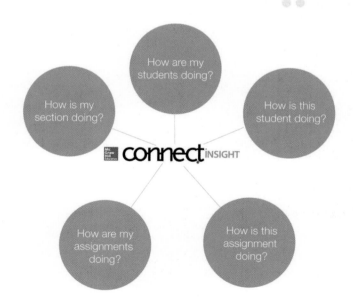

With Connect, the educational possibilities are limitless

TRADITIONS & ENCOUNTERS: A BRIEF GLOBAL HISTORY: VOLUME 1: TO 1500, FOURTH EDITION

Published by McGraw-Hill Education, 2 Penn Plaza, New York, NY 10121. Copyright © 2016 by McGraw-Hill Education. All rights reserved. Printed in the United States of America. Previous editions © 2014, 2010, and 2008. No part of this publication may be reproduced or distributed in any form or by any means, or stored in a database or retrieval system, without the prior written consent of McGraw-Hill Education, including, but not limited to, in any network or other electronic storage or transmission, or broadcast for distance learning.

Some ancillaries, including electronic and print components, may not be available to customers outside the United States.

This book is printed on acid-free paper.

2 3 4 5 6 7 8 9 RMN 21 20 19 18 17 16

ISBN 978-1-259-277276
MHID 1-259-277275

Senior Vice President, Products & Markets: *Kurt L. Strand*
Vice President, General Manager, Products & Markets: *Michael Ryan*
Vice President, Content Design & Delivery: *Kimberly Meriwether David*
Managing Director: *Gina Boedeker*
Brand Manager: *Jason Seitz*
Director, Product Development: *Meghan Campbell*
Executive Marketing Manager: *April Cole*
Executive Market Development Manager: *Stacy Ruel*
Marketing Manager: *Alexandra Schultz*
Lead Product Developer: *Rhona Robbin*
Director, Content Design & Delivery: *Terri Schiesl*
Program Manager: *Marianne Musni*
Content Project Managers: *Rick Hecker/Katie Klochan*
Buyer: *Sandy Ludovissy*
Design: *Matt Backhaus*
Content Licensing Specialists: *Carrie Burger/Ann Marie Jannette*
Cover Image: © *Andrey Prokhorov/Getty Images*
Compositor: *Aptara®, Inc.*
Printer: *R.R. Donnelley*

All credits appearing on page or at the end of the book are considered to be an extension of the copyright page.

The Internet addresses listed in the text were accurate at the time of publication. The inclusion of a website does not indicate an endorsement by the authors or McGraw-Hill Education, and McGraw-Hill Education does not guarantee the accuracy of the information presented at these sites.

mheducation.com/highered

BriefContents

Contents

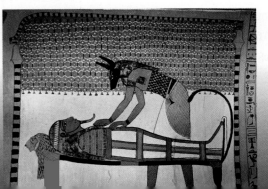

PART 4

AN AGE OF CROSS-CULTURAL INTERACTION, 1000 TO 1500 C.E.   252

Preface

How do the themes of traditions and encounters help make sense of the entire human past?

World history is about both diversity and connections. We began this text with a simple goal: to help our students understand the unique histories of the world's rich variety of peoples while allowing them to see the long histories of connections and interactions that have shaped all human communities for millennia. To do this, we have written a story around the dual themes of traditions and encounters, so that we can highlight the many different religions and customs embraced by the world's peoples while also exploring the encounters with other cultures that brought about inevitable change.

The interaction of these traditions and encounters provides the key to making sense of our past. Human communities furthered themselves not by remaining isolated, but by interacting with others and exploring the benefits and risks of reaching out. The vitality of history—and its interpretation—lies in understanding the nature of individual traditions and the scope of encounters that punctuated every significant event in human history.

Traditions & Encounters: A Brief Global History provides a global vision of history that is increasingly meaningful in a shrinking world. The theme of *traditions* draws attention to the formation, maintenance, and sometimes collapse of individual societies. Because the world's peoples have also interacted regularly with one another since the earliest days of human history, the theme of *encounters* directs attention to communications, interactions, networks, and exchanges that have linked individual societies to their neighbors and others in the larger world.

The themes of traditions and encounters are at the heart of every chapter in the text. They provide a lens through which to interpret the affairs of humankind and the pressures that continue to shape history. All aspects of the text support these themes—from the organization of chapters, engaging stories of the world's peoples, to the robust map program and critical-thinking features.

Organization: Seven Eras of Global History

We discuss the world's development through time by organizing it into seven eras of global history. These eras, treated successively in the seven parts of this book, represent coherent epochs that form the larger architecture of world history as we see it. Every region of the world is discussed in each of the seven eras. The eras owe their coherence in large part to the networks of transportation, communication, and exchange that have linked peoples of different societies at different times in the past. This structure allows us to make cross-cultural comparisons that help frame world history for students to put events in a perspective that renders them more understandable.

Highlights of the Fourth Edition

In preparing this fourth edition of *Traditions and Encounters: A Brief Global History,* we have revised and updated the text to stay current with recent world historical scholarship and to stay true to the goals of a brief textbook. Significant modifications to the fourth edition include new material on the ancient peoples of South and Central Asia, revised material on the 16th century Americas, additional material on the Ottoman Empire during World War I, new scholarship on the Communist International, and thoroughly updated material on the 21st century. In addition, the visual art program has been extensively refreshed, and the Sources of the Past feature in each chapter includes a variety of new sources.

Additional significant changes to the fourth edition include the following:

Chapter 1, "The Foundations of Complex Societies": revised to reflect current scholarship on nomadic peoples as well as the centrality of religion to Sumerian culture.

Chapter 3, "Early Societies in South and East Asia": revised to reflect current scholarship on early South Asian peoples.

Chapter 18, "Cross-Cultural Interactions": New "Thinking about Traditions" about comparative cultural revivals in Ming China and Renaissance Europe. New "Thinking about Encounters" box about long-distance travel and cross-cultural exchange.

Primary Source Documents

*Items marked with an asterisk are new to this edition.

ConnectingtheSourcesDocuments

Acknowledgments

M any individuals have contributed to this book, and the authors take pleasure in recording deep thanks for all the comments, criticism, advice, and suggestions that helped to improve the work. Special thanks to the editorial, marketing, and production teams at McGraw-Hill: Laura Wilk, Rhona Robbin, Nomi Sofer, and Rick Hecker, who provided crucial support by helping the authors work through difficult issues and solving the innumerable problems of content, style, organization, and design that arise in any project to produce a history of the world.

Academic Reviewers

This edition continues to reflect many discerning suggestions made by instructors of the world history course. We would like to acknowledge the contributions of the following reviewers who suggested many of the changes implemented in this print and digital program:

Heather J. Abdelnur
Blackburn College

Wayne Ackerson
Salisbury University

Valerie Adams
Arizona State University

Patrick Albano
Fairmont State University

William H. Alexander
Norfolk State University

Michael Balyo
Chemeketa Community College

Diane Barefoot
Caldwell Community College, Watauga Campus

Gene Barnett
Calhoun Community College

Christopher M. Bellitto
Kean University

Michael J. Bennett
Winston Salem State University

Patricia Boelhower
Marian University

John Boswell
San Antonio College

Beau Bowers
Central Piedmont Community College

Jeff Bowersox
University of Southern Mississippi

W. H. Bragg
Georgia College and State University

Kathryn Braund
Auburn University

David Brosius
U.S. Air Force Academy/USAFA

Robert Brown
UNC Pembroke

Gayle Brunelle
California State University, Fullerton

Samuel Brunk
University of Texas, El Paso

Marybeth Carlson
University of Dayton

Kay J. Carr
Southern Illinois University

Robert Carriedo
U.S. Air Force Academy/USAFA

Annette Chamberlin
Virginia Western Community College

Jim Chelsvig
MacMurray College

Patricia Colman
Moorpark College

John Davidann
Hawaii Pacific University

Kevin Dougherty
University of Southern Mississippi

Tim Dowling
Virginia Military Institute

Mike Downs
Tarrant County College Southeast

Christopher Drennan
Clinton Community College

Mitch Driebe
Andrew College

Shawn Dry
Oakland Community College

Shannon Duffy
Loyola University of New Orleans

Peter Dykema
Arkansas Technical University

Ken Faunce
Washington State University

Robert J. Flynn
Portland Community College

Deanna D. Forsman
North Hennepin Community College

Sarah Franklin
University of Southern Mississippi

Kristine Frederickson
Brigham Young University

James Fuller
University of Indianapolis

Jessie Ruth Gaston
California State University, Sacramento

George W. Gawrych
Baylor University

Deborah Gerish
Emporia State University

Gary G. Gibbs
Roanoke College

Margaret Gillikin
Tiffin University

Philip Grace
Grand Valley State University

Candace Gregory
California State University, Sacramento

Ernie Grieshaber
Minnesota State University-Mankato

Casey Harison
University of Southern Indiana

Jillian Hartley
Arkansas Northeastern College

James M. Hastings
Wingate University

Gregory Havrilcsak
The University of Michigan, Flint

Timothy Hawkins
Indiana State University

John K. Hayden
Southwest Oklahoma State University

Susan M. Hellert
University of Wisconsin, Platteville

Mark C. Herman
Edison State College

Paul Isherwood
Ohio University

Theodore Kallman
San Joaquin Delta Community College

David Katz
Mohawk Valley Community College

Richard Kennedy
Mount Olive College

Xurong Kong
Kean University

Janine Lanza
Wayne State University

Jodie N. Mader
Thomas More College

David Massey
Bunker Hill Community College

Jason McCollom
University of Arkansas

Mark W. McLeod
University of Delaware

Eileen Moore
Miles College

Kelli Yoshie Nakamura
Kapiolani Community College

Lance Nolde
Kapiolani Community College

Nathan Orgill
Georgia Gwinnett College

Anne Osborne
Rider University

Charles Parker
Saint Louis University

Bobby Peak
Shawnee Community College

Brian Plummer
Asuza Pacific University

Julie Rancilio
Kapiʻolani Community College

Kayla Reno
University of Memphis; Northeast Texas Community College

William Rodner
Tidewater Community College

Pamela Sayre
Henry Ford Community College

David Schmidt
Bethel College

Ron Schultz
University of Wyoming

Jerry Sheppard
Mount Olive College

Brett S. Shufelt
Copiah-Lincoln Community College

Kyle Smith
Grand Valley State University

Michael Snodgrass
Indiana University–Purdue University Indianapolis

Paul Steeves
Stetson University

Kurt Stiegler
Nicholls State University

Clif Stratton
Washington State University

Elisaveta Todorova
University of Cincinnati

Sarah Trembanis
Immaculata University

Eric Engel Tuten
Slippery Rock University of PA

Katya Vladimirov
Kennesaw State University

Judith Walden
College of the Ozarks

Ron Wallenfels
Kean University

Kathleen Warnes
Grand Valley State University

Kurt Werthmuller
Azusa Pacific University

Sherri West
Brookdale Community College

Kenneth Wilburn
East Carolina University

Jeffrey Wilson
University of New Orleans

Mary Clingerman Yaran
Grand Valley State University

William Zogby
Mohawk Valley Community College

In addition, we would like to thank the following individuals who participated in McGraw-Hill history symposia and focus groups and on the Connect Board of Advisors; these individuals helped shape our digital program:

Gisela Ables
Houston Community College

Sal Anselmo
Delgado Community College

Simon Baatz
John Jay College

Mario A. J. Bennekin
Georgia Perimeter College

Manu Bhagavan
Hunter College

C. J. Bibus
Wharton County Junior College

Olwyn M. Blouet
Virginia State University

Michael Botson
Houston Community College

Cathy Briggs
Northwest Vista College

Brad Cartwright
University of Texas at El Paso

Roger Chan
Washington State University

June Cheatham
Richland College

Karl Clark
Coastal Bend College

Bernard Comeau
Tacoma Community College

Kevin Davis
North Central Texas College

Michael Downs
Tarrant County College–Southeast

Laura Dunn
Brevard Community College

Arthur Durand
Metropolitan Community College

David Dzurec
University of Scranton

Amy Forss
Metropolitan Community College

Jim Good
Lone Star College–North Harris

R. David Goodman
Pratt Institute

Wendy Gunderson
Colin County Community College

Debbie Hargis
Odessa College

John Hosler
Morgan State University

James Jones
Prairie View A & M University

Mark Jones
Central Connecticut State University

Philip Kaplan
University of North Florida

Stephen Katz
Philadelphia University

Carol A. Keller
San Antonio College

Greg Kelm
Dallas Baptist University

Michael Kinney
Calhoun Community College

Jessica Kovler
John Jay College

David Lansing
Ocean County College

Benjamin Lapp
Montclair State University

Julian Madison
Southern Connecticut State University

David Marshall
Suffolk County Community College

Meredith R. Martin
Collin College

Linda McCabe
North Lake College

George Monahan
Suffolk County Community College

Tracy Musacchio
John Jay College

Mikal Nash
Essex County College

Sandy Norman
Florida Atlantic University

Michelle Novak
Houston Community College–Southeast

Veena Oldenburg
Baruch College

Jessica Patton
Tarrant County College–Northwest

Edward Paulino
John Jay College

Craig Pilant
County College of Morris

Robert Risko
Trinity Valley Community College

Esther Robinson
Lone Star College–Cyfair

Geri Ryder
Ocean County College

Linda Scherr
Mercer County Community College

Susan Schmidt-Horning
St. John's University

Donna Scimeca
College of Staten Island

Jeffrey Smith
Lindenwood University

Rachel Standish
San Joaquin Delta College

Matthew Vaz
City College of New York

Roger Ward
Colin County Community College–Plano

Christian Warren
Brooklyn College

Don Whatley
Blinn College

Scott M. Williams
Weatherford College

Carlton Wilson
North Carolina Central University

Geoffrey Willbanks
Tyler Junior College

Chad Wooley
Tarrant County College

Connect Board of Advisors

Michael Downs
University of Texas–Arlington

Jim Halverson
Judson University

Reid Holland
Midlands Technical College

Stephen Katz
Rider University

David Komito
Eastern Oregon University

Wendy Sarti
Oakton Community College

Linda Scherr
Mercer County Community College

Eloy Zarate
Pasadena City College

About The Authors

Jerry H. Bentley was professor of history at the University of Hawai'i and editor of the *Journal of World History*. His research on the religious, moral, and political writings of Renaissance humanists led to the publication of *Humanists and Holy Writ: New Testament Scholarship in the Renaissance* (Princeton, 1983) and *Politics and Culture in Renaissance Naples* (Princeton, 1987). More recently, his research was concentrated on global history and particularly on processes of cross-cultural interaction. His book *Old World Encounters: Cross-Cultural Contacts and Exchanges in Pre-Modern Times* (New York, 1993) examines processes of cultural exchange and religious conversion before the modern era, and his pamphlet *Shapes of World History in Twentieth-Century Scholarship* (Washington, D.C., 1996) discusses the historiography of world history. His most recent publication is *The Oxford Handbook of World History* (Oxford, 2011), and he served as a member of the editorial team preparing the forthcoming *Cambridge History of the World*. Jerry Bentley passed away in July 2012.

Herbert F. Ziegler is an associate professor of history at the University of Hawai'i. He has taught world history since 1980 and currently serves as director of the world history program at the University of Hawai'i. He also serves as book review editor of the *Journal of World History*. His interest in twentieth-century European social and political history led to the publication of *Nazi Germany's New Aristocracy* (1990). He is at present working on a study that explores from a global point of view the demographic trends of the past ten thousand years, along with their concomitant technological, economic, and social developments. His other current research project focuses on the application of complexity theory to a comparative study of societies and their internal dynamics.

Heather E. Streets-Salter is department chair and director of world history programs at Northeastern University. She is the author of *Martial Races: The Military, Martial Races, and Masculinity in British Imperial Culture, 1857–1914* (2004), *Empires and Colonies in the Modern World: A Global Perspective* (2015) *with* Trevor Getz, and *Southeast Asia and the First World War* (forthcoming 2016). Her current research focuses on communist and anti-communist networks in interwar East and Southeast Asia.

PART 1

THE EARLY COMPLEX SOCIETIES, 3500 TO 500 B.C.E.

About 12,000 years ago, humans crossed an important threshold when they began to experiment with agriculture. It quickly became clear that cultivation of crops provided a larger and more reliable food supply than foraging. Groups that turned to agriculture experienced rapid population growth, and they settled into permanent communities. Some of these developed into cities and became the world's first complex societies.

The Development of Complex Societies

The term *complex society* refers to a form of large-scale social organization in which productive agricultural economies produced surplus food. That surplus allowed some people to devote their time to specialized tasks other than food production and to congregate in urban settlements. During the centuries from 3500 to 500 B.C.E., complex societies arose independently in several regions of the world, including Mesopotamia, Egypt, northern India, China, Mesoamerica, and the central Andean region of South America. Each

established political authorities, built states with formal governmental institutions, collected surplus agricultural production in the form of taxes or tribute, and redistributed wealth. Complex societies also traded with other peoples, and they often sought to extend their authority to surrounding territories.

Increased Social Distinctions

Complex societies were able to generate and preserve much more wealth than smaller societies. When bequeathed to heirs and held within particular families, this accumulated wealth became the foundation for social distinctions. These societies developed different kinds of social distinctions, but all recognized several classes of people, including ruling elites, common people, and slaves.

Bronze bust of a Mesopotamian king often thought to represent Sargon of Akkad. The sculpture dates to about 2350 B.C.E. and reflects high levels of expertise in the working of bronze.

The Growth of Sophisticated Cultural Traditions

All early complex societies also created sophisticated cultural traditions. Most of them either invented or borrowed a system of writing, which quickly came to be used to construct traditions of literature, learning, and reflection. All the complex societies organized systems of formal education that introduced intellectual elites to skills such as writing and astronomical observation deemed necessary for their societies' survival. In addition, all of these societies explored the nature of humanity, the world, and the gods.

Anubis, the jackal-headed Egyptian god of mummification, prepares the mummy of a deceased worker for burial. This painting comes from the wall of a tomb built about the thirteenth century B.C.E.

cultural, political, social, and economic traditions of its own. These distinctions were based, at least initially, on geographical differences and the differing availability of resources. For instance, the absence or presence of large supplies of fresh water, of river or ocean transport, of mountains or desert, or of large draft animals or domesticable plants helped structure the shape of early economic activities, cultural beliefs, and state structures. As a result, early complex societies in different parts of the world grew into a variety of rich and unique cultures.

Differences Between Complex Societies

Although all the early complex societies shared some common features, each nevertheless developed distinct

In this Maya mural from Bonampak in the southern part of modern Mexico, war captives prepare to be sacrificed by their captors.

Connections Between Complex Societies

At the same time, none of the early complex societies developed their distinct cultures in complete isolation. Indeed, each interacted with neighboring peoples, with whom they traded valuable items, fought, married, and borrowed ideas about government, philosophy, or religion. In many ways, these encounters were crucial to the development of early complex societies. Because of this, it seems clear that, even in the earliest complex societies, connections between peoples were an important part of the human story.

1. *What factors provided the catalyst for the development of the first complex societies?*

2. *What needs prompted people in most complex societies to interact with neighboring societies, and what might have been the result of these interactions?*

The Foundations
of Complex Societies
CHAPTER 1

A wall relief from an Assyrian palace of the eighth century B.C.E. depicts a heroic figure thought to be Gilgamesh holding a lion.

EYEWITNESS:
Gilgamesh: The Man and the Myth

By far, the most familiar individual of ancient Mesopotamian society was a man named Gilgamesh. According to historical sources, Gilgamesh was the fifth king of the city of Uruk. He ruled about 2750 B.C.E., and he led his community in its conflicts with Kish, a nearby city that was the principal rival of Uruk.

Gilgamesh was a figure of Mesopotamian mythology and folklore as well as history. He was the subject of numerous poems and legends, and Mesopotamian bards made him the central figure in a cycle of stories known collectively as the *Epic of Gilgamesh.* As a figure of legend, Gilgamesh became the greatest hero figure of ancient Mesopotamia. According to the stories, the gods granted Gilgamesh a perfect body and endowed him with super-human strength and courage. The legends declare that he constructed the massive city walls of Uruk as well as several of the city's magnificent temples to Mesopotamian deities.

The stories that make up the *Epic of Gilgamesh* recount the adventures of this hero and his cherished friend Enkidu as they sought fame. They killed an evil monster, rescued Uruk from a ravaging bull, and matched wits with the gods. In spite of their heroic deeds, Enkidu offended the gods and fell under a sentence of death. His loss profoundly affected Gilgamesh, who sought for some means to cheat death and gain eternal life. He eventually found a magical plant that had the power to confer immortality, but a serpent stole the plant and carried it away, forcing Gilgamesh to recognize that death is the ultimate fate of all human beings. Thus, while focusing on the activities of Gilgamesh and Enkidu, the stories explored themes of friendship, loyalty, ambition, fear of death, and longing for immortality. In doing so they reflected the interests and concerns of the complex, urban-based society that had recently emerged in Mesopotamia.

Yet such interests and concerns had their foundation deep in the human past. By the time Mesopotamian society emerged, our own species of human, *Homo sapiens,* had existed for about two hundred thousand years. These humans, who themselves descended from earlier hominids, were already accomplished problem solvers and thinkers long before urban societies developed. In fact, early human communities were responsible for laying the social, economic, and cultural foundations on which their descendants built increasingly complex societies—especially through the domestication of plants and animals and by establishing agricultural economies.

Indeed, productive agricultural economies supported the development of the first known complex societies during the fourth millennium B.C.E. Such societies, in which sizable numbers of people lived in cities and extended their political, social, economic, and cultural influence over large regions, emerged first in southwest Asia, particularly in Mesopotamia. As these complex societies developed and grew, people found that they needed to resolve disputes that inevitably arose as individual and group interests conflicted. In Mesopotamia, settled agricultural peoples in search of order recognized political authorities and built states. The establishment of states

---

Uruk (OO-rook)

hominid (HAW-mih-nihd)

CHRONOLOGY

4 million–1 million years ago	Era of first hominids, *Australopithecus*
2.5 million–200,000 years ago	Era of *Homo erectus*
200,000 years ago	Early evolution of *Homo sapiens*
40,000 years ago	First appearance of *Homo sapiens sapiens*
10,000–8000 B.C.E.	Early experimentation with agriculture
4000–3500 B.C.E.	Appearance of cities in southwest Asia
3200–2350 B.C.E.	Era of Sumerian dominance in Mesopotamia
3000 B.C.E.–1000 C.E.	Era of Indo-European migrations
2350–1600 B.C.E.	Era of Babylonian dominance in Mesopotamia
2334–2315 B.C.E.	Reign of Sargon of Akkad
1792–1750 B.C.E.	Reign of Hammurabi
1450–1200 B.C.E.	Era of Hittite dominance in Anatolia
1000–612 B.C.E.	Era of Assyrian dominance in Mesopotamia
1000–970 B.C.E.	Reign of Israelite king David
970–930 B.C.E.	Reign of Israelite king Solomon
722 B.C.E.	Assyrian conquest of the kingdom of Israel
605–562 B.C.E.	Reign of Nebuchadnezzar
600–550 B.C.E.	New Babylonian empire
586 B.C.E.	New Babylonian destruction of the first temple in Judah

Apart from stimulating the establishment of states, urban society in Mesopotamia also promoted the emergence of social classes, thus giving rise to increasingly complex social and economic structures. Cities fostered specialized labor, and the efficient production of high-quality goods in turn stimulated trade. Furthermore, early Mesopotamia developed distinctive cultural traditions as Mesopotamians invented a system of writing and supported organized religions.

Mesopotamian and other peoples regularly interacted with one another, which helped further the geographic reach of Mesopotamian society. Some Indo-European peoples also had direct dealings with their Mesopotamian contemporaries, with effects crucial for both Indo-European and Mesopotamian societies. Other Indo-European peoples probably never heard of Mesopotamia, but they employed Mesopotamian inventions, such as wheels and metallurgy, when undertaking extensive migrations that profoundly influenced historical development throughout much of Eurasia from western Europe to India and beyond.

in turn encouraged the creation of empires, as some states sought to extend their power by imposing their rule on neighboring lands. Even in the earliest days of city life, the world was the site of frequent and intense interaction between peoples of different societies.

THE TRANSITION TO AGRICULTURE

Between twelve and six thousand years ago, humans crossed a critical threshold of immense significance for the species, and the earth more generally, when they began to domesticate plants and animals. That transition to agriculture led to a population explosion, which enabled human communities to establish themselves in far greater numbers around the world than ever before. Agriculture also led to new forms of social organization, which ultimately resulted in the birth of the world's first urban centers.

Homo sapiens (HOH-moh SAY-pyans)
Homo sapiens sapiens (HOH-moh SAY-pyans SAY-pyans)

The Paleolithic Era

Homo sapiens *Homo sapiens* ("consciously thinking human")—the direct ancestor of our own subspecies, *Homo sapiens sapiens*—evolved about two hundred thousand years ago from a hominid ancestry that originated in east Africa about four to five million years ago. *Homo sapiens* possessed larger brains and greater intelligence than earlier hominids—a feature that enabled them to adapt to widely varying environmental conditions and to displace earlier hominid species. More than one hundred thousand years ago, communities of *Homo sapiens* began to spread throughout the temperate lands of the eastern hemisphere. Using their intelligence to make warm clothes and shelters, *Homo sapiens* soon established communities in progressively colder regions. Then, between sixty and fifteen thousand years ago, *Homo sapiens* took advantage of land bridges exposed by lowered sea levels and spread to Indonesia, New Guinea, Australia, and,

finally, the Americas. Thus by about fifteen thousand years ago, communities of *Homo sapiens* had appeared in almost every habitable region of the world.

For most of human existence—indeed, from the evolution of the first hominids until about twelve thousand years ago—our ancestors foraged for their food. In other words, they hunted wild animals or gathered edible products of naturally growing plants. That reliance on foraging characterized what historians and archaeologists call the *paleolithic era,* or the "old stone age."

The conditions of foraging economies decisively influenced all dimensions of the human experience during the paleolithic era. For instance, because of constant mobility in the search for food, a foraging economy virtually prohibits individuals from accumulating private property and basing social distinctions on wealth. In the absence of accumulated wealth, hunters and gatherers of paleolithic times probably lived a relatively egalitarian existence. Some scholars believe that this relative social equality also extended to relations between the sexes, because all members of a paleolithic group made important contributions to the survival of the community. Although meat from the hunt (provided by men) was the most highly prized item in the paleolithic diet, plant foods (provided by women) were essential to survival and sustained communities when the hunt did not succeed. Because of the thorough interdependence of the sexes from the viewpoint of food production, paleolithic society probably did not encourage the domination of one sex by the other.

The Neolithic Era

Between twelve and six thousand years ago, human communities in a variety of locations underwent profound economic, social, and political changes when they began to experiment with the domestication of plants and animals. Scientists refer to this period as the *neolithic era,* or "new stone age," because of the polished stone tools associated with peoples who relied on cultivation for subsistence.

Neolithic peoples sought to ensure themselves more regular food supplies by encouraging the growth of edible crops and bringing wild animals into dependence on human keepers. Many scholars believe that women most likely began the systematic care of plants. As the principal gatherers in foraging communities, women in neolithic societies probably began to nurture plants instead of simply collecting available foods in the wild. Meanwhile, instead of just stalking game with the intention of killing it for meat, neolithic men began to capture animals and domesticate them by providing for their needs and supervising their breeding. Over a period of decades and centuries, these practices gradually led to the formation of agricultural economies.

The Early Spread of Agriculture The transition to agriculture—including both the cultivation of crops and the domestication of animals—emerged independently in several parts of the world. The earliest evidence of agricultural activity discovered so far dates to the era after 9000 B.C.E. in southwest Asia (modern-day Iraq, Syria, and Turkey). Between 9000 and 7000 B.C.E., agriculture also emerged among African peoples inhabiting the southeastern margin of the Sahara desert (modern-day Sudan), and then among the peoples of sub-Saharan west Africa (in the vicinity of modern Nigeria) between 8000 and 6000 B.C.E. In east Asia, residents of the Yangzi River valley began to cultivate crops as early as 6500 B.C.E., and their neighbors to the north in the Yellow River valley did the same after 5500 B.C.E. In southeast Asia the cultivation of crops dates from an indeterminate but very early time, probably 3000 B.C.E. or earlier. In the western hemisphere, inhabitants of Mesoamerica (central Mexico) cultivated plants as early as 4000 B.C.E., and residents of the central Andean region of South America (modern Peru) followed suit after 3000 B.C.E. It is also possible that the Amazon River valley was yet another site of independently invented agriculture.

Once established, agriculture spread rapidly. As a result, foods originally cultivated in only one region also spread widely, as merchants, migrants, or other travelers carried knowledge of these foods to agricultural lands that previously had relied on different crops. However, agriculture did not spread rapidly because it was easier than foraging. On the contrary, agriculture involved long hours of hard physical labor—clearing land, preparing fields, planting seeds, pulling weeds, and harvesting crops—and thus probably required more work than paleolithic foraging. Yet over time, agriculture made possible the production of abundant food supplies, which in turn allowed human populations to grow to unprecedented levels. For example, historians estimate that before agriculture, about 10,000 B.C.E., the earth's human population was about four million. By 500 B.C.E., after agriculture had spread to most world regions, the human population had risen to about one hundred million.

The Development of Social Distinctions Such rapidly increasing populations encouraged neolithic peoples to adopt new forms of social organization. Because they devoted their time to cultivation rather than to foraging, neolithic peoples did not continue the migratory life of their paleolithic predecessors but, rather, settled near their fields in permanent villages. Most people in neolithic villages cultivated crops or kept animals, and many even

---

paleolithic (pey-lee-oh-LITH-ik)
neolithic (nee-uh-LITH-ik)

continued to hunt and forage for wild plants. But a surplus of food enabled some individuals to concentrate their time and talents on enterprises that had nothing to do with the production of food, especially pottery making, metallurgy, and textile production. Moreover, the concentration of people into permanent settlements and the increasing specialization of labor provided the first opportunity for individuals to accumulate considerable wealth. The institutionalization of privately owned landed property—which occurred at an uncertain date after the introduction of agriculture—enhanced the significance of accumulated wealth. Because land was (and remains) the ultimate source of wealth in any agricultural society, ownership of land carried enormous economic power. When especially successful individuals managed to consolidate wealth in their families' hands and kept it there for several generations, clearly defined social classes emerged.

Çatal Hüyük Within four thousand years of its introduction, agriculture had dramatically transformed the face of the earth. Human beings multiplied prodigiously, congregated in densely populated quarters, placed the surrounding lands under cultivation, and domesticated several species of animals. Besides altering the physical appearance of the earth, agriculture transformed the lives of human beings. Even a modest neolithic village dwarfed a paleolithic band of a few dozen hunters and gatherers. In larger villages and towns, with their populations of several thousand people, their specialized labor, and their craft industries, social relationships became more complex than would have been conceivable during paleolithic times.

Excavations carried out at Çatal Hüyük, one of the best-known neolithic settlements, have helped confirm that view. Located in south-central Anatolia (modern Turkey), Çatal Hüyük grew from a small village to a bustling town of five thousand inhabitants between its settlement in 7250 B.C.E. and its abandonment in 5400 B.C.E. Archaeological evidence indicates that because the site was close to large obsidian deposits, Çatal Hüyük became a center for production and trade in obsidian tools. The wealth generated from such trade in turn allowed increasing specialization of labor, so that residents eventually manufactured and traded pots, textiles, leather, beads, and jewelry at the site. Gradually, dense populations, specialized labor, and complex social relations such as those that developed at Çatal Hüyük gave rise to an altogether new form of social organization—the city.

Çatal Hüyük (chat-l-hoo-yook)
Sumerians (soo-MEHR-ee-uhns)
Semitic (suh-MIHT-ihk)

THE QUEST FOR ORDER

The earliest known cities grew out of agricultural villages and towns in the valleys of the Tigris and Euphrates rivers in Mesopotamia (modern-day Iraq). During the fourth millennium B.C.E., human population increased rapidly in the area, which in turn presented inhabitants with the challenge of keeping order in a large-scale society. Over time, by experimentation and adaptation, they created states and governmental machinery that brought political and social order to their territories. Moreover, effective political and military organization enabled them to build regional empires and extend their authority to neighboring peoples.

Mesopotamia: "The Land between the Rivers"

The place-name *Mesopotamia* comes from two Greek words meaning "the land between the rivers." This was one of four river-valley regions in which ancient civilizations were established. Each shared important geographical features, including dry soils, an environment that was slowly drying and warming following the end of the last ice age, and seasonally flooding rivers that made irrigation agriculture possible. So, although Mesopotamia received little rainfall, the Tigris and Euphrates brought large volumes of fresh water to the region. Early cultivators realized that by tapping these rivers, building reservoirs, and digging canals, they could irrigate fields of barley, wheat, and peas. Small-scale irrigation began in Mesopotamia soon after 6000 B.C.E.

Sumer Artificial irrigation led to increased food supplies, which in turn supported a rapidly increasing human population and attracted migrants from other regions. Human numbers grew especially fast in the land of Sumer in the southern half of Mesopotamia. By about 5000 B.C.E. the Sumerians were constructing elaborate irrigation networks that helped them realize abundant agricultural harvests. By 3000 B.C.E. the population of Sumer approached one hundred thousand—an unprecedented concentration of people in ancient times—and the Sumerians were the dominant people of Mesopotamia.

Semitic Migrants While supporting a growing population, the wealth of Sumer also attracted migrants from other regions. Most of the new arrivals were Semitic peoples—so called because they spoke tongues in the Semitic family of languages, including Akkadian, Aramaic, Hebrew, and Phoenician. Semitic peoples were nomadic herders who went to Mesopotamia from the Arabian and Syrian deserts to the south and west. They often intermarried with the Sumerians, and they largely adapted to Sumerian ways.

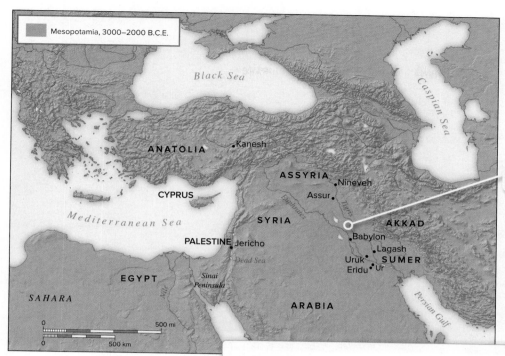

MAP 1.1

Early Mesopotamia, 3000–2000 B.C.E. Note the locations of Mesopotamian cities in relation to the Tigris and Euphrates rivers.

In what ways were the rivers important for Mesopotamian society?

Sumerian City-States Beginning about 4000 B.C.E., as human numbers increased in southern Mesopotamia, the Sumerians built the world's first cities. These cities differed markedly from the neolithic villages that preceded them. Unlike the earlier settlements, the Sumerian cities were centers of political and military authority, and their jurisdiction extended into the surrounding regions. Moreover, bustling marketplaces that drew buyers and sellers from near and far turned the cities into economic centers as well. Finally, the cities also served as cultural centers where priests maintained organized religions and scribes developed traditions of writing and formal education. For almost a millennium, from 3200 to 2350 B.C.E., a dozen Sumerian cities—Eridu, Ur, Uruk, Lagash, Nippur, Kish, and others—dominated public affairs in Mesopotamia.

These cities all experienced internal and external pressures that prompted them to establish states—formal governmental institutions that wielded authority throughout their territories. Internally, the cities needed recognized authorities to maintain order and ensure that inhabitants cooperated on community projects. With their expanding populations, the cities also needed to prevent conflicts between urban residents from escalating into serious civic disorder. In addition, because agriculture was crucial to the welfare of urban residents, the cities all

became city-states: they not only controlled public life within the city walls but also oversaw affairs in surrounding agricultural regions.

While preserving the peace, recognized authorities were also needed to organize work on projects of value to the entire community. Palaces, temples, and defensive walls dominated all the Sumerian cities. Particularly impressive were the ziggurats—distinctive stepped pyramids that housed temples and altars to the principal local deity. More important, however, were the irrigation systems that supported productive agriculture and urban society. As their population grew, the Sumerians expanded their networks of reservoirs and canals, whose construction and maintenance required untold thousands of laborers and provided precious water for Sumerian crops.

Sumerian Kings As the wealth of Sumerian cities grew, they began to face increasing external problems from raiders outside the cities. The cities responded to that threat by building defensive walls and organizing military forces. Thus the need to recruit, train, equip, maintain, and deploy military forces created another demand for recognized authority. To answer that demand, the earliest

ziggurats (ZIG-uh-rahts)

Sumerian Ziggurat.
The massive temple of the moon god Nanna-Suen (sometimes known as Sin) dominated the Sumerian city of Ur. Constructing temples of this size required a huge investment of resources and thousands of laborers.

As some of the largest human-built structures of the time, how might such temples have impressed Mesopotamian peoples?

Sumerian governments were probably made up of assemblies of prominent men who made decisions on behalf of the whole community. By about 3000 B.C.E., however, most Sumerian cities were ruled by individual kings (known as *lugals*) who claimed absolute authority within their realms. By 2500 B.C.E. city-states ruled by kings dominated public life in Sumer.

The Course of Empire

Conflicts between city-states often led to war between ambitious or aggrieved kings. However, after 2350 B.C.E. a series of conquerors sought to put an end to these constant conflicts by building empires that supervised the affairs of numerous subject cities and peoples.

Sargon of Akkad The first of these conquerors was Sargon of Akkad. A talented administrator and brilliant warrior, Sargon (2370–2315 B.C.E.) began his career as a minister to the king of Kish. About 2334 B.C.E. he organized a coup against the king, recruited an army, and went on the offensive against the Sumerian city-states.

He conquered the cities one by one, destroyed their defensive walls, and placed them under his own governors and administrators. Sargon financed his empire by seizing control of trade routes and taxing the goods that traveled along them, which allowed him to transform his capital at Akkad into the wealthiest and most powerful city in the world. At the high point of his reign, his empire embraced all of Mesopotamia, and his armies had ventured as far afield as the Mediterranean and the Black Sea.

By about 2150 B.C.E. Sargon's empire had collapsed in the midst of rebellion from within and invasion from outsiders. Yet the memory of his deeds, recorded in legends and histories as well as in his own works of propaganda, inspired later conquerors to follow his example. Most prominent of these later conquerors was the Babylonian Hammurabi (reigned 1792–1750 B.C.E.), who styled himself "king of the four quarters of the world." Hammurabi improved on Sargon's administrative techniques by relying on centralized bureaucratic rule and regular taxation rather than on suppression and plunder.

Law in Hammurabi's Babylon By these means Hammurabi developed a more efficient and predictable government than his predecessors and also spread its costs more evenly over the population. Hammurabi also sought to

Sin (seen)
Hammurabi (hahm-uh-RAH-bee)

maintain his empire by providing it with a code of law, which became the most extensive and complete Mesopotamian law code up to that point. In the prologue to his laws, Hammurabi proclaimed that the gods had chosen him "to promote the welfare of the people, . . . to cause justice to prevail in the land, to destroy the wicked and evil, [so] that the strong might not oppress the weak, to rise like the sun over the people, and to light up the land (Harper 1904)." Hammurabi's laws established high standards of behavior and stern punishments for violators. They prescribed death penalties for murder, theft, fraud, false accusations, sheltering of runaway slaves, failure to obey royal orders, adultery, and incest. Civil laws regulated prices, wages, commercial dealings, marital relationships, and the conditions of slavery.

The code relied heavily on the principle that offenders should suffer punishments resembling their violations. However, the code did not treat all social classes equally and demanded lesser punishments for those of higher classes who committed crimes against those of lower classes. In addition, local judges did not always follow the prescriptions of Hammurabi's code: indeed, they frequently relied on their own judgment when deciding cases that came before them. Nevertheless, Hammurabi's laws established a set of common standards that lent some degree of cultural unity to the far-flung Babylonian empire.

Eventually, the wealth of the Babylonian empire attracted invaders. Foremost among them were the Hittites, who had built a powerful empire in Anatolia (modern-day Turkey). By about 1595 B.C.E. the Babylonian empire had crumbled before Hittite assaults. For several centuries after the fall of Babylon, southwest Asia was a land of considerable turmoil, as regional states competed for power and position while migrants and invaders struggled to establish footholds for themselves in Mesopotamia and neighboring regions.

MAP 1.2

Mesopotamian empires, 1800–600 B.C.E. Mesopotamian empires facilitated interactions between peoples from different societies. Consider the various land, river, and sea routes by which peoples of Mesopotamia, Anatolia, and Egypt were able to communicate with one another in the second and first millennia B.C.E.

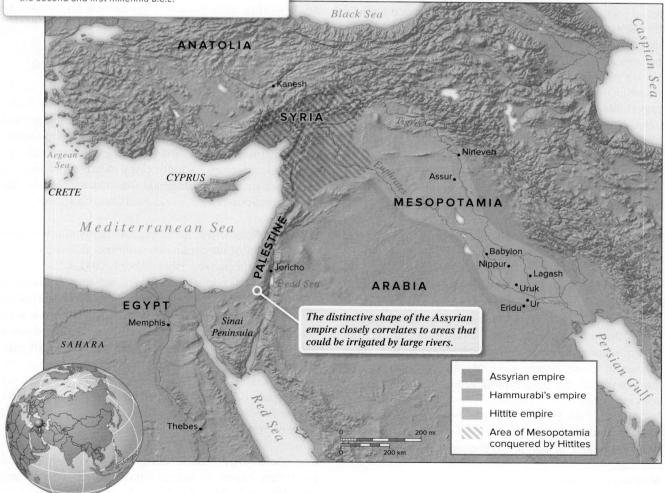

The distinctive shape of the Assyrian empire closely correlates to areas that could be irrigated by large rivers.

- Assyrian empire
- Hammurabi's empire
- Hittite empire
- Area of Mesopotamia conquered by Hittites

The Assyrian Empire Imperial rule returned to Mesopotamia with the Assyrians, a people from northern Mesopotamia who had built a compact state in the Tigris River valley during the nineteenth century B.C.E. Taking advantage of their location on trade routes running both north-south and east-west, the Assyrians built flourishing cities at Assur and Nineveh. They built a powerful and intimidating army by organizing their forces into standardized units and placing them under the command of professional officers chosen on the basis of merit and skill. They supplemented infantry with cavalry forces and light, swift, horse-drawn chariots, which they borrowed from the Hittites. These chariots were devastating instruments of war that allowed archers to attack their enemies from rapidly moving platforms.

Many states jockeyed for power following the collapse of the Babylonian empire, but after about 1300 B.C.E. the Assyrians gradually extended their authority to much of southwest Asia. At its high point, during the eighth and seventh centuries B.C.E., the Assyrian empire embraced not only Mesopotamia but also Syria, Palestine, much of Anatolia, and most of Egypt.

Like most other Mesopotamian peoples, the Assyrians relied on the administrative techniques pioneered by their Babylonian predecessors, and they followed laws much like those enshrined in the code of Hammurabi. They also preserved a great deal of Mesopotamian literature in huge libraries maintained at their large and lavish courts. Yet Assyrian domination was extremely unpopular and proved impossible to maintain. In 612 B.C.E. a combination of internal unrest and external assault brought the empire down.

The New Babylonian Empire For half a century, from 600 to 550 B.C.E., Babylon once again dominated Mesopotamia during the New Babylonian empire, sometimes called the Chaldean empire. King Nebuchadnezzar (reigned 605–562 B.C.E.) lavished wealth and resources on his capital city. Babylon occupied some 850 hectares (more than 2,100 acres), and the city's defensive walls were reportedly so thick that a four-horse chariot could turn around on top of them. Within the walls there were enormous palaces and 1,179 temples, some of them faced with gold and decorated with thousands of statues. When one of the king's wives longed for flowering shrubs from her mountain homeland, Nebuchadnezzar had them planted in terraces above the city walls, and the hanging gardens of Babylon have symbolized the city's luxuriousness ever since.

By this time, however, peoples beyond Mesopotamia had acquired advanced weapons and were experimenting with techniques of administering large territories. As a result, in the mid–sixth century B.C.E. Mesopotamians largely lost control of their affairs, and foreign conquerors absorbed them into their own empires.

THE FORMATION OF A COMPLEX SOCIETY AND SOPHISTICATED CULTURAL TRADITIONS

With the emergence of cities and the congregation of dense populations in urban spaces, specialized labor proliferated. The Mesopotamian economy became increasingly diverse, and trade linked the region with distant peoples. Clearly defined social classes emerged, as small groups of people concentrated wealth and power in their own hands, and Mesopotamia developed into a patriarchal society that vested authority largely in adult males. Mesopotamians also allocated some of their resources to individuals who worked to develop sophisticated cultural traditions, including the invention of writing, which enabled them to record information for future retrieval. Indeed, writing soon became a foundation for education, science, literature, and religious reflection.

Economic Specialization and Trade

When large numbers of people began to congregate in cities and work at tasks other than agriculture, they vastly expanded the stock of human skills. Craftsmen refined techniques inherited from earlier generations and experimented with new ways of doing things. Pottery making, textile manufacture, woodworking, leather production, brick making, stonecutting, and masonry all became distinct occupations in the world's earliest cities.

Bronze Metallurgy Metallurgical innovations ranked among the most important developments that came about because of specialized labor. About 3500 B.C.E. experimentation with copper metallurgy led to the invention of bronze when Mesopotamian metalworkers learned to alloy copper with tin. Unlike pure copper, bronze is both hard and strong, and it quickly became the preferred metal for military weaponry as craftsmen turned out swords, spears, axes, shields, and armor made of the recently invented metal. And although bronze was expensive, over a long period Mesopotamian farmers also began to use bronze knives and bronze-tipped plows instead of tools made of bone, wood, stone, or obsidian.

Iron Metallurgy After about 1000 B.C.E. Mesopotamian craftsmen began to manufacture effective tools and weapons with iron as well as bronze. Whereas early

---

Assyrians (uh-SEER-ee-uhns)
Nebuchadnezzar (neb-uh-kud-NEZ-er)

Sumerian shipbuilding.
A silver model of a boat discovered in a royal tomb at Ur sheds light on Sumerian transportation of grain and other goods on the rivers, canals, and marshes of southern Mesopotamia about 2500 B.C.E.

experimentation with iron metallurgy resulted in products that were too brittle for heavy-duty uses, by about 1300 B.C.E. craftsmen from Hittite society in Anatolia (discussed later in this chapter) developed techniques of forging exceptionally strong iron tools and weapons. As knowledge of those techniques spread, Assyrian conquerors made particularly effective use of them by forging iron weapons to build their empire. Iron also had the advantage of being less expensive than bronze, which quickly made it the metal of choice for weapons and tools.

The Wheel Other craftsmen focused on devising efficient means of transportation based on wheeled vehicles and sailing ships, both of which facilitated long-distance trade. Sumerians first invented the wheel in about 3500 B.C.E., and they were building wheeled carts by 3000 B.C.E. Wheeled carts and wagons enabled people to haul heavy loads of bulk goods over much longer distances than human porters or draft animals could manage. The wheel rapidly diffused from Sumer to neighboring lands, and within a few centuries it had become a standard means of overland transportation.

Shipbuilding Sumerians also experimented with technologies of maritime transportation. By 3500 B.C.E. they had built watercraft that allowed them to venture into the Persian Gulf and beyond. By 2300 B.C.E. they were trading regularly with merchants of Harappan society in the Indus River valley of northern India (discussed in chapter 3), which they reached by sailing through the Persian Gulf and the Arabian Sea. Until about 1750 B.C.E. Sumerian merchants shipped woolen textiles, leather goods, sesame oil, and jewelry to India in exchange for copper, ivory, pearls, and semiprecious stones. During the time of the Babylonian empire, Mesopotamians traded extensively with peoples in all directions: they imported silver from Anatolia, cedarwood from Lebanon, copper from Arabia, gold from Egypt, tin from Persia, lapis lazuli from Afghanistan, and carnelian from Gujarat.

Trade Networks Archaeological excavations have shed bright light on one Mesopotamian trade network in particular. During the early second millennium B.C.E., Assyrian merchants traveled regularly by donkey caravan some 1,600 kilometers (1,000 miles) from their home of Assur in northern Mesopotamia to Kanesh (modern Kültepe) in Anatolia. Surviving correspondence shows that during the forty-five years from 1810 to 1765 B.C.E., merchants transported at least eighty tons of tin and one hundred thousand textiles from Assur and returned from Kanesh with no less than ten tons of silver. The correspondence also shows that the merchants and their families operated a well-organized business. Merchants' wives and children manufactured textiles in Assur and sent them to their menfolk who lived in trading colonies at Kanesh. The merchants responded with orders for textiles in the styles desired at Kanesh.

Reverberations ● ● ● ● ● ● ● ● ●

The Role of Urbanization in the Creation of Patriarchy

Some events or processes in the global past are so momentous that they produce social, political, economic, or environmental changes for centuries—even in places thousands of miles from their points of origin. In other words, we can see the *reverberations* of these events or processes in multiple places and in multiple timelines after they occur. Understanding the spectrum of consequences spurred by such momentous events and processes can help us trace the historical connections between the world's people and places, even when such connections may not have been obvious to people living at the time.

large-scale agriculture similarly led to the development of cities in Central and South America (chapter 4). In all of these locations, early urbanization involved the establishment of states that localized power in the hands of a small group of people, organized military protection, made laws to control large populations, oversaw the development of large-scale infrastructure such as irrigation, and exerted control over the surrounding countryside. Also in all these locations, urbanization appears to have resulted in the decline of women's status over time and in the creation of patriarchy, or the institutional domination of men over women.

Urbanization and Patriarchy

The creation of the first cities in human history was one of these momentous processes. Between 4000 and 2350 B.C.E., cities emerged in the fertile region of Mesopotamia. After 2350 B.C.E., Mesopotamian leaders of city-states also built empires to dominate ever-larger regions, which spread the values and practices of these urban centers across Mesopotamia, Anatolia, and Egypt. Yet peoples in North Africa (chapter 2), India (chapter 3), and East Asia (chapter 3) also built cities independently beginning in about 3100 B.C.E., 3000 B.C.E., and 2200 B.C.E., respectively. Near the turn of the first millennium C.E.,

Why Patriarchy?

Scholars believe the emergence of patriarchy was closely linked to early urbanization. Although evidence from the deep human past is limited, many historians and archeologists believe that urbanization created a set of similar pressures that led societies to develop patriarchal practices in many different areas. Once established, these practices spread as cities and city-states increased their influence over surrounding regions—with long-lasting and profound effects on the development of human societies for thousands of years.

Scholars suggest a variety of reasons why urbanization might have encouraged the development of patriarchy. Some argue that the transition to intensive agriculture characteristic of early cities led to practices that emphasized women's roles as producers of children, who could provide

The Emergence of a Stratified Patriarchal Society

With their increasingly specialized labor and long-distance trade, cities provided many more opportunities for the accumulation of wealth than ever before. As a result, social distinctions in Mesopotamia became much more sharply defined than those in neolithic villages.

Social Classes In early Mesopotamia the ruling classes originally consisted of kings and nobles who were elected to their positions because of their valor and success as warriors. However, royal status soon became hereditary,

as kings arranged for their sons to succeed them. Nobles were mostly members of royal families and other close supporters of the kings and thus controlled significant wealth and power. Members of the ruling class displayed their high status through large-scale construction projects and by lavishly decorating their capital cities.

Temple Communities Closely allied with the ruling elites were priests and priestesses, many of whom were younger relatives of the rulers. The principal role of the priestly elites was to intervene with the gods to ensure good fortune for their communities. In exchange for those services, priests and priestesses lived in temple communities

the workforce necessary for such large-scale agriculture. At the same time, this emphasis on producing large numbers of children may have led women to have less time and energy for heavy agricultural work—particularly once plows had been introduced. Other scholars argue that increased militarization of agricultural societies—in order to protect resources from outside invaders—led to a decline in women's status, since pregnancy and child-rearing tended to prevent most women from soldiering. In fact, some scholars speculate that this may be why the status of women in the early cities of the Nile River valley (chapter 2) and the Indus River valley (chapter 3) was higher than in the cities of Mesopotamia and East Asia (chapter 3): since early cities in the former two areas were more militarily secure—and thus less militarized—than their counterparts in Mesopotamia and East Asia, they also may have been less patriarchal. Still other scholars argue that as power and wealth grew concentrated in the hands of a small class of elites, the desire to keep such power and wealth within particular families led to increased anxieties about ensuring the lineage of all family members. Since it was impossible for men to ensure the paternity of their children, paternity was increasingly ensured by controlling women's

movements, morality, and access to other men through the assumption of political control (chapters 1–4), laws (chapters 1 and 3), veiling (chapter 1), and seclusion (chapters 1 and 3).

Patriarchy did not develop overnight in ancient urban areas, and it seems clear that gender stratification was already developing among farming villages by the time cities first emerged. However, by 1000 B.C.E. patriarchal practices, enshrined both in custom and law, had become a way of life for urbanized peoples in Mesopotamia, the Nile, the Indus River valley, and east Asia. In the Americas, patriarchal practices also seem to have emerged in early cities, although evidence of their particular shape is quite limited. For these reasons, many scholars view the development of patriarchy as an integral part of the development of urbanization. When reading subsequent chapters, consider the effects patriarchal structures have had on societies around the world over the very long term.

Hammurabi's Laws. Hammurabi's Code of Laws demonstrate that women already occupied a subordinate legal and social position in ancient Mesopotamia nearly 4,000 years ago.

and received offerings of food, drink, and clothing from city inhabitants. Temples also generated income from the vast tracts of land that they owned and large workshops that they maintained. Because of their wealth, temples provided comfortable livings for their inhabitants, and they also served the needs of the larger community. For instance, temples functioned as banks where individuals could store wealth, and they helped underwrite trading ventures to distant lands. They also helped those in need by taking in orphans, supplying grain in times of famine, and providing ransoms for community members captured in battle.

Apart from the ruling and priestly elites, Mesopotamian society included less privileged classes of free commoners,

dependent clients, and slaves. Free commoners mostly worked as peasant cultivators in the countryside on land owned by their families, although some also worked in the cities as builders, craftsmen, or professionals. Dependent clients possessed no property and usually worked as agricultural laborers on estates owned by others. Free commoners and dependent clients all paid taxes—usually in the form of surplus agricultural production—that supported the ruling classes, military forces, and temple communities. In addition, free commoners and dependent clients were subject to conscription by ruling authorities to provide labor services for large-scale construction projects such as roads, city walls, irrigation systems, temples, and public buildings.

Commoners in Mesopotamia.
Gypsum carving of an elderly couple from the city of Nippur about 2500 B.C.E.

How does this figure give us insight into daily life among the Sumerians?

Slaves Slaves came from three main sources: prisoners of war, convicted criminals, and heavily indebted individuals who sold themselves into slavery to satisfy their obligations. Some slaves worked as agricultural laborers on the estates of nobles or temple communities, but most were domestic servants in wealthy households. Many masters granted slaves their freedom, often with a financial bequest, after several years of good service.

In addition to recognizing differences of rank, wealth, and social status, Mesopotamians built a patriarchal society that vested authority over public and private affairs in adult men. Men made most of the important decisions within households and dominated public life as well. In effect, men ruled as kings, and decisions about policies and public affairs rested almost entirely in their hands.

Gender Roles Hammurabi's laws throw considerable light on sex and gender relations in ancient Mesopotamia. The laws recognized men as heads of their households and entrusted all major family decisions to their judgment. Men even had the power to sell their wives and children into slavery to satisfy their debts. In the interests of protecting the reputations of husbands and the legitimacy of offspring, the laws prescribed death by drowning as the punishment for adulterous wives, as well as for their partners, while permitting men to engage in consensual sexual relations with concubines, slaves, or prostitutes without penalty.

In spite of their subordinate legal status, women made their influence felt in Mesopotamian society. At ruling courts women sometimes advised kings and their governments. A few women wielded great power as high priestesses who managed the enormous estates belonging to their temples. Others obtained a formal education and worked as scribes—literate individuals who prepared administrative and legal documents for governments and private parties. Women also pursued careers as midwives, shopkeepers, brewers, bakers, tavern keepers, and textile manufacturers.

During the second millennium B.C.E., however, Mesopotamian men progressively tightened their control over the social and sexual behavior of women. To protect family fortunes and guarantee the legitimacy of heirs, Mesopotamians insisted on the virginity of brides at marriage, and they forbade casual socializing between married women and men outside their family. By 1500 B.C.E. and probably even earlier, married women in Mesopotamian cities had begun to wear veils when they ventured beyond their own households in order to discourage the attention of men from other families. This concern to control women's social and sexual behavior spread throughout much of southwest Asia and the Mediterranean basin, where it reinforced patriarchal social structures.

The Development of Written Cultural Traditions

The world's earliest known writing came from Mesopotamia. Sumerians invented a system of writing about the middle of the fourth millennium B.C.E. to keep track of commercial transactions and tax collections. They first experimented with pictographs representing animals, agricultural products, and trade items that figured prominently in tax and commercial transactions. By 3100 B.C.E. conventional signs representing specific words had spread throughout Mesopotamia.

A writing system that depends on pictures is useful for purposes such as keeping records, but it is a cumbersome way to communicate abstract ideas. Beginning about 2900 B.C.E. the Sumerians developed a more flexible system of writing that used graphic symbols to represent sounds, syllables, and ideas as well as physical objects. By combining pictographs and other symbols, the Sumerians created a powerful writing system.

Cuneiform Writing When writing, a Sumerian scribe used a stylus fashioned from a reed to impress symbols on wet clay. Because the stylus left lines and wedge-shaped marks, Sumerian writing is known as *cuneiform,* a term that comes from two Latin words meaning "wedge-shaped." When dried in the sun or baked in an oven, the clay hardened and preserved a permanent record of the scribe's message. Babylonians, Assyrians, and other peoples later adapted the Sumerians' script to their own languages, and the tradition of cuneiform writing continued for more than three thousand years.

Though originally invented for purposes of keeping records, writing clearly had potential that went far beyond the purely practical matter of storing information. Mesopotamians relied on writing to communicate complex ideas about the world, the gods, human beings, and their relationships with one another. Indeed, writing made

SourcesfromthePast

The Flood Story from the Epic of Gilgamesh

The Epic of Gilgamesh *is the oldest surviving epic poem in history, dating from about 2500 B.C.E. As part of his adventures, Gilgamesh seeks the secret of immortality from a wise man named Ut-napishtim. During the visit, Ut-napishtim tells him how the god Ea alerted him to a plot by the gods to destroy humankind by a massive flood. Here, Ut-napishtim recounts the story to Gilgamesh.*

    In its circuit (the boat measured) 14 measures
    I placed its roof on it (and) I enclosed it
    I rode in it, for the sixth time;
    I (rode in it) for the seventh time into the restless deep.
    Its planks the waters within it admitted,
    I saw breaks and holes.
    Three measures of bitumen I poured over the outside,
    Three measures of bitumen I poured over the inside.
    The men carrying its baskets . . . fixed an altar;
    I unclosed the altar for an offering.
    The material of the ship (was) completed;
    Reeds I spread above and below.
    All I possessed I collected it, all I possessed I collected of silver,
    All I possessed I collected of gold,
    All I possessed I collected of the seed of life, the whole.
    I caused to go up into the ship, all my male and female servants,
    The beasts of the field, the animals of the field,
    And the sons of the army all of them, I caused to go up.
    A flood Shamas made, and he spoke saying in the night,
    'I will cause it to rain from heaven heavily;
    Enter to the midst of the ship, and shut thy door.'
    A flood he raised, and he spoke saying in the night,
    'I will cause it to rain from heaven heavily.'
    In the day that I celebrated his festival, the day that he had appointed; fear I had.
    I entered to the midst of the ship, and shut my door . . .
    The raging of a storm in the morning arose,
    From the horizon of heaven extending and wide . . .

    The bright earth to a waste was turned;
    The surface of the earth (was) swept.
    It destroyed all life, from the face of the earth.
    The strong tempest over the people, reached to heaven.
    Brother saw not his brother, it did not spare the people . . .
    Six days and nights passed, the wind tempest and storm overwhelmed.
    On the seventh day in its course, was calmed the storm, and all the tempest which had destroyed like an earthquake, quieted.
    The sea he caused to dry, and the wind and tempest ended.
    I was carried through the sea.
    The doer of evil, and the whole of mankind who turned to sin, like reeds their corpses floated.
    I opened the window and the light broke in, over my refuge it passed . . .
    On the seventh day . . . I sent forth a dove, and it left.
    The dove went and searched and a resting place it did not find, and it returned.
    I sent forth a swallow, and it left.
    The swallow went and searched and a resting place it did not find, and it returned.
    I sent forth a raven, and it left.
    The raven went, and the corpses on the waters it saw, And it did eat, it swam, and wandered away, and did not return.
    I sent the animals forth to the four winds;
    I poured out a libation;
    I built an altar on the peak of the mountain.

For Further Reflection

■ Think about the similarities between the flood story above and the story of Noah's Ark from the Old Testament. Which features appear in both stories? Why do you think these stories are so similar?

Source: Thomas Sanders et al. *Encounters in World History: Sources and Themes from the Global Past,* Vol. I. Boston: McGraw-Hill, 2006, pp. 40–41.

possible the emergence of a distinctive cultural tradition that shaped Mesopotamian values for almost three millennia.

Astronomy and Mathematics Literacy led to a rapid expansion of knowledge. Mesopotamian scholars devoted themselves to the study of astronomy and mathematics—both important sciences for agricultural societies. Knowledge of astronomy helped them prepare accurate calendars, which in turn enabled them to chart the rhythms of the seasons and determine the appropriate times for planting and harvesting crops. They used their mathematical skills to survey agricultural lands and allocate them to the proper owners or tenants. Some Mesopotamian conventions persist to the present day: Mesopotamian scientists divided the year into twelve months, for example, and they divided the hour into sixty minutes, each composed of sixty seconds.

The Epic of Gilgamesh Mesopotamians also used writing to communicate abstract ideas, investigate intellectual and religious problems, and reflect on human beings and their place in the world. Best known of the reflective literature from Mesopotamia is the *Epic of Gilgamesh,* completed after 2000 B.C.E. In recounting the experiences of Gilgamesh and Enkidu, the epic explored themes of friendship, relations between humans and the gods, and especially the meaning of life and the inevitability of death. The stories of Gilgamesh and Enkidu resonated so widely that for some two thousand years—from the time of the Sumerian city-states to the fall of the Assyrian empire—they were the principal vehicles for Mesopotamian reflections on moral issues.

THE BROADER INFLUENCE OF MESOPOTAMIAN SOCIETY

While building cities and regional states, Mesopotamians deeply influenced the development and experiences of peoples living far beyond their own lands. Often their wealth and power attracted the attention of neighboring peoples. Sometimes Mesopotamians projected their power to foreign lands and imposed their ways by force. Occasionally migrants left Mesopotamia and carried their inherited traditions to new lands. Mesopotamian influence did not completely transform other peoples and turn them into carbon copies of Mesopotamians. On the contrary, other peoples adopted Mesopotamian ways selectively and adapted them to their own needs and interests. Yet the broader impact of Mesopotamian society shows that, even in early times, complex agricultural societies organized around cities had strong potential to influence the development of distant human communities.

Hebrews, Israelites, and Jews

The best-known cases of early Mesopotamian influence involved Hebrews, Israelites, and Jews, who preserved memories of their historical experiences in an extensive collection of sacred writings. Hebrews were speakers of the ancient Hebrew language. Israelites formed a branch of Hebrews who settled in Palestine (modern-day Israel) after 1300 B.C.E. Jews descended from southern Israelites who inhabited the kingdom of Judah. For more than two thousand years, Hebrews, Israelites, and Jews interacted constantly with Mesopotamians and other peoples as well, with profound consequences for the development of their own societies.

The Early Hebrews The earliest Hebrews were pastoral nomads who inhabited lands between Mesopotamia and

monotheism (mah-noh-THEE-iz'm)
Yahweh (YAH-way)

Egypt during the second millennium B.C.E. As Mesopotamia prospered, some of the Hebrews settled in the region's cities. According to the Hebrew scriptures (the Old Testament of the Christian Bible), the Hebrew patriarch Abraham came from the Sumerian city of Ur, but he migrated to northern Mesopotamia about 1850 B.C.E. Abraham's descendants continued to recognize many of the deities, values, and customs common to Mesopotamian peoples. Hebrew law, for example, borrowed heavily from Hammurabi's code. The Hebrews also told the story of a devastating flood that had destroyed all early human society, which was a variation on similar flood stories related from the earliest days of Sumerian society. One early version of the story made its way into the *Epic of Gilgamesh.* The Hebrews altered the story and adapted it to their own interests and purposes, but their familiarity with the flood story shows that they participated fully in the larger society of Mesopotamia.

Migrations and Settlement in Palestine According to their scriptures, some Hebrews migrated from Palestine to Egypt during the eighteenth century B.C.E. About 1300 B.C.E., however, this branch of the Hebrews departed under the leadership of Moses and returned to Palestine. Organized into a loose federation of twelve tribes, those Hebrews, known as the Israelites, fought bitterly with other inhabitants of Palestine and carved out a territory for themselves. Eventually the Israelites abandoned their inherited tribal structure in favor of a Mesopotamian-style monarchy that brought all their twelve tribes under unified rule. During the reigns of King David (1000–970 B.C.E.) and King Solomon (970–930 B.C.E.), Israelites dominated the territory between Syria and the Sinai peninsula. They built an elaborate and cosmopolitan capital city at Jerusalem and entered into diplomatic and commercial relations with Mesopotamians, Egyptians, and Arabian peoples. Like other peoples of southwest Asia, the Israelites made use of iron technology to strengthen their military forces and produce tough agricultural implements.

Moses and Monotheism After the time of Moses, however, the religious beliefs of the Israelites developed along increasingly distinctive lines. Whereas the early Hebrews had recognized many of the same gods as their Mesopotamian neighbors, Moses embraced monotheism: he taught that there was only one god, known as Yahweh, who was a supremely powerful deity, the creator and sustainer of the world. Yahweh expected his followers to worship him alone, and he demanded that they observe high moral and ethical standards. In the Ten Commandments, a set of religious and ethical principles that Moses announced to the Israelites, Yahweh warned his followers against destructive and antisocial behavior such as lying, theft, adultery, and murder. Between about 1000 and 400 B.C.E.,

Thinking about **TRADITIONS**

Differences between Early Complex Societies

In the period between 3500 and 500 B.C.E., peoples such as the Sumerians, Assyrians, Hittites, and Phoenicians independently developed distinctive characteristics in terms of architecture, economic pursuits, and technology. *What were some of the defining characteristics that marked these societies as different from one another, and why might these differences have arisen? Think carefully here about geographical location, the presence or absence of plants and animals, and the availability of resources.*

the Israelites' religious leaders compiled their teachings in a set of holy scriptures known as the Torah (Hebrew for "doctrine" or "teaching"), which laid down Yahweh's laws and outlined his role in creating the world and guiding human affairs. The Torah taught that Yahweh would reward those who obeyed his will and punish those who did not.

Assyrian and Babylonian Conquests The Israelites placed increasing emphasis on devotion to Yahweh as they experienced a series of political and military setbacks. Following King Solomon's reign, tribal tensions led to the division of the community into a large kingdom of Israel in the north and a smaller kingdom of Judah in the land known as Judea to the south. In 722 B.C.E. Assyrian forces conquered the northern kingdom and deported many of its inhabitants to other regions, causing many of the deported to lose their identity as Israelites. In 586 B.C.E., the New Babylonian empire toppled the kingdom of Judah and destroyed Jerusalem, forcing many residents into exile. Unlike their cousins to the north, however, most of these Israelites maintained their religious identity, and many of the deportees eventually returned to Judea, where they became known as Jews.

Ironically, perhaps, the Israelites' devotion to Yahweh intensified during this era of turmoil. Between the ninth and sixth centuries B.C.E., a series of prophets urged the Israelites to rededicate themselves to their faith and obey Yahweh's commandments. Failure to do so, they warned, would be punished by Yahweh in the form of conquest by foreigners. Many Israelites took the Assyrian and Babylonian conquests as proof that the prophets accurately represented Yahweh's mind and will.

The exiles who returned to Judea after the Babylonian conquest did not abandon hope for a state of their own, and even organized several small Jewish states as tributaries to the larger empires that dominated the area. But the returnees also built a distinctive religious community based on their conviction that they had a special relationship with Yahweh. This conviction enabled the Jews to

maintain a strong sense of identity as a people distinct from others, even as they participated fully in the development of a larger complex society in southwest Asia. Over the longer term, Jewish monotheism, scriptures, and moral concerns also profoundly influenced the development of Christianity and Islam.

The Phoenicians

Phoenician Trade Networks North of the Israelites' kingdom in Palestine, the Phoenicians occupied a narrow coastal plain between the Mediterranean Sea and the Lebanon Mountains. They spoke a Semitic language, referring to themselves as Canaanites and their land as Canaan. (The term *Phoenician* comes from early Greek references.) Sometime after 3000 B.C.E., the Phoenicians established a series of city-states ruled by local kings, the most important of which were Tyre, Sidon, Beirut, and Byblos. Though not a numerous or militarily powerful people, the Phoenicians influenced societies throughout the Mediterranean basin because of their trade and communication networks. Their meager lands did not permit development of a large agricultural society, so after about 2500 B.C.E. the Phoenicians turned increasingly to industry and trade. Although the Phoenicians traded overland, they were also excellent sailors, and they built the best ships of their times. Between 1200 and 800 B.C.E., they dominated Mediterranean trade. They established commercial colonies in Rhodes, Cyprus, Sicily, Sardinia, Spain, and north Africa. They sailed far and wide in search of raw materials, which took them well beyond the Mediterranean: Phoenician merchant ships visited the Canary Islands, coastal ports in Portugal and France, and even the distant British Isles, and adventurous Phoenician mariners made exploratory voyages to the Azores Islands and down the west coast of Africa as far as the Gulf of Guinea.

Alphabetic Writing Like the Hebrews, the Phoenicians largely adapted Mesopotamian cultural traditions to their own needs. Their gods, for example, were mostly adapted from Mesopotamian gods. The Phoenicians also creatively adapted the Mesopotamian practice of writing by experimenting with simpler alternatives to cuneiform. By 1500 B.C.E. Phoenician scribes had devised an early alphabetic script consisting of twenty-two symbols representing consonants (the Phoenician alphabet had no symbols for vowels). Learning twenty-two letters and building words with them was much easier than memorizing the hundreds of symbols employed in cuneiform.

Phoenicians (fi-NEE-shins)

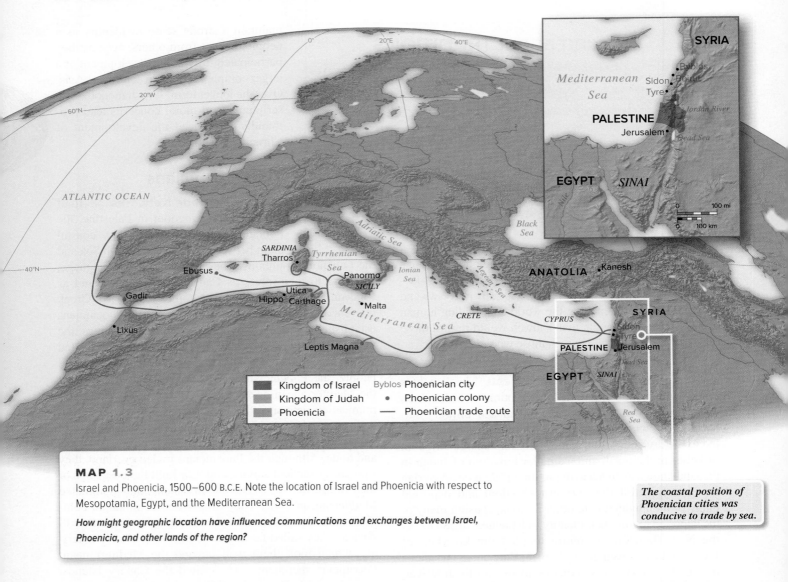

MAP 1.3

Israel and Phoenicia, 1500–600 B.C.E. Note the location of Israel and Phoenicia with respect to Mesopotamia, Egypt, and the Mediterranean Sea.

How might geographic location have influenced communications and exchanges between Israel, Phoenicia, and other lands of the region?

The coastal position of Phoenician cities was conducive to trade by sea.

Because alphabetic writing required much less investment in education than did cuneiform writing, more people were able to become literate than ever before.

Alphabetic writing spread widely as the Phoenicians traveled and traded throughout the Mediterranean basin. About the ninth century B.C.E., for example, Greeks modified the Phoenician alphabet and added symbols representing vowels. Romans later adapted the Greek alphabet to their own language and passed it along to their cultural heirs in Europe. In later centuries alphabetic writing spread to central Asia, south Asia, and southeast Asia, and ultimately throughout most of the world.

THE INDO-EUROPEAN MIGRATIONS

After 3000 B.C.E. Mesopotamia was a prosperous, productive region where peoples from many different communities mixed and mingled. But Mesopotamia was only one region in a much larger world of interaction and exchange. Mesopotamians and their neighbors all dealt frequently with peoples from regions far beyond southwest Asia. Among the most influential of these peoples in the third and second millennia B.C.E. were those who spoke various Indo-European languages. Their migrations throughout much of Eurasia profoundly influenced historical development in both southwest Asia and the larger world.

Indo-European Origins

Indo-European Languages During the eighteenth and nineteenth centuries, linguists noticed that many languages of Europe, southwest Asia, and India featured remarkable similarities in vocabulary and grammatical structure. Ancient languages displaying these similarities included Sanskrit (the sacred language of ancient India), Old Persian, Greek, and Latin. Because of the geographic regions where these tongues are found, scholars refer to

| NORTHWEST SEMITIC | | | GREEK | | ETRUSCAN | LATIN | |
EARLY PHOENICIAN	EARLY HEBREW	PHOENICIAN	EARLY	CLASSICAL	EARLY	EARLY	CLASSICAL
Ϙ	Ϝ	Ϟ	ᐊ	A	Ⱶ	A	A
9	9	9	9	B	Ꞵ	B	B
7	٦	7	1	Γ	٦		C
△	٩	٩	△	△	◠	◠	D

Phoenician, Greek, Hebrew, and Roman Letters.

them as Indo-European languages. Major subgroups of the Indo-European family of languages include Indo-Iranian, Greek, Balto-Slavic, Germanic, Italic, and Celtic. English belongs to the Germanic subgroup of the Indo-European family of languages.

After noticing linguistic similarities, scholars sought a way to explain the close relationship between the Indo-European languages. The only persuasive explanation for the high degree of linguistic coincidence was that speakers of Indo-European languages were all descendants of ancestors who spoke a common tongue and migrated from their original homeland. As migrants established separate communities and lost touch with one another, their languages evolved along different lines, adding new words, pronunciations, and spellings but retaining the basic grammatical structure of their original speech.

The Indo-European Homeland The original homeland of Indo-European speakers was probably the steppe region of modern-day Ukraine and southern Russia, where the earliest of them built a society between about 4500 and 2500 B.C.E. A central feature of Indo-European society was the domestication of wild horses from the Eurasian steppe about 4000 B.C.E. Horses were initially used for food and soon thereafter for riding as well. When

Sumerian knowledge of bronze metallurgy spread to the Indo-European homeland about 3000 B.C.E., Indo-European speakers devised ways to hitch horses to carts, wagons, and chariots. The possession of domesticated horses vastly magnified the power of the Indo-Europeans. Horses enabled them to develop transportation technologies that were much faster and more efficient than other alternatives. Furthermore, because of their strength and speed, horses provided Indo-European speakers with a tremendous military advantage over peoples they encountered. It is perhaps significant that many groups of Indo-European speakers considered themselves superior to other peoples: the terms *Aryan, Iran,* and *Eire* (the official name of the modern Republic of Ireland) all derive from the Indo-European word *aryo,* meaning "nobleman" or "lord."

Indo-European Expansion and Its Effects

The Nature of Indo-European Migration Horses also provided Indo-European speakers with a means of expanding far beyond their original homeland. As they flourished in southern Russia, Indo-European speakers experienced a population explosion, which prompted

TABLE 1.1	Similarities in Vocabulary Indicating Close Relationships between Select Indo-European Languages				
English	**German**	**Spanish**	**Greek**	**Latin**	**Sanskrit**
father	vater	padre	pater	pater	pitar
one	ein	uno	hen	unus	ekam
fire	feuer	fuego	pyr	ignis	agnis
field	feld	campo	agros	ager	ajras
sun	sone	sol	helios	sol	surya
king	könig	rey	basileus	rex	raja
god	gott	dios	theos	deus	devas

some of them to move into the sparsely inhabited eastern steppe or even beyond the grasslands altogether. The earliest Indo-European migrations began about 3000 B.C.E. and continued until about 1000 B.C.E. Like early movements of other peoples, these were not mass migrations so much as gradual and incremental processes that resulted in the spread of Indo-European languages and ethnic communities, as small groups of people established settlements in new lands, which then became foundations for further expansion.

The Hittites The most influential Indo-European migrants in ancient times were the Hittites. About 1900 B.C.E. the Hittites migrated to the central plain of Anatolia, where they imposed their language and rule on the region's inhabitants. During the seventeenth and sixteenth centuries B.C.E., they built a powerful kingdom and established close relations with

Mesopotamian peoples. They traded with Babylonians and Assyrians, adapted cuneiform writing to their Indo-European language, and accepted many Mesopotamian deities into their own pantheon. In 1595 B.C.E. the Hittites toppled the mighty Babylonian empire of Mesopotamia, and for several centuries thereafter they were the dominant power in southwest Asia. Between 1450 and 1200 B.C.E. their authority extended to eastern Anatolia, northern Mesopotamia, and Syria down to Phoenicia. After 1200 B.C.E. the unified Hittite state dissolved, but a Hittite identity survived, along with the Hittite language, throughout the era of the Assyrian empire and beyond.

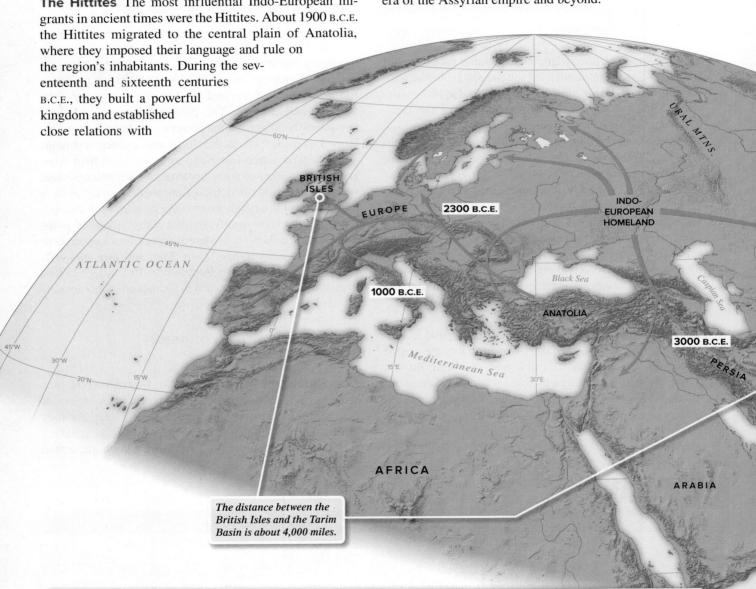

The distance between the British Isles and the Tarim Basin is about 4,000 miles.

MAP 1.4

Indo-European migrations, 3000–1000 B.C.E. Consider the vast distances over which Indo-European migrants established communities.

Would it have been possible for speakers of Indo-European languages to spread so widely without the aid of domesticated horses?

Thinking about **ENCOUNTERS**

Interactions between Early Complex Societies

Despite important differences between the early complex societies, it is nevertheless clear that significant interaction occurred among them. *What were the mechanisms by which such interaction occurred (i.e., trade, transport), and what evidence do scholars have that these early societies influenced one another?*

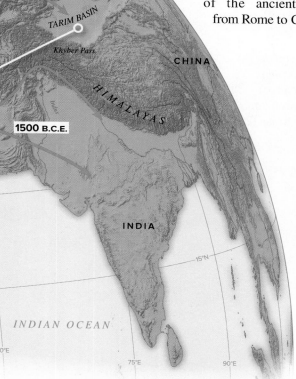

2000 B.C.E.

TARIM BASIN

Khyber Pass

CHINA

H I M A L A Y A S

1500 B.C.E.

INDIA

15°N

INDIAN OCEAN

60°E

75°E

90°E

War Chariots The Hittites were responsible for two technological innovations—the construction of light, horse-drawn war chariots, and the refinement of iron metallurgy—that greatly strengthened their own society and influenced other peoples throughout much of the ancient world. The Hittites' speedy chariots were crucial in their campaign to establish a state in Anatolia. Following the Hittites' example, Mesopotamians soon added chariot teams to their own armies, and Assyrians made especially effective use of chariots in building their empire. Indeed, chariot warfare was so effective— and its techniques spread so widely—that charioteers became the elite strike forces in armies throughout much of the ancient world from Rome to China.

Iron Metallurgy After about 1300 B.C.E. the Hittites also refined the technology of iron metallurgy, which enabled them to produce effective weapons cheaply and in large quantities. Hittite methods of iron production diffused rapidly and eventually spread throughout all of Eurasia. (Peoples of sub-Saharan Africa and also probably China independently invented iron metallurgy.) Hittites were not the original inventors either of horse-drawn chariots or of iron metallurgy: in both cases they built on Mesopotamian precedents. But in both cases they clearly improved on existing technologies and introduced innovations that other peoples readily adopted.

Indo-European Migrations to the West, East, and South While the Hittites were building a state in Anatolia, other Indo-European speakers migrated from the steppe to different regions. Some went east into central Asia, venturing as far as the Tarim Basin (now western China) by 2000 B.C.E. Meanwhile, other Indo-European migrants moved west. One wave of migration took Indo-European speakers into Greece after 2200 B.C.E., with their descendants moving into central Italy by 1000 B.C.E. Another migratory wave established an Indo-European presence farther to the west. By 2300 B.C.E. some Indo-European speakers had made their way from southern Russia into central Europe (modern Germany and Austria), by 1200 B.C.E. to

Hittite chariot.
A stone carving from about 1200 B.C.E. depicts a Hittite chariot with spoked wheels during a lion hunt. A horse pulls the chariot bearing one driver and one archer.

western Europe (modern France), and shortly thereafter to the British Isles, the Baltic region, and the Iberian peninsula. Yet another, later, wave of migrations established an Indo-European presence in Iran and India.

Aryans (AYR-ee-uhns)

About 1500 B.C.E. the Medes and the Persians migrated into the Iranian plateau, while the people sometimes called Indo-Aryans began filtering into northern India. As in earlier migrations, Indo-European migrants borrowed from, influenced, and mixed with the settled peoples they discovered and in so doing shaped future historical developments in each area.

SUMMARY

Building on neolithic foundations, Mesopotamian peoples constructed societies much more complex, powerful, and influential than those of their predecessors. Through their city-states, kingdoms, and regional empires, Mesopotamians created formal institutions of government that extended the authority of ruling elites to all corners of their states, and they occasionally mobilized forces that projected their power to distant lands. They generated several distinct social classes. Specialized labor fueled productive economies and encouraged the establishment of long-distance trade networks. They devised systems of writing, which enabled them to develop sophisticated cultural traditions. They deeply influenced other peoples, such as the Hebrews and the Phoenicians, throughout southwest Asia and the eastern Mediterranean basin. They had frequent dealings also with Indo-European peoples. Although Indo-European society emerged far to the north of Mesopotamia, speakers of Indo-European languages migrated widely and established societies throughout much of Eurasia. Sometimes they drew inspiration from Mesopotamian practices, and sometimes they developed their own practices that influenced Mesopotamians and others as well. Thus, already in remote antiquity, the various peoples of the world profoundly influenced one another through cross-cultural interaction and exchange.

STUDY TERMS

Aryans (24)
Assyrians (12)
bronze (12)
Çatal Hüyük (8)
chariot (12)
cuneiform (16)
Gilgamesh (5)
Hammurabi (10)
Hebrews (18)
Hittites (22)
hominid (5)
Homo sapiens (6)
Homo sapiens sapiens (6)
Indo-European migrations (20)

Israelites (18)
Mesopotamia (8)
monotheism (18)
Nebuchadnezzar (12)
neolithic era (7)
New Babylonian empire (12)
paleolithic era (6)
Phoenician (19)
Sargon of Akkad (10)
Semitic (8)
Sumerians (8)
Uruk (5)
wheel (13)
Yahweh (18)
ziggurats (9)

FOR FURTHER READING

David W. Anthony. *The Horse, the Wheel, and Language: How Bronze-Age Riders from the Eurasian Steppes Shaped the Modern World.* Princeton, 2007. Brilliant study of early Indo-European speakers and the uses they made of domesticated horses.

Elizabeth Wayland Barber. *Women's Work: The First 20,000 Years.* New York, 1994. Fascinating study of ancient textiles, which the author argues was a craft industry dominated by women from the earliest times.

Trevor Bryce. *The Kingdom of the Hittites.* New ed. Oxford, 2005. A solid, scholarly account of Hittite history, with an emphasis on political issues.

Israel Finkelstein and Neil Asher Silberman. *The Bible Unearthed: Archaeology's New Vision of Ancient Israel and the Origin of Its Sacred Texts.* New York, 2001. Interprets the Hebrew scriptures and early Israelite history in light of numerous archaeological discoveries.

Andrew George, trans. *The Epic of Gilgamesh.* London, 1999 (Reprinted with revisions 2003). A careful study and fresh translation of the best-known Mesopotamian literary work prepared on the basis of recently discovered texts.

Pita Kelekna. *The Horse in Human History.* Cambridge, 2009. Fascinating analysis of horses' roles in human history.

J. P. Mallory. *In Search of the Indo-Europeans.* London, 1991. Classic investigation of the probable origins and migrations of the Indo-Europeans.

J. P. Mallory and Victor H. Mair. *The Tarim Mummies: Ancient China and the Mystery of the Earliest Peoples from the West.* London, 2000. A cautious analysis of the Indo-European migrants to the Tarim Basin, drawing heavily on linguistic evidence.

Hans J. Nissen and Peter Heine. *From Mesopotamia to Iraq: A Concise History.* Chicago, 2009. An authoritative discussion of ancient Mesopotamia viewed in the context of the longer history of Iraq.

Michael Roaf. *Cultural Atlas of Mesopotamia and the Ancient Near East.* New York, 1990. Richly illustrated volume with well-informed essays on all dimensions of Mesopotamian history.

Marc van de Mieroop. *A History of the Ancient Near East, ca. 3000–323 B.C.* Oxford, 2004. A concise and readable history of ancient Mesopotamia and neighboring societies.

Early African Societies and the Bantu Migrations

CHAPTER **2**

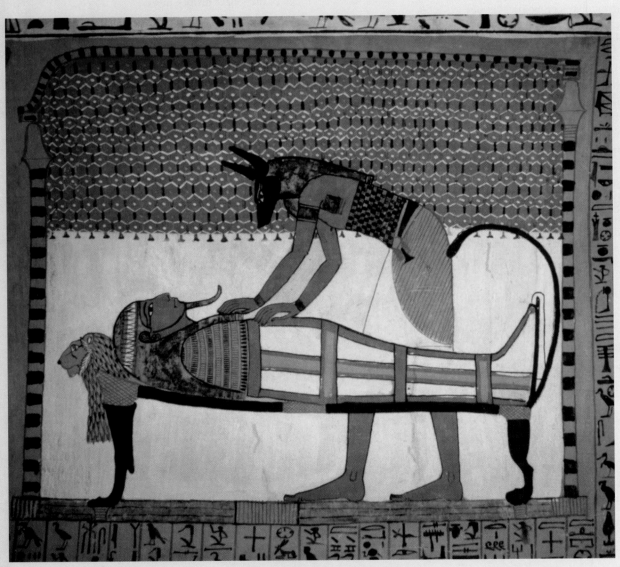

Anubis, the jackal-headed Egyptian god of mummification, prepares the mummy of a deceased worker for burial. This painting comes from the wall of a tomb built about the thirteenth century B.C.E.

EYEWITNESS:

Herodotus and the Making of a Mummy

For almost three thousand years, Egyptian embalmers preserved the bodies of deceased individuals through a process of mummification. Egyptian records rarely mention the techniques of mummification, but the Greek historian Herodotus probably traveled in Egypt about 450 B.C.E. and briefly explained the craft. The embalmer first used a metal hook to draw the brain of the deceased out through a nostril, then removed the internal organs through an incision made alongside the abdomen, washed them in palm wine, and sealed them with preservatives in stone vessels. Next, the embalmer washed the body, filled it with spices and aromatics, and covered it for about two months with natron, a naturally occurring salt substance. When the natron had extracted all moisture from the body, the embalmer cleansed it again and wrapped it with strips of fine linen covered with resin. Adorned with jewelry, the preserved body then went into a coffin bearing a painting or a sculpted likeness of the deceased.

Careful preservation of the body was only a part of the funerary ritual for prominent Egyptians. Ruling elites, wealthy individuals, and sometimes common people as well laid their deceased to rest in expensive tombs equipped with furniture, tools, weapons, and ornaments that the departed would need in their next lives. Relatives periodically brought food and wine to nourish the deceased in their new dimension of existence.

Egyptian funerary customs were reflections of both deeply held religious beliefs, but also of a prosperous agricultural society. Food offerings consisted mostly of local agricultural products, and scenes painted on tomb walls often depicted workers preparing fields or cultivating crops. Moreover, bountiful harvests explained the accumulation of wealth that supported elaborate funerary practices, and they also enabled some individuals to devote their efforts to specialized tasks such as embalming. Agriculture even influenced religious beliefs. Egyptians believed fervently in a life beyond the grave, and they likened the human experience of life and death to the agricultural cycle in which crops grow, die, and come to life again in another season.

As Mesopotamians built a productive agricultural society in southwest Asia and as Indo-European peoples introduced domesticated horses to much of Eurasia, cultivation and herding also transformed African societies. African agriculture first took root in the Sudan, then moved into the Nile River valley and also to most parts of sub-Saharan Africa. Agriculture flourished particularly in the fertile Nile valley, and abundant harvests soon supported fast-growing populations. That agricultural bounty underwrote the development of Egypt, the most prosperous and powerful of the early agricultural societies in Africa, and also of Nubia, Egypt's neighbor to the south.

Distinctive Egyptian and Nubian societies began to take shape in the valley of the Nile River during the late fourth millennium B.C.E., shortly after the emergence of complex society in Mesopotamia. Like their Mesopotamian counterparts, Egyptians and Nubians drew on agricultural surpluses to organize formal states, support specialized laborers, and develop distinctive cultural traditions. Also like Mesopotamians, Egyptian and Nubian residents of the Nile valley had regular dealings with peoples from other societies. They drew inspiration for political

Nubia (NOO-bee-uh)

CHRONOLOGY

9000 B.C.E.	Origins of Sudanic herding
7500 B.C.E.	Origins of Sudanic cultivation
3100 B.C.E.	Unification of Egypt
3100–2660 B.C.E.	Archaic Period of Egyptian history
2660–2160 B.C.E.	Egyptian Old Kingdom
2600–2500 B.C.E.	Era of pyramid building in Egypt
2500–1450 B.C.E.	Early kingdom of Kush with capital at Kerma
2040–1640 B.C.E.	Egyptian Middle Kingdom
2000 B.C.E.	Beginnings of Bantu migrations
1550–1070 B.C.E.	Egyptian New Kingdom
1479–1425 B.C.E.	Reign of Pharaoh Tuthmosis III
1473–1458 B.C.E.	Reign of Queen Hatshepsut (coruler with Tuthmosis III)
1353–1335 B.C.E.	Reign of Pharaoh Amenhotep IV (Akhenaten)
900 B.C.E.	Invention of iron metallurgy in sub-Saharan Africa
760 B.C.E.	Conquest of Egypt by King Kashta of Kush

and social organization both from Mesopotamia and from their African neighbors to the south. In addition, they both traded with and competed against Mesopotamians, Phoenicians, Africans, and others, which resulted in increasing connections with other societies as well as intermittent military conflict.

Indeed, like their counterparts in Mesopotamia, Egyptian and Nubian societies developed from their earliest days in a larger world of interaction and exchange. Just as the peoples of southwest Asia influenced one another, so inhabitants of the Nile valley mixed and mingled with peoples from the eastern Mediterranean, southwest Asia, and sub-Saharan Africa. Just as Indo-European peoples migrated to new lands and established communities that transformed much of Eurasia, so Bantu peoples migrated from their original homeland in west Africa and established settlements that brought profound change to much of sub-Saharan Africa. By no means were Egypt and Nubia isolated centers of social development. Instead, they were only a small part of a much larger world of interacting societies.

EARLY AGRICULTURAL SOCIETY IN AFRICA

Egypt was the most prominent of early African societies, but it was by no means the only agricultural society, or even the only complex, city-based society of ancient Africa. On the contrary, Egypt emerged alongside Nubia and other agricultural societies in sub-Saharan Africa. Indeed, agricultural crops and domesticated animals reached Egypt from sub-Saharan Africa by way of Nubia as well as from southwest Asia. Favorable geographic conditions enabled Egyptians to build an especially productive agricultural economy that supported a powerful state, while Nubia became home to a somewhat less prosperous but nonetheless sophisticated society. After taking shape as distinctive societies, Egypt had regular dealings with both eastern Mediterranean and southwest Asian peoples, and Nubia linked Egypt and the eastern Mediterranean basin with the peoples and societies of sub-Saharan Africa.

Climatic Change and the Development of Agriculture in Africa

African agriculture emerged in the context of gradual but momentous changes in climatic conditions. About 10,000 B.C.E., after the end of the last ice age, the area now occupied by the Sahara desert was mostly a grassy steppe with numerous lakes, rivers, and streams. Indeed, climatic and geographic conditions were similar to those of the Sudan—a region of savanna and grassland that stretches across the African continent between the Sahara to the north and the tropical rain forest to the south.

Early Sudanic Agriculture After about 9000 B.C.E., peoples of the eastern Sudan domesticated cattle and became nomadic herders but also continued to collect wild grains. After 7500 B.C.E. they established permanent settlements and began to cultivate sorghum. Meanwhile, after about 8000 B.C.E., inhabitants of the western Sudan began to cultivate yams in the region between the Niger and Congo rivers. Sudanic agriculture became increasingly diverse over the following centuries: sheep and goats arrived from southwest Asia after 7000 B.C.E., and Sudanic peoples began to cultivate gourds, watermelons, and cotton after 6500 B.C.E.

Agricultural productivity—and the need for order—led Sudanic peoples to organize small-scale states. By about 5000 B.C.E. many Sudanic peoples had formed small monarchies ruled by kings who were viewed as divine or semidivine beings. Sudanic peoples also developed religious beliefs that reflected their agricultural society. They recognized a single divine force as the

Bantu (BAHN-too)

source of good and evil, and they associated it with rain—a matter of concern for any agricultural society.

Climatic Change After 5000 B.C.E. the northern half of Africa became much hotter and drier than before. The Sahara desert in particular became increasingly arid and uninhabitable. This process of desiccation drove both humans and animals to regions that offered reliable sources of water such as lakes and rivers. One of those regions was the valley of the Nile River, the principal source of water flowing through north Africa.

The Nile River Valley Fed by rain and snow in the mountains of east Africa, the Nile, which is the world's longest river, courses some 6,695 kilometers (4,160 miles) from its source at Lake Victoria to its outlet through the delta to the Mediterranean Sea. Each spring, rain and melting snow swell the river, which surges north through the Sudan and Egypt. Until the completion of the high dam at Aswan in 1968, every year the Nile flooded the plains downstream. When the waters receded, they left behind a layer of rich, fertile alluvial deposits that supported a remarkably productive agricultural economy throughout the Nile River valley.

Egypt and Nubia: "Gifts of the Nile"

Agriculture transformed the entire Nile River valley, with effects that were most dramatic in Egypt. In ancient times, Egypt referred not to the territory embraced by the modern state of Egypt but, rather, to the ribbon of land bordering the lower third of the Nile between the Mediterranean and the river's first cataract (an unnavigable stretch of rapids and waterfalls) near Aswan. Egypt enjoyed a much larger floodplain than most of the land to the south known as Nubia, the middle stretches of the Nile valley between the river's first and sixth cataracts. As the Sahara became increasingly arid, cultivators flocked to the Nile valley and established societies that depended on intensive agriculture. Because of their broad floodplains, Egyptians were able to take better advantage of the Nile's annual floods than their neighbors to the

south, and they turned Egypt into an especially productive agricultural region that was capable of supporting a much larger population than were Nubian lands. Because of its prosperity, the Greek historian Herodotus proclaimed Egypt the "gift of the Nile."

Early Agriculture in the Nile Valley Geography ensured that Egypt and Nubia would come under the influence of both sub-Saharan Africa and the eastern Mediterranean basin, since the Nile River links the two regions. About 10,000 B.C.E. migrants from the Red Sea hills in northern Ethiopia traveled down the Nile valley and introduced to Egypt and Nubia the practice of collecting wild grains as well as their language, which became the language of ancient Egypt. After 5000 B.C.E., as the African climate grew hotter and drier, Sudanic peoples moved down the Nile, introducing Egypt and Nubia to crops such as gourds and watermelons and domesticated animals such as cattle and donkeys. About the same time, wheat and barley reached Egypt and Nubia from Mesopotamia by traveling up the Nile from the Mediterranean.

Both Egyptians and Nubians relied heavily on agriculture at least by 5000 B.C.E. Egyptian cultivators went

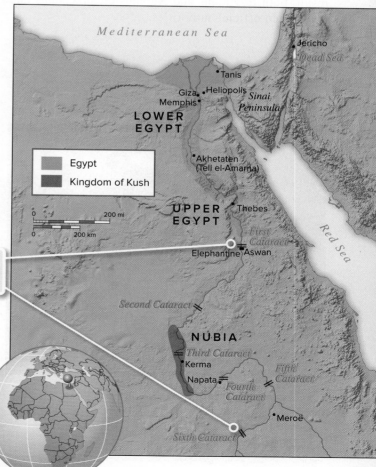

The region between the first and sixth cataracts was known as Nubia.

MAP 2.1

The Nile valley, 3000–2000 B.C.E. Note the difference in size between the kingdom of Egypt and the kingdom of Kush.

What geographical conditions favored the establishment of large states north of the first cataract of the Nile River?

into the floodplains in the late summer, after the recession of the Nile's annual flood, sowed their seeds without extensive preparation of the soil, allowed their crops to mature during the cool months of the year, and harvested them during the winter and early spring. With less-extensive floodplains, Nubians relied more on prepared fields and irrigation by waters diverted from the Nile. As in Mesopotamia, high agricultural productivity led to a rapid increase in population throughout the Nile valley. Demographic pressures soon forced Egyptians in particular to develop more intense and sophisticated methods of agriculture as cultivators found it necessary to move beyond the Nile's immediate floodplains to areas that required careful preparation and irrigation. By 4000 B.C.E. agricultural villages dotted the Nile's shores from the Mediterranean in the north to the river's fourth cataract in the south. As in Mesopotamia, dense human population in Egypt and Nubia brought a need for formal organization of public affairs. Although geographical barriers in the form of seas and desert meant that neither area faced external dangers to the extent that Mesopotamia did, the two areas still needed to maintain order and organize community projects. As a result, both Egyptians and Nubians created states and recognized official authorities.

Menes (mee-neez)

Early agriculture in Egypt.
A painting from the tomb of a priest who lived about the fifteenth century B.C.E. depicts agricultural workers plowing and sowing crops in southern Egypt.

The earliest Egyptian and Nubian states were small kingdoms much like those instituted in the Sudan after 5000 B.C.E. Indeed, it is likely that the notion of divine or semidivine rulers reached Egypt and Nubia from the eastern and central Sudan. In any case, small kingdoms appeared first in southern Egypt and Nubia after 4000 B.C.E., and by 3300 B.C.E. small local kingdoms organized public life throughout Egypt as well as Nubia.

The Unification of Egypt

Menes By 3500 B.C.E. political and economic competition fueled numerous skirmishes and small-scale wars between the Nile kingdoms. Some kingdoms overcame their neighbors and gradually expanded until they controlled sizable territories. About 3100 B.C.E. Egyptian rulers drew on the considerable agricultural and demographic advantages of Egypt's large population and broad floodplains to forge all the territory between the Nile delta and the river's first cataract into a powerful and unified kingdom. Tradition suggests that unified rule came to Egypt in the person of a conqueror named Menes (sometimes identified with an early Egyptian ruler called Narmer). Menes was an ambitious minor official from southern Egypt (known as Upper Egypt, since the Nile flows north) who rose to power and extended his authority north and into the delta (known as Lower Egypt). According to tradition, Menes founded the city of Memphis, near modern Cairo, which stood at the junction of Upper and Lower Egypt. Memphis served as Menes' capital and eventually became the cultural as well as the political center of ancient Egypt.

Menes and his successors built a centralized state ruled by the pharaoh, the Egyptian king. The early pharaohs claimed to be gods living on the earth in human form, the owners and absolute rulers of all the land. In that respect, they continued the tradition of divine kingship inherited from the early agricultural societies of the Sudan. Over time, Egyptians viewed rulers as offspring of Amon, a sun god. They considered the ruling pharaoh a human sun overseeing affairs on the earth, just as Amon was the sun supervising the larger cosmos, and they believed that after his death the pharaoh actually merged with Amon.

The Archaic Period and the Old Kingdom The power of the pharaohs was greatest during the first millennium of Egyptian history—the eras known as the Archaic Period (3100–2660 B.C.E.) and the Old Kingdom (2660–2160 B.C.E.). The most enduring symbols of their authority and divine status are the massive pyramids constructed during the Old Kingdom as royal tombs, most of them during the century from 2600 to 2500 B.C.E. These enormous monuments stand today at Giza, near Cairo, as testimony to the pharaohs' ability to marshal Egyptian resources. The largest is the pyramid of Khufu (also known as Cheops), which involved the precise cutting and fitting of 2.3 million limestone blocks weighing up to 15 tons, with an average weight of 2.5 tons. Scholars estimate that construction of Khufu's pyramid required the services of some eighty-four thousand laborers working eighty days per year for twenty years.

Relations between Egypt and Nubia Even after the emergence of the strong pharaonic state, the fortunes of Egypt and Nubia remained closely intertwined. Egyptians had strong interests in Nubia for both political and commercial reasons: they were wary of Nubian kingdoms that might threaten Upper Egypt, and they desired products such as gold, ivory, ebony, and precious stones that were available only from southern lands. Meanwhile, Nubians had equally strong interests in Egypt: they wanted to protect their independence from their large and powerful neighbor to the north, and they sought to profit by controlling trade down the Nile.

The Early Kingdom of Kush Tensions led to frequent violence between Egypt and Nubia throughout the Archaic Period and the Old Kingdom. Indeed, Egypt dominated Lower Nubia (the land between the first and second cataracts of the Nile) for more than half a millennium, from about 3000 to 2400 B.C.E. This Egyptian presence in the north forced Nubian leaders to concentrate their efforts at political organization farther to the south in Upper Nubia. By about 2500 B.C.E. they had established a powerful kingdom, called Kush, with a capital at Kerma, about 700 kilometers (435 miles) south of Aswan. Though not as powerful as united Egypt, the kingdom of Kush became a formidable and wealthy state in its own right.

In spite of constant tension and frequent hostilities, Egypt and Nubia remained connected in many ways. About 2300 B.C.E., for example, the Egyptian explorer Harkhuf made four expeditions to Nubia. He returned from one of his trips with a caravan of some three hundred donkeys bearing exotic products from tropical Africa, as well as a dancing dwarf, and his cargo stimulated Egyptian desire for trade with southern lands. Meanwhile, by the end of the Old Kingdom, Nubian mercenaries had become quite prominent in Egyptian armies. In fact, they often married Egyptian women and assimilated into Egyptian society.

Turmoil and Empire

The Middle Kingdom Toward the end of the Old Kingdom, high agricultural productivity made several regions of Egypt so prosperous and powerful that they were able to ignore the pharaohs and pursue their own interests. As a result, the central state declined and eventually disappeared altogether during a long period of upheaval and unrest (2160–2040 B.C.E.). Pharaonic authority returned with the establishment of the Middle Kingdom (2040–1640 B.C.E.). Pharaohs of the Middle Kingdom were not as powerful as their predecessors of the Old Kingdom, but they effectively stabilized Egypt and supervised relations with neighboring lands.

The Hyksos Gradually, however, Egypt came under the pressure of foreign peoples from southwest Asia, particularly a Semitic people whom Egyptians called the Hyksos ("foreign rulers"). Little information survives about the Hyksos, but it is clear that they were horse-riding nomads. Indeed, their horse-drawn chariots, which they learned about from Hittites and Mesopotamians, provided them with a significant military advantage over Egyptian forces. They enjoyed an advantage also in their weaponry: the Hyksos used bronze weapons and bronze-tipped arrows, whereas Egyptians relied mostly on wooden weapons and arrows with stone heads. About 1674 B.C.E. the Hyksos captured Memphis and levied tribute throughout Egypt.

Hyksos rule provoked a strong reaction especially in Upper Egypt, where disgruntled nobles organized revolts against the foreigners. They adopted horses and chariots for their own military forces. They also equipped their troops with bronze weapons. Working from Thebes and later from Memphis, Egyptian leaders gradually pushed the Hyksos out of the Nile delta and founded a powerful state known as the New Kingdom (1550–1070 B.C.E.).

Pharaohs of the New Kingdom presided over a prosperous and productive society. Agricultural surpluses supported a population of perhaps four million people as well as an army and an elaborate bureaucracy that divided responsibilities among different offices.

Egyptian Imperialism Pharaohs of the New Kingdom also worked to extend Egyptian authority well beyond the Nile valley and the delta. After expelling the Hyksos, they sought to prevent new invasions by seizing control of regions that might pose threats in the future. Most vigorous of the New Kingdom pharaohs

Kush (kuhsh)

Hyksos (HICK-sohs)

SourcesfromthePast

Harkhuf's Expeditions to Nubia

Many Egyptians wrote brief autobiographies that they or their descendants had carved into their tombs. One of the most famous autobiographies from the Old Kingdom is that of Harkhuf, a royal official who became governor of Upper Egypt before 2300 B.C.E. The inscriptions in his tomb mention his four expeditions to Nubia to seek valuable items and report on political conditions there. The inscriptions also include the text of a letter from the boy-pharaoh Neferkare expressing his appreciation for Harkhuf's fourth expedition and his desire to see the dancing dwarf that Harkhuf brought back from Nubia.

His Majesty [Pharaoh] Mernera, my Lord, sent me with my father Ara . . . to the [Nubian] land of Amam to open up a road into this country. I performed the journey in seven months. I brought back gifts of all kinds from that place . . . there was very great praise to me for it. His Majesty sent me a second time by myself . . . I came back . . . in a period of eight months . . . and I brought very large quantities of offerings from this country. Never were brought such things to this land. . . His Majesty sent me a third time to Amam . . . I came back . . . with three hundred asses laden with incense, ebony, heknu, grain, panther skins, ivory . . . and valuable products of every kind.

[The letter from Pharaoh Nefekare to Harkuf]: Royal despatch to the . . . governor of the caravan, Herkhuf. I have understood the words of this letter, which you have written to the king in his chamber to make him to know that you have returned in peace from Amam, together with the soldiers who were with thee. You say in this . . . letter that there have been brought back . . . beautiful offerings of all kinds . . . like the pygmy whom the seal-bearer of the god Baurtet brought back from Punt in the time of Assa. Thou say to [my] Majesty, "The like of him has never been brought back by any other person who has visited Amam."

Behold, every year you perform what thy Lord wishes and praises. Behold, you pass your days and nights meditating about doing what thy Lord orders, wishes, and praises.

And His Majesty will confer on you so many splendid honors, which shall give renown to your grandson for ever, that all the people shall say when they have heard what [my] Majesty hath done for thee, "Was there ever anything like this that has been done for . . . Harkhuf when he came back from Amam because of the attention . . . he displayed in doing what his Lord commanded, and wished for, and praised?"

Come down the river at once to the Capital. Bring with you this pygmy whom you have brought from the Land of the Spirits, alive, strong, and healthy, to dance the dance of the god, and to cheer and gratify the heart of the King of the South and North. . . When he comes down with you in the boat, cause trustworthy men to be about him on both sides of the boat, to prevent him from falling into the water. When he is asleep at night cause trustworthy men to sleep by his side on his bedding.

See [that he is there] ten times [each] night. [My] Majesty wishes to see this pygmy more than any offering of the countries of Ba and Punt. If when you arrive at the Capital, this pygmy who is with you is alive, and strong, and in good health, [my] Majesty will confer upon you a greater honor than that which was conferred upon the bearer of the seal Baurtet in the time of Assa, and as great is the wish of [my] Majesty to see this pygmy orders have been brought to . . . the overseer of the priests, the governor of the town . . . to arrange that rations for him shall be drawn from every station of supply, and from every temple that has not been exempted.

For Further Reflection

■ How do Harkhuf's autobiography and the letter from the pharaoh illuminate early Egyptian interest in Nubia and the processes by which Egyptians of the Old Kingdom developed knowledge about Nubia?

Source: E. A. Wallis Budge. *The Literature of the Ancient Egyptians,* London: J. M. Dent & Sons Limited, Aldine House, Bedford Street, W. C. Project Guttenberg 1914.

---

was Tuthmosis III (reigned 1479–1425 B.C.E.). After seventeen campaigns that he personally led to Palestine and Syria, Tuthmosis dominated the coastal regions of the eastern Mediterranean as well as north Africa. Rulers of the New Kingdom also turned their attention to the south and restored Egyptian dominance in Nubia. Thus for half a millennium Egypt was an imperial power throughout much of the eastern Mediterranean basin and southwest Asia as well as most of the Nile River valley, meaning that it imposed its political and economic will on other areas through the forcible acquisition of territory.

After the New Kingdom, Egypt entered a long period of political and military decline. Just as Hyksos rule provoked a reaction in Egypt, so Egyptian rule provoked reactions in the regions subdued by pharaonic armies. Local resistance drove Egyptian forces out of Nubia and southwest Asia; then Kushite and Assyrian armies invaded Egypt itself.

Tuthmosis (tuh-MOE-sis)

Chapter 2 ■ Early African Societies and the Bantu Migrations   **33**

Nubian tribute to Egypt.
A wall painting from the tomb of an Egyptian imperial official in Nubia depicts a delegation of Nubians bringing tribute in the forms of exotic beasts, animal skins, and rings of gold.

Why might these cultural gifts have been welcome tribute for Egyptians?

The Revived Kingdom of Kush By 1100 B.C.E. Egyptian forces were in full retreat from Nubia, and in the tenth century B.C.E. Nubian leaders organized a new kingdom of Kush with a capital at Napata, located just below the Nile's fourth cataract. By the eighth century B.C.E., rulers of this revived kingdom of Kush were powerful enough to invade Egypt. King Kashta conquered Thebes about 760 B.C.E. and founded a Kushite dynasty that ruled Egypt for almost a century. Kashta's successors consolidated Kushite authority in Upper Egypt, claimed the title of pharaoh, and eventually extended their rule to the Nile delta and beyond.

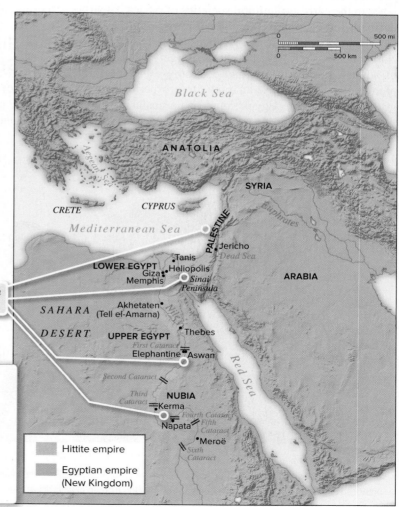

Areas of Egyptian expansion during the New Kingdom.

MAP 2.2
Imperial Egypt, 1400 B.C.E. Compare the territory ruled by the New Kingdom with the earlier kingdom of Egypt as represented in Map 2.1.

Why was the New Kingdom able to expand so dramatically to the north and south? Why did it not expand to the east and west also?

Meanwhile, as Kushites pushed into Egypt from the south, Assyrian armies equipped with iron weapons bore down from the north. During the mid–seventh century B.C.E., while building their vast empire, the Assyrians invaded Egypt, campaigned as far south as Thebes, drove out the Kushites, and subjected Egypt to Assyrian rule. After the mid–sixth century B.C.E., like Mesopotamia, Egypt fell to a series of foreign conquerors who built vast empires throughout southwest Asia and the eastern Mediterranean region.

Reverberations of ● ● ● ● ● ● ●
Urbanization and the Creation of Patriarchy

Recall from chapter 1 that some scholars have attempted to explain the relatively high status of Egyptian and Nubian women by arguing that their societies were less militarized than those of Mesopotamia, and thus not as predisposed to valuing male warriors. Given the evidence of frequent warfare between Egypt and Nubia from the Archaic period through the Middle Kingdom, can you think of other reasons why women of the Nile might have had more influence than their counterparts in Mesopotamia?

THE FORMATION OF COMPLEX SOCIETIES AND SOPHISTICATED CULTURAL TRADITIONS

As in Mesopotamia, cities and the congregation of dense populations encouraged the emergence of specialized labor in the early agricultural societies of Africa. Clearly defined social classes emerged throughout the Nile valley, and both Egypt and Nubian lands built patriarchal societies that placed authority largely in the hands of adult males. The Egyptian economy was especially productive, and because of both its prosperity and its geographic location, Egypt figured as a center of trade, linking lands in southwest Asia, the eastern Mediterranean, and sub-Saharan Africa. Meanwhile, like southwest Asia, the Nile valley was a site of sophisticated cultural development. Writing systems appeared in both Egypt and Nubia, and writing soon became a principal medium of literary expression and religious reflection as well as a means for preserving governmental records and commercial information.

The Emergence of Cities and Stratified Societies

Cities of the Nile Valley Cities were not as prominent in early societies of the Nile River valley as they were in ancient Mesopotamia. Nevertheless, several major cities

Social stratification in Egyptian society.
Building pyramids and other large structures involved heavy work, especially by the less privileged classes. Here an Egyptian manuscript painting produced about 1000 B.C.E. depicts a supervisor overseeing a group of laborers as they drag a sled loaded with stone building blocks.

Thinking about TRADITIONS

Environment, Climate, and Agriculture

Agriculture is possible only if environmental and climatic conditions are favorable for the cultivation of crops. *What environmental and climatic conditions made it possible for Egyptians and Nubians to build agricultural societies in the Nile river valley?*

emerged and guided affairs in both Egypt and Nubia. In Egypt, Memphis, Thebes, Heliopolis, and Tanis all became important political, administrative, or cultural centers. In Nubia, Kerma, Napata, and Meroë all took their turn as political capitals between about 2500 B.C.E. and 100 C.E.

Social Classes In Egypt and Nubia alike, ancient cities were centers of considerable accumulated wealth, which encouraged the development of social distinctions and hierarchies. Like the Mesopotamians, ancient Egyptians recognized a series of well-defined social classes. Egyptian peasants and slaves played roles in society similar to those of their Mesopotamian counterparts: they supplied the hard labor that made complex agricultural society possible. The organization of the ruling classes, however, differed considerably between Mesopotamia and Egypt. Instead of a series of urban kings, as in Mesopotamia, Egyptians recognized the pharaoh as a supreme central ruler. In addition, rather than depending on nobles who owed their positions to their birth, Egypt relied on professional military forces and an elaborate bureaucracy of administrators and tax collectors who served the central government. Thus, in Egypt much more than in Mesopotamia, individuals of common birth could attain high positions in society through government service.

Surviving information illuminates Egyptian society much better than Nubian, but it is clear that Nubia also was the site of a complex, hierarchical society in ancient times. Indeed, cemeteries associated with Nubian cities clearly reveal social and economic distinctions. Tombs of wealthy and powerful individuals were often elaborate structures—comfortable dwelling places tastefully decorated with paintings and filled with expensive goods such as gold jewelry, gems, fine furniture, and abundant supplies of food. In contrast, graves of commoners were much simpler, although they usually contained jewelry, pottery, personal ornaments, and other goods to accompany the departed.

Patriarchal Society Like their Mesopotamian counterparts, both Egyptian and Nubian peoples built patriarchal societies that vested authority over public and private affairs in their men. With rare exceptions men were the rulers in both Egyptian and Nubian private as well as public

life, and decisions about government policies rested mostly in men's hands.

Yet women made their influence felt in ancient Egyptian and Nubian societies much more than in contemporary Mesopotamia. In Egypt, women of the royal family sometimes served as regents for young rulers. In one notable case, a woman took power as pharaoh herself: Queen Hatshepsut (reigned 1473–1458 B.C.E.) served as coruler with her stepson Tuthmosis III. However, the notion of a female ruler may have been unsettling to many Egyptians. In what seems to have been an effort to present her in unthreatening guise, a monumental statue of Queen Hatshepsut depicts her wearing the stylized beard traditionally associated with the pharaohs. In Nubia, in contrast, there is abundant evidence of many women rulers in the kingdom of Kush. Some ruled in their own right, others reigned jointly with male kings, and many governed also in the capacity of regents. Meanwhile, other women wielded considerable power as priestesses in the numerous religious cults observed in Egypt and Nubia. A few women also obtained a formal education and worked as scribes.

Economic Specialization and Trade

With the formation of complex, city-based societies, peoples of the Nile valley were able to draw on a rapidly expanding stock of human skills. Bronze metallurgy made its way from Mesopotamia to both Egypt and Nubia, and by 1000 B.C.E. Sudanic peoples independently developed a technology of iron production that eventually spread to most parts of sub-Saharan Africa. Pottery, textile manufacture, woodworking, leather production, stonecutting, and masonry all became distinct occupations in cities throughout the Nile valley. Specialized labor and the invention of efficient transportation technologies encouraged the development of trade networks that linked the Nile valley to a much larger world.

Bronze Metallurgy Nile societies were much slower than their Mesopotamian counterparts to adopt metal tools and weapons. Whereas the production of bronze flourished in Mesopotamia by 3000 B.C.E., use of bronze implements became widespread in Egypt only after the seventeenth century B.C.E., when the Hyksos relied on bronze weapons to impose their authority on the Nile delta. Although Egyptians equipped their own forces with bronze weapons after expelling the Hyksos, the high cost of copper and tin kept bronze out of the hands of most people. Indeed, bronze was considered so valuable that

Hatshepsut (hat-SHEP-soot)

Connecting
the Sources

Thinking about non-elites in the ancient Egyptian past

In order to write about the past, historians must find and interpret **primary sources**. Primary sources can include **material objects, archeological evidence, oral traditions, texts (including official documents, letters, accounts, newspapers), or images**. They provide the evidence on which historical narratives rest. This exercise highlights some of the challenges of interpreting original primary sources by asking you to consider the kinds of contextual information you might need in order to interpret such documents accurately, and by asking you to consider what individual documents can and cannot tell you.

The problem   Writing about the ancient past poses multiple problems for historians. Among these is the problem of *preservation,* since many potential sources for historical documentation simply have not survived over thousands of years. For textual sources there is also the problem of *language and script,* since ancient societies used languages and forms of writing very different from our own. In addition, even when sources have been preserved and historians are able to decipher ancient texts, there is the problem of *selectivity*— meaning that the sources most likely to have been preserved were those generated by elites.

Fortunately for historians, ancient Egyptian peoples left many textual, material, and archaeological sources behind. The arid climate helped to preserve many textual sources written on papyrus, while the use of stone allowed many monuments to withstand thousands of years of exposure to the elements. Despite the abundance of primary sources, however, much less is known about the lives of everyday Egyptians than is known about Egyptian monarchs, nobles, political elites, and religious authorities. Historians know that most Egyptians were farmers, but few surviving sources tell their story from their own perspective. In the following two documents, which were generated centuries apart, think about what historians can and cannot infer about the lives of non-elites in ancient Egypt.

The documents   Read the documents below, and consider carefully the questions that follow.

Document 1: *Stela (inscribed stone) from the tomb of a man named Mentuhotep, from the 11th Dynasty (2133–1991 B.C.E.). Mentuhotep is depicted to the left, with his parents and his son. To the right are Mentuhotep's other children and his servants.*

(1) *O ye who live and are upon the earth and who shall pass by this tomb, who love life and hate death, say ye: "May Osiris, head of the Westerners [people of the underworld], glorify Menthotpe."*

(2) *Now I was first among my contemporaries, the foreman of my gang [man of the people], one who discovered the statement about which he had been asked, and answered (it) appropriately,*

(3) *cool(-headed), one who obtained bread in its (due) season, one whose (own) counsel replaced for him a mother at home, a father making the family*

Document 1: Stela from the tomb of Mentuhotep.

fortune (??), and a son of good disposition, one whom his (own) nature instructed as (it were) a child growing up with its father.

(4) *Now although I was become an orphan, I acquired cattle and got oxen (?) and developed my business in goats; I built a house and excavated a (garden-) pond, the priest Menthotpe.*

Translated by Alan Gardiner. From W. M. F. Petrie Tombs of the Courtiers and Oxyrhynkhos, 1922

Document 2: *The following comes from a declaration freeing slaves, from the 20th Dynasty (1185–1070 B.C.E.)*

Year 28, 1st month of Inundation, day 10, under the Majesty of the King of Upper and Lower Egypt, Ramesses (XI). On this day, declaration made by the stable-master Neb-nufe and his wife the musician of Seth of Spermeru Rennufe, to wit:

"We purchased the female slave Dini-huiry and she gave birth to these three children, one male and two female, in all three. And I [i.e., Rennufe] took them and nourished them and brought them up, and I have reached this day with them without their doing evil towards me, but they dealt well with me, I having no son or daughter except them. And the stable-master Padiu entered my house and took Ta-Amon-no, their elder sister, to wife, he being related to me and being my younger brother. And I accepted him for her and he is with her at this day.

"Now behold, I have made her a freewoman of the land of Pharaoh, and if she bears either son or daughter, they shall be freemen of the land of Pharaoh in exactly the same way, they being with the stable-master Padiu, this younger brother of mine. And the children shall be with their elder sister in the house of Padiu, this stable-master, this younger brother of mine, and today I make him a son of mine exactly like them."

And she said: "As Amun endures, and the Ruler endures, I (hereby) make the people whom I have put on record freemen of the land of Pharaoh, and if any son, daughter, brother, or sister of their mother and their father should contest their rights, except Padiu this son of mine—for they are indeed no longer with him as servants, but are with him as younger siblings, being freemen of the land <of Pharaoh>—may a donkey copulate with him and a donkey with his wife, whoever it be that shall call any of them a servant.

"And if I have fields in the country, or if I have any property in the world, or if I have merchants (?), these shall be divided among my four children, Padiu being one of them. And as for these matters of which I have spoken, they are entrusted in their entirety to Padiu, this son of mine, who dealt well with me when I was a widow and when my husband had died."

Before many and numerous witnesses . . . (both men and women).

Source: Alan H. Gardiner, "Adoption Extraordinary," Journal of Egyptian Archaeology 26 (1940) 23–29. Text reproduced courtesy of the Egypt Exploration Society. http://www.reshafim.org.il/ad/egypt/texts/adoption_papyrus.htm

Questions

- What can these sources definitively tell you about the lives of the people who produced them? What **facts** can be gleaned from these sources?

- In Document 1, what is the life story of Mentuhotep, according to the inscription in the stela? Does the inscription indicate that the social mobility described by Mentuhotep was common or uncommon during the 11th Dynasty?

- Also in Document 1, do the figures on the right offer clues about the daily lives of people in Mentuhotep's household?

- In Document 2, why does Rennufe want to free the three slaves under question? Does this document offer any clues about the experience of slavery in Egypt during the 20th Dynasty?

- Also in Document 2, does this document allow speculation about the status of women in Egypt during the 20th Dynasty? If so, in what ways?

- Taking both documents together, what can each of them tell us about the experience of non-elites in ancient Egypt? What kinds of additional contextual information would you need in order to gauge this question more fully?

- Sources such as these can give historians tantalizing evidence about the lives of everyday people, even in the ancient past. To understand them accurately, however, historians must place individual sources in their larger historical context in order to decide whether they represent broad trends or historical exceptions.

Source Website: **Document 1:** http://www.reshafim.org.il/ad/egypt/texts/mentuhotep_stela.htm. **Document 2:** http://www.reshafim.org.il/ad/egypt/texts/adoption_papyrus.htm

officers weighed the bronze tools issued to workers at royal tombs to ensure that craftsmen did not shave slivers off them for personal uses.

Iron Metallurgy Bronze was even less prominent in Nubian societies than in Egypt. During the centuries after 1000 B.C.E., however, the southern Nile societies made up for their lack of bronze with the emergence of large-scale iron production. Furnaces churned out iron implements both in Nubia and in west Africa at least by 500 B.C.E. Meroë in particular became a site of large-scale iron production. Indeed, archaeologists who excavated Meroë in the early twentieth century C.E. found enormous mounds of slag still remaining from ancient times.

Transportation Nile craftsmen also worked from the early days of agricultural society to devise efficient means of transportation. Before 3500 B.C.E. Egyptians already traveled up and down the Nile with ease. Because the Nile flows north, boats could ride the currents from Upper to Lower Egypt. Meanwhile, prevailing winds blow almost year-round from the north, so that by raising a sail, boats could easily make their way upriver from Lower to Upper Egypt. Soon after 3000 B.C.E. Egyptians sailed beyond the Nile into the Mediterranean, and by about 2000 B.C.E. they had also thoroughly explored the waters of the Red Sea, the Gulf of Aden, and the western portion of the Arabian Sea. Egyptians also made use of Mesopotamian-style wheeled vehicles for local transport as well as donkey caravans for overland transport.

In Nubia, navigation on the Nile was less convenient than in Egypt because unnavigable cataracts made it necessary to transport goods overland before continuing on the river. Moreover, sailing ships heading upriver could not negotiate a long stretch of the Nile around the fourth cataract because winds blow the same direction that currents flow. As a result, Nubian societies had to rely more than Egyptians on overland transport by wheeled vehicles and donkey caravan.

Egyptian river transport.
A wooden model found in a tomb shows how Egyptians traveled up and down the Nile River. Produced about 2000 B.C.E., this sculpture depicts a relatively small boat with a mast, sail, rudder, and poles to push the vessel through shallow waters. Many wall and tomb paintings confirm the accuracy of this model.

Why is the figure in front trying to gauge the water's depth?

Trade Networks In both Egypt and Nubia, specialized labor and efficient means of transportation encouraged the development of long-distance trade. By the time of the Old Kingdom, trade flowed regularly between Egypt and Nubia. Exotic African goods such as ivory, ebony, leopard skins, ostrich feathers, gemstones, gold, and slaves went down the Nile in exchange for pottery, wine, honey, and finished products from Egypt. Among the most prized Egyptian exports were fine linen textiles woven from the flax that flourished in the Nile valley as well as high-quality decorative and ornamental objects such as boxes, furniture, and jewelry produced by skilled artisans.

Egyptian merchants looked north as well as south. They traded with Mesopotamians as early as 3500 B.C.E., and after 3000 B.C.E. they were active throughout the eastern Mediterranean basin. Since Egypt has very few trees, Egyptian ships regularly imported huge loads from Lebanon. Pharaohs especially prized aromatic cedar for their tombs, and one record from about 2600 B.C.E. mentions an expedition of forty ships hauling cedar logs.

In exchange for cedar, Egyptians offered gold, silver, linen textiles, leather goods, and dried foods such as lentils.

After the establishment of the New Kingdom, Egyptians also traded through the Red Sea and the Gulf of Aden with an east African land they called Punt—probably modern-day Somalia and Ethiopia. From Punt they imported gold, ebony, ivory, cattle, aromatics, and slaves. Thus, as in southwest Asia, specialization of labor and efficient technologies of transportation not only quickened the economies of complex societies in Egypt and Nubia but also encouraged their interaction with peoples of distant lands.

Early Writing in the Nile Valley

Hieroglyphic Writing Writing appeared in Egypt at least by 3200 B.C.E., possibly as a result of Mesopotamian influence. As in Mesopotamia, the earliest Egyptian writing was pictographic, but Egyptians soon supplemented their pictographs with symbols representing sounds and ideas. Early Greek visitors to Egypt marveled at the large and handsome pictographs that adorned Egyptian monuments and buildings. Since the symbols were particularly prominent on temples, the visitors called them hieroglyphs, from two Greek words meaning "holy inscriptions." Hieroglyphic writing also survives on sheets of papyrus, a paper-like material fashioned from the insides of papyrus reeds, which flourish along the Nile River. The hot, dry climate of Egypt has preserved large numbers of papyrus texts bearing administrative and commercial records as well as literary and religious texts.

Although striking and dramatic, hieroglyphs were also somewhat cumbersome. Egyptians went to the trouble of using hieroglyphs for formal writing and monumental inscriptions, but for everyday affairs they commonly relied on the hieratic ("priestly") script, a simplified, cursive form of hieroglyphs. Hieratic appeared in the early centuries of the third millennium B.C.E., and Egyptians made extensive use of the script for more than three thousand years, from about 2600 B.C.E. to 600 C.E. Hieratic largely disappeared after the middle of the first millennium C.E., when Egyptians adapted the Greek alphabet to their own language and developed alphabetic scripts known as the demotic ("popular") and Coptic ("Egyptian") scripts.

Meroitic Writing Nubian peoples spoke their own languages, but all early writing in Nubia was Egyptian hieroglyphic writing. Indeed, over the centuries, Egypt wielded great cultural influence in Nubia, especially during times when Egyptian political and military influence was strong in southern lands. After about the fifth century B.C.E., however, Egyptian cultural influence declined noticeably in Nubia. After the transfer of the Kushite capital from Napata to Meroë, Nubian scribes even devised an alphabetic script for the Meroitic language. They borrowed Egyptian hieroglyphs but used them to represent sounds rather than ideas and so created a flexible writing system. Many Meroitic inscriptions survive, both on monuments and on papyrus. However, although scholars have ascertained the sound values of the alphabet, the Meroitic language itself is so different from other known languages that no one has been able to decipher Meroitic texts.

---

hieroglyphics (heye-ruh-GLIPH-iks)
hieratic (hahy-uh-RAT-tik)

The cult of Osiris.
Osiris (seated at right) receives a recently deceased individual, while attendants weigh the heart of another individual against a feather. This illustration comes from a papyrus copy of the *Book of the Dead* that was buried with a royal mummy.

The Development of Organized Religious Traditions

Amon and Re Like their counterparts in other world regions, Egyptians and Nubians believed that deities played prominent roles in the world and that proper cultivation of the gods was an important community responsibility. The principal gods revered in ancient Egypt were Amon and Re. Amon was originally a local Theban deity associated with the sun, creation, fertility, and reproductive forces, and Re was a sun god worshiped at Heliopolis. During the Old Kingdom and the Middle Kingdom, priests increasingly associated the two gods with each other and honored them in the combined cult of Amon-Re. At Heliopolis a massive temple complex supported priests who tended to the cult of Amon-Re and studied the heavens for astronomical purposes. When Egypt became an imperial power during the New Kingdom, some devotees suggested that Amon-Re might even be a universal god who presided over all the earth.

Aten and Monotheism For a brief period the cult of Amon-Re faced a monotheistic challenge from the god Aten, another deity associated with the sun. Aten's champion was Pharaoh Amenhotep IV (reigned 1353–1335 B.C.E.), who changed his name to Akhenaten in honor of his preferred deity. Akhenaten considered Aten the world's "sole god, like whom there is no other." Thus, unlike the priests of Amon-Re, most of whom viewed their god as one among many, Akhenaten and others devoted to Aten considered their deity the one and only true god. Their faith represented one of the world's earliest expressions of monotheism—the belief that a single god rules over all creation.

Akhenaten built a new capital city called Akhetaten ("Horizon of Aten," located at modern Tell el-Amarna), where broad streets, courtyards, and open temples allowed unobscured vision and constant veneration of the sun. He also dispatched agents to all parts of Egypt with instructions to encourage the worship of Aten and to chisel out the names of Amon, Re, and other gods from inscriptions on temples and public buildings. As long as Akhenaten lived, the cult of Aten flourished. But when the pharaoh died, traditional priests mounted a fierce counterattack, restored the cult of Amon-Re to privileged status, and nearly annihilated the worship and even the memory of Aten.

Mummification Whereas Mesopotamians believed with Gilgamesh that death brought an end to an individual's

Thinking about ENCOUNTERS

Encounters in Early African Societies

Egyptian and Nubian kingdoms were positioned in such a way that they provided crucial links between the Mediterranean basin on the one hand and sub-Saharan Africa on the other. *In what ways did trade and contact with distant regions shape Egyptian and Nubian ideas about religion, written expression, technology, and agriculture?*

existence, many Egyptians believed that death was not an end so much as a transition to a new dimension of existence. The yearning for immortality helps to explain the Egyptian practice of mummifying the dead. During the Old Kingdom, Egyptians believed that only the ruling elites would survive the grave, so they mummified only pharaohs and their close relatives. During the Middle and New Kingdoms, however, Egyptians came to think of eternal life as a condition available to normal mortals as well as members of the ruling classes. Mummification never became general practice in Egypt, but with or without preservation of the body, a variety of religious cults promised to lead individuals of all classes to immortality.

Cult of Osiris The cult of Osiris attracted particularly strong popular interest. According to the myths surrounding the cult, Osiris's evil brother Seth murdered him and scattered his dismembered parts throughout the land, but the victim's loyal wife, Isis, retrieved his parts and gave her husband a proper burial. Impressed by her devotion, the gods restored Osiris to life as god of the underworld, the dwelling place of the departed.

Egyptians also associated Osiris with immortality and honored him through a religious cult that demanded observance of high moral standards. Following their deaths, individual souls faced the judgment of Osiris, who had their hearts weighed against a feather symbolizing justice. Those with heavy hearts carrying a burden of evil and guilt did not merit immortality, whereas those of pure heart and honorable deeds gained the gift of eternal life. Thus Osiris's cult held out hope of eternal reward for those who behaved according to high moral standards.

Nubian Religious Beliefs Nubian peoples observed their own religious traditions, but very little written information survives to throw light on their religious beliefs. The most prominent of the Nubian deities was the lion-god Apedemak, often depicted with a bow and arrows, who served as war god for the kingdom of Kush. Another deity, Sebiumeker, was a creator god and divine guardian of his human devotees. Alongside native traditions, Egyptian religious cults were quite prominent in Nubia, especially after the aggressive pharaohs of the New Kingdom imposed Egyptian rule on the southern

Amon-Re (AH-mohn RAY)

Akhenaten (ahk-eh-NAH-ton)

Sebiumeker (sehb-ih-meh-kur)

lands. Nubian peoples did not mummify the remains of their deceased, but they built pyramids similar to those of Egypt, although smaller, and they embraced several Egyptian gods. Amon was the preeminent Egyptian deity in Nubia as in Egypt itself. Osiris was also popular in Nubia, where he sometimes appeared in association with the native deity Sebiumeker. However, Egyptian gods did not displace native gods so much as they joined them in the Nubian pantheon. Indeed, Nubians often identified Egyptian gods with their own deities or endowed the foreign gods with traits important in Nubian society.

BANTU MIGRATIONS AND EARLY AGRICULTURAL SOCIETIES OF SUB-SAHARAN AFRICA

Like their counterparts in southwest Asia, Egyptian and Nubian societies participated in a much larger world of interaction and exchange. Mesopotamian societies developed under the strong influences of long-distance trade, diffusions of technological innovations, the spread of cultural traditions, and the far-flung migrations of Semitic and Indo-European peoples. Similarly, quite apart from their dealings with southwest Asian and Mediterranean peoples, Egyptian and Nubian societies developed in the context of widespread interaction and exchange in sub-Saharan Africa. The most prominent processes unfolding in sub-Saharan Africa during ancient times were the migrations of Bantu-speaking peoples and the establishment of agricultural societies in regions where Bantu speakers settled. Just as Sudanic agriculture spread to the Nile valley and provided an economic foundation for the development

of Egyptian and Nubian societies, it also spread to most other regions of Africa south of the Sahara and supported the emergence of distinctive agricultural societies.

The Dynamics of Bantu Expansion

The Bantu Among the most influential peoples of sub-Saharan Africa in ancient times were those who spoke Bantu languages. The original Bantu language was one of many related tongues in the larger Niger-Congo family of languages widely spoken in west Africa after 4000 B.C.E. The earliest Bantu speakers inhabited a region embracing the eastern part of modern Nigeria and the southern part of modern Cameroon. Members of this community referred to themselves as *bantu* (meaning "persons" or "people"). The earliest Bantu speakers settled mostly along the banks of rivers, which they navigated in canoes, and in open areas of the region's forests. They cultivated yams and oil palms, and in later centuries they added millet and sorghum. They also kept goats and raised guinea fowl. They lived in clan-based villages headed by chiefs who conducted religious rituals and represented their communities in dealings with neighboring villages. They

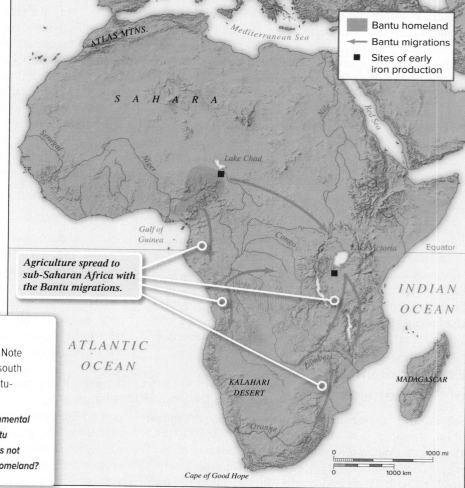

Agriculture spread to sub-Saharan Africa with the Bantu migrations.

MAP 2.3

Bantu migrations, 2000 B.C.E.–1000 C.E. Note that Bantu migrations proceeded to the south and east of the original homeland of Bantu-speaking peoples.

To what extent do technological and environmental factors help to explain the extent of the Bantu migrations? Why did Bantu-speaking peoples not migrate also to the north and west of their homeland?

traded regularly with hunting and gathering peoples who inhabited the tropical forests. Bantu cultivators provided these forest peoples with pottery and stone axes in exchange for meat, honey, and other forest products.

Bantu Migrations Unlike most of their neighbors, the Bantu displayed an early readiness to migrate to new territories. By 3000 B.C.E. they were slowly spreading south into the west African forest, and after 2000 B.C.E. they expanded rapidly to the south toward the Congo River basin and east toward the Great Lakes, absorbing local populations of hunting, gathering, and fishing peoples into their own agricultural societies. Over the centuries, as some groups of Bantu speakers settled and others moved on to new territories, their languages differentiated into more than five hundred distinct but related tongues. (Today more than ninety million people speak Bantu languages, which collectively constitute the most prominent family of languages in sub-Saharan Africa.) Like the Indo-European migrations discussed in chapter 1, the Bantu migrations were not mass movements of peoples. Instead, they were intermittent and incremental processes that resulted in the gradual spread of Bantu languages and ethnic communities, as small groups moved to new territories and established settlements, which then became foundations for further expansion. By 1000 C.E. Bantu-speaking peoples occupied most of Africa south of the equator.

The precise motives of the early Bantu migrants are unknown, but it seems likely that population pressures drove the migrations. When settlements grew uncomfortably large and placed strains on available resources, small groups left their parent communities and moved to new territories. As they moved, Bantu migrants placed pressures on the forest dwellers, sometimes clashing with them over land resources but often intermarrying and absorbing them into Bantu agricultural society.

Iron and Migration After about 1000 B.C.E., the pace of Bantu migrations quickened, as Bantu peoples began to produce iron tools and weapons. Iron tools enabled Bantu cultivators to clear land and expand the zone of agriculture more effectively than before, while iron weapons strengthened the hand of Bantu groups against adversaries and competitors for land or other resources. Thus iron metallurgy supported rapid population growth among the Bantu while also lending increased momentum to their continuing migrations.

Early Agricultural Societies of Sub-Saharan Africa

Several smaller migrations took place alongside the spread of Bantu peoples in sub-Saharan Africa. Between 3500 and 1000 B.C.E., southern Kushite herders pushed into parts of east Africa (modern-day Kenya and Tanzania), while Sudanese cultivators and herders moved into the upper reaches of the Nile River (now southern Sudan and northern Uganda). Meanwhile, Mande-speaking peoples who cultivated African rice established communities along the Atlantic estuaries of west Africa, and other peoples speaking Niger-Congo languages spread the cultivation of okra from forest regions throughout much of west Africa.

Spread of Agriculture Among the most important effects of Bantu and other migrations was the establishment of agricultural societies throughout most of sub-Saharan Africa. Between 1000 and 500 B.C.E., cultivators extended the cultivation of yams and grains deep into east and south Africa (modern-day Kenya, Malawi, Mozambique, Zimbabwe, and South Africa), while herders introduced sheep and cattle to the region. About the same time, Bantu and other peoples speaking Niger-Congo languages spread the intensive cultivation of yams, oil palms, millet, and sorghum throughout west and central Africa while also introducing sheep, pigs, and cattle to the region. By the late centuries B.C.E., agriculture had reached almost all of sub-Saharan Africa except for densely forested regions and deserts.

As cultivation and herding spread throughout sub-Saharan Africa, agricultural peoples built distinctive societies and cultural traditions. Most Bantu and other peoples lived in communities of a few hundred individuals led by chiefs. Many peoples recognized groups known as age sets, or age grades, consisting of individuals born within a few years of one another. Members of each age set jointly assumed responsibility for tasks appropriate to their levels of strength, energy, maturity, and experience. During their early years, for example, members of an age set might perform light public chores. At maturity, members jointly underwent elaborate initiation rites that introduced them to adult society. Older men cultivated fields and provided military service, and women tended to domestic chores and sometimes traded at markets. In later years, members of age sets served as community leaders and military officers.

African Cultivators African cultivators and herders also developed distinctive cultural and religious traditions. Both Sudanic and Niger-Congo peoples (including Bantu speakers), for example, held monotheistic religious beliefs by 5000 B.C.E. Sudanic peoples recognized a single, impersonal divine force that they regarded as the source of both good and evil. They believed that this divine force could take the form of individual spirits, and they often addressed the divine force through prayers to intermediary spirits. The divine force itself, however, was ultimately responsible for rewards and punishments meted out to human beings. For their part, Niger-Congo peoples recognized a single god originally called Nyamba who created the world and established the principles that would govern its development, then stepped back and allowed the world to proceed on its own. Individuals did not generally address this distant creator god directly but, rather, offered their prayers to ancestor spirits and local territorial spirits believed to inhabit the world and influence the fortunes of living humans. Proper attention to these spirits would ensure them good fortune, they believed, whereas their neglect would bring punishment or adversity from disgruntled spirits.

Individual communities frequently borrowed religious elements from other communities and adapted their beliefs to changing circumstances or fresh understandings of the world. Migrations of Bantu and other peoples in particular resulted in a great deal of cultural mixing and

mingling, and religious beliefs often spread to new communities in the wake of population movements. After 1000 B.C.E., for example, as they encountered Sudanic peoples and their reverence of a single divine force that was the source of good and evil, many Bantu peoples associated the god Nyamba with goodness. As a result, this formerly distant creator god took on a new moral dimension that brought him closer to the lives of individuals. Thus changing religious beliefs sometimes reflected widespread interactions among African societies.

SUMMARY

Like other world regions, Africa was a land in which peoples of different societies regularly traded, communicated, and interacted with one another from ancient times. African agriculture and herding first emerged in the Sudan, then spread both to the Nile River valley and to arable lands throughout sub-Saharan Africa. Agricultural crops and domesticated animals from southwest Asia soon made their way into the Nile valley. With its broad floodplains, Egypt became an especially productive land, while Nubia supported a smaller but flourishing society. Throughout the Nile valley, abundant agricultural surpluses supported dense populations and the construction of prosperous societies with sophisticated cultural traditions. Elsewhere in sub-Saharan Africa, populations were less dense, but the migrations of Bantu and other peoples facilitated the spread of agriculture, and later iron metallurgy as well, throughout most of the region. Meanwhile, the Nile River served as a route of trade and communication linking Egypt and the Mediterranean basin to the north with the Sudan and sub-Saharan Africa to the south. Only in the context of migration, trade, communication, and interaction is it possible to understand the early development of African societies.

FOR FURTHER READING

Basil Davidson. *Lost Cities of Africa*. Rev. ed. Boston, 1970. Popular account with discussions of Kush and Meroë.

Christopher Ehret. *The Civilizations of Africa: A History to 1800*. Charlottesville, Va., 2001. An important contribution that views Africa in the context of world history.

John L. Foster. *Ancient Egyptian Literature: An Anthology*. Austin, 2001. A useful and readily accessible selection of literary works from ancient Egypt.

Zahi Hawass. *Silent Images: Women in Pharaonic Egypt*. New York, 2000. A prominent archaeologist draws on both textual and artifactual evidence in throwing light on women's experiences in ancient Egypt.

T. G. H. James. *Pharaoh's People: Scenes from Life in Imperial Egypt*. London, 1984. Draws on archaeological and literary scholarship in reconstructing daily life in ancient Egypt.

Barry J. Kemp. *Ancient Egypt: Anatomy of a Civilization*. New York, 2006. Wide-ranging and reflective analysis emphasizing Egyptian identity.

Roderick James McIntosh. *The Peoples of the Middle Niger: The Island of Gold*. Oxford, 1998. Fascinating volume emphasizing the environmental context of west African history.

Catharine H. Roehrig, Renée Dreyfus, and Cathleen A. Keller, eds. *Hatshepsut: From Queen to Pharaoh*. New York, 2005. Brilliantly illustrated volume focusing on the reign of the New Kingdom's female pharaoh.

Jan Vansina. *Paths in the Rainforests: Toward a History of Political Tradition in Equatorial Africa*. Madison, 1990. A brilliant synthesis concentrating on central Africa by one of the world's foremost historians of Africa.

Derek A. Welsby. *The Kingdom of Kush: The Napatan and Meroitic Empires*. London, 1996. Draws on both written and archaeological sources in tracing the development of ancient Nubia and charting its relationship with Egypt.

STUDY TERMS

Akhenaten (40)
Amon-Re (40)
Archaic Period (31)
Aten (40)
Bantu (28)
Bantu migrations (42)
cult of Osiris (40)
Egypt (29)
Hatshepsut (35)
hieratic script (39)
hieroglyphics (39)
Hyksos (31)
Kush (31)

Menes (30)
Meroitic writing (39)
Middle Kingdom (31)
mummification (27)
New Kingdom (32)
Nile River (29)
Nubia (27)
Old Kingdom (31)
pharaoh (31)
pyramids (31)
Sebiumeker (40)
Tuthmosis III (32)

Early Societies in South and East Asia
CHAPTER 3

A unicorn seal from Harappan society, dating from about 2400 B.C.E.

EYEWITNESS:

Warrior Gods and Sage Kings: Heroes in South and East Asia

For a god, Indra was a very rambunctious fellow. According to the stories told about him by the Aryans (Sanskrit for "noble ones"), Indra had few if any peers in fighting, feasting, or drinking. The Aryans were a nomadic and herding people who spoke an Indo-European language and who migrated to south Asia over a prolonged period after about 1500 C.E. In the early days of their migrations they took Indra as their chief deity. The Aryans told dozens of stories about Indra and sang hundreds of hymns in his honor. One favorite story described how Indra brought rain to the earth by killing a dragon who lived in the sky and hoarded water in the clouds. When the dragon fell to earth, its weight caused such turmoil in the atmosphere that it rained enough to fill seven rivers in northern India. Those rivers, in turn, brought life-giving waters to inhabitants of the region.

A warrior such as Indra was a useful god for the Aryans, because as they migrated into south Asia they fought among themselves and may have come into conflict with indigenous peoples already living there. For a thousand years and more, Aryans looked on the rowdy, raucous war god as a ready source of inspiration as they sought to build a society in an already occupied land.

In ancient China, heroic figures were quite different. Legends tell stories of heroes who invented agriculture, domesticated animals, taught people to marry and live in families, created music, introduced the calendar, and instructed people in the arts and crafts. Most dashing of those heroes was a sage-king named Yu, who helped lay the foundations of Chinese society by rescuing China from the devastating floodwaters of the Yellow River. Rather than dam the river as his predecessors had done, Yu dredged it and dug canals parallel to the river to allow the floodwaters to flow harmlessly out to sea.

The legends say that Yu worked on the river for thirteen years without ever returning home. Once, he passed by the gate to his home and heard his wife and children crying out of loneliness, but he continued on his way rather than interrupt his flood-control work. Because he tamed the Yellow River, Yu became a popular hero, and poets praised the man who protected fields and villages from deadly and destructive floods. By exalting Yu as an exemplar of virtue, Chinese moralists promoted the values of social harmony and selfless, dedicated work that the sage-king represented.

Archaeological excavations show that China was a site of paleolithic communities as early as four hundred thousand years ago. In south Asia, humans appeared at least two hundred thousand years ago, long before the Aryans introduced Indra to south Asia. Yet, as in Mesopotamia and Egypt, population pressures in both east and south Asia induced human groups to begin experimenting with agriculture. By 7000 B.C.E. agriculture had taken root in India's Indus River valley, and by 3000 B.C.E. it had spread throughout much of the Indian subcontinent. In roughly the same period, between 7000 and 5000 B.C.E., people in China's Yangzi River valley domesticated and became dependent on rice, while people farther north in the Yellow River valley learned to cultivate and depend on millet.

Yu (yoo)

CHRONOLOGY

SOUTH ASIA

8000–7000 B.C.E.	Beginnings of agriculture in south Asia
2500–2000 B.C.E.	High point of Harappan society
1900 B.C.E.	Beginning of Harappan decline
1500 B.C.E.	Beginning of Aryan migration to India
1500–500 B.C.E.	Vedic age
1400–900 B.C.E.	Composition of the *Rig Veda*
1000 B.C.E.	Early Aryan migrations into the Ganges River valley
1000 B.C.E.	Emergence of *varna* distinctions
1000–500 B.C.E.	Formation of regional kingdoms in northern India
800–400 B.C.E.	Composition of the principal Upanishads
750 B.C.E.	Establishment of first Aryan cities in the Ganges valley
500 B.C.E.	Aryan migrations to the Deccan Plateau

EAST ASIA

2200–1766 B.C.E.	Xia dynasty
1766–1122 B.C.E.	Shang dynasty
1122–256 B.C.E.	Zhou dynasty
403–221 B.C.E.	Period of the Warring States

In both south and east Asia, agricultural surpluses encouraged the growth of complex societies. Indeed, people in both locations developed bustling cities. By 3000 B.C.E. people in India's Indus River valley built south Asia's first cities in what has come to be known as *Harappan* society. Harappan society collapsed about 1500 B.C.E., and it seems probable that Indo-European Aryan migrations into India increased in intensity at around the same time. Eventually, it seems clear that Aryan peoples interacted and intermarried with the indigenous peoples of India, and that combination led to the development of a distinctive society and a rich cultural tradition. In China, three dynastic states based in the Yellow River valley brought much of China under their authority during the second millennium B.C.E. In the process they forged many local communities into a larger Chinese society. At the same time, all three dynasties had frequent dealings with neighboring peoples to the west, who linked China to other societies and brought knowledge and technologies from afar. As in early Mesopotamia and Egypt, then, complex society in both south and east Asia promoted the development of distinctive social and cultural traditions in the context of cross-cultural interaction and exchange.

HARAPPAN SOCIETY

Like societies in Mesopotamia and Egypt, the earliest urban society in south Asia was built by indigenous Indian peoples in the valley of a river, the Indus, whose waters were available for irrigation of crops. This society—called Harappan society after one of its two chief cities—thrived between about 3000 B.C.E. and 1900 B.C.E. Scholars believe that as Harappan society fell into decline over the next four hundred years, Indo-European migrants from the northwest began to settle in south Asia. Over time, the two groups mixed and became indistinguishable from each other. In the process, they created a unique social and religious order that helped shape south Asian society until modern times.

Although scholars know that cities were evolving in the Indus region by 3000 B.C.E., it is impossible to follow the development of Harappan society in detail. One reason is that many of the earliest Harappan physical remains lie below the existing water table and thus are inaccessible to archaeologists. Another reason is the lack of deciphered written records, because scholars have so far been unable to understand the complex pictographic Harappan script. As a result, our understanding of Harappan society depends entirely on the study of accessible material remains.

The Indus River If the Greek historian Herodotus had known of Harappan society, he might have called it "the gift of the Indus." Like the Nile, the Indus draws its waters from rain and melting snow in towering mountains—in this case, the Hindu Kush and the Himalayas. As the waters reach the lowlands, the Indus deposits huge quantities of silt on its banks. Although the Indus periodically caused extensive destruction from flooding, it did make agricultural society possible in northern India. Early cultivators sowed their crops along its banks in September, after the flood receded, and harvested their crops the following spring.

As in Mesopotamia and Egypt, agricultural surpluses in India vastly increased the food supply, stimulated population growth, and supported the establishment of cities and specialized labor. Between 3000 and 2500 B.C.E., the agricultural

Harappan (huh-RUHP-puhn)
Indus (IN-duhs)

surplus of the Indus valley fed two large cities, Harappa and Mohenjo-daro, as well as subordinate cities and a vast agricultural hinterland. Harappan society embraced much of modern-day Pakistan and a large part of northern India as well—a territory of about 1.3 million square kilometers (502,000 square miles)—and thus was considerably larger than either Mesopotamian or Egyptian society.

Harappa and Mohenjo-daro No evidence survives concerning the Harappan political system, although archaeological excavations do not suggest a royal or imperial authority. However, both Harappa and Mohenjo-daro had city walls, a fortified citadel, and a large granary, suggesting that they served as centers of political authority and sites for the collection and redistribution of taxes paid in the form of grain. The two cities represented a considerable investment of human labor and other resources: both featured marketplaces, temples, public buildings, extensive residential districts, and broad streets laid out on a carefully planned grid.

The two cities clearly established the patterns that shaped the larger society: weights, measures, architectural styles, and even brick sizes were consistent throughout the land. This standardization no doubt reflects the prominence of Harappa and Mohenjo-daro as powerful and wealthy cities whose influence touched all parts of Harappan society,

as well as the degree to which the Indus River facilitated trade, travel, and communication among the far-flung regions of Harappan society.

Specialized Labor and Trade Like other complex societies in ancient times, Harappa engaged in trade, both domestic and foreign. Pottery, tools, and decorative items produced in Harappa and Mohenjo-daro found their way to all corners of the Indus valley, while the cities imported precious metals and stones from neighboring peoples in Persia and the Hindu Kush mountains. During the period about 2300 to 1750 B.C.E., they also traded with Mesopotamians, mostly via ships that followed the coastline of the Arabian Sea between the mouth of the Indus River and the Persian Gulf.

Harappan Society and Culture

Social Distinctions Like societies in Mesopotamia and Egypt, Harappan society generated considerable wealth. Excavations at Mohenjo-daro show that at its high point, from about 2500 to 2000 B.C.E., the city was a thriving economic center with a population of about forty thousand. The wealth of Harappan society, like that in Mesopotamia and Egypt, encouraged the formation of social distinctions. It is clear from Harappan dwellings that rich and poor lived in very different styles. In Mohenjo-daro, for example, many people lived in one-room tenements in barracks-like structures, but there were also individual houses of two and three stories with a dozen rooms and an interior courtyard, as well as a few even larger houses. Almost all houses had

MAP 3.1

Harappan society and its neighbors, ca. 2000 B.C.E. Compare Harappan society with its Mesopotamian and Egyptian contemporaries with respect to size.

What conditions would have been necessary to enable trade to flow between the Indus River valley and Mesopotamia?

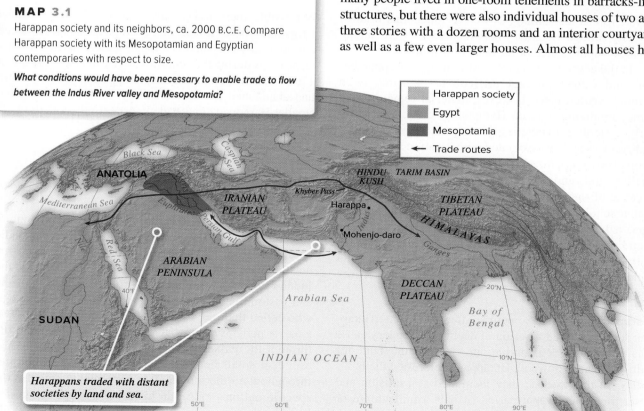

Harappans traded with distant societies by land and sea.

Mohenjo-daro.
This aerial view of the excavations at Mohenjo-daro illustrates the careful planning and precise layout of the city.

What does the layout of this city suggest about the planning abilities of the city's builders?

private rooms for bathing, as well as toilets that drained into city sewage systems, which themselves were among the most sophisticated of the ancient world.

In the absence of deciphered writing, Harappan beliefs and values are very difficult to interpret. Even without written texts, however, material remains shed some tantalizing light on Harappan society. Like other early agricultural societies, Harappans venerated gods and goddesses they associated with creation and procreation. They recognized a mother goddess and a horned fertility god, and they held trees and animals sacred because of their associations with vital forces. In fact, many scholars believe that some Harappan deities survived the collapse of the larger society and later found places in the Hindu pantheon, because they have noticed striking similarities between Harappan and Hindu deities—especially those associated with fertility and procreation.

Harappan Decline Sometime after 1900 B.C.E. Harappan society entered a period of decline. A primary cause was ecological degradation: in clearing the land for cultivation and firewood, Harappans deforested the Indus valley. In the process, they facilitated soil erosion and desertification. Over a period of half a millennium or more, most of the Indus valley became a desert: agriculture

is possible there today only with the aid of artificial irrigation. These climatic and ecological changes reduced agricultural yields, and Harappan society faced a subsistence crisis during the centuries after 1900 B.C.E. By about 1700 B.C.E. the populations of Harappa and Mohenjo-daro had abandoned the cities, and by 1500 B.C.E. even the smaller Harappan cities had almost entirely collapsed.

THE INDO-EUROPEAN MIGRATIONS AND EARLY VEDIC INDIA

Some scholars believe that during the second millennium B.C.E., as Harappan society declined, bands of nomadic herders filtered into the Indian subcontinent from the northwest mountain passes and settled throughout the Indus valley and beyond. Most prominent were nomadic and pastoral peoples speaking Indo-European languages who called themselves Aryans ("noble ones"). By 1500 B.C.E. or perhaps somewhat earlier, they had begun to file through the passes of the Hindu Kush mountains and establish small herding and agricultural communities throughout northern India. It is important to note that the specific outlines of Aryan history are deeply contested by contemporary scholars. Disagreements are especially strong between linguists who trace Aryan migrations via the traces left through language, archeologists who have found little material evidence of Aryan artifacts, and some Indian classical scholars who have argued that the theory of Aryan migration was a false narrative concocted by European imperialists to divide the Indian people. In spite of these controversies, however, most scholars still believe that Indo-Aryan migrants did filter into India around or before 1500 B.C.E., and that they then played a prominent role in shaping Indian society in the centuries afterward.

Although there is much scholars don't yet know about Indo-Aryan migrations, they appear to have taken place over several centuries: by no means did the arrival of the Aryans constitute an invasion or an organized military campaign. It is likely that Indo-Aryan migrants sometimes clashed with peoples already settled in India, but there is no indication that they conquered or destroyed Harappan society. By the time the Indo-Aryans entered India, internal problems had already brought Harappan society to the point of collapse. During the centuries after 1500 B.C.E., indigenous and Indo-Aryan peoples intermarried, interacted, and laid social and cultural foundations that would influence Indian society to the present day.

The Aryans and India

The Early Aryans When they entered India, the Aryans depended heavily on a pastoral economy. They especially prized their horses and herds of cattle. Horses were quite valuable because of their expense and rarity: horses do not breed well in India, so it was necessary for Aryans to replenish their stock by importing animals from central Asia. Like their Indo-European cousins to the north, the Aryans harnessed horses to carts, and they also hitched them to chariots for use in warfare. Meanwhile, cattle became the principal measure of wealth in early Aryan society. The Aryans consumed both dairy products and beef, and they often calculated prices in terms of cattle.

The Vedas The early Aryans did not use writing but instead preserved extensive collections of religious and literary works by transmitting them orally from one generation to another in their sacred language, Sanskrit. The earliest of these orally transmitted works were the *Vedas,* which were collections of hymns, songs, prayers, and rituals honoring the various gods of the Aryans. There are four *Vedas,* the earliest and most important of which is the *Rig Veda,* a collection of 1,028 hymns addressed to Aryan gods. Although it was compiled between about 1400 and 900 B.C.E., Aryan priests committed the *Rig Veda* to writing only in about 600 B.C.E.

While the *Vedas* represent a priestly perspective on affairs because of their function in transmitting religious knowledge, they also shed considerable light on early Aryan society in India. Indeed, in view of their importance as historical sources, scholars refer to Indian history during the millennium between 1500 and 500 B.C.E. as the Vedic age.

The Vedic Age The *Vedas* reflect a boisterous society in which the Aryans clashed repeatedly with indigenous peoples—referred to in the texts as *dasas,* meaning "enemies" or "subject peoples"—already living in India. The *Vedas* identify Indra, the Aryan war god and military hero, as one who ravaged citadels, smashed dams, and destroyed forts the way age consumes cloth garments. These characterizations in the *Vedas* suggest that competition over land and resources fueled intermittent conflict between Aryan and indigenous peoples, although scholars have found little archeological evidence of such clashes. The Aryans also fought ferociously among themselves. They did not have a state or common government but, rather, formed hundreds of chiefdoms organized around herding communities and agricultural villages. Because of their close proximity, this practice encouraged competition for resources and created enormous potential for conflict.

Aryan Migrations in India During the early centuries of the Vedic age, Aryan groups settled in the Punjab, the upper Indus River valley that straddles the modern-day border between northern India and Pakistan. After 1000 B.C.E. they began to settle in the area between the Himalayan foothills and the Ganges River, where they learned to make iron tools and to practice agriculture. Agricultural surpluses encouraged larger populations and more complex social organization, and by about 750 B.C.E., Aryans had established the first small cities in the Ganges River valley. Population growth also encouraged further migration. Thus, by 500 B.C.E. Aryan groups had migrated as far south as the northern Deccan, a plateau region in the southern cone of the Indian subcontinent about 1,500 kilometers (950 miles) south of the Punjab.

As they settled into permanent communities and began to rely more on agriculture than on herding, the Aryans gradually lost the tribal political organization they had brought into India and instead evolved more formal political institutions. Indeed, between 1000 and 500 B.C.E., tribal chiefdoms increasingly developed into regional kingdoms, and for centuries these became the most common form of political organization on the subcontinent.

Aryan (AIR-ee-uhn)
Vedas (VAY-duhs)

Origins of the Caste System

Although the Aryans did not build large imperial states, they did construct a well-defined social order. In fact, in some ways their social hierarchy served to maintain the order and stability that states and political structures guaranteed in other societies. The Aryan social structure, known today as the caste system, rested on sharp hereditary distinctions between individuals and groups, according to their occupations and roles in society.

Caste and Varna Caste identities developed gradually as the Aryans established settlements throughout India. Initially, increased interaction with indigenous peoples probably prompted Aryans to base social distinctions on either Aryan or indigenous ancestry. In part, those distinctions may have arisen from differences in complexion between the Aryans, who referred to themselves as "wheat-colored," and the darker-skinned people native to India. Indeed, the Aryan term *varna,* which refers to the major social divisions, comes from the Sanskrit word meaning "color." However, over time Aryans and indigenous peoples mixed, mingled, interacted, and intermarried to the point that distinguishing between them was impossible.

After about 1000 B.C.E. the Aryans increasingly recognized four main *varnas: brahmins* (priests), *kshatriyas* (warriors and aristocrats), *vaishyas* (cultivators, artisans, and merchants), and *shudras* (landless peasants and serfs). Some centuries later, probably about the end of the Vedic age, they added the category of the *untouchables*—people who performed dirty or unpleasant tasks, such as butchering animals or handling dead bodies, and who theoretically became so polluted from their work that their very touch could defile individuals of higher status.

Subcastes and Jati Until about the sixth century B.C.E., the four *varnas* described Vedic society reasonably well. Because they did not live in cities and did not yet pursue many specialized occupations, the Aryans had little need for a more complicated social order. Over the longer term, however, a much more elaborate scheme of social classification emerged. As Vedic society became more complex and generated increasingly specialized occupations, the caste system served as the umbrella for a complicated hierarchy of subcastes known as *jati,* which were hereditary categories largely determined by occupation. By the eighteenth and nineteenth centuries C.E., in its most fully articulated form, the system featured several

varna (VUHR-nuh)
brahmins (BRAH-minz)
kshatriyas (SHUHT-ree-uhs)
vaishyas (VEYESH-yuhs)
shudras (SHOO-druhs)

thousand *jati,* which prescribed individuals' roles in society in minute detail.

Castes and subcastes deeply influenced the lives of individual Indians through much of history. Members of a *jati* ate with one another and intermarried, and they cared for those who became ill or fell on hard times. Elaborate rules dictated forms of address and specific behavior appropriate for communication between members of different castes and subcastes. Violation of *jati* rules could result in expulsion from the larger group. That penalty was serious, since an outcast individual could not function well and sometimes could not even survive when shunned by members of the larger society.

Caste and Social Mobility The caste system never functioned in an absolutely rigid or inflexible manner but, rather, operated so as to accommodate social change. Individuals sometimes prospered on the basis of their own initiative, or else they could fall on hard times and move down in the social hierarchy. More often, however, social mobility came about as members of a *jati* improved their condition collectively. Achieving upward mobility was not an easy matter—it often entailed moving to a new area, or at least taking on a new line of work—but the possibility of improving individual or group status helped to dissipate social tensions. In addition, the caste system enabled foreign peoples to find a place in Indian society by allowing newcomers to organize into well-defined groups that eventually came to adopt caste identities.

By the end of the Vedic age, caste distinctions had become central institutions in Aryan India. Whereas in other lands states and empires maintained public order, in India the caste system served as a principal foundation of social stability. Individuals have often identified more closely with their *jati* than with their cities or states, and castes have played a large role in maintaining social discipline in India.

The Lawbook of Manu While building an elaborate social hierarchy on the foundations of caste and *varna* distinctions, the Aryans also constructed a strongly patriarchal social order on the basis of gender distinctions. At the time of their migrations into India, men already dominated Aryan society. All priests, warriors, and tribal chiefs were men, and the Aryans recognized descent through the male line. Women influenced affairs within their own families but enjoyed no public authority. As the Aryans settled in agricultural communities throughout India, they maintained this thoroughly patriarchal society. Only males could inherit property, unless a family had no male heirs, and only men could preside over family rituals that honored departed ancestors.

A text from about the first century B.C.E., called the *Lawbook of Manu,* illustrates the patriarchal ideologies that helped structure Indian society. Although composed after the Vedic age, the *Lawbook of Manu* reflected the society constructed earlier under Aryan influence. The author advised men to treat women with honor and respect, but he insisted that women remain subject to the guidance of the principal men in their lives. The *Lawbook* also specified that the most important duties of women were to bear children and maintain wholesome homes for their families.

RELIGION IN THE VEDIC AGE

As the caste system emerged and helped to organize Indian society, distinctive cultural and religious traditions also took shape. The Aryans entered India with traditions and beliefs that met the needs of a mobile and often violent society. As they spread throughout India and mixed with indigenous peoples, however, the Aryans encountered new religious ideas they considered intriguing and persuasive. The resulting fusion of Aryan traditions with indigenous beliefs and values laid the foundation for Hinduism, a faith immensely popular in India and parts of southeast Asia for more than two millennia.

Aryan Religion

As in Mesopotamia, Egypt, and other lands, religious values in India reflected the larger society. For example, during the early centuries following the Aryan migrations, the focus on Indra the war god testified to the instability and turbulence of early Vedic society. Also important to those early beliefs was the proper performance of ritual sacrifices. Through sacrifices, Aryans hoped to win the favor of the gods to ensure military success, large families, long life, and abundant herds of cattle. But those rewards required constant attention to religious ritual: proper honor for the gods called for households to have brahmins perform no fewer than five sacrifices per day—a time-consuming and expensive obligation.

Spirituality As the centuries passed, many Aryans became dissatisfied with the sacrificial cults of the *Vedas,* which increasingly seemed like sterile rituals rather than a genuine means of communicating with the gods. Beginning about 800 B.C.E. many thoughtful individuals left their villages and retreated to the forests of the Ganges valley, where they lived as hermits

Aryan woman and child.
This greenish blue schist carving illustrates the devotion of a mother to her child.

and reflected on the relationships between human beings, the world, and the gods. These mystics drew considerable inspiration from the religious beliefs of indigenous peoples, who often worshiped nature spirits that they associated with fertility and the generation of new life. Some scholars also argue that indigenous people may have believed that human souls took on new physical forms after the deaths of their bodily hosts, although the evidence is limited. Nevertheless, over time the notion that souls could experience transmigration and reincarnation— that an individual soul could depart one body at death and become associated with another body through a new birth—intrigued thoughtful people and encouraged them to try to understand the principles that governed the fate of souls. As a result, a remarkable tradition of religious speculation emerged.

The Blending of Aryan and Indigenous Values

This tradition achieved its fullest development in a body of works known as the *Upanishads,* which began to appear late in the Vedic age, about 800 to 400 B.C.E. The word *upanishad* literally means "a sitting in front of," and it refers to the practice of disciples gathering before a sage for discussion of religious issues. The Upanishads often took the form of dialogues that explored the *Vedas* and the religious issues that they raised.

Brahman, the Universal Soul The Upanishads taught that each person participates in a larger cosmic order and is one with a universal soul, known as *Brahman.* Whereas the physical world is a theater of change, instability, and illusion, *Brahman* is an eternal, unchanging, permanent foundation for all things that exist—hence the only genuine reality. The authors of the Upanishads believed that individual souls were born into the physical world, not once, but many times: they believed that souls appeared most often as humans, but sometimes as animals, and possibly even occasionally as plants or other vegetable matter.

Teachings of the Upanishads The Upanishads developed several specific doctrines that helped to explain this line of thought. One was the doctrine of *samsara,* which held that upon death, individual souls go temporarily to the World of the Fathers and then return to earth in a new

Upanishads (oo-pah-NIH-shuhds)
samsara (suhm-SAH-ruh)

Thinking about **TRADITIONS**

Traditions in Early Societies in South and East Asia

In the period between 3000 and 500 B.C.E., sophisticated, stratified, and wealthy states developed in both China and India. Although each society shared concerns with morality and ethics, their approaches to religion and social organization were quite distinct. *What were the main differences between the two sets of societies with respect to political, economic, and social organization?*

incarnation. Another was the doctrine of *karma,* which accounted for the specific incarnations that souls experienced. According to this doctrine, individuals who lived virtuous lives and fulfilled all their duties could expect rebirth into a purer and more honorable existence—for example, into a higher and more distinguished caste. Those who accumulated a heavy burden of karma, however, would suffer in a future incarnation by being reborn into a difficult existence, or perhaps even into the body of an animal or an insect.

The Upanishads also encouraged the cultivation of personal integrity—a self-knowledge that would incline individuals naturally toward both ethical behavior and union with Brahman. In addition, they taught respect for all living things, animal as well as human. Animal bodies, after all, might well hold incarnations of unfortunate souls suffering the effects of a heavy debt of karma. A vegetarian diet thus became a common feature of the ascetic regime.

Yet even under the best of circumstances, the cycle of rebirth involved a certain amount of pain and suffering. The authors of the Upanishads sought to escape the cycle altogether and attain the state of *moksha,* which they characterized as a deep, dreamless sleep that came with permanent liberation from physical incarnation. This goal was difficult to reach, since it entailed severing all ties to the physical world and identifying with the ultimate reality of Brahman, the universal soul. The two principal means to the goal were asceticism and meditation, which could help individuals purge themselves of desire for the comforts of the physical world.

Religion and Vedic Society Just as the Aryan focus on Indra reflected early Aryan society, so the religious views of the Upanishads dovetailed with the social order of

the late Vedic age. Indeed, the doctrines of samsara and karma certainly reinforced the Vedic social order: they explained why individuals were born into their castes, and they encouraged individuals to observe their caste duties in hopes of enjoying a more comfortable and honorable incarnation in the future. However, these doctrines were not simply cynical means of controlling Vedic society. Indeed, the sages who gave voice to these doctrines were conscientiously attempting to deal with meaningful spiritual and intellectual problems. Like Greek philosophers, Christian theologians, and many others, the authors of the Upanishads sought ultimate truth and certain knowledge in an ideal world that transcends our own.

POLITICAL ORGANIZATION IN EARLY CHINA

As in the Indus River valley of India, fertile river valleys in China allowed villages and towns to flourish along their banks. The most important of these valleys were those of the Yellow and Yangzi rivers, which supported settlements of agriculturalists after about 7000 B.C.E. By the late years of the third millennium B.C.E., these small settlements began to give way to much larger regional states. Among the most notable were perhaps those of the Xia, and certainly the powerful Shang, and Zhou dynasties, which progressively brought much of China under their authority and laid a political foundation for the development of a distinctive Chinese society.

The Yellow River Like the Indus, the Yellow River is boisterous and unpredictable. It rises in the mountains bordering the high plateau of Tibet, and it courses almost 4,700 kilometers (2,920 miles) before emptying into the Yellow Sea. It takes its name, Huang He, meaning "Yellow River," from the vast quantities of light-colored soil that it picks up along its route. So much soil becomes suspended in the Yellow River that the water turns yellow. The soil gradually builds up, raising the river bed and forcing the water out of its established path, periodically unleashing tremendous floods. The Yellow River has caused so much destruction that it has earned the nickname "China's Sorrow." Despite the periodic damage caused by the Yellow River, however, the soil it deposits is extremely fertile and easy to work, so even before the introduction of metal tools, cultivators using wooden implements could bring in generous harvests. As in India, agricultural surpluses resulted in increased population, which eventually gave rise to complex societies.

karma (KAHR-mah)

moksha (MOHK-shuh)

Yangzi (YAHNG-zuh)

Xia (shyah)

Zhou (JOH)

Bronze vessel.
The delicate design of this bronze wine vessel displays the high level of craftsmanship during the late Shang dynasty.

Why did the elite classes prefer objects made of bronze?

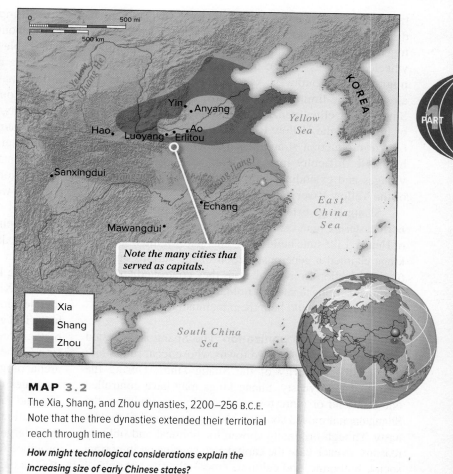

Note the many cities that served as capitals.

Xia
Shang
Zhou

MAP 3.2
The Xia, Shang, and Zhou dynasties, 2200–256 B.C.E. Note that the three dynasties extended their territorial reach through time.

How might technological considerations explain the increasing size of early Chinese states?

Chinese legends speak of three ancient dynasties—the Xia, the Shang, and the Zhou—that arose before the Qin and Han dynasties brought China under unified rule in the third century B.C.E. These dynasties were hereditary states that extended their control over progressively larger regions, although none of them embraced all the territory claimed by later Chinese dynasties.

The Xia and Shang Dynasties

The Xia Dynasty The Xia dynasty emerged about 2200 B.C.E. and was one of the earliest to organize public life in China on a large scale. Ancient legends credit the dynasty's founder, the sage-king Yu, with the organization of effective flood-control projects on the Yellow River: thus here, as in Mesopotamia and Egypt, the need to organize large-scale public works projects helped to establish recognized authorities and formal political institutions. Although no information survives about the political institutions of the Xia, the dynasty's rulers probably exercised power throughout the middle Yellow River valley by controlling the leaders of individual villages. By extending formal control over this region, the Xia dynasty established a precedent for hereditary monarchical rule in China.

The Shang Dynasty According to the legends, the last Xia king was an oppressive despot who lost his realm to the founder of the Shang dynasty. In fact, the Xia state probably gave way gradually before the Shang, which arose in a region to the south and east of the Xia realm. Tradition assigns the Shang dynasty to the period 1766 to 1122 B.C.E., and archaeological discoveries have largely confirmed those dates. Because the Shang dynasty left written records as well as material remains, the basic features of early Chinese society come into much clearer focus than they did during the Xia.

Bronze Metallurgy and Chariots Technology helps to explain the rise and success of the Shang dynasty. Bronze metallurgy transformed Chinese society during Shang

Qin (Chin)

times and indeed may well have enabled Shang rulers to displace the Xia dynasty. Some scholars believe metallurgy—together with horses, horse-drawn chariots, and other wheeled vehicles—came to China with Indo-European migrants from southwest Asia. Although the Xia dynasty already made limited use of bronze tools and weapons, Shang ruling elites managed to monopolize the production of bronze in the Yellow River valley. Thus, control over bronze production strengthened Shang forces, and they had little difficulty imposing their rule on agricultural villages and extending their influence throughout much of the Yellow River valley.

Shang kings extended their rule to a large portion of northeastern China centered on the modern-day province of Henan. Like state builders in other parts of the world, the kings claimed a generous portion of the surplus agricultural production from the regions they controlled and then used that surplus to support military forces, political allies, and others who could help them maintain their rule.

Shang Political Organization The Shang state rested on a vast network of walled towns whose local rulers recognized the authority of the Shang kings. During the course of the dynasty, Shang kings may have controlled one thousand or more towns. According to tradition, the Shang capital moved six times during the course of the dynasty. Though originally chosen for political and military reasons, in each case the capital also became an important social, economic, and cultural center—the site not only of administration and military command but also of bronze foundries, arts, crafts, trade, and religious observances.

The Shang Capital at Yin Excavations have revealed much about the workings of the Shang dynasty. One remarkable site is Yin, near modern Anyang, which was the Shang capital during the last two or three centuries of the dynasty. Archaeologists working at Yin have identified a complex of royal palaces, archives with written documents, several residential neighborhoods, two large bronze foundries, several workshops used by craftsmen, and scattered burial grounds. Eleven large and lavish tombs constructed for Shang kings have received particular attention. The graves included thousands of objects—chariots, weapons, bronze goods, pottery, carvings, and sacrificial victims, including dogs, horses, and scores of human beings intended to serve the deceased royals in another existence. One tomb alone contained skeletons of more than three hundred sacrificial victims who joined the Shang king in death.

The Xia and Shang dynasties were not the only states that developed in ancient China, although legendary and historical accounts paid special attention to them because of their location in the Yellow River valley, where the first Chinese imperial states rose in later times. Indeed, archaeological excavations are making it clear that similar states dominated other regions at the same time the Xia and the Shang ruled the Yellow River valley. Recent excavations, for example, have unearthed evidence of a very large city at Sanxingdui in modern-day Sichuan province (southwestern China). Occupied about 1700 to 1000 B.C.E., the city was roughly contemporaneous with the Shang dynasty, and it probably served as the capital of a regional kingdom.

Zhou burial site.
A tomb from the early Zhou dynasty containing the remains of horses and war chariots, which transformed military affairs in ancient China. Survivors sacrificed the horses and buried them along with the chariots for use by the tomb's occupant after his death.

Reverberations of ●●●●●●●● ●

Urbanization and the Creation of Patriarchy

Recall that scholars debate the reasons why urbanization and the creation of large states seem to have led to patriarchy in diverse regions of the world. In light of what you have read about early Chinese societies, do any of the explanations—agricultural, military, or the protection of resources—seem to fit best in this instance?

The Zhou Dynasty

The Rise of the Zhou Although little information survives to illustrate the principles of law, justice, and administration by which Shang rulers maintained order, the picture becomes more clear in the practices of the Zhou dynasty, which succeeded the Shang as the preeminent political authority in northern China. Dwelling in the Wei River valley of northwestern China (modern Shaanxi province), the Zhou were a tough people who battled Shang forces and eventually won recognition as kings of the western regions. But the ambitions of the two dynasties collided in the late twelfth century B.C.E. According to Zhou accounts, the last Shang king was a criminal fool who gave himself over to wine, women, tyranny, and greed. As a result, many of the towns and political districts subject to the Shang transferred their loyalties to the Zhou, who toppled the Shang king's government in 1122 B.C.E. and replaced it with their own state. The new dynasty ruled most of northern and central China, at least nominally, until 256 B.C.E.

The Mandate of Heaven In justifying the deposition of the Shang, spokesmen for the Zhou dynasty articulated a set of principles that influenced Chinese thinking about government and political legitimacy until the twentieth century. The Zhou theory of politics rested on the assumption that heavenly powers granted the right to govern—"the mandate of heaven"—to an especially deserving individual known as the son of heaven. The ruler had the duty to govern conscientiously, to observe high standards of honor and justice, and to maintain order and harmony within his realm. As long as he did so, the heavenly powers would approve of his work, the cosmos would enjoy stability, and the ruling dynasty would retain its mandate to govern. If a ruler failed in his duties, however, chaos and suffering would afflict his realm, the cosmos would fall out of balance, and the displeased heavenly powers would withdraw the mandate to rule and transfer it to a more deserving candidate. On the basis of that reasoning, spokesmen for the new dynasty explained the fall of the Shang and the transfer of the mandate of heaven to the Zhou.

Political Organization The Zhou state was much larger than the Shang. In fact, it was so extensive that a single central court could not rule the entire land effectively. As a result, Zhou rulers relied on a decentralized administration: they entrusted power, authority, and responsibility to subordinates who in return owed allegiance, tribute, and military support to the central government. During the early centuries of the dynasty, that system worked reasonably well. Gradually, however, subordinates established their own bases of power, which allowed them to become more independent of the Zhou dynasty. In addition, iron production spread rapidly across China in the first millennium B.C.E., and Zhou subordinates took advantage of the technology to outfit their own forces with weapons to resist the central government.

Decline of the Zhou After the early eighth century B.C.E., Zhou rule deteriorated as nomadic invaders forced the royal court from their capital at Hao. Although the dynasty survived, it never regained its authority, and competing states fought ferociously with one another in hopes of establishing themselves as leaders of a new political order. So violent were the last centuries of the Zhou dynasty that they are known as the Period of the Warring States (403–221 B.C.E.). The Zhou dynasty officially ended in 256 B.C.E. when the last king abdicated his position under pressure from his ambitious subordinate, the king of Qin. Only with the establishment of the Qin dynasty in 221 B.C.E. did effective central government return to China.

SOCIETY AND FAMILY IN ANCIENT CHINA

In China, as in India, the introduction of agriculture enabled individuals to accumulate wealth and preserve it within their families. Social distinctions began to appear during neolithic times, and after the establishment of the Xia, Shang, and Zhou dynasties the distinctions became even sharper. Throughout China the patriarchal family emerged as the institution that most directly influenced individuals' lives and their roles in the larger society.

The Social Order

Ruling Elites Already during the Xia dynasty, but especially under the Shang and the early Zhou, the royal family and allied noble families occupied the most honored positions in Chinese society. They resided in large, palatial compounds made of pounded earth, and they lived on the agricultural surplus and taxes delivered by their subjects.

Sourcesfromthe**Past**

Peasants' Protest

Peasants in ancient China mostly did not own land. Instead, they worked as tenants on plots allotted to them by royal or aristocratic owners, who took sizable portions of the harvest. In the following poem from the Book of Songs, *a collection of verses dating from Zhou times, peasants liken their lords to rodents, protest the bite lords take from the peasants' agricultural production, and threaten to abandon the lords' lands for a neighboring state where conditions were better.*

> Large rats! Large rats!
> Do not eat our millet.
> Three years have we had to do with you.
> And you have not been willing to show any regard
>   for us.
> We will leave you,
> And go to that happy land.
> Happy land! Happy land!
> There shall we find our place.
> Large rats! Large rats!
> Do not eat our wheat.
> Three years have we had to do with you.

> And you have not been willing to show any kindness
>   to us.
> We will leave you,
> And go to that happy state.
> Happy state! Happy state!
> There shall we find ourselves aright.
> Large rats! Large rats!
> Do not eat our springing grain!
> Three years have we had to do with you,
> And you have not been willing to think of our toil.
> We will leave you,
> And go to those happy borders.
> Happy borders! Happy borders!
> Who will there make us always to groan?

For Further Reflection

■ How might you go about judging the extent to which these verses throw reliable light on class relations in ancient China?

Source: James Legge, trans. *The Chinese Classics,* 5 vols. London: Henry Frowde, 1893, 4:171–72.

One of the hallmarks of these elites was their conspicuous consumption of bronze, which was far too expensive for most people to afford. Indeed, ruling elites controlled much of the bronze weaponry that existed in northern China and also supplied their households with elaborately decorated cast-bronze utensils and vessels. Ruling elites consumed bronze in such staggering quantities that the tomb of Yi of Zeng, a provincial governor of the late Zhou dynasty, contained a collection of bronze weapons and decorative objects that weighed almost eleven tons.

A privileged class of hereditary aristocrats rose from the military allies of Shang and Zhou rulers. These aristocrats possessed extensive landholdings, and their standard of living was much more refined than that of the commoners and slaves who worked their fields and served their needs. They were served by a small class of free artisans and craftsmen, including bronzesmiths, jewelers, jade workers, and silk manufacturers, who enjoyed a reasonably comfortable existence because of aristocratic patronage.

Peasants Far less comfortable was a large class of semiservile peasants who populated the Chinese countryside. They owned no land but provided agricultural, military, and labor services for their lords in exchange for plots to cultivate, security, and a portion of the harvest. They lived like their neolithic predecessors in small, partially subterranean houses excavated to a depth of about one meter (three feet) and protected from the elements by thatched walls and roofs. Women's duties included mostly indoor activities such as wine making, weaving, and cultivation of silkworms, whereas men spent most of their time outside working in the fields, hunting, and fishing.

Slaves Finally, there was a sizable class of slaves, most of whom were enemy warriors captured during battles between the many competing states of ancient China. Slaves performed hard labor, such as the clearing of new fields or the building of city walls, that required a large workforce.

Family and Patriarchy

Throughout human history the family has served as the principal institution for the socialization of children and the preservation of cultural traditions. In China the extended family emerged as a particularly influential institution during neolithic times, and it continued to play a prominent role in shaping both private and public affairs after the appearance of the Xia, Shang, and Zhou states. Indeed, the early dynasties ruled their territories largely through family and kinship groups.

Thinking about ENCOUNTERS

Encounters in Early Societies in South and East Asia

Both Chinese and Indian (Aryan) societies developed in the context of interactions with peoples outside their own territories or social groupings: in China with nomads to the north and west, and in India with indigenous peoples. *How did these interactions influence the development of Chinese and Indian trade, social structure, or culture?*

Veneration of Ancestors One reason for the pronounced influence of the Chinese family was the veneration of ancestors, a practice with roots in neolithic times. This practice was based on the belief that dead ancestors had the power to support and protect their surviving families, but only if their descendants displayed proper respect and ministered to the spirits' needs. The strong sense of ancestors' presence and continuing influence in the world led to an equally strong ethic of family solidarity. A family could expect to prosper only if all its members—dead as well as living—worked cooperatively toward common interests. The family became an institution linking departed generations to the living and even to those yet unborn—an institution that wielded enormous influence over both the private and the public lives of its members.

In the absence of organized religion or official priesthood in ancient China, the patriarchal head of the family presided at rites and ceremonies honoring ancestors' spirits. As mediator between the family's living members and its departed relatives, the family patriarch possessed tremendous authority. He officiated not only at ceremonies honoring ancestors of his household but also at memorials for collateral and subordinate family branches that might include hundreds of individuals.

Patriarchal Society Chinese society vested authority principally in elderly males who headed their households. Like its counterparts in other regions, Chinese society took on a strongly patriarchal character—one that intensified with the emergence of large states. During neolithic times Chinese men wielded public authority, but they won their rights to it by virtue of the female line of their descent. Even if it did not vest power and authority in women, this system provided solid reasons for a family to honor its female members. As late as Shang times, two queens posthumously received the high honor of having temples dedicated to their memories.

Women's Influence Women occasionally played prominent roles in public life during Shang times. Fu Hao, for example, the consort of King Wu Ding, whose tomb has thrown important light on Shang royal society, ventured beyond the corridors of the Shang palace to play prominent roles in public life. Documents from her tomb indicate that Fu Hao supervised her estate and presided over sacrificial ceremonies that were usually the responsibility of men who were heads of their households. She even served as general on several military campaigns and once led thirteen thousand troops in a successful operation against a neighboring state.

During the later Shang and Zhou dynasties, however, women came to live increasingly in the shadow of men. Large states brought the military and political contributions of men into sharp focus. The ruling classes performed elaborate ceremonies publicly honoring the spirits of departed ancestors, particularly males who had guided their families and led especially notable lives. Gradually, the emphasis on men became so intense that Chinese society lost its matrilineal character. After the Shang dynasty, not even queens and empresses merited temples dedicated exclusively to their memories: at most, they had the honor of being remembered in association with their illustrious husbands.

EARLY CHINESE WRITING AND CULTURAL DEVELOPMENT

Early Chinese myths and legends explained the origins of the world, the human race, agriculture, and the various arts and crafts. But Chinese thinkers saw no need to organize those ideas into systematic religious traditions. Although they often spoke of an impersonal heavenly power, they did not recognize a personal supreme deity who intervened in human affairs or took special interest in human behavior. Nor did ancient China support a large class of priests like those of Mesopotamia, Egypt, and India. As a result, it was family patriarchs who represented the interests of living generations to the spirits of departed ancestors.

In that environment, writing served as the foundation for a distinctive secular cultural tradition in ancient China. Surviving evidence suggests that writing came into extensive use during the Shang dynasty. As in other lands, writing in east Asia quickly became an indispensable tool of government as well as a means of expressing ideas and offering reflections on human beings and their world.

patriarch (PAY-tree-ahrk)

Oracle Bones and Early Chinese Writing

In Mesopotamia and India, merchants pioneered the use of writing. In China, however, the earliest known writing served the interests of rulers rather than traders. Writing in China goes back at least to the early part of the second millennium B.C.E. Surviving records indicate that scribes at the Shang royal court kept written accounts of important events on strips of bamboo or pieces of silk. Unfortunately, almost all those materials have perished, along with their messages. Yet one medium employed by ancient Chinese scribes has survived the ravages of time. Recognized just over a century ago, inscriptions on oracle bones have thrown tremendous light both on the Shang dynasty and on the early stages of Chinese writing.

Oracle Bones Oracle bones were the principal instruments used by fortune-tellers in ancient China. Diviners inscribed a question on a specially prepared broad bone—such as the shoulder blade of a sheep—and then subjected it to heat. When heated, the bone developed networks of splits and cracks. The fortune-teller then studied the patterns and determined the answer to the question inscribed on the bone. Often the diviner recorded the answer on the bone, and later scribes occasionally added further information about the events that actually came to pass.

Most of the oracle bones have come from royal archives, and the questions posed on them clearly reveal the day-to-day concerns of the Shang royal court. Will the season's harvest be abundant or poor? Will the queen bear a son or a daughter? Taken together, bits of information preserved on the oracle bones have allowed historians to piece together an understanding of the political and social order of Shang times.

Even more important, the oracle bones offer the earliest glimpse into the tradition of Chinese writing. The earliest form of Chinese writing, like Sumerian and Egyptian writing, was the pictograph—a conventional or stylized representation of an object. The characters used in contemporary Chinese writing are direct descendants of those used in Shang times. Scholars have identified more than two thousand characters inscribed on oracle bones, most of which have a modern counterpart. Over the centuries, written Chinese characters have undergone considerable modification: generally speaking, they have become more stylized, conventional, and abstract. Yet the affinities between Shang and later Chinese written characters are apparent at a glance.

The political interests of the Shang kings may have accounted for the origin of Chinese writing, but once established, the technology was available for other uses. Because Shang writing survives only on oracle bones and a small number of bronze inscriptions, however, evidence for the expanded uses of writing comes only from the Zhou dynasty and later times.

Zhou Literature Indeed, the Zhou dynasty produced books of poetry and history, manuals of divination and ritual, and essays dealing with moral, religious, philosophical, and political themes. Best known of these works are the reflections of Confucius and other late Zhou thinkers (discussed in chapter 6), which served as the intellectual foundation of classical Chinese society. But many

Chinese oracle bone.
Oracle bone from Shang times with an inscribed question and cracks caused by exposure of the bone to heat.

	Turtle	Horse
Oracle bone script of the Shang dynasty (16th century– 11th century B.C.E.)		
Zhou dynasty script (11th century– 3rd century B.C.E.)		
Qin dynasty script (221–207 B.C.E.)		
Han dynasty script (207 B.C.E.–220 C.E.)		
Modern script (3rd century C.E.–present)		
Contemporary script, People's Republic of China (1950–the present)		

Chinese Writing.

The evolution of Chinese characters from the Shang dynasty to the present.

In what ways did these characters change over time?

works won recognition in Zhou society, including the popular *Book of Changes* (a manual instructing diviners in the art of foretelling the future), the *Book of History* (a collection of documents that justified the Zhou state), the *Book of Etiquette* (a manual in the arts of polite behavior), and—most notable of all—the *Book of Songs* (a collection of verses).

Unfortunately, most other Zhou writings have perished. One important reason for this is that when the imperial house of Qin ended the chaos of the Period of the Warring States and brought all of China under tightly centralized rule in 221 B.C.E., the victorious emperor ordered the destruction of all writings that did not have some immediate utilitarian value. Only a few items escaped, hidden away for a decade or more until scholars and writers could once again work without

fear of persecution. These few survivors represent the earliest development of Chinese literature and moral thought.

ANCIENT CHINA AND THE LARGER WORLD

High mountain ranges, forbidding deserts, and turbulent seas stood between China and other early societies of the eastern hemisphere. These geographic features did not entirely prevent communication between China and other lands, but they hindered the establishment of direct long-distance trade relations such as those linking Mesopotamia with Harappan India or those between the Phoenicians and other peoples of the Mediterranean basin. Nevertheless, like other early societies, ancient China developed in the context of a larger world of interaction and exchange. Trade, migration, and the expansion of Chinese agricultural society all ensured that peoples of the various east Asian and central Asian societies would have regular dealings with one another. Chinese cultivators had particularly intense relations—sometimes friendly and sometimes hostile—with their neighbors to the north, the west, and the south.

Relations with Nomadic Peoples of Central Asia

Steppe Nomads From the valley of the Yellow River, Chinese agriculture spread to the north and west. As this expansion occurred, Chinese cultivators encountered nomadic peoples who had built pastoral societies in the grassy steppes of central Asia. These lands were too arid to sustain large agricultural societies, but their grasses supported large herds of livestock. By 2200 B.C.E. these nomads were already experienced horseback riders, had learned the technology of bronze metallurgy, and had introduced large numbers of heavy wagons into the steppes. After about 1000 B.C.E. several clusters of nomadic peoples organized powerful militarized herding societies on the Eurasian steppes.

Nomadic Society Nomadic peoples did little farming but instead concentrated on herding their animals, driving them to regions where they could find food and water. Because nomadic peoples ranged widely over the grassy steppes of central Asia, they served as links between agricultural societies to the east and west. They were prominent intermediaries in trade networks spanning central Asia. Nomadic peoples depended on agricultural societies for grains and finished products, such as textiles and metal goods, which they could not readily produce for themselves. In exchange for those products, they offered

Chinese agriculture.
Terraced rice paddies in the river valleys of southern China have long produced abundant harvests.

What is the advantage of terraces in agriculture?

horses, which flourished on the steppes, and their services as links to other societies. Yet the Chinese and nomadic peoples always had tense relations. Indeed, they often engaged in bitter wars, and nomadic raids posed a constant threat to the northern and western regions of China.

The Southern Expansion of Chinese Society

The Yangzi Valley Chinese influence spread to the south as well as to the north and west. There was no immediate barrier to cultivation in the south: indeed, the valley of the Yangzi River supports even more intensive agriculture than is possible in the Yellow River basin. In fact, the moist, subtropical climate of southern China lent itself readily to the cultivation of rice: ancient cultivators sometimes raised two crops of rice per year.

But intensive cultivation of rice depended on the construction and maintenance of an elaborate irrigation system that allowed cultivators to flood their paddies and release the waters at the appropriate time. The Shang

and Zhou states provided sources of authority that could supervise a complex irrigation system, and harvests in southern China—along with the population—increased dramatically during the second and first millennia B.C.E.

The State of Chu Agricultural surpluses and growing populations led to the emergence of cities, states, and complex societies in the Yangzi as well as the Yellow River valley. During the late Zhou dynasty, the powerful state of Chu, situated in the central region of the Yangzi, governed its affairs autonomously and challenged the Zhou for supremacy. By the end of the Zhou dynasty, Chu and other states in southern China were in regular communication with their counterparts in the Yellow River valley. They adopted Chinese political and social traditions as well as Chinese writing, and they built societies closely resembling those of the Yellow River valley. As a result, although only the northern portions of the Yangzi River valley fell under the authority of the Shang and Zhou states, by the end of the Zhou dynasty all of southern China formed part of an emerging larger Chinese society.

SUMMARY

Agricultural peoples in south and east Asia built complex societies that in broad outline were much like those to the west. Particularly in the valleys of the Yellow River, the Yangzi River, and the Indus River, early Chinese and Indian cultivators organized states, developed social distinctions, and established sophisticated cultural traditions. Their languages, writing, beliefs, and values differed considerably from one another and from those of their contemporaries in other societies, and these cultural elements lent distinctiveness to both Chinese and Indian society. Moreover, inhabitants of both ancient China and India managed to trade and communicate with peoples of other societies. As a result, wheat cultivation, bronze and iron metallurgy, horse-drawn chariots, and wheeled vehicles all made their way from southwest Asia in ancient times. Thus, in south and east Asia, as in other parts of the eastern hemisphere, agriculture demonstrated its potential to provide a foundation for large-scale social organization and to support interaction and exchange between peoples of different societies.

STUDY TERMS

Aryans (45)	samsara (51)
Brahman (51)	Shang dynasty (53)
brahmins (50)	shudras (50)
caste (50)	untouchables (50)
Harappan (46)	Upanishads (51)
Indus River (46)	vaishyas (50)
jati (50)	*varna* (50)
karma (52)	*Vedas* (49)
kshatriyas (50)	Vedic age (49)
mandate of heaven (55)	Xia dynasty (53)
moksha (52)	Yangzi (52)
oracle bones (58)	Yellow River (52)
patriarch (55)	Yu (45)
Qin (53)	Zhou dynasty (55)

FOR FURTHER READING

Bridget and Raymond Allchin. *The Rise of Civilization in India and Pakistan.* Cambridge, 1982. A detailed and authoritative survey of early Indian society based largely on archaeological evidence.

Kwang-chih Chang. *The Archaeology of Ancient China.* 4th ed. New Haven, 1986. Brings the results of archaeological excavations to bear on ancient Chinese history.

Patricia Ebrey. *The Cambridge Illustrated History of China.* Cambridge, 2000. A splendid collection of images and superb text makes this one of the finest resources available on Chinese history and culture.

Ainslie T. Embree, ed. *Sources of Indian Tradition.* 2 vols. 2nd ed. New York, 1988. An important collection of primary sources in translation.

Michael Loewe and Edward L. Shaughnessy, eds. *The Cambridge History of Ancient China: From the Origins of Civilization to 221 B.C.* Cambridge, 1999. Presents fourteen detailed essays by leading scholars.

Victor H. Mair, Nancy S. Steinhardt, and Paul R. Goldin, eds. *Hawai`i Reader in Traditional Chinese Culture.* Honolulu, 2005. An imaginative selection of primary sources in English translation.

J. P. Mallory. *In Search of the Indo-Europeans: Language, Archaeology, and Myth.* London, 1989. Carefully reviews modern theories about early Indo-European speakers in light of both the linguistic and the archaeological evidence.

Gregory Possehl. *The Indus Civilization.* Walnut Creek, CA, 2002. An excellent summary of recent thinking about Indus/Harappan Civilization by one of the world's leading specialists in the field.

Conrad Schirokauer et al. *A Brief History of Chinese and Japanese Civilizations.* 3rd ed. New York, 2006. Written by a team of experts, this is a sweeping overview of the history of Chinese and Japanese culture, with a particular emphasis on art, religion, philosophy, and literature.

Romila Thapar. *Early India: From the Origins to A.D.* 1300. Berkeley, 2003. A fresh view by one of the leading scholars of early Indian history.

Early Societies in the Americas and Oceania
CHAPTER **4**

In this Maya mural from Bonampak in modern Mexico, war captives prepare to be sacrificed by their captors.

EYEWITNESS:
Chan Bahlum Spills Blood to Honor the Gods

In early September of the year 683 C.E., a Maya man named Chan Bahlum grasped a sharp obsidian knife and cut three deep slits into the skin of his penis. He inserted into each slit a strip of paper made from beaten tree bark so as to encourage a continuing flow of blood. His younger brother Kan Xul performed a similar rite, and other members of his family also drew blood from their own bodies.

The bloodletting observances of September 683 C.E. were political and religious rituals, acts of deep piety performed as Chan Bahlum presided over funeral services for his recently deceased father, Pacal, king of the Maya city of Palenque in the Yucatan peninsula. The Maya believed that the shedding of royal blood was essential to the world's survival. Thus, as Chan Bahlum prepared to succeed his father as king of Palenque, he let his blood flow copiously.

Throughout Mesoamerica, Maya and other peoples performed similar rituals for a millennium and more. Maya rulers and their family members regularly spilled their own blood. Men commonly drew blood from the penis, like Chan Bahlum, and women often drew from the tongue. Both sexes occasionally drew blood also from the earlobes, lips, or cheeks, and they sometimes increased the flow by pulling long, thick cords through their wounds.

According to Maya priests, the gods had shed their own blood to water the earth and nourish crops of maize, and they expected human beings to honor them by imitating their sacrifice. By spilling human blood the Maya hoped to please the gods and ensure that life-giving waters would bring bountiful harvests to their fields. By inflicting painful wounds not just on their enemies but on their own bodies as well, the Maya demonstrated their conviction that bloodletting rituals were essential to the coming of rain and the survival of their agricultural society.

This agricultural society was the product of a distinctive tradition. Human groups migrated to the Americas and Oceania long after they had established communities throughout most of the eastern hemisphere, but long before any people began to experiment with agriculture. Their migrations took place during the last ice age, when glaciers locked up much of the earth's water, causing sea levels all over the world to decline precipitously—sometimes by as much as 300 meters (984 feet). For thousands of years, temporary land bridges joined regions that both before and after the ice ages were separated by the seas. One land bridge linked Siberia with Alaska. Another joined the continent of Australia to the island of New Guinea. Human groups took advantage of those bridges by migrating to new lands.

When the earth's temperature rose and the glaciers melted, beginning about eighteen thousand years ago, the waters returned and flooded low-lying lands around the world. Eventually, the seas once again divided Asia from America by the body of water known as the Bering Strait, and they also separated Australia and New Guinea. By that time, however, human communities had become well established in each of those areas.

Maya (MY-uh)
Yucatan (yoo-kah-TAN)

CHRONOLOGY

AMERICAS

13,000 B.C.E.	Human migration to North America from Siberia
8000–7000 B.C.E.	Origins of agriculture in Mesoamerica
4000 B.C.E.	Origins of maize cultivation in Mesoamerica
3000 B.C.E.	Origins of agriculture in South America
1200–100 B.C.E.	Olmec society
1000–300 B.C.E.	Chavín cult
200 B.C.E.–750 C.E.	Teotihuacan society
300–1100 C.E.	Maya society
300–700 C.E.	Mochica society

OCEANIA

60,000 B.C.E.	Human migration to Australia and New Guinea
3000 B.C.E.	Origins of agriculture in New Guinea
3000 B.C.E.	Austronesian migrations to New Guinea
1500–500 B.C.E.	Lapita society
1500 B.C.E.–700 C.E.	Austronesian migrations to Pacific islands

The return of high waters did not put an end to human migrations. Human groups fanned out from Alaska and ventured to all corners of North, Central, and South America. Beginning about 3000 B.C.E. coastal peoples of southeast Asia built large sailing canoes and established human settlements in the previously uninhabited islands of the Pacific Ocean. By about 700 C.E. human beings had established communities in almost every habitable part of the world.

Although they were separated by large bodies of water, by no means did human migrants to the Americas and Oceania lead completely isolated lives. On the contrary, there were frequent and sometimes regular interactions between peoples of different societies within the Americas and within Oceania. It is likely that at least fleeting encounters took place as well between peoples of the eastern and western hemispheres, although very little evidence survives to throw light on the nature of those encounters in early times. Yet even as they dealt with peoples of other societies, the first inhabitants of the Americas and Oceania also established distinctive societies of their own.

Despite their different origins and their distinctive political, social, and cultural traditions, peoples of the Americas and Oceania built societies that in some ways resembled those of the eastern hemisphere. Human communities independently discovered agriculture in several regions of North America and South America, and migrants introduced cultivation to the inhabited Pacific islands as well. With agriculture came increasing populations, settlement in towns, specialized labor, formal political authorities, hierarchical social orders, long-distance trade, and organized religious traditions. The Americas also generated large, densely populated societies featuring cities, monumental public works, imperial states, and sometimes traditions of writing as well. Thus, like their counterparts in the eastern hemisphere, the earliest societies of the Americas and Oceania reflected a common human tendency toward the development of increasingly complex social structures.

EARLY SOCIETIES OF MESOAMERICA

Much is unclear about the early population of the Americas by human communities. The first large wave of migration from Siberia to Alaska probably took place about 13,000 B.C.E. But small numbers of migrants may have crossed the Bering land bridge earlier, and it is also possible that some migrants reached the western hemisphere by watercraft, sailing or drifting with the currents from northeast Asia down the west coast of North America. In the view of some scholars, it is also possible that some migrants crossed the Atlantic Ocean and established communities on the eastern coast of North America. Several archaeological excavations at widely scattered sites in both North America and South America have yielded remains that scholars date to 15,000 B.C.E. or earlier, suggesting that at least a few human groups made their way to the Americas before the beginning of large-scale migration from Siberia. In any case, after 13,000 B.C.E. migrants arrived in large numbers, and they quickly populated all habitable regions of the western hemisphere. By 9500 B.C.E. they had reached the southernmost part of South America, more than 17,000 kilometers (10,566 miles) from the Bering land bridge.

The earliest human inhabitants of the Americas lived exclusively by hunting and gathering. Beginning about 8000 B.C.E., however, large game animals became scarce, partly because they did not adapt well to the rapidly warming climate and partly because of overhunting by expanding human communities. By 7500 B.C.E. many species of large animals in the Americas were well on the road to extinction. To survive, some human communities supplemented the foods they gathered with fish and small game.

Others turned to agriculture, and they gave rise to the first complex societies in the Americas.

The Olmecs

Early Agriculture in Mesoamerica By 8000 to 7000 B.C.E. the peoples of Mesoamerica—the region from the central portion of modern Mexico to Honduras and El Salvador—had begun to experiment with the cultivation of beans, chili peppers, avocados, squashes, and gourds. By 4000 B.C.E. they had discovered the agricultural potential of maize, which soon became the staple food of the region. Later they added tomatoes to the crops they cultivated. Agricultural villages appeared soon after 3000 B.C.E., and by 2000 B.C.E. agriculture had spread throughout Mesoamerica.

Early Mesoamerican peoples had a diet rich in cultivated foods, but they did not keep as many animals as their counterparts in the eastern hemisphere. Their domesticated animals included turkeys and small, barkless dogs, both of which they consumed as food. They had no cattle, sheep, goats, or swine, so far less animal protein was available to them than to their counterparts in the eastern hemisphere. In addition, most large animals of the western hemisphere were not susceptible to domestication. For

that reason, Mesoamericans were unable to harness animal energy as did the peoples of the eastern hemisphere. As a result, human laborers prepared fields for cultivation, and human porters carried trade goods on their backs. Mesoamericans had no need for wheeled vehicles, which would have been useful only if draft animals had been available to pull them.

Ceremonial Centers Toward the end of the second millennium B.C.E., the tempo of Mesoamerican life quickened as elaborate ceremonial centers with monumental pyramids, temples, and palaces arose alongside the agricultural villages. These were not cities like those that existed in the eastern hemisphere, because only members of the ruling elite, priests, and those who tended to their needs were permanent residents. Instead, most people lived in surrounding villages and gathered in the ceremonial centers only on special occasions or on market days.

Olmecs: The "Rubber People" The earliest known ceremonial centers of the ancient Americas appeared on the coast of the Gulf of Mexico, near the modern Mexican city of Veracruz, and they served as the nerve center of the Olmecs, the first complex society of the Americas. Historians and archaeologists have systematically studied Olmec society only since the 1940s, and many questions about them remain unanswered. Even their proper name is

---

Mesoamerica (mez-oh-uh-MER-i-kuh)

MAP 4.1

Early Mesoamerican societies, 1200 B.C.E.–1100 C.E. *Describe the different geographical settings of the early Mesoamerican societies represented here. Consider the extent to which geographical and environmental conditions influenced the historical development and daily life of these societies.*

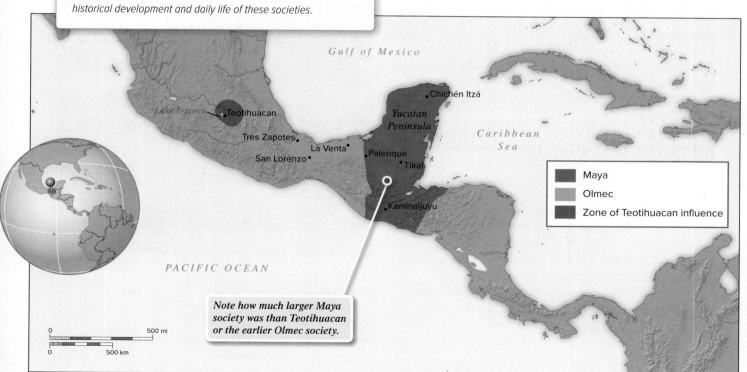

Note how much larger Maya society was than Teotihuacan or the earlier Olmec society.

Maya
Olmec
Zone of Teotihuacan influence

unknown: the term *Olmec* (meaning "rubber people") did not come from the ancient people themselves but derives instead from the rubber trees that flourish in the region they inhabited. Nevertheless, some of the basic features of Olmec society have become reasonably clear, and it is certain that Olmec cultural traditions influenced all complex societies of Mesoamerica until the arrival of European peoples in the sixteenth century C.E.

The first Olmec ceremonial center arose about 1200 B.C.E. on the site of the modern town of San Lorenzo, and it served as their capital for some four hundred years. When the influence of San Lorenzo waned, leadership passed to new ceremonial centers at La Venta (800–400 B.C.E.) and Tres Zapotes (400–100 B.C.E.). These sites defined the heartland of Olmec society, where agriculture produced rich harvests. The entire region receives abundant rainfall; so, like the Harappans, the Olmecs constructed elaborate drainage systems to divert waters that otherwise might have flooded their fields or destroyed their settlements.

Olmec Society Olmec society was probably authoritarian in nature. Common subjects delivered a portion of their harvests for the maintenance of the elite classes living in the ceremonial centers and provided labor for large-scale construction projects. Indeed, untold thousands of laborers were required to build the temples, pyramids, altars, sculptures, and tombs that characterized each Olmec ceremonial center.

Common subjects also provided appropriate artistic adornment for the elites in Olmec capitals. The most distinctive artistic creations of the Olmecs were colossal human heads—possibly likenesses of rulers—sculpted from basalt rock. The largest of these sculptures stands 3 meters (almost 10 feet) tall and weighs some twenty tons. In the absence of draft animals and wheels, human laborers had to move rocks to the ceremonial centers. The largest sculptures required the services of about one thousand laborers.

Trade in Jade and Obsidian Olmec influence extended to much of the central and southern regions of modern Mexico and beyond to modern Guatemala and El Salvador. The Olmecs spread their influence partly by military force, but trade was a prominent link between the Olmec heartland and the other regions of Mesoamerica. Indeed, the Olmecs obtained both jade and obsidian—used for decorative objects and for cutting tools, respectively—from distant regions in the interior of Mesoamerica.

Among the many mysteries surrounding the Olmecs, one of the most perplexing concerns the decline and fall of their society. The Olmecs systematically destroyed their

ceremonial centers at both San Lorenzo and La Venta and then deserted the sites. Archaeologists studying those sites found statues broken and buried, monuments defaced, and the capitals themselves burned. Although intruders may have ravaged the ceremonial centers, many scholars believe that the Olmecs deliberately destroyed their capitals, perhaps because of civil conflicts or doubts about the effectiveness and legitimacy of the ruling classes. In any case, by about 400 B.C.E. Olmec society had fallen on hard times, and soon thereafter societies in other parts of Mesoamerica eclipsed it altogether.

Nevertheless, Olmec traditions deeply influenced later Mesoamerican societies. Olmecs made astronomical observations and created a calendar to help them keep track of the seasons. They invented a system of writing, although unfortunately little of it survives beyond calendrical inscriptions. They also carried out rituals involving human sacrifice and invented a distinctive ball game. Later Mesoamerican peoples adopted all these Olmec traditions as well as their cultivation of maize and their construction of ceremonial centers with temple pyramids. The later and better-known societies of Mesoamerica stood largely on Olmec foundations.

Heirs of the Olmecs: The Maya

During the thousand years following the Olmecs' disappearance about 100 B.C.E., complex societies arose in several Mesoamerican regions and carried on many of the

Olmec colossal head.
This particular head was carved from basalt rock between 1000 and 600 B.C.E. and discovered at La Venta. Olmecs carved similar heads for their ceremonial centers at San Lorenzo and Tres Zapotes.

In the absence of wheeled vehicles, how could human laborers have moved these enormous sculptures?

La Venta (lah BEHN-tah)
Tres Zapotes (TRACE-zah-POE-tace)

legacies of the Olmecs. Human population grew dramatically, and ceremonial centers cropped up at sites far removed from the Olmec heartland. Some of them evolved into genuine cities that attracted large populations of permanent residents and encouraged increasing specialization of labor. Networks of long-distance trade linked the new urban centers and extended their influence to all parts of Mesoamerica. Within the cities themselves, priests devised written languages and compiled a body of astronomical knowledge. In short, Mesoamerican societies developed in a manner roughly parallel to that of their counterparts in the eastern hemisphere.

The Maya The earliest heirs of the Olmecs were the Maya, who created a remarkable society in the region now occupied by southern Mexico, Guatemala, Belize, Honduras, and El Salvador. Although Maya society originally appeared in the fertile Guatemalan highlands beginning in the third century B.C.E., after the fourth century C.E. it flourished mostly in the poorly drained Mesoamerican lowlands, where thin, tropical soils quickly lost their fertility. To enhance the agricultural potential of their region, the Maya built terraces designed to trap silt carried by the numerous rivers passing through the lowlands. By artificially retaining rich earth, they dramatically increased the agricultural productivity of their lands. They harvested maize in abundance, and they also cultivated cotton, from which they wove fine textiles highly prized both in their own society and by trading partners in other parts of Mesoamerica. Maya cultivators also raised cacao, the large bean that is the source of chocolate. Cacao was a precious commodity consumed mostly by nobles in Maya society. They whisked powdered cacao into water to create a stimulating beverage, and they sometimes even ate the bitter cacao beans as snacks. The product was so valuable that the Maya used cacao beans as money.

Tikal The Maya organized themselves politically into scores of small city-kingdoms. From about 300 to 900 C.E., the Maya built more than eighty large ceremonial centers in the lowlands—all with pyramids, palaces, and temples—as well as numerous smaller settlements. Some of the larger centers attracted dense populations and evolved into genuine cities. Foremost among them was Tikal, the most important Maya political center between the fourth and ninth centuries C.E. At its height, roughly 600 to 800 C.E., Tikal

Maya Temple of the Giant Jaguar.
This temple, built in the city of Tikal, served as the funerary pyramid for Lord Cacao, a prominent Maya ruler of the late sixth and early seventh centuries C.E.

What kind of message might a monument of this size have been trying to convey?

was a wealthy and bustling city with a population approaching forty thousand. It boasted enormous paved plazas and scores of temples, pyramids, palaces, and public buildings. The Temple of the Giant Jaguar, a stepped pyramid rising sharply to a height of 47 meters (154 feet), dominated the skyline and represented Tikal's control over the surrounding region, which had a population of about five hundred thousand.

Maya Warfare The Maya kingdoms fought constantly with one another. Victors generally destroyed the peoples they defeated and took over their ceremonial centers, but the purpose of Maya warfare was not so much to kill enemies as to capture them in hand-to-hand combat on the battlefield. Warriors won enormous prestige when they brought back important captives from neighboring kingdoms. Ultimately, most captives ended their lives either as slaves or as sacrificial victims to Maya gods. High-ranking captives in particular often underwent ritual torture and sacrifice in public ceremonies on important occasions.

Tikal (tee-KAHL)

Chichén Itzá Bitter conflicts between small kingdoms were a source of constant tension in Maya society. Only about the ninth century C.E. did the state of Chichén Itzá in the northern Yucatan peninsula seek to construct a larger society by integrating captives into their own society instead of killing them. Some captives refused the opportunity and went to their deaths as proud warriors, but many agreed to recognize the authority of Chichén Itzá. Between the ninth and eleventh centuries C.E., Chichén Itzá organized a loose empire that brought a measure of political stability to the northern Yucatan.

Maya Decline By about 800 B.C.E., however, most Maya populations had begun to desert their cities. Within a century Maya society was in full decline everywhere except the northern Yucatan, where Chichén Itzá continued to flourish. Historians have suggested many possible causes of the decline, including invasion, internal dissension and civil war, failure of the system of water control, ecological problems caused by destruction of the forests, the spread of epidemic diseases, and natural catastrophes such as earthquakes. Possibly several problems combined to destroy Maya society. It is likely that debilitating civil conflict and excessive siltation of agricultural terraces caused particularly difficult problems for the Maya. In any case, the population declined, the people abandoned their cities, and long-distance trade came to a halt. Meanwhile, the tropical jungles of the lowlands encroached on human settlements and gradually smothered the cities, temples, pyramids, and monuments of a once-vibrant society.

Maya Society and Religion

In addition to kings and ruling families, Maya society included a large class of priests who maintained an elaborate calendar and transmitted knowledge of writing, astronomy, and mathematics. A hereditary nobility owned most land and cooperated with the kings and the priests by organizing military forces and participating in religious rituals. Maya merchants also came from the ruling and noble classes, because they served not only as traders but also as ambassadors to neighboring lands and allied peoples. Maya society also generated several other distinct social classes. Professional architects and sculptors oversaw construction of large monuments and public buildings. Artisans specialized in the production of pottery, tools, and cotton textiles. Finally, large classes of peasants and slaves fed the entire society and provided physical labor for the construction of cities and monuments.

Building on the achievements of their Olmec predecessors, Maya priests studied astronomy and mathematics, and they devised both a sophisticated calendar and an elaborate system of writing. They understood the movements of heavenly bodies well enough to plot planetary cycles and to predict eclipses of the sun and the moon. They invented the concept of zero and used a symbol to represent zero mathematically, which facilitated their manipulation of large numbers. By combining their astronomical and mathematical observations, Maya priests calculated the length of the solar year at 365.242 days—about seventeen seconds shorter than the figure reached by modern astronomers.

The Maya Calendar Maya priests constructed the most elaborate calendar of the ancient Americas, which reflected a powerful urge to identify meaningful cycles of time. The Maya calendar interwove two kinds of year: a solar year of 365 days governed the agricultural cycle, and a ritual year of 260 days governed daily affairs by organizing time into twenty "months" of 13 days apiece. The Maya believed that each day derived certain specific characteristics from its position in both the solar and the ritual calendar and that the combined attributes of each day would determine the fortune of activities undertaken on that day. It took fifty-two years for the two calendars to work through all possible combinations of days and return simultaneously to their respective starting points. Maya priests carefully studied the various opportunities and dangers that would come together on a given day in hopes that they could determine which activities were safe to initiate. The Maya attributed especially great significance to the fifty-two-year periods in which the two calendars ran.

Maya Writing The Maya also expanded on the Olmec tradition of written inscriptions. In doing so they created the most flexible and sophisticated of all the early American systems of writing. The Maya script contained both ideographic elements (like Chinese characters) and symbols for syllables. Scholars have begun to decipher this script only since the 1960s, and it has become clear that writing was just as important to the Maya as it was to early complex societies in the eastern hemisphere. Most Maya writing survives today in the form of inscriptions on temples and monuments, because sixteenth-century Spanish conquerors and missionaries destroyed untold numbers of books in hopes of undermining native religious beliefs. Today only four books of the ancient Maya survive, all dealing with astronomical and calendrical matters.

Maya Creation Myths Surviving inscriptions and other writings shed considerable light on Maya religious and cultural traditions. The *Popol Vuh,* a Maya creation myth, taught that the gods had created human beings out of maize and water, the ingredients that became human flesh and blood. Thus Maya religious thought reflected the fundamental role of agriculture in their society, much like religious thought in early complex societies of the eastern hemisphere. Maya

Popol Vuh (paw-pawl vuh)

Reverberations of ● ● ● ● ● ● ●

Urbanization and the Creation of Patriarchy

In Eurasia, there is abundant textual and material evidence that patriarchal systems developed over time in most urban areas and centralized states. Since scholars do not have as much textual evidence of patriarchy among the Maya, what kinds of material evidence would be most convincing of its existence: pictures of elites on stelae, ceramics, or other objects, or excavations of living and burial spaces?

priests also taught that the gods kept the world going and maintained the agricultural cycle in exchange for honors and sacrifices performed for them by human beings.

Bloodletting Rituals The most important of those sacrifices involved the shedding of human blood, which the Maya believed would prompt the gods to send rain to water their crops of maize. Some bloodletting rituals centered on war captives. Before sacrificing the victims by decapitation, their captors cut off the ends of their fingers or lacerated their bodies so as to cause a copious flow of blood in honor of the gods. Yet the Maya also frequently and voluntarily shed their own blood as a means of displaying reverence to their gods.

The Maya Ball Game Apart from the calendar and sacrificial rituals, the Maya also inherited a distinctive ball game from the Olmecs. The game usually involved teams of two to four members apiece. Its object was for players to score points by propelling a rubber ball through a ring or onto a marker without using their hands. The Maya used a solid rubber ball about 20 centimeters (8 inches) in diameter, which was both heavy and hard. Players needed great dexterity and skill to maneuver it accurately using only their feet, legs, hips, torso, shoulders, or elbows. The game was extremely popular: almost all Maya ceremonial centers, towns, and cities had stone-paved courts on which players performed publicly.

The Maya played the ball game for several reasons. Sometimes individuals competed for sporting purposes, and sometimes the game was used as a ritual that honored the conclusion of treaties. High-ranking captives often engaged in forced public competition in which the stakes were their very lives: losers became sacrificial victims and faced torture and execution immediately following the match. Alongside some ball courts were skull racks that bore the decapitated heads of losing players. Thus Maya concerns to please the gods by shedding human blood extended even to the realm of sport.

Gender Roles in Maya Society Because the Spanish destroyed nearly all Maya texts, not as much is known

about gender relations among the Maya as it is about ancient Mesopotamia, Egypt, or China. Many inscriptions on stone stelae survive, but these are concerned almost solely with elite matters. Nevertheless, inscriptions on such stelae indicate the importance of women in forging marriage alliances among ruling families. Material evidence, which includes pictorial representations of men and women, the living spaces of families, and the graves of Maya people offer further clues about the gender roles of women and men. For example, representations of elite men and women together give men priority of position. In addition, only elite men are depicted in scenes of war, playing the ball game, or smoking, suggesting that women did not take part in such activities and that men dominated court life. When women are depicted in these representations, they commonly appear in their roles as mothers and as male companions. Representations also frequently depict women as weavers, suggesting that textile production was the reserve of women. While pictorial representations generally represent the concerns of elites, excavations of living sites have led scholars to conclude that ordinary men and women collaborated on agricultural work. Examinations of skeletal remains do not indicate that men were better nourished than women. Thus, while it seems clear that men dominated politics, warfare, and court life, the extent to which men sought to control women through law codes and ideas about morality is not. Based on the limited evidence provided by inscriptions, representations,

A limestone altar carved in 796 C.E. depicts two Maya kings playing a ritual ball game to celebrate the negotiation of an agreement.

Sourcesfromthe Past

The Creation of Humanity According to the Popol Vuh

The Popol Vuh, *a Maya creation myth, describes how, after several failed attempts, the Maya gods finally created humans out of maize and water. The maize, along with many other delicious foods, including chocolate, was revealed to the gods by two animals and two birds. Human flesh was made from the maize, and water became the blood of humanity. The following excerpt from the myth concludes by naming the first four humans, describing them as "our first mothers and fathers." The version of the work that survives today dates from the mid-sixteenth century, but it reflects beliefs of a much earlier era.*

THIS, then, is the beginning of the conception of humanity, when that which would become the flesh of mankind was sought. Then spoke they who are called She Who Has Borne Children and He Who Has Begotten Sons, the Framer and the Shaper, Sovereign and Quetzal Serpent:

"The dawn approaches, and our work is not successfully completed. A provider and a sustainer have yet to appear—a child of light, a son of light. Humanity has yet to appear to populate the face of the earth," they said.

Thus they gathered together and joined their thoughts in the darkness, in the night. They searched and they sifted. Here they thought and they pondered. Their thoughts came forth bright and clear. They discovered and established that which would become the flesh of humanity. This took place just a little before the appearance of the sun, moon, and stars above the heads of the Framer and the Shaper.

It was from within the places called Paxil and Cayala that the yellow ears of ripe maize and the white ears of ripe maize came.

THESE were the names of the animals that obtained their food—fox and coyote, parakeet and raven. Four, then, were the animals that revealed to them the yellow ears of maize and the white ears of maize. They came from Paxil and pointed out the path to get there.

Thus was found the food that would become the flesh of the newly framed and shaped people. Water was their blood. It became the blood of humanity. The ears of maize entered into their flesh by means of She Who Has Borne Children and He Who Has Begotten Sons.

Thus they rejoiced over the discovery of that excellent mountain that was filled with delicious things, crowded with yellow ears of maize and white ears of maize. It was crowded as well with pataxte and chocolate, with countless zapotes and anonas, with jocotes and nances, with matasanos and honey. From within the places called Paxil and Cayala came the sweetest foods in the citadel. All the small foods and great foods were there, along with the small and great cultivated fields. The path was thus revealed by the animals.

The yellow ears of maize and the white ears of maize were then ground fine with nine grindings by Xmucane. Food entered their flesh, along with water to give them strength. Thus was created the fatness of their arms. The yellowness of humanity came to be when they were made by they who are called She Who Has Borne Children and He Who Has Begotten Sons, by Sovereign and Quetzal Serpent.

Thus their frame and shape were given expression by our first Mother and our first Father. Their flesh was merely yellow ears of maize and white ears of maize. Mere food were the legs and arms of humanity, of our first fathers. And so there were four who were made, and mere food was their flesh.

These are the names of the first people who were framed and shaped: the first person was Balam Quitze, the second was Balam Acab, the third was Mahucutah, and the fourth was Iqui Balam. These, then, were the names of our first mothers and fathers.

For Further Reflection

■ To what extent does this account of human creation reflect the influences on Maya society of both agriculture and the untamed natural world?

Source: Allen J. Christenson, trans. *Popol Vuh.* Sacred Book of the Quiché Maya People, pp. 180–184. Copyright © 2003 by John Hunt Publishing. Reprinted by permission.

and archeology, some scholars hypothesize that gender relations among the Maya were conceived as deeply complementary and that they were perhaps more egalitarian than in Eurasian societies.

Heirs of the Olmecs: Teotihuacan

While the Maya flourished in the Mesoamerican lowlands, a different society arose to the north in the highlands of Mexico. For most of human history, the valley of central Mexico, situated some two kilometers (more than a mile) above sea level, was the site of several large lakes fed by the waters coming off the surrounding mountains. Although environmental changes have caused most of the lakes to disappear, in earlier times their abundant supplies of fresh water, fish, and waterfowl attracted human settlers.

The earliest settlers in the valley of Mexico channeled some of the waters from the mountain streams into their fields and established a productive agricultural society.

Thinking about **TRADITIONS**

The Consequences of Isolation

As a result of geographical distance across vast expanses of ocean, the earliest complex societies in both the Americas and Oceania developed in complete isolation from those in Africa and Eurasia. *In what ways did this isolation lead to unique social, political, cultural, or economic formations? In what ways did societies in the Americas and Oceania develop similarly to those in Africa and Eurasia in spite of such isolation?*

The earliest center of this society was the large and bustling city of Teotihuacan, located about 50 kilometers (31 miles) northeast of modern Mexico City.

The City of Teotihuacan Teotihuacan was probably a large agricultural village by 500 B.C.E., but by the end of the millennium its population approached fifty thousand. By the year 100 C.E., the city's two most prominent monuments, the colossal pyramids of the sun and the moon, dominated the skyline. The Pyramid of the Sun is the largest single structure in Mesoamerica. It occupies nearly as much space as the pyramid of Khufu in Egypt, though it stands only half as tall. At its high point, about 400 to 600 C.E., Teotihuacan was home to almost two hundred thousand inhabitants, a thriving metropolis with scores of temples, several palatial residences, neighborhoods with small apartments for the masses, busy markets, and hundreds of workshops for artisans and craftsmen.

The organization of a large urban population, along with the hinterland that supported it, required a recognized source of authority. Unfortunately, scholars have little information about the character of that authority, since books and written records from the city did not survive. Yet paintings and murals suggest that Teotihuacan was a theocracy of sorts. Priests figure prominently in the works of art, and scholars interpret many figures as representations of deities.

The Society of Teotihuacan Apart from rulers and priests, Teotihuacan's population included cultivators, artisans, and merchants. Artisans of Teotihuacan were especially famous for their obsidian tools and fine orange pottery. Professional merchants traded the products of

Teotihuacan (tay-oh-tee-wa-KAHN)

Teotihuacan.
Aerial view of Teotihuacan, looking toward the Pyramid of the Moon (top center) from the Pyramid of the Sun (bottom left). Shops and residences occupied the spaces surrounding the main street and the pyramids.

Teotihuacan throughout Mesoamerica, from the region of modern Guatemala City in the south to Durango and beyond in the north.

Until about 500 C.E. there was little sign of military organization in Teotihuacan. The city did not have defensive walls, and works of art rarely depicted warriors. Yet the influence of Teotihuacan extended to much of modern Mexico and beyond. Apparently, the city's influence derived less from military might than from its ability to produce fine manufactured goods that appealed to consumers in distant markets.

Cultural Traditions Like the Maya, the residents of Teotihuacan built on cultural foundations established by the Olmecs. They played the ball game, adapted the Olmec calendar to their own uses, and expanded the Olmecs' graphic symbols into a complete system of writing. Unfortunately, because their books have all perished, it is impossible to know exactly how they viewed the world and their place in it. Works of art suggest that they recognized an earth god and a rain god, and it is certain that they carried out human sacrifices during their religious rituals.

Decline of Teotihuacan Teotihuacan began to experience increasing military pressure from other peoples about 500 C.E. About the middle of the eighth century, invaders sacked and burned the city, destroying its books and monuments. After that catastrophe most residents deserted Teotihuacan, and the city slowly fell into ruin.

EARLY SOCIETIES OF SOUTH AMERICA

By about 12,000 B.C.E. hunting and gathering peoples had made their way across the narrow isthmus of Central America and into South America. Those who migrated into the region of the northern and central Andes mountains hunted deer, llama, alpaca, and other large animals. Both the mountainous highlands and the coastal regions below benefited from a cool and moist climate that provided natural harvests of squashes, gourds, and wild potatoes. Beginning about 8000 B.C.E., however, the climate of this whole region became increasingly warm and dry, and the changes placed pressure on natural food supplies. To maintain their numbers, the human communities of the region began to experiment with agriculture. Here, as elsewhere, agriculture encouraged population growth, the establishment of villages and cities, the building of states, and the elaboration of organized cultural traditions. During the centuries after 1000 B.C.E., the central Andean region generated complex societies parallel to those of Mesoamerica.

Early Andean Society and the Chavín Cult

Although they were exact contemporaries, early Mesoamerican and Andean societies developed largely independently. Geography discouraged the establishment of communications between the Andean region and Mesoamerica because neither society possessed abundant pack animals or a technology to facilitate long-distance transportation. Although some agricultural products and technologies diffused slowly from one area to the other, neither the Andes mountains nor the lowlands of modern Panama and Nicaragua offered an attractive highway linking the two regions.

Geography made even communications within the central Andean region difficult. Deep valleys crease the western flank of the Andes mountains as rivers drain waters from the highlands to the Pacific Ocean, so transportation and communication between the valleys have always been very difficult. Nevertheless, powerful Andean states sometimes overcame the difficulties and influenced human affairs over a broad geographical range.

Most of the early Andean heartland came under cultivation between 2500 and 2000 B.C.E. The coastal regions probably developed complex societies first, since cultivators there experienced abundant harvests as a result of crops such as beans, peanuts, and sweet potatoes, and supplemented them with the rich marine life of the Pacific Ocean. Settlements likely appeared somewhat later in the Andean highlands, but it is clear that potatoes were being cultivated in the region after about 2000 B.C.E. By 1800 B.C.E. peoples in all the Andean regions had begun to fashion distinctive styles of pottery and to build temples and pyramids in large ceremonial centers.

The Chavín Cult Shortly after the year 1000 B.C.E., a new spiritual belief appeared in the central Andes. The Chavín cult, which enjoyed enormous popularity during the period 900 to 800 B.C.E., spread through most of the territory occupied by modern Peru and then vanished about 300 B.C.E. Although scholars do not understand the precise significance of the cult, it is clear that Andean society became increasingly complex during this period. Weavers devised techniques of producing elaborate, intricately patterned cotton textiles. Artisans manufactured large, light, and strong fishnets from cotton string. Craftsmen experimented with minerals and discovered techniques of gold, silver, and copper metallurgy and used them to make jewelry as well as small tools.

Early Cities There is no evidence to suggest that Chavín cultural and religious beliefs led to the establishment of a state or any organized political order. Indeed, they probably inspired the building of ceremonial centers rather than the making of true cities. As the population increased and society became more complex, however, cities began to appear shortly after the disappearance of the Chavín cult. Beginning about 200 B.C.E. large cities emerged at the modern-day sites of Huari, Pucara, and Tiahuanaco. Each of these early Andean cities had a population exceeding ten thousand, and each also featured large public buildings, ceremonial plazas, and extensive residential districts.

MAP 4.2

Early societies of Andean South America, 1000 B.C.E.–700 C.E. The early societies of Andean South America occupied long, narrow territories between the Andes Mountains and the Pacific Ocean.

Why did these societies not occupy territories to the east?

Caribbean Sea

Equator

Orinoco

Napo

Amazon

Chavín de Huántar

Lake Titicaca

PACIFIC
OCEAN

ANDES MOUNTAINS

	Moche and Chimu
	Huari
	Tiahuanaco

0   500   1000 mi

0   1000 km

Early Andean societies had to cope with extremely mountainous territories.

Early Andean States: Mochica

Along with cities there appeared regional states. The earliest Andean states arose in the many valleys on the western side of the mountains. These states emerged when conquerors unified the valleys and organized them into integrated societies. They coordinated the building of irrigation systems so that the lower valleys could support intensive agriculture, and they established trade and exchange networks that tied the highlands, the central valleys, and the coastal regions together. Each region contributed its own products to the larger economy of the valley: from the highlands came potatoes, llama meat, and alpaca wool; the central valleys supplied maize, beans, and squashes; and the coasts provided sweet potatoes, fish, and cotton.

The Mochica State   Because early Andean societies did not make use of writing, their beliefs, values, and ways of life remain largely hidden. Surviving fortifications as well as art suggest that early Andean states relied heavily on arms to introduce order and maintain stability within their realms. In addition, art from the early Andean state of Mochica—which dominated the coasts and valleys of northern Peru from about 300 to 700 C.E.—offers a detailed and expressive depiction of early Andean society in all its variety. Most Mochica art survives in the form of pottery vessels, many of which depict individuals' heads or represent the major gods and various subordinate deities and demons. Most interesting, perhaps,

Mochica (moh-CHEE-kah)

Many Mochica pots and jars portray human figures and often depict distinctive characteristics of individuals or typical scenes from daily life. This blackware effigy jar portrays a musician playing a conch shell trumpet.

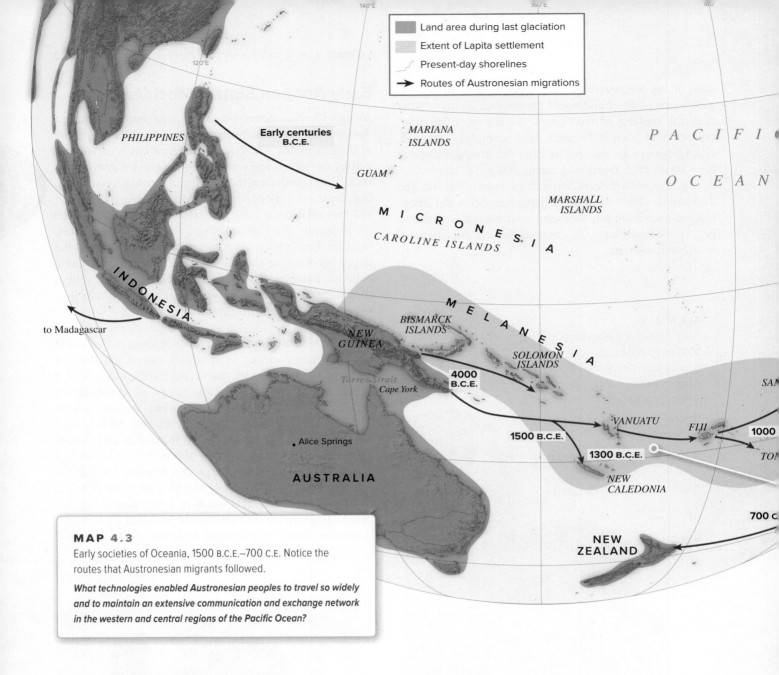

Land area during last glaciation

Extent of Lapita settlement

Present-day shorelines

Routes of Austronesian migrations

PHILIPPINES

Early centuries B.C.E.

MARIANA ISLANDS

GUAM

PACIFIC

OCEAN

MARSHALL ISLANDS

M I C R O N E S I A

CAROLINE ISLANDS

INDONESIA

to Madagascar

M E L A N E S I A

BISMARCK ISLANDS

NEW GUINEA

SOLOMON ISLANDS

4000 B.C.E.

Torres Strait

Cape York

SAM

VANUATU

FIJI

1000

1500 B.C.E.

1300 B.C.E.

TO

• Alice Springs

NEW CALEDONIA

AUSTRALIA

700 c

NEW ZEALAND

MAP 4.3

Early societies of Oceania, 1500 B.C.E.–700 C.E. Notice the routes that Austronesian migrants followed.

What technologies enabled Austronesian peoples to travel so widely and to maintain an extensive communication and exchange network in the western and central regions of the Pacific Ocean?

are those that illustrate scenes in the everyday life of the Mochica people: warriors leading captives bound by ropes, women working in a textile factory under the careful eye of a supervisor, and beggars looking for handouts on a busy street. Even in the absence of writing, Mochica artists left abundant evidence of a complex society with considerable specialization of labor.

Mochica was only one of several large states that dominated the central Andean region during the first millennium C.E. Although they integrated the regional economies of the various Andean valleys, none of these early states was able to impose order on the entire region or even to dominate a portion of it for very long. The exceedingly

difficult geographical barriers posed by the Andes mountains presented challenges that ancient technology and social organization simply could not meet. As a result, at the end of the first millennium C.E., Andean society exhibited regional differences much sharper than those of Mesoamerica and early complex societies in the eastern hemisphere.

EARLY SOCIETIES OF OCEANIA

Human migrants entered Australia and New Guinea at least 50,000 years ago, and possibly earlier than that. They arrived in watercraft—probably canoes fitted with

HAWAII

Early centuries
C.E.

P
O
L
Y
N
E
S
I
A

MARQUESAS

300 C.E.

to Easter
Island

Late centuries
B.C.E.

TAHITI

160°W · 140°W · 20°N · Equator · 0° · 20°S

Thinking about **ENCOUNTERS**

The Persistence of Interactions

Although all of the early complex societies in the Americas and Oceania engaged in long-distance trade with neighboring societies, it seems clear that such interactions were more difficult to sustain over the long term than they were in the complex societies of Africa and Eurasia. *What factors contributed to these difficulties? What might the existence of such interactions—despite such difficulties—tell us about early complex societies more generally?*

PART 1

> *Note how many centuries it took for humans to populate most of the islands in the Pacific Ocean.*

sails—but because of the low sea levels of that era, the migrants did not have to cross large stretches of open ocean. These earliest inhabitants of Oceania also migrated—perhaps over land when sea levels were still low—to the Bismarcks, the Solomons, and other small island groups near New Guinea. Beginning about 5,000 years ago, seafaring peoples from southeast Asia settled the northern coast of New Guinea and then ventured farther and established communities in the island groups of the western Pacific Ocean. By the middle centuries of the first millennium C.E., their descendants had established communities in all the habitable islands of the Pacific Ocean.

Early Societies in Australia and New Guinea

Human migrants reached Australia and New Guinea long before any people had begun to cultivate crops or keep herds of domesticated animals. As a result, the earliest inhabitants of Australia and New Guinea lived by hunting and gathering. Once rising seas covered the land bridge connecting Australia and New Guinea about 10,000 years ago, however, human societies in each area followed radically different paths. While the aboriginal peoples of Australia continued as hunting and gathering societies, in New Guinea communities turned to agriculture: beginning about 3000 B.C.E. the cultivation of root crops such as yams and taro and the

keeping of pigs and chickens spread rapidly throughout the island.

Early Hunting and Gathering Societies in Australia
Like hunting and gathering peoples elsewhere, the aboriginal Australians lived in small, mobile communities that undertook seasonal migrations in search of food. Over the centuries, they learned to exploit the resources of the various ecological regions of Australia. Plant foods, including fruits, berries, roots, nuts, seeds, shoots, and green leaves, constituted the bulk of their diet. To supplement their plant-based diet, they used axes, spears, clubs, nets, lassos, snares, and boomerangs to bring down animals ranging in size from rats to giant kangaroos, which

Windjana figures (cloud and rain spirits) loom from a rock painting produced about 12,000 years ago by inhabitants of the Chamberlain Gorge region in western Australia.

Austronesian migration.
Austronesian mariners sailed double-hulled voyaging canoes much like this one from Raʻiatea in the Society Islands, drawn in 1769 by an artist who accompanied Captain James Cook on his first voyage in the Pacific Ocean.

What features allowed these canoes to travel across such huge expanses of open ocean?

grew to a height of 3 meters (almost 10 feet), and to catch fish, waterfowl, and small birds.

Austronesian Peoples In New Guinea, seafaring peoples from southeast Asia introduced agriculture to the island about 5,000 years ago when they began to establish trading and settlement communities on the northern coast. These sailors spoke Austronesian languages (whose modern relatives include Malayan, Indonesian, and Polynesian) and were highly skilled in seafaring technologies. They sailed the open ocean in large canoes equipped with outriggers, which stabilized their craft and reduced the risks of long voyages. By paying close attention to winds, currents, stars, cloud formations, and other natural indicators, they learned how to find distant lands reliably and return home safely.

Early Agriculture in New Guinea Austronesian seafarers came from societies that depended on the cultivation of root crops and the herding of animals. When they settled in New Guinea, they introduced yams, taro, pigs, and chickens to the island, and the indigenous peoples themselves soon followed suit. Within a few centuries agriculture and herding had spread to all parts of New Guinea. There, as in other lands, agriculture brought population growth and specialization of labor: after the change to agriculture, permanent settlements, pottery, and carefully crafted tools appeared throughout the island.

The Peopling of the Pacific Islands

Austronesian Migrations to Polynesia Austronesian-speaking peoples possessed a sophisticated maritime technology as well as agricultural expertise, and they established human settlements in the islands of the Pacific Ocean. Their outrigger canoes enabled them to sail safely over long distances of open ocean, and their food crops and domesticated animals enabled them to establish agricultural societies in the islands. Once they had established coastal settlements in New Guinea, Austronesian seafarers sailed easily to the Bismarck and Solomon islands east of New Guinea. From there they undertook exploratory voyages that led them to previously unpopulated islands.

By about 1500 B.C.E. Austronesian mariners had arrived at Vanuatu (formerly called New Hebrides) and New Caledonia, by 1300 B.C.E. at Fiji, and by 1000 B.C.E. at Tonga and Samoa. During the late centuries of the first millennium B.C.E., they established settlements in Tahiti and the Marquesas. From there they launched ventures that took them to the most remote outposts of Polynesia, which required them to sail over thousands of nautical miles of blue water. They reached the islands of Hawai`i in the early centuries C.E., Easter Island by 300 C.E., and the large islands of New Zealand by 700 C.E.

Austronesian Migrations to Micronesia and Madagascar

While one branch of the Austronesian-speaking peoples populated the islands of Polynesia, other branches sailed in different directions. From the Philippines some ventured to the region of Micronesia, which includes small islands and atolls such as the Mariana, Caroline, and Marshall islands of the western Pacific. Others looked west from their homelands in Indonesia, sailed throughout the Indian Ocean, and became the first human settlers of the large island of Madagascar off the east African coast.

The Lapita Peoples

The earliest Austronesian migrants to sail out into the blue water of the Pacific Ocean and establish human settlements in Pacific islands are known as the Lapita peoples. No one knows what they called themselves: the name Lapita comes from a beach in New Caledonia where some of the earliest recognizable Lapita artifacts came to the attention of archaeologists. It is clear, however, that between about 1500 and 500 B.C.E., Lapita peoples maintained communication and exchange networks throughout a large region extending about 4,500 kilometers (2,800 miles) from New Guinea and the Bismarck Archipelago to Samoa and Tonga.

Wherever they settled, Lapita peoples established agricultural villages where they raised pigs and chickens and introduced the suite of crops they inherited from their Austronesian ancestors. They supplemented their crops and domesticated animals with fish and seaweed from nearby waters, and they soon killed off most of the large land animals and birds that were suitable for human consumption. They left abundant evidence of their presence

in the form of their distinctive pottery decorated with stamped geometric designs.

For about 1,000 years, Lapita peoples maintained extensive networks of trade and communication across vast stretches of open ocean. Their agricultural settlements were largely self-sufficient, but they placed high value on some objects from distant islands. Their pottery was a principal item of long-distance exchange, as was high-quality obsidian, which they sometimes transported over thousands of kilometers, since it was available at only a few sites of Lapita settlement. Other trade items brought to light by archaeologists include shell jewelry and stone tools. Indeed, it is clear that, like their counterparts in other regions of the world, the earliest inhabitants of the Pacific islands maintained regular contacts with peoples well beyond their own societies.

Chiefly Political Organization

After about 500 B.C.E. Lapita trade networks fell into disuse, probably because the various Lapita settlements had grown large enough that they could supply their own needs. By the middle part of the first millennium B.C.E., Lapita and other Austronesian peoples had established hierarchical chiefdoms in the Pacific islands. Contests for power and influence between ambitious subordinates frequently caused tension and turmoil, but the possibility of migration offered an alternative to conflict. Indeed, the spread of Austronesian peoples throughout the Pacific islands came about partly because of population pressures and conflicts that encouraged small parties to seek fresh opportunities in more hospitable lands.

Over the longer term, descendants of Lapita peoples built strong, chiefly societies, particularly on large islands with relatively dense populations, such as those of the Tongan, Samoan, and Hawaiian groups. In Hawai`i, for example, militarily skilled chiefs cooperated closely with priests, administrators, soldiers, and servants in ruling their districts. Chiefs and their retinues claimed a portion of the agricultural surplus produced by their subjects, and they sometimes required subjects to deliver additional products, such as fish, birds, or timber. Chiefs and their administrators also vied with the ruling classes of neighboring districts, led public ritual observances, and oversaw irrigation systems that watered the taro plants that were crucial to the survival of Hawaiian society. Eventually, the chiefly and aristocratic classes became so entrenched and powerful that they regarded themselves as divine or semidivine, and the law of the land prohibited common subjects from even gazing directly at them.

Lapita (lah-PEE-tah)

SUMMARY

Very little writing survives to illuminate the historical development of early societies in the Americas and Oceania. Thus it is impossible to offer the sort of richly detailed account of their political organization, social structures, and cultural traditions that historians commonly provide for societies of the eastern hemisphere. Nevertheless, it is clear that migrations to the Americas and Oceania represented continuations of population movements that began with *Homo erectus* and early *Homo sapiens,* resulting eventually in the establishment of human communities in almost all habitable parts of the earth. Moreover, it is clear that the earliest inhabitants of the Americas and Oceania built productive and vibrant societies whose development roughly paralleled that of their counterparts in the eastern hemisphere. Many communities depended on an agricultural economy, and with their surplus production they supported dense populations, engaged in specialized labor, established formal political authorities, constructed hierarchical social orders, carried on long-distance trade, and formed distinctive cultural traditions. The early historical development of the Americas and Oceania demonstrates once again the tendency of agriculture to encourage human communities to construct ever more elaborate and complex forms of social organization.

STUDY TERMS

Austronesian peoples (76)	Mochica (73)
bloodletting rituals (63)	Oceania (74)
cacao (67)	Olmecs (65)
Chavín cult (72)	*Popol Vuh* (68)
Chichén Itzá (68)	San Lorenzo (66)
colossal heads (66)	Temple of the Giant
Lapita peoples (77)	Jaguar (67)
La Venta (66)	Teotihuacan (70)
maize (65)	Tikal (67)
Maya (63)	Tres Zapotes (66)
Maya ball game (69)	Yucatan (63)
Mesoamerica (64)	

FOR FURTHER READING

Peter Bellwood. *The Polynesians: Prehistory of an Island People.* Rev. ed. London, 1987. Well-illustrated popular account emphasizing the origins and early development of Polynesian societies.

Richard A. Diehl. *The Olmecs: America's First Civilization.* London, 2004. The best brief introduction to Olmec society.

Peter Hiscock. *Archaeology of Ancient Australia.* London, 2008. The most up-to-date account of the key archaeological evidence for Australia's ancient peoples by one of the foremost specialists in the field.

K. R. Howe. *The Quest for Origins: Who First Discovered and Settled the Pacific Islands?* Honolulu, 2003. Reviews the numerous theories advanced to explain the arrival of human populations and the establishment of human societies in the remote islands of the Pacific Ocean.

Patrick V. Kirch. *On the Road of the Winds: An Archaeological History of the Pacific Islands before European Contact.* Berkeley, 2000. A valuable synthesis of scholarship by the foremost contemporary archaeologist of the Pacific islands.

Charles C. Mann. 1491: *New Revelations of the Americas before Columbus.* New York, 2006. Summarizes a great deal of archaeological research on the pre-Columbian Americas.

Simon Martin and Nikolai Grube. *Chronicle of the Maya Kings and Queens: Deciphering the Dynasties of the Ancient Maya.* London, 2000. Offers an important synthesis of Maya political history on the basis of both inscriptions and archaeological discoveries.

Michael E. Mosley. *The Incas and Their Ancestors: The Archaeology of Peru.* Rev. ed. London, 2001. A comprehensive survey of Andean history through the era of the Incas.

Linda Schele and Mary Ellen Miller. *The Blood of Kings: Dynasty and Ritual in Maya Art.* New York, 1986. A richly illustrated volume that explores Maya society through works of art and architecture as well as writing.

David Webster. *The Fall of the Ancient Maya: Solving the Mystery of the Maya Collapse.* London, 2002. A careful and readable analysis of the difficulties that confronted Maya society.

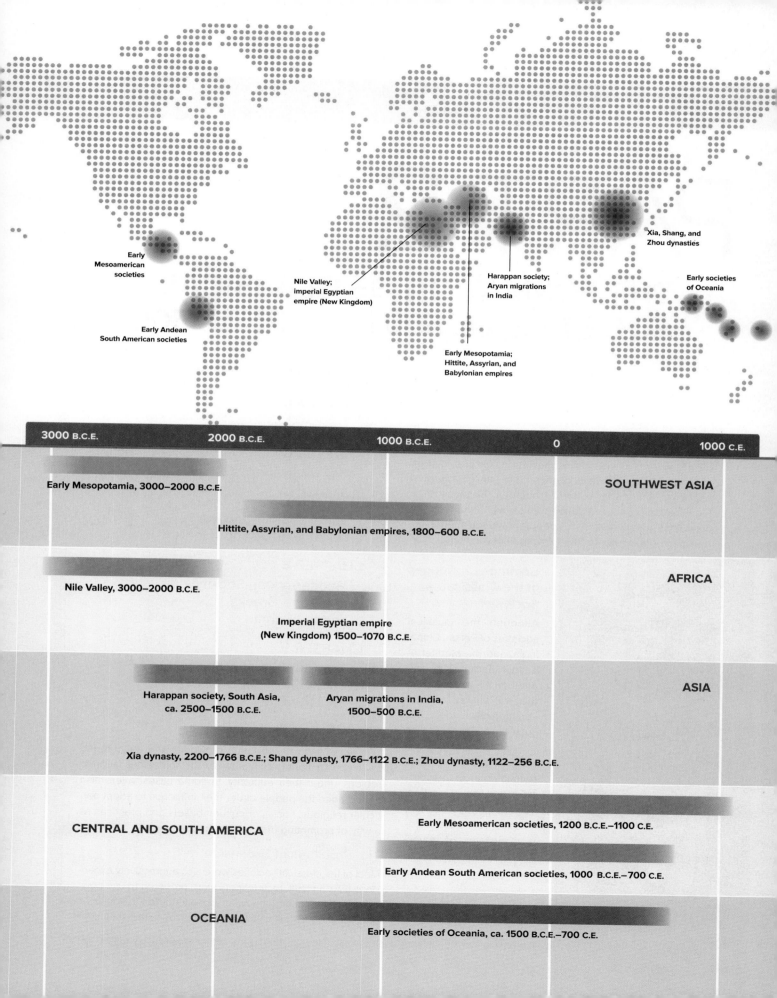

Early Mesoamerican societies

Nile Valley; imperial Egyptian empire (New Kingdom)

Early Andean South American societies

Early Mesopotamia; Hittite, Assyrian, and Babylonian empires

Harappan society; Aryan migrations in India

Xia, Shang, and Zhou dynasties

Early societies of Oceania

| 3000 B.C.E. | 2000 B.C.E. | 1000 B.C.E. | 0 | 1000 C.E. |

SOUTHWEST ASIA

Early Mesopotamia, 3000–2000 B.C.E.

Hittite, Assyrian, and Babylonian empires, 1800–600 B.C.E.

AFRICA

Nile Valley, 3000–2000 B.C.E.

Imperial Egyptian empire (New Kingdom) 1500–1070 B.C.E.

ASIA

Harappan society, South Asia, ca. 2500–1500 B.C.E.

Aryan migrations in India, 1500–500 B.C.E.

Xia dynasty, 2200–1766 B.C.E.; Shang dynasty, 1766–1122 B.C.E.; Zhou dynasty, 1122–256 B.C.E.

CENTRAL AND SOUTH AMERICA

Early Mesoamerican societies, 1200 B.C.E.–1100 C.E.

Early Andean South American societies, 1000 B.C.E.–700 C.E.

OCEANIA

Early societies of Oceania, ca. 1500 B.C.E.–700 C.E.

PART 2

THE FORMATION OF CLASSICAL SOCIETIES, ca. 500 B.C.E. TO ca. 500 C.E.

In the millennium between about 500 B.C.E. and 500 C.E., several early complex societies achieved particularly high degrees of internal organization, extended their authority over extremely large regions, and elaborated especially influential cultural traditions. Because their legacies have endured so long and have influenced the ways that literally billions of people have led their lives, historians often refer to them as classical societies.

Common Challenges in the Classical Societies

Although the classical societies of Persia, China, India, and the Mediterranean differed from one another in many ways, they all shared several common challenges. One such challenge was that of administering vast territories without advanced technologies of transportation and communication. To meet that challenge, classical rulers standardized systems of governance, law, and taxation; built roads and transportation networks; and encouraged trade and communication between the sometimes far-flung regions under their authority. In some cases, rulers also encouraged the people under their influence to adopt particular religious, social, or cultural beliefs and practices as a way of promoting unity within their realms.

The Problems of Expansion

Most of the classical societies were also aggressively expansionist. As a result, their leaders were prepared to use powerful armies to conquer new areas, to fend off the advances of competing states, and to quell rebellion within their own

A limestone sculpture depicts a serene Buddha as he preaches a sermon to his followers.

territories. Indeed, one of the central problems most classical societies faced was how to balance the need to create loyalty and unity among their diverse subjects with the realities of authoritarian, foreign, and often unwanted rule. Heavy taxation and stiff labor requirements were particularly distasteful to many subjects of the classical societies, and these sometimes contributed to rebellions and civil wars that threatened the very survival of the societies themselves.

Long-Distance Trade

Another shared feature of all the classical societies was that each sponsored and maintained a vast system of roads and ports, which resulted in a dramatic increase in long-distance trade. This trade encouraged economic integration within and between societies, and various regions came to depend on one another for agricultural products and manufactured items. In fact, long-distance trade was such an important feature of the classical societies that a well-established network of land and sea routes, known collectively as the Silk Roads, linked lands as distant as China and Europe.

Cultural and Religious Traditions

Finally, all the classical societies generated sophisticated cultural and religious traditions that offered guidance on moral, religious, political, and social issues. Because of the extensive trade networks that linked distant regions, many of these traditions spread along the trade routes and shaped peoples and cultures in societies far from their origin. Thus, even though each of the classical societies adopted

A marble relief sculpture of about 100 C.E. depicts a crew of men working in a treadmill that powers a crane used in construction of a Roman temple.

outside traditions selectively, for most of the classical period cultural borrowing was more widespread than it had been in the period of the early complex societies.

Epidemic Disease

Accelerated interaction also carried the seeds of disintegration because disease pathogens traveled the trade routes alongside people, goods, and ideas. In the second and third centuries C.E., epidemic diseases afflicted most societies along the silk roads, disrupting long-distance trade and creating severe social unrest. As a result, many societies turned inward and sacrificed long-distance connections for local and regional concerns.

Over the centuries since the height of their influence, many of the specific political, social, economic, and cultural features of the classical societies have disappeared. Yet their legacies deeply influenced future societies and in many ways continue to influence the lives of the world's peoples. Appreciation of the legacies of classical societies is thus crucial to understanding the world's historical development.

A cave painting from the late seventh century C.E. depicts the Chinese emperor Han Wudi (seated on horse) as he dispatches Zhang Qian (kneeling at left) on his mission to western lands in search of an alliance against the Xiongnu.

1. *What were some of the features common to most of the classical societies?*

2. *In what ways do the legacies of the classical societies continue to influence the world's peoples?*

The Empires of Persia
CHAPTER **5**

A procession of envoys with offerings for the king makes its way up a ceremonial stairway in the ancient city of Persepolis in modern Iran, one of four capitals of the Achaemenid Persian empire.

EYEWITNESS:

King Croesus and the Tricky Business of Predicting the Future

The Greek historian Herodotus relished a good story, and he related many a tale about the Persian empire and its conflicts with other peoples, including Greeks. One story had to do with a struggle between Cyrus, leader of the expanding Persian realm, and Croesus, ruler of the powerful and wealthy kingdom of Lydia in southwestern Anatolia (modern Turkey). Croesus noted the growth of Persian influence with concern and asked the Greek oracle at Delphi whether to go to war against Cyrus. The oracle responded that an attack on Cyrus would destroy a great kingdom.

Overjoyed, Croesus lined up his allies and prepared for war. In 546 B.C.E. he provoked Cyrus to engage the formidable Lydian cavalry. The resulting battle was hard fought but inconclusive. Because winter was approaching, Croesus disbanded his troops and returned to his capital at Sardis, expecting Cyrus to retreat as well. But Cyrus was a vigorous and unpredictable warrior, and he pursued Croesus to Sardis. When he learned of the pursuit, Croesus hastily assembled an army to confront the invaders. Cyrus threw it into disarray, however, by advancing a group of warriors mounted on camels, which spooked the Lydian horses and sent them into headlong flight. Cyrus's army then surrounded Sardis and took the city after a siege of only two weeks. Croesus was taken captive and afterward became an advisor to Cyrus. Herodotus could not resist pointing out that events proved the Delphic oracle right: Croesus's attack on Cyrus did indeed lead to the destruction of a great kingdom—his own.

The victory over Lydia was a major turning point in the development of the Persian empire. Lydia had a reputation as a kingdom of fabulous wealth, partly because it conducted maritime trade with Greece, Egypt, and Phoenicia as well as overland trade with Mesopotamia and Persia. Lydian wealth and resources gave Cyrus tremendous momentum as he extended Persian authority to new lands and built the earliest of the vast imperial states of classical times.

Classical Persian society began to take shape during the sixth century B.C.E. when warriors conquered an enormous region from the Indus River to Egypt and southeastern Europe. Indeed, the very size of the Persian empire created political and administrative problems for its rulers. Once they solved those problems, however, a series of Persian-based empires governed much of the territory between India and the Mediterranean Sea for more than a millennium—from the mid–sixth century B.C.E. until the early seventh century C.E.—and brought centralized political organization to many distinct peoples living over vast geographic spaces.

In organizing their realm, Persian rulers relied heavily on Mesopotamian techniques of administration, but they also created institutions and administrative procedures of their own. In addition, they invested resources in

Cyrus (SIGH-ruhs)
Croesus (CREE-suhs)

CHRONOLOGY

7th–6th centuries B.C.E.	Life of Zarathustra
558–330 B.C.E.	Achaemenid dynasty
558–530 B.C.E.	Reign of Cyrus the Achaemenid
521–486 B.C.E.	Reign of Darius
334–330 B.C.E.	Invasion and conquest of the Achaemenid empire by Alexander of Macedon
323–83 B.C.E.	Seleucid dynasty
247 B.C.E.–224 C.E.	Parthian dynasty
224–651 C.E.	Sasanid dynasty

the construction of roads and highways to improve communications and mobility across the empire. As a result of those efforts, central administrators were able to send instructions throughout the empire, dispatch armies in times of turmoil, and ensure that local officials would carry out imperial policies.

The organization of the vast territories embraced by the classical Persian empires had important social, economic, and cultural implications. Because high agricultural productivity allowed more people to work at tasks other than cultivation, classes of bureaucrats, administrators, priests, craftsmen, and merchants increased in number. Meanwhile, social extremes between the wealthy and the poor became more pronounced. In addition, good roads across the empire allowed Persian society to serve as a commercial and cultural bridge between Indian and Mediterranean societies. As a result, Persia became an important link in long-distance trade networks as well as a conduit for the exchange of philosophical and religious ideas. Indeed, Persian religious traditions inspired religious thinkers subject to Persian rule and deeply influenced Judaism, Christianity, and Islam.

THE PERSIAN EMPIRES

The empires of Persia arose in the arid land of Iran. For centuries Iran had developed under the shadow of the wealthier and more productive Mesopotamia to the west while absorbing migrations and invasions of nomadic peoples coming out of central Asia. During the sixth century B.C.E., rulers of the province of Persia in southwestern Iran embarked on a series of conquests that resulted in the formation of an enormous empire. For more than a millennium, four ruling dynasties—the Achaemenids (558–330 B.C.E.), the Seleucids (323–83 B.C.E.), the Parthians (247 B.C.E.–224 C.E.), and the Sasanids (224–651 C.E.)—maintained a continuous tradition of imperial rule in much of southwest Asia.

The Achaemenid Empire

The Medes and the Persians The origins of classical Persian society trace back to the late stages of Mesopotamian society. During the centuries before 1000 B.C.E., two closely related Indo-European peoples known as the Medes and the Persians migrated from central Asia to Persia, where they lived in loose subjection to the Babylonian and Assyrian empires. The Medes and the Persians shared many cultural traits with their distant cousins the Aryans, who had migrated into India. Like

the Aryans, they were mostly pastoralists, although they also practiced a limited amount of agriculture. They also possessed considerable military power: like other Indo-Europeans, they were skilled equestrians and expert archers. They also organized themselves by clans rather than by states, although they did recognize leaders who collected taxes and delivered tribute to their Mesopotamian overlords.

Cyrus's Conquests When the Assyrian and Babylonian empires weakened in the sixth century B.C.E., the Medes and the Persians launched their first bid for empire in the person of Cyrus the Achaemenid (reigned 558–530 B.C.E.). Cyrus proved to be a tough, wily leader and an outstanding military strategist, whose conquests laid the foundation for the first Persian empire. In 558 B.C.E. Cyrus became king of the Persian tribes, which he ruled from his mountain fortress at Pasargadae. In 553 B.C.E. he initiated a rebellion against his Median overlord, whom he crushed within three years. By 548 B.C.E. he had brought all of Iran under his control, and he began to look for opportunities to expand. In 546 B.C.E., as we know, he conquered the powerful kingdom of Lydia in Anatolia. Between 545 B.C.E. and 539 B.C.E. he campaigned in central Asia and Bactria (modern Afghanistan). In a swift campaign of 539 B.C.E., he seized Babylonia, whose vassal states immediately recognized him as their lord. Within twenty years Cyrus went from minor regional king to ruler of an empire that stretched from India to the borders of Egypt. Had he lived long enough, Cyrus no doubt would have mounted a campaign against Egypt, the largest and wealthiest

---

Achaemenid (ah-KEE-muh-nid)
Medes (meeds)
Pasargadae (pah-SAR-gah-dee)

neighboring state outside his control. But in 530 B.C.E. he fell, mortally wounded, while protecting his northeastern frontier from nomadic raiders.

Darius Cyrus's empire survived and expanded during the reigns of his successors. His son Cambyses (reigned 530–522 B.C.E.) conquered Egypt in 525 B.C.E. His younger kinsman Darius (reigned 521–486 B.C.E.) then extended the empire both east and west. Indeed, Darius's armies pushed into northwestern India as far as the Indus River, absorbing parts of northern India, while also capturing Thrace, Macedonia, and the western coast of the Black Sea in southeastern Europe. By the late sixth century B.C.E., Darius presided over an empire stretching some 3,000 kilometers (1,865 miles) from the Indus River in the east to the Aegean Sea in the west and 1,500 kilometers (933 miles) from Armenia in the north to the first cataract of the Nile River in the south. With a population of some thirty-five million, Darius's realm was by far the largest empire the world had yet seen.

Yet Darius was more important as an administrator than as a conqueror. Governing a far-flung empire of so many ethnic groups, languages, and traditions was a much more difficult challenge than conquering it. To maintain their empire, the Achaemenids needed to establish lines of communication with all parts of their realm and design institutions that would enable them to administer their territories efficiently. Their solutions not only made it possible for the Achaemenid empire to survive but also pioneered administrative techniques that would outlast their own dynasty and influence political life in southwestern Asia for centuries to come.

Persepolis Soon after his rise to power, Darius began to centralize his administration. About 520 B.C.E. he started to build a new capital of astonishing magnificence at Persepolis. Darius intended Persepolis to serve not only as an administrative center but also as a monument to the Achaemenid dynasty. From the time of Darius to the end of the Achaemenid dynasty in 330 B.C.E., Persepolis served as

Cambyses (kam-BIE-sees)
Aegean (ih-GEE-an)
Persepolis (per-SEP-uh-lis)

MAP 5.1

The Achaemenid and Seleucid empires, 558–83 B.C.E. Observe how much larger the Achaemenid and Seleucid empires were compared to the earlier Mesopotamian and Egyptian empires discussed in chapters 1 and 2.

What role did the Royal Road and other highways play in the maintenance of the Achaemenid empire?

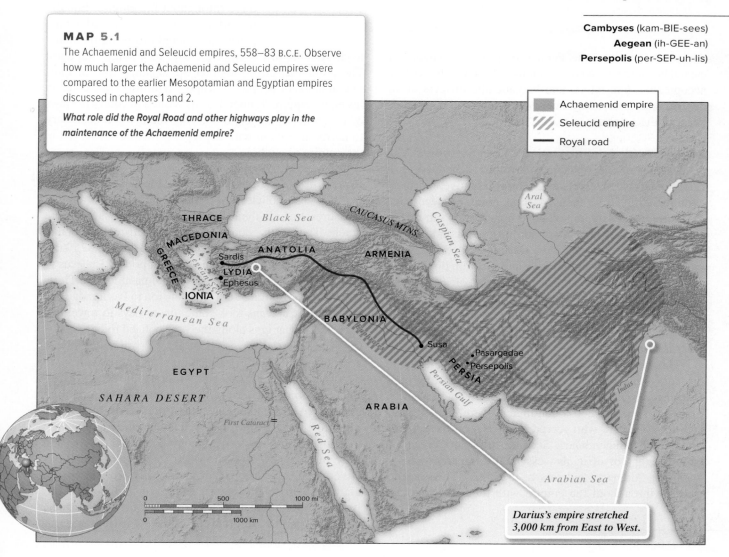

Achaemenid empire
Seleucid empire
Royal road

Darius's empire stretched 3,000 km from East to West.

Ruins of Persepolis.
This image shows the ruins of a variety of buildings from the imperial city. Try to imagine the size and grandeur of the buildings these columns supported.

forces, conducting surprise audits of accounts and procedures in the provinces and collecting intelligence reports. Taken together, these two strategies helped prevent the vast Achaemenid empire from splitting into a series of independent kingdoms.

Taxation and Law Darius also sought to improve administrative efficiency by regularizing tax levies and standardizing laws. Instead of exacting irregular tribute payments from subject lands as his predecessors had done, Darius instituted regular, formal tax levies. Each satrapy was now required to pay a set quantity of silver to the imperial court every year. To simplify the process, Darius issued standardized coins—a move that also fostered trade throughout his empire. Equally important, beginning in 520 B.C.E., Darius also sought to bring the many

the nerve center of the Persian empire—a resplendent capital bustling with advisors, ministers, diplomats, scribes, accountants, translators, and bureaucratic officers of all descriptions. Even today, massive columns and other ruins bespeak the grandeur of Darius's capital.

legal systems of his empire closer to a single standard. The point was not to abolish the existing laws of individual lands or peoples to impose a uniform law code on his entire empire. Rather, Darius wished to codify the laws of his subject peoples, modifying them when necessary to harmonize them with the legal principles observed in the empire as a whole.

Achaemenid Administration: The Satrapies The government of the Achaemenid empire depended on a finely tuned balance between central initiative and local administration. Like their Mesopotamian predecessors, the Achaemenids appointed governors (called satraps) to serve as agents of the central administration and oversee affairs in the various regions. Darius divided his realm into twenty-three administrative and taxation districts he called satrapies, with each governed by an official satrap. Yet the Achaemenids did not try to push direct rule on their subjects: although most satraps were Persian, the Achaemenids recruited local officials to fill almost all other administrative posts.

The Achaemenid rulers employed two strategies to discourage distant satraps from allying with local groups or trying to become independent of Achaemenid authority. First, each satrapy had a contingent of military officers and tax collectors who served as checks on the satraps' power and independence. Second, the rulers created a new category of officials—essentially imperial spies—known as "the eyes and ears of the king." These agents traveled throughout the empire with their own military

Roads and Communications Alongside administrative and legal policies, the Achaemenid rulers took other measures to knit their far-flung realm into a coherent whole. They built good roads across their realm, notably the Persian Royal Road, which stretched some 2,575 kilometers (1,600 miles) from the Aegean port of Ephesus to Sardis in Anatolia, through Mesopotamia along the Tigris River, to Susa in Iran, with an extension to Pasargadae and Persepolis. Caravans took some ninety days to travel this road, lodging at inns along the well-policed route.

The imperial government also organized a courier service and built 111 postal stations at intervals of 40 to 50 kilometers (25 to 30 miles) along the Royal Road. Each station kept a supply of fresh horses, enabling couriers to speed from one end of the Royal Road to the other in a week's time. The Achaemenids also improved existing routes between Mesopotamia and Egypt, and they built a new road between Persia and the Indus River to link the imperial center with the satrapy of Gandhara in northwestern India. In addition to improving communications, these roads facilitated trade, which helped to integrate the empire's various regions into a larger economy.

satraps (SAY-traps)

Stone carving from Persepolis.
This carving shows an enthroned Darius (with his son Xerxes standing behind him) receiving a high court official, as incense burners perfume the air.

In what ways does the official's posture indicate respect and submission to the emperor?

Decline of the Achaemenid Empire

The Achaemenid Commonwealth The Achaemenids' roads and administrative machinery enabled them to govern a vast empire and extend Persian influences throughout their territories. Persian concepts of law and justice administered by trained imperial officials linked peoples from the Mediterranean Sea to the Indus River in a larger Persian society. Political stability made it possible to undertake enormous public works projects such as the construction of *qanat* (underground canals), which led to enhanced agricultural production and population growth. Iron metallurgy spread to all parts of the empire, and by the end of the Achaemenid dynasty, iron tools were common in Persian agricultural communities. Peoples in the various regions of the Achaemenid empire maintained their ethnic identities, but all participated in a larger Persian commonwealth.

Eventually, however, difficulties between rulers and subject peoples undermined the integrity of the empire. Cyrus and Darius both consciously pursued a policy of toleration in administering their vast multicultural empire: they took great care to respect the values and cultural traditions of the peoples they ruled. In Mesopotamia, for example, they portrayed themselves not as Persian conquerors but, rather, as legitimate Babylonian rulers and

representatives of Marduk, the patron deity of Babylon. Cyrus also won high praise from Jews in the Achaemenid empire, since he allowed them to return to Jerusalem and rebuild the temple that Babylonian conquerors had destroyed in 586 B.C.E.

Darius's successor, Xerxes (reigned 486–465 B.C.E.), had more difficult relations with subject peoples. The burden of Persian rule became particularly heavy in Mesopotamia and Egypt—regions with sophisticated cultural traditions and long histories of independence—and subject peoples there frequently rose up in rebellion. Xerxes did not seek to impose specifically Persian values in Mesopotamia and Egypt, but he harshly repressed rebellions and thereby gained a reputation for cruelty and insensitivity to the concerns of subject peoples.

The Persian Wars In fact, efforts to control their ethnic Greek subjects helped to bring about the collapse of the Achaemenid empire. Ethnic Greeks inhabited many of the cities in Anatolia—particularly in the region of Ionia on the Aegean coast of western Anatolia—and they maintained close economic and commercial ties with their cousins in

---

qanat (kah-NAHT)

the peninsula of Greece. The Ionian Greeks fell under Persian domination during the reign of Cyrus. They became restive under Darius's Persian governors who oversaw their affairs, and in 500 B.C.E. the Ionian cities rebelled, expelled or executed their governors, and asserted their independence. Their rebellion launched a series of conflicts known as the Persian Wars (500–479 B.C.E.).

The conflict between the Ionian Greeks and the Persians expanded considerably when the cities of peninsular Greece sent fleets to aid their kinsmen in Ionia. Darius managed to put down the rebellion and reassert Achaemenid authority, but he and his successors became entangled in a difficult and ultimately destructive effort to extend their authority to the Greek peninsula. Indeed, after some initial successes against the Greeks, the Persians suffered a rout at the battle of Marathon (490 B.C.E.), and they returned home without achieving their goals. Ten years later, in 480 B.C.E., a renewed Persian attempt to conquer the Greek cities ended in costly defeats for the Persians. Thereafter, for almost 150 years the Persian empire continued to spar intermittently with the Greek cities without achieving victory.

Alexander of Macedon The standoff ended with the rise of Alexander of Macedon, often called Alexander the Great (discussed more fully in chapter 8). In 334 B.C.E. Alexander invaded Persia with an army of some forty-eight thousand tough, battle-hardened Macedonians. Though far smaller than the Persian army in numbers, the well-disciplined Macedonians carried heavier arms and employed more sophisticated military tactics than their opponents. As a result, they sliced through the Persian empire and dealt their adversaries a series of devastating defeats. In 331 B.C.E. Alexander shattered Achaemenid forces at the battle of Gaugamela, and within a year the empire founded by Cyrus had dissolved.

Alexander led his forces into Persepolis and proclaimed himself heir to the Achaemenid rulers. After a brief season of celebration, Alexander and his forces ignited a blaze—perhaps intentionally—that destroyed Persepolis. The conflagration was so great that when archaeologists first began to explore the ruins of Persepolis in the eighteenth century, they found layers of ash and charcoal up to 1 meter (3 feet) deep.

A gold coin from the early Hellenistic era depicting the Macedonian conqueror, Alexander.

The Achaemenid empire had crumbled, but its legacy was by no means exhausted. Alexander portrayed himself in Persia and Egypt as a legitimate successor of the Achaemenids who observed their precedents and deserved their honors. He retained the Achaemenid administrative structure, and he even confirmed the appointments of many satraps and other officials. As it happened, Alexander had little time to enjoy his conquests, because he died in 323 B.C.E. after a brief effort to extend his empire to India. But the states that succeeded him— the Seleucid, Parthian, and Sasanid empires—continued to employ a basically Achaemenid structure of imperial administration.

The Seleucid, Parthian, and Sasanid Empires

The Seleucids After Alexander died, his chief generals carved his empire into three large realms, which they divided among themselves. The choicest realm, which included most of the former Achaemenid empire, went to Seleucus (reigned 305–281 B.C.E.), who had commanded an elite corps of guards in Alexander's army. Like Alexander, Seleucus and his successors retained the Achaemenid systems of administration and taxation as well as the imperial roads and postal service. The Seleucids also founded new cities throughout the realm and attracted Greek colonists to occupy them. These new cities greatly stimulated trade and economic development both within the Seleucid empire and beyond.

As foreigners, the Seleucids faced opposition from native Persians. Satraps often revolted against Seleucid rule and tried to establish their independence. The Seleucids soon lost their holdings in northern India, and the semi-nomadic Parthians progressively took over Iran during the third century B.C.E. The Seleucids continued to rule a truncated empire until 83 B.C.E., when Roman conquerors put an end to their empire.

The Parthians Meanwhile, the Parthians established themselves as rulers of a powerful empire based in Iran that they extended to Mesopotamia. The Parthians had occupied the region of eastern Iran around Khurasan since Achaemenid times. They retained many of the customs and traditions of nomadic peoples from the steppes of central Asia. They did not have a centralized government, for example, but organized themselves into a federation of clans. They were also skillful warriors, accustomed

Macedon (MAS-ih-don)
Gaugamela (GAW-guh-mee-luh)
Seleucids (sih-LOO-sihds)

Thinking about **TRADITIONS**

Cultural Traditions and the Imposition of Foreign Rule

One of the problems of the Achaemenids, Seleucids, Parthians, and Sasanids was that some of the peoples each empire conquered strongly resented what they viewed as rule by foreigners. At times, such resentment contributed to the toppling of one empire for another. *How did the Persian-based empires try to balance the imposition of their rule from above with the cultural and ethnic identities of the people they conquered, and why did this balance sometimes fail?*

nomadic peoples who had to forage on the steppes in winter. The larger Parthian horses could then support heavily armed warriors outfitted with metal armor, which served as an effective shield against the arrows of the steppe nomads. Indeed, few existing forces could stand up to Parthian heavy cavalry.

As early as the third century B.C.E., the Parthians began to wrest their independence from the Seleucids. The Parthian satrap revolted against his Seleucid overlord in 238 B.C.E., and during the following decades his successors gradually enlarged their holdings. Mithradates I, the Parthians' greatest conqueror, came to the throne about 171 B.C.E. and transformed his state into a mighty empire. By about 155 B.C.E. he had consolidated his hold on Iran and had also extended Parthian rule to Mesopotamia.

to defending themselves against constant threats from nomadic peoples farther east.

As they settled and turned increasingly to agriculture, the Parthians discovered that they could resist nomadic invasions better by feeding their horses on alfalfa during the winter. The alfalfa allowed the animals to grow much larger and stronger than the small horses and ponies of

Mithradates (mihth-rah-DAY-teez)

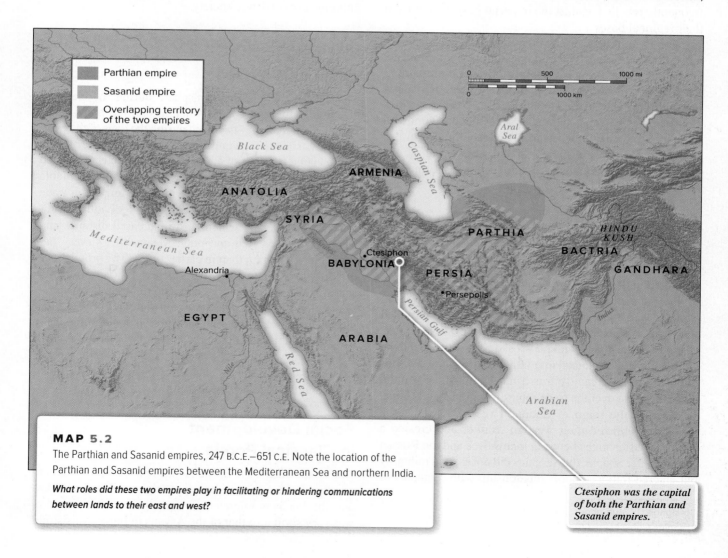

MAP 5.2

The Parthian and Sasanid empires, 247 B.C.E.–651 C.E. Note the location of the Parthian and Sasanid empires between the Mediterranean Sea and northern India.

What roles did these two empires play in facilitating or hindering communications between lands to their east and west?

Ctesiphon was the capital of both the Parthian and Sasanid empires.

Parthian Government The Parthians portrayed themselves as enemies of the foreign Seleucids and as restorers of rule in the Persian tradition. To some extent that characterization was accurate. The Parthians largely followed the example of the Achaemenids in structuring their empire: they governed through satraps, employed Achaemenid techniques of administration and taxation, and built a lavish capital city. But the Parthians also retained elements of their own steppe traditions. For example, they did not develop nearly as centralized a regime as the Achaemenids or the Seleucids but, rather, vested a great deal of authority and responsibility in their clan leaders. These men—who frequently served as satraps—could be troublesome, because they frequently rebelled against the imperial government from their regional bases.

For about three centuries the Parthians presided over a powerful empire between India and the Mediterranean. Beginning in the first century C.E., they faced pressure in the west from the expanding Roman empire. On three occasions in the second century C.E., Roman armies captured the Parthian capital at Ctesiphon. Combined with internal difficulties caused by rebellious satraps, Roman pressure contributed to the weakening of the Parthian state. During the early third century C.E., internal rebellion brought it down.

The Sasanids Once again, though, the tradition of imperial rule continued, this time under the Sasanids, who came from Persia and claimed direct descent from the Achaemenids. The Sasanids toppled the Parthians in 224 C.E. and ruled until 651 C.E., re-creating much of the splendor of the Achaemenid empire. From their cosmopolitan capital at Ctesiphon, the Sasanid "king of kings" provided strong rule from Parthia to Mesopotamia. Sasanid merchants traded actively with peoples to both the east and the west, and they introduced into Iran the cultivation of crops such as rice, sugarcane, citrus fruits, eggplant, and cotton that came west over the trade routes from India and China.

During the reign of Shapur I (239–272 C.E.), the Sasanids stabilized their western frontier and created a series of buffer states between themselves and the Roman empire. After Shapur, the Sasanids did not expand militarily but entered into a standoff relationship with remnants of

Ctesiphon (TES-uh-phon)
Sasanids (suh-SAH-nids)

Parthian sculpture.
Gold sculpture of a nomadic horseman discharging an arrow. This figurine dates from the fifth or fourth century B.C.E. and might well represent a Parthian.

the Kushan empire in the east and the Roman and Byzantine empires in the west. None of those large empires was strong enough to overcome the others, but they contested border areas and buffer states, sometimes engaging in lengthy and bitter disputes that sapped the energies of all involved.

These continual conflicts seriously weakened the Sasanid empire in particular. The empire came to an end in 651 C.E. when Arab warriors killed the last Sasanid ruler, overran his realm, and incorporated it into their rapidly expanding Islamic empire. Yet even conquest by external invaders did not end the legacy of classical Persia, since Arab conquerors adopted Persian administrative techniques and cultural traditions for their own use in building a new Islamic society.

IMPERIAL SOCIETY AND ECONOMY

Throughout the eastern hemisphere during the classical era, public life and social structure became much more complicated than they had been during the days of the early complex societies. Centralized imperial governments needed large numbers of administrative officials, which led to the emergence of educated classes of bureaucrats. Stable empires also enabled many individuals to engage in trade or other specialized labor. Some of these individuals accumulated vast wealth, which led to increased distance and tensions between rich and poor. Meanwhile, slavery became more common than in earlier times. The prominence of slavery had to do partly with the expansion of imperial states, which often enslaved conquered foes, but it also reflected the increasing gulf between rich and poor, which placed such great economic pressure on some individuals that they had to give up their freedom in order to survive. All these developments had implications for the social structures of classical societies in Persia as well as China, India, and the Mediterranean basin.

Social Development in Classical Persia

During the early days of the Achaemenid empire, Persian society reflected its nomadic steppe origins. When the Medes and the Persians migrated to Iran, their social structure was very similar to that of the Aryans in India, consisting

Chapter 5 ■ The Empires of Persia 93

primarily of warriors, priests, and peasants. Family and clan relationships were extremely important in the organization of Persian political and social affairs. Male warriors headed the clans, which retained much of their influence long after the establishment of the Achaemenid empire.

Imperial Bureaucrats The development of a cosmopolitan empire and the requirements of imperial administration, however, called for a new class of educated bureaucrats, who to a large extent undermined the position of the old warrior elite. Although the bureaucrats did not directly challenge the patriarchal warriors, their crucial role in running the day-to-day affairs of the empire guaranteed them a prominent and comfortable place in Persian society. By the time of the later Achaemenids and the Seleucids, Persian cities were home to masses of administrators, tax collectors, and record keepers. The bureaucracy even included a substantial corps of translators, who facilitated communications among the empire's many linguistic groups. Imperial survival depended on these literate professionals, and high-ranking bureaucrats came to share power and influence with warriors and clan leaders.

Free Classes The bulk of Persian society consisted of free individuals such as artisans, craftspeople, farmers, merchants, and low-ranking civil servants. Priests and priestesses were also prominent urban residents, along with servants who maintained the temple communities in which they lived. In Persian society, as in earlier Mesopotamian societies, members of the free classes participated in religious observances conducted at local temples, and they had the right to share in the income that temples generated from their agricultural operations and from craft industries such as textile production that the temples organized. The weaving of textiles was mostly the work of women, who received rations of grain, wine, beer, and sometimes meat from the imperial and temple workshops that employed them.

In the countryside the free classes included peasants who owned land as well as landless cultivators who worked on properties owned by the state, temple communities, or other individuals. Free residents of rural areas had the right to marry and move as they wished, and they could seek better opportunities in the cities or in military service. The Persian empires embraced a great deal of parched land that received little rainfall, and free residents of the countryside contributed much of the labor that went into the building and maintenance of irrigation systems. Most remarkable of those systems were underground canals known as *qanat*, which allowed cultivators to distribute water to fields without losing large quantities to evaporation through exposure to the sun and open air. Numerous *qanat* crisscrossed the Iranian plateau in the heartland of the Persian empire, where extreme scarcity of water justified the enormous investment of human labor required to build the canals. Although they had help from slaves, free residents of the countryside contributed much of the labor that went into the excavation and maintenance of the *qanat*.

Slaves A large class of slaves also worked in both the cities and the countryside. Individuals passed into slavery by two main routes. Most were prisoners of war who became slaves as the price of survival. Other slaves came from the ranks of free subjects who accumulated debts that they could not satisfy. In the cities, for example, merchants, artisans, and craftsmen borrowed funds to purchase goods or open shops, while in the countryside small farmers facing competition from large-scale cultivators borrowed against their property and liberty to purchase

Staircase from Persepolis.
In this sculpture from Persepolis, Persian nobles dressed in fine cloaks and hats ascend the staircase leading to the imperial reception hall.

What kinds of feelings might these sculptures have elicited from visitors to the reception hall?

Reverberations ●●●●●●●●

Long-Distance Trade Networks

Long-Distance Trade Networks

Between about 500 B.C.E. and 500 C.E., peoples across Eurasia and North Africa established long-distance trade networks on an unprecedented scale. Although we saw in Part I that peoples in the early complex societies had established trade networks in earlier times, the scale of long-distance trade networks in the classical societies was far greater and of even more lasting consequence. The vast empires of Persia, China, and Rome that arose in this period helped to create the relative political stability that allowed trade to flourish. These large empires also facilitated long-distance trade by issuing standardized coins, by building and maintaining new roads and ports, and by supporting large markets and urban areas. As a result, trade networks in this period extended by land and by sea from Europe to China, from Persia to north Africa and central Asia, and from India to China, southeast Asia, and the Mediterranean basin. Their existence, in turn, had profound long-term consequences because they allowed the diffusion of foodstuffs and the exchange of commodities, and because they laid the foundation for the spread of religions and epidemic disease far from their points of origin.

The Diffusion of Foodstuffs and the Exchange of Commodities

In this chapter, we have already seen that the trade routes of the Persian empires facilitated the diffusion of Egyptian grains and textiles, Indian gold and ivory, and metals from Anatolia to diverse parts of the empire. At roughly the same time, fine Chinese silks were being carried across trade routes from the east and became coveted items in Persia, India, Mesopotamia, and the Roman empire (chapter 6). Pepper, meanwhile, was carried across both land and sea routes from India to China, central Asia, and the Mediterranean (chapter 7), while spices from southeast Asia were carried west from China and India (chapter 9). The spread of such commodities and foodstuffs had long-term social and economic consequences in the lands to which they diffused. For example, long-distance trade in coveted luxury items like silk, jewels, gold, and spices became markers of social distinction in the societies where they were traded, meaning that the possession of such items came to symbolize high status and helped to delineate social boundaries. In addition, the numerous markets and ports necessary to maintain such extensive trade networks encouraged urban growth

tools, seed, or food. Failure to repay those debts in a timely fashion often forced the borrowers not only to forfeit their property but also to sell their children, their spouses, or themselves into slavery.

Economic Foundations of Classical Persia

Agriculture was the economic foundation of classical Persian society. Like other classical societies, Persia needed large agricultural surpluses to support military forces and administrative specialists as well as residents of cities who were artisans, crafts workers, and merchants rather than cultivators. The Persian empires embraced several regions of exceptional fertility—notably Mesopotamia, Egypt, Anatolia, and northern India—and they prospered by mobilizing the agricultural surpluses of those lands.

Agricultural Production Barley and wheat were the grains cultivated most commonly in the Persian empires. Peas, lentils, mustard, garlic, onions, cucumbers, dates, apples, pomegranates, pears, and apricots supplemented

the cereals in diets throughout Persian society, and beer and wine were the most common beverages. In most years agricultural production far exceeded the needs of cultivators, making sizable surpluses available for sale in the cities or for distribution to state servants through the imperial bureaucracy. Vast quantities of produce flowed into the imperial court from state-owned lands. Even though they are incomplete, surviving records show that in 500 B.C.E., during the middle period of Darius's reign, the imperial court received almost eight hundred thousand liters of grain, quite apart from vegetables, fruits, meat, poultry, fish, oil, beer, wine, and textiles. Officials distributed some of this produce to the imperial staff as wages in kind, but much of it also found its way into the enormous banquets that Darius organized for as many as ten thousand guests.

Trade Agriculture was the foundation of the Persian economy, but long-distance trade grew rapidly during the course of the Persian empires and linked lands from India to Egypt in a vast commercial zone. Each region of the Persian empire contributed particular products to the

around the hubs of trade networks, allowing for population growth and a new range of urban creature comforts (chapter 8).

The Spread of Religions

Of course, commodities and foodstuffs did not move by themselves: individual people traveled along portions of the trade routes, carrying goods and items back and forth over sizeable distances. In the process, individuals from a variety of religious backgrounds and cultural traditions encountered one another and exchanged ideas. Some of the most important ideas people exchanged along these trade networks were about salvation. Along the silk roads, which linked vast portions of Eurasia, merchants who had converted to the Indian religion of Buddhism (chapter 7) invited Buddhist monks to establish monasteries across the oasis towns of central Asia (chapter 9). Similarly, adherents of both Christianity and Manichaeism took advantage of stable long-distance trade networks to establish communities of believers in the Mediterranean and southwest Asia (chapter 9). Over the long term, the spread of these religions of

Camels laden with goods

salvation had profound effects on the cultures of the regions to which they spread.

The Spread of Epidemic Disease

While the establishment of long-distance trade networks in this period allowed unprecedented exchanges of goods and ideas, they also created the conditions that allowed epidemic disease to travel much farther—and much faster—than ever before. During the second and third centuries C.E., epidemics of smallpox, measles, and perhaps bubonic plague tore through both the Roman empire and China, resulting in dramatic population losses and reductions in trade. Over the long term, the epidemic diseases—ironically made possible by long-distance trade routes—contributed to the political instability that destroyed both the western Roman and Han empires (chapter 9).

When reading chapters in subsequent Parts, try to keep in mind the often dramatic and long-term social, political, and economic consequences of long-distance trade for all participating societies.

imperial economy, from the gold and ivory of India to the semiprecious stones of Iran, and from the metals of Anatolia to the textiles and grain of Egypt. Several conditions promoted the growth of trade: the relative political stability maintained by the Persian empires, the general prosperity of the realm, the use of standardized coins, and the availability of good trade routes, including long-established routes, newly constructed highways such as the Persian Royal Road, and sea routes through the Red Sea, the Persian Gulf, and the Arabian Sea. Markets operated regularly in all the larger cities of the Persian empires, and the largest cities, such as Babylon, also were home to banks and companies that invested in commercial ventures.

Long-distance trade of this sort became especially prominent during the reigns of Alexander of Macedon and his Seleucid successors. The cities they established and the colonists they attracted stimulated trade throughout the whole region from the Mediterranean to northern India. Indeed, Greek migrants facilitated cultural as well as commercial exchanges by encouraging the mixing and mingling of religious faiths, art styles, and philosophical speculation throughout the Persian realm.

RELIGIONS OF SALVATION IN CLASSICAL PERSIAN SOCIETY

Cross-cultural influences were especially noticeable in the development of Persian religion. Persians came from the family of peoples who spoke Indo-European languages, and their earliest religion closely resembled that of the Aryans of India. During the classical era, however, the new faith of Zoroastrianism emerged and became widely popular in Iran and to a lesser extent also in the larger Persian empires. Zoroastrianism reflected the cosmopolitan society of the empires, and it profoundly influenced the beliefs and values of Judaism, Christianity, and Islam.

Zarathustra and His Faith

The earliest Persian religion recognized many of the same gods as the ancient Aryans, and their priests performed sacrifices similar to those conducted by the brahmins in India. Like the Aryans, the ancient Persians glorified

Zoroastrianism (zohr-oh-ASS-tree-ahn-iz'm)

Thinking about ENCOUNTERS

Imperial Connections

Between the mid–sixth century B.C.E. and the early seventh century C.E., Persian-based empires ruled a variety of diverse peoples and territories between India and the Mediterranean Sea. *What effects did these empires have on the movement of people and goods across their territories, and how did such movement alter or modify the ways people thought about themselves and others?*

strength and martial virtues, and the cults of both peoples sought principally to bring about a comfortable material existence for their practitioners.

Zarathustra   During the classical era Persian religion underwent considerable change, as moral and religious thinkers sought to adapt their messages to the circumstances of a complex, cosmopolitan society. One result was Zoroastrianism, which emerged from the teachings of Zarathustra. Though Zarathustra was undoubtedly a historical person, little certain information survives about his life and career. It is not even clear when he lived, though most scholars date his life to the late seventh and early sixth centuries B.C.E. He came from an aristocratic family, and he probably was a priest who became disenchanted with the traditional religion. In any case, when he was about twenty years old, Zarathustra left his family and home in search of wisdom. After about ten years of travel, he experienced a series of visions and became convinced that the supreme god, whom he called Ahura Mazda (the "wise lord"), had chosen him to serve as his prophet and spread his message.

The *Gathas*   Like his life, Zarathustra's doctrine remains largely unknown, since many of the earliest Zoroastrian teachings were not preserved in writing. Only during the Seleucid dynasty did Zoroastrian priests, known as *magi,* begin to preserve religious texts in writing, and only under the Sasanids did they compile their scriptures in a holy book known as the *Avesta.* Nevertheless, many of Zarathustra's own compositions survive because of the diligence by which magi preserved them through oral transmission. Known as the *Gathas,* Zarathustra's

Zoroastrian divine image.
A gold clasp or button of the fifth century B.C.E. with the symbol of Ahura Mazda as a winged god.

Zarathustra (zar-uh-THOO-struh)
Gathas (GATH-uhs)

works were hymns that he composed in honor of the various deities that he recognized. Apart from the *Gathas,* ancient Zoroastrian literature included a wide variety of hymns, liturgical works, and treatises on moral and theological themes. Though some of these works survive, the arrival of Islam in the seventh century C.E. and the subsequent decline of Zoroastrianism resulted in the loss of most of the Avesta and later Zoroastrian works.

Zoroastrian Teachings   Zarathustra and his followers recognized Ahura Mazda as a supreme deity and the creator of all good things, but Zarathustra also praised six lesser deities in the *Gathas.* Furthermore, he believed that Ahura Mazda engaged in a cosmic conflict with an independent adversary, an evil and malign spirit known as Angra Mainyu (often also referred to as Ahriman the "destructive spirit" or "hostile spirit"). Following a struggle of some twelve thousand years, Zarathustra believed, Ahura Mazda and the forces of good would ultimately prevail, and Angra Mainyu and the principle of evil would disappear forever. At that time individual human souls would undergo judgment and would experience the rewards or punishments they deserved.

Zarathustra did not call for ascetic renunciation of the world in favor of a future heavenly existence. On the contrary, he considered the material world a blessing that reflected the benevolent nature of Ahura Mazda. His moral teachings allowed human beings to enjoy the world and its fruits—including wealth, sexual pleasure, and social prestige—as long as they did so in moderation and behaved honestly toward others. Zoroastrians have often summarized their moral teachings in the simple formula "good words, good thoughts, good deeds."

Popularity of Zoroastrianism   Zarathustra's teachings began to attract large numbers of followers during the sixth century B.C.E., particularly among Persian aristocrats and ruling elites. Wealthy patrons donated land and established endowments for the support of Zoroastrian temples. The Achaemenid era saw the emergence of a sizable priesthood, whose members conducted religious rituals, maintained a calendar, taught Zoroastrian values, and preserved Zoroastrian doctrine through oral transmission.

Beginning with Darius, the Achaemenid emperors closely associated

SourcesfromthePast

Zarathustra on Good and Evil

Like many other religious faiths of classical times, Zoroastrianism encouraged the faithful to observe high moral and ethical standards. In this hymn from the Gathas, *Zarathustra relates how Ahura Mazda and Angra Mainyu— representatives of good and evil, respectively—made choices about how to behave based on their fundamental natures. Human beings did likewise, according to Zarathustra, and ultimately all would experience the rewards and punishments that their choices merited.*

In the beginning, there were two Primal Spirits, Twins
   spontaneously active;
These are the Good and the Evil, in thought, and in
   word, and in deed:
Between these two, let the wise choose aright;
Be good, not base.
And when these Twin Spirits came together at first,
They established Life and Non-Life,
And so shall it be as long as the world shall last;
The worst existence shall be the lot of the followers
   of evil,
And the Good Mind shall be the reward of the followers
   of good.
Of these Twin Spirits, the Evil One chose to do
   the worst;
While the bountiful Holy Spirit of Goodness,
Clothing itself with the mossy heavens for a garment,
   chose the Truth;

And so will those who [seek to] please Ahura Mazda
   with righteous deeds, performed with faith in Truth. . . .
And when there cometh Divine Retribution for the
   Evil One,
Then at Thy command shall the Good Mind establish
   the Kingdom of Heaven, O Mazda,
For those who will deliver Untruth into the hands of
   Righteousness and Truth.
Then truly cometh the blow of destruction on Untruth,
And all those of good fame are garnered up in the
   Fair Abode,
The Fair Abode of the Good Mind, the Wise Lord, and
   of Truth!
O ye mortals, mark these commandments—
The commandments which the Wise Lord has given, for
   Happiness and for Pain;
Long punishment for the evil-doer, and bliss for the
   follower of Truth,
The joy of salvation for the Righteous ever afterwards!

For Further Reflection

■ What assumptions does Zarathustra make about human nature and the capacity of human beings to make morally good choices out of their own free will?

Source: D. J. Irani. *The Divine Songs of Zarathustra.* London: George Allen & Unwin, 1924.

themselves with Ahura Mazda and claimed divine sanction for their rule. Darius ordered stone inscriptions celebrating his achievements, and in those monuments he clearly revealed his devotion to Ahura Mazda and his opposition to the principle of evil. In one of his inscriptions, Darius praised Ahura Mazda as the great god who created the earth, the sky, and humanity and who moreover elevated Darius himself to the imperial honor. With the aid of imperial sponsorship, Zoroastrian temples cropped up throughout the Achaemenid realm. The faith was most popular in Iran, but it attracted sizable followings also in Mesopotamia, Anatolia, Egypt, and other parts of the Achaemenid empire even though there was no organized effort to spread it beyond its original homeland.

Religions of Salvation in a Cosmopolitan Society

The arrival of Alexander of Macedon inaugurated a difficult era for the Zoroastrian community. During his Persian

campaign, Alexander's forces burned many temples and killed numerous magi. Because at that time the magi still transmitted Zoroastrian doctrines orally, an untold number of hymns and holy verses disappeared. The Zoroastrian faith survived, however, and the Parthians cultivated it to rally support against the Seleucids.

Officially Sponsored Zoroastrianism During the Sasanid dynasty, however, Zoroastrianism experienced a revival. As self-proclaimed heirs to the Achaemenids, the Sasanids identified closely with Zoroastrianism and supported it zealously. Indeed, the Sasanids often persecuted other faiths if they seemed likely to become popular enough to challenge the supremacy of Zoroastrianism.

With generous imperial backing, the Zoroastrian faith and the magi flourished as never before. Theologians prepared written versions of the holy texts and collected them in the Avesta. They also explored points of doctrine and addressed difficult questions of morality and theology. Ordinary people flocked to Zoroastrian temples, where they prayed to Ahura Mazda and participated in rituals. The Zoroastrian faith faced severe difficulties in the seventh century C.E. when Islamic conquerors toppled the Sasanid empire. The conquerors did not outlaw the religion altogether, but they placed political and financial pressure on the magi and Zoroastrian temples. Some Zoroastrians fled their homeland and found refuge in India, where their descendants, known as Parsis ("Persians"), continue even today to observe Zoroastrian traditions. But most Zoroastrians remained in Iran and eventually converted to Islam. Only a few thousand faithful maintain a Zoroastrian community in modern-day Iran.

Other Faiths Meanwhile, even though Zoroastrianism ultimately declined in its homeland, the cosmopolitan character of the Persian realm offered it opportunities to influence other religious faiths. Numerous Jewish communities had become established in Mesopotamia, Anatolia, and Persia after the Hebrew kingdom of David and Solomon fell in 930 B.C.E. During the Seleucid, Parthian, and Sasanid eras, the Persian empire attracted merchants, emissaries, and missionaries from the whole

---

Parsis (pahr-SEES)
Manichaeism (man-ih-KEE-iz'm)

region between the Mediterranean and India. Three religions of salvation—Buddhism, Christianity, and Manichaeism, all discussed in later chapters—found a footing alongside Judaism and attracted converts. Indeed, Christianity and Manichaeism became extremely popular faiths in spite of intermittent rounds of persecution organized by Sasanid authorities.

Influence of Zoroastrianism Jews living in Persia during Achaemenid times adopted several specific teachings of Zoroastrianism, which later found their way into the faiths of Christianity and Islam as well. These teachings included the notion that an omnipotent and beneficent deity was responsible for all creation, the idea that a purely evil being worked against the creator god, the conviction that the forces of good will ultimately prevail over the forces of evil after a climactic struggle, the belief that human beings must strive to observe the highest moral standards, and the doctrine that individuals will undergo judgment, after which the morally upright will experience rewards in paradise while evildoers will suffer punishments in hell. These teachings, which have profoundly influenced Judaism, Christianity, and Islam, all derived ultimately from the faith of Zarathustra and his followers.

SUMMARY

The Achaemenid empire inaugurated a new era of world history. The Achaemenids borrowed military and administrative techniques devised earlier by Babylonian and Assyrian rulers, but they applied those techniques on a much larger scale than did any of their Mesopotamian predecessors. In doing so they conquered a vast empire and then governed its diverse lands and peoples with tolerable success for more than two centuries. The Achaemenids demonstrated how it was possible to build and maintain a massive imperial state, and their example inspired later efforts to establish similar large-scale imperial states based in Persia and other Eurasian lands as well. The Achaemenid and later Persian empires integrated much of the territory from the Mediterranean Sea to the Indus River into a commonwealth in which peoples of different regions and ethnic groups participated in a larger economy and society. By sponsoring regular and systematic interactions between peoples of different communities, the Persian empires wielded tremendous cultural as well as political, social, and economic influence. Indeed, Persian religious beliefs helped to shape moral and religious thought throughout much of southwest Asia and the Mediterranean basin. Zoroastrian teachings were particularly influential: although Zoroastrianism declined after the Sasanid dynasty, its doctrines decisively influenced the fundamental teachings of Judaism, Christianity, and Islam.

STUDY TERMS

Achaemenids (86)
Aegean (87)
Ahura Mazda (96–97)
Alexander of Macedon (90)
Avesta (96–97)
battle of Marathon (90)
Cambyses (87)
Croesus (85)

Ctesiphon (92)
Cyrus (85)
Darius (87–89, 94, 97)
Gathas (96)
Gaugamela (90)
Macedon (90)
magi (96–98)
Manichaeism (98)

Medes (86)
Mithradates I (91)
Parsis (98)
Parthians (88)
Pasargadae (86)
Persepolis (87)
Persian Royal Road (88, 95)
Persian Wars (89)

qanat (89)
Sasanids (92)
satraps (88)
Seleucids (90)
Shapur I (90)
Xerxes (89)
Zarathustra (96)
Zoroastrianism (95)

FOR FURTHER READING

Lindsay Allen. *The Persian Empire*. Chicago, 2005. A valuable survey of the Achaemenid empire with special attention to archaeological discoveries.

Mary Boyce, ed. *Textual Sources for the Study of Zoroastrianism*. Totowa, N.J., 1984. Sources in translation with numerous explanatory comments by the author.

Maria Brosius. *The Persians: An Introduction*. London, 2006. Perhaps the best short account of the Persian empires.

———. *Women in Ancient Persia, 559–331 B.C.* Oxford, 1996. Carefully examines both Persian and Greek sources for information about women and their role in Achaemenid society.

Vesta Sarkosh Curtis and Sarah Stewart, eds. *The Age of the Parthians*. London, 2007. Different scholars explore the history and legacy of the Parthians from a range of perspectives in this fascinating new collection.

Muhammad A. Dandamaev and Vladimir G. Lukonin. *The Culture and Social Institutions of Ancient Iran*. Ed. by P. L. Kohl. Cambridge, 1989. Scholarly account that brings the results of Russian research to bear on the Achaemenid empire.

Richard C. Foltz. *Spirituality in the Land of the Noble: How Iran Shaped the World's Religions*. Oxford, 2004. Includes an accessible discussion of the Zoroastrian faith.

Richard N. Frye. *The Heritage of Central Asia: From Antiquity to the Turkish Expansion*. Princeton, 1996. Briefly sketches the history of various Persian-speaking peoples in the steppes of central Asia as well as on the Iranian plateau.

The Unification of China
CHAPTER 6

The Great Wall of China, the first version of which was constructed by the first emperor of the Qin, stretches across the mountains of northern China.

EYEWITNESS:
Sima Qian: Speaking Truth to Power in Han China

In about the year 99 B.C.E., Chinese imperial officials sentenced the historian Sima Qian to punishment by castration. For just over a decade, Sima Qian had worked on a project that he had inherited from his father, a history of China from earliest times to his own day. That project brought Sima Qian high prominence at the imperial court. Thus, when he spoke in defense of a dishonored general, his views attracted widespread attention. The emperor reacted furiously when he learned that Sima Qian had publicly expressed opinions that contradicted the ruler's judgment and ordered the historian to undergo his humiliating punishment.

Human castration was by no means uncommon in premodern times. Thousands of boys and young men of undistinguished birth underwent voluntary castration in China and many other lands as well to pursue careers as eunuchs. Ruling elites often appointed eunuchs, rather than nobles, to sensitive posts because eunuchs did not sire families and so could not build power bases to challenge established authorities. As personal servants of ruling elites, eunuchs sometimes came to wield enormous power.

Castration was not an appealing alternative, however, to educated elites and other prominent individuals: indeed, Chinese men of honor normally avoided the penalty by taking their own lives. Yet Sima Qian chose to endure his punishment. In a letter to a friend he explained that suicide would mean that his work would go forever unwritten. To transmit his understanding of the Chinese past, then, Sima Qian opted to live and work in disgrace until his death about 90 B.C.E.

During his last years Sima Qian completed a massive work consisting of 130 chapters, most of which survive. He composed historical accounts of the emperors' reigns and biographical sketches of notable figures, including ministers, statesmen, generals, empresses, aristocrats, scholars, officials, merchants, and rebels. He even described the societies of neighboring peoples with whom the Chinese sometimes conducted trade and sometimes made war. As a result, Sima Qian's efforts still provide the best information available about the development of early imperial China.

A rich body of political and social thought prepared the way for the unification of China under the Qin and Han dynasties. Confucians, Daoists, Legalists, and others formed schools of thought and worked to bring political and social stability to China during the chaotic years of the late Zhou dynasty and the Period of the Warring States. Legalist ideas contributed directly to unification by outlining means by which rulers could strengthen their states. The works of the Confucians and the Daoists were not directly concerned with unification, but both schools of thought profoundly influenced Chinese political and cultural traditions over the long term.

Rulers of the Qin and Han dynasties adopted Legalist principles and imposed centralized imperial rule on all of China. Like the Achaemenids of Persia, the Qin and Han emperors ruled through an elaborate bureaucracy, and

Qin (chin)

CHRONOLOGY

sixth century B.C.E. (?)	Laozi
551–479 B.C.E.	Confucius
403–221 B.C.E.	Period of the Warring States
390–338 B.C.E.	Shang Yang
372–289 B.C.E.	Mencius
298–238 B.C.E.	Xunzi
280–233 B.C.E.	Han Feizi
221–207 B.C.E.	Qin dynasty
206 B.C.E.–9 C.E.	Early Han dynasty
141–87 B.C.E.	Reign of Han Wudi
9–23 C.E.	Reign of Wang Mang
25–220 C.E.	Later Han dynasty

they built roads that linked the various regions of China. They went further than the Persian emperors in their efforts to foster cultural unity in their realm. They imposed a common written language throughout China and established an educational system based on Confucian thought and values. For almost 450 years the Qin and Han dynasties guided the fortunes of China and established a strong precedent for centralized imperial rule.

Especially during the Han dynasty, political stability brought economic prosperity. High agricultural productivity supported the development of iron and silk industries, and Chinese goods found markets in central Asia, India, the Persian empire, and even the Mediterranean basin. In spite of economic prosperity, however, later Han society experienced deep divisions between rich landowners and poor peasants. Those divisions eventually led to civil disorder and the emergence of political factions, which ultimately brought the Han dynasty to an end.

IN SEARCH OF POLITICAL AND SOCIAL ORDER

The late centuries of the Zhou dynasty led eventually to the chaos associated with the Period of the Warring States (403–221 B.C.E.). Yet the political turmoil of that period also resulted in a remarkable cultural flowering, because it forced thoughtful people to reflect on the proper roles of human beings in society. Some sought to identify principles that would restore political and social order. Others concerned themselves with a search for individual tranquility apart from society. Three schools of thought that emerged during those centuries of confusion and chaos—Confucianism, Daoism, and Legalism—exercised a particularly deep influence on Chinese political and cultural traditions.

Confucianism

Confucius The first Chinese thinker who addressed the problem of political and social order in a straightforward and self-conscious way was Kong Fuzi (551–479 B.C.E.)—"Master Philosopher Kong," as his disciples called him, or Confucius, as he is known in English. He came from an aristocratic family in the state of Lu in northern China, and for many years he sought an influential post at the Lu court. But Confucius was a strong-willed man who often did not get along well with others. He could be quite cantankerous: he was known to lodge bitter complaints, for example, if someone undercooked or overcooked his rice. Not surprisingly, then, he refused to compromise his beliefs in the interest of political expediency, and he insisted on observing principles that frequently clashed with state policy. As a result, Confucius was unable to obtain a high position at the Lu court. Confucius then sought employment with other courts in northern China but after a decade of travel found none willing to accept his services. In 484 B.C.E., bitterly disappointed, he returned to Lu, where he died five years later.

Although Confucius never realized his ambition, he left an enduring mark on Chinese society through his work as an educator and a political advisor. He attracted numerous disciples who aspired to political careers, and those disciples compiled the master's sayings and teachings in a book known as the *Analects*—a work that has profoundly influenced Chinese political and cultural traditions.

Confucian Ideas Confucius's thought was fundamentally moral, ethical, and political in character. It was also thoroughly practical: Confucius did not address philosophical or religious questions but focused instead on the proper ordering of human relationships. In an age when bureaucratic institutions were not yet well developed, Confucius believed that the best way to promote good government was to fill official positions with individuals who were both well educated and extraordinarily conscientious. Thus Confucius concentrated on the formation of what he called *junzi*—"superior individuals"—who did not allow personal interests to influence their judgments.

Zhou (joh)

Confucianism (kuhn-FEW-shuhn-iz'm)

junzi (juhn-zee)

In the absence of an established educational system and a formal curriculum, Confucius had his disciples study works of poetry and history that provided insight into human nature. He and his students carefully examined works produced during the Zhou dynasty, such as the *Book of Songs,* the *Book of History,* and the *Book of Rites,* concentrating especially on their practical value for prospective administrators. As a result of Confucius's influence, literary works of the Zhou dynasty became the core texts of the traditional Chinese education. For more than two thousand years, until the early twentieth century C.E., talented Chinese seeking government posts followed a program of study deriving from the one developed by Confucius in the fifth century B.C.E.

Confucian Values

For Confucius, though, ideal government officials needed more than an advanced education: they also needed a strong sense of moral integrity and a capacity to deliver wise and fair judgments.

Confucius.

No contemporary portrait of Confucius survives, but artists have used their imaginations and depicted him in many ways over the years. This portrait of 1735 identifies Confucius as "the Sage and Teacher" and represents him in the distinctive dress of an eighteenth-century Confucian scholar-bureaucrat.

Several qualities were particularly important to Confucius. One of them he called *ren,* by which he meant an attitude of kindness and benevolence or a sense of humanity. Confucius explained that individuals possessing *ren* were courteous, respectful, diligent, and loyal—characteristics desperately needed in government officials. Another quality of central importance was *li,* a sense of propriety, which called for individuals to behave appropriately: they should treat all other human beings with courtesy, while showing special respect and deference to elders or superiors. Yet another quality that Confucius emphasized was *xiao,* filial piety, which obliged children to respect their parents and other family elders, look after their welfare, support them in old age, and remember them along with other ancestors after their deaths.

Confucius emphasized personal qualities such as *ren, li,* and *xiao* because he believed that individuals who

possessed those traits would gain influence in the larger society and in the process would lead others by their example. Only through enlightened leadership by morally strong individuals, Confucius believed, was there any hope for the restoration of political and social order in China. Thus his goal was not simply the cultivation of personal morality for its own sake but also the creation of *junzi* who could bring order and stability to China.

Because Confucius expressed his thought in general terms, later disciples could adapt it to the particular problems of their times. Indeed, the flexibility of Confucian thought helps to account for its remarkable longevity and influence in China. Two later disciples of Confucius—Mencius and Xunzi—illustrate especially well the ways in which Confucian thought lent itself to adaptation.

Mencius

Mencius (372–289 B.C.E.) was the most learned man of his age and the principal spokesman for the Confucian school. During the Period of the Warring States, he traveled widely throughout China as a political advisor. Mencius firmly believed that human nature was basically good; thus he placed special emphasis on the Confucian virtue of *ren* and advocated government by benevolence and humanity. This principle implied that rulers would levy light taxes, avoid wars, support education, and encourage harmony and cooperation. In his lifetime, Mencius's advice had little practical effect, and critics charged that his views about human nature were naïve. Over the long term, however, his ideas deeply influenced the Confucian tradition. Since about the tenth century C.E., many Chinese scholars have considered Mencius the most authoritative of Confucius's early expositors.

Mencius (MEN-shi-us)

SourcesfromthePast

Confucius on Good Government

Confucius did not record his teachings in formal writings, but scholars believe his disciples collected his often pithy remarks into a work known as the Analects (Sayings) *soon after his death in 479 B.C.E. Many scholars believe that Confucian disciples and adherents continued to add to the* Analects *for two or three centuries after Confucius's death, and thus that they represent the evolution of Confucian thought rather than a verbatim record. In the following selection from the* Analects, *Confucius is referred to as "the Master." This selection highlights the consistent Confucian argument that only good men possessing moral authority could rule effectively.*

The Master said, "He who exercises government by means of his virtue may be compared to the north polar star, which keeps its place, while all the stars turn toward it. . . ."

The Master said, "If the people be led by laws, and uniformity be imposed on them by punishments, they will try to avoid the punishment, but will have no sense of shame."

"If they be led by virtue, and uniformity be provided for them by the rules of propriety, they will have the sense of shame, and moreover will become good. . . ."

The duke Ai asked, saying, "What should be done in order to secure the submission of the people?" Confucius replied, "Advance the upright and set aside the crooked, and then the people will submit. Advance the crooked and set aside the upright, and then the people will not submit."

Ji Kang asked how to cause the people to reverence their ruler, to be faithful to him, and to go on to seek virtue. The Master said, "Let him preside over them with gravity; then they will reverence him. Let him be filial and kind to all; then they will be faithful to him. Let him advance the good and teach the incompetent; then they will eagerly seek to be virtuous. . . ."

Zigong asked about government. The Master said, "The requisites of government are that there be sufficiency of food, sufficiency of military equipment, and the confidence of the people in their ruler." Zigong said, "If it cannot be helped, and one of these must be dispensed with, which of the three should be foregone first?" "The military equipment," said the Master.

Zigong again asked, "If it cannot be helped, and one of the remaining two must be dispensed with, which of them should be foregone?" The Master answered, "Part with the food. From olden times, death has been the lot of all men; but if the people have no faith in their rulers, there is no standing for the state. . . ."

Ji Kang asked Confucius about government, saying, "What do you say to killing the unprincipled for the good of the principled?" Confucius replied, "Sir, in carrying on your government, why should you use killing at all? Let your evinced desires be for what is good, and the people will be good. The relation between superiors and inferiors is like that between the wind and the grass. The grass must bend when the wind blows across it. . . ."

The Master said, "When a prince's personal conduct is correct, his government is effective without the issuing of orders. If his personal conduct is not correct, he may issue orders, but they will not be followed."

For Further Reflection

■ In what ways does this selection from the *Analects* highlight the importance of Confucian ideas about *ren* (benevolence and humanity), *li* (propriety), and *xiao* (filial piety) in the creation of *junzi* (superior individuals)?

Source: James Legge, trans. *The Chinese Classics,* 7 vols. Oxford: Clarendon Press, 1893, 1:145, 146, 152, 254, 258–59, 266. (Translations slightly modified.)

Xunzi Like Confucius and Mencius, Xunzi (298–238 B.C.E.) was a man of immense learning, but unlike his predecessors, he also served for many years as a government administrator. His practical experience encouraged him to develop a less optimistic view of human nature than Mencius's. Xunzi believed that human beings selfishly pursued their own interests and resisted making any voluntary contribution to the larger society. He considered strong social discipline the best means to bring order to society. Thus, whereas Mencius emphasized the Confucian quality of *ren*, Xunzi emphasized *li*. He advocated the establishment of clear, well-publicized standards of conduct that would set limits on the pursuit of individual

interests and punish those who neglected their obligations to the larger society.

Like Confucius and Mencius, however, Xunzi also believed that it was possible to improve human beings and restore order to society. That fundamental optimism was a basic characteristic of Confucian thought. It explains the high value that Confucian thinkers placed on education and public behavior, and it accounts also for their activist approach to public affairs. Confucians involved themselves in society: they sought government positions and made conscientious efforts to solve political and social problems and to promote harmony in public life. By no means, however, did the Confucians win universal praise for their efforts: to some of their contemporaries, Confucian activism represented little more than misspent energy.

Xunzi (SHOON-dzuh)

Daoism

Among the most prominent of these critics were the Daoists. Like Confucianism, Daoism developed in response to the turbulence of the late Zhou dynasty and the Period of the Warring States. But unlike the Confucians, the Daoists considered it pointless to waste time on social activism. Instead, the Daoists devoted their energies to reflection and introspection in hopes that they could understand how to live in harmony with the natural principles that governed the world. The Daoists believed that, over time, this approach would bring harmony to society as a whole, as people ceased to meddle in affairs that they could not understand or control.

Laozi and the Daodejing   According to Chinese tradition, the founder of Daoism was a sage named Laozi who lived during the sixth century B.C.E. Although there might have been a historical Laozi, it is almost certain that several thinkers contributed to the *Daodejing* (*Classic of the Way and of Virtue*), the basic exposition of Daoist beliefs traditionally ascribed to Laozi, and that the book acquired its definitive form over several centuries. After the *Daodejing,* the most important Daoist work was the *Zhuangzi,* named after its author, the philosopher Zhuangzi (369–286 B.C.E.), who provided a well-reasoned compendium of Daoist views.

The Dao   Daoism represented an effort to understand the fundamental character of the world and nature. The central concept of Daoism is the elusive concept of *dao,* meaning "the way," or more specifically "the way of nature" or "the way of the cosmos." In the *Daodejing, dao* figures as the original force of the cosmos, an eternal principle that governs all the workings of the world. The Daodejing envisioned *dao* as a passive force that acted in perfect harmony with the principles of nature. Thus *dao* resembles water, which is soft and yielding, yet is also so powerful that it eventually erodes even the hardest rock placed in its path. *Dao* also resembles the cavity of a pot: although it is nothing more than an empty space, it makes the pot a useful tool.

Daoists believed that human beings should live in harmony with the passive and yielding nature of *dao.* To the Daoists, that meant retreating from the world of politics and administration. Ambition and activism had only brought the world to a state of chaos. The proper response to that situation was to cease frantic striving and with a sense of selfless detachment.

Laozi.
A jade statue produced about the tenth century C.E. depicts the sage Laozi on an ox. Legends reported that Laozi rode a blue ox from China to central Asia while spreading his teachings.

Why would simple dress and transport be appropriate for Laozi?

The Doctrine of Wuwei   Thus early Daoists recognized as the chief moral virtue the trait of *wuwei*—disengagement from active involvement in worldly affairs. *Wuwei* required that individuals refrain from advanced education and personal striving, and that they live simply, unpretentiously, and in harmony with nature.

Wuwei also had implications for state and society: the less government, the better. Instead of expansive kingdoms, the *Daodejing* envisioned a world of tiny, self-sufficient communities where people had no desire to conquer their neighbors or even to trade or visit with them.

Although Daoist thought opposed the activism of Confucianism, in fact the Daoist encouragement of self-knowledge appealed strongly to many Confucians. And, since neither Confucianism nor Daoism was an exclusive faith, it was possible for individuals to study the Confucian curriculum and take administrative posts in the government while devoting their private hours to reflection on human nature and the place of humans in the larger world—to live as Confucians by day, as it were, and Daoists by night.

Daoism (DOW-iz'm)
Daodejing (DOW-DAY-JIHNG)
Zhuangzi (joo-wong-dz)
wuwei (woo-WAY)

Thinking about TRADITIONS

Cultural Unity in Qin and Han China

Although the Qin and Han dynasties built large empires that encompassed a variety of peoples and languages, they insisted on a cultural unity that emphasized the primacy of Chinese customs and traditions over other traditions. *What measures did the two dynasties use to impose this cultural unity, and how successful were they?*

Legalism

Ultimately, neither Confucian activism nor Daoist retreat was able to solve the problems of the Period of the Warring States. Order returned to China only after the emergence of a third school of thought—that of the Legalists—which promoted a practical and ruthlessly efficient approach to statecraft. Unlike the Confucians, the Legalists did not concern themselves with ethics, morality, or propriety. Unlike the Daoists, the Legalists cared nothing about the place of human beings in nature. Instead, they devoted their attention exclusively to the state, which they sought to strengthen and expand at all costs.

Shang Yang and Han Feizi Legalist doctrine emerged from the insights of men who were active in Chinese political affairs during the late fourth century B.C.E. Most notable of them was Shang Yang (ca. 390–338 B.C.E.), who served as chief minister to the duke of the Qin state in western China. His policies survive in a work titled *The Book of Lord Shang*. Though a clever and efficient administrator, Shang Yang was despised because of his power and ruthlessness. Thus, when his patron died, Shang's enemies at court executed him, mutilated his body, and annihilated his family. Another Legalist theorist, Han Feizi (ca. 280–233 B.C.E.) also fell afoul of ambitious men at the Qin court. During his life, Han Feizi synthesized Legalist ideas in a collection of powerful and well-argued essays on statecraft. However, his enemies forced him to commit suicide by taking poison. Thus, the Legalist state itself consumed the two foremost exponents of Legalist doctrine.

Legalist Doctrine   Shang Yang, Han Feizi, and other Legalists reasoned that the foundations of a state's strength were agriculture and armed forces. Since both lines of work directly advanced the interests of the state, Legalists sought to channel as many individuals as possible into cultivation or military service. Meanwhile, they discouraged others from pursuing what they believed were less useful careers as merchants, entrepreneurs, scholars, educators, philosophers, poets, or artists.

The Legalists expected to harness subjects' energy by means of clear and strict laws—hence the name "Legalist." Their faith in laws distinguished the Legalists clearly from the Confucians, who relied on education and example to induce individuals to behave appropriately. The Legalists believed that this was not enough: to persuade individuals to serve the needs of the state, they imposed a strict legal regimen that clearly outlined expectations and provided severe punishment for violators. They believed that if people feared to commit small crimes, they would hesitate all the more before committing great crimes. Thus Legalists imposed harsh penalties for even minor infractions: individuals could suffer amputation of their hands or feet, for example, for disposing of trash in the street. The Legalists also established the principle of collective responsibility before the law, whereby all members of a family or a community were liable to be punished along with the actual violator.

The Legalists' principles of government did not win them much popularity. Yet Legalist doctrine lent itself readily to practical application, and Legalist principles of government quickly produced remarkable results for rulers who adopted them. In fact, Legalist methods put an end to the Period of the Warring States and brought about the unification of China.

THE UNIFICATION OF CHINA

During the Period of the Warring States, rulers of several regional states adopted elements of the Legalist program. Legalist doctrines met the most enthusiastic response in the state of Qin, in western China, where Shang Yang and Han Feizi oversaw the implementation of Legalist policies. The Qin state soon dominated its neighbors and imposed centralized imperial rule throughout China. Qin rule survived for only a few years, but the succeeding Han dynasty followed the Qin example by governing China through a centralized imperial administration.

The Qin Dynasty

The Kingdom of Qin During the fourth and third centuries B.C.E., the Qin state underwent a remarkable round of economic, political, and military development. Shang Yang encouraged peasant cultivators to migrate to the sparsely populated state by granting them private plots. That policy dramatically boosted agricultural production while it simultaneously weakened the economic position of the hereditary aristocratic classes. As a result, Qin rulers found fewer obstacles to establishing centralized, bureaucratic

Han Feizi (hahn-fay-zi)

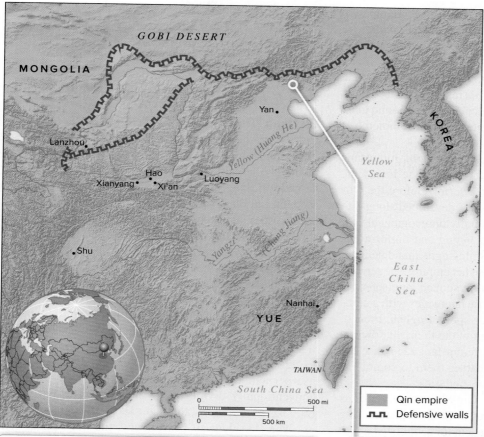

MAP 6.1
China under the Qin dynasty, 221–207 B.C.E. Compare the size of Qin territories to those of earlier Chinese kingdoms depicted in Map 3.2.

How might historians account for the greater reach of the Qin dynasty?

These defensive walls were precursors to China's Great Wall, which was built during the Ming dynasty (1368–1644 C.E.)

Like his ancestors in the kingdom of Qin, the First Emperor of China ignored the nobility and ruled his empire through a centralized bureaucracy. He governed from his capital at Xianyang, near the modern city of Xi'an. The remainder of China he divided into administrative provinces and districts, and he entrusted the implementation of his policies to officers of the central government who served at his pleasure. He disarmed regional military forces, and he built roads to facilitate communications and the movement of armies. He also drafted laborers by the hundreds of thousands to build a massive defensive barrier that was a precursor to the Great Wall of China.

Resistance to Qin Policies
It is likely that many Chinese welcomed the political stability introduced by the Qin dynasty, but it did not win universal acceptance. Confucians, Daoists, and others launched a vigorous campaign of criticism. In an effort to reassert his authority, Qin Shihuangdi ordered execution for those who criticized his regime. In the year following this decree, for example, he is said to have sentenced some 460 scholars residing in the capital to be buried alive for their criticism of his regime. Qin Shihuangdi also demanded that all books of philosophy, ethics, history, and literature be burned. Although he spared some works on medicine, fortune-telling, and agriculture on the grounds that they had some utilitarian value, many classical literary or philosophical works were lost.

rule throughout their state. Meanwhile, they devoted their newfound wealth to the organization of a powerful army equipped with the most effective iron weapons available. During the third century B.C.E., Qin rulers attacked one state after another, absorbing each new conquest into their centralized structure, until finally they had brought China for the first time under the sway of a single state.

The First Emperor In 221 B.C.E., Qin Shihuangdi, the king of Qin (reigned 221–210 B.C.E.), proclaimed himself the First Emperor and decreed that his descendants would reign for thousands of generations. In fact, the dynasty lasted only fourteen years, dissolving in 207 B.C.E. because of civil insurrections. Yet the Qin dynasty had a significance out of proportion to its short life, because like the Achaemenid empire in Persia, the Qin dynasty established a tradition of centralized imperial rule that later rulers sought to emulate.

Qin Centralization The First Emperor launched several initiatives that enhanced the unity of China. In keeping with his policy of centralization, he standardized the laws, currencies, weights, and measures of the various regions of China. Previously, regional states had organized their

Qin Shihuangdi (chin she-huang-dee)
Xianyang (SHYAHN-YAHNG)
Xi'an (shee-ahn)

own legal and economic systems, which often hampered commerce and communications across state boundaries. Uniform coinage and legal standards encouraged the integration of China's various regions into a society more tightly knit than ever before. The roads and bridges that Qin Shihuangdi built throughout his realm, like those built in other classical societies, also encouraged economic integration because they facilitated interregional commerce.

Standardized Script   Perhaps even more important than his legal and economic policies was the First Emperor's standardization of Chinese script. Before the Qin dynasty, regional Chinese scripts had developed along different lines and had become mutually unrecognizable. In hopes of ensuring better understanding and uniform application of his policies, Qin Shihuangdi mandated the use of a common script throughout his empire. The regions of China continued to use different spoken languages, as they do today, but they wrote those languages with a common script—just as if Europeans spoke English, French, German, and other languages but wrote them all down in Latin. In China, speakers of different languages use the same written symbols, which enables them to communicate in writing across linguistic boundaries.

In spite of his ruthlessness, Qin Shihuangdi ranks as one of the most important figures in Chinese history. The First Emperor established a precedent for centralized imperial rule, which remained the norm in China until the early twentieth century. He also pointed China in the direction of political and cultural unity, and with some periods of interruption, China has remained politically and culturally unified to the present day.

Tomb of the First Emperor   Qin Shihuangdi died in 210 B.C.E. His final resting place was a lavish tomb constructed by some seven hundred thousand drafted laborers as a permanent monument to the First Emperor. Rare and expensive grave goods accompanied the emperor in burial, along with sacrificed slaves, concubines, and many of the craftsmen who designed and built the tomb. Qin Shihuangdi was laid to rest in an elaborate underground palace lined with bronze and protected by traps and crossbows rigged to fire at intruders. Buried in the vicinity of the tomb itself was an entire army of magnificently detailed life-size pottery figures to guard the emperor in death.

The terra-cotta army of Qin Shihuangdi protected his tomb, but it could not save his successors or his empire. The First Emperor had conscripted millions of laborers from all parts of China to work on massive public works projects. Although these projects increased productivity and promoted the integration of China's various regions, they also generated tremendous ill will among the drafted laborers.

Revolts began in the year after Qin Shihuangdi's death, and in 207 B.C.E. waves of rebels overwhelmed the Qin court, slaughtering government officials and burning state buildings. The Qin dynasty quickly dissolved in chaos.

The Early Han Dynasty

Liu Bang   The bloody end of the Qin dynasty might well have ended the experiment with centralized imperial rule in China. However, centralized rule returned almost immediately, largely because of a determined commander named Liu Bang. Judging from the historian Sima Qian's account, Liu Bang was not a colorful or charismatic figure, but he was a persistent man and a methodical planner. He surrounded himself with brilliant advisors and enjoyed the unwavering loyalty of his troops. By 206 B.C.E. he had restored order throughout China and established himself at the head of a new dynasty.

Liu Bang called the new dynasty the Han, in honor of his native land. The Han dynasty turned out to be one of the longest and most influential in all of Chinese history. It lasted for more than four hundred years, from 206 B.C.E. to 220 C.E., although for a brief period (9–23 C.E.) a usurper temporarily displaced Han rule. Thus historians conventionally divide the dynasty into the Early Han (206 B.C.E.–9 C.E.) and the Later Han (25–220 C.E.).

The Han dynasty consolidated the tradition of centralized imperial rule that the Qin dynasty had pioneered. During the Early Han, emperors ruled from Chang'an, a cosmopolitan city near modern Xi'an that became the cultural capital of China. During the Later Han, the emperors moved their capital east to Luoyang, also a cosmopolitan city and second in importance only to Chang'an throughout much of Chinese history.

Early Han Policies   During the early days of the Han dynasty, Liu Bang attempted to follow a middle path between the decentralized political alliances of the Zhou dynasty and the tightly centralized state of the Qin to reap the advantages and avoid the excesses of both. On the one hand, he allotted large landholdings to members of the imperial family, in the expectation that they would provide a reliable network of support for his rule. On the other hand, he divided the empire into administrative districts governed by officials who served at the emperor's pleasure.

Liu Bang learned quickly that reliance on his family did not guarantee support for the emperor. In 200 B.C.E. an army of nomadic Xiongnu warriors besieged Liu Bang and almost captured him. He managed to escape—but without receiving the support he had expected from his family members. From that point forward, Liu Bang and his successors followed a policy of centralization. They reclaimed lands from family members, absorbed those lands into the imperial domain, and entrusted political responsibilities to

Xiongnu (SHE-OONG-noo)

The tomb of Qin Shihuangdi.
One detachment of the formidable, life-size, terra-cotta army buried in the vicinity of Qin Shihuangdi's tomb to protect the emperor after his death.
What does the construction of such an elaborate tomb tell us about Qin Shihuangdi's ability to command resources?

an administrative bureaucracy. Thus, despite a brief flirtation with a decentralized government, the Han dynasty left as its principal political legacy a tradition of centralized imperial rule.

The Martial Emperor: Han Wudi Much of the reason for the Han dynasty's success was the long reign of the dynasty's greatest and most energetic emperor, Han Wudi, the "Martial Emperor," who occupied the throne for fifty-four years, from 141 to 87 B.C.E. Han Wudi ruled his empire with vision and vigor. He pursued two policies in particular: administrative centralization and imperial expansion.

Han Centralization Domestically, Han Wudi worked strenuously to increase the authority and prestige of the central government. He built an enormous bureaucracy to administer his empire, and he relied on Legalist principles of government. He also continued the Qin policy of building roads and canals to facilitate trade and communication

between China's regions. To finance the vast machinery of his government, he levied taxes on agriculture, trade, and craft industries, and he established imperial monopolies on the production of essential goods such as iron and salt. In building such an enormous governmental structure, Han Wudi faced a serious problem of recruitment. He needed thousands of reliable, intelligent, educated individuals to run his bureaucracy, but there was no institutionalized educational system in China that could provide a continuous supply of such people.

The Confucian Educational System Han Wudi addressed that problem in 124 B.C.E. by establishing an imperial institute of higher learning that prepared young men for government service. Personally, the Martial Emperor cared little for learning. In that respect he resembled all the other early Han emperors: Liu Bang once emptied his bladder in the distinctive cap worn by Confucian scholars in order to demonstrate his contempt for academic pursuits. Yet

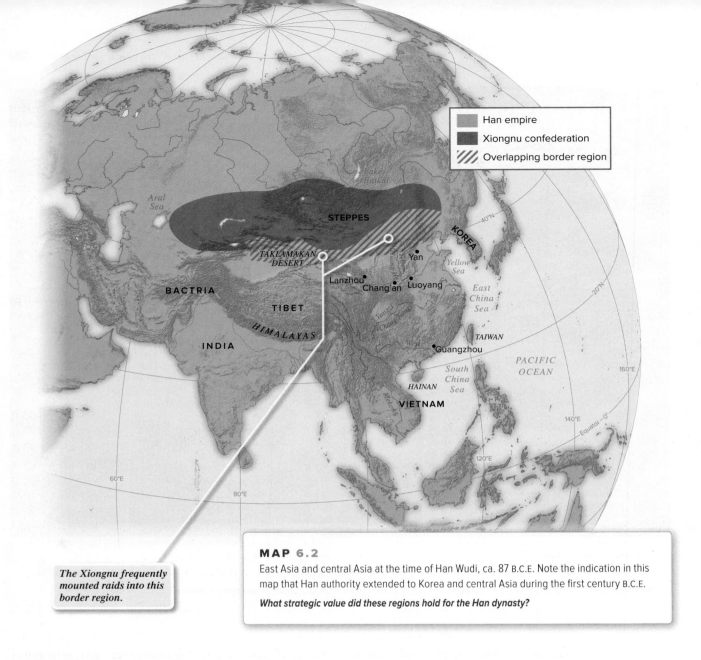

Han empire

Xiongnu confederation

Overlapping border region

STEPPES

KOREA

Yan

Yellow
Sea

Lanzhou
Chang'an Luoyang

East
China
Sea

TAKLAMAKAN
DESERT

Aral
Sea

Lake
Baikal

BACTRIA

TIBET

HIMALAYAS

INDIA

TAIWAN

Guangzhou

PACIFIC
OCEAN

South
China
Sea

HAINAN

VIETNAM

The Xiongnu frequently mounted raids into this border region.

MAP 6.2

East Asia and central Asia at the time of Han Wudi, ca. 87 B.C.E. Note the indication in this map that Han authority extended to Korea and central Asia during the first century B.C.E.

What strategic value did these regions hold for the Han dynasty?

Han Wudi recognized that the success of his efforts at bureaucratic centralization would depend on a corps of educated officeholders. The imperial institute of higher learning took Confucianism—the only Chinese cultural tradition developed enough to provide rigorous intellectual discipline—as the basis for its curriculum. Ironically, then, although he partially relied on Legalist principles of government, Han Wudi ensured the long-term survival of the Confucian tradition by establishing it as the official imperial ideology.

Han Imperial Expansion While he moved aggressively to centralize power and authority at home, Han Wudi pursued an equally vigorous foreign policy of imperial expansion. He invaded northern Vietnam and Korea, subjected them to Han rule, and brought them into the orbit of Chinese society. He ruled both lands through a Chinese-style government, and Confucian values followed the Han armies into the new colonies. Over the course of

the centuries, the educational systems of both northern Vietnam and Korea drew their inspiration almost entirely from Confucianism.

The Xiongnu The greatest foreign challenge that Han Wudi faced came from the Xiongnu, a nomadic people from the steppes of central Asia. Like most of the other nomadic peoples of central Asia, the Xiongnu were superb horsemen. Although their weaponry was not as sophisticated as that of the Chinese, their mobility offered the Xiongnu a distinct advantage. When they could not satisfy their needs through peaceful trade, they mounted sudden raids into villages or trading areas, where they commandeered supplies and then rapidly departed. Because they had no cities or settled places to defend, the Xiongnu could quickly disperse when confronted by a superior force.

During the reign of Modu (210–174 B.C.E.), their most successful leader, the Xiongnu ruled a vast federation

of nomadic peoples that stretched from the Aral Sea to the Yellow Sea. Modu brought strict military discipline to the Xiongnu. According to Sima Qian, Modu once instructed his forces to shoot their arrows at whatever target he himself selected. He aimed in succession at his favorite horse, one of his wives, and his father's best horse, and he summarily executed those who failed to discharge their arrows. When his forces reliably followed his orders, Modu targeted his father, who immediately fell under a hail of arrows, leaving Modu as the Xiongnu chief.

With its highly disciplined army, the Xiongnu empire was a source of concern to the Han emperors. During the early days of the dynasty, they attempted to pacify the Xiongnu by paying them tribute—providing them with food and finished goods in hopes that they would refrain from mounting raids in China—or by arranging marriages between the ruling houses of the two peoples in hopes of establishing peaceful diplomatic relations. Neither method succeeded for long.

Han Expansion into Central Asia Ultimately, Han Wudi decided to go on the offensive against the Xiongnu. He invaded central Asia with vast armies and brought much of the Xiongnu empire under Chinese military control. He pacified a long central Asian corridor extending almost to Bactria (modern Afghanistan), which served as the lifeline of a trade network that linked much of the Eurasian landmass. He even planted colonies of Chinese cultivators in the oasis communities of central Asia. As a result of those efforts, the Xiongnu empire soon fell into disarray. For the moment, the Han state enjoyed uncontested hegemony in both east Asia and central Asia. Before long, however, economic and social problems within China brought serious problems for the Han dynasty itself.

FROM ECONOMIC PROSPERITY TO SOCIAL DISORDER

Already during the Xia, Shang, and Zhou dynasties, a productive agricultural economy supported the emergence of complex society in China. High agricultural productivity continued during the Qin and Han dynasties, and it supported the development of craft industries such as the forging of iron tools and the weaving of silk textiles. During the Han dynasty, however, China experienced serious social and economic problems as land became concentrated in the hands of a small, wealthy elite class. Social tensions generated banditry, rebellion, and even the temporary deposition of the Han state itself. Although Han rulers regained the throne, they presided over a much-weakened realm. By the early third century C.E., social and political problems brought the Han dynasty to an end.

Productivity and Prosperity during the Early Han

Patriarchal Social Order The structure of Chinese society during the Qin and Han dynasties was similar to that of the Zhou era. Patriarchal households averaged five inhabitants, although several generations of aristocratic families sometimes lived together in large compounds. During the Han dynasty, moralists sought to enhance the authority of patriarchal family heads by emphasizing the importance of filial piety and women's subordination to their menfolk. The anonymous Confucian *Classic of Filial Piety,* composed probably in the early Han dynasty, taught that children should obey and honor their parents as well as other superiors and political authorities.

Ban Zhao, Woman Scholar An equally influential treatise was *Lessons for Women* by Ban Zhao (45–120 C.E.), perhaps the most famous woman scholar in Chinese history. Ban Zhao was born into a prominent literary and political family. Her father was a famous scholar and educator. She had two brothers, who were twins. One was a powerful general, and the other followed in the footsteps of Sima Qian as the foremost historian of the later Han dynasty. Ban Zhao herself enjoyed an advanced education and argued in *Lessons for Women* that education should be available to all children—girls as well as boys. Yet Ban Zhao agreed with the *Classic of Filial Piety* and Confucian morality in general that the virtues most appropriate for women were humility, obedience, subservience, and devotion to their fathers, husbands, and sons. From the time of its composition around 100 C.E. to the early twentieth century, *Lessons for Women* was one of the most popular and most widely read statements on the role of women in Chinese society.

Iron Metallurgy During the Han dynasty, the iron industry entered a period of rapid growth. Han artisans experimented with production techniques and learned to

Connecting
the Sources

Prescriptive Literature and the lives of Chinese Women during the Han Dynasty

The problem   Writing about culture and social relationships in the distant past poses specific challenges for historians. Even in societies like China, where literary traditions were already highly sophisticated by the time of the Han dynasty (206 B.C.E.–220 C.E.), available sources illuminating particular cultural attitudes or social relations were nevertheless limited. Existing textual sources tended to be written by educated elites rather than by the peasant farmers or laborers who made up the majority of the population. As a result, historians often have to rely on sources that tell us what educated people said about the ways culture and social relationships should be. Historians call these types of texts **prescriptive literature,** because they *prescribe* how things should be, at least according to their authors. But what can prescriptive literature tell us about how real people actually interacted? Did prescriptive literature *reflect* what culture and social relationships were like for ordinary people, or did people write prescriptive literature in order to *shape* those aspects of society?

When exploring the effects of Confucianism on women's lives in Han China, for example, historians must rely on a relatively small body of textual sources. Two of the most commonly known of these sources—the *Analects* of Confucius and Ban Zhao's *Lessons for Women*—were written by highly educated elites centuries apart from one another. Read the following two documents and think about what historians can and cannot understand about the lives of women in Han China by reading prescriptive literature.

The documents   Read the documents below, and consider carefully the questions that follow.

Document 1: The *Analects* of Confucius do not specifically address the subject of women in many places, although women were implicitly included in Confucius's vision of a moral and ethical society. This short selection, titled "On Women and Servants," is one place where women are mentioned explicitly.

The text reads:

> *17:25 Women and servants are most difficult to nurture. If one is close to them, they lose their reserve, while if one is distant, they feel resentful.*

Document 2: This is an excerpt from Ban Zhao's *Lessons for Women,* written in about 80 C.E.

The text reads:

> *Being careless, and by nature stupid, I taught and trained my children without system. . . .*
>
> *But I do grieve that you, my daughters, just now at the age for marriage, have not at this time had gradual training and advice; that you still have not learned the proper customs for married women. I fear that by failure in good manners in other families you will humiliate both your ancestors and your clan . . . in order that you may have something wherewith to benefit your persons, I wish every one of you, my daughters each to write out a copy for yourself.*
>
> *From this time on every one of you strive to practice these lessons.*
>
> **HUMILITY**
> *On the third day after the birth of a girl the ancients observed three customs: first to place the baby below the bed; second to give her a potsherd [pottery piece] with which to play; and third to announce her birth to her ancestors by an offering. Now to lay the baby below the bed plainly indicated that she is lowly and weak, and should regard it as her primary duty to humble herself before others. To give her potsherds with which to play indubitably signified that she should practice labor and consider it her primary duty to be industrious. To announce her birth before her ancestors clearly meant that she ought to esteem as her primary duty the continuation of the observance of worship in the home.*
>
> *These three ancient customs epitomize woman's ordinary way of life and the teachings of the traditional ceremonial rites and regulations. Let a woman modestly yield to others; let her respect others; let her put others first, herself last. Should she do something good, let her not mention it; should she do something bad let her*

not deny it. Let her bear disgrace; let her even endure when others speak or do evil to her. Always let her seem to tremble and to fear. When a woman follows such maxims as these then she may be said to humble herself before others.

. . .

No woman who observes these three fundamentals of life has ever had a bad reputation or has fallen into disgrace. If a woman fails to observe them, how can her name be honored; how can she but bring disgrace upon herself?

. . .

WOMANLY QUALIFICATIONS

A woman ought to have four qualifications: (1) womanly virtue; (2) womanly words; (3) womanly bearing; and (4) womanly work. Now what is called womanly virtue need not be brilliant ability, exceptionally different from others. Womanly words need be neither clever in debate nor keen in conversation. Womanly appearance requires neither a pretty nor a perfect face and form. Womanly work need not be work done more skillfully than that of others.

To guard carefully her chastity; to control circumspectly her behavior; in every motion to exhibit modesty; and to model each act on the best usage, this is womanly virtue.

To choose her words with care; to avoid vulgar language; to speak at appropriate times; and nor to weary others with much conversation, may be called the characteristics of womanly words.

To wash and scrub filth away; to keep clothes and ornaments fresh and clean; to wash the head and bathe the body regularly, and to keep the person free from disgraceful filth, may be called the characteristics of womanly bearing.

With whole-hearted devotion to sew and to weave; to love not gossip and silly laughter; in cleanliness and order to prepare the wine and food for serving guests, may be called the characteristics of womanly work.

These four qualifications characterize the greatest virtue of a woman. No woman can afford to be without them. In fact they are very easy to possess if a woman only treasure them in her heart. The ancients had a saying: "Is love afar off? If I desire love, then love is at hand!" So can it be said of these qualifications.

Questions

- What can these sources definitively tell you about the lives of the people who produced them? What *facts* can be gleaned from these sources?

- In Document 1, is it significant that Confucius grouped women together with servants when describing the difficulty of nurturing both?

- What might this indicate about Confucius's attitude toward women?

- In Document 2, what is the primary role of women, according to Ban Zhao? What kinds of behaviors should women cultivate if they wish to maintain good virtue and harmonious relationships with others? Do you believe that Ban Zhao was trying to represent women's behavior as she normally observed it, or that she was trying to provide a model to which women should aspire but had not yet reached?

- Taking both documents together, what can they tell us about the effects of Confucianism on the lives of actual women in Han China?

- Do you believe that many women in Han China fulfilled the ideals of womanly virtue as represented by Ban Zhao?

- Sources such as these can help historians understand attitudes about women in Han China, especially when read in conjunction with other textual and material evidence. At the same time, it is important to remember that prescriptive literature is only part of the story: in order to understand the experiences of the majority of women in Han China, we must know more about the conditions of their lives and whether the ideas embodied in prescriptive literature influenced their day-to-day experiences.

Source: Document 1: From Sources of Chinese Tradition, compiled by Wm. Theodore de Bary and Irene Bloom. New York: Columbia University Press (1999), 62. Document 2: Swann, Nancy Lee. Pan Chao: Foremost Woman Scholar of China. New York: Century Co. (1932) pp. 82–90. ©The East Asian Library and the Gest Collection, Princeton University. Reprinted by permission.

Reverberations of
Long-Distance Trade Networks

As we saw in chapter 5, the creation and maintenance of large empires helped to create the conditions for greatly expanded networks of long-distance trade during the classical period. Chinese silk became one of the most highly coveted items of trade over vast areas of Eurasia in this period. Think about the ways that Han state policies were connected to the enormous popularity of Chinese silk in places as far afield as the Mediterranean basin. How was it that so many people were able to discover the beauty of Chinese silk in this period? How might the demand for Chinese silk have affected regional Chinese economies during the Han dynasty?

helps to explain the success of Chinese armies against the Xiongnu and other nomadic peoples.

Silk Textiles Textile production—particularly sericulture, the manufacture of silk—became an especially important industry. The origins of sericulture date to the fourth millennium B.C.E., but only in Han times did sericulture expand from its original home in the Yellow River valley to most parts of China. Although silkworms inhabited much of Eurasia, Chinese silk was especially fine because of advanced sericulture techniques. Chinese producers bred their silkworms, fed them on finely chopped mulberry leaves, and carefully unraveled their cocoons so as to obtain long fibers of raw silk that they wove into light, strong, lustrous fabrics. (In other lands, producers relied on wild silkworms that ate a variety of leaves and chewed through their cocoons, leaving only short fibers that yielded lower-quality fabrics.) Chinese silk became a prized commodity in India, Persia, Mesopotamia, and

craft fine utensils for both domestic and military uses. Iron pots, stoves, knives, needles, axes, hammers, saws, and other tools became standard fixtures in households that could not have afforded more expensive bronze utensils. The ready availability of iron also had important military implications. Craftsmen designed suits of iron armor to protect soldiers against arrows and blows, which

Model of a luxury chariot of the kind used by high imperial officials in the Qin and Han dynasties. Crafted from bronze with silver inlay, this model is about one-third life size.

even the distant Roman empire. Commerce in silk and other products led to the establishment of an intricate network of trade routes known collectively as the Silk Roads (discussed in chapter 9).

Paper While expanding the iron and silk industries, Han craftsmen also invented paper. In earlier times Chinese scribes had written mostly on bamboo strips and silk fabrics, but about 100 C.E. Chinese craftsmen began to fashion hemp, bark, and textile fibers into sheets of paper. Although wealthy elites continued to read books written on silk rolls, paper soon became the preferred medium for most writing.

Population Growth High agricultural productivity supported rapid demographic growth and general prosperity during the early part of the Han dynasty. Historians estimate that about 220 B.C.E., just after the founding of the Qin dynasty, the Chinese population was twenty million. By the year 9 C.E., at the end of the Early Han dynasty, it had tripled to sixty million. Meanwhile, taxes claimed only a small portion of production, yet state granaries bulged so much that their contents sometimes spoiled before they could be consumed.

Economic and Social Difficulties

In spite of general prosperity, China began to experience economic and social difficulties in the Early Han period. The military adventures and the central Asian policy of Han Wudi caused severe economic strain. To finance his ventures, Han Wudi raised taxes and confiscated land

and personal property from wealthy individuals, sometimes on the pretext that they had violated imperial laws. Those measures discouraged investment in manufacturing and trading enterprises, which in turn had a dampening effect on the larger economy.

Social Tensions Distinctions between rich and poor hardened during the course of the Han dynasty. Wealthy individuals wore fine silk garments and ate rich foods, whereas the poor classes made do with rough hemp clothing and a diet of mostly grain. By the first century B.C.E., social and economic differences had generated serious tensions, and peasants in hard-pressed regions began to organize rebellions in hopes of gaining a larger share of Han society's resources.

Land Distribution A particularly difficult problem concerned the distribution of land. Economic problems forced many small landowners to sell their property under unfavorable conditions or even to forfeit it in exchange for cancellation of their debts. In extreme cases, individuals had to sell themselves and their families into slavery to satisfy their creditors. Owners of large estates not only increased the size of their holdings by absorbing the property of their less fortunate neighbors but also increased the efficiency of their operations by employing cheap labor.

By the end of the first century B.C.E., land had accumulated in the hands of a relatively small number of individuals who owned vast estates, while ever-increasing numbers of peasant cultivators led difficult lives with few prospects for improvement. Landless peasants became

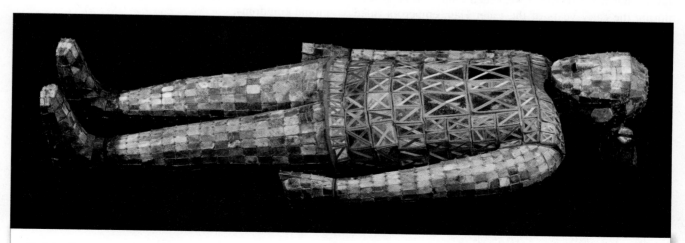

Burial suit.

In Han times the wealthiest classes enjoyed the privilege of being buried in suits of jade plaques sewn together with gold threads, like the burial dress of Tou Wan, wife of Liu Sheng, who lived in the second century B.C.E. at Manzheng in Hebei Province. Legend held that jade prevented decomposition of the deceased's body. Scholars have estimated that a jade burial suit like this one required ten years' labor.

What can such a suit tell us about the lives of the Chinese elite during the Han dynasty?

restive, and Chinese society faced growing problems of banditry and sporadic rebellion.

The Reign of Wang Mang Tensions came to a head during the early first century C.E. when a powerful and respected Han minister named Wang Mang undertook a thoroughgoing program of reform. In 6 C.E. a two-year-old boy inherited the Han imperial throne. Because the boy was unable to govern, Wang Mang served as his regent. Many officials regarded Wang as more capable than members of the Han family and urged him to claim the imperial honor for himself. In 9 C.E. he did just that: announcing that the mandate of heaven had passed from the Han to his family, he seized the throne. Wang Mang then introduced a series of wide-ranging reforms that have prompted some historians to refer to him as the "socialist emperor."

The most important reforms concerned landed property: Wang Mang limited the amount of land that a family could hold and ordered officials to break up large estates, redistribute them, and provide landless individuals with property to cultivate. Despite his good intentions, the socialist emperor attempted to impose his policy without adequate preparation and communication. The result was confusion: landlords resisted a policy that threatened their holdings, and even peasants found its application inconsistent and unsatisfactory. After several years of chaos, in 23 C.E. a coalition of disgruntled landlords and desperate peasants ended both his dynasty and his life.

The Later Han Dynasty

Within two years a recovered Han dynasty returned to power, but it ruled over a weakened realm. Nevertheless, during the early years of the Later Han, emperors ruled vigorously in the manner of Liu Bang and Han Wudi. They regained control of the centralized administration and reorganized the state bureaucracy. They also maintained the Chinese presence in central Asia, continued to keep the Xiongnu in submission, and exercised firm control over the silk roads.

However, the Later Han emperors did not seriously address the problem of land distribution that had helped to bring down the Early Han dynasty. The wealthy classes still lived in relative luxury while peasants worked under difficult conditions. The empire continued to suffer the effects of banditry and rebellions organized by desperate peasants with few opportunities to improve their lot.

Collapse of the Han Dynasty In addition, the Later Han emperors were unable to prevent the development of factions at court that paralyzed the central government. Factions of imperial family members, Confucian scholar-bureaucrats, and court eunuchs sought to increase their influence, protect their own interests, and destroy their rivals. On several occasions relations between the various factions became so strained that they made war against one another. In 189 C.E., for example, a faction led by an imperial relative descended on the Han palace and slaughtered more than two thousand eunuchs in an effort to destroy them as a political force. In that respect the attack succeeded. From the unmeasured violence of the operation, however, it is clear that the Later Han dynasty had reached a point of internal weakness from which it could not easily recover. Indeed, early in the next century, the central government disintegrated, and for almost four centuries China remained divided into several large regional kingdoms.

SUMMARY

The Qin state lasted for a short fourteen years, but it opened a new era in Chinese history. Qin conquerors imposed unified rule on a series of politically independent kingdoms and launched an ambitious program to forge culturally distinct regions into a larger Chinese society. The Han dynasty that followed the Qin endured for more than four centuries and largely completed the project of unifying China. Using a combination of Legalism and Confucianism, two of the most important philosophies that had emerged during the Late Zhou Dynasty, Han rulers built a centralized bureaucracy that administered a unified empire. Han emperors worked particularly closely with Confucian moralists who organized a system of advanced education that provided recruits for the imperial bureaucracy. Moreover, on the basis of a highly productive economy stimulated by technological innovations, Han rulers projected Chinese influence abroad to Korea, Vietnam, and central Asia. Thus, like classical societies in Persia, India, and the Mediterranean basin, Han China produced a set of distinctive political and cultural traditions that shaped Chinese and neighboring societies over the long term.

STUDY TERMS

Analects (102, 104, 112)
Confucianism (102)
Daodejing (105)
Daoism (105)
Early Han (111, 115–116)
Han dynasty (108–111, 116)
Han Feizi (106)
Han Wudi (109–111)
junzi (102)
Laozi (105)
Later Han (116)
Legalism (106)
Liu Bang (108)
Modu (110–111)

Mencius (103)
Qin (101)
Qin Shihuangdi (107)
ren (103)
Sima Qian (101)
Wang Mang (116)
wuwei (105)
Xi'an (107)
Xianyang (107)
Xiongnu (108, 110)
Xunzi (104)
Zhou (102)
Zhuangzi (105)

FOR FURTHER READING

Sebastian DeGrazia, ed. *Masters of Chinese Political Thought from the Beginnings to the Han Dynasty.* New York, 1973. A valuable collection of primary sources in translation, all of them bearing on political themes.

Nicola Di Cosmo. *Ancient China and Its Enemies: The Rise of Nomad Power in East Asian History.* Cambridge, 2002. Outstanding analysis of the relationship between ancient China and its militarized nomadic neighbors, particularly between the Han dynasty and the Xiongnu.

Cho-yun Hsu. *Han Agriculture: The Formation of Early Chinese Agrarian Economy (206 B.C.–A.D. 220).* Seattle, 1980. Studies the development of intensive agriculture in Han China and provides English translations of more than two hundred documents illustrating the conditions of rural life.

Mark Edward Lewis. *The Early Chinese Empires: Qin and Han.* Cambridge, Mass., 2007. Emphasizes the long-term influence of imperial rule established by the Qin and Han dynasties.

Simon Leys, trans. *The Analects of Confucius.* New York, 1997. A modern, fluent, and very readable translation of the classic work of Confucianism.

Frederick W. Mote. *Intellectual Foundations of China.* 2nd ed. New York, 1989. A compact and concise introduction to the cultural history of classical China.

Michele Pirazzoli-t'Serstevens. *The Han Dynasty.* Trans. by J. Seligman. New York, 1982. An excellent and well-illustrated survey of Han China that draws on archaeological discoveries.

Benjamin I. Schwartz. *The World of Thought in Ancient China.* Cambridge, Mass., 1985. A synthesis of classical Chinese thought by a leading scholar.

Arthur Waldron. *The Great Wall of China: From History to Myth.* Cambridge, 1989. Places the modern Great Wall in the tradition of Chinese wall building from Qin times forward.

Burton Watson, trans. *Records of the Grand Historian.* Rev. ed. 2 vols. New York, 1993. Excellent translation of Sima Qian's history, the most important narrative source for Han China.

State, Society, and the Quest for Salvation in India

CHAPTER 7

A sculpture of the Buddha in gray schist, from the Gandhara region of modern Pakistan.

PART

EYEWITNESS:

A Greek Perspective on Classical India

The earliest description of India by a foreigner came from the pen of a Greek ambassador named Megasthenes. As the diplomatic representative of the Seleucid emperor, Megasthenes lived in India for many years during the late fourth and early third centuries B.C.E., and he traveled throughout much of northern India. Although Megasthenes' book, the *Indika,* has long been lost, many quotations from it survive in Greek and Latin literature. These fragments clearly show that Megasthenes had great respect for the Indian land, people, and society.

Like travel writers of all times, Megasthenes included a certain amount of spurious information in his account of India. He wrote, for example, of ants the size of foxes that mined gold from the earth and fiercely defended their hoards from any humans who tried to steal them. Only by distracting them with slabs of meat, Megasthenes said, could humans safely make away with their treasure. He also reported races of monstrous human beings: some with no mouth who survived by breathing in the odors of fruits, flowers, and roots, others with the heads of dogs who communicated by barking.

Beyond the tall tales, Megasthenes offered a great deal of reliable information. He portrayed India as a fertile land that supported two harvests of grain per year. He described the capital of Pataliputra as a rectangle-shaped city situated along the Ganges River and surrounded by a moat and a massive timber wall with 570 towers and sixty-four gates. He mentioned large armies that used elephants as war animals. He pointed out the strongly hierarchical character of Indian society. He noted that two main schools of "philosophers" (Hindus and Buddhists) enjoyed special prominence as well as exemption from taxes, and he described the ascetic lifestyles and vegetarian diets followed by particularly devout individuals. In short, Megasthenes portrayed India as a wealthy land that supported a distinctive society with well-established cultural traditions.

In India as in Persia and China, the centuries after 500 B.C.E. witnessed the development of a classical society whose influence has persisted over the centuries. Its most prominent features were a well-defined social structure, which left individuals with few doubts about their position and role in society, and several popular religious traditions that helped to shape Indian beliefs and values. Two religions, Buddhism and Hinduism, also appealed strongly to peoples beyond the subcontinent.

For the most part, classical India fell under the sway of regional kingdoms rather than centralized empires. Yet the empires that did arise were crucial for the consolidation of Indian cultural traditions, because they sponsored cultural leaders and promoted their ideals throughout the subcontinent and beyond. The spread of Buddhism is a case in point: imperial support helped the faith secure its position in India and attract converts in other lands. Thus, even in the absence of a continuous imperial tradition like that of Persia or China, the social and cultural traditions of classical India not only shaped the lives and experiences of the subcontinent's inhabitants but also influenced peoples in distant lands.

CHRONOLOGY

599–527 B.C.E.	Life of Vardhamana Mahavira
563–483 B.C.E.	Life of Siddhartha Gautama, the Buddha
520 B.C.E.	Invasion of India by Darius of Persia
327 B.C.E.	Invasion of India by Alexander of Macedon
321–185 B.C.E.	Mauryan dynasty
321–297 B.C.E.	Reign of Chandragupta Maurya
268–232 B.C.E.	Reign of Ashoka Maurya
182 B.C.E.–1 C.E.	Bactrian rule in northern India
1–270 C.E.	Kushan empire in northern India and central Asia
127–153 C.E.	Reign of Kushan emperor Kanishka
320–550 C.E.	Gupta dynasty

THE FORTUNES OF EMPIRE IN CLASSICAL INDIA

Following their migrations to India after 1500 B.C.E., the Aryans established a series of small kingdoms throughout the subcontinent. By the sixth century B.C.E., wars of expansion between these small kingdoms had resulted in the consolidation of several large regional kingdoms that dominated much of the subcontinent. Despite strenuous efforts, none of these kingdoms was able to establish hegemony over the others until the classical era, when the Mauryan and the Gupta dynasties founded centralized, imperial states that embraced much of India. However, neither empire survived long enough to establish centralized rule as a lasting feature of Indian political life.

The Mauryan Dynasty and the Temporary Unification of India

The unification of India came about partly as a result of intrusion from beyond the subcontinent. About 520 B.C.E. the Persian emperor Darius I crossed the Hindu Kush Mountains, conquered parts of northwestern India, and made the kingdom of Gandhara (the northern part of modern-day Pakistan and southern modern-day Afghanistan) a province of the Achaemenid empire. Almost two centuries later, in 327 B.C.E., after overrunning the Persian empire, Alexander of Macedon crossed the Indus River and crushed the states he found there. Alexander remained in India for only two years, and he did not make a deep impression on the Punjabi people. Yet his campaign had an important effect on Indian history, since he created a political vacuum in northwestern India by destroying the existing states and then withdrawing his forces.

Kingdom of Magadha Poised to fill the vacuum was the dynamic kingdom of Magadha, located in the central portion of the Ganges plain. By about 500 B.C.E. Magadha had emerged as the most important state in northeastern India. During the next two centuries, the kings of Magadha conquered the neighboring states and gained control of Indian commerce passing through the Ganges valley as well as overseas trade between India and Burma passing across the Bay of Bengal. The withdrawal of Alexander from the Punjab presented Magadha with a rare opportunity to expand.

Chandragupta Maurya During the late 320s B.C.E., an ambitious adventurer named Chandragupta Maurya exploited that opportunity and laid the foundation for the Mauryan empire, the first state to bring a centralized, unified government to most of the Indian subcontinent. Chandragupta began by seizing control of small, remote regions of Magadha and then worked his way gradually toward the center. By 321 B.C.E. he had overthrown the ruling dynasty and consolidated his hold on the kingdom. He then moved into the Punjab and brought northwestern India under his control. Next he ventured beyond the Indus River and conquered the Greek state in Bactria a large region incorporating most of modern Afghanistan and some regions to the north. By the end of the fourth century B.C.E., Chandragupta's empire embraced all of northern India from the Indus to the Ganges.

Chandragupta's Government A careful and systematic advisor named Kautalya devised procedures for the governance of Chandragupta's realm. Some of Kautalya's advice survives in the ancient Indian political handbook known as the *Arthashastra*. The *Arthashastra* outlined

Chandragupta Maurya (chuhn-dra-GOOP-tah MORE-yuh)

Kautalya (KAHT-ahl-yah)

Arthashastra (UHRR-th-sha-strah)

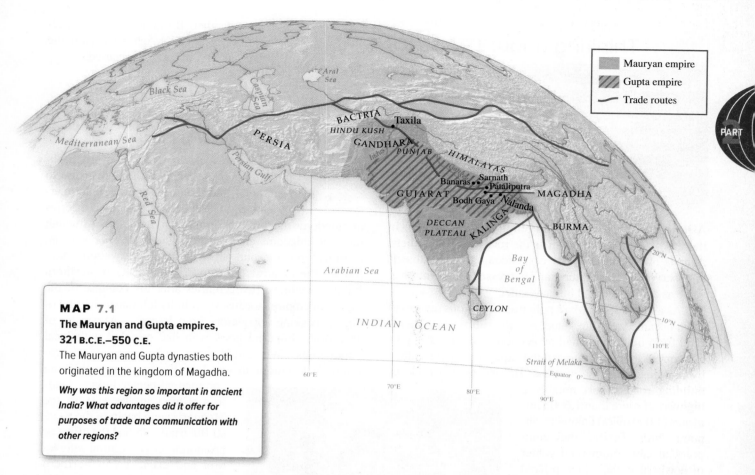

MAP 7.1

The Mauryan and Gupta empires, 321 B.C.E.–550 C.E.

The Mauryan and Gupta dynasties both originated in the kingdom of Magadha.

Why was this region so important in ancient India? What advantages did it offer for purposes of trade and communication with other regions?

methods of administering the empire, overseeing trade and agriculture, collecting taxes, maintaining order, conducting foreign relations, and waging war. Kautalya also advised Chandragupta to make abundant use of spies, even including prostitutes in his stable of informants. Like the emperors of Persia and China, Chandragupta and Kautalya built a bureaucratic administrative system that enabled them to implement policies throughout the state.

Ashoka Maurya Tradition holds that Chandragupta abdicated his throne to become a Jain monk and led such an ascetic life that he starved himself to death. Whether that report is true or not, it is certain that his son succeeded him in 297 B.C.E. and added much of southern India to the growing empire. The high point of the Mauryan empire, however, came during the reign of Chandragupta's grandson Ashoka.

Ashoka began his reign (268–232 B.C.E.) as a conqueror. When he came to power, the only major region that remained independent of the Mauryan empire was the kingdom of Kalinga (modern Orissa) in the east-central part of the subcontinent. Kalinga was desirable territory for Ashoka because it controlled both land and sea trade routes between the Ganges plain and southern India. Thus Ashoka's first major undertaking as emperor was to conquer Kalinga and bring it under Mauryan control,

which he did in a bloody campaign in 260 B.C.E. By Ashoka's estimate, 100,000 Kalingans died in the fighting, 150,000 were driven from their homes, and untold numbers of others perished in the ruined land.

In spite of that campaign, Ashoka is much better known as a governor than as a conqueror. With Kalinga subdued, Ashoka ruled almost the entire subcontinent—only the southernmost region escaped his control—and he turned his attention to the responsible government of his realm. As heir to the administrative structure that Chandragupta and Kautalya had instituted, Ashoka ruled through a tightly organized bureaucracy. He established his capital at the fortified and cosmopolitan city of Pataliputra (near modern Patna), where a central administration developed policies for the whole empire. A central treasury oversaw the efficient collection of taxes—a hallmark of Kautalya's influence—which supported legions of officials, accountants, clerks, soldiers, and other imperial employees. Ashoka communicated his policies throughout his realm by inscribing edicts in natural stone formations or on pillars that he ordered erected. As we will see later in this chapter,

---

Ashoka (ah-SHOW-kuh)

Pataliputra (pah-tal-ih-puh-trah)

Ashoka also converted to the religion of Buddhism. In those promulgations, known as the rock and pillar edicts, Ashoka issued imperial decrees, encouraged his subjects to observe Buddhist values, and expressed his intention to serve as a fair, just, and humane ruler.

As a result of Ashoka's policies, the various regions of India became well integrated, and the subcontinent benefited from both an expanding economy and a stable government. Ashoka encouraged the expansion of agriculture by building irrigation systems. He encouraged trade by building roads, most notably a highway of more than 1,600 kilometers (1,000 miles) linking Pataliputra with Taxila, the chief political and commercial center of northern India, which offered access to Bactria, Persia, and other points west. Ashoka also provided comforts for administrators, merchants, and other travelers by planting banyan trees to offer shade, digging wells, and establishing inns along the roads.

Decline of the Mauryan Empire Ashoka's policies did not long survive his rule, nor did his empire. Ashoka died in 232 B.C.E., and decline set in almost immediately. During its later years the Mauryan empire suffered from acute financial and economic difficulties. The empire depended on a strong army and a large corps of officials to administer imperial policy. Salaries for soldiers and bureaucrats were very expensive, and administrative costs soon outstripped the revenues that flowed into the central treasury. Because of their financial difficulties, the later Mauryan emperors were unable to hold the

Stone column from the reign of Ashoka.
As a symbol of his rule, Ashoka had this sculpture of four lions mounted atop a column about 20 meters (66 feet) tall. The lion capital is the official symbol of the modern Republic of India.

Why might Ashoka have chosen the lion as a symbol of his rule?

realm together. By about 185 B.C.E., almost fifty years after Ashoka's death, the Mauryan empire had disappeared.

The Emergence of Regional Kingdoms and the Revival of Empire

Bactrian Rule in Northwestern India

Although the Mauryan empire came to an end, India did not crumble into anarchy. Instead, local rulers formed a series of kingdoms that brought order to large regions. Although regional kingdoms emerged throughout the subcontinent, historical records and archaeological excavations have thrown the clearest light on developments in northern India. For almost two centuries after the collapse of the Mauryan empire, northwestern India fell under the rule of Greek-speaking conquerors from Bactria—Alexander of Macedon's imperial heirs who had mingled with local populations since establishing an independent Greco-Bactrian kingdom in ca. 250. Bactria was a thriving commercial center linking lands from China in the east to the Mediterranean basin in the west, so Bactrian rule had the effect of promoting cross-cultural interaction and exchange in northern India. Large volumes of trade provided sources of revenue for the Bactrian rulers, and the city of Taxila flourished because of its strategic location on trade routes leading from northern India to Bactria.

The Kushan Empire Beginning in the late second century B.C.E., several groups of nomadic conquerors from central Asia attacked Bactria and eventually put an end to the Greco-Bactrian kingdom there. The most successful of those conquerors were the Kushans, who ruled a sizable empire embracing much of northern India and central Asia from about 1 to 270 C.E. Under Kanishka, the most prominent of the Kushan emperors (reigned 127–153 C.E.), the Kushan empire included modern-day Pakistan, Afghanistan, parts of Uzbekistan and Tajikistan, and northern India to the central part of the Ganges valley.

Like the Greco-Bactrians, the Kushans facilitated commerce between India and lands to the north. Indeed, the Kushan empire played a crucial role in the silk roads network (discussed in chapter 12) by pacifying much of the large region between Persia and China, thus making it possible for merchants to travel safely across long distances. Participation in extensive networks enabled Kushan rulers to serve as cultural intermediaries. They generously patronized Bactrian and Indian artists who employed Greek styles of painting and sculpture in the depiction of local subjects. Because many of the Kushan kings were enthusiastic supporters of Buddhism, they commissioned the artists of the so-called Gandharan and Mathuran traditions to create the first ever depictions of the Buddha, which was a crucial development in facilitating the spread of Buddhism from India into central and east Asia. On several occasions the Kushans and other rulers of northern India faced ambitious kings who sought to expand their realms and imitate the Mauryas by building an empire based in the Indian subcontinent. Only with the Guptas, however, did any of them approach the realization of their imperial ambitions.

The Gupta Dynasty In about 320 C.E., a new power—the Guptas—arose in the Ganges region and established a dynamic kingdom. Like the Mauryas, the Guptas based their state in Magadha, a crucial region because of its wealth, its dominance of the Ganges valley, and its role as intermediary between the various regions of the subcontinent. The empire was founded by Chandra Gupta (not related to Chandragupta Maurya), who forged alliances with powerful families in the Ganges region. His successors, Samudra Gupta (reigned 335–375 C.E.) and Chandra Gupta II (reigned 375–415 C.E.), took the former Mauryan capital of Pataliputra as their own, conquered many of the regional kingdoms of India, and established tributary alliances with others that elected not to fight. Only the Deccan Plateau and the southernmost part of the subcontinent remained outside the orbit of Gupta influence.

The Gupta empire was somewhat smaller in size than the Mauryan, and it also differed considerably in organization. Ashoka had insisted on knowing the details of regional affairs, which he closely monitored from his court at Pataliputra. The Guptas left local government and administration, and even the making of basic policy, in the hands of their allies in the various regions of their empire. Nevertheless, during the late fourth and early fifth centuries C.E., the Gupta dynasty brought stability and prosperity to much of the subcontinent.

Gupta Decline The Guptas were eventually overcome, however, by the White Huns, a nomadic people from central Asia. For the first half of the fifth century, the Guptas repelled the Huns as they tried to invade across the Hindu Kush mountains from Bactria, but the defense cost them dearly in resources and eventually weakened their state. By the end of the fifth century, the Huns moved across the Hindu Kush almost at will and had established several kingdoms in northern and western India.

The Gupta dynasty continued in name only: regional governors progressively usurped imperial rights and powers, and contemporary documents do not even record the names of all the later Gupta emperors. Once again, imperial government survived only for a short term in India. Not until the establishment of the Mughal dynasty in the sixteenth century C.E. did any state rule as much of India as the Mauryan and Gupta empires ruled. Memories of empire remained, to be sure, but for the most part large regional kingdoms dominated political life in India during the millennium between the Gupta and the Mughal dynasties.

ECONOMIC DEVELOPMENT AND SOCIAL DISTINCTIONS

After spreading across northern India, Aryan migrants turned increasingly from herding to agriculture. Once they learned the techniques of iron metallurgy after about 1000 B.C.E., they used iron axes and tools to advance into previously inaccessible regions, notably the jungle-covered valley of the Ganges River. Agricultural surpluses from these fertile lands supported large-scale states such as the regional kingdoms and the Mauryan and Gupta empires that organized Indian public life.

Agricultural surpluses also encouraged the emergence of towns, the growth of trade, and further development of the caste system.

Towns and Trade

After about 600 B.C.E. towns dotted the Indian countryside, especially in the northwestern corner of the subcontinent.

A gold Kushan coin depicts King Kanishka on one side and one of the earliest known representations of the Buddha on the other.

Gupta (GOOP-tah)

Reverberations of ● ● ● ● ● ● ● ●
Long-Distance Trade Networks

The long-distance trade networks of the classical period allowed the introduction of foodstuffs and commodities to regional cuisines thousands of miles from their points of origin. Indian black pepper was one of the most sought-after foodstuffs in these long-distance networks and was traded over the land routes to central Asia and China as well as over sea routes to the Mediterranean and Southeast Asia. At the time, pepper was used for far more than a condiment to enliven dull food. Instead, pepper was an important preservative for meat and was also used for its medicinal properties to alleviate stomach and other ailments. *What might have been the long-term impact of the introduction of pepper as a preservative across Eurasia?*

These towns served the needs of a productive agricultural society by providing manufactured products for local consumption—pots, textiles, iron tools, and other metal utensils—as well as luxury goods such as jewelry destined for the wealthy and elite classes.

Flourishing towns maintained marketplaces and encouraged the development of trade. Within the subcontinent itself trade was most active along the Ganges River, although trade routes also passed through the Ganges delta east to Burma and down the east Indian coast to the Deccan and southern India. Roads built by Ashoka also facilitated overland commerce within the subcontinent.

Long-Distance Trade Meanwhile, the volume of long-distance trade also grew as large imperial states in China, southwest Asia, and the Mediterranean basin provided a political foundation enabling merchants to deal with their counterparts in distant lands. From India, long-distance trade passed overland in two directions: through the Hindu Kush mountains and the Gandharan capital of Taxila to Persia and the Mediterranean basin, and across the Silk Roads of central Asia to markets in China. Cotton, aromatics, black pepper, pearls, and gems were the principal Indian exports, in exchange for which Indian merchants imported horses and bullion from western lands and silk from China.

Trade in the Indian Ocean Basin
During the Mauryan era merchants continued to use land routes, but they increasingly turned to the sea to transport their goods. Seaborne trade benefited

especially from the rhythms of the monsoon winds that govern weather and the seasons in the Indian Ocean basin. During the spring and summer, the winds blow from the southwest, and during the fall and winter, they blow from the northeast. Once mariners recognized these rhythms, they could sail easily and safely before the wind to any part of the Indian Ocean basin.

As early as the fifth century B.C.E., Indian merchants had traveled to the islands of Indonesia and the southeast Asian mainland, where they exchanged pearls, cotton, black pepper, and Indian manufactured goods for spices and exotic local products. Many of those goods then traveled west through the Arabian Sea to the lands bordering the Persian Gulf and the Red Sea. Indian products also found markets in the Mediterranean basin. Indian pepper became so popular there that the Romans established direct commercial relations and built several trading settlements in southern India. Archaeologists in southern India have unearthed hoards of Roman coins that testify to the large volume of trade between classical India and Mediterranean lands.

Gupta-era painting.
Jewel-bedecked flying goddesses drop flowers on the earth from their perch in the heavens. Their gems and personal adornments reflect the tastes of upper-class women during the Gupta dynasty. This painting on a rock wall, produced about the sixth century C.E., survives in modern Sri Lanka.

Family Life and the Caste System

Gender Relations In the midst of urban growth and economic development, Indian moralists sought to promote stability by encouraging respect for strong patriarchal families and to promote the maintenance of a social order in which all members played well-defined roles. Although most people lived with members of their nuclear family, among the higher castes several generations of a family often lived in large compounds ruled by powerful patriarchs. Literary works suggest that women were largely subordinate to men. The two great Indian epics, the *Mahabharata* and the *Ramayana,* commonly portrayed women as weak-willed and emotional creatures and exalted wives who devoted themselves to their husbands.

During the early centuries C.E., patriarchal dominance became more pronounced in India. By the Gupta era child marriage was common: when girls were age eight or nine, their parents betrothed them to men in their twenties. Formal marriage took place just after the girls reached puberty. Wives often came to dominate domestic affairs in their households, but the practice of child marriage placed them under the control of older men and encouraged them to devote themselves to family matters rather than to public affairs in the larger society.

Social Order After their arrival in India, the Aryans recognized four main castes, or classes of people: *brahmins* (priests), *kshatriyas* (warriors and aristocrats), *vaishyas* (peasants and merchants), and *shudras* (serfs). Brahmins in particular endorsed this social order, which brought them honor, prestige, and sometimes considerable wealth as well.

Castes and Guilds However, as trade and industrial activity expanded, new groups of artisans, craftsmen, and merchants appeared, many of whom did not fit easily into the established structure. Individuals working in the same craft or trade usually joined together to form a guild, a corporate body that supervised prices and wages in a given industry and provided for the welfare of members and their families. Guild members lived in the same quarter of town, socialized with one another, intermarried, and cared for the group's widows, orphans, and needy.

In effect, the guilds functioned as subcastes based on occupation, known as *jati*. These *jati,* in turn, assumed much of the responsibility for maintaining social order in India. *Jati* regularly organized their own courts, through which they disciplined members, resolved differences, and regulated community affairs. Individuals who did not abide by group rules were liable to expulsion from the community. Thus Indian guilds and *jati* performed services that central governments provided in other lands. The tendency for individuals and their families to associate closely with others of the same occupation remained a prominent feature of Indian society well into modern times.

Buddhist temple sculpture.
Buddhist art often depicted individuals as models of proper social relationships. Here a sculpture from a Buddhist temple at Karli, produced about the first century C.E., represents an ideal Buddhist married couple.

What does the position of the images imply about the ideal relationship between husband and wife?

Wealth and the Social Order Beyond encouraging further development of the caste system, economic development in the subcontinent also generated tremendous wealth, which posed a serious challenge to the social order that arose in India following the Aryan migrations. Traditional social theory accorded special honor to the brahmins and the kshatriyas because of the worthy lives they had led during previous incarnations and the heavy responsibilities

Mahabharata (mah-hah-BAH-'rah-tah)
Ramayana (rah-MAY-yuh-nah)
kshatriyas (kuh-SHAT-tree-uhs)
vaishyas (VEYESH-yuhs)
shudras (SHOO-druhs)

they assumed as priests, warriors, and rulers during their current incarnations. Members of the vaishya and shudra castes, on the other hand, had the obligation to work as directed by the higher castes. During the centuries after 600 B.C.E., however, trade and industry brought prosperity to many vaishyas and even shudras, who sometimes became wealthier and more influential in society than their brahmin and kshatriya contemporaries.

Economic development and social change in classical India had profound implications for the established cultural as well as the social order. The beliefs, values, and rituals that were meaningful in early Aryan society—especially the ritual sacrifices offered by brahmins—seemed increasingly irrelevant during the centuries after 600 B.C.E. Along with emerging towns, growing trade, increasing wealth, and a developing social structure, classical India saw the appearance of new religions that addressed the needs of the changing times.

RELIGIONS OF SALVATION IN CLASSICAL INDIA

During the sixth and fifth centuries B.C.E., new religions and philosophies appealed to the interests of new social classes. Some of them tended toward atheistic materialism: members of the Charvaka sect, for example, believed that the gods were figments of the imagination, that brahmins were charlatans who enriched themselves by hoodwinking others, and that human beings came from dust and returned to dust like any other animal in the natural world. Others, such as the Jains, the Buddhists, and the Hindus, turned to intense spirituality as an alternative to the mechanical rituals of the brahmins.

Jainism and the Challenge to the Established Cultural Order

Vardhamana Mahavira Among the most influential of the new religions was Jainism. Although Jainist doctrines first appeared during the seventh century B.C.E., they became popular only when the great teacher Vardhamana Mahavira turned to Jainism in the late sixth century B.C.E. Mahavira (the "great hero") was born in northern India about 599 B.C.E. to a prominent kshatriya family. According to the semilegendary accounts of his life, he left home at age thirty to seek salvation by escaping from the cycle of incarnation. For twelve years he led an ascetic life wandering

Charvaka (CHAHR-vah-kuh)

Jainism (JEYEN-iz'm)

Vardhamana (vahr-duh-MAH-nuh)

Upanishads (oo-pan-NIH-shuhds)

ahimsa (uh-HIM-suh)

Jain sculpture.
Mahavira with his disciples. Representations of the early Jains often depicted them in the nude because of their ascetic way of life.

throughout the Ganges valley, after which he gained enlightenment. He abandoned all his worldly goods, even his clothes, and taught an ascetic doctrine of detachment from the world. For the next thirty years, until his death about 527 B.C.E., he expounded his thought to a group of disciples who formed a monastic order to perpetuate and spread his message. These disciples referred to Mahavira as *Jina* (the "conqueror"), and borrowing from this title his followers referred to themselves as *Jains*.

Much of the inspiration for Jainist doctrine came from the Upanishads. Jains believed that virtually everything in the universe—humans, animals, plants, the air, bodies of water, and even inanimate physical objects—possessed a soul. As long as they remained trapped in terrestrial bodies, these souls experienced both physical and psychological suffering. Only by purification from selfish behavior could souls gain release from their imprisonment and attain a state of bliss.

Jainist Ethics Individuals underwent purification by observing the principle of *ahimsa,* or nonviolence to other souls. Devout Jainist monks went to extremes to avoid harming the millions of souls they encountered each day. They swept the ground before them as they walked to avoid causing harm to insects; they strained their drinking water through cloth filters to remove tiny animals they might unwittingly consume; they followed an abstemious and strictly vegetarian diet; they even wore masks and avoided making sudden movements so that they would not bruise or otherwise disturb the tiny souls inhabiting the surrounding air.

Jainist ethics were so demanding that few people other than devout monks could hope to observe them closely. For certain groups, however, Jainism represented an attractive alternative to the traditional cults. Indeed, since Jains believed all creatures had souls that should be protected equally, Jains did not recognize human social hierarchies based on caste or *jati.* It is not surprising, then, that their faith became popular especially among members of lower castes who did not command much respect in the traditional social order. These people provided substantial lay support for the Jainist monks and helped to maintain the ideal of ahimsa as a prominent concern of Indian ethics. Indeed, the doctrine of ahimsa has been an especially influential teaching over the long term, both in India and beyond. Quite apart from some 4.2 million Indian individuals who maintain Jainist traditions in the present day, many Buddhists and Hindus recognize ahimsa as a fundamental element of their beliefs, and prominent reformers of the twentieth century c.e. such as Mohandas K. Gandhi and Martin Luther King Jr. relied on the doctrine of ahimsa when promoting social reform by nonviolent means.

In spite of the moral respect it has commanded and the influence it has wielded through the centuries, however, Jainism has always been the faith of a small minority. It has simply been too difficult for most people to observe. A more popular and practical alternative to the brahmins' cults came in the form of Buddhism.

Early Buddhism

Siddhartha Guatama Like Mahavira, the founder of Buddhism, Siddhartha Gautama came from a kshatriya family but gave up his position and inheritance to seek salvation. He was born about 563 B.C.E. in a small tribal state governed by his father in the foothills of the Himalayas. According to early accounts, Gautama lived a pampered and sheltered life in palaces and parks, because his father had determined that Gautama would never know misery. He married his cousin and excelled in the program of studies that would prepare him to succeed his father as governor.

Eventually, however, Gautama became dissatisfied with his comfortable life. One day, according to an early legend, while riding toward a park in his chariot, Gautama saw a man made miserable by age and infirmity. When he asked for an explanation of this unsettling sight, Gautama learned from his chariot driver that all human beings grow old and weak. On later outings Gautama learned that disease and death were also inevitable features of the human condition. When he then came into contact with a monk traveling by foot, Gautama learned that some individuals withdraw from the active life of the world to lead holy lives. Inspired, Gautama determined to take up a similar life for himself in the hope that it would help him to understand the phenomenon of suffering.

Gautama's Search for Enlightenment About 534 B.C.E. Gautama left his wife and family and the comforts of home to lead the existence of a holy man. He wandered throughout the Ganges valley searching for spiritual enlightenment and an explanation for suffering. He sought enlightenment first by means of intense meditation and later through the rigors of extreme asceticism. None of those tactics satisfied him. Then, according to Buddhist legends, as he sat one day beneath a large pipal (*ficus religiosa*) tree in Bodh Gaya, southwest of Pataliputra, Gautama decided that he would remain exactly where he was until he understood the problem of suffering. For forty-nine days he sat in meditation as various demons tempted and threatened him to shake his resolution. On the forty-ninth day Gautama prevailed and received enlightenment: he understood both the problem of suffering and the means by which humans could eliminate it from the world. At that point, Gautama became the Buddha—the "enlightened one."

The Buddha and His Followers The Buddha publicly announced his doctrine for the first time about 528 B.C.E. at the Deer Park of Sarnath, near the city of Banaras (modern Varanasi), in a sermon delivered to friends. Buddhists refer to this sermon as the "Turning of the Wheel of the Law" because it represented the beginning of the Buddha's quest to promulgate the law of righteousness. His teachings quickly attracted attention, and disciples came from all parts of the Ganges valley. He organized them into a community of monks who owned only their yellow robes and their begging bowls. For more than forty years, the Buddha led his disciples throughout much of northern India in hopes of bringing spiritual enlightenment to others.

Buddhist Doctrine: The Dharma The core of the Buddha's doctrine, known as the Four Noble Truths, teaches that all life involves suffering; that desire is the

---

Buddhism (BOO-diz'm)
Siddhartha Gautama (sih-DHAR-tuh GAHW-tah-mah)
Buddha (BOO-duh)
dharma (DHUHR-muh)

Painting of the Buddha.
A painting produced in the late fifth century C.E. depicts the Buddha seated under a pavilion as servants attend to his needs and anoint him with holy water.

cause of suffering; that elimination of desire brings an end to suffering; and that a disciplined life conducted in accordance with the Noble Eightfold Path brings the elimination of desire. The Noble Eightfold Path calls for individuals to lead balanced and moderate lives, rejecting both devotion to luxury and to regimes of extreme asceticism. Specifically, the Noble Eightfold Path demands right belief, right resolve, right speech, right behavior, right occupation, right effort, right contemplation, and right meditation. Taken together, the teachings of the Four Noble Truths and the Noble Eightfold Path constitute the Buddhist *dharma*—the basic doctrine shared by Buddhists of all sects.

Ultimately, Buddhists believed that a lifestyle based on the Buddhist dharma would lead to personal salvation, which meant an escape from the cycle of incarnation and attainment of *nirvana,* a state of perfect spiritual independence. Like the Jains, the Buddhists sought to escape the

cycle of incarnation without depending on the services of the brahmins. Like the Jains, too, they did not recognize social distinctions based on caste or *jati.* As a result, their message appealed strongly to members of lower castes. Yet, because it did not demand the rigorous asceticism of Jainism, Buddhism became far more popular, especially with merchants.

Appeal of Buddhism Apart from the social implications of the doctrine, there were several other reasons for the popularity of early Buddhism in India. One has to do with language. Following the example of the Buddha himself, early Buddhist monks and preachers avoided the use of Sanskrit, the literary language of the *Vedas* that the brahmins employed in their rituals, in favor of vernacular tongues that reached a much larger popular audience. Furthermore, early Buddhists recognized holy sites that served as focal points for devotion. Even in the early days of Buddhism, pilgrims flocked to Bodh Gaya, where Gautama received enlightenment, and the Deer Park of Sarnath, where as the Buddha he preached his first sermon. Also popular with the faithful were stupas—shrines housing relics of the Buddha and his first disciples that pilgrims venerated while meditating on Buddhist values.

Yet another reason for the early popularity of Buddhism was the organization of the Buddhist movement. The most enthusiastic and highly motivated converts joined monastic communities where they dedicated their lives to the search for enlightenment and to preaching the Buddhist dharma to lay audiences. During the centuries following the Buddha's death, this monastic organization proved to be extremely efficient at spreading the Buddhist message and winning converts to the faith.

Ashoka's Support The early Buddhist movement also benefited from the official patronage and support of the Mauryan dynasty. The precise reason for Ashoka's conversion to Buddhism is unclear. Ashoka's own account, as preserved in one of his edicts, explains that the emperor adopted Buddhism about 260 B.C.E. after the war against Kalinga. Saddened by the violence of the war and the suffering of the Kalingans, Ashoka said that he decided to pursue his aims henceforth by means of virtue, benevolence, and humanity rather than arms. Quite apart from his sincere religious convictions, it is also likely that Ashoka found Buddhism appealing as a faith that could lend unity to his culturally diverse and far-flung realm. In any case, in honor of ahimsa, the doctrine of nonviolence, Ashoka banned animal sacrifices in Pataliputra, gave up his beloved hunting expeditions, and eliminated most meat dishes from the tables of his court. Ashoka rewarded Buddhists with grants of land, and he encouraged them to spread their faith throughout India. He built monasteries and stupas and made pilgrimages to the holy sites of

nirvana (ner-VAHN-nah)
stupas (STOO-pahs)

The Buddhist Stupa at Sanchi.
This stupa was originally built by Ashoka and enlarged in later times. It is a domed shrine—representing the dome of heaven over the earth—intended to contain sacred relics of the Buddha.

Buddhism. Ashoka also sent missionaries to Bactria and Ceylon (modern Sri Lanka), thus inaugurating a process by which Buddhism attracted large followings in central Asia, east Asia, and southeast Asia.

Mahayana Buddhism

From its earliest days Buddhism attracted merchants, artisans, and others of low rank in the traditional Indian social order. Its appeal was due both to its disregard for social classes and to its concern for ethical behavior instead of complicated ceremonies. Yet, even though it vastly simplified religious observances, early Buddhism made heavy demands on individuals seeking to escape from the cycle of incarnation. A truly righteous existence involved considerable sacrifice: giving up personal property, forsaking the search for social standing, and resolutely detaching oneself from the charms of family and the world. Although perhaps more

attractive than the religion of the *brahmins,* Buddhism did not promise to make life easy for its adherents.

Development of Buddhism Between the third century B.C.E. and the first century C.E., however, three new developments in Buddhist thought and practice reduced obligations of believers, opened new avenues to salvation, and brought explosive popularity to the faith. In the first place, whereas the Buddha had not considered himself divine, some of his later followers began to worship him as a god. Thus Buddhism acquired a devotional focus that helped converts channel their spiritual energies. In the second place, theologians articulated the notion of the *bodhisattva,* an enlightened being. Bodhisattva were individuals who had reached spiritual perfection and merited the reward of nirvana, but who intentionally delayed

bodhisattva (BOH-dih-SAT-vuhs)

Thinking about ENCOUNTERS

Trade and Culture

Throughout the classical period, India was tied to vast overland trading networks linking it to central and east Asia, as well as ocean trading networks linking it to southeast and east Asia. *How did the interactions promoted by these networks alter Indian society, and to what extent did these same networks allow for the diffusion of Indian cultural beliefs and practices?*

their entry into nirvana to help others who were still struggling. Like Christian saints, bodhisattva served as examples of spiritual excellence, and they provided a source of inspiration. Finally, Buddhist monasteries began to accept gifts from wealthy individuals and to regard the bequests as acts of generosity that merited salvation. Thus wealthy individuals could avoid the sacrifices demanded by early Buddhist teachings and still ensure their salvation.

The Spread of Mahayana Buddhism   Because these innovations opened the road to salvation for large numbers of people, their proponents called their faith the *Mahayana* (the "greater vehicle," which could carry more people to salvation), as opposed to the *Hinayana* (the "lesser vehicle"), a pejorative term for the earlier and stricter doctrine known also as Theravada Buddhism. During the early centuries C.E., Mahayana Buddhism spread rapidly throughout India and attracted many converts. In later centuries Mahayana Buddhism became established also in central Asia, China, Japan, and Korea. The stricter Theravada faith did not disappear, but since the first century C.E. most of the world's Buddhists have practiced Mahayana Buddhism.

Nalanda   Mahayana Buddhism flourished partly because of educational institutions that promoted the faith. During the Vedic era, Indian education was mostly an informal affair involving a sage and his students. When Jains and

Mahayana (mah-huh-YAH-nah)
Hinayana (HEE-nah-yah-nuh)
Theravada (thehr-ah-VAH-dah)
Bhagavad Gita (BHUHG-vuhd GEE-tuh)

Buddhists organized monasteries, however, they began to establish educational institutions. Most monasteries provided basic education, and larger communities offered advanced instruction as well. Best known of all was the Buddhist monastery at Nalanda, founded during the Gupta dynasty in the Ganges River valley near Pataliputra. At Nalanda it was possible to study not only Buddhism but also the *Vedas,* Hindu philosophy, logic, mathematics, astronomy, and medicine. Nalanda soon became famous, and by the end of the Gupta dynasty, several thousand students may have been in residence there.

The Emergence of Popular Hinduism

As Buddhism generated new ideas and attracted widespread popular interest, Hinduism underwent a similar evolution that transformed it into a popular religion of salvation. Although drawing inspiration from the *Vedas* and the Upanishads, popular Hinduism increasingly departed from the older traditions of the brahmins to meet the needs of ordinary people.

The Bhagavad Gita   A short poetic work known as the *Bhagavad Gita* ("song of the lord") best illustrates both the expectations that Hinduism made of individuals and the promise of salvation that it held out to them. Scholars have dated the work at various points between 300 B.C.E. and 300 C.E., and it most likely underwent several rounds of revision before taking on its final form about 400 C.E. Yet it eloquently evokes the cultural climate of India between the Mauryan and the Gupta dynasties.

The work is a self-contained episode of the *Mahabharata,* one of the great epic poems of India. It presents a dialogue

Gandharan sculpture.
This carving dates from the second or third century C.E. It may represent Avalokitesvara, also known as the Lord of Compassion. Almost as perfect as the Buddha, Avalokitesvara had a reputation for protecting merchants and sailors, helping women conceive, and turning enemies into kindhearted friends.

SourcesfromthePast

Ashoka Adopts and Promotes Buddhism

Ashoka, grandson of Chandragupta and the greatest of all Mauryan rulers, spent the early part of his reign consolidating and expanding the Mauryan empire through waging war. After a particularly bloody campaign against the large eastern state of Kalinga, Ashoka, apparently sickened by the violence, adopted Buddhism and promoted it throughout the empire. He then communicated his reasons for adopting Buddhism, and his imperial policies, by having edicts carved in natural stone or on pillars that were erected all over his realm. In the 13th Major Rock Edict below, Ashoka explains the reasons for his renunciation of violence and his adoption of Buddhism (which he calls Dhamma).

13th Major Rock Edict of Ashoka. Beloved-of-the-Gods, King Piyadasi, conquered the Kalingas eight years after his coronation. One hundred and fifty thousand were deported, one hundred thousand were killed and many more died (from other causes). After the Kalingas had been conquered, Beloved-of-the-Gods came to feel a strong inclination towards the Dhamma, a love for the Dhamma and for instruction in Dhamma. Now Beloved-of-the-Gods feels deep remorse for having conquered the Kalingas.

Indeed, Beloved-of-the-Gods is deeply pained by the killing, dying and deportation that take place when an un-conquered country is conquered. But Beloved-of-the-Gods is pained even more by this—that Brahmans, ascetics, and householders of different religions who live in those countries, and who are respectful to superiors, to mother and father, to elders, and who behave properly and have strong loyalty towards friends, acquaintances, companions, relatives, servants and employees—that they are injured, killed or separated from their loved ones. Even those who are not affected (by all this) suffer when they see friends, acquaintances, companions and relatives affected. These misfortunes befall all (as a result of war), and this pains Beloved-of-the-Gods.

There is no country, except among the Greeks, where these two groups, Brahmans and ascetics, are not found, and there is no country where people are not devoted to one or another religion. Therefore the killing, death or deportation of a hundredth, or even a thousandth part of those who died during the conquest of Kalinga now pains Beloved-of-the-Gods. Now Beloved-of-the-Gods thinks that even those who do wrong should be forgiven where forgiveness is possible. . . .

I have had this Dhamma edict written so that my sons and great-grandsons may not consider making new conquests, or that if military conquests are made, that they be done with forbearance and light punishment, or better still, that they consider making conquest by Dhamma only, for that bears fruit in this world and the next. May all their intense devotion be given to this, which has a result in this world and the next.

For Further Reflection

■ Why would Ashoka make such an extraordinary public confession? What message was he trying to impart in this edict to his subjects, and to his successors?

Source: Ven. S. Dhammika, trans. *The Wheel Publication,* no. 386/387. Kandy Sri Lanka: Buddhist Publication Society, 1993. Copyright 1993 Ven. S. Dhammika. DharmaNet Edition 1994. Electronic edition offered for free distribution via DharmaNet by arrangement with the publisher.

---

between Arjuna, a kshatriya about to enter battle, and his charioteer Krishna, who was in fact a human incarnation of the god Vishnu. The immediate problem addressed in the work was Arjuna's reluctance to fight: the enemy included many of his friends and relatives, and even though he recognized the justice of his cause, he shrank from the conflict. In an effort to persuade the warrior to fight, Krishna presented Arjuna with several lines of argument. In the first place, he said, Arjuna must not worry about harming his friends and relatives, because the soul does not die with the human body, and Arjuna's weapons did not have the power to touch the soul.

Krishna also held that Arjuna's caste imposed specific moral duties and social responsibilities on him. The duty of shudras was to serve, of vaishyas to work, of brahmins to learn the scriptures and seek wisdom. Similarly,

Krishna argued, the duty of kshatriyas was to govern and fight. Indeed, Krishna went further and held that failure to fulfill caste duties was a grievous sin, whereas their observance brought spiritual benefits.

Finally, Krishna taught that Arjuna would attain everlasting peace if he devoted himself to the love, adoration, and service of Krishna himself. Arjuna should abandon his selfish and superficial personal concerns and surrender to the deeper wisdom of the god. As a reward, Arjuna would receive eternal salvation through unity with his god. Alongside understanding of the soul and caste duties, then, unquestioning faith and devotion would put Arjuna in the proper state of mind for the conflict by aligning his actions with divine wisdom and will. Krishna's teaching that faith would bring salvation helped inspire a tradition of ecstatic and unquestioning devotion in popular Hinduism.

Hindu Ethics Hindu ethics thus differed considerably from those of earlier Indian moralists. The Upanishads had taught that only through renunciation and detachment from the world could individuals escape the cycle of incarnation. As represented in the *Bhagavad Gita,* however, Hindu ethical teachings also held out the promise of salvation to those who participated actively in the world and met their caste responsibilities. To be sure, Krishna taught that individuals should meet their responsibilities in detached fashion and that they should not strive for material reward or recognition. Rather, they should perform their duties faithfully, with no thought as to their consequences.

Other works by early Hindu moralists acknowledged even more openly than did the *Bhagavad Gita* that individuals could lead honorable lives in the world. Indeed, Hindu ethics commonly recognized four principal aims of human life: *dharma,* obedience to religious and moral laws; *artha,* the pursuit of economic well-being and honest prosperity; *kama,* the enjoyment of social, physical, and sexual pleasure; and *moksha,* the salvation of the soul. According to Hindu moral precepts, a proper balance of *dharma, artha,* and *kama* would help an individual to attain *moksha.*

As devotional Hinduism evolved and became increasingly distinct from the teachings of the Upanishads and the older traditions of the brahmins, it also enhanced its appeal to all segments of Indian society. Hinduism offered salvation to masses of people who, as a matter of practical necessity, had to lead active lives in the world and thus could not hope to achieve the detachment envisioned in the Upanishads.

Popularity of Hinduism Hinduism gradually displaced Buddhism as the most popular religion in India. Later Buddhist monks did not seek to communicate their message to the larger society in the zealous way of their predecessors but increasingly confined themselves to the comforts of monasteries richly endowed by wealthy patrons. Meanwhile, devotional Hinduism attracted political support and patronage, particularly from the Gupta emperors. The Guptas and their successors bestowed grants of land on Hindu *brahmins* and supported an educational system that promoted Hindu values. Just as Ashoka Maurya had advanced the cause of Buddhism, the Guptas and their successors later helped Hinduism become the dominant religious and cultural tradition in India. By about 1000 C.E., Buddhism had entered a noticeable decline in India, while Hinduism was growing in popularity. Within a few centuries devotional Hinduism and the more recently introduced faith of Islam almost completely eclipsed Buddhism in its homeland.

SUMMARY

In India, as in classical Persia and China, a robust agricultural economy supported the creation of large-scale states and interregional trade. Although an imperial state did not become a permanent feature of Indian political life, the peoples of the subcontinent maintained an orderly society based on the caste system and regional states. Indian cultural and religious traditions reflected the conditions of the larger society in which they developed. Mahayana Buddhism and devotional Hinduism in particular addressed the needs of the increasingly prominent lay classes, and the two faiths profoundly influenced the religious life of Asian peoples over the long term of history.

STUDY TERMS

ahimsa (126)
artha (132)
Arthashastra (120)
Ashoka (121)
Bhagavad Gita (130)
bodhisattva (129)
brahmin (125–126)
Buddha (127)
Buddhism (127)
Chandragupta Maurya (120)
Charvaka (126)
dharma (127)
Four Noble Truths (127–128)
Gupta dynasty (123)
Hinayana Buddhism (130)
Jainism (126)
kama (132)

Kautalya (120)
kshatriya (125)
Kushan empire (122–123)
Magadha (120)
Mahabharata (125)
Mahayana Buddhism (130)
Mauryan dynasty (120)
moksha (132)
nirvana (128)
Pataliputra (121)
Ramayana (125)
shudra (125)
Siddhartha Gautama (127)
stupas (128)
Theravada Buddhism (130)
Upanishads (126)
vaishya (125)
Vardhamana (126)

FOR FURTHER READING

Karen Armstrong. *Buddha*. New York, 2001. An accessible introduction to the Buddha by a prominent scholar of Indian religions.

Jeannine Auboyer. *Daily Life in Ancient India*. Trans. by S. W. Taylor. London, 2002. An excellent introduction to Indian social history during the classical era.

William Theodore De Bary, ed. *Sources of Indian Tradition*. 2 vols. 2nd ed. New York, 1988. Important collection of sources in translation.

Kautalya. *The Kautilya Arthashastra*. 3 vols. 2nd ed. Ed. by R. P. Kangle. Bombay, 1960–69. Translation of the most important political treatise of classical India.

Xinru Liu. *Ancient India and Ancient China: Trade and Religious Exchanges, A.D. 1–600*. Delhi, 1988. Important study exploring the early spread of Buddhism from India to central Asia and China.

Juan Mascaró, trans. *The Bhagavad Gita*. Harmondsworth, 1962. Brilliant and evocative English version by a gifted translator.

K. M. Sen. *Hinduism*. London, 2005. Reissue of a classic interpretation with a new foreword by Amartya Sen drawing out the contemporary implications of the study.

John S. Strong. *The Legend of King Ashoka: A Study and Translation of the Ashokavadana*. Princeton, 1983. Valuable translation of an important early Buddhist account of King Ashoka's life and reign.

Romila Thapar. *Early India: From the Origins to A.D. 1300*. Berkeley, 2003. A fresh view by one of the leading scholars of early Indian history.

Stanley Wolpert. *A New History of India*. 7th ed. New York, 2004. A concise and readable survey of Indian history.

Mediterranean Society under the Greeks and the Romans

CHAPTER 8

Pericles organized the construction of numerous marble buildings, partly with funds collected from poleis belonging to the Delian League. Most notable of his projects was the Parthenon, a temple dedicated to the goddess Athena, which symbolizes the prosperity and grandeur of classical Athens.

EYEWITNESS:

Homer and Paul of Tarsus: The Cosmopolitan Worlds of Greeks and Romans

For a man who perhaps never existed, Homer has been a profoundly influential figure. According to tradition, Homer composed the two great epic poems of ancient Greece, the *Iliad* and the *Odyssey*. In fact, scholars now know that bards recited both poems for generations before Homer, and some believe that Homer was simply a convenient name for the otherwise anonymous scribes who committed the *Iliad* and the *Odyssey* to writing. Whether Homer ever really lived or not, the epics attributed to him deeply influenced the development of classical Greek thought and literature. The *Iliad* offered a Greek perspective on a campaign waged by a band of Greek warriors against the city of Troy in Anatolia during the twelfth century B.C.E. The *Odyssey* recounted the experiences of the Greek hero Odysseus as he sailed home after the Trojan War. The two works described scores of difficulties faced by Greek warriors, including battles, monsters, and conflicts among themselves. Between them, the two epics preserved a rich collection of stories that literary figures mined for more than a millennium.

The *Iliad* and the *Odyssey* also testify to the frequency and normality of travel, communication, and interaction in the Mediterranean basin during the second and first millennia B.C.E. Both works portray Greeks as expert and fearless seamen, almost as comfortable aboard their ships as on land, who did not hesitate to venture into the waters of what Homer called the "wine-dark sea." Homer lovingly described the sleek galleys in which Greek warriors raced across the waters, and he even had Odysseus construct a sailing ship single-handedly when he found himself shipwrecked on an island inhabited only by a goddess. The *Iliad* and the *Odyssey* make it clear that maritime links touched peoples throughout the Mediterranean basin in Homer's time and, further, that Greeks were among the most prominent seafarers of the age.

The maritime links established by the Greeks lived on long after the decline of classical Greek society. Indeed, the Romans took advantage of those links and used them to build a powerful society that dominated the whole Mediterranean basin by the first century C.E. By that time, Roman citizens found themselves living in a cosmopolitan world in which Roman administrators oversaw affairs from Anatolia and Palestine in the east to Spain and Morocco in the west.

Just as Homer's epics recall the world of the Greeks, the story of Paul of Tarsus reflects the cosmopolitan world of the Romans. Born in the first century C.E., Paul was a devout Jew from Anatolia who accepted the Christian teachings of Jesus of Nazareth. Paul was a principal figure in the development of Christianity to an independent religious faith, largely because of his zealous missionary efforts to attract converts from outside as well as within the Jewish community. While promoting his adopted faith in Jerusalem about 55 C.E., however, Paul was attacked

CHRONOLOGY

2200–1100 B.C.E.	Minoan society
1600–1100 B.C.E.	Mycenaean society
800–338 B.C.E.	Era of the classical Greek polis
509 B.C.E.	Establishment of the Roman republic
500–479 B.C.E.	Persian Wars
470–399 B.C.E.	Life of Socrates
443–429 B.C.E.	Pericles' leadership in Athens
431–404 B.C.E.	Peloponnesian War
430–347 B.C.E.	Life of Plato
384–322 B.C.E.	Life of Aristotle
359–336 B.C.E.	Reign of Philip II of Macedon
336–323 B.C.E.	Reign of Alexander of Macedon
264–146 B.C.E.	Roman expansion in the Mediterranean basin
106–43 B.C.E.	Life of Marcus Tullius Cicero
first century B.C.E.	Civil war in Rome
46–44 B.C.E.	Rule of Gaius Julius Caesar as dictator
31 B.C.E.–14 C.E.	Rule of Augustus
4 B.C.E.–early 30s C.E.	Life of Jesus of Nazareth
first century C.E.	Life of Paul of Tarsus
66–70 C.E.	Jewish War

by a crowd of his enemies who believed his views were a threat to Judaism. The disturbance was so severe that Roman authorities intervened to restore order.

Under normal circumstances, Roman authorities would have delivered Paul to the leaders of his own ethnic community, where he would be dealt with according to custom. But knowing that Jewish leaders would probably execute him, Paul asserted his rights as a Roman citizen to appeal his case in Rome. Paul had never been to Rome, but this Anatolian traveling in Palestine called on the laws of the imperial center to determine his fate. Paul traveled across the Mediterranean to Rome, but his appeal did not succeed. Tradition holds that he was executed by imperial authorities out of concern that Christianity was a threat to the peace and stability of the empire.

Under both the Greeks and the Romans, the Mediterranean basin became much more tightly integrated than before as both societies organized commercial exchange and sponsored interaction throughout the region. In fact, under Greek and then Roman supervision, the Mediterranean served not as a barrier but, rather, as a highway. Moreover, this highway carried more than soldiers, citizens, and goods: it also carried ideas. Indeed, Greek philosophy—which generated a remarkable body of moral thought and philosophical reflection—shaped the cultural foundations of the Roman republic and empire, as educated Roman thinkers drew inspiration from their neighbors to the east. Later, this highway carried the Christian religion to all corners of the Roman empire.

Yet Greek and Roman societies also differed substantially, both in organization and in outlook. Early in the classical era, the Greeks lived in independent, autonomous city-states. Only after the late third century B.C.E. did they play prominent roles in the large, centralized empire established by their neighbors to the north in Macedon. Until then, the Greeks had integrated the societies and economies of distant lands mainly through energetic commercial activity over the Mediterranean sea-lanes. In contrast to the Greeks, the Romans built an extensive, centralized land empire. At its high point the Roman empire dominated the entire Mediterranean basin and parts of southwest Asia as well as north Africa and much of continental Europe and Britain. In addition, whereas Greek authorities did not sponsor an evangelical religion, Christianity eventually became the official religion of the Roman empire, which allowed the new religion to spread much more effectively than before. In spite of their differences, however, exploring Greek and Roman societies together makes it possible to understand the growing integration of the Mediterranean basin—and its increasing interconnectedness with a wide swath of Eurasia and North Africa—over the millennium just prior to the start of the Common Era.

EARLY DEVELOPMENT OF GREEK SOCIETY

During the third millennium B.C.E., the peoples of the Balkan region and the Greek peninsula increasingly met and mingled with peoples from different societies who traveled and traded in the Mediterranean basin. As a result, early inhabitants of the Greek peninsula built their societies under the influence of Mesopotamians, Egyptians, Phoenicians, and others active in the region. Beginning in the ninth century B.C.E., the Greeks organized a series of city-states, which served as the political context for the development of classical Greek society.

Minoan and Mycenaean Societies

Knossos During the late third millennium B.C.E., a sophisticated society arose on the island of Crete. Scholars refer to it as Minoan society, after Minos, a legendary king of ancient Crete. Between 2000 and 1700 B.C.E., the inhabitants of Crete built a series of lavish palaces throughout the island, most notably the enormous complex at Knossos decorated with vivid frescoes depicting Minoans at work and play. These palaces were the nerve centers of Minoan society: they were residences of rulers, and they also served as storehouses where officials collected taxes in kind from local cultivators.

Between 2200 and 1450 B.C.E., Crete was a principal center of Mediterranean commerce. By 2200 B.C.E. Cretans were traveling aboard advanced sailing craft of Phoenician

design. Minoan ships sailed to Greece, Anatolia, Phoenicia, and Egypt, where they exchanged Cretan wine, olive oil, and wool for grains, textiles, and manufactured goods. After 1600 B.C.E. Cretans established colonies on Cyprus and many islands in the Aegean Sea.

Decline of Minoan Society After 1700 B.C.E. Minoan society experienced a series of earthquakes, volcanic eruptions, and tidal waves. Between 1600 and 1450 B.C.E., Minoans embarked on a new round of palace building to replace structures destroyed by those natural catastrophes: they built luxurious complexes with indoor plumbing and drainage systems and even furnished some of them with flush toilets. After 1450 B.C.E., however, the wealth of Minoan society attracted a series of invaders, and by 1100 B.C.E. Crete had fallen under foreign domination. Yet Minoan traditions deeply influenced the inhabitants of nearby Greece.

Minoan (mih-NOH-uhn)

MAP 8.1

Classical Greece, 800–350 B.C.E. Note the mountainous topography of the Greek peninsula and western Anatolia.

To what extent did geography encourage Greeks to venture into the Mediterranean Sea?

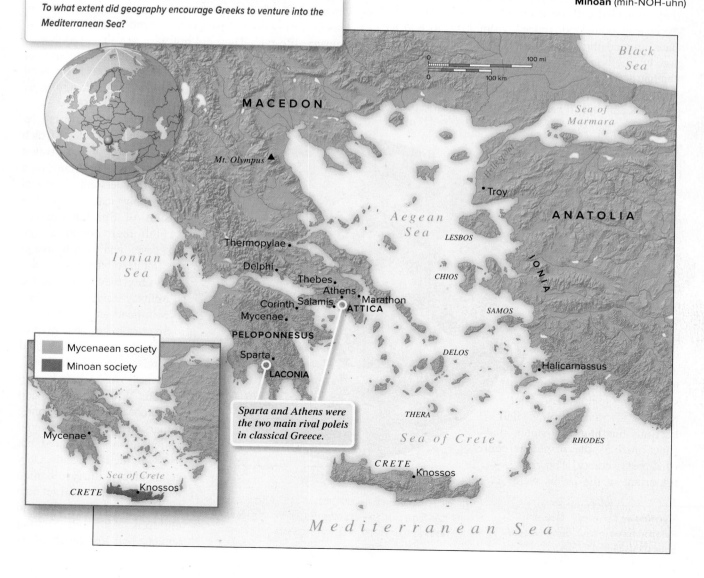

Sparta and Athens were the two main rival poleis in classical Greece.

Mycenaean society
Minoan society

Mycenaean Society Beginning about 2200 B.C.E. migratory Indo-European peoples filtered into the Greek peninsula. By 1600 B.C.E. they had begun to trade with Minoan merchants and visit Crete, where they learned about writing and large-scale construction. After 1450 B.C.E. they also built massive stone fortresses and palaces throughout the southern part of the Greek peninsula, known as the Peloponnesus. Because the fortified sites offered protection, they soon attracted settlers, who built small agricultural communities. Their society is known as Mycenaean, after Mycenae, one of their most important settlements.

Chaos in the Eastern Mediterranean From 1500 to 1100 B.C.E., the Mycenaeans expanded their influence beyond peninsular Greece. They largely overpowered Minoan society, and they took over the Cretan palaces. The Mycenaeans also established settlements in Anatolia, Sicily, and southern Italy. About 1200 B.C.E. the Mycenaeans engaged in a conflict with the city of Troy in Anatolia. This Trojan War, which Homer recalled from a Greek perspective in his *Iliad,* coincided with invasions of foreign mariners in the Mycenaean homeland. Indeed, from 1100 to 800 B.C.E., chaos reigned throughout the eastern Mediterranean region. Invasions and civil disturbances made it impossible to maintain stable governments or even productive agricultural societies. Mycenaean palaces fell into ruin, the population sharply declined, and people abandoned most settlements.

The World of the Polis

In the absence of a centralized state or empire, local institutions took the lead in restoring political order in Greece after the decline of Mycenaean society. The most important institution was the *polis,* or city-state. Over time, many of these *poleis* (the plural of *polis*) became lively commercial centers. They took on an increasingly urban character and extended their authority over surrounding regions. By about 800 B.C.E. many poleis had become bustling city-states that functioned as the principal centers of Greek society. The most important of the poleis were

Sparta and Athens, whose contrasting constitutions help to illustrate the variety of political structures in classical Greece. Indeed, as we will see, the contrasts between Sparta and Athens led to simmering tensions between the two poleis, which later erupted in a fierce civil conflict known as the Peloponnesian War (431–404 B.C.E.).

Sparta Sparta was situated in a fertile region of the Greek peninsula, whose lands the Spartans exploited by forcing neighboring peoples to perform agricultural labor. These *helots,* or servants of the Spartan state, were not slaves, but neither were they free to leave the land. Their role in society was to keep Sparta supplied with food. By the sixth century B.C.E., the helots probably outnumbered the Spartan citizens by more than ten to one, which meant that the Spartans constantly had to guard against rebellion. As a result, the Spartans devoted most of their resources to maintaining a powerful and disciplined military.

Spartan Society In theory, Spartan citizens were equal in status. To discourage the development of economic and social distinctions, Spartans observed an extraordinarily austere lifestyle. They did not wear jewelry or elaborate clothes, nor did they pamper themselves with luxuries or accumulate private wealth on a large scale. It is for good reason, then, that our adjective *spartan* refers to a lifestyle characterized by simplicity, frugality, and austerity.

Distinction among the ancient Spartans came by prowess, discipline, and military talent, which the Spartan educational system cultivated from an early age. All Spartans, men and women, underwent a rigorous regime of physical training. The sons of Spartan citizens left their homes at age seven and went to live in military barracks. At age twenty they began active military service, which they continued until retirement. Spartan authorities also prescribed vigorous physical exercise for girls in hopes that they would bear strong children. When they reached age eighteen to twenty, young women married and had occasional sexual relations, but did not live with their husbands. Only at about age thirty did men leave the barracks and set up a household with their wives and children. Although Spartan society had lost much of its

Painted Spartan vessel.
This painted cup produced in Sparta about 550 B.C.E. depicts hunters attacking a boar. Spartans regarded hunting as an exercise that helped to sharpen fighting skills and aggressive instincts.

Mycenaean (meye-suh-NEE-uhn)
Peloponnesus (pell-uh-puh-NEE-suhs)
polis (POH-lihs)

ascetic rigor by the fourth century B.C.E., Spartan institutions nevertheless continued to reflect the larger society's commitment to military values. In effect, Sparta sought to maintain public order by creating a military state that could crush any threat.

Athens Whereas Sparta sought to impose order by military means, Athens sought to negotiate order by considering the interests of the polis's various constituencies. It is important to note, however, that while the principles of Athenian government were exceptionally democratic in the context of their own time, ideas about what constitutes a democracy have changed over time and vary from place to place. For example, citizenship in Athens was not open to all residents: only free adult males from this polis itself were allowed to play a role in public affairs, leaving foreigners, slaves, and women with no direct voice in government. Nevertheless, in seeking to resolve social problems, Athenians opened government offices to all male citizens and broadened the base of political participation in classical Greece.

Athenian Society During the seventh century B.C.E., the gap between rich and poor around Athens widened considerably as increased trade brought prosperity to wealthy landowners. By the early sixth century B.C.E., a large class of underprivileged people were unhappy enough to wage war against their wealthy neighbors. To avert civil war, an Athenian aristocrat named Solon devised a solution to class conflict in Attica, the region around Athens.

Solon and Athenian Democracy Solon forged a compromise between the classes. He allowed aristocrats to keep their lands, but he cancelled debts, forbade debt slavery, and liberated those already enslaved for debt. Solon also introduced the idea of individual rights that would be protected by law, which in theory assumed the worth of individual persons regardless of class. In addition, Solon provided representation for the common classes in the Athenian government by opening the councils of the polis to any citizen wealthy enough to devote time to public affairs. During the late sixth and fifth centuries B.C.E., these reforms went even further as Athenian leaders paid salaries to officeholders so financial hardship would not exclude anyone from service.

Pericles These reforms gradually transformed Athens into

a more democratic state. The high tide of Athenian democracy came under the leadership of the statesman Pericles, who became the most popular Athenian leader from 461 B.C.E. until his death in 429 B.C.E. He wielded enormous personal influence in a government with hundreds of officeholders from the common classes, and he supported building programs that provided employment for thousands of construction workers and laborers. Under the leadership of Pericles, Athens became the most sophisticated of the poleis, with a vibrant community of scientists, philosophers, poets, dramatists, artists, and architects. Little wonder, then, that in a moment of civic pride, Pericles boasted that Athens was "the education of Greece."

GREECE AND THE LARGER WORLD

As the poleis prospered, Greeks became increasingly prominent in the larger world of the Mediterranean basin. They established colonies along the shores of the Mediterranean Sea and the Black Sea, and they traded throughout the region. Eventually, their political and economic interests brought them into conflict with the expanding Persian empire. After a century of intermittent war, in the fourth century B.C.E. Alexander of Macedon toppled the Achaemenid empire and built an empire stretching from India to Egypt and Greece. His conquests created a vast zone of trade and communication that encouraged commercial and cultural exchange on an unprecedented scale.

Greek Colonization

By about 800 B.C.E. the poleis were emerging as centers of political organization in Greece. During the next century increasing population strained the resources available in the rocky and mountainous Greek peninsula. To relieve population pressures, the Greeks began to establish colonies in other parts of the Mediterranean basin. Between the mid-eighth and the late sixth centuries B.C.E., they founded more than four hundred colonies along the shores of the Mediterranean Sea and the Black Sea.

The Greeks established their first colonies in the central Mediterranean during the early eighth century B.C.E. The

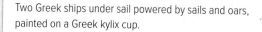
Two Greek ships under sail powered by sails and oars, painted on a Greek kylix cup.

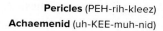
Pericles (PEH-rih-kleez)
Achaemenid (uh-KEE-muh-nid)

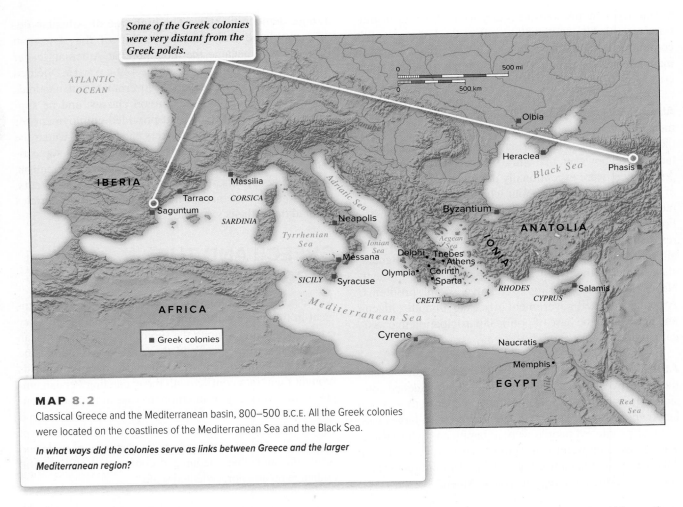

Some of the Greek colonies were very distant from the Greek poleis.

MAP 8.2

Classical Greece and the Mediterranean basin, 800–500 B.C.E. All the Greek colonies were located on the coastlines of the Mediterranean Sea and the Black Sea.

In what ways did the colonies serve as links between Greece and the larger Mediterranean region?

most popular sites were Sicily and southern Italy, particularly the region around modern Naples, which was itself originally a Greek colony called Neapolis ("new polis"). These colonies provided merchants not only with fertile fields that yielded large agricultural surpluses but also with convenient access to the copper, zinc, tin, and iron ores of central Italy. By the sixth century B.C.E., Greek colonies dotted the shores of Sicily and southern Italy, and more Greeks lived in these colonies than in the Greek peninsula itself. By 600 B.C.E. the Greeks had ventured even farther west and established the important colony of Massalia (modern Marseilles) in what is now southern France.

Greek Colonies Greek colonies arose also in the eastern Mediterranean and the Black Sea. Hundreds of islands in the Aegean Sea beckoned to a maritime people such as the Greeks. Colonists also settled in Anatolia, where their Greek cousins had established communities during the centuries of political turmoil after 1100 B.C.E. During the eighth and seventh centuries B.C.E., Greeks ventured into the Black Sea in large numbers and established colonies all along its shores. These settlements offered merchants access to rich supplies of grain, fish, furs, timber, honey,

wax, gold, and amber as well as slaves captured in southern Russia and transported to markets in the Mediterranean.

Unlike their counterparts in classical Persia, China, and India, the Greeks did not build a centralized imperial state. Greek colonization was not a process controlled by a central government so much as an ad hoc response of individual poleis to population pressures. Colonies often did not take guidance from the poleis from which their settlers came but, rather, relied on their own resources and charted their own courses.

Effects of Greek Colonization Nevertheless, Greek colonization sponsored more communication, interaction, and exchange than ever before among Mediterranean lands and peoples. From the early eighth century B.C.E., colonies facilitated trade between their regions and the poleis in peninsular Greece and Anatolia. At the same time, colonization spread Greek language and cultural traditions throughout the Mediterranean basin. Moreover, the Greek presence quickened the tempo of social life, especially in the western Mediterranean and the Black Sea. Except for a few urban districts surrounding Phoenician colonies in the western Mediterranean, these regions were home mostly to small-scale agricultural societies organized by clans. As Greek merchants brought wealth into these societies, local clan leaders built small states in areas such as Sicily, southern Italy, southern France, the Crimean peninsula, and southern Russia where trade was especially strong. Thus Greek colonization had important political and social effects throughout the Mediterranean basin.

Conflict with Persia

During the fifth century B.C.E., their links abroad brought the poleis of the Greek peninsula into direct conflict with the Persian empire in a long struggle known as the Persian Wars (500–479 B.C.E.). As the Persian emperors Cyrus and Darius I tightened their grip on Anatolia, the Greek cities on the Ionian coast became increasingly restless. In 500 B.C.E. they revolted against Persian rule and expelled the Achaemenid administrators. In support of their fellow Greeks and commercial partners, the Athenians sent a fleet of ships to aid the Ionian effort.

The Persian Wars Despite Athenian assistance, Darius I repressed the Ionian rebellion in 493 B.C.E. Three years later, he mounted a campaign against peninsular Greece to punish them for their interference. Although greatly outnumbered, the Athenians routed the Persian army at the battle of Marathon and then marched back to Athens in time to fight off the Persian fleet. In spite of success in individual battles, however, neither side could secure a definitive victory over the other, and for more than a century Greeks and Persians continued to skirmish intermittently without decisive results.

The Delian League Yet the Persian Wars did initiate serious conflict among the Greek poleis themselves. The cause was an alliance between the poleis known as the Delian League, which was formed to discourage further Persian actions in Greece. Because of its superior fleet, Athens became the leader of the alliance, benefiting greatly from the financial contributions of other poleis. However, once it was clear that the Persian threat no longer existed, the other poleis resented having to make contributions that seemed to benefit only the Athenians.

The Peloponnesian War Ultimately, the tensions resulted in a bitter civil conflict known as the Peloponnesian War (431–404 B.C.E.). Poleis divided into two armed camps under the leadership of Athens and Sparta, the principal contenders for hegemony in the Greek world. By 404 B.C.E. the Spartans and their allies had forced the Athenians to unconditional surrender. However, Sparta's victory soon generated new jealousies, and new conflicts quickly broke out between the poleis. During the decades following Athenian surrender, hegemony in the Greek world passed to Sparta, Thebes, Corinth, and other poleis.

The Peloponnesian War was both a debilitating and a demoralizing conflict. Athenians bullied smaller communities, disregarded the interests and concerns of other poleis, insisted that allies resolutely toe the Athenian line, and subjected insubordinate communities to severe punishments. When the small island of Melos refused to acknowledge the authority of Athens, for example, Athenian forces reportedly conquered the island, massacred all the men of military age, and sold the women and children into slavery. As a result of that and other atrocities, Athens lost its reputation as the moral and intellectual leader of the Greek people and gained notoriety as an arrogant, insensitive imperialist power. Meanwhile, as the Peloponnesian War divided and weakened the world of the Greek poleis, a formidable power took shape to the north.

The Macedonians and the Coming of Empire

The Kingdom of Macedon Until the fourth century B.C.E., the kingdom of Macedon was a frontier state north of peninsular Greece. During the reign of King Philip II (359–336 B.C.E.), however, Macedon became a powerful, unified state with an impressive military. When Philip had consolidated his hold on Macedon, he turned his attention to two larger prizes: Greece and the Persian empire. Greece proved relatively easy to conquer: the Peloponnesian War had poisoned the poleis against one another, which hampered organized resistance. Thus in 338 B.C.E., after a campaign of twelve years, Philip had all of Greece under his control.

Alexander of Macedon Philip intended to use his conquest of Greece as a launching pad for an invasion of Persia but was prevented from doing so because he was assassinated by one of his bodyguards in 336 B.C.E. The invasion of Persia thus fell to his twenty-year-old son, Alexander of Macedon, often called Alexander

Wearing a lion skin around his head, Alexander the warrior plunges into battle with Persian forces in this carving on a stone sarcophagus.

Peloponnesian (pell-uh-puh-NEE-suhn)

the Great. Alexander soon assembled an army to invade the Persian empire. Alexander was a brilliant strategist and an inspired leader, and he inherited a well-equipped and highly spirited veteran force from his father. By 333 B.C.E. Alexander had subjected Ionia and Anatolia to his control; within another year he held Syria, Palestine, and Egypt; by 331 B.C.E. he controlled Mesopotamia and prepared to invade the Persian homeland. He took Pasargadae and burned the Achaemenid palace at Persepolis late in 331 B.C.E., and in 330 B.C.E. Alexander established himself as the new emperor of Persia.

Alexander's Conquests By 327 B.C.E. Alexander had larger ambitions: he took his army into India but was forced to return home when his troops refused to proceed any farther. By 324 B.C.E. Alexander and his army had returned to Susa in Mesopotamia. In June of 323 B.C.E., however, after an extended round of feasting and drinking, he suddenly fell ill and died at age thirty-three. Thus, although Alexander proved to be a brilliant conqueror, he did not live long enough to develop a system of administration for his vast realm.

The Hellenistic Era

Historians refer to the age of Alexander and his successors as the Hellenistic age—an era when Greek cultural traditions expanded their influence (*Hellas*) to a much larger world. Indeed, the Hellenistic empires governed cosmopolitan societies and sponsored interactions between peoples from Greece to India. Like imperial states in classical Persia, China, and India, the Hellenistic empires facilitated trade, and they made it possible for beliefs, values, and religions to spread over greater distances than ever before.

The Hellenistic Empires When Alexander died, his generals divided the empire into three large states. Antigonus took Greece and Macedon, which his Antigonid successors ruled until replaced by the Romans in the second century B.C.E. Ptolemy took Egypt, which the Ptolemaic

MAP 8.3

Boundaries of Alexander's former empire and of the Hellenistic empires that succeeded it about the year 275 B.C.E. Notice the difference in size between the three Hellenistic empires.

What would have been the economic and political advantages and disadvantages of each?

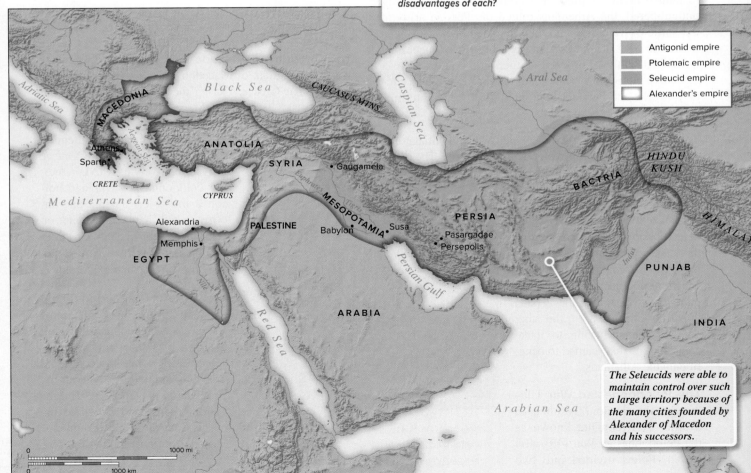

The Seleucids were able to maintain control over such a large territory because of the many cities founded by Alexander of Macedon and his successors.

dynasty ruled until the Roman conquest of Egypt in 31 B.C.E. Seleucus took the largest portion, the former Achaemenid empire stretching from Bactria to Anatolia, which his successors ruled until the Parthians displaced them during the second century B.C.E.

The Antigonid Empire Although the Antigonid realm of Greece and Macedon was the smallest of the Hellenistic empires, it benefited handsomely from the new order. There was continual tension between the Antigonid rulers and the Greek cities, which sought to retain their independence by forming defensive leagues that stoutly resisted Antigonid efforts to control the Greek peninsula. The poleis often struck bargains with the Antigonids, offering to recognize their rule in exchange for tax relief and local autonomy. Internal social tensions also flared, as Greeks wrestled with the perennial problem of land and its equitable distribution. Yet cities such as Athens and Corinth flourished during the Hellenistic era as enormous volumes of trade passed through their ports. Moreover, the overpopulated Greek peninsula sent large numbers of colonists to newly founded cities, especially in the Seleucid empire.

The Ptolemaic Empire All the Hellenistic empires benefited handsomely from the new order through the supervision of extensive trade networks and efficient tax collection. Yet perhaps the wealthiest of the Hellenistic empires was Ptolemaic Egypt. Greek and Macedonian overlords did not interfere in Egyptian society, contenting themselves with the efficient organization of agriculture, industry, and tax collection. They maintained the irrigation networks and monitored the cultivation of crops and the payment of taxes. They also established royal monopolies over the most lucrative industries, such as textiles, salt making, and the brewing of beer.

The City of Alexandria Much of Egypt's wealth flowed to the Ptolemaic capital of Alexandria. Founded by Alexander at the mouth of the Nile, Alexandria served as the Ptolemies' administrative headquarters, but it became much more than a bureaucratic center. Alexandria's enormous harbor was able to accommodate 1,200 ships simultaneously, and the city soon became the most important port in the Mediterranean. Alongside Greeks, Macedonians, and Egyptians lived sizable communities of Phoenicians, Jews, Arabs, and Babylonians. The city was indeed an early megalopolis, where peoples of different ethnic, religious, and cultural traditions conducted their affairs. Under the Ptolemies, Alexandria also became the cultural capital of the Hellenistic world. It was the site of the famous Alexandrian Museum—a state-financed institute of higher learning where philosophical, literary, and scientific scholars carried on advanced research—and of the equally famous Alexandrian Library, which supported the scholarship sponsored by the museum and which, by the first century B.C.E., boasted a collection of more than seven hundred thousand works.

The Seleucid Empire It was in the Seleucid realm, however, that Greek influence reached its greatest extent. The principal channels of that influence were the numerous cities that Alexander and his successors founded in the former Persian empire. Greek and Macedonian colonists flocked to these cities, where they created a Mediterranean-style urban society that left its mark on lands as distant as Bactria and India. Many Seleucids became familiar with Greek language, dress, literature, philosophy, art, and architecture. Emperor Ashoka of India himself had his edicts promulgated in Greek and Aramaic, the two most commonly used languages of the Hellenistic empires. Indeed, although the societies under Hellenistic domination did not lose their own customs, the Hellenistic empires, like classical states in Persia, China, and India, nevertheless brought distant lands into interaction by way of trade and cultural exchange.

THE FRUITS OF TRADE: GREEK ECONOMY AND SOCIETY

The mountainous and rocky terrain of the Greek peninsula yielded only small harvests of grain, and the southern Balkan mountains hindered travel and communication. Indeed, until the construction of modern roads, much of Greece was more accessible by sea than by land. As a result, early Greek society depended heavily on maritime trade.

Trade and the Integration of the Mediterranean Basin

Trade Although it produced little grain, much of Greece is ideally suited to the cultivation of olives and grapes. After the establishment of the poleis, the Greeks discovered that they could profitably concentrate their efforts on the production of olive oil and wine. Greek merchants traded these products around the Mediterranean, returning with abundant supplies of grain and other items as well.

By the early eighth century B.C.E., trade had generated considerable prosperity in the Greek world. Merchants and mariners linked Greek communities throughout the Mediterranean world—not only those in the Greek peninsula but also those in Anatolia, the Mediterranean islands, and the Black Sea region. These trade links contributed to a sense of a larger Greek community. Colonists recognized the same gods as their cousins in the Greek peninsula. They spoke Greek dialects, and they maintained commercial relationships with their native communities.

Antigonus (an-TIG-uh-nuhs)
Ptolemaic (TAWL-oh-may-ihk)
Seleucid (sih-LOO-sid)

The Olympic Games Greeks from all parts gathered periodically to participate in panhellenic festivals that reinforced their common bonds. Many of these festivals featured athletic, literary, or musical contests in which individuals sought to win glory for their polis. Best known of the panhellenic festivals were the Olympic Games. According to tradition, in 776 B.C.E. Greek communities from all parts of the Mediterranean sent their best athletes to the polis of Olympia to engage in contests of speed, strength, and skill. Events included footracing, long jump, boxing, wrestling, javelin tossing, and discus throwing. Winners of events received olive wreaths, and they became celebrated heroes in their home poleis. The ancient Olympic Games took place every four years for more than a millennium before quietly disappearing from Greek life. So, although they were not united politically, by the sixth century B.C.E. Greek communities had nevertheless established a sense of collective identity.

Family and Society

Patriarchal Society With the establishment of poleis in the eighth century B.C.E., the nature of Greek family and society came into focus. Like urban societies in southwest Asia and Anatolia, the Greek poleis adopted strictly patriarchal family structures. Male family heads ruled their households, and fathers even had the right to decide whether to keep infants born to their wives. Greek women fell under the authority of their fathers, husbands, or sons. Upper-class Greek women spent most of their time in the family home and frequently wore veils when they ventured outside. In most of the poleis, women could not own landed property, but they sometimes operated small businesses such as shops and food stalls. The only public position open to Greek women was that of priestess of a religious cult. Sparta was something of a special case when it came to gender relations: there women participated in athletic contests, went about town by themselves, and sometimes even took up arms to defend the polis. Even in Sparta, however, men were family authorities, and men alone determined state policies.

The Diskobolos, or discus thrower, attributed to Myron (C. 450 B.C.E.) captures the athlete's powerful muscular motion and illustrates the Greeks' appreciation for the human body and athletic endeavor.

Slavery Throughout the Greek world, as in other classical societies, slavery was a prominent means of mobilizing labor. Slaves came from several different backgrounds. Some entered slavery because they could not pay their debts. Many were soldiers captured in war. A large number came from the peoples with whom the Greeks traded: slave markets at Black Sea ports sold seminomadic Scythians captured in Russia, and Egyptians provided African slaves.

Greek law regarded all slaves as the private chattel property of their owners, and the conditions of slaves' lives depended on the needs and the temperament of their owners. In general, however, slaves who possessed special skills fared better than unskilled slaves. A slave named Pasion, for example, worked first as a porter and then as a clerk at a prominent Athenian bank during the late fifth and early fourth centuries B.C.E. Ultimately, Pasion gained his freedom, took over management of the bank, outfitted five warships from his own pocket, and won a grant of Athenian citizenship.

THE CULTURAL LIFE OF CLASSICAL GREECE

During the eighth and seventh centuries B.C.E., as Greek merchants ventured throughout the Mediterranean basin, they became acquainted with the sophisticated cultural traditions of Mesopotamia and Egypt. They learned astronomy, science, mathematics, medicine, and magic from the Babylonians as well as geometry, medicine, and divination from the Egyptians. They also drew inspiration from the myths, religious beliefs, art motifs, and architectural styles of Mesopotamia and Egypt. About 800 B.C.E. they adapted the Phoenician alphabet to their own language. To the Phoenicians' consonants they added symbols for vowels and thus created an exceptionally flexible system for representing human speech in written form.

During the fifth and fourth centuries B.C.E., the Greeks combined those borrowed cultural elements with their own intellectual interests to elaborate a rich cultural tradition that exercised enormous influence in the Mediterranean basin and western Europe. The most distinctive feature of classical Greek culture was the effort to construct a consistent system of philosophy based purely on human reason.

Pasion (pahs-ee-on)

Sources from the Past

Socrates' View of Death

In one of his earliest dialogues, the Apology, Plato offered an account of Socrates' defense of himself during his trial before a jury of Athenian citizens. After the jury had convicted him and condemned him to death, Socrates reflected on the nature of death and reemphasized his commitment to virtue rather than to wealth or fame.

And if we reflect in another way we shall see that we may well hope that death is a good thing. For the state of death is one of two things: either the dead man wholly ceases to be and loses all sensation; or, according to the common belief, it is a change and a migration of the soul unto another place. And if death is the absence of all sensation, like the sleep of one whose slumbers are unbroken by any dreams, it will be a wonderful gain. For if a man had to select that night in which he slept so soundly that he did not even see any dreams, and had to compare with it all the other nights and days of his life, and then had to say how many days and nights in his life he had slept better and more pleasantly than this night, I think that a private person, nay, even the great king of Persia himself, would find them easy to count, compared with the others. If that is the nature of death, I for one count it a gain. For then it appears that eternity is nothing more than a single night.

But if death is a journey to another place, and the common belief be true, that all who have died dwell there, what good could be greater than this, my judges? Would a journey not be worth taking if at the end of it, in the other world, we should be released from the self-styled judges of this world, and should find the true judges who are said to sit in judgment below? . . . It would be an infinite happiness to converse with them, and to live with them, and to examine them. Assuredly there they do not put men to death for doing that. For besides the other

ways in which they are happier than we are, they are immortal, at least if the common belief be true.

And you too, judges, must face death with a good courage, and believe this as a truth, that no evil can happen to a good man, either in life, or after death. His fortunes are not neglected by the gods, and what has come to me today has not come by chance. I am persuaded that it is better for me to die now, and to be released from trouble. . . . And so I am hardly angry with my accusers, or with those who have condemned me to die. Yet it was not with this mind that they accused me and condemned me, but rather they meant to do me an injury. Only to that extent do I find fault with them.

Yet I have one request to make of them. When my sons grow up, visit them with punishment, my friends, and vex them in the same way that I have vexed you if they seem to you to care for riches or for anything other than virtue: and if they think that they are something when they are nothing at all, reproach them as I have reproached you for not caring for what they should and for thinking that they are great men when in fact they are worthless. And if you will do this, I myself and my sons will have received our desserts at your hands.

But now the time has come, and we must go hence: I to die, and you to live. Whether life or death is better is known to God, and to God only.

For Further Reflection

■ How does Socrates' understanding of personal morality and its rewards compare and contrast with the Zoroastrian, Buddhist, and Hindu views discussed in earlier chapters?

Source: F. J. Church, trans. *The Trial and Death of Socrates,* 2nd ed. London: Macmillan, 1886, pp. 76–78. (Translation slightly modified.)

Rational Thought and Philosophy

Socrates The pivotal figure in the development of philosophy was Socrates (470–399 B.C.E.), a thoughtful Athenian driven by a powerful urge to understand human beings in all their complexity. Socrates did not commit his thought to writing, but his disciple Plato later composed dialogues that represented Socrates' views. He suggested that honor was far more important than wealth, fame, or other superficial attributes. He scorned those who preferred public accolades to personal integrity, and he insisted on the need to reflect on the purposes and goals of life. In elaborating those views, Socrates often subjected traditional ethical teachings to critical scrutiny. That outraged

some of his fellow citizens, who brought him to trial on charges that he corrupted the Athenian youths who joined him in the marketplace to discuss moral and ethical issues. A jury of Athenian citizens decided that Socrates had indeed passed the bounds of propriety and condemned him to death. In 399 B.C.E. Socrates drank a potion of hemlock sap and died in the company of his friends.

Plato Socrates' influence survived in the work of his most zealous disciple, Plato (430–347 B.C.E.), and in

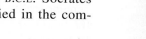
Socrates (SAHK-rah-teez)

Plato.

A mosaic from the Italian town of Pompeii, near Naples, depicts Plato (standing at left) discussing philosophical issues with students. Produced in the early first century C.E., this illustration testifies to the popularity of Greek philosophy in classical Roman society.

would work at functions for which their talents best suited them.

Aristotle During the generation after Plato, Aristotle elaborated a systematic philosophy that equaled Plato's work in its long-term influence. Unlike Plato, Aristotle believed that philosophers could rely on their senses to provide accurate information about the world and then depend on reason to sort out its mysteries. His work provided such a coherent and comprehensive vision of the world that his later disciples called him "the master of those who know."

The Greek philosophers deeply influenced the development of European and Islamic cultural traditions. Until the seventeenth century C.E., most European philosophers regarded the Greeks as intellectual authorities. Christian and Islamic theologians alike went to great lengths to harmonize their religious convictions with the philosophical views of Plato and Aristotle. Thus, like philosophical and religious figures in other classical societies, Plato and Aristotle provided a powerful intellectual framework that shaped thought about the world and human affairs for two millennia and more.

Popular Religion and Greek Drama

Deities Because most Greeks of the classical era did not have an advanced education, they turned to traditions of popular culture and popular religion rather than philosophy to seek guidance for human behavior. The Greeks did not recognize a single, exclusive, all-powerful god. Rather, they believed that in the beginning there was the formless void of chaos out of which emerged the earth, the mother and creator of all things. The earth then generated the sky, and together they produced night, day, sun, moon, and other natural phenomena. Struggles between the deities led to bitter heavenly battles, and ultimately Zeus, grandson of the earth and sky gods, emerged as paramount ruler of the divine realm. Zeus's heavenly court included scores of subordinate deities who had various responsibilities: the god Apollo promoted wisdom and justice, for example; the goddess Fortune brought unexpected opportunities and difficulties; and the Furies wreaked vengeance on those who violated divine law.

Religious Cults Like religious traditions in other lands, Greek myths sought to explain the world and the forces that shape it. They served also as foundations for religious cults based on individual poleis that contributed to a powerful sense of community in classical Greece. These religious

Plato's disciple Aristotle (384–322 B.C.E.). Inspired by his mentor's reflections, Plato elaborated a systematic philosophy of great subtlety. He presented his thought in a series of dialogues in which Socrates figured as the principal speaker.

The cornerstone of Plato's thought was his theory of Forms, or Ideas. It disturbed Plato that he could not gain satisfactory intellectual control over the world. The quality of virtue, for example, meant different things in different situations, as did honesty, courage, truth, and beauty. How was it possible, then, to understand virtue as an abstract quality? In seeking an answer to that question, Plato developed his belief that the world in which we live is not the world of genuine reality, but only a pale and imperfect reflection of the world of Forms or Ideas. The secrets of this world, Plato argued, were available only to philosophers—those who applied their rational faculties to the pursuit of wisdom. In works like his dialogue the *Republic,* Plato thus came to advocate an intellectual aristocracy in which the philosophical elite would rule while less-educated classes

Aristotle (AHR-ih-stot-uhl)

Thinking about TRADITIONS

Institutions and Identity in the Mediterranean World

Both Greeks and Romans maintained multiple and consistent connections with a wide variety of peoples and places in the classical period. *Given such interaction, what cultural, political, and social institutions helped both Greeks and Romans maintain a sense of their own unique identities?*

cults varied widely: many conducted ritual observances in special places, for example, and some were open to only one sex. Before the fifth century B.C.E., many cults inspired emotional displays and spirited—sometimes frenzied—song and dance.

Tragic Drama During the fifth century B.C.E., however, as the poleis strengthened their grip on public and political life, the religious cults became progressively more tame. Instead of festivals, religious cults marked the year with the presentation of plays that examined relations between humans and the gods or reflected on ethics and morality. That transformation set the stage for the emergence of Greek dramatic literature, which sought to engage audiences in subtle reflection on complicated themes. The great tragedians—Aeschylus, Sophocles, and Euripides, whose lives spanned the fifth century B.C.E.—explored the possibilities and limitations of human action. Comic dramatists such as Aristophanes also dealt with serious issues of human striving and responsible behavior by ridiculing the foibles of prominent public figures and calling attention to the absurd consequences of ill-considered action.

Hellenistic Philosophy and Religion

As the Hellenistic empires seized the political initiative in the Mediterranean basin and eclipsed the poleis, residents ceased to regard their polis as the focus of individual and religious loyalties. Instead, they increasingly looked toward cultural and religious alternatives that ministered to the needs and interests of individuals living in a cosmopolitan society.

The Hellenistic Philosophers The most popular Hellenistic philosophers—the Epicureans, the Skeptics, and the Stoics—addressed individual needs by searching for personal tranquility and serenity. Epicureans, for example, identified pleasure as the greatest good. By *pleasure* they meant not unbridled hedonism but, rather, a state of quiet satisfaction that would shield them from the pressures of the Hellenistic world. Skeptics refused to take strong positions on political, moral, and social issues because they

doubted the possibility of certain knowledge. The most respected and influential of the Hellenistic philosophers, however, were the Stoics. Unlike the Epicureans and the Skeptics, the Stoics did not seek to withdraw from the pressures of the world. Rather, they taught that individuals had the duty to aid others and lead virtuous lives in harmony with reason and nature.

Religions of Salvation Whereas the philosophers' doctrines appealed to educated elites, religions of salvation spread across the trade routes of the Hellenistic empires and enjoyed surging popularity in Hellenistic society. Mystery religions promised eternal bliss for initiates who observed their rites and lived in accordance with their doctrines. Some of these faiths spread across the trade routes and found followers far from their homelands. The Egyptian cult of Osiris, for example, became extraordinarily popular because it promised salvation for those who led honorable lives. Cults from Persia, Mesopotamia, Anatolia, and Greece also attracted disciples throughout the Hellenistic world.

Many of the mystery religions involved the worship of a savior whose death and resurrection would lead the way to eternal salvation for devoted followers. Some philosophers and religious thinkers speculated that a single, universal god might rule the entire universe, and that this god had a plan for the salvation of all humankind. Like the Hellenistic philosophies, then, religions of salvation addressed the interests of individuals searching for security in a complex world. Indeed, those interests continued to be of concern to peoples in the Mediterranean basin long after political dominance passed from the Greek to the Italian peninsula.

ROME: FROM KINGDOM TO REPUBLIC

Founded in the eighth century B.C.E., the city of Rome was originally a small city-state ruled by a single king. In 509 B.C.E., however, the city's aristocrats deposed the king, ended the monarchy, and instituted a republic—a form of government in which delegates represent the interests of various constituencies. The Roman republic survived for more than five hundred years, and it was under the republican constitution that Rome came to establish itself as the dominant power in the Mediterranean basin.

Aeschylus (ES-kuh-luhs)
Epicureans (ehp-ih-KYOOR-eeuhns)
Stoics (STOH-ihks)

The Etruscans and Rome

Romulus and Remus According to legend, the city of Rome was founded by Romulus, who—along with his twin brother, Remus—was abandoned as a baby by an evil uncle near the flooded Tiber River. Before the infants could drown, a kindly she-wolf found them and nursed them to health. The boys grew strong and courageous, and in 753 B.C.E. Romulus founded the city and established himself as its first king.

Modern scholars do not tell so colorful a tale, but they do agree that bands of Indo-European migrants crossed the Alps and settled throughout the Italian peninsula beginning about 2000 B.C.E. Like their distant cousins in India, Greece, and northern Europe, these migrants blended with the neolithic inhabitants of the region, adopted agriculture, and established tribal federations. Sheepherders and small farmers occupied much of the Italian peninsula, including the future site of Rome. Bronze metallurgy appeared about 1800 B.C.E. and iron about 900 B.C.E.

The Etruscans The Etruscans, a dynamic people, dominated much of Italy between the eighth and fifth centuries B.C.E. The Etruscans probably migrated to Italy from Anatolia. They settled first in Tuscany, the region around modern Florence, but they soon controlled much of Italy. They built thriving cities and established political and economic alliances between their settlements. They manufactured high-quality bronze and iron goods, and they worked gold and silver into jewelry. They built a fleet and traded actively in the western Mediterranean. During the late sixth century B.C.E., however, the Etruscans encountered a series of challenges from other peoples, and their society began to decline.

The Kingdom of Rome The Etruscans deeply influenced the early development of Rome. Like the Etruscan cities, Rome was a monarchy during the early days after its foundation, and several Roman kings were Etruscans. The kings ruled Rome through the seventh and sixth centuries B.C.E., and they provided the city with paved streets, public buildings, defensive walls, and large temples.

Etruscan merchants drew a large volume of traffic to Rome, thanks partly to the city's geographical advantages. Rome enjoyed easy access to the Mediterranean by way of the Tiber River, but since it was not on the coast, it did not run the risk of invasion or attack from the sea. Already during the period of Etruscan dominance, trade routes from all parts of Italy converged on Rome. When Etruscan society declined, Rome was in a strong position to play a more prominent role both in Italy and in the larger Mediterranean world.

Romulus (ROM-yuh-luhs)
Remus (REE-muhs)
Etruscans (ih-TRUHS-kuhns)
plebeians (plih-BEE-uhns)

The Roman Republic and Its Constitution

Establishment of the Republic When the Roman nobility deposed the last Etruscan king and replaced him with a republic, they built the Roman forum at the heart of the city—a political and civic center filled with temples and public buildings where leading citizens tended to government business. They also instituted a republican constitution that entrusted executive responsibilities to two consuls who wielded civil and military power. Consuls were elected by an assembly dominated by the noble classes, known in Rome as the patricians, and they served one-year terms. The powerful Senate, whose members were mostly aristocrats with extensive political experience, advised the consuls and ratified all major decisions. When faced with crises, however, the Romans appointed an official, known as a dictator, who wielded absolute power for a term of six months. By providing for strong leadership during times of extraordinary difficulty, the republican constitution enabled Rome to maintain a reasonably stable society throughout most of the republic's history.

Conflicts between Patricians and Plebeians Because the consuls and the Senate both represented the interests of the patricians, there was constant tension between the wealthy classes and the common people, known as the plebeians. Indeed, during the early fifth century B.C.E., relations between the classes became so strained that the plebeians threatened to secede from Rome. To maintain the integrity of the Roman state, the patricians granted plebeians the right to elect officials, known as tribunes, who represented their interests in the Roman government. Originally plebeians chose two tribunes, but the number eventually rose to ten. Tribunes had the power to intervene in all political matters, and they possessed the right to veto measures that they judged unfair.

Although tensions between the classes never disappeared, during the fourth century B.C.E. plebeians became eligible to hold almost all state offices and gained the right to have one of the consuls come from their ranks. By the early third century, plebeian-dominated assemblies won the power to make decisions binding on all of Rome. Thus, like fifth-century Athens, republican Rome gradually broadened the base of political participation.

The Expansion of the Republic

Between the fourth and second centuries B.C.E., the people of Rome transformed their city from a small and vulnerable city-state to the center of an enormous empire. They began by consolidating their power in the Italian peninsula itself. Indeed, by the later fourth century they had emerged as the predominant power in the Italian peninsula. Roman success in the peninsula was partly a matter of military power and partly a matter of generous policies toward the peoples they conquered. Instead of ruling them as vanquished subjects, the Romans allowed conquered people to govern their internal affairs as long as they provided military support and did not enter into hostile alliances. In addition, conquered peoples were allowed to trade in Rome, to take Roman spouses, and even to gain Roman citizenship. These policies both provided Rome with essential support and eased the pain of conquest.

Expansion in the Mediterranean With Italy under its control, Rome began to play a major role in the affairs of the larger Mediterranean basin and to experience conflicts with other Mediterranean powers. The principal power in the western Mediterranean during the fourth and third centuries B.C.E. was the city-state of Carthage, located near modern Tunis. Originally established as a Phoenician colony, Carthage enjoyed a strategic location that enabled it to trade actively throughout the Mediterranean. From the wealth generated by this commerce, Carthage became the dominant political power in north Africa (excluding Egypt), the southern part of the Iberian peninsula, and the western region of grain-rich Sicily as well. Meanwhile, the three Hellenistic empires that succeeded Alexander of Macedon continued to dominate the eastern Mediterranean.

The Punic Wars Economic and political competition brought the Romans into conflict with Carthage first. Between 264 and 146 B.C.E., they fought three devastating conflicts known as the Punic Wars with the Carthaginians,

in which Rome and Carthage struggled for regional supremacy. The rivalry ended after Roman forces subjected Carthage to a long siege, conquered and burned the city, and forced some fifty thousand survivors into slavery. The Romans then annexed Carthaginian possessions in north Africa and Iberia—rich in grain, oil, wine, silver, and gold—and used those resources to finance continued imperial expansion.

Shortly after the beginning of the Carthaginian conflict, Rome became embroiled in conflicts with the Antigonids and the Seleucids in the eastern Mediterranean. Between 215 and 148 B.C.E., Rome fought five major wars, mostly in Macedon and Anatolia, against these opponents. As a result of these conflicts, Rome emerged as the preeminent power in the eastern as well as the western Mediterranean by the middle of the second century B.C.E.

FROM REPUBLIC TO EMPIRE

Imperial expansion brought wealth and power to Rome, but these brought problems as well as benefits. Unequal distribution of wealth aggravated class tensions and gave rise to conflict over political and social policies. Meanwhile, the need to administer conquered lands efficiently strained the capacities of the republican constitution. During the first century B.C.E. and the first century C.E., Roman civil and military leaders gradually dismantled the republican constitution and imposed a centralized imperial form of government on the city of Rome and its empire.

Ruins of the Roman Forum.
Political leaders conducted public affairs in the forum during the era of the republic.

Imperial Expansion and Domestic Problems

In Rome, as in classical China and Greece, patterns of land distribution caused serious political and social tensions. Conquered lands fell largely into the hands of wealthy elites, who organized enormous plantations known as *latifundia*. Because they enjoyed economies of scale and often employed slave labor, owners of latifundia operated at lower costs than did owners of smaller holdings, who often had to sell out to their wealthier neighbors.

Carthage (KAHR-thihj)
latifundia (lah-tee-FOON-dya)

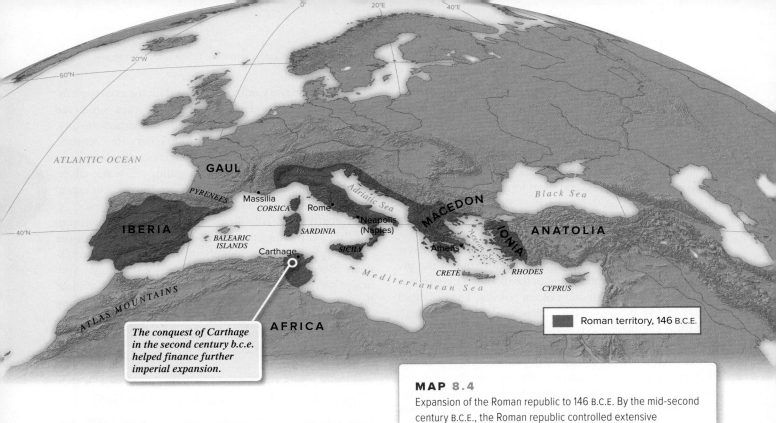

The conquest of Carthage in the second century b.c.e. helped finance further imperial expansion.

Roman territory, 146 B.C.E.

MAP 8.4

Expansion of the Roman republic to 146 B.C.E. By the mid-second century B.C.E., the Roman republic controlled extensive territories outside Italy.

In what ways did Roman expansion encourage interactions and exchanges throughout the Mediterranean region?

Civil War During the second and first centuries B.C.E., relations between the classes became so strained that they led to violent social conflict and civil war. Roman politicians and generals jockeyed for power in support of either social reform or the privileged position of the wealthy elites, with bloody results on both sides. By the middle of the first century B.C.E., it had become increasingly clear that the Roman republic was not suitable for a large and growing empire. In this chaotic context Gaius Julius Caesar inaugurated the process by which Rome replaced its republican constitution with a centralized imperial form of government.

The Foundation of Empire

Julius Caesar recognized the need for social reform and favored liberal policies that would ease the suffering of the poor. During the decade of the 60s B.C.E., he played an active role in Roman politics. He spent enormous sums of money sponsoring public spectacles—such as battles between gladiators and wild animals—which helped him build a reputation and win election to posts in the republican government. This activity kept him in the public eye and helped to publicize his interest in social reform. During the next decade Caesar led a Roman army to Gaul, which he conquered and brought into the still-growing Roman empire.

In 49 B.C.E. Caesar turned his army toward Rome itself after conservative leaders in the city sought to maneuver him out of power. By early 46 B.C.E. he had made himself master of the Roman state and named himself dictator—an office that he claimed for life rather than for the constitutional six-month term. Caesar then centralized military and political functions and brought them

under his own control. He confiscated property from conservatives and distributed it to veterans of his armies and other supporters. He launched large-scale building projects in Rome as a way to provide employment for the urban poor. He also extended Roman citizenship to peoples in the imperial provinces.

Augustus Caesar never had the chance to consolidate his government, however, because in 44 B.C.E. members of the Roman elite stabbed him to death in the hopes of reestablishing the republic. Instead, they plunged Rome into thirteen more years of civil conflict. When the struggles ended, power belonged to Octavian, Caesar's grandnephew and adopted son. In a naval battle at Actium in Greece (31 B.C.E.), Octavian defeated his principal rival, Mark Antony, who had joined forces with Cleopatra, last of the Ptolemaic rulers of Egypt. Octavian then moved quickly to consolidate his rule. In 27 B.C.E. the Senate bestowed on him the title Augustus, a term with strong religious connotations suggesting the divine or semidivine nature of its holder.

Augustus's Administration Augustus's government was a monarchy disguised as a republic. He preserved traditional republican offices and forms of government and included members of the Roman elite in his government while at the same time fundamentally altering the nature of that government. He accumulated vast powers for himself and ultimately

Thinking about ENCOUNTERS

The Relationship between Expansion and Integration

Both Greek and Roman society expanded well beyond their borders at the height of their respective influence in Mediterranean affairs. *In what ways did Greek colonization and Roman empire-building facilitate and encourage the movement of goods, ideas, and people in the Mediterranean region?*

took responsibility for all important governmental functions. He reorganized the military system, creating a new standing army with commanders who owed allegiance directly to himself. He also was careful to place individuals loyal to him in all important positions. During his forty-five years of virtually unopposed rule, Augustus fashioned an imperial government that guided Roman affairs for the next three centuries.

Continuing Expansion and Integration of the Empire

During the two centuries following Augustus's rule, Roman armies conquered distant lands and integrated them into a larger economy and society. At its high point, during the early second century C.E., the Roman empire embraced much of Britain and continental Europe as well as a continuous belt of possessions surrounding the Mediterranean and extending to rich agricultural regions inland, including Mesopotamia.

Roman Roads Within the boundaries of the Roman empire itself, a long era of peace—known as the *pax romana,* or "Roman peace"—facilitated economic and political integration from the first to the middle of the third century C.E. Like their Persian, Chinese, Indian, and Hellenistic counterparts, the Romans integrated their empire by building networks of transportation and communication. Indeed, roads linked all parts of the Roman empire. One notable highway stretched more than 2,500 kilometers (1,554 miles) along the northeast imperial frontier from the Black Sea to the North Sea, parallel to the Danube and Rhine rivers. The roads permitted urgent travel and messages to proceed with remarkable speed: Tiberius, successor of Augustus as Roman emperor, once traveled 290 kilometers (180 miles) in a single day over Roman roads.

Sea-Lanes Where roads came to the water's edge, Romans made use of sea-lanes throughout the Mediterranean Sea and the Black Sea. Established sea-lanes linked ports from Syria and Palestine to Spain and north Africa. Indeed, the Mediterranean became essentially a Roman lake, which the Romans themselves called *mare nostrum* ("our sea"). Thus, by sea as well as by land, Romans found ways to maintain communications with all regions of their empire.

Roman Law As armies spread Roman influence throughout the Mediterranean, jurists also worked to construct a rational body of law that would apply to all peoples under Roman rule. During the late republic and especially during the empire, the jurists articulated standards of justice and gradually applied them throughout Roman territory. They established the

Augustus.

In this statue, which emphasizes his civil and military leadership in Rome, Augustus wears the uniform of a Roman general. How would you characterize the image of Augustus projected in this statue?

nostrum (NAHS-truhm)

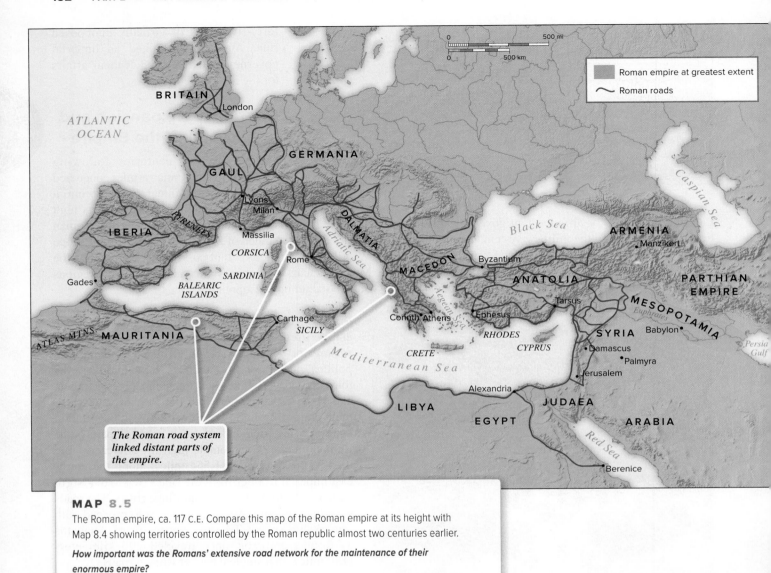

The Roman road system linked distant parts of the empire.

MAP 8.5

The Roman empire, ca. 117 C.E. Compare this map of the Roman empire at its height with Map 8.4 showing territories controlled by the Roman republic almost two centuries earlier.

How important was the Romans' extensive road network for the maintenance of their enormous empire?

principle that defendants were innocent until proven guilty, and they ensured that defendants had a right to challenge their accusers before a judge in a court of law. Like transportation and communication networks, Roman law helped to integrate the diverse lands that made up the empire, and the principles of Roman law continued to shape Mediterranean and European society long after the empire had disappeared.

ECONOMY AND SOCIETY IN THE ROMAN MEDITERRANEAN

The rapid expansion of Roman influence and the imposition of Roman imperial rule brought economic and social changes to peoples throughout the Mediterranean basin. Good roads and the pax romana encouraged trade between

regions. Existing cities benefited handsomely from the wealth generated by trade, and in the lands they conquered, the Romans founded new cities to serve as links between local regions and the larger Mediterranean economy. Meanwhile, like most other peoples of classical times, the Romans built a strictly patriarchal society and made extensive use of slave labor.

Trade and Urbanization

Commercial Agriculture   As the Roman empire became more integrated, agricultural production grew increasingly commercialized as well as specialized. Because it was possible to import grain at favorable prices from lands that routinely produced large surpluses, other regions could concentrate on the cultivation of fruits and vegetables or on the production of manufactured items. Greece, for example,

Reverberations of ● ● ● ● ● ● ● ●
Long-Distance Trade Networks

The long-distance trade networks in which the Romans took part facilitated the movement of people and products around a vast area of Eurasia. But long-distance trade also encouraged the transformation of fixed locations, like capital cities and ports, as a result of the money such networks could bring in from profits and taxes. Consider carefully the ways long-distance trade networks of the classical period were linked to architectural innovation, artistic expression, and the development of new cultural forms both in Roman cities as well as in the cities of other classical empires.

concentrated on olives and vines. Syria and Palestine produced fruits, nuts, and wool fabrics. Gaul produced grain, while Spain produced olive oil, wine, horses, and precious metals. Italy became a center for the production of pottery, glassware, and bronze goods.

Mediterranean Trade Specialized production of agricultural commodities and manufactured goods set the stage for vigorous trade over the Mediterranean sea lanes. Roman military and naval power kept the seas largely free of pirates so that sizable cargoes could move safely over long distances, barring foul weather. As Roman military forces, administrators, tax collectors, and other officials traveled throughout the empire carrying out their duties, they joined the merchants in linking the Mediterranean's regions into a well-integrated network of communication and exchange. Archaeologists have discovered that even in remote rural areas, peasants routinely used high-quality pottery, ate food off fine tableware, consumed wines and oils imported from afar, and slept under tiled roofs. Beyond the Mediterranean, the port of Berenice on the Red Sea coast of Egypt offered access to the Indian Ocean and distant markets. Sometime about the first century C.E., an anonymous Roman subject composed a remarkable work called the *Periplus maris erythraei* (meaning a "sailing itinerary of the Red Sea"),

which provided a description of the ports on the Red Sea itself as well as east African and Indian ports that Roman merchants commonly visited.

The City of Rome Much of the profit from Mediterranean trade flowed to Rome, where it fueled remarkable urban development. In the first century C.E., some ten thousand statues and seven hundred pools decorated the city. The Roman state financed the construction of temples, bathhouses, public buildings, stadiums, and, perhaps most important of all, aqueducts—built with concrete invented by Roman engineers—that brought fresh water into the city from the neighboring mountains.

Roman Cities and Their Attractions In addition to the spectacular growth of Rome, urban growth and development took place in cities all over the empire. And, as wealth concentrated in the cities, urban residents came to

A Roman port city.
A wall painting from Stabiae (a small community near Pompeii destroyed by the eruption of Vesuvius in 79 C.E.) depicts an Italian harbor with ships, wharves, warehouses, markets, and decorative columns topped by statues.

expect a variety of comforts not available in rural areas. Roman cities enjoyed abundant supplies of fresh water and elaborate sewage and plumbing systems. All sizable cities and even many smaller towns had public baths and often swimming pools and gymnasia as well. Enormous circuses, stadiums, and amphitheaters provided sites for the entertainment of the urban masses. Entertainment in stadiums often took forms now considered coarse and cruel—battles to the death between gladiators or between humans and wild animals—but urban populations flocked to such events, which they looked on as exciting diversions from daily routine. The Roman Colosseum, a magnificent marble stadium and sports arena opened in 80 C.E., provided seating for about fifty thousand spectators.

Family and Society in Roman Times

The Paterfamilias Roman law vested immense authority in male heads of families, known as the *paterfamilias*— "father of the family." Roman law gave the paterfamilias the authority to arrange marriages for his children, determine the work or duties they would perform, and punish them for offenses. He had rights also to sell them into slavery and even to execute them.

Although the paterfamilias was legally endowed with extraordinary powers, women usually supervised domestic affairs in Roman households, and by the time they reached middle age they generally wielded considerable influence within their families. Also, although Roman law placed strict limits on the ability of women to receive inheritances, clever individuals found ways to evade the law. During the third and second centuries B.C.E., women came to possess a great deal of property, and by the first century B.C.E., many women supervised the financial affairs of family businesses and wealthy estates.

Slavery Roman society made extensive use of slave labor: by the second century C.E., slaves may have represented as much as one-third of the population of the Roman empire. In the countryside they worked mostly on latifundia under extremely harsh conditions, often chained together in teams. In fact, discontent among rural slaves led to several large-scale revolts, especially during the second and first centuries B.C.E. During the most serious uprising, in 73 B.C.E., the escaped slave Spartacus assembled an army of seventy thousand rebellious slaves. The Roman army dispatched eight legions, comprising more than forty thousand well-equipped, veteran troops, to quell the revolt.

---

paterfamilias (PAH-tehr-fah-MEE-lyas)
Spartacus (SPAHR-tah-cus)
Cicero (SIHS-er-oh)

In the cities, conditions were much less difficult. Female slaves commonly worked as domestic servants while males toiled as servants, laborers, craftsmen, shopkeepers, or business agents for their owners. As in Greece, slaves who had an education or possessed some particular talent had the potential to lead comfortable lives. In urban areas it was also common, though not mandatory, for masters to free slaves about the time they reached age thirty. Until freed, however, slaves remained under the strict authority of their masters, who had the right to sell them, arrange their family affairs, punish them, and even execute them for serious offenses.

THE COSMOPOLITAN MEDITERRANEAN

The integration of the Mediterranean basin had important effects not only for the trade and economy of the Roman empire but also for its cultural and religious traditions. Roads and communication networks favored the spread of new popular religions. Most important of these over the long run was Christianity, which became the official religion of the Roman empire and the predominant faith of the Mediterranean basin.

Greek Philosophy and Religions of Salvation

Roman Deities During the early days of their history, the Romans recognized many gods and goddesses, who they believed intervened directly in human affairs. Jupiter was the principal god, lord of the heavens, and Mars was the god of war, Ceres the goddess of grain, Janus the god who watched the threshold of individual houses, and Vesta the goddess of the hearth. In addition to those major deities, most Roman households honored tutelary deities, gods who looked after the welfare of individual families.

As the Romans expanded their political influence and built an empire, they encountered the religious and cultural traditions of other peoples. Often they adopted the deities of other peoples and used them for their own purposes. From the Etruscans, for example, they learned of Juno, the moon goddess, and Minerva, the goddess of wisdom, as well as certain religious practices, such as divination of the future through examination of the internal organs of ritually sacrificed animals.

Greek Influence The Romans also drew deep inspiration from the Greek tradition of rational thought and philosophy, especially Stoicism. The Stoics' desire to identify a set of universal moral standards based on nature and reason appealed strongly to Roman intellectuals. Indeed, thinkers such as Marcus Tullius Cicero (106–43 B.C.E.)

Roman Pantheon.
Built between 118 and 125 C.E., the Pantheon in Rome was a temple honoring all gods, and it survives as one of the outstanding examples of Roman architecture. With a diameter of 43 meters (141 feet), the building's dome was the largest constructed until the twentieth century.

What feelings might such a structure have evoked in worshipers?

republic as well as during the empire. Many originated in the far-flung realms of the empire, including the popular Anatolian cult of Mithras, the Anatolian cult of the mother goddess Cybele, and the Egyptian cult of the goddess Isis.

Mithraism The Mithraic religion provided divine sanction for human life and especially for purposeful moral behavior. It brought together a community that welcomed and nurtured like-minded individuals. Finally, it offered hope for individuals who conscientiously observed the cult's teachings by promising them ecstatic and mysterious union with Mithras—who was strongly associated with military virtues such as strength, courage, and discipline—himself. During the late republic, Mithraic altars and temples appeared in military garrisons throughout the empire. During the early centuries C.E., administrators and merchants also became enchanted with Mithras, and his cult attracted followers among the male populations of all sizable communities and commercial centers in the Roman empire.

Cult of Isis The cult of Mithras did not admit women, but cults dedicated to the Anatolian mother goddess Cybele, the Egyptian goddess Isis, and other deities made a place for both men and women. Indeed, the cult of Isis may have been the most popular of all the Mediterranean religions of salvation before the rise of Christianity. Devotees built temples to Isis throughout the Roman empire, and they adored the Egyptian goddess as a benevolent and protective deity who nurtured her worshipers and helped them cope with the stresses of life in cosmopolitan society. Like the Mithraic religion, the cult of Isis and other religions of salvation attracted followers in Rome and other cities throughout the Mediterranean basin. The immense popularity of these religions of salvation provides a context that helps to explain the remarkable success of Christianity in the Roman empire.

Judaism and Early Christianity

The Jews and the Empire After the dissolution of the Jewish kingdom of David and Solomon in the early tenth century B.C.E., the Jewish people maintained their faith and their communities under various imperial regimes. At times, Jewish communities clashed with their imperial overlords, especially because monotheistic Jews refused to revere emperors as gods. As the Romans extended their empire in the eastern Mediterranean and brought the Jews in Palestine under their control, relations between the two became especially tense. Between 66 and 70 C.E., relations deteriorated to such a point that Palestinian Jews rose in rebellion against the Romans in what became known as the Jewish War.

Jesus of Nazareth The Jews were decisively defeated in the war, which prompted some Jews to found new sects

readily adopted Stoic values. His letters and treatises emphasized the individual's duty to live in accordance with nature and reason. He argued that the pursuit of justice was the individual's highest public duty, and he scorned those who sought to accumulate wealth or to become powerful through immoral, illegal, or unjust means. Through his speeches and especially his writings, Cicero helped to establish Stoicism as the most prominent school of moral philosophy in Rome.

Religions of Salvation Whereas educated thinkers drew inspiration from the Greeks, the masses found comfort in religions of salvation that established their presence throughout the Mediterranean basin and beyond. These religions became prominent features in Rome during the late

that looked for saviors to deliver them from Roman rule so they could practice their faith without interference. The early Christians were one such sect. The Christians formed their community around Jesus of Nazareth, a charismatic Jewish teacher whom they recognized as their savior. Born about the year 4 B.C.E., Jesus grew up at a time of high tension between Roman overlords and their Jewish subjects. He was a peaceful man who taught devotion to God and love for fellow human beings. He attracted large crowds because of a reputation for wisdom and miraculous powers, especially the ability to heal the sick.

Yet Jesus alarmed the Romans because he also taught that "the kingdom of God is at hand." To Jesus, the kingdom of God was a spiritual realm in which God would gather those faithful to him. To Roman administrators, however, his message sounded like a threat to Roman rule in Palestine, especially since crowds routinely accompanied Jesus. In an effort to forestall a new round of rebellion, Roman administrators executed Jesus by fixing him to a cross in the early 30s C.E.

Jesus' Early Followers Jesus' crucifixion did not put an end to his movement. Even after his execution Jesus' close followers strongly felt his presence and proclaimed that he had triumphed over death by rising from his grave. They called him "Christ," meaning "the anointed one," the savior who would bring individuals into the kingdom of God. They taught that he was the son of God and that his sacrifice served to offset the sins of those who had faith in him. They taught further that, like Jesus, the faithful would survive death and would experience eternal life in the spiritual kingdom of God. Following Jesus' teachings, the early Christians observed a demanding moral code and devoted themselves uncompromisingly to God. They also compiled a body of writings—accounts of Jesus' life, reports of his followers' works, and letters outlining Christian teachings—that gained recognition as the New Testament. Together with the Jews' Hebrew scriptures, which Christians referred to as the Old Testament, the New Testament became the holy book of Christianity.

Paul of Tarsus Jesus and his earliest followers were all Jews. Beginning about the middle of the first century C.E., however, some Christians avidly sought converts from non-Jewish communities in the Hellenistic world and the Roman empire. The principal figure in the expansion of Christianity beyond Judaism was Paul of Tarsus, a Jew from Anatolia who zealously preached his faith, especially in the Greek-speaking eastern region of the Roman empire. Paul taught a Christianity that attracted the urban masses in the same way as other religions of salvation that spread widely in the Roman empire. His doctrine called for individuals to observe high moral standards and to place their faith ahead of personal and family interests. His teaching also explained the world and human history as the results of God's purposeful activity so that it provided a framework of meaning for individuals' lives. Furthermore, Paul's doctrine promised a glorious future existence for those who conscientiously observed the faith.

Early Christian Communities Yet for two centuries after the crucifixion of Jesus, there was no central authority for the fledgling church. Rather, individual communities selected their own supervisors, known as *bishops,* who oversaw priests and governed their jurisdictions according to their own best understanding of Christian doctrine. As a result, until the emergence of Rome as the principal seat of church authority in the third century C.E., Christians held doctrinal views and followed practices that varied considerably from one community to the next. Some religious leaders taught that Jesus had literally risen from the dead and come back to life, for example, and others held that his resurrection was spiritual rather than physical. Only gradually did believers agree to recognize certain texts as authoritative scripture—the New Testament—and adopt them as fundamental guides for Christian doctrine and practice.

The Growth of Early Christianity Like the Jews from whose ranks they had sprung, the early Christians refused to honor the Roman state cults or revere the emperor as a god. As a result, Roman imperial authorities launched sporadic campaigns of persecution designed to eliminate Christianity as a threat to the empire. In spite of this repression, Christian numbers grew rapidly. During the first three centuries of the faith's existence, Christianity found its way to almost all parts of the Roman empire, and Christians established thriving communities throughout the Mediterranean basin and farther east in Mesopotamia and Iran. The remarkable growth of Christianity reflected the new faith's appeal particularly to the lower classes, urban populations, and women. Christianity accorded honor and dignity to individuals who did not enjoy high standing in Roman society, and it endowed them with a sense of spiritual freedom more meaningful than wealth, power, or social prominence. It taught the spiritual equality of the sexes and welcomed the contributions of both men and women. And it provided a promise of future glory for those who placed their faith in Jesus. Thus, although Christianity originated as a minor sect of Judaism, urban populations in the Roman empire embraced the new faith with such enthusiasm that by the third century C.E. it had become the most dynamic and influential religious faith in the Mediterranean basin.

SUMMARY

Under Greek and Roman influence, the Mediterranean region became a tightly integrated society. Although the Greeks did not build a centralized empire, they dotted the Mediterranean and Black Sea shorelines with their colonies, and their merchant fleets stimulated both commercial and cultural interactions between peoples of distant lands. Greek merchants, soldiers, and administrators also played prominent roles in the extensive empires of Alexander and the Hellenistic rulers, and they left a remarkably rich and enduring cultural legacy. Building in part on both the cultural and the economic legacies of the Greeks, the Romans proceeded to construct a republic, and then an empire, that eventually administered lands as distant as Mesopotamia and Britain. Highly organized trade networks enabled peoples throughout the empire to concentrate on specialized agricultural or industrial production. Popular religions spread widely and attracted enthusiastic converts. Like Confucianism and Buddhism in classical China and India, rational philosophy and Christianity became prominent sources of intellectual and religious authority in the classical Mediterranean and continued to influence cultural development in the Mediterranean, Europe, and southwest Asia over the centuries that followed.

STUDY TERMS

Achaemenid (139)
Aeschylus (147)
Alexander of Macedon (141–143)
Antigonus (142)
Aristotle (146)
Athens (138–139, 141)
Augustus (150–151)
Carthage (149)
Christians (156)
Cicero (154)
cult of Isis (155)
Delian League (141)
Epicureans (147)
Etruscans (148)
Jesus of Nazareth (155)
Jewish War (155)
Julius Caesar (150)

latifundia (149)
mare nostrum (151)
Minoan society (137)
Mithraism (155)
Mycenaean society (137)
Olympic Games (144)
Pasion (144)
paterfamilias (154)
pax romana (151)
Peloponnesian War (141)
Peloponnesus (138)
Pericles (139)
Persian Wars (141)
Plato (145–146)
plebeians (148)
polis (138)
Ptolemaic (143)
Punic Wars (149)

Remus (148)
Romulus (148)
Seleucids (143)
Senate (148)
Skeptics (147)

Socrates (145)
Sparta (138)
Spartacus (154)
Stoics (147)

FOR FURTHER READING

Keith R. Bradley. *Discovering the Roman Family: Studies in Roman Social History*. New York, 1991. A provocative analysis of Roman family life with illustrations from individual experiences.

Peter Brown. *The Rise of Western Christendom: Triumph and Diversity, A.D. 200–1000*. 2nd ed. Oxford, 2003. A landmark analysis of early Christian history by an unusually perceptive scholar.

Walter Burkert. *Babylon, Memphis, Persepolis: Eastern Contexts of Greek Culture*. Cambridge, Mass., 2004. Explores Mesopotamian, Egyptian, and Persian influences on Greek literature, philosophy, and science.

Lionel Casson. *The Ancient Mariners: Seafarers and Sea Fighters of the Mediterranean in Ancient Times*. 2nd ed. Princeton, 1991. Draws on discoveries of underwater archaeologists in reconstructing the maritime history of the ancient Mediterranean.

F. M. Cornford. *Before and After Socrates*. Cambridge, 1965. A short but brilliant synthesis of classical Greek philosophy.

Barry Cunliffe. *Greeks, Romans, and Barbarians: Spheres of Interaction*. New York, 1988. Draws on archaeological evidence in assessing the effects of the Roman presence in Gaul, Britain, and Germany.

W. V. Harris, ed. *Rethinking the Mediterranean*. New York, 2005. A collection of scholarly essays exploring issues that linked the various lands bordering the Mediterranean in premodern times.

Ramsay MacMullen. *Christianizing the Roman Empire*. New Haven, 1984. Scholarly study of the processes by which Christianity became established in the Roman empire.

Sarah B. Pomeroy. *Goddesses, Whores, Wives, and Slaves: Women in Classical Antiquity*. New York, 1975. Outstanding study analyzing the status and role of women in classical Greece and Rome.

Romolo Augusto Staccioli. *The Roads of the Romans*. Los Angeles, 2003. A well-illustrated volume that surveys the entire Roman road system.

Cross-Cultural Exchanges on the Silk Roads During the Late Classical Era
CHAPTER 9

Tomb figure of a camel and a foreign rider. The majority of the silk road trade was handled by the nomadic peoples of central and western Asia.

EYEWITNESS:
Zhang Qian: An Early Traveler on the Silk Roads

Around the year 139 B.C.E., the Chinese emperor Han Wudi sent an envoy named Zhang Qian on a mission to lands west of China. The emperor's purpose was to find allies who could help combat the nomadic Xiongnu, who menaced the northern and western borders of the Han empire. From captives he had learned that other nomadic peoples in far western lands bore grudges against the Xiongnu, and he reasoned that they might ally with Han forces to pressure their common enemy.

The problem for Zhang Qian was that to communicate with potential allies against the Xiongnu, he had to pass directly through lands they controlled. Soon after Zhang Qian left Han territory, Xiongnu forces captured him. For ten years the Xiongnu held him in comfortable captivity: they allowed him to keep his personal servant, and they provided him with a Xiongnu wife, with whom he had a son. When suspicions about him subsided, however, Zhang Qian escaped with his family and servant. He even had the presence of mind to keep with him the yak tail that Han Wudi had given him as a sign of his ambassadorial status. He fled to the west and traveled as far as Bactria, but he did not succeed in lining up allies against the Xiongnu. While returning to China, Zhang Qian again fell into Xiongnu hands but managed to escape after one year's detention when the death of the Xiongnu leader led to a period of turmoil. In about 126 B.C.E. Zhang Qian and his party returned to China and a warm welcome from Han Wudi.

Although his diplomatic efforts did not succeed, Zhang Qian's mission had far-reaching consequences. Apart from political and military intelligence about western lands and their peoples, Zhang Qian also brought back information of immense commercial value. While in Bactria about 128 B.C.E., he noticed Chinese goods—textiles and bamboo articles—offered for sale in local markets. Upon inquiry he learned that they had come from southwest China by way of Bengal. From that information he deduced the possibility of establishing trade relations between China and Bactria through India.

Han Wudi responded enthusiastically to this idea and dreamed of trading with peoples inhabiting lands west of China. From 102 to 98 B.C.E., he mounted an ambitious campaign that broke the power of the Xiongnu and pacified parts of central Asia. His conquests simplified trade relations, since it became unnecessary to route commerce through India. The intelligence that Zhang Qian gathered during his travels thus contributed to the opening of the silk roads—the network of trade routes that linked lands as distant as China and the Roman empire—and more generally to the establishment of relations between China and lands to the west.

China and other classical societies, including the Parthian and Kushan Empires, imposed political and military control over vast territories. They promoted trade and communication within their own empires, bringing regions that had previously been self-sufficient into a larger economy and society. They also fostered the spread of cultural,

Zhang Qian (jung-chen)
Han Wudi (hahn-woo-dee)

CHRONOLOGY

third century B.C.E.	Spread of Buddhism and Hinduism to southeast Asia
second century B.C.E.	Introduction of Buddhism to central Asia
139–126 B.C.E.	Travels of Zhang Qian in central Asia
first century B.C.E.	Introduction of Buddhism to China
second century C.E.	Spread of Christianity in the Mediterranean basin and southwest Asia
184 C.E.	Yellow Turban rebellion
216–272 C.E.	Life of Mani
220 C.E.	Collapse of the Han dynasty
284–305 C.E.	Reign of Diocletian
313–337 C.E.	Reign of Constantine
313 C.E.	Edict of Milan and the legalization of Christianity in the Roman empire
325 C.E.	Council of Nicaea
451 C.E.	Council of Chalcedon
476 C.E.	Collapse of the western Roman empire

religious, and political traditions to distant regions, and they encouraged the construction of institutional frameworks that promoted the long-term survival of those traditions.

The classical societies established a broad zone of communication and exchange throughout much of the earth's eastern hemisphere. Trade networks crossed the deserts of central Asia and the depths of the Indian Ocean. Long-distance trade passed through much of Eurasia and north Africa, from China to the Mediterranean basin, and to parts of sub-Saharan Africa as well. That long-distance trade profoundly influenced the experiences of peoples and the development of societies throughout the eastern hemisphere. It brought wealth and access to foreign products, and it facilitated the spread of religious traditions beyond their original homelands. It also facilitated the transmission of disease. Indeed, the transmission of disease over the silk roads helped bring an end to the classical societies, since infectious and contagious diseases sparked devastating epidemics that caused political, social, and economic havoc. Long-distance trade thus had deep political, social, and cultural as well as economic and commercial implications for classical societies.

LONG-DISTANCE TRADE AND THE SILK ROADS NETWORK

Ever since the earliest days of history, human communities have traded with one another, sometimes over long distances. Before classical times, however, long-distance trade was a risky venture. Ancient societies often policed their own realms effectively, but extensive regions were difficult to control. Trade passing between societies was therefore liable to interception by bandits or pirates. That risk increased the costs of long-distance transactions in ancient times.

During the classical era, two developments reduced the risks associated with travel and stimulated long-distance trade. First, rulers invested heavily in the construction of roads and bridges. They undertook these expensive projects primarily for military and administrative reasons, but roads also had the effect of encouraging trade within individual societies and facilitating exchanges between different societies. Second, classical societies pacified large stretches of Eurasia and north Africa. As a result, merchants did not face such great risk as in previous eras, the costs of long-distance trade dropped, and its volume rose dramatically.

Trade Networks of the Hellenistic Era

The tempo of long-distance trade increased noticeably during the Hellenistic era, partly because of the many colonies established by Alexander of Macedon and the Seleucid rulers in Persia and Bactria. Though originally populated by military forces and administrators, these settlements soon attracted Greek merchants and bankers who linked the recently conquered lands to the Mediterranean basin. The Seleucid rulers controlled land routes linking Bactria, which offered access to Indian markets, to Mediterranean ports in Syria and Palestine.

Like the Seleucids, the Ptolemies maintained land routes—in their case, routes going south from Egypt to the kingdom of Nubia and Meroë in east Africa—but they also paid close attention to sea-lanes and maritime trade. They ousted pirates from sea-lanes linking the Red Sea to the Arabian Sea and the Indian Ocean. They also built several new ports, the most important being Berenice on the Red Sea, while Alexandria served as their principal window on the Mediterranean.

The Monsoon System Even more important, perhaps, mariners from Ptolemaic Egypt learned from Arab and Indian seamen about the monsoon winds that governed sailing and shipping in the Indian Ocean. During the summer the winds blow regularly from the southwest, whereas in the winter they come from the northeast. Knowledge of these winds enabled mariners to sail safely and reliably to all parts of the Indian Ocean basin.

Trade in the Hellenistic World Establishment and maintenance of these trade routes was an expensive affair calling for substantial investment in military forces, construction, and bureaucracies to administer the commerce that passed over the routes. But the investment paid handsome dividends. Long-distance trade stimulated economic development within the Hellenistic realms themselves, bringing benefits to local economies throughout the empires. Moreover, Hellenistic rulers closely supervised foreign trade and levied taxes on it, thereby deriving income even from foreign products. Thus with official encouragement, a substantial trade developed throughout the Hellenistic world, from Bactria and India in the east to the Mediterranean basin in the west.

Indeed, maritime trade networks through the Indian Ocean linked not only the large classical societies of Eurasia and north Africa but also smaller societies in east Africa. During the late centuries B.C.E., the port of Rhapta (located near Dar es Salaam in Tanzania) emerged as the principal commercial center on the east African coast. With increasing trade, groups of professional merchants and entrepreneurs emerged at Rhapta, and coins came into general use on the east African coast. Merchants of Rhapta imported iron goods such as spears, axes, and knives from southern Arabia and the eastern Mediterranean region in exchange for ivory, rhinoceros horn, tortoise shell, and slaves obtained from interior regions.

The Silk Roads

The establishment of classical empires greatly expanded the scope of long-distance trade, as much of Eurasia and north Africa fell under the sway of one classical society or another. The Han empire maintained order in China and pacified much of central Asia, including a sizable corridor offering access to

Glass Goblet.
An enameled glass goblet produced in about the second century C.E. in Begram (modern-day Afghanistan) depicts a party harvesting dates in a grove of palms. The production technique is Roman, testifying to Mediterranean influence in central Asia.

Bactria and western markets. The Parthian empire displaced the Seleucids in Persia and extended its authority to Mesopotamia. The Roman empire brought order to the Mediterranean basin. With the decline of the Mauryan dynasty, India lacked a strong imperial state, but the Kushan empire and other regional states provided stability and security, particularly in northern India, which favored long-distance trade.

Overland Trade Routes As the classical empires expanded, merchants and travelers created an extensive network of trade routes that linked much of Eurasia and north Africa. Historians refer to these routes collectively as the silk roads, since high-quality silk from China was one of the principal commodities exchanged over the roads. The overland silk roads took caravan trade from China to the Roman empire, thus linking the extreme ends of the Eurasian landmass. From the Han capital of Chang'an, the main silk road went west until it arrived at the Taklamakan desert, located in the Tarim Basin. The silk road then split into two main branches that skirted the desert proper and passed through oasis towns that ringed it to the north and south. The branches came together at Kashgar (now known as Kashi, located in the westernmost corner of modern China). From there the reunited road went west to Bactria, now under the control of the Kushan Empire, where a branch forked off to offer access to Taxila and northern India, while the principal route continued across northern Iran. There it joined with roads to ports on the Caspian Sea and the Persian Gulf and proceeded to Palmyra (in modern Syria), where it met roads coming from Arabia and ports on the Red Sea. Continuing west, it terminated at the Mediterranean ports of Antioch (in modern Turkey) and Tyre (in modern Lebanon).

Sea-Lanes and Maritime Trade The silk roads also included a network of sea-lanes that sustained maritime commerce throughout much of the eastern hemisphere. From Guangzhou in southern China, sea-lanes through the South China Sea linked the east Asian seaboard to the mainland and the islands of southeast Asia. Routes linking southeast Asia with Ceylon (modern Sri Lanka)

Ptolemaic (TAWL-oh-may-ihk)
Chang'an (chahng-ahn)
Tyre (tah-yer)

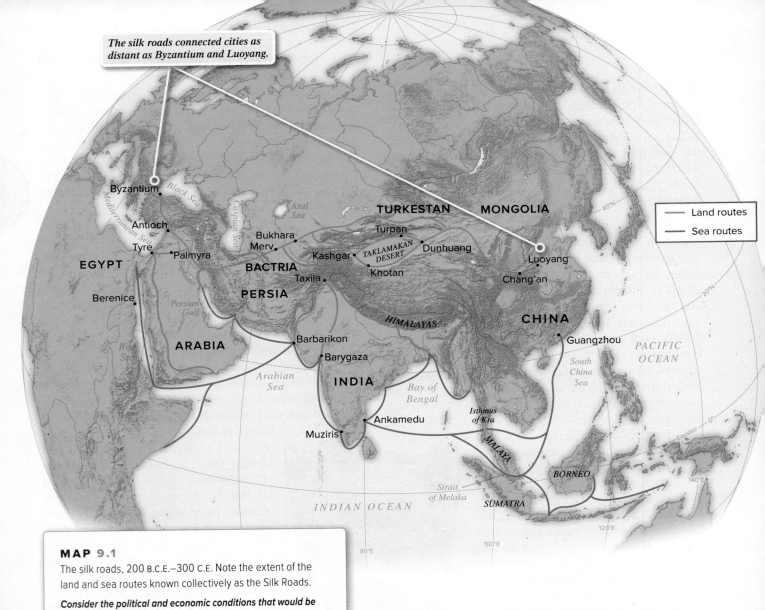

The silk roads connected cities as distant as Byzantium and Luoyang.

Land routes

Sea routes

MAP 9.1

The silk roads, 200 B.C.E.–300 C.E. Note the extent of the land and sea routes known collectively as the Silk Roads.

Consider the political and economic conditions that would be necessary for regular travel and trade across the silk roads.

and India were especially busy during classical times. From India, sea-lanes passed through the Arabian Sea to Persia and Arabia, and through the Persian Gulf and the Red Sea they offered access to land routes and the Mediterranean basin, which already possessed a well-developed network of trade routes.

Trade Goods A wide variety of manufactured products and agricultural commodities traveled over the silk roads. Silk and spices traveled west from producers in southeast Asia, China, and India to consumers in central Asia, Iran, Arabia, and the Roman empire. Silk came mostly from China, and the fine spices—cloves, nutmeg, mace, and cardamom—all came from southeast Asia. Ginger came from China, cinnamon from China and southeast Asia, pepper from India, and sesame oil from India, Arabia, and southwest Asia. Spices were extremely important

commodities in classical times because they had many more uses than they do in the modern world. They served not only as condiments and flavoring agents but also as drugs, anesthetics, aphrodisiacs, perfumes, aromatics, and magical potions. For the silk and spices they imported, western lands exchanged a variety of manufactured goods and other commodities, including horses and jade from central Asia and glassware, jewelry, textiles, and pottery from the Roman empire.

Zhang Qian was only one of many individuals who made very long journeys during classical times. Indeed, records indicate that merchants and diplomats from central Asia, China, India, southeast Asia, and the Roman empire traveled long distances in pursuit of trade and diplomacy. On a few occasions individuals even traveled across much or all of the eastern hemisphere between China and the Roman empire. A Chinese ambassador named Gang Ying embarked on a mission to distant western lands in 97 C.E. and proceeded as far as Mesopotamia before reports of the long and dangerous journey ahead persuaded him to return home. And Chinese sources reported the arrival in 166 C.E. of a delegation claiming to represent the Roman emperor Marcus Aurelius.

The Organization of Long-Distance Trade Individual merchants did not usually travel from one end of Eurasia to the other, either by land or by sea. Instead, they handled long-distance trade in stages. On the caravan routes between China and Bactria, for example, Chinese and central Asian peoples, such as the Kushans, dominated trade. Farther west, however, the Parthians took advantage of their power and geographic position to control overland trade within their boundaries. Once merchandise reached Palmyra, it passed mostly into the hands of Roman subjects such as Greeks, Jews, and Armenians, who were especially active in the commercial life of the Mediterranean basin.

On the seas, the situation was similar: Malay and Indian mariners dominated trade in southeast Asian and south Chinese water, Persians and subjects of the Roman empire dominated the Arabian Sea, Parthians controlled the Persian Gulf, and the Roman empire dominated the Red Sea. Indeed, after Roman emperors absorbed Egypt in the first century C.E., their subjects carried on an especially brisk trade between India and the Mediterranean. The Greek geographer Strabo reported in the early first century C.E. that as many as 120 ships departed annually from the Red Sea for India. Meanwhile, since the mid-first century C.E., the Romans also had dominated both the eastern and the western regions of mare nostrum, the Mediterranean.

It is impossible to determine the quantity or the value of trade that passed over the silk roads in classical times, but it clearly made a deep impression on contemporaries. By the first century C.E., pepper, cinnamon, and other spices graced the tables of the wealthy classes in the Roman empire, where silk garments had become items of high fashion. Some Romans fretted that see-through silk attire would lead to moral decay, and others worried that hefty expenditures for luxury items would ruin the imperial economy. In both cases their anxieties testified to the powerful attraction of imported silks and spices for Roman consumers.

As it happened, long-distance trade more likely stimulated rather than threatened local economies. Yet long-distance trade did not occur in a vacuum. Commercial exchanges encouraged cultural and biological exchanges, some of which had large implications for classical societies.

Roman coin.

This Roman coin, dated 189 C.E., depicts a merchant ship near the lighthouse at Alexandria. Ships like this regularly picked up pepper and cinnamon from India along with other cargoes.

CULTURAL AND BIOLOGICAL EXCHANGES ALONG THE SILK ROADS

The silk roads served as magnificent highways for merchants and their commodities, but others also took advantage of the opportunities they offered to travel in relative safety over long distances. Merchants, missionaries, and other travelers carried their beliefs, values, and religious convictions to distant lands: Buddhism, Hinduism, and Christianity all traveled the silk roads and attracted converts far from their original homelands. Meanwhile, invisible travelers such as disease pathogens also crossed the silk roads and touched off devastating epidemics when they found fresh populations to infect. Toward the end of the classical era, epidemic disease that was spread over the silk roads caused dramatic demographic decline, especially in China and the Mediterranean basin and to a lesser extent in other parts of Eurasia as well.

The Spread of Buddhism and Hinduism

By the third century B.C.E., Buddhism had become well established in northern India, and with the sponsorship of the emperor Ashoka the faith spread to Bactria and Ceylon. Buddhism was particularly successful in attracting merchants as converts. When they traveled, Buddhist merchants observed their faith among themselves and explained it to others. Gradually, Buddhism made its way along the silk roads to Iran, central Asia, China, and southeast Asia.

Buddhism in Central Asia Buddhism first established a presence in the oasis towns along the silk roads where merchants and their caravans found food, rest, lodging, and markets. The oases depended heavily on trade for their prosperity, and they allowed merchants to build monasteries and invite monks and scribes into their communities. Because they hosted travelers who came from different lands, spoke different languages, and observed different religious practices, the oasis towns became cosmopolitan centers. As early as the second century B.C.E., many residents of the oases themselves adopted Buddhism, which was the most prominent faith of silk roads merchants for almost a millennium, from about 100 B.C.E. to 800 C.E.

Buddhism (BOO-diz'm)

Buddhism in China From the oasis communities, Buddhism spread to the steppe lands of central Asia and to China via the nomadic peoples who visited the oases to trade. In the early centuries C.E., they increasingly responded to the appeal of Buddhism, and by the fourth century C.E., they had sponsored the spread of Buddhism throughout much of central Asia. Foreign merchants also brought their faith to China in about the first century B.C.E. Although the religion remained unpopular among native Chinese for several centuries, the presence of Buddhist monasteries and missionaries in China's major cities did attract some converts. Then, in about the fifth century C.E., the Chinese began to respond enthusiastically to Buddhism. Indeed, during the postclassical era Buddhism became the most popular religious faith throughout all of east Asia, including Japan and Korea as well as China.

Buddhism and Hinduism in Southeast Asia As Buddhism spread north from India into central Asia and China, both Buddhism and Hinduism also began to attract a following in southeast Asia. Once again, merchants traveling the silk roads—in this case the sea-lanes through the Indian Ocean—played prominent roles in spreading these faiths. By the first century C.E., clear signs of Indian cultural influence had appeared in many parts of southeast Asia. Many rulers converted to Buddhism, and others promoted the Hindu cults of Shiva and Vishnu. They built walled cities around lavish temples constructed in the Indian style, they adopted Sanskrit as a means of written communication, and they appointed Buddhist or Hindu advisors.

The Spread of Christianity

Early Christians faced intermittent persecution from Roman officials. During the early centuries C.E., Roman authorities launched a series of campaigns to stamp out Christianity, because most Christians refused to observe the state cults that honored emperors as divine beings. Imperial officials also considered Christianity a menace to society because zealous missionaries attacked other religions and generated sometimes violent conflict. Nevertheless, Christian missionaries took full advantage of the Romans' magnificent network of roads and sea-lanes,

Early Buddhist sculpture.
This sculpture from Bactria reflects the influence of Mediterranean and Greek artistic styles. This seated Buddha from the first or second century C.E. bears Caucasian features and wears Mediterranean-style dress.

which enabled them to carry their message throughout the Roman empire and the Mediterranean basin.

Christianity in the Mediterranean Basin During the second and third centuries C.E., countless missionaries worked zealously to attract converts. One of the more famous was Gregory the Wonderworker, a tireless missionary with a reputation for performing miracles, who popularized Christianity in central Anatolia during the mid-third century C.E. Contemporaries reported that Gregory not only preached Christian doctrine but also had access to impressive supernatural powers. Gregory and his fellow missionaries helped to make Christianity an enormously popular religion of salvation in the Roman empire. By the late third century C.E., in spite of continuing imperial opposition, devout Christian communities flourished throughout the Mediterranean basin in Anatolia, Syria, Palestine, Egypt, and north Africa as well as in Greece, Italy, Spain, and Gaul.

Christianity in Southwest Asia The young faith also traveled the trade routes and found followers beyond the Mediterranean basin. By the second century C.E., sizable Christian communities flourished throughout Mesopotamia and Iran, and a few Christian churches had appeared as far away as India. Christians also attracted large numbers of converts in southwest Asia and came to constitute—along with Jews and Zoroastrians—one of the major religious communities in the region.

Christian communities in Mesopotamia and Iran deeply influenced Christian practices in the Roman empire. To demonstrate utter loyalty to their faith, Christians in southwest Asia often followed strict ascetic regimes and sometimes even withdrew from family life and society. By the third century C.E., some Mediterranean Christians were so impressed by these practices that they began to live as hermits in isolated locations or to live exclusively among like-minded individuals who devoted their efforts to prayer and praise of God. Thus ascetic practices of Christians living in lands east of the Roman empire helped to inspire the formation of Christian monastic communities in the Mediterranean basin.

After the fifth century C.E., Christian communities in southwest Asia and the Mediterranean basin increasingly went separate ways. Most of the faithful in southwest Asia

Zoroastrian (zohr-oh-ASS-tree-ahn)

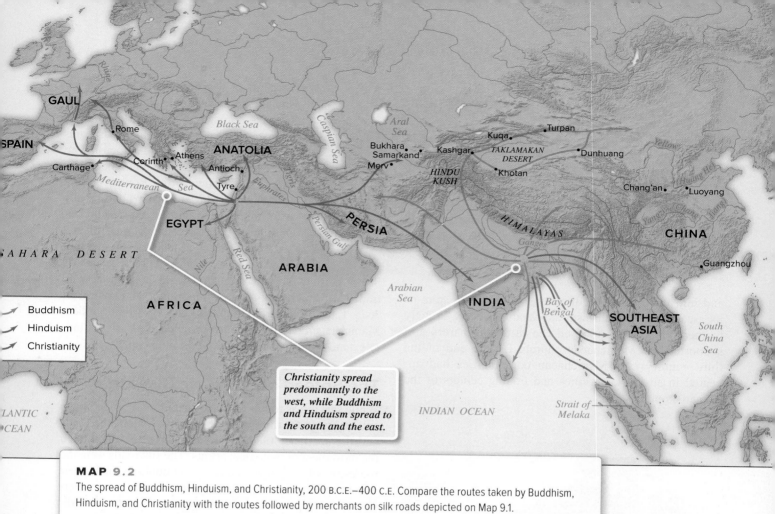

GAUL

SPAIN

Rome

Black Sea

Caspian Sea

Aral Sea

Kuqa

Turpan

Dunhuang

Carthage

Corinth

Athens

ANATOLIA

Antioch

Bukhara
Samarkand

Merv

Kashgar

TAKLAMAKAN
DESERT

Khotan

Tyre

Mediterranean Sea

Euphrates

EGYPT

SAHARA DESERT

Nile

Red Sea

Persian Gulf

PERSIA

ARABIA

HINDU
KUSH

HIMALAYAS

Ganges

Chang'an

Luoyang

CHINA

Yellow

Huang He

Guangzhou

Yangzi

Arabian Sea

AFRICA

INDIA

Bay of Bengal

SOUTHEAST
ASIA

South China Sea

ATLANTIC OCEAN

INDIAN OCEAN

Strait of Melaka

Buddhism

Hinduism

Christianity

Christianity spread predominantly to the west, while Buddhism and Hinduism spread to the south and the east.

MAP 9.2

The spread of Buddhism, Hinduism, and Christianity, 200 B.C.E.–400 C.E. Compare the routes taken by Buddhism, Hinduism, and Christianity with the routes followed by merchants on silk roads depicted on Map 9.1.

How might you account for the similarities?

became Nestorians—followers of the Greek theologian Nestorius, who lived during the early fifth century and emphasized the human as opposed to the divine nature of Jesus. Mediterranean church authorities rejected Nestorius's views, and many of his disciples departed for Mesopotamia and Iran. Although they had limited dealings with Mediterranean Christians, the Nestorians spread their faith east across the silk roads, and by the early seventh century they had established communities in central Asia, India, and China.

The Spread of Manichaeism

Mani and Manichaeism The explosive spread of Manichaeism dramatically illustrated how missionary religions made effective use of the silk roads trading network. Manichaeism was the faith derived from the prophet Mani (216–272 C.E.), a devout Zoroastrian from Babylon in Mesopotamia who also drew deep inspiration from Christianity and Buddhism. Because of the intense interaction between peoples of different societies, Mani promoted a syncretic blend of Zoroastrian, Christian, and Buddhist elements as a religious faith that would serve the needs of a cosmopolitan world.

Manichaean Ethics Mani was a dualist: he viewed the world as the site of a cosmic struggle between the forces of light and darkness, good and evil. He urged his followers to reject worldly pleasures and to observe high ethical standards. Devout Manichaeans, known as "the elect," abstained from marriage, sexual relations, and personal comforts, dedicating themselves instead to prayer, fasting, and ritual observances. Less zealous Manichaeans, known as "hearers," led more conventional lives, but they followed a strict moral code and provided food and gifts to sustain the elect. Mani's doctrine had strong appeal because it offered a rational explanation for the presence of good and evil in the world while also providing a means for individuals to achieve personal salvation.

Mani was a fervent missionary and traveled widely to promote his faith. He also created a Manichaean church with its own services, rituals, hymns, and liturgies. His doctrine attracted converts first in Mesopotamia, and before Mani's death it had spread throughout the Sasanid empire

---

Nestorian (neh-STOHR-eeuhn)

Manichaeism (man-ih-KEE-iz'm)

Sasanid (suh-SAH-nid)

Thinking about ENCOUNTERS

The Exchange of Religions along the Silk Roads

During the classical era, large empires and regional states maintained order across large portions of Eurasia and north Africa, which allowed long-distance trade to expand dramatically. In addition to exchanges of material goods, travelers along the trade routes exchanged ideas about religious salvation as well. *What was it about Buddhism, Hinduism, Christianity, and Manichaeism that converts from foreign lands found attractive?*

and into the eastern Mediterranean region. In spite of its asceticism, Manichaeism appealed especially strongly to merchants, who adopted the faith as hearers and supported the Manichaean church. By the end of the third century C.E., Manichaean communities had appeared in all the large cities and trading centers of the Roman empire.

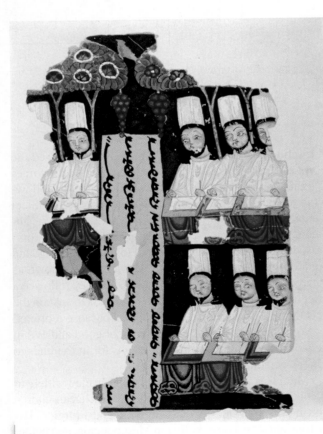

Manichaean painting.
A manuscript fragment from about the eleventh century C.E. depicts a group of devout Manichaean faithful, whose austere regimen called for them to dress in plain white garments and keep their hair uncut and beards untrimmed.

Decline of Manichaeism Manichaeism soon came under tremendous pressure in both the Zoroastrian Sasanid state and the Roman empire. Mani himself died in chains as a prisoner of the Sasanid emperor, who saw Manichaeism as a threat to the public order. Authorities in the Roman empire also persecuted Manichaeans and largely exterminated the faith in the Mediterranean basin over the course of the fifth and sixth centuries. Yet Manichaeism survived in central Asia, where it attracted converts among nomadic Turkish peoples who traded with merchants from China, India, and southwest Asia. Like Buddhism, Hinduism, and Christianity, then, Manichaeism relied on the trade routes of classical times to extend its influence to new lands and peoples.

The Spread of Epidemic Disease

While serving as routes for the distribution of trade goods and highways for the spread of religious beliefs, the roads and the sea-lanes of the classical world also facilitated the movement of biological agents. The silk roads were the routes by which grapes, camels, and donkeys made their way from the Mediterranean region to China, while cherries, apricots, peaches, and walnuts traveled in the other direction, from central Asia and China to the Mediterranean. Alongside the fruits and nuts were some less welcome traveling companions—infectious and contagious diseases that sparked ferocious epidemics when they found their way to previously unexposed populations.

Information about human populations in classical times is scanty and full of gaps. Scholars often do not have records to work with and must draw inferences about population size from the area enclosed by city walls, the number of houses discovered in a settlement, the agricultural potential of a region, and similar considerations. As a result, population estimates for premodern societies are rough approximations rather than precise figures. Moreover, within a single society, individual regions often had very different demographic experiences. Nevertheless, even for classical times, the general outlines of population history are reasonably clear.

Epidemic Diseases During the second and third centuries C.E., the Han and Roman empires suffered large-scale outbreaks of epidemic disease. The most destructive of these diseases were probably smallpox and measles, and epidemics of bubonic plague may also have erupted. All three diseases are devastating when they break out in populations without resistance, immunities, or medicines to combat them. As disease ravaged the two empires, Chinese and Roman populations declined sharply.

Sources from the Past

St. Cyprian on Epidemic Disease in the Roman Empire

St. Cyprian, bishop of Carthage, was an outspoken proponent of Christianity during the early and middle decades of the third century C.E. When epidemic disease struck the Roman empire in 251 C.E., imperial authorities blamed the outbreak on Christians who refused to honor pagan gods. Cyprian refuted this charge in his treatise On Mortality, *which described the symptoms of epidemic disease and reflected on its significance for the Christian community.*

It serves as validation of the [Christian] faith when the bowels loosen and drain the body's strength, when fever generated in bone marrow causes sores to break out in the throat, when continuous vomiting roils the intestines, when blood-shot eyes burn, when the feet or other bodily parts are amputated because of infection by putrefying disease, when through weakness caused by injuries to the body either mobility is impeded, or hearing is impaired, or sight is obscured. It requires enormous greatness of heart to struggle with resolute mind against so many onslaughts of destruction and death. It requires great loftiness to stand firm amidst the ruins of the human race, not to concede defeat with those who have no hope in God, but rather to rejoice and embrace the gift of the times. With Christ as our judge, we should receive this gift as the reward of his faith, as we vigorously affirm our faith and, having suffered, advance toward Christ by Christ's narrow path. . . .

Many of us [Christians] are dying in this epidemic—that is, many of us are being liberated from the world. The epidemic is a pestilence for the Jews and the pagans and the enemies of Christ, but for the servants of God it is a welcome event.

True, without any discrimination, the just are dying alongside the unjust, but you should not imagine that the evil and the good face a common destruction. The just are called to refreshment, while the unjust are herded off to punishment: the faithful receive protection, while the faithless receive retribution. We are unseeing and ungrateful for divine favors, beloved brethren, and we do not recognize what is granted to us. . . .

How suitable and essential it is that this plague and pestilence, which seems so terrible and ferocious, probes the justice of every individual and examines the minds of the human race to determine whether the healthy care for the ill, whether relatives diligently love their kin, whether masters show mercy to their languishing slaves, whether physicians do not abandon those seeking their aid, whether the ferocious diminish their violence, whether the greedy in the fear of death extinguish the raging flames of their insatiable avarice, whether the proud bend their necks, whether the shameless mitigate their audacity, whether the rich will loosen their purse strings and give something to others as their loved ones perish all around them and as they are about to die without heirs.

For Further Reflection

- To what extent do you think St. Cyprian was effective in his efforts to bring inherited Christian teachings to bear on the unprecedented conditions he and his followers faced?

Source: Wilhelm von Hartel, ed. *S. Thasci Caecili Cypriani opera omnia in Corpus scriptorum ecclesiasticorum latinorum.* Vienna, 1868, vol. 3, pp. 305–6. (Translation by Jerry H. Bentley.)

During the reign of Augustus, the population of the Roman empire stood at about sixty million people. During the second century C.E., epidemics reduced Roman population to forty-five million. Most devastating was an outbreak of smallpox that spread throughout the Mediterranean basin during the years 165 to 180 C.E. In combination with war and invasions, by 400 C.E. continuing outbreaks caused the population to decline even further, to about forty million. Whereas population in the eastern Mediterranean probably stabilized by the sixth century C.E., western Mediterranean lands experienced demographic stagnation until the tenth century.

Epidemics appeared slightly later in China than in the Mediterranean region. From fifty million people at the beginning of the millennium, Chinese population rose to sixty million in 200 C.E. As diseases found their way east, however, Chinese numbers fell back to fifty million by 400 C.E. and to forty-five million by 600 C.E. Thus by 600 C.E.

both Mediterranean and Chinese populations had fallen by a quarter to a third from their high points during classical times.

Effects of Epidemic Diseases Demographic decline in turn brought economic and social change. Trade within the empires declined, and both the Chinese and the Roman economies contracted. Both economies also moved toward regional self-sufficiency: whereas previously the Chinese and Roman states had integrated the various regions of their empires into a larger network of trade and exchange, after about 200 C.E. they increasingly embraced several smaller regional economies that concentrated on their own needs instead of the larger imperial market. Indeed, epidemic disease contributed to serious instability in China after the collapse of the Han dynasty, and in weakening Mediterranean society, it helped bring about the collapse of the western Roman empire.

Reverberations of ● ● ● ● ● ● ● ●
Long-Distance Trade Networks

The long-distance trade networks of the classical period introduced people across Eurasia and North Africa to diverse foods, commodities, ideas, and religions for many centuries. Yet the same networks that allowed for the diffusion of things and people also allowed for the rapid diffusion of microbes. Is it possible to argue that by creating the conditions in which disease could ravage huge areas with greater speed than ever before, the very success and stability of these networks paved the way for the undoing of the classical-era states and empires?

CHINA AFTER THE HAN DYNASTY

By the time epidemic diseases struck China, internal political problems had already begun to weaken the Han dynasty. By the late second century C.E., Han authorities had largely lost their ability to maintain order. Early in the third century C.E., the central government dissolved, and a series of autonomous regional kingdoms took the place of the Han state. With the disappearance of the Han dynasty, China experienced significant cultural change, most notably an increasing interest in Buddhism.

Internal Decay of the Han State

The Han dynasty collapsed largely because of internal problems that its rulers could not solve. One problem involved the development of factions within the ranks of the ruling elites. The desire of some elites to advance their own prospects in the imperial government at the cost of others led to constant infighting and backstabbing among the ruling elites, which reduced the effectiveness of the central government. An even more difficult problem had to do with the perennial issue of land and its equitable distribution. In the last two centuries of the Han dynasty, large landowners gained new influence in the government. They reduced their share of taxes and shifted the burden onto peasants. They even formed private armies to advance the interests of their class.

Peasant Rebellion These developments provoked widespread unrest among peasants, who found themselves under increasing economic pressure with no means to influence the government. Pressures became particularly acute during the late second and third centuries when epidemics began to take their toll. In 184 C.E. peasant discontent fueled a large-scale uprising known as the Yellow Turban rebellion, so called because the rebels wore yellow headbands that represented the color of the Chinese earth and symbolized their peasant origins. Although quickly suppressed, the rebellion proved to be only the first in a series of insurrections that plagued the late Han dynasty.

Collapse of the Han Dynasty Meanwhile, Han generals increasingly usurped political authority. By 190 C.E. the Han emperor had become a mere puppet, and the generals effectively ruled the regions controlled by their armies. They allied with wealthy landowners of their regions and established themselves as warlords who maintained a kind of rough order based on force of arms. In 220 C.E. they abolished the Han dynasty altogether and divided the empire into three large kingdoms.

Once the dynasty had disappeared, large numbers of nomadic peoples migrated into China, especially the northern regions, and they helped to keep China disunited for more than 350 years. Between the fourth and sixth centuries C.E., nomadic peoples established large kingdoms that dominated much of northern China as well as the steppe lands.

Cultural Change in Post-Han China

In some ways the centuries following the fall of the Han dynasty present a spectacle of chaos and disorder. One kingdom toppled another, only to fall in its turn to a temporary successor. War and nomadic invasions led to population decline in much of northern China. By the mid-fifth century, contemporaries reported, the Early Han capital of Chang'an had no more than one hundred households and the Later Han capital of Luo-yang resembled a trash heap more than a city.

Cultural Adaptation of Nomadic Peoples Beneath the disorderly surface of political events, however, several important social and cultural changes were taking place. First, nomadic peoples increasingly adapted to the Chinese environment and culture, and as the generations passed, distinctions between peoples of nomadic and Chinese ancestry became less and less obvious. Partly because of that development, a new imperial dynasty was eventually able to reconstitute a centralized imperial state in north China.

Second, with the disintegration of political order, the Confucian tradition lost much of its credibility. The original goal of Confucius and his early followers was to find some means to move from chaos to stability during the Period of the Warring States. When the Han dynasty

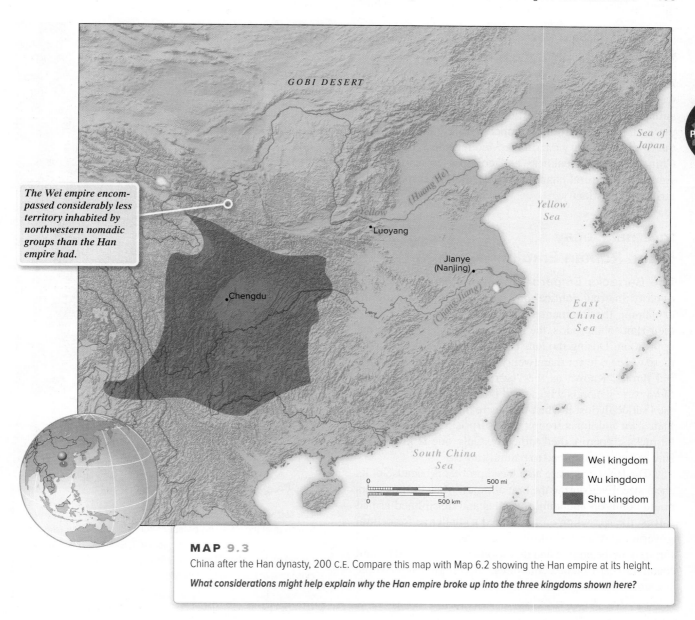

The Wei empire encompassed considerably less territory inhabited by northwestern nomadic groups than the Han empire had.

	Wei kingdom
	Wu kingdom
	Shu kingdom

MAP 9.3

China after the Han dynasty, 200 C.E. Compare this map with Map 6.2 showing the Han empire at its height.

What considerations might help explain why the Han empire broke up into the three kingdoms shown here?

collapsed, Confucianism seemed both ineffective and irrelevant.

Individuals who in earlier centuries might have committed themselves to Confucian values turned instead to Daoism and Buddhism. Daoism, from its origins in the Period of the Warring States, had originally appealed mostly to an educated elite. After the fall of the Han, however, Daoist sages widened its appeal by promising salvation to those who observed their doctrines and rituals and by offering the use of elixirs made of spices, herbs, and drugs that supposedly conferred health and immortality. Daoism attracted widespread interest among a population afflicted by war and disease and became much more popular than before, especially because it faced less competition from the Confucian tradition.

Popularity of Buddhism Even more important than Daoism for Chinese cultural history was Buddhism. After the fall of the Han empire, Buddhism received strong support from nomadic peoples who migrated into northern China and who in many cases had long been familiar with Buddhism in central Asia. Meanwhile, as a result of missionary efforts, the Indian faith began to attract a following among native Chinese as well. Indeed, between the fourth and sixth centuries C.E., Buddhism became well established in China. When a centralized imperial state took shape in the late sixth century C.E., Buddhism provided an important cultural foundation for the restoration of a unified political order.

Daoism (dow-ism)
Confucianism (kuhn-FEW-shun-iz'm)

THE COLLAPSE OF THE WESTERN ROMAN EMPIRE

A combination of internal problems and external pressures weakened the Roman empire and brought an end to its authority in the western portion of the empire, whereas in the eastern Mediterranean imperial rule continued until the fifteenth century C.E. In the Mediterranean basin as in China, imperial weakness and collapse coincided with significant cultural change, notably the increasing popularity of Christianity.

Internal Decay in the Roman Empire

The Barracks Emperors As in the case of the Han dynasty, internal political problems go a long way toward explaining the fragmentation of the Roman empire. Like their Han counterparts, the Roman emperors faced internal opposition. During the half century from 235 to 284 C.E., there were no fewer than twenty-six claimants to the imperial throne. Known as the "barracks emperors," most of them were generals who seized power, held it briefly, and then suddenly lost it when they were displaced by rivals or their own mutinous troops. Not surprisingly, most of the barracks emperors died violently. Only one is known for sure to have succumbed to natural causes.

The Roman empire also faced problems because of its sheer size. Even during the best of times, when the emperors could count on abundant revenues and disciplined armed forces, the sprawling empire posed a challenge for central governors. After the third century, as epidemics spread throughout the empire and its various regions moved toward local, self-sufficient economies, the empire as a whole became increasingly unmanageable.

The Tetrarchs.
Sculpture of the tetrarchs, or four co-rulers of the Roman empire, during the late third century C.E.; from left, Galerius, Constantius, Diocletian, and Maximian. What message is the apparent closeness of the tetrarchs intended to convey?

The Emperor Diocletian The emperor Diocletian (reigned 284–305 C.E.) attempted to deal with this problem by dividing the empire into two administrative districts: one in the east and one in the west. A co-emperor ruled each district with the aid of a powerful lieutenant, and the four officials, known as the tetrarchs, were able to administer the vast empire more effectively than an individual emperor could. Diocletian was a skillful administrator. He managed to bring Rome's many armies, including unpredictable maverick forces, under firm imperial control. He also tried to deal with a crumbling economy by strengthening the imperial currency, forcing the government to adjust its expenditures to its income, and imposing price caps to dampen inflation. His economic measures

Diocletian (dah-yuh-KLEE-shuhn)

were less successful than his administrative reforms, but they helped stabilize an economy ravaged by half a century of civil unrest.

Yet Diocletian's reforms encouraged ambition among the tetrarchs and their generals, and his retirement from the imperial office in 305 C.E. set off a round of internal struggles and bitter civil war. Already in 306 C.E. Constantine, son of Diocletian's coruler Constantius, moved to stake his claim as sole emperor. Once he had consolidated his grip on power in 324 C.E., Constantine ordered the construction of a new capital city, Constantinople, at a strategic site overlooking the Bosporus, the strait linking the Black Sea to the Sea of Marmara and beyond to the wealthy eastern Mediterranean. After 340 C.E. Constantinople became the capital of a united Roman empire.

Constantine Constantine himself was an able emperor. With the reunion of the eastern and western districts of the empire, however, he and his successors faced the same sort of administrative difficulties that Diocletian had attempted to solve by dividing the empire. As population declined and the economy contracted, emperors found it increasingly difficult to marshal the resources needed to govern and protect the vast Roman empire.

Germanic Invasions and the Collapse of the Western Roman Empire

Apart from internal problems, the Roman empire faced a formidable military threat from migratory Germanic peoples. Indeed, during the fifth century C.E., Germanic invasions brought an end to Roman authority in the western half of the empire, although imperial rule survived for an additional millennium in the eastern Mediterranean.

Germanic Migrations Germanic peoples had migrated from their homelands in northern Europe and lived on the eastern and northern borders of the Roman empire since the second century C.E. Most notable were the Visigoths, who came originally from Scandinavia and Russia. Like the nomadic peoples who moved into northern China after the fall of the Han dynasty, the Visigoths settled, adopted agriculture, and drew deep inspiration from Roman society. In the interests of social order, however, the Romans discouraged settlement of the Visigoths and other Germanic peoples within the empire, preferring that they constitute buffer societies outside imperial borders.

The Huns During the late fourth century, the relationship between Visigoths and Romans changed dramatically when the nomadic Huns began an aggressive westward migration from their homeland in central Asia. The Huns were probably cousins of the nomadic Xiongnu who inhabited the central Asian steppe lands west of China. During the mid-fifth century C.E., the warrior-king Attila organized the Huns into a virtually unstoppable military juggernaut. Under Attila, the Huns invaded Hungary, probed Roman frontiers in the Balkan region, menaced Gaul and northern Italy, and attacked Germanic peoples living on the borders of the Roman empire.

Collapse of the Western Roman Empire Attila did not create a set of political institutions or a state structure, and the Huns disappeared as a political and military force soon after his death in 453 C.E. By that time, however, the Huns had placed such pressure on Visigoths and other Germanic peoples that they streamed en masse into the Roman empire in search of refuge. Once inside imperial boundaries, they encountered little effective resistance and moved around almost at will. They established settlements throughout the western half of the empire—Italy, Gaul, Spain, Britain, and north Africa—where populations were less dense than in the eastern Mediterranean. Under the command of Alaric, the Visigoths even stormed and sacked Rome in 410 C.E. By the middle of the fifth century, the western part of the Roman empire was in a shambles. In 476 C.E. imperial authority came to an ignominious end when the Germanic general Odovacer deposed Romulus Augustulus, the last of the Roman emperors in the western half of the empire.

Unlike the Han dynasty, the Roman empire did not entirely disintegrate. As we will see in Chapter 16, imperial authority survived for another millennium in the eastern half of the empire, known after the fifth century C.E. as the Byzantine empire. In the western half, however, Roman authority dissolved, and nomadic peoples built successor states in regions formerly subject to Rome. Vandals and then Visigoths governed Spain, Franks ruled Gaul, Angles and Saxons invaded Britain, and Italy fell under the sway of a variety of peoples, including Visigoths, Vandals, and Lombards.

Cultural Change in the Late Roman Empire

In the Roman empire, as in China, the collapse of the imperial state coincided with important social and cultural changes. The Germanic peoples who toppled the empire looked to their own traditions for purposes of organizing society and government. When they settled in the regions of the former empire, however, they absorbed a good deal of Roman influence. Over time, the mingling of Roman and Germanic traditions led to the emergence of an altogether new society—medieval Europe.

Prominence of Christianity Christianity was perhaps the most prominent survivor of the western Roman empire. During the fourth century C.E., several developments enhanced its influence throughout the Mediterranean basin. In the first place, Christianity won recognition as a legitimate religion in the Roman empire. In 312 C.E., while seeking to establish himself as sole Roman emperor, Constantine experienced a vision that impressed upon him the power of the Christian God. He believed that the Christian God helped him to prevail over his rivals, and he promulgated the Edict of Milan, which allowed Christians to practice their faith openly in the Roman empire. At some point during his reign, perhaps after his edict, Constantine himself converted to Christianity, and in 380 C.E. the emperor Theodosius proclaimed

Constantine (KAHN-stuhn-teen)

Odovacer (AHD-oh-vah-cer)

Byzantine (BIHZ-uhn-teen)

Theodosius (thee-hu-DOH-see-uhs)

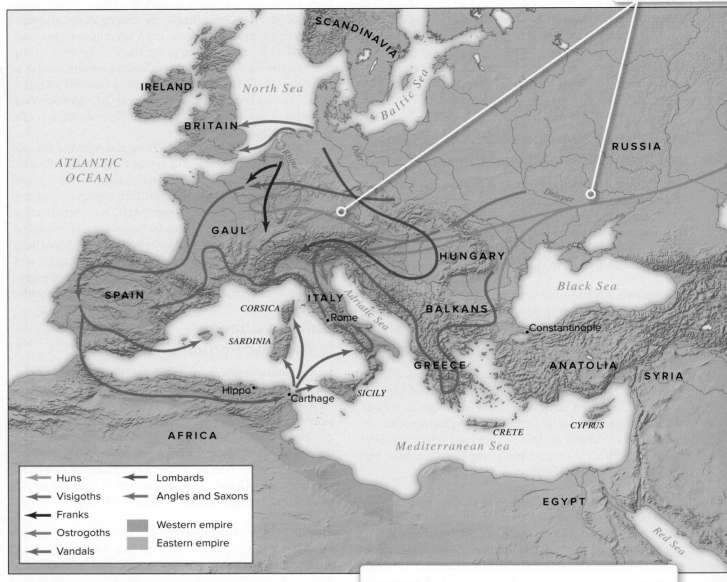

Routes of Hun invasions

Legend:
- Huns
- Visigoths
- Franks
- Ostrogoths
- Vandals
- Lombards
- Angles and Saxons
- Western empire
- Eastern empire

MAP 9.4

Germanic invasions and the collapse of the western Roman empire between 450 and 476 C.E. Notice the many different groups that moved into western Roman territory in this period.

What might have motivated such movement, and why couldn't the western Roman empire prevent it?

Christianity the official religion of the Roman empire. By the mid-fourth century, Christians held important political and military positions, and imperial sponsorship helped their faith to attract more converts than ever before.

Christianity also began to attract thoughtful and talented converts who articulated a Christian message for the intellectual elites of the Roman empire. The earliest Christians had come largely from the ranks of ordinary working people, and for three centuries the new faith grew as a popular religion of salvation favored by the masses, rather than as a reasoned doctrine of intellectual substance. During the fourth century, however, intellectual elites began to articulate Christianity in terms that were familiar and persuasive to the educated classes.

St. Augustine The most important and influential of those figures was St. Augustine (354–430 C.E.), bishop of the north African city of Hippo (modern-day Annaba in Algeria). Augustine had a fine education, and he was conversant with the leading intellectual currents of the day. During his youth he drew great inspiration from Stoicism and Platonism, and for nine years he belonged to a community of Manichaeans. Eventually he became disillusioned

Thinking about TRADITIONS

The Evolution of Christianity

In the first century C.E., Christianity could claim only small numbers of believers. By the fourth century, the religion had attracted even emperors to its community. *How did Christianity extend its appeal to political elites? How did decisions taken at the Councils of Nicaea and Chalcedon reflect and preserve changes in the Christian religious tradition between the first and fifth centuries?*

St. Augustine.
This fifteenth century painting by Sandro Botticelli depicts St. Augustine in his study. In his voluminous writings, Augustine sought to explain the meaning of history from a Christian perspective.

The Institutional Church Besides winning the right to practice their faith openly and attracting intellectual talent, Christian leaders constructed an institutional apparatus that transformed a popular religion of salvation into a powerful church. In the absence of recognized leadership, the earliest Christians generated a range of conflicting and sometimes contradictory doctrines. To standardize their faith, Christian leaders instituted a hierarchy of church officials. At the top were five religious authorities—the bishop of Rome and the patriarchs of Jerusalem, Antioch, Alexandria, and Constantinople—who resided in the most important spiritual and political centers of the Roman empire. Subordinate to the five principal authorities were bishops, who presided over religious affairs in their districts, known as dioceses, which included all the prominent cities of the Roman empire. When theological disputes arose, the patriarchs and the bishops assembled in church councils to determine which views would prevail as official doctrine. The councils at Nicaea (325 C.E.) and Chalcedon (451 C.E.), for example, took up the difficult and contentious issue of Jesus' nature. Delegates at these councils proclaimed that Jesus was both fully human and fully divine at the same time, in contrast to Nestorians, Arians, and other Christian groups who held that Jesus was either primarily human or primarily divine.

As Roman imperial authority crumbled, the bishop of Rome, known as the pope (from the Latin *papa,* meaning "father"), emerged as spiritual leader of Christian communities in the western regions of the empire. As the only sources of established and recognized authority, the popes and the bishops of other important cities organized local government and defensive measures for their communities. They also mounted missionary campaigns to convert Germanic peoples to Christianity. Although Roman imperial authority disappeared, Roman Christianity survived and served as a foundation for cultural unity in lands that had formerly made up the western half of the Roman empire.

Nicaea (nahy-SEE-uh)
Chalcedon (KAL-suh-dawn)

with both the Hellenistic philosophical school and Manichaeism, and in 387 C.E., while studying in Italy, he converted to Christianity. For the remainder of his life, he worked to reconcile Christianity with Greek and Roman philosophical traditions. More than any others, Augustine's writings helped make Christianity an intellectually respectable alternative to Hellenistic philosophy and to popular religions of salvation.

SUMMARY

Between the last centuries of the first millennium B.C.E. and the first few centuries of the new millennium, the classical societies established a broad zone of exchange throughout much of Eurasia and north Africa. Long-distance trade along what has come to be known as the silk roads profoundly shaped the societies involved. Products like silk, jewels, and spices found new markets in far-distant regions, while ideas and religious beliefs from Buddhism to Christianity found new adherents and converts. Long-distance trade also facilitated the spread of epidemic disease, and by the second and third centuries C.E. disease had wreaked havoc among most of the classical societies. Indeed, coupled with severe internal conflicts as well as external threats, the disorder caused by epidemic disease helped contribute to the collapse of the Han, Kushan, Parthian and Roman dynasties as well as the western Roman empire.

STUDY TERMS

Attila the Hun (171)
Buddhism (163)
Byzantine empire (171)
Chalcedon (173)
Chang'an (161)
Christianity (164, 167, 171–172)
Confucianism (168)
Constantine (171)
Constantinople (170)
Council of Chalcedon (173)
Council of Nicaea (173)
Daoism (169)
Diocletian (170)
Edict of Milan (171)
epidemic disease (166–167)
Gregory the Wonderworker (164)
Han dynasty (167–169)

Han Wudi (159)
Mani (165)
Manichaeism (165)
Nestorians (165)
Nicaea (173)
Odovacer (171)
pope (173)
Ptolemaic (161)
Sasanid (165)
silk roads (159–160)
St. Augustine (172)
tetrarchs (170)
Theodosius (171)
Tyre (161)
Visigoths (171)
Yellow Turban rebellion (168)
Zhang Qian (159)
Zoroastrian (164)

FOR FURTHER READING

Thomas J. Barfield. *The Perilous Frontier: Nomadic Empires and China*. Cambridge, Mass., 1989. Provocative study of the Xiongnu and other central Asian peoples.

Jerry H. Bentley. *Old World Encounters: Cross-Cultural Contacts and Exchanges in Pre-Modern Times*. New York, 1993. Studies the spread of cultural and religious traditions before 1500 C.E.

Averil Cameron. *The Mediterranean World in Late Antiquity, A.D. 395–600*. London, 1993. A lively and well-informed synthesis.

C. D. Gordon, ed. *The Age of Attila: Fifth-Century Byzantium and the Barbarians*. Ann Arbor, 1972. Translations of primary sources on the society and history of nomadic and migratory peoples.

Mark Edward Lewis. *China between Empires: The Northern and Southern Dynasties*. Cambridge, Mass., 2009. Discusses social and cultural change in China after the collapse of the Han dynasty.

Samuel Hugh Moffett. *A History of Christianity in Asia,* vol. 1. San Francisco, 1992. An important volume that surveys the spread of early Christianity east of the Roman empire.

Elaine Pagels. *Beyond Belief: The Secret Gospel of Thomas*. New York, 2003. Discusses the emergence of orthodox Christianity and the recognition of the New Testament as a body of canonical writings.

Jonathan Tucker. *The Silk Road: Art and History*. London, 2003. Lavishly illustrated volume exploring Silk Roads history and geography.

Susan Whitfield. *Life along the Silk Road*. Berkeley, 1999. Focuses on the experiences of ten individuals who lived or traveled along the Silk Roads.

Francis Wood. *The Silk Road: Two Thousand Years in the Heart of Asia*. Berkeley, 2002. A brilliantly illustrated volume discussing the history of the Silk Roads from antiquity to the twentieth century.

PART 2 THE FORMATION OF CLASSICAL SOCIETIES, ca. 500 B.C.E. TO ca. 500 C.E.

In Part II, we have seen that the classical societies that developed in Persia, China, India, and the Mediterranean built on many of the traditions established by the early complex societies discussed in Part I. By the last half-millennium B.C.E., however, the classical societies had surpassed their predecessors in complexity, organization, and sophistication. As a result, they were able to expand further, to control more people and resources, and to trade longer distances than any human societies in the past.

The increased reach of classical societies created an ever-stronger need for rulers to impose their will efficiently across long distances, especially when their territories included diverse and potentially rebellious conquered peoples. Some, like the Achaemenid dynasty of Persia, established carefully designed administrations that divided oversight of their wide realms into manageable portions headed by loyal administrators. Many, including the Achaemenids, the Romans, and the Han dynasty of China, standardized systems of law and taxation as a means of encouraging uniformity throughout their realms. Others, like the rulers of Han China, established a uniform educational system from which all imperial administrators would be drawn.

Classical rulers also sought to impose their will and to promote unity within their realms by sponsoring particular philosophies, cultural practices, or religious beliefs. Thus, Greeks encouraged a sense of commonality between the diverse poleis and colonies by sponsoring the Olympic Games. In India, the Mauryan dynasty advocated Buddhism as a unifying system of belief, the Persian Sasanids sponsored Zoroastrianism as a state religion, and the Romans actively promoted Christianity after 380 C.E. Finally, all the classical societies sought to increase the efficiency of their administrations by establishing long-distance transportation and communication networks. While these networks aided imperial administration, they also allowed for a dramatic increase in long-distance trade. In turn, long-distance trade encouraged both the spread of religions such as Buddhism, Hinduism, and Christianity as well as the diffusion of disease pathogens that ultimately contributed to the disintegration of the classical societies.

By 500 C.E. classical societies in Persia, China, India, and the Mediterranean basin had either collapsed or fallen into decline. Yet all the classical societies left rich legacies that shaped political institutions, social orders, and cultural traditions for centuries to come. Moreover, by sponsoring commercial and cultural relations between different peoples, the classical societies laid a foundation for intensive and systematic cross-cultural interaction in later times.

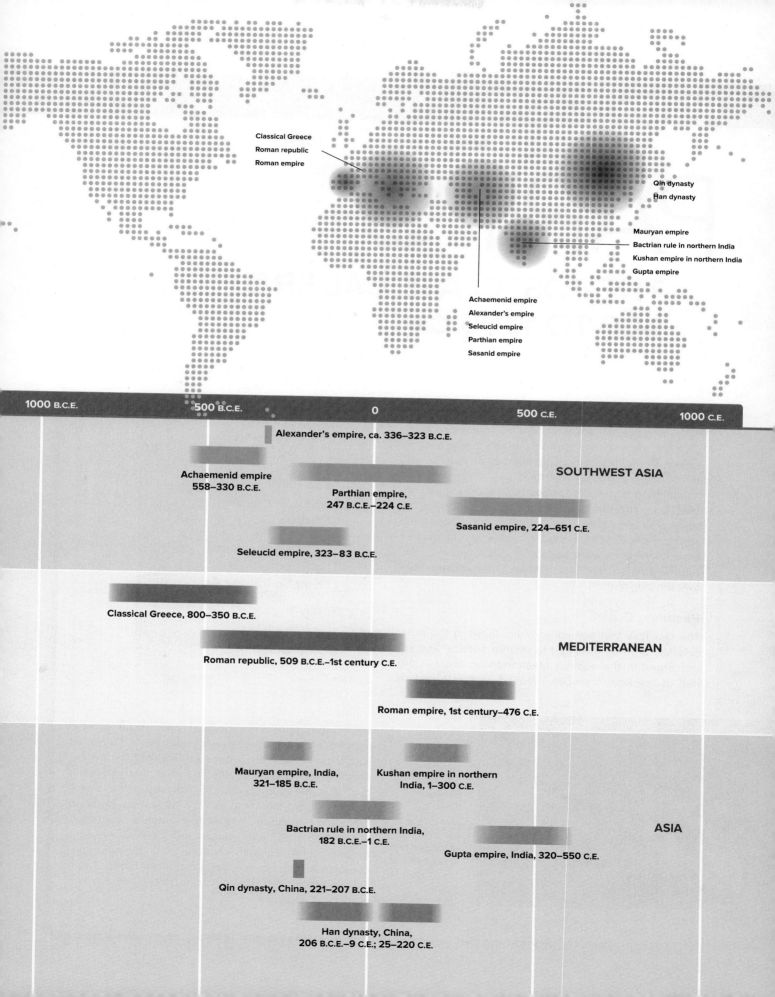

Classical Greece
Roman republic
Roman empire

Qin dynasty
Han dynasty

Mauryan empire
Bactrian rule in northern India
Kushan empire in northern India
Gupta empire

Achaemenid empire
Alexander's empire
Seleucid empire
Parthian empire
Sasanid empire

| 1000 B.C.E. | 500 B.C.E. | 0 | 500 C.E. | 1000 C.E. |

Alexander's empire, ca. 336–323 B.C.E.

Achaemenid empire
558–330 B.C.E.

Parthian empire,
247 B.C.E.–224 C.E.

SOUTHWEST ASIA

Sasanid empire, 224–651 C.E.

Seleucid empire, 323–83 B.C.E.

Classical Greece, 800–350 B.C.E.

MEDITERRANEAN

Roman republic, 509 B.C.E.–1st century C.E.

Roman empire, 1st century–476 C.E.

Mauryan empire, India,
321–185 B.C.E.

Kushan empire in northern
India, 1–300 C.E.

Bactrian rule in northern India,
182 B.C.E.–1 C.E.

ASIA

Gupta empire, India, 320–550 C.E.

Qin dynasty, China, 221–207 B.C.E.

Han dynasty, China,
206 B.C.E.–9 C.E.; 25–220 C.E.

PART 3

THE POSTCLASSICAL ERA, 500 TO 1000 C.E.

The postclassical era was a period of major readjustment for societies throughout the eastern hemisphere. During the early centuries C.E., disease as well as both internal and external pressures brought serious instability to classical societies in China, India, southwest Asia, and the Mediterranean basin. Most of the classical empires collapsed under the strain. During the postclassical era the settled societies of the eastern hemisphere underwent political, social, economic, and cultural change that would shape their experiences over the long term.

Restoring Order

The first task that settled societies faced in the postclassical era was the need to restore political and social order. In the eastern Mediterranean the eastern half of the Roman empire survived as the Byzantine

A painting on silk depicts anxious candidates taking the civil service examinations at the time of the emperor Song Renzong (reigned 1023–1031).

empire but underwent political and social reorganization in order to deal with external pressures. In southwest Asia, Arab conquerors inspired by the recently founded Islamic faith asserted their authority over vast areas in southwest Asia and north Africa, and introduced their faith to India as well as Iberia. In China the Sui and Tang dynasties restored centralized imperial authority after almost four centuries of rule by competing regional kingdoms and nomadic conquerors. In India, in contrast, centralized imperial rule did not return: authority devolved instead to a series of regional kingdoms.

Economic Growth

The reestablishment of political and social order enabled postclassical societies to revive networks of long-distance trade and participate more actively in processes of cross-cultural communication and exchange. As a result, the postclassical era was a time of rapid economic growth in most of the eastern hemisphere. Meanwhile, increased trade facilitated biological and technological as well as commercial exchanges: agricultural crops migrated far beyond the lands of their origin, and improved techniques of irrigation and cultivation spread through much of Eurasia. As agricultural production increased, so did human population, which allowed growing numbers of people to devote their efforts to trade and manufacturing rather than cultivation.

The Spread of Religious Traditions

The postclassical era was also crucially important for the formation and development of cultural and religious traditions. Islam first appeared during the postclassical era, and it soon became the foundation of an expansive empire stretching from north Africa to northern India. Buddhism expanded beyond the Indian subcontinent and central Asia, attracting converts in east and southeast Asia. Christianity was the official faith of the Byzantine empire, where the Eastern Orthodox church emerged and gave shape to a distinctive form of Christianity that eventually spread to much of eastern Europe and Russia.

A fourteenth-century manuscript illustration shows St. Benedict meeting with two monks beside a fishpond at their monastery.

Legacies of the Postclassical Era

The empires and regional states of the postclassical era disappeared long ago, but the social, economic, and cultural legacies of the age are noticeable even today. Most notable, perhaps, religious and cultural traditions continue to flourish in lands where they first attracted converts in postclassical times. In some ways, then, the postclassical age survives even in the modern world.

1. *What factors allowed the spread of religious traditions outside their regions of origin in this period?*

2. *In what specific ways might the legacies of the postclassical era survive in the present day?*

In a thirteenth-century manuscript illustration, a fictional Muslim traveler passes a lively agricultural village. On the right a woman spins cotton thread. Sheep, goats, chickens, and date palms figure prominently in the local economy.

The Christian Commonwealth of Byzantium

CHAPTER 10

The church of Hagia Sophia ("Holy Wisdom") rises above the modern city of Istanbul. Originally a Christian church, the building then became an Islamic mosque and finally a museum.

EYEWITNESS:

Procopius on the Spread of Chinese Sericulture to Byzantium

According to the Byzantine historian Procopius, two Christian monks from Persia set out on a momentous journey about the middle of the sixth century C.E. The result of their travels was the introduction of high-quality silk production to the eastern Mediterranean. Although local crafts workers had long produced coarse fabrics from the cocoons of wild silkworms, fine silks had come to the Mediterranean only from China, where manufacturers closely guarded both their carefully bred strains of silkworms and the complex technology that yielded high-quality textiles. Mediterranean consumers obtained silk not directly from Chinese producers but, rather, through intermediaries subject to the Sasanid empire of Persia.

According to Procopius's account, the two Christian monks observed the techniques of silk production during the course of a mission to China. Upon departure they hollowed out their walking staffs and filled them with silkworm eggs, which they smuggled out of China, through their native land of Persia, and into the Byzantine empire.

The monks' motives are unknown. Whatever they may have been, though, it is certain that the monks by themselves could not have introduced a full-blown silk industry to Byzantium. The production of fine, Chinese-style silks required more than a few silkworm eggs. It also required understanding sophisticated technologies and elaborate procedures that must have reached the Byzantine empire by several different routes. Thus it seems that Procopius simplified a much more complex story.

In any case, Byzantine crafts workers did indeed learn how to produce high-quality silk fabrics. By the late sixth century, Byzantine silks matched Chinese silks in quality. Mediterranean consumers no longer relied on Chinese producers and Persian intermediaries, and local production of high-quality silk greatly strengthened the Byzantine economy. Thus Procopius's anonymous monks participated in a momentous transfer of technology between distant lands. Their efforts contributed to the vibrance of Byzantine society, and their story highlights the significance of cross-cultural interactions during the postclassical era.

During the centuries after 200 C.E., most of the classical societies faced a series of problems—epidemic disease, declining population, economic contraction, social and political turmoil, and military threats—that brought about their collapse. Only in the eastern Mediterranean did a classical empire survive. The eastern half of the Roman empire, known as the Byzantine empire, withstood the various problems that brought down other classical societies and survived for almost a millennium after the collapse of the western Roman empire in the fifth century C.E.

The Byzantine empire did not reconstitute the larger Mediterranean society of classical times. The Roman empire had dominated an integrated Mediterranean basin; the Byzantine empire mostly faced a politically and culturally fragmented Mediterranean region. After the seventh century C.E., Islamic states controlled lands to

Procopius (proh-KOH-pee-uhs)
Byzantine (BIHZ-uhn-teen)

CHRONOLOGY

313–337	Reign of Constantine
325	Council of Nicaea
329–379	Life of St. Basil of Caesarea
340	Transfer of Roman government to Constantinople
527–565	Reign of Justinian
717–741	Reign of Leo III
726–843	Iconoclastic controversy
ninth century	Missions of St. Cyril and St. Methodius to the Slavs
976–1025	Reign of Basil II, "the Bulgar-Slayer"
989	Conversion of Prince Vladimir of Kiev to Orthodox Christianity
1054	Beginning of the schism between the eastern and western Christian churches
1071	Battle of Manzikert
1202–1204	Fourth crusade
1453	Fall of Constantinople

the east and south of the Mediterranean, Slavic peoples dominated lands to the north, and western Europeans organized increasingly powerful states in lands to the west.

Nevertheless, the Byzantine empire was a political and economic powerhouse of the postclassical era. Until the twelfth century, Byzantine authority dominated the wealthy and productive eastern Mediterranean region. Manufactured goods from the Byzantine empire enjoyed a reputation for high quality in markets from the Mediterranean basin to India. The Byzantine empire also deeply influenced the historical development of the Slavic peoples of eastern Europe and Russia by introducing writing, Christianity, codified law, and sophisticated political organization into their lands. Because Byzantine political, economic, and cultural influence stretched so far, historians often refer to it as the "Byzantine commonwealth." Just as Greek and Roman initiative brought Mediterranean lands into a larger integrated society during classical times, Byzantine policies led to the formation of a large, multicultural zone of trade, communication, interaction, and exchange in eastern Europe and the eastern Mediterranean basin during the postclassical era.

THE EARLY BYZANTINE EMPIRE

The Byzantine empire takes its name from Byzantion—latinized as Byzantium—a modest village that occupied a site of enormous strategic significance. Situated on a defensible peninsula and blessed with a magnificent natural harbor known as the Golden Horn, Byzantion had the potential to control the Bosporus, the strait of water leading from the Black Sea to the Sea of Marmara and beyond to the Dardanelles, the Aegean Sea, and the Mediterranean. Apart from its maritime significance, Byzantion also offered convenient access to the rich lands of Anatolia, southwestern Asia, and southeastern Europe.

Because of its strategic value, the Roman emperor Constantine designated Byzantion as the site of a new imperial capital, which he named Constantinople ("city of Constantine"). The imperial government moved to Constantinople in 340 C.E., and the new capital rapidly reached metropolitan dimensions. By the late fourth century, it was the most important political and military center of the eastern Roman empire, and it soon became the dominant economic and commercial center in the eastern Mediterranean basin. The city kept the name Constantinople until 1453 C.E.,

when it fell to the Ottoman Turks, who renamed it Istanbul. By convention, however, historians refer to the realm governed from Constantinople between the fifth and fifteenth centuries C.E. as the Byzantine empire, or simply as Byzantium, in honor of the original settlement.

The Later Roman Empire and Byzantium

The Byzantine empire originated as the eastern half of the classical Roman empire, which survived the collapse of the western Roman empire in the fifth century C.E. In its early days the Byzantine empire embraced Greece, the Balkan region, Anatolia, Syria, Palestine, Egypt, and northeast Africa. During the seventh and eighth centuries C.E., however, the southern regions of the empire fell into the hands of Arab Muslim conquerors. Nevertheless, Byzantium figured as a major power of the eastern Mediterranean basin until the thirteenth century C.E.

The Later Roman Empire As the western Roman empire crumbled, the eastern half of the empire remained intact, complete with roads, communications, lines of authority, and a set of functioning imperial institutions, all

Aegean (ih-JEE-uhn)

inherited from Roman predecessors. Yet the early Byzantine emperors faced challenges different from those of their predecessors, and they built a state significantly different from the classical Roman empire.

The principal challenges that confronted the late Roman and early Byzantine empires were the consolidation of the dynamic Sasanid dynasty (226–641 C.E.) in Persia and the invasions of migratory peoples from the north and east. The Sasanid emperors sought to rebuild the Achaemenid empire of classical Persia, a goal that brought them into conflict with Roman forces in Mesopotamia and Syria. Germanic invasions also menaced the late Roman empire. Because they did not have adequate resources to respond strongly to the threat on all fronts, Roman authorities concentrated on maintaining the integrity of the wealthy eastern portion of the empire.

The Early Byzantine State The Byzantine emperors built a distinctive tradition of statecraft. Its most important feature was tightly centralized rule that concentrated power in the hands of a highly exalted emperor. This characteristic was already noticeable in the time of Constantine, who built his new capital to lavish standards.

He filled it with libraries, museums, and artistic treasures, and he constructed magnificent marble structures—all in an effort to create a new Rome fit for the ruler of a mighty empire.

Caesaropapism Constantine also set a precedent by hedging his rule with an aura of divinity. Although he did not claim divine status as some of his imperial predecessors had, as the first Christian emperor he did claim divine favor and sanction for his rule. He intervened in theological disputes and used his political position to support views that he considered orthodox and condemn those he regarded as heretical. Constantine initiated a policy that historians call *caesaropapism*, whereby the emperor not only ruled as secular lord but also played an active and prominent role in ecclesiastical affairs.

Particularly after the sixth century, Byzantine emperors became absolute rulers. According to Roman law, emperors stood above the law: theoretically, they wielded absolute authority in political, military, judicial, financial, and religious

Sasanid (suh-SAH-nid)
Achaemenid (uh-KEE-muh-nihd)

MAP 10.1

The Byzantine empire and its neighbors, 527–554 C.E. Compare this map with Map 8.5 showing the Roman empire at its height.

How did the territories of the Byzantine empire differ from those of the classical Roman empire?

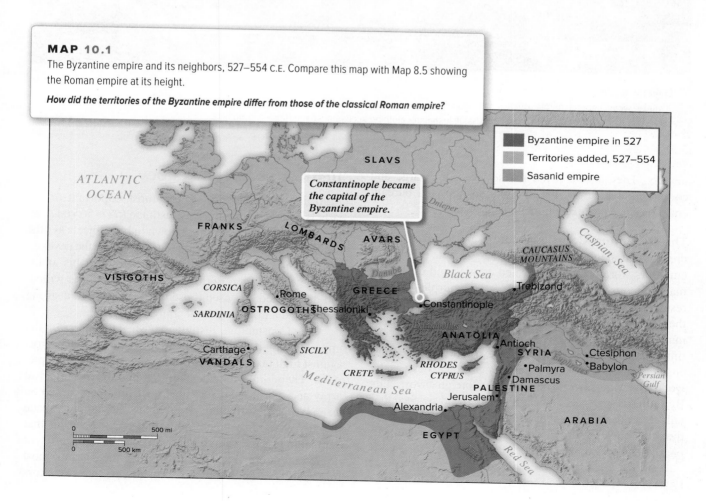

Emperor Justinian.
Justinian wears imperial purple robes in this mosaic from the church of San Vitale in Ravenna. He is pictured in the company of ecclesiastical, military, and court officials. Notice the richness of Justinian's clothing in comparison to those around him.

matters. They also enjoyed the services of a large and complex bureaucracy. In combination, law and bureaucracy produced an exceptionally centralized state.

The Byzantine Court Even dress and court etiquette drew attention to the lofty status of Byzantine rulers. The emperors wore heavily bejeweled crowns and dressed in magnificent silk robes dyed a dark, rich purple—a color reserved strictly for imperial use. High officials presented themselves to the emperor as slaves and before taking up matters of business prostrated themselves before him three times and kissed his hands and feet. By the tenth century, engineers had contrived a series of mechanical devices that worked dazzling effects and impressed foreign envoys at the Byzantine court: mechanical lions roared and swished their tails as ambassadors approached the emperor, and sometimes the imperial throne itself moved up and down to emphasize the awesome splendor of the emperor.

Hagia Sophia (HAH-yah soh-FEE-uh)

Justinian and His Legacy

Justinian and Theodora The most important of the early Byzantine emperors was Justinian (527–565 C.E.), an energetic and tireless worker known to his subjects as "the sleepless emperor," who profoundly influenced the development of the Byzantine empire with the aid of his ambitious wife Theodora. Both were intelligent, strong willed, and disciplined and used those qualities to build a strong empire and a grand imperial court.

Like Constantine, Justinian lavished resources on the imperial capital. During the early years of his rule, riots against high taxes had destroyed much of Constantinople. After Theodora persuaded him to deploy the imperial army and quash the disturbances, Justinian embarked on an ambitious construction program that thoroughly remade the city. The most notable building erected during that campaign was the church of Hagia Sophia, a magnificent domed structure that ranks as one of the world's most important examples of Christian architecture. Visitors

marveled at the church's enormous dome, which they likened to the heavens encircling the earth, and they expressed awe at the gold, silver, and gems that decorated and illuminated Hagia Sophia. Over time, the church even acquired a reputation for working miraculous cures: its columns and doors reportedly healed the illnesses of people who stood beside them or touched them.

Justinian's Code Justinian's most significant political contribution was his codification of Roman law. Almost immediately on taking the throne, Justinian ordered a thorough and systematic review of Roman law. On the basis of that work, he issued the *Corpus iuris civilis (Body of the Civil Law),* which immediately won recognition as a definitive work. Later emperors updated Roman law by adding new provisions, but Justinian's code continued to serve as a source of legal inspiration and went on to influence civil law codes throughout much of western Europe.

Belisarius and Byzantine Conquests Justinian's most ambitious venture was his effort to reconquer the western Roman empire from Germanic peoples and reestablish Roman authority throughout the Mediterranean basin. Beginning in 533 he sent his brilliant general Belisarius on military campaigns that returned Italy, Sicily,

northwestern Africa, and southern Spain to imperial hands. By the end of his reign in 565, Justinian had reconstituted a good portion of the classical Roman empire.

Justinian's accomplishment, however, did not long survive his own rule. Byzantium simply did not possess the resources to sustain Belisarius's conquests. Although Byzantium managed to hold on to a few areas in the Italian peninsula, Justinian's dream of restoring Roman authority throughout the Mediterranean basin soon faded. Indeed, Justinian's efforts clearly showed that the classical Roman empire was beyond recovery. While Justinian devoted his attention to the western Mediterranean, the Sasanids threatened Byzantium from the east and Slavic peoples approached from the north. Justinian's successors had no choice but to withdraw their resources from the western Mediterranean and redeploy them in the east. Even though Belisarius's reconquest of the western Roman empire was a spectacular military accomplishment, it was also something of an anachronism, since the lands of the eastern and western Mediterranean had already begun to follow different historical trajectories.

Corpus iuris civilis (KOR-poos EW-rees sih-VEE-lees)

Belisarius (bel-uh-SAIR-ee-uhs)

Interior of the Hagia Sophia.
The interior of the church of Hagia Sophia ("Holy Wisdom"), built by Justinian and transformed into a mosque in the fifteenth century. The dome rises almost 60 meters (197 feet) above the floor, and its windows allow abundant light to enter the massive structure.

Islamic Conquests and Byzantine Revival

After the seventh century C.E., the emergence of Islam and the development of a powerful and expansive Islamic state (topics discussed in chapter 11) posed a serious challenge to Byzantium. Inspired by their Islamic faith, Arab peoples conquered the Sasanid empire and overran Byzantine Syria, Palestine, Egypt, and north Africa. During the late seventh and early eighth centuries, Islamic forces even subjected Constantinople to prolonged siege (in 674–678 and again in 717–718). Byzantium resisted this northern thrust of Islam partly because of military technology. Byzantine forces used a weapon known as Greek fire—a highly effective incendiary weapon whose ingredients were a state secret that has since been lost—which they launched at both the fleets and the ground forces of the invaders. Greek fire burned even when floating on water and thus created a serious hazard when deployed around wooden ships. On land it caused panic among enemy forces because it was very difficult to extinguish and often burned troops to death. As a result of this defensive effort, the Byzantine empire retained its hold on Anatolia, Greece, and the Balkan region.

Imperial Organization Though much reduced by the Islamic conquests, the Byzantine empire after the eighth century was also more compact and manageable. Also, Byzantine rulers initiated political and social adjustments that strengthened the empire that remained in their hands. The most important innovation was the reorganization of Byzantine society under the *theme* (imperial province) system. This system placed a *theme* under the jurisdiction of a general, who assumed responsibility for both its military defense and its civil administration. Generals received their appointments from the imperial government, which closely supervised their activities to prevent decentralization of power and authority. Generals recruited armies from the ranks of free peasants, who received allotments of land in exchange for military service. The armies proved to be effective military forces, and the system as a whole strengthened the class of free peasants, which in turn solidified Byzantium's agricultural economy. The *theme* system enabled Byzantine forces to mobilize quickly and resist

further Islamic advances and also undergirded the political order and the social organization of the empire from the eighth through the twelfth century.

Indeed, Byzantium vastly expanded its influence between the late ninth and the late eleventh centuries. During the tenth century Byzantine forces shored up defenses in Anatolia and reconquered Syria from Arab Muslims. During the reign of Basil II (976–1025 C.E.), known as "Basil the Bulgar-Slayer," Byzantine armies turned west and crushed the neighboring Bulgars, who had built a large kingdom in the Balkans. After his victory at the battle of Kleidion in 1014 C.E., Basil reportedly commanded his forces to blind fourteen thousand Bulgarian survivors, though he spared one eye in a few, who then guided the others home. By the mid–eleventh century the Byzantine empire embraced lands from Syria and Armenia in the east to southern Italy in the west, from the Danube River in the north to Cyprus and Crete in the south. Byzantine expansion brought in so much wealth that Basil was able to waive the collection of taxes for two years. Once again, Byzantium dominated the eastern Mediterranean.

Byzantium and Western Europe

Tensions between Byzantium and Western European States While they went to war with their Arab Muslim and pagan Slavic neighbors, Byzantines also experienced tense relations with their Christian counterparts in the western Mediterranean. The Christian church of Constantinople conducted its affairs in Greek and was heavily influenced by the will of the caesaropapist emperors, whereas the Christian church of Rome conducted its affairs in Latin and rejected imperial interference in ecclesiastical matters. Church authorities in Byzantium

Byzantine manuscript illustration.
This illustration depicts Byzantine naval forces turning Greek fire on their Arab enemies.

regarded Roman Christians as poorly educated and un-couth. In return, church leaders in Rome considered their Byzantine counterparts insincere and insufficiently wary of heresy.

Political grievances also strained relations between Byzantium and western European lands. During the fifth and sixth centuries, imperial authorities could do little more than watch as Germanic peoples established successor states to the western Roman empire—lands that Byzantine emperors regarded as their rightful inheritance. Worse yet, some of the upstart powers claimed imperial authority for themselves. In 800, for example, the Frankish ruler Charlemagne received an imperial crown from the pope in Rome, thereby directly challenging Byzantine claims to imperial authority over western lands. Charlemagne's empire soon dissolved, but in 962 Otto of Saxony lodged his own claim to rule as emperor over the western lands of the former Roman empire. Adding injury to insult, Otto then attacked lands in southern Italy that had been in Byzantine possession since the days of Justinian.

BYZANTINE ECONOMY AND SOCIETY

Byzantium dominated the political and military affairs of the eastern Mediterranean largely because of its strong economy. Ever since classical times, the territories embraced by the Byzantine empire had produced abundant agricultural surpluses, supported large numbers of crafts workers, and participated in trade with lands throughout the Mediterranean. Even after the collapse of the Roman empire, those territories continued to provide a solid material foundation for Byzantium, and they helped to make the Byzantine empire an economic powerhouse of the postclassical era.

Rural Economy and Society

Until its conquest by Arab forces, Egypt was the major source of grain for Byzantium. Afterward, Anatolia and the lower Danube region served as the imperial breadbasket. All those lands produced reliable and abundant harvests of wheat, which supported large populations in Byzantium's major cities. Indeed, between the fifth and the early thirteenth centuries, Constantinople's population alone approached or exceeded one million people.

The Peasantry Byzantine economy and society were strongest when the empire supported a large class of free peasants who owned small plots of land. Besides serving as the backbone of the Byzantine military system, free peasants cultivated their land intensively in hopes of improving their families' fortunes. As in other

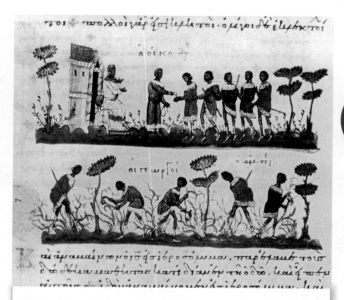

Byzantine peasants.
Peasants—probably sharecroppers—receive seeds and tend to vineyards in this painting from a Byzantine manuscript. What does this illustration suggest about the relationship between the two landowners or overseers (left, in the top register) and the five laborers?

societies, however, wealthy families sought to accumulate land and to control the labor of peasants for their own interests. Especially in the early centuries of the Byzantine empire, wealthy cultivators worked to bind peasants to their estates or to force them into share-cropping arrangements from which it was difficult to break free.

However, the invasions of the sixth and seventh centuries broke up many large estates and afforded peasants an opportunity to rebuild small holdings. The *theme* system strengthened the free peasantry by making land available to those who performed military service. The imperial government also made periodic efforts to prevent wealthy landowners from gaining control over peasant lands. Over the long term, however, wealthy landowners built ever-larger estates. From the eleventh century onward, they transformed the peasants into an increasingly dependent class, and by the thirteenth century free peasants accounted for only a small portion of the rural population.

Decline of the Free Peasantry The accumulation of landholdings in the hands of the wealthy had important implications for financial and military affairs. For one thing, large estates often received tax exemptions and so did not contribute their fair share to imperial coffers.

Charlemagne (SHAHR-leh-mane)

Thinking about TRADITIONS

Legacies of Greece and Rome

From the time of the transfer of Roman government to Constantinople until the city's fall in 1453, the people of the Byzantine empire drew heavily from their historical association with both the western Roman empire as well as classical Greece. *In which areas of Byzantine culture and politics were these influences most apparent?*

Moreover, the decline of the free peasantry diminished the pool of recruits available for service in military forces organized under the *theme* system. Thus, the concentration of land and rural resources worked against the financial interests of the central government, and it caused political, military, and economic difficulties for the Byzantine state during the last three centuries of its existence.

Industry and Trade

In spite of social and economic problems, Byzantium remained a wealthy land. Byzantine prosperity derived both from the empire's productive capacity and from the importance of Constantinople as a center of trade.

Manufacturing Enterprises Indeed, Constantinople was home to many artisans and crafts workers who enjoyed a reputation especially for their glassware, linen and woolen textiles, gems, jewelry, and fine work in gold and silver. In addition, after the arrival of silkworms, crafts workers added high-quality silk textiles to the list of products manufactured in the Byzantine empire. Silk was a most important addition to the economy, and Byzantium became the principal supplier of this fashionable fabric to lands in the Mediterranean basin. The silk industry was so important to the Byzantine economy that the government closely supervised every step in its production and sale. Regulations allowed individuals to participate in only one activity—such as weaving, dyeing, or sales—to prevent the creation of a monopoly in the industry by a few wealthy or powerful entrepreneurs.

Trade Situated astride routes going east and west as well as north and south, Constantinople also served as the main clearinghouse for trade in the western part of Eurasia. The merchants of Constantinople maintained direct commercial links with manufacturers and merchants in central Asia, Russia, Scandinavia, northern Europe, and the lands of the Black Sea and the Mediterranean basin. Byzantium dominated trade to such an extent that trading peoples recognized the Byzantine gold coin, the *bezant,* as the standard currency of the Mediterranean basin for more than half a millennium, from the sixth through the twelfth century.

Byzantium drew enormous wealth simply from the control of trade and the levying of customs duties on merchandise that passed through its lands. More important, Byzantium served as the western anchor of a Eurasian trading network that revived the silk roads of classical times. Silk and porcelain came to Constantinople from China, spices from India and southeast Asia. Carpets arrived from Persia, woolen textiles from western Europe, and timber, furs, honey, amber, and slaves from Russia and Scandinavia.

The Organization of Trade Banks helped to fuel Byzantine trade by advancing loans to individuals seeking to launch business ventures, and Byzantine merchants often formed partnerships that allowed them to pool their resources and limit their risks. Although neither banking nor partnership was an altogether new technique, Byzantine

Byzantine art: women weaving.
Women studying medical plants (top) and weaving at a loom: Byzantine manuscript illumination, 1368.

Sourcesfromthe**Past**

The Wealth and Commerce of Constantinople

The Spanish rabbi Benjamin of Tudela traveled throughout Europe, north Africa, and southwest Asia between 1165 and 1173 C.E. He may have ventured as far as India, and he mentioned both India and China in his travel account. His main purpose was to record the conditions of Jewish communities, but he also described the many lands and about three hundred cities that he visited. His travels took place during an era of political decline for the Byzantine empire, yet he still found Constantinople a flourishing and prosperous city.

The circumference of the city of Constantinople is eighteen miles; half of it is surrounded by the sea, and half by land, and it is situated upon two arms of the sea, one coming from the sea of Russia [the Black Sea], and one from the sea of Sepharad [the Mediterranean].

All sorts of merchants come here from the land of Babylon, from the land of Shinar [Mesopotamia], from Persia, Media [western Iran], and all the sovereignty of the land of Egypt, from the land of Canaan [Palestine], and the empire of Russia, from Hungary, Patzinakia [Ukraine], Khazaria [southern Russia], and the land of Lombardy [northern Italy] and Sepharad [Spain].

Constantinople is a busy city, and merchants come to it from every country by sea or land, and there is none like it in the world except Baghdad, the great city of Islam. In Constantinople is the church of Hagia Sophia, and the seat of the pope of the Greeks, since Greeks do not obey the pope of Rome. There are also as many churches as there are days of the year. . . . And in this church [Hagia Sophia] there are pillars of gold and silver, and lamps of silver and gold more than a man can count.

Close to the walls of the palace is also a place of amusement belonging to the emperor, which is called the Hippodrome, and every year on the anniversary of the birth of Jesus the emperor gives a great entertainment there. And in that place men from all the races of the world come before the emperor and empress with jugglery and without jugglery, and they introduce lions, leopards, bears, and wild asses, and they engage them in combat with one another; and the same thing is done with birds. No entertainment like this is to be found in any other land. . . .

From every part of the Byzantine empire tribute is brought here every year, and they fill strongholds with garments of silk, purple, and gold. Like unto these storehouses and this wealth there is nothing in the whole world to be found. It is said that the tribute of the city amounts every year to 20,000 gold pieces, derived both from the rents of shops and markets and from the tribute of merchants who enter by sea or land.

The Greek inhabitants are very rich in gold and precious stones, and they go clothed in garments of silk and gold embroidery, and they ride horses and look like princes. Indeed, the land is very rich in all cloth stuffs and in bread, meat, and wine.

Wealth like that of Constantinople is not to be found in the whole world. Here also are men learned in all the books of the Greeks, and they eat and drink, every man under his vine and his fig-tree.

For Further Reflection

■ How is it possible to account for the prosperity that Benjamin of Tudela found in Constantinople?

Source: Benjamin of Tudela. *The Itinerary of Benjamin of Tudela.* Trans. by M. N. Adler. London: H. Frowde, 1907. (Translation slightly modified.)

---

businessmen made much more extensive use of them than their predecessors had. In doing so, they both supported and stimulated a dynamic commercial economy.

Urban Life

Constantinople had no rival among Byzantine cities. Subjects of the Byzantine empire referred to it simply as "the City." The heart of the City was the imperial palace, which employed twenty thousand workers as palace staff. Peacocks strutted through gardens filled with sculptures and fountains. Most famous was a gold fountain in the shape of a pineapple that spouted wine for imperial guests.

Housing in Constantinople Aristocrats maintained enormous palaces that included courtyards, reception halls, libraries, and chapels. Women lived in separate apartments and did not receive male visitors from outside the household. Indeed, women often did not participate in banquets and parties, especially when wine flowed freely or when the affairs were likely to become so festive that they could compromise a woman's honor.

The less privileged classes of Constantinople occupied less splendid dwellings. Artisans and crafts workers usually lived in rooms above their shops, and clerks and government officials lived in multistory apartment buildings. Workers and the poor occupied dangerous and rickety tenements, sharing kitchens and sanitary facilities with their neighbors.

Attractions of Constantinople Even for the poor, though, the City had its attractions. As the heir to Rome, Constantinople was a city of baths, which were sites of relaxation and exercise as well as hygienic bathing. Taverns and restaurants offered settings for social gatherings—checkers, chess, and dice games were especially popular activities at taverns—and theaters provided entertainment in the form of song, dance, and striptease. Mass entertainment took place in the Hippodrome, a large stadium adjacent to the imperial palace. There Byzantine subjects watched chariot races, athletic matches, contests between wild animals, and circuses featuring clowns, jugglers, acrobats, and dwarfs.

CLASSICAL HERITAGE AND ORTHODOX CHRISTIANITY

The first Christian emperor of the Roman empire gave both his name and his faith to Constantinople. Like the Byzantine state, however, Byzantine Christianity developed along distinctive lines, and it became a faith different from the early Christianity of the Roman empire. For one thing, the philosophy and literature of classical Greece had a much deeper influence in Byzantium than in western Europe. Byzantine church leaders also disagreed with their western counterparts on matters of doctrine, ritual, and church authority. By the mid–eleventh century, differences between the eastern and western churches had become so great that their leaders formally divided Mediterranean Christianity into the Eastern Orthodox and Roman Catholic churches.

The Legacy of Classical Greece

Although local inhabitants spoke Greek, the official language of early Constantinople was Latin, the language of Rome. After the sixth century, however, Greek replaced Latin as the language of government in the Byzantine empire. Byzantine scholars often did not learn to read Latin, and they drew intellectual inspiration from the New Testament (originally composed in Greek) and the philosophy and literature of classical Greece rather than classical Rome.

Byzantine Education The legacy of classical Greece was especially noticeable in Byzantine education. The Byzantine state considered education vitally important, since its bureaucracy called for large numbers of literate individuals to administer the empire. As a result, the state organized a school system that offered a primary education in reading, writing, and grammar, followed by studies of classical Greek literature, philosophy, and science. Because of this, basic literacy was widespread in Byzantine society.

Byzantine Scholarship Like the educational system, Byzantine scholarship reflected the cultural legacy of classical Greece. Byzantine scholars concentrated on the humanities—literature, history, and philosophy—rather than on the natural sciences or medicine. Byzantines with a literary education considered themselves the direct heirs of classical Greece, and they went to great lengths to preserve and transmit the classical legacy. Indeed, almost all literary and philosophical works of classical Greece that survive have come down to the present in copies made between the tenth and twelfth centuries in the Byzantine empire.

The Byzantine Church

Church and State The most distinctive feature of Byzantine Christianity was its close relationship with the imperial government. From the time of Constantine on, caesaropapist emperors participated actively in religious and theological matters. In 325 C.E., for example, Constantine organized the Council of Nicaea, which brought together bishops, spokesmen, and leaders from all the important Christian churches to consider the views of the Arians, who believed that Jesus had been a mortal human rather than a divine being coeternal with God. Although Constantine originally favored Arian views, he came to accept the view that Jesus was both human and divine and personally attended sessions of the Council of Nicaea to support it. His presence encouraged the council to endorse his preferred view as orthodox and to condemn Arianism as heresy.

The Byzantine emperors, in fact, treated the church as a department of state. They appointed individuals to serve as patriarch of Constantinople—the highest ecclesiastical official in the Byzantine church, counterpart of the pope in Rome—and they instructed patriarchs, bishops, and priests to deliver sermons that supported imperial policy. This caesaropapism was a source of constant conflict between imperial and ecclesiastical authorities, and sometimes even between emperors and their subjects. For example, Emperor Leo III (reigned 717–741 C.E.) sparked riots throughout the empire when he embarked on a policy of iconoclasm (literally, "the breaking of icons") in an attempt to prohibit the use of religious images and icons in churches. Although the policy was ultimately unsuccessful, it generated tremendous bitterness among ordinary people who were deeply attached to the religious imagery in their churches.

Greek Philosophy and Byzantine Theology In its theology, Byzantine Christianity reflected the continuing influence of classical Greek philosophy. Theologians invested a great deal of time and intellectual energy in the examination of religious questions from a philosophical point of view. They looked to classical philosophy, for example, when seeking to understand the nature of Jesus and the extent to which he possessed both human and divine characteristics. Although these debates often became extremely technical, they illustrated an effort to understand Christian doctrine in light of the terms and concepts

Nicaea (nahy-SEE-uh)
patriarch (PAY-tree-ahrk)
iconoclasm (eye-KAHN-oh-klasm)

that classical philosophers had employed in their analysis of the world. A school maintained by the patriarch of Constantinople provided instruction for clergy and church officials in advanced theology of this sort. Thus, although it differed in many ways from Mediterranean society of classical times, Byzantium built its own cultural and religious traditions on a solid classical foundation.

Monasticism and Popular Piety

Caesaropapist emperors, powerful patriarchs, and other high church officials concerned themselves with theological and ritual matters and rarely dealt directly with the lay population of the Byzantine church. Nor did the Byzantine laity have much interest in fine points of theology, and they positively resented policies such as iconoclasm that infringed on cherished patterns of worship. For religious inspiration, then, the laity looked not to the church hierarchy but to the local monasteries.

Asceticism Byzantine monasticism grew out of the efforts of devout individuals to lead especially holy lives. Drawing inspiration from early Christian ascetics in Egypt, Mesopotamia, and Persia, these individuals observed regimes of extreme asceticism and self-denial. During the fifth century, for example, a few men and at least two women demonstrated their ascetic commitments by perching for years at a time atop tall pillars. Because of the extreme dedication of ascetics, disciples often gathered around them and established communities of men and women determined to follow their example. These communities became the earliest monasteries of the Byzantine church. They had few rules until St. Basil of Caesarea (329–379 C.E.), the patriarch of Constantinople during the mid–fourth century, urged them to give up their personal possessions and live communally, to observe the rule of elected superiors, and to devote themselves to work and prayer. After the fourth century, Basilian monasticism spread rapidly throughout the Byzantine empire.

Byzantine Monasticism Unlike their counterparts in western Europe and other lands, Byzantine monasteries for the most part did not become centers of education, study, learning, and scholarship. Yet monasteries under the rule of St. Basil had a reputation for piety and devotion that endeared them to the Byzantine laity. Basilian monks went to great lengths in search of mystical union with God through meditation and prayer. Some retired to remote destinations to lead lives of strict asceticism. The devotion of Basilian monks, in turn, inspired piety among the Byzantine laity because they represented a religious faith more immediate and meaningful than that of the theologians and ecclesiastical bureaucrats of Constantinople.

Monks and nuns also provided social services to their communities. They provided spiritual counsel to local laity,

and they organized relief efforts by bringing food and medical attention to communities struck by disasters. They won the support of the Byzantine populace, too, when they vigorously opposed the policy of iconoclasm and fought to restore icons to churches and monasteries. Indeed, by setting examples of devotion and by tending to the needs and interests of the laity, monks helped to maintain support for their faith in the Byzantine empire.

Tensions between Eastern and Western Christianity

Byzantine Christianity developed in tension particularly with the Christian faith of western Europe. During the centuries following Constantine's legalization of Christianity, church leaders in Jerusalem, Alexandria, Antioch, Constantinople, and Rome exercised great influence in the larger Christian community. Yet after Arab peoples conquered most of southwest Asia and introduced Islam there in the seventh century, the influence of the patriarchs in Jerusalem, Alexandria, and Antioch declined, leaving only Constantinople and Rome as the principal centers of Christian authority.

Constantinople and Rome The specific issues that divided the two Christian communities in Constantinople and Rome were religious and theological. Some ritual and doctrinal differences were relatively minor concerns over forms of worship and the precise wording of theological teachings. Byzantine theologians objected, for example, to the fact that western priests shaved their beards and used unleavened instead of leavened bread when saying Mass. Other differences concerned substantive theological matters, such as the precise relationship between God, Jesus, and the Holy Spirit.

Schism Alongside these ritual and doctrinal differences, the Byzantine patriarchs and Roman popes disputed their respective rights and powers. Patriarchs argued for the autonomy of all major Christian jurisdictions, including that of Constantinople, whereas popes asserted the primacy of Rome as the sole seat of authority for all Christendom. Ultimately, relations became so strained that the eastern and western churches went separate ways. In 1054 C.E. the patriarch and the pope excommunicated each other, each refusing to recognize the other's church as properly Christian. Despite efforts at reconciliation, the resulting schism between eastern and western churches persists to the present day. In recognition of the split, historians refer to the eastern Christian church after 1054 as the Eastern Orthodox church and its western counterpart as the Roman Catholic church.

asceticism (uh-SET-uh-siz-uhm)

Thinking about ENCOUNTERS

Cultural Influence as a Result of Interaction

Although the Mediterranean world inhabited by the Byzantines was more politically fragmented than it had been under the Roman empire, the Byzantine empire nevertheless sustained both hostile and friendly encounters with Islamic peoples to the south and east, Slavic peoples to the north, and Europeans to the west. *In what ways did these various encounters shape the Byzantine empire, and in what ways did Byzantine influence shape societies beyond imperial borders?*

THE INFLUENCE OF BYZANTIUM IN EASTERN EUROPE

By the second millennium C.E., a dynamic society founded on the Islamic faith had seized control of the lands on the Mediterranean's southern and eastern rims, and Byzantines and western Europeans contested the northern rim. Hemmed in and increasingly pressured by Islamic and western European societies, Byzantium entered a period of decline beginning about the late eleventh century.

As its Mediterranean influence waned, however, Byzantium turned its attention to eastern Europe and Russia. Through political, commercial, and cultural relations, Byzantium decisively influenced the history of Slavic peoples. The Byzantine state itself came to an end in the fifteenth century C.E. But because of the Byzantine commonwealth—the larger collection of societies in eastern Europe and the eastern Mediterranean basin that developed under Byzantine influence—the legacy of Byzantium survives and continues to shape the lives of millions of people in Russia and eastern Europe.

Domestic Problems and Foreign Pressures

When Basil II, "the Bulgar-Slayer," died in 1025 C.E., the Byzantine empire was a political, military, and economic dynamo. Within fifty years, however, the empire was suffering from serious internal weaknesses and had endured a series of military reverses. Both domestic and foreign problems help to explain this decline.

Social Problems Domestic problems arose, ironically, from the success of the *theme* system. Generals who governed the *themes* were natural allies of local aristocrats who held large tracts of land, and together they began to resist the policies of the imperial government. At times, they even mounted rebellions against central authorities. Moreover, by the mid–eleventh century aristocrats had accumulated vast estates that placed the free peasantry under increasing pressure. Since peasants provided the backbone of Byzantium's military system and agricultural economy, this caused both fiscal and military problems for the imperial government.

Challenges from the West As domestic problems mounted, Byzantium also faced fresh foreign challenges. From the west came the Normans—a Scandinavian people who had seized and settled in Normandy (in northern France). During the early eleventh century, they established themselves as an independent power in southern Italy, and by mid-century they had taken control of southern Italy and expelled Byzantine authorities there.

During the twelfth and thirteenth centuries, the Normans and other western European peoples mounted a series of crusades—vast military campaigns intended to recapture Jerusalem and other sites holy to Christians from Muslims—and took the opportunity to carve out states in the heart of the Byzantine empire. They even conquered and sacked Constantinople in 1204. Although Byzantine forces recaptured the capital in 1261, the destruction of Constantinople dealt the Byzantine empire a blow from which it never completely recovered.

Challenges from the East As Europeans expanded into Byzantine territory from the west, nomadic Turkish peoples invaded from the east. Most important among them were the Muslim Saljuqs, who beginning in the eleventh century sent waves of invaders into Anatolia. Given the military and financial problems of the Byzantine empire, the Saljuqs found Anatolia ripe for plunder. In 1071 they subjected the Byzantine army to a demoralizing defeat at the Battle of Manzikert. Byzantine factions then turned on one another in civil war, allowing the Saljuqs almost free rein in Anatolia. By the late twelfth century, the Saljuqs had seized much of Anatolia, and crusaders from western Europe held most of the remainder.

The loss of Anatolia—the principal source of Byzantine grain, wealth, and military forces—sealed the fate of the Byzantine empire. A territorially truncated Byzantium survived until the mid–fifteenth century, but the late Byzantine empire enjoyed little autonomy and

Saljuqs (sahl-JYOOKS)

continually faced fresh challenges from Italian merchants, western European adventurers, and Turkish nomads. In 1453, after a long era of decline, the Byzantine empire came to an end when Ottoman Turks captured Constantinople and absorbed its territories into their own expanding realm.

Early Relations between Byzantium and Slavic Peoples

By the time Constantinople fell, Byzantine traditions had deeply influenced the political and cultural development of Slavic peoples in eastern Europe and Russia. Close relations between Byzantium and Slavic peoples date from the sixth century. When Justinian deployed Byzantium's military resources in the western Mediterranean, Slavic peoples from the north took advantage of the opportunity to move into Byzantine territory. Serbs and Croats moved into the Balkan peninsula, and Bulgars established a powerful kingdom in the lower Danube region.

Relations between Byzantium and Bulgaria were especially tense. By the eighth century, however, Byzantium had begun to influence Bulgarian politics and society. Byzantium and Bulgaria entered into political, commercial, and cultural relations. Members of Bulgarian ruling families often went to Constantinople for a formal education in Greek language and literature and followed Byzantine examples in organizing their court and capital.

Cyril and Methodius Byzantium also sent missionaries to Balkan lands, and Bulgars and other Slavic peoples began to convert to Orthodox Christianity. The most famous of the missionaries to the Slavs were Saints Cyril and Methodius, two brothers from Thessaloniki in Greece. During the mid–ninth century Cyril and Methodius conducted missions in Bulgaria and Moravia (which included much of the modern Czech, Slovakian, and Hungarian territories). While there, they devised an alphabet, known as the Cyrillic alphabet, for the previously illiterate Slavic peoples. Though adapted from written Greek, the Cyrillic alphabet represented the sounds of Slavic languages more precisely than did the Greek, and it remained in use in much of eastern Europe until supplanted by the Roman alphabet in the twentieth century. In Russia and most other parts of the former Soviet Union, the Cyrillic alphabet survives to the present day.

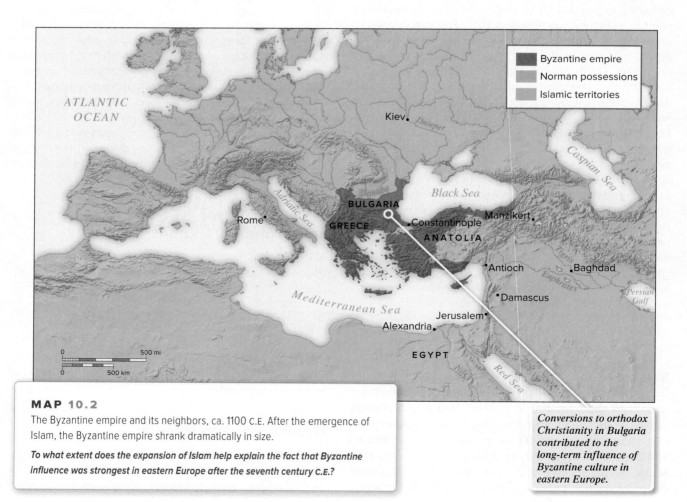

MAP 10.2

The Byzantine empire and its neighbors, ca. 1100 C.E. After the emergence of Islam, the Byzantine empire shrank dramatically in size.

To what extent does the expansion of Islam help explain the fact that Byzantine influence was strongest in eastern Europe after the seventh century C.E.?

Conversions to orthodox Christianity in Bulgaria contributed to the long-term influence of Byzantine culture in eastern Europe.

Reverberations ● ● ● ● ● ● ● ●

The Spread of Religious Traditions

One of the defining characteristics of the postclassical era was that the religions of Christianity, Buddhism, Islam, and Hinduism each won large numbers of converts far beyond their regions of origin. As a result, the values and doctrines of each religion profoundly shaped the societies where it won converts. At the same time, individual societies also shaped the contours of each religion, so that Christianity, Buddhism, Islam, and Hinduism were all at least partially made over in the image of the new societies that adopted them. The consequences of these processes—which in most cases occurred gradually as a result of revived trade networks and the work of missionaries—had deep and long-lasting consequences that can still be seen in the religious distribution of the world's peoples today.

New Homes for Religious Traditions

In this chapter we have already seen how the Orthodox Christianity of Byzantium was adopted by Slavic peoples in eastern Europe on a massive scale during the ninth and tenth centuries, largely due to the political influence of Byzantium and the self-conscious efforts of Byzantine missionaries to proselytize amongst the Slavs. But Orthodox Christianity was only one of several religious traditions to win converts in distant lands in this period. Indeed, from the seventh to the sixteenth centuries Islam spread far from its origins in the Arabian peninsula, attracting converts in central and southwest Asia, north Africa, Iberia, India, and southeast Asia (chapters 11 and 13). Even as Islam was attracting converts in parts of India, traders and religious figures from India encouraged a variety of states and kingdoms in southeast Asia to adopt either Buddhism or Hinduism between the sixth and fifteenth centuries (chapter 13). Meanwhile, Buddhism—which originated in India but had already spread along the Silk Roads in Central Asia—began to attract large numbers of converts in China from the seventh to the tenth centuries (chapter 12). Chinese influence, in turn, encouraged the spread of Buddhism to Korea, Vietnam, and Japan. By 1000 C.E., in fact, Buddhism had become a minority religion in its region

of origin, but continues to thrive in its adopted region of east Asia up to the present. Over the course of the postclassical period, then, the spread of Orthodox Christianity, Buddhism, Islam, and Hinduism from their regions of origin resulted in dramatic changes in the religious faith of millions of people.

The Influence of Religious Traditions on Culture and Society

The spread of these religious traditions deeply influenced social, cultural, and political developments in the lands where they were adopted. For example, the Cyrillic alphabet devised by Byzantine monks in the ninth century to represent the Slavic language in translations of Christian literature became the primary vehicle for printed works in eastern Europe, and continues to be used in Russia and other states of the former Soviet Union in the present (this chapter). In lands where Islam was widely adopted, shared beliefs in the values expressed by the Quran, the system of Islamic law (*sharia*), and the circulation of judges (*quadis*) and legal scholars (*ulama*) qualified to interpret such law contributed to a shared sense of cultural unity across many parts of Eurasia (chapter 11). In China, the concerns of Mahayana Buddhism with logical thought and the nature of the soul were so influential on Confucian thought that the two blended to become a new tradition known as neo-Confucianism—which itself influenced societies in east Asia for more than a millennium (chapter 12). And in southeast Asia, rulers of a variety of states borrowed Indian Hindu notions of political authority by assuming the title of *raja,* adopted the Indian epic story of the *Ramayana* as their own, and built monumental architecture closely modeled on Indian styles (chapter 13).

The Influence of Societies on Religious Traditions

At the same time, the societies into which new religious traditions spread also had an impact on the shape of the religions themselves. For example, as Islam spread it was also

Mission to the Slavs The Cyrillic alphabet stimulated conversion to Orthodox Christianity. Missionaries translated the Christian scriptures and church rituals into Slavonic, and Cyrillic writing helped them explain Christian values and ideas in Slavic terms. Meanwhile, schools organized by missionaries ensured that Slavs would receive religious instruction alongside their introduction to basic literacy. As a result, Orthodox

Christianity deeply influenced the cultural traditions of many Slavic peoples.

Byzantium and Russia

North of Bulgaria another Slavic people began to organize large states: the Russians. About the mid–ninth century Russians created several principalities governed

deeply influenced by Persian literary traditions, Indian scientific and mathematic traditions, Greek philosophy, and patriarchal traditions from the eastern Mediterranean (chapter 11). When Islam spread to southeast Asia, its expression was modified both by Hindu elements that had already shaped the region as well as by indigenous mystical traditions (chapter 13). Additionally, when Buddhism was adopted on a large scale by Chinese adherents, it was modified in ways that appealed to Chinese Daoist beliefs about spiritual life and in ways that complemented the primacy of the family in

Chinese tradition (chapter 12). As a result of their adoption in lands far from their regions of origin, then, the religions discussed in Part III each took on new forms of expression that remained influential for many centuries, and in some cases to the present day.

These are only a small sampling of the historical reverberations of the spread of religious traditions in the postclassical era. When reading subsequent chapters, try to identify additional short- and long-term consequences that resulted from these momentous processes.

T'ang Dynasty Buddhist Temple in China.

from thriving trading centers, notably Kiev. Strategically situated on the Dnieper River along the main trade route linking Scandinavia and Byzantium, Kiev became a wealthy and powerful center, and it dominated much of the territory between the Volga and the Dnieper from the tenth to the thirteenth century. Russian merchants visited Constantinople in large numbers and became well acquainted with Byzantine society. Russian princes sought

alliances with Byzantine rulers and began to express an interest in Orthodox Christianity.

The Conversion of Prince Vladimir About 989 Prince Vladimir of Kiev converted to Orthodox Christianity and ordered his subjects to follow his example. After his conversion, Byzantine influences flowed rapidly into Russia. Cyrillic writing, literacy, and Orthodox missions all spread quickly throughout Russia. Byzantine teachers traveled north to establish schools, and Byzantine priests conducted services for Russian converts. For two centuries Kiev served as a conduit for the spread of Byzantine cultural and religious influence in Russia. Indeed, Byzantine art and architecture dominated Kiev and other Russian cities. The onion domes that are a distinctive feature of early Russian churches were the result of architects' efforts to imitate the domed structures of Constantinople using wood as their principal building material.

The Growth of Kiev The princes of Kiev established firm, caesaropapist control over the Russian Orthodox church—so called to distinguish it from the Eastern Orthodox church of the Byzantine empire. They also drew inspiration from Byzantine legal tradition and compiled a written law code for their lands. By controlling trade with Byzantium and other lands, they gained financial resources to build a flourishing society.

Eventually, Russians even claimed to inherit the imperial mantle of Byzantium. According to a popular theory of the sixteenth century, Moscow was the world's third Rome: the first Rome had fallen to Germanic invaders in the fifth century, whereas the second Rome, Constantinople, had fallen to the Turks a thousand years later. Moscow survived as the third Rome, the cultural and religious beacon that would guide the world to Orthodox Christian righteousness. Inspired by that theory, missionaries took their Russian Orthodox faith to distant lands. Thus, long after the collapse of the eastern Roman empire, the Byzantine legacy continued to work its influence through the outward reach of the Russian Orthodox church.

Bulgarians in Byzantium.
This illustration from a twelfth-century manuscript depicts ninth-century incursions of Bulgarians into Byzantine territory, culminating in a lecture by the Bulgarian king to the Byzantine emperor, shown here with bound hands.

SUMMARY

The Byzantine empire originated as a survivor of the classical era. Byzantium inherited a hardy economy, a set of governing institutions, an imperial bureaucracy, an official religion, an established church, and a rich cultural tradition from classical Mediterranean society and the Roman empire. Byzantine leaders drew heavily on that legacy as they dealt with new challenges. Throughout Byzantine history, classical inspiration was especially noticeable in the imperial office, the bureaucracy, the church, and the educational system. Yet in many ways Byzantium changed profoundly over the course of its thousand-year history. After the seventh century the Byzantine empire shrank dramatically in size, and after the eleventh century it faced relentless foreign pressure from western Europeans and nomadic Turkish peoples. Changing times also brought transformations in Byzantine social and economic organization. Yet from the fifth to the twelfth century and beyond, Byzantium brought political stability and economic prosperity to the eastern Mediterranean basin, and Byzantine society served as a principal anchor supporting commercial and cultural exchanges in the postclassical world. Through its political, economic, and cultural influence, Byzantium also helped shape the development of the larger Byzantine commonwealth in eastern Europe and the eastern Mediterranean basin.

STUDY TERMS

Achaemenid (183)
Aegean (182)
Arians (190)
asceticism (191)
Basil the Bulgar-Slayer (186)
Basilian monasticism (191)
Battle of Manzikert (192)
Belisarius (185)
bezant (188)
Bosporus (182)
Byzantine (181)
caesaropapism (183)
Charlemagne (187)
Constantinople (182, 184, 186–192)
Council of Nicaea (190)
Corpus iuris civilis (185)
Cyrillic alphabet (193)
Eastern Orthodox church (179)
Hagia Sophia (184)
Hippodrome (189)
iconoclasm (190–191)
Justinian (184–185)
Normans (192)
patriarch (190)
Prince Vladimir of Kiev (195)
Procopius (181)
Saljuqs (192)
Sasanid (183)
theme system (186–188, 192)
Theodora (184)

FOR FURTHER READING

Averil Cameron. *The Mediterranean World in Late Antiquity, A.D. 395–600.* London, 1993. A thoughtful synthesis that places Byzantium in the context of the late Roman empire.

Helen C. Evans, ed. *Byzantium: Faith and Power (1261–1557).* New York, 2004. A lavishly illustrated volume exploring religious life in the late Byzantine empire.

John V. A. Fine Jr. *The Early Medieval Balkans: A Critical Survey from the Sixth to the Late Twelfth Century.* Ann Arbor, 1983. An excellent introduction to Balkan history in the postclassical era.

Garth Fowden. *Empire to Commonwealth: Consequences of Monotheism in Late Antiquity.* Princeton, 1993. A provocative volume that interprets Byzantine political and cultural development as a monotheist Christian society.

Deno John Geanakoplos. *Byzantium: Church, Society, and Civilization Seen through Contemporary Eyes.* Chicago, 1984. Rich collection of translated documents that throw light on all aspects of Byzantine society.

Judith Herrin. *Byzantium: The Surprising Life of a Medieval Empire.* Princeton, 2009. A judicious survey of Byzantine history.

J. M. Hussey. *The Byzantine World.* London, 1982. A brief and reliable survey.

Dimitri Obolensky. *The Byzantine Commonwealth: Eastern Europe, 500–1453.* New York, 1971. A well-informed overview of early Slavic history and relations between Byzantine and Slavic peoples.

Procopius. *History of the Wars, Secret History, and Buildings.* Trans. by A. Cameron. New York, 1967. Translations of writings by the most important historian in the time of Justinian.

Mark Whittow. *The Making of Byzantium, 600–1025.* Berkeley, 1996. Concentrates on Byzantine military and political relations with neighboring societies.

The Expansive Realm of Islam

CHAPTER 11

A sixteenth-century Turkish manuscript depicts pilgrims praying at Mecca in the mosque surrounding the Ka'ba.

EYEWITNESS:
Season of the Mecca Pilgrimage

In 632 C.E. the prophet Muhammad visited his native city of Mecca from his home in exile at Medina, and in doing so he set an example that devout Muslims have sought to emulate ever since. The *hajj*—the holy pilgrimage to Mecca—draws Muslims by the hundreds of thousands from all parts of the world to Saudi Arabia. Each year Muslims travel to Mecca by land, sea, and air to make the pilgrimage and visit the holy sites of Islam.

In centuries past the numbers of pilgrims were smaller, but their observance of the hajj was no less conscientious. By the ninth century, pilgrimage had become so popular that Muslim rulers went to some lengths to meet the needs of travelers passing through their lands. With the approach of the pilgrimage season, crowds gathered at major trading centers such as Baghdad, Damascus, and Cairo. There they lived in tent cities, surviving on food and water provided by government officials, until they could join caravans bound for Mecca. Muslim rulers invested considerable sums in the maintenance of roads, wells, cisterns, and lodgings that accommodated pilgrims—as well as police forces that protected travelers—on their journeys to Mecca and back.

The hajj was not only solemn observance but also an occasion for joy and celebration. Muslim rulers and wealthy pilgrims often made lavish gifts to caravan companions and others they met en route to Mecca. During her famous hajj of 976–977, for example, the Mesopotamian princess Jamila bint Nasir al-Dawla provided food and fresh green vegetables for her fellow pilgrims and furnished five hundred camels for handicapped travelers. She also purchased freedom for five hundred slaves and distributed fifty thousand fine robes among the common people of Mecca.

Most pilgrims did not have the resources to match Jamila's generosity, but for common travelers, too, the hajj became a special occasion. Merchants and craftsmen arranged business deals with pilgrims from other lands. Students and scholars exchanged ideas during their weeks of traveling together. For all pilgrims, participation in ritual activities lent new meaning and significance to their faith.

The word *Islam* means "submission," signifying obedience to the rule and will of Allah, the only deity recognized in the strictly monotheistic Islamic religion. An individual who accepts the Islamic faith is a *Muslim,* meaning "one who has submitted." Though it began as one man's expression of unqualified faith in Allah, Islam quickly attracted followers. During the first century of the new faith's existence, Islam reached far beyond its Arabian homeland, bringing Sasanid Persia and parts of the Byzantine empire into its orbit. By the eighth century the realm of Islam stood alongside the Byzantine empire as a political and economic anchor of the postclassical world.

Islamic society originally reflected the nomadic and mercantile Arabian society from which Islam arose. Yet over time, Muslims drew deep inspiration from other societies as well. After toppling the Sasanid dynasty, Muslim conquerors adopted Persian techniques of government and finance to administer their lands. Persian literature, science, and religious values also found a place in Islamic society. During later centuries Muslims drew inspiration from Greek and Indian traditions as well.

---

hajj (HAHJ)

CHRONOLOGY

570–632	Life of Muhammad
622	The *hijra*
632	Muhammad's hajj
650s	Compilation of the Quran
661–750	Umayyad dynasty
750–1258	Abbasid dynasty
1050s	Establishment of Saljuq control over the Abbasid dynasty
1126–1198	Life of Ibn Rushd

While drawing influence from other societies, however, the Islamic faith thoroughly transformed the cultural traditions that it absorbed. The expansive realm of Islam eventually provided a political framework for trade and diplomacy over a vast portion of the eastern hemisphere, from west Africa to the islands of Southeast Asia. Many lands of varied cultural backgrounds thus became part of a larger society often called the *dar al-Islam*—an Arabic term that means the "house of Islam" and that refers to lands under Islamic rule.

A PROPHET AND HIS WORLD

Islam arose in the Arabian peninsula, and the new religion faithfully reflected the social and cultural conditions of its homeland. Desert covers most of the peninsula, and agriculture is possible only in the well-watered area of Yemen in the south and in a few other places, such as the city of Medina, where oases provide water. Yet human communities have occupied Arabia for millennia. Nomadic peoples known as bedouin migrated through the deserts to find grass and water for their herds of sheep, goats, and camels. The bedouin organized themselves in family and clan groups. Individuals and their immediate families depended heavily on those kinship networks for support in times of need. In an environment as harsh and unforgiving as the Arabian desert, cooperation with kin often made the difference between life and death. As a result, bedouin peoples developed a strong sense of loyalty to their clans. Indeed, clan loyalties survived for centuries after the appearance of Islam.

Arabia also figured prominently in the long-distance trade networks of the postclassical era. Commodities arrived at ports on the Persian Gulf (near modern Bahrain), the Arabian Sea (near modern Aden), and the Red Sea (near Mecca), and then traveled overland by camel caravan to Palmyra or Damascus, which offered access to the Mediterranean basin. After the third century C.E., Arabia became an increasingly important link in long-distance trade networks. With the weakening of classical empires, trade routes across central Asia became increasingly insecure. In response, merchants abandoned the overland routes in favor of sea-lanes connecting with land routes in the Arabian peninsula. In the process, their trade allowed Arabian cities to thrive.

bedouin (BEHD-oh-ihn)
Muhammad (muh-HAHM-mahd)

Muhammad and His Message

Muhammad's Early Life The prophet Muhammad came into this world of nomadic bedouin herders and merchants. Born about 570 C.E. into a reputable family of merchants in Mecca, Muhammad ibn Abdullah lost both of his parents as a young child. His grandfather and his uncle raised him and provided him with an education, but Muhammad's early life was difficult. As a young man, he worked for a woman named Khadija, a wealthy widow whom he married about the year 595. Through this marriage he gained wealth and a position of some prominence in Meccan society.

By age 30 Muhammad had established himself as a merchant. He made a comfortable life for himself in Arabian society, where peoples of different religious and cultural traditions regularly dealt with one another. Most Arabs recognized many gods, goddesses, demons, and nature spirits, whose favor they sought through prayers and sacrifices. Large communities of Jewish merchants also worked throughout Arabia, and many Arabs had converted to Christianity by Muhammad's time. Although he was not deeply knowledgeable about Judaism or Christianity, Muhammad had a basic understanding of both faiths. He may even have traveled by caravan to Syria, where he would certainly have dealt with Jewish and Christian merchants.

Muhammad's Spiritual Transformation About 610 C.E., as he approached age 40, Muhammad underwent a profound spiritual experience that transformed his life and left a deep mark on world history. His experience left him with the convictions that in all the world there was only one true deity, Allah ("God"), that he ruled the universe, that idolatry and the recognition of other gods amounted to wickedness, and that Allah would soon bring his judgment on the world. Muhammad experienced visions, which he understood as messages or revelations from Allah,

200

delivered through the archangel Gabriel (also recognized by Jews and Christians as a special messenger of God), instructing him to explain his faith to others. He did not set out to construct a new religion by combining elements of Arab, Jewish, and Christian beliefs. In light of his cultural context, however, it is not surprising that he shared numerous specific beliefs with Jews and Christians—and indeed with Zoroastrians, whose views had profoundly influenced the development of both Judaism and Christianity. In any case, in accordance with instructions transmitted to him by Gabriel, Muhammad began to expound his faith to his family and close friends. Gradually, others showed interest in his message, and by about 620 C.E. a zealous and expanding minority of Mecca's citizenry had joined his circle.

The Quran Muhammad originally presented oral recitations of the revelations he received during his visions. As the Islamic community grew, his followers prepared written texts of his teachings. During the early 650s devout Muslims compiled these written versions of Muhammad's revelations and issued them as the Quran ("recitation"), the holy book of Islam. A work of magnificent poetry, the Quran communicates in powerful and moving terms Muhammad's understanding of Allah and his relation to the world, and it serves as the definitive authority for Islamic religious doctrine and social organization.

Apart from the Quran, several other sources have provided moral and religious guidance for the Islamic community. Most important after the Quran itself are traditions known as *hadith,* which include sayings attributed to Muhammad and accounts of his deeds. Regarded as less authoritative than the Quran and the *hadith,* but still important as inspirations for Islamic thought, were early works describing social and legal customs, biographies of Muhammad, and pious commentaries on the Quran.

Muhammad's Migration to Medina

Conflict at Mecca The growing popularity of Muhammad's preaching brought him into conflict with the ruling elites at Mecca. Muhammad's insistence that Allah was the only divine power in the universe struck many polytheistic Arabs as offensive and dangerous, since it disparaged long-recognized deities and spirits thought to wield influence over human affairs. The tensions also had a personal dimension. Mecca's ruling elites, who were also the city's wealthiest merchants, took it as a personal affront when Muhammad denounced greed as moral wickedness that Allah would punish.

Muhammad's attack on idolatry also represented an economic threat to those who owned and profited from the many shrines to deities that attracted merchants and pilgrims to Mecca. The best known of these shrines was a large black rock long considered to be the dwelling of a powerful deity. Housed in a cube-shaped building known as the Ka'ba, it drew worshipers from all over Arabia and brought considerable wealth to Mecca. As Muhammad relentlessly condemned the idolatry officially promoted at the Ka'ba and other shrines, the ruling elites of Mecca began to persecute the prophet and his followers.

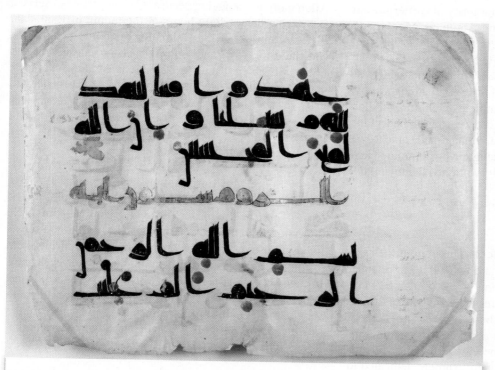

The Quran.
Current Islamic doctrine forbids artistic representations of Muhammad and Allah to prevent the worship of their images as idols. Although artists of previous centuries occasionally produced paintings of Muhammad, Islamic art has emphasized geometric design and calligraphy. This handsome page from a Quran written on vellum dates from the ninth or early tenth century.

Quran (koorr-AHN)
Ka'ba (KAH-bah)

The Hijra The pressure became so great that Muhammad and his followers were forced to migrate from Mecca in 622 C.E. They established themselves in Yathrib, a rival trading city north of Mecca, which they renamed Medina ("the city," meaning "the city of the prophet"). Known as the *hijra* ("migration"), Muhammad's move to Medina serves as the starting point of the official Islamic calendar.

The Umma Once in Medina, Muhammad found himself at the head of a small but growing society in exile that needed guidance in practical as well as spiritual affairs. He organized his followers into a cohesive community called the *umma* ("community of the faithful") and provided it with a comprehensive legal and social code. He led this community both in daily prayers to Allah and in battle with enemies at Medina, Mecca, and other places. Remembering the difficult days of his own youth, he provided relief for widows, orphans, and the poor, and he made almsgiving a prime moral virtue.

The "Seal of the Prophets" Muhammad's understanding of his religious mission expanded during his years at Medina. He began to refer to himself as a prophet, indeed as the "seal of the prophets"—the final prophet through whom Allah would reveal his message to humankind. Muhammad accepted the authority of earlier Jewish and Christian prophets, including Abraham, Moses, and Jesus, and he held the Hebrew scriptures and the Christian New Testament in high esteem. He also believed that Allah was one and the same as the Jews' Yahweh and the Christians' God. Muhammad taught, however, that the message entrusted to him was a more complete revelation of Allah and his will than Jewish and Christian faiths had made available. Thus, while at Medina, Muhammad came to see himself consciously as the messenger who communicated Allah's wishes and his plan for the world to all humankind.

The Establishment of Islam in Arabia

Muhammad's Return to Mecca Throughout their sojourn at Medina, Muhammad and his followers planned ultimately to return to their home in Mecca. In 629 C.E. they arranged with the authorities to participate in the annual pilgrimage to the Ka'ba, but they were not content with a short visit. In 630 they attacked Mecca and conquered the city. They forced the elites to adopt Muhammad's faith, and they imposed a government dedicated to Allah. They also destroyed the pagan shrines and replaced them with mosques, buildings that sought to instill a sense of sacredness and community where Muslims gathered for prayers. Only the Ka'ba escaped their efforts to cleanse Mecca of pagan monuments.

Muhammad and his followers denied that the Ka'ba was the home of a deity, but they preserved the black rock and its housing—cleansed of all the idols that had once been worshipped inside—because they maintained that it had originally been built by the prophet Abraham and his son Ishmael as a place for monotheistic worship. In 632 Muhammad himself led the first Islamic pilgrimage to the Ka'ba, thus establishing the hajj as an example for all devout Muslims. Building on the conquest of Mecca, Muhammad and his followers launched campaigns against other towns and bedouin clans, and by the time of the prophet's death in 632, shortly after his hajj, they had brought most of Arabia under their control.

The Five Pillars of Islam Muhammad's faith and his personal leadership decisively shaped the values and the development of the Islamic community. The foundation of the Islamic faith as elaborated by Muhammad consists of obligations known as the Five Pillars of Islam: (1) Muslims must acknowledge Allah as the only god and Muhammad as his prophet. (2) They must pray to Allah daily while facing Mecca. (3) They must observe a fast during the daylight hours of the month of Ramadan. (4) They must contribute alms for the relief of the weak and the poor. (5) Finally, those who are physically and financially able must undertake the hajj and make at least one pilgrimage to Mecca. Although Islam has generated many schools and sects in the centuries since its appearance, the Five Pillars of Islam constitute a powerful framework that has bound the *umma* as a whole into a cohesive community of faith.

Jihad Some Muslims, though by no means all, have taken *jihad* as an additional obligation for the faithful. The term *jihad* literally means "struggle," and Muslims have understood its imperatives in various ways. In one sense, jihad imposes obligations on Muslims by requiring them to combat vice and evil, both within the self and externally. In another sense, jihad calls on Muslims to struggle against unbelief by spreading the word of Islam and seeking converts to the faith. In some circumstances, jihad also obliges Muslims to take up the sword and wage war against unbelievers who threaten Islam.

Islamic Law: The Sharia Beyond the general obligations prescribed by the Five Pillars, Islamic holy law, known as the *sharia,* emerged during the centuries after Muhammad and offered detailed guidance on proper behavior in almost every aspect of life. Inspired by the Quran and elaborated by jurists and legal scholars, the sharia

---

hijra (HIHJ-ruh)

umma (UM-mah)

jihad (jih-HAHD)

sharia (shah-REE-ah)

Sourcesfrom**the Past**

The Quran on Allah and His Expectations of Humankind

The foundation of the Islamic faith is the understanding of Allah, his nature, and his plan for the world as outlined in the Quran. Through his revelations Muhammad came to understand Allah as the one and only God, the creator and sustainer of the world in the manner of the Jews' Yahweh and the Christians' God. Those who rejected Allah and his message would suffer eternal punishment, but those who recognized and obeyed him would receive his mercy and secure his blessings.

1. The Prologue

In the name of Allah, most benevolent, ever-merciful.
All praise be to Allah,
Lord of all the worlds,

2. Most beneficent, ever-merciful,
3. King of the Day of Judgement.
4. You alone we worship, and to You alone turn for help.
5. Guide us (O Lord) to the path that is straight,
6. The path of those You have blessed,
7. Not of those who have earned Your anger,
   nor those who have gone astray. . . .

Surah 33: The Allied Troops

35. Verily men and women who have come to submission,
    men and women who are believers,
    men and women who are devout,
    truthful men and women,
    men and women with endurance,
    men and women who are modest,
    men and women who give alms,
    men and women who observe fasting,
    men and women who guard their private parts,
    and those men and women who remember God a
      great deal,
    for them God has forgiveness and a great reward.
36. No believing men and women have any choice in a matter
    after God and His Apostle [i.e., Muhammad] have
      decided it.
    Whoever disobeys God and His Apostle has clearly
      lost the way and gone astray. . . .

41. O you who believe, remember God a great deal,
42. And sing His praises morning and evening.
43. It is He who sends His blessings on you,
    as (do) His angels, that He may lead you out of
      darkness into light,
    for He is benevolent to the believers. . . .

Surah 93: Early Hours of Morning

In the name of Allah, most benevolent, ever-merciful.
I call to witness
the early hours of the morning,

2. And the night when dark and still,
3. Your Lord has neither left you,
   nor despises you.
4. What is to come is better for you than what has
   gone before;
5. For your Lord will certainly give you,
   and you will be content.
6. Did He not find you an orphan and take care of you?
7. Did He not find you perplexed. . . .
8. Did He not find you poor and enrich you?
9. So do not oppress the orphan,
10. And do not drive the beggar away,
11. And keep recounting the favours of your Lord. . . .

Surah 112: Pure Faith

Say: "He is God the one the most unique,

2. God the immanently indispensable.
3. He has begotten no one,
   and is begotten of none.
4. There is no one comparable to Him."

For Further Reflection

■ Based on these passages, what kind of god is Allah for
his believers? Is he an angry or a caring god?

Source: Ali, Ahmed (trans), *Al-Qur'an: A Contemporary Translation.*
Copyright © 1984 by Princeton University Press. Used with
permission.

offered precise guidance on matters as diverse as marriage and family life, inheritance, slavery, business relationships, political authority, and crime. Through the sharia, Islam became more than a religious doctrine: it developed into a way of life.

THE EXPANSION OF ISLAM

After Muhammad's death the Islamic community might well have unraveled and disappeared. Muhammad had made no provision for a successor, and there was serious

division within the *umma* concerning the selection of a new leader. Many of the towns and bedouin clans that had recently accepted Islam took the opportunity of Muhammad's death to renounce the faith, reassert their independence, and break free from Mecca's control. Within a short time, however, the Islamic community had embarked on a stunningly successful round of military expansion that extended its political and cultural influence far beyond the boundaries of Arabia. Those conquests laid the foundation for the rapid growth of Islamic society.

Thinking about TRADITIONS

The Prophet and the Principles of Islam

The Muslim community received the basic teachings of Islam through the prophet Muhammad. Consider Muhammad's understanding of Judaism and Christianity as well as his life, career, and family circumstances. *In what ways did the religious beliefs and practices of Islam reflect the personal experiences of Muhammad?*

The Early Caliphs and the Umayyad Dynasty

The Caliph Because Muhammad was the "seal of the prophets," it was inconceivable that another prophet should succeed him. Shortly after Muhammad's death his advisors selected Abu Bakr, a genial man who was one of the prophet's closest friends and most devoted disciples, to serve as *caliph* ("deputy"). Thus Abu Bakr and later caliphs led the *umma* not as prophets but as substitutes for Muhammad.

Abu-Bakr (a-BOO BAK-uhr)
caliph (KHA-leef)

Abu Bakr became head of state for the Islamic community as well as chief judge, religious leader, and military commander, echoing the kind of marriage between religious and secular authority exercised by the Byzantine rulers in Chapter 10. Under the new caliph's leadership, the *umma* went on the offensive against people who had renounced Islam after Muhammad's death, and within a year it had compelled them to recognize the faith of Islam and the rule of the caliph.

The Expansion of Islam Indeed, during the century after Muhammad's death, Islamic armies carried their religion and authority throughout Arabia into Byzantine and Sasanid territories and beyond. Although much less powerful than either the Byzantine empire or the Sasanid empire, Muslim armies fought with particular effectiveness because

MAP 11.1

The expansion of Islam, 632–733 C.E. During the seventh and eighth centuries, the new faith of Islam expanded rapidly and dramatically beyond its Arabian homeland.

What environmental, political, and social circumstances facilitated the rapid spread of the new faith? What were the cultural and political effects of the expansion of Islam?

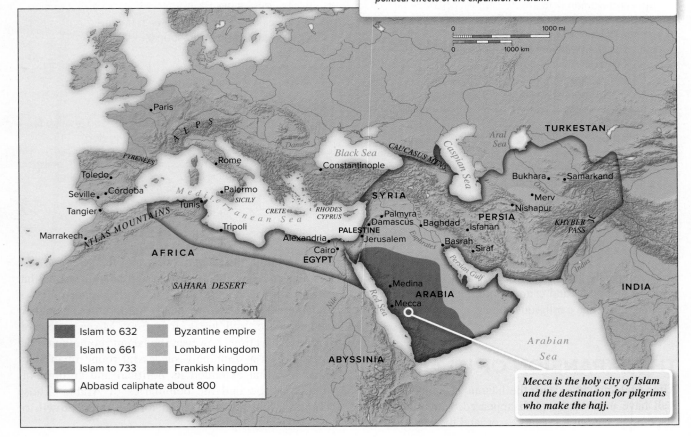

Islam to 632
Islam to 661
Islam to 733
Abbasid caliphate about 800
Byzantine empire
Lombard kingdom
Frankish kingdom

Mecca is the holy city of Islam and the destination for pilgrims who make the hajj.

their leaders had unified tribal groups into a powerful state under the banner of Islam. Moreover, they attacked at a moment when the larger empires were preoccupied with internal difficulties. Between 633 and 637 C.E., Muslim forces seized Byzantine Syria and Palestine and took most of Mesopotamia from the Sasanids. During the 640s they conquered Byzantine Egypt and north Africa. In 651 they toppled the Sasanid dynasty and incorporated Persia into their expanding empire. In 711 they conquered the Hindu kingdom of Sind in northwestern India. Between 711 and 718 they extended their authority to northwest Africa and crossed the Strait of Gibraltar, conquering most of the Iberian peninsula and threatening the Frankish kingdom in Gaul. By the mid–eighth century an immense Islamic empire ruled lands from India and the central Asian steppe lands in the east to northwest Africa and Iberia in the west.

During this rapid expansion the empire's rulers encountered problems of governance and administration. One problem had to do with the selection of caliphs. During the early decades after Muhammad's death, leaders of the most powerful Arab clans appointed the first four caliphs. Political ambitions, personal differences, and clan loyalties, however, soon led to the rise of factions and parties within the Islamic community.

The Shia Disagreements over succession led to the emergence of the Shia sect, the most important and enduring of all the alternatives to the faith observed by the majority of Muslims, known as Sunni Islam. The Shia sect originated as a party supporting the appointment of Ali—a cousin and son-in-law of Muhammad—and his descendants as caliphs. Ali did serve briefly as the fourth caliph (656–661 C.E.), but his enemies assassinated him, killed many of his relatives, and imposed their own candidate as caliph. Partisans of Ali then organized the Shia ("party") and furiously struggled to return the caliphate to the line of Ali. Although persecuted, the Shia survived and strengthened its identity by adopting doctrines and rituals distinct from those of the Sunnis ("traditionalists"), who accepted the legitimacy of the early caliphs. Shia partisans, for example, observed holy days in honor of their leaders and martyrs to their cause, and they taught that descendants of Ali were infallible, sinless, and divinely appointed to rule the Islamic community.

The Umayyad Dynasty After the assassination of Ali, the establishment of the Umayyad dynasty (661–750 C.E.) temporarily solved the problem of succession. The Umayyads ranked among the most prominent of the Meccan merchant clans, and their reputation and network of alliances helped them bring stability to the Islamic community. Despite their association with Mecca, the Umayyads established their capital at Damascus, a thriving commercial city in Syria, whose central location enabled them to maintain better communication with the vast and still-expanding Islamic empire.

Islamic expansion.
The early expansion of Islam was a bloody affair. This illustration from an Arabic manuscript of the thirteenth century depicts a battle between Muhammad's cousin Ali and his adversaries.

Policy toward Conquered Peoples Although the Umayyads' dynasty solved the problem of succession, their tightly centralized rule and the favor they showed to their fellow Arabs generated an administrative problem. The Umayyads ruled the *dar al-Islam* as conquerors, and their policies favored the Arab military aristocracy by distributing both lands and positions of power among this privileged class. Such policies caused severe discontent among the scores of ethnic and religious groups encompassed within the Umayyad empire. In addition, although the Arabs

Shia (SHEE-'ah)

Sunni (SOON-nee)

Umayyad (oo-MEYE-ah)

mostly allowed conquered peoples to observe their own religions, they levied a special head tax, called the *jizya,* on those who did not convert to Islam. Moreover, even those who converted did not enjoy access to wealth and positions of authority, which the Umayyads reserved almost exclusively for members of the Arab military aristocracy.

Umayyad Decline Beginning in the early eighth century, the Umayyad caliphs became alienated even from other Arabs as they devoted themselves increasingly to luxurious living rather than to moral leadership of the *umma.* By midcentury the Umayyad caliphs faced not only the continued resistance of the Shia faction but also the discontent of conquered peoples throughout their empire and even the disillusionment of Muslim Arab military leaders.

The Abbasid Dynasty

Abu al-Abbas Rebellion in Persia brought the Umayyad dynasty to an end. The chief leader of the rebellion was Abu al-Abbas, a descendant of Muhammad's uncle. Although he was a Sunni Arab, Abu al-Abbas allied readily with Shias and with non-Arab Muslims. During the 740s Abu al-Abbas's party seized control of Persia and Mesopotamia. In 750 his army shattered Umayyad forces in a great battle. Afterward Abu al-Abbas invited the remaining members of the Umayyad clan to a banquet under the pretext of reconciling their differences. Instead, during the festivities his troops slaughtered the Umayyads and annihilated the clan. Abu al-Abbas then founded the Abbasid dynasty, which was the principal source of authority in the *dar al-Islam* until the Mongols toppled it in 1258 C.E.

The Abbasid Dynasty The Abbasid dynasty differed considerably from the Umayyad. For one thing, the Abbasid rulers did not show special favor to the Arab military aristocracy. Arabs continued to play a large role in government, but Persians, Egyptians, Mesopotamians, and others also rose to positions of wealth and power.

The Abbasid dynasty differed from the Umayyad also in that it was not a conquering dynasty. The Abbasids did clash intermittently with the Byzantine empire and nomadic peoples from central Asia, and in 751 they defeated a Chinese army at Talas River near Samarkand. The battle of Talas River was exceptionally important: it ended the expansion of China's Tang dynasty into central Asia (discussed in chapter 12), and it opened the door for the spread of Islam among Turkish peoples. Overall, however, the Abbasids did not expand their empire by conquest. The *dar al-Islam* as a whole continued to grow during the Abbasid era, but that was a result of largely autonomous Islamic forces rather than the policies of the caliphs. During the ninth

and early tenth centuries, for example, largely autonomous Islamic forces from distant Tunisia mounted naval expeditions throughout the Mediterranean, seizing various island territories as well as territories in southern Italy and southern France. Meanwhile, Muslim merchants introduced Islam to southern India and sub-Saharan Africa (discussed in chapters 13 and 15).

Abbasid Administration Instead of conquering new lands, the Abbasids largely contented themselves with administering the empire they inherited—a considerable challenge given the empire's diversity of linguistic, ethnic, and cultural groups. In designing their administration, the Abbasids relied heavily on Persian techniques of statecraft whereby rulers devised policies, built capital cities to oversee affairs, and organized their territories through regional governors and bureaucracies.

Baghdad Central authority came from the court at the magnificent new city of Baghdad (capital of modern Iraq). By building this new center of government to replace the Umayyad capital at Damascus, the Abbasids associated themselves with the cosmopolitan environment of Mesopotamia. Baghdad was a round city protected by three round walls. At the heart of the city was the caliph's green-domed palace, from which instructions flowed to the distant reaches of the Abbasid realm. In the provinces, governors represented the caliph and implemented his political and financial policies.

Learned officials known as *ulama* ("people with religious knowledge") and *qadis* ("judges") set moral standards in local communities and resolved disputes. *Ulama* and *qadis* were not priests—Islam does not recognize priests—but they had a formal education that emphasized study of the Quran and the sharia. *Ulama* were pious scholars who sought to develop public policy in accordance with the Quran and the sharia. *Qadis* heard cases at law and rendered decisions based on the Quran and the sharia. Because of their moral authority, *ulama* and *qadis* became extremely influential officials who helped to ensure widespread observance of Islamic values. The Abbasid caliphs also kept a standing army, maintained the network of roads they inherited from the Sasanids, and established bureaucratic ministries in charge of taxation, finance, coinage, and postal services.

Harun al-Rashid The high point of the Abbasid dynasty came during the reign of the caliph Harun al-Rashid (786–809 C.E.). By the late eighth century, Abbasid authority had lost some of its force in provinces distant from Baghdad, but it remained strong enough to bring reliable tax revenues from most parts of the empire. Flush with wealth, Baghdad became a center of banking, commerce, crafts, and industrial production, a metropolis with a population of several hundred thousand people. According to stories from his time, Harun al-Rashid provided liberal support

jizya (JIHZ-yah)
Abbasid (ah-BAH-sih)

for artists and writers, bestowed lavish and luxurious gifts on his favorites, and distributed money to the poor and the common classes by tossing coins into the streets of Baghdad. Once, he sent an elephant and a collection of rich presents as gifts to his contemporary Charlemagne, who ruled the Carolingian empire of western Europe.

Abbasid Decline In the early ninth century, however, the Abbasid empire entered a period of decline, and disputes over succession seriously damaged its authority. Provincial governors took advantage of disorder in the ruling house by acting independently of the caliphs and building up local bases of power. Meanwhile, popular uprisings and peasant rebellions further weakened the empire.

As a result of these difficulties, the Abbasid caliphs became mere figureheads long before the Mongols extinguished the dynasty in 1258. In 945 members of a Persian noble family seized control of Baghdad and established their clan as the power behind the Abbasid throne. Later, imperial authorities in Baghdad fell under the control of the Saljuq Turks, a nomadic people from central Asia who also invaded the Byzantine empire. In response to rebellions mounted by peasants and provincial governors, authorities in Baghdad allied with the Saljuqs, who began to enter the Abbasid realm and convert to Islam in about the mid-tenth century. By the mid–eleventh century the Saljuqs effectively controlled the Abbasid empire. During the 1050s they took possession of Baghdad, and during the following decades they extended their authority to Syria, Palestine, and Anatolia. They retained Abbasid caliphs as nominal sovereigns, but for two centuries, until the arrival of the Mongols, the Saljuq *sultan* ("ruler") was the true source of power in the Abbasid empire.

ECONOMY AND SOCIETY OF THE EARLY ISLAMIC WORLD

In the *dar al-Islam,* as in other agricultural societies, peasants tilled the land while manufacturers and merchants supported a thriving urban economy. Here, as in other lands, the creation of large empires had dramatic economic implications. The Umayyad and Abbasid empires created a zone of trade, exchange, and communication stretching from India to Iberia. Commerce throughout this zone served as a vigorous economic stimulus for both the countryside and the cities of the early Islamic world.

New Crops, Agricultural Experimentation, and Urban Growth

The Spread of Food and Industrial Crops As soldiers, administrators, diplomats, and merchants traveled throughout the *dar al-Islam,* they encountered plants, animals, and agricultural techniques peculiar to the empire's

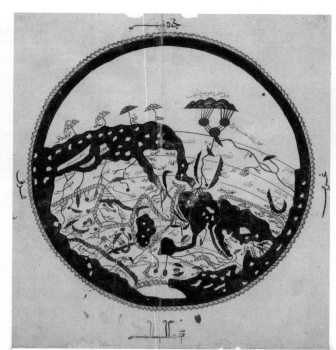

Islamic map.

A map produced in the eleventh century by the Arab geographer al-Idrisi shows the lands known and reported by Muslim merchants and travelers. Note that, in accordance with Muslim cartographic convention, this map places south at the top and north at the bottom.

various regions. They often introduced particularly useful crops to new regions. The most important of the transplants traveled west from India and included staple crops such as sugarcane, rice, and new varieties of sorghum and wheat; vegetables such as spinach and artichokes; fruits such as oranges, bananas, coconuts, and mangoes; and industrial crops such as cotton, indigo, and henna.

Effects of New Crops The introduction of these crops into the western regions of the Islamic world had wide-ranging effects. New food crops led to a richer and more varied diet. They also increased quantities of food available because they enabled cultivators to extend the growing season: since most of the transplanted crops grew well in high heat, cultivators in southwest Asia and other hot zones could plant an additional crop in the summer months instead of leaving their fields fallow. The result was a dramatic increase in food supplies.

Agricultural Experimentation Travel and communication in the *dar al-Islam* also encouraged experimentation with agricultural methods. Cultivators paid close attention to methods of irrigation, fertilization, crop rotation, and the like, and they outlined their findings in hundreds of agricultural manuals. The combined effect of new crops and improved techniques was a far more productive agricultural economy, which in turn supported vigorous economic growth throughout the *dar al-Islam.*

Urban Growth Increased agricultural production contributed to the rapid growth of cities in all parts of the Islamic world from India to Spain. All these cities—including, for example, Delhi, Merv, Isfahan, Damascus, Cairo, Córdoba, and Tangier—had flourishing markets supporting thousands of artisans, craftsmen, and merchants. Most of them were also important centers of industrial production, particularly of textiles, pottery, glassware, leather, iron, and steel.

One new industry appeared in Islamic cities during the Abbasid era: paper manufacture. When Arab forces defeated a Chinese army at the battle of Talas River in 751, they took prisoners skilled in paper production and learned the technique from them. Paper soon became popular throughout the Islamic world. Paper facilitated the keeping of administrative and commercial records, and it made possible the dissemination of books and treatises in larger quantities than ever before. By the tenth century, mills produced paper in Persia, Mesopotamia, Arabia, Egypt, and Spain, and the industry soon spread to western Europe.

The Formation of a Hemispheric Trading Zone

From its earliest days Islamic society drew much of its prosperity from commerce. Muhammad himself was a merchant, and he held merchants in high esteem. By the time of the Abbasid caliphate, elaborate trade networks linked all the regions of the Islamic world and joined it to a larger, hemispheric economy.

Overland Trade When they overran the Sasanid empire, Muslim conquerors brought the prosperous trading cities of central Asia under control of the expanding *dar al-Islam.* Muslim merchants were then able to take advantage of the extensive road networks originally built during the classical era by imperial authorities in India,

Persia, and the Mediterranean basin. To be sure, Umayyad and Abbasid rulers maintained the roads for military and administrative purposes, but those same roads also made excellent highways for merchants as well as missionaries and pilgrims.

Camels and Caravans Overland trade traveled mostly by camel caravan. Although they are uncooperative beasts, camels endure the rigors of desert travel much better than horses or donkeys. Moreover, when fitted with a well-designed saddle, camels can carry heavy loads. During the early centuries C.E., the manufacture of camel saddles spread throughout Arabia, north Africa, southwest Asia, and central Asia, and camels became the favored beasts of burden in deserts and other dry regions. As camel transport became more common, the major cities of the Islamic world and central Asia built and

Muslim travelers.

In a thirteenth-century manuscript illustration, a fictional Muslim traveler passes a lively agricultural village. On the right a woman spins cotton thread. Sheep, goats, chickens, and date palms figure prominently in the local economy.

maintained caravanserais—inns offering lodging for caravan merchants as well as food, water, and care for their animals.

Maritime Trade Meanwhile, innovations in nautical technology contributed to a steadily increasing volume of maritime trade in the Red Sea, Persian Gulf, Arabian Sea, and Indian Ocean. Arab and Persian mariners borrowed the compass from its Chinese inventors and used it to guide them on the high seas. From southeast Asian and Indian mariners they borrowed the lateen sail, a triangular sail that increased a ship's maneuverability. From the Hellenistic Mediterranean they borrowed the astrolabe, an instrument that enabled them to calculate latitude. Thus equipped, Arab and Persian mariners ventured throughout the Indian Ocean basin.

Banks Banking also stimulated the commercial economy of the Islamic world. Banks had operated since classical antiquity, but Islamic banks of the Abbasid period conducted business on a much larger scale than their predecessors. They not only lent money to entrepreneurs but also served as brokers for investments and exchanged different currencies. They established multiple branches that honored letters of credit known as *sakk* drawn on the parent bank. Thus merchants could settle accounts with distant business partners without having to deal in cash.

The Organization of Trade Trade benefited also from refined techniques of business organization. Usually Islamic businessmen preferred not to embark on solo ventures, since an individual could face financial ruin if an entire cargo of commodities fell prey to pirates or went down with a ship that sank in a storm. Instead, like their counterparts in other postclassical societies, Abbasid entrepreneurs often pooled their resources in a variety of group investments designed to distribute individual risks.

As a result of improved transportation, expanded banking services, and refined techniques of business organization, long-distance trade surged in the early Islamic world. Muslim merchants dealt in silk and ceramics from China, spices and aromatics from India and southeast Asia, and jewelry and fine textiles from the Byzantine empire. Merchants also ventured beyond settled societies in China, India, and the Mediterranean basin to distant lands that previously had not engaged systematically in long-distance trade. They crossed the Sahara desert by camel caravan to trade salt, steel, copper, and glass for gold and slaves from the kingdoms of west Africa. They visited the coastal regions of east Africa, where they obtained slaves and exotic local commodities such as animal skins. They engaged in trade with Russia and

The mosque at Córdoba.

This mosque was originally built in the late eighth century and enlarged during the ninth and tenth centuries. One of the largest structures in the *dar al-Islam*, the mosque rests on 850 columns and features nineteen aisles.

Why are there no representations of Allah in the mosque?

Scandinavia by way of the Dnieper and Volga rivers and obtained commodities such as animal skins, furs, honey, amber, and slaves as well as bulk goods such as timber and livestock. The vigorous economy of the Abbasid empire thus helped to establish networks of communication and exchange throughout much of the eastern hemisphere.

Al-Andalus The prosperity of Islamic Spain, known as al-Andalus, illustrates the far-reaching effects of long-distance trade during the Abbasid era. Most of the Iberian peninsula had fallen into the hands of Muslim

sakk (sahk)

al-Andalus (al-ahn-duh-LUHS)

Berber conquerors from north Africa during the early eighth century. As allies of the Umayyads, the governors of al-Andalus refused to recognize the Abbasid dynasty, and beginning in the tenth century they styled themselves caliphs in their own right rather than governors subject to Abbasid authority. Despite political and diplomatic tensions, al-Andalus participated actively in the commercial life of the larger Islamic world, which enabled merchants and manufacturers in al-Andalus to conduct thriving businesses in cities such as Córdoba, Toledo, and Seville.

The Changing Status of Women

A patriarchal society had emerged in Arabia long before Muhammad's time, but Arab women enjoyed rights not accorded to women in many other lands. They could legally inherit property, divorce husbands on their own initiative, and engage in business ventures. Khadija, the first of Muhammad's four wives, managed a successful commercial business.

The Quran and Women In some respects the Quran enhanced the security of women in Arabian society. It outlawed female infanticide, and it provided that dowries go directly to brides rather than to their husbands and male guardians. It portrayed women not as the property of their menfolk but as honorable individuals, equal to men before Allah, with their own rights and needs. Muhammad's own kindness and generosity toward his wives also served as an example that may have improved the lives of Muslim women.

For the most part, however, the Quran—and later the sharia as well—reinforced male dominance. The Quran and Islamic holy law recognized descent through the male line, and to guarantee proper inheritance, they placed a high premium on genealogical purity. To ensure the legitimacy of heirs, they subjected the social and sexual lives of women to the strict control of male guardians. The Quran and the sharia also permitted men to take up to four wives, whereas women could have only one husband. The Quran and the sharia thus provided a religious and legal foundation for a decisively patriarchal society.

Veiling of Women When Islam expanded into the Byzantine and Sasanid empires, it encountered strong patriarchal traditions, and Muslims readily adopted long-standing customs such as the veiling of women. Social and family pressures had induced upper-class urban women to veil themselves in Mesopotamia as early as the thirteenth century B.C.E., and long before Muhammad the practice of veiling had spread to Persia and the eastern Mediterranean. When Muslim Arabs conquered these lands, they adopted the practice. A conspicuous symbol of male authority thus found a prominent place in the early Islamic community.

Although the Quran served as the preeminent source of authority in the Islamic world, over the centuries jurists and legal scholars interpreted the Quran in ways that progressively limited the rights of women. To a large extent the increased emphasis on male authority in Islamic law reflected the influence of the strongly hierarchical and patriarchal societies of Mesopotamia, Persia, and eastern Mediterranean lands as Islam developed from a local faith to a large-scale complex society.

ISLAMIC VALUES AND CULTURAL EXCHANGES

Since the seventh century C.E., the Quran has served as the cornerstone of Islamic society. Arising from a rich tradition of bedouin poetry and song, the Quran established Arabic as a flexible and powerful medium of communication. When carrying their faith to new lands during the era of Islamic expansion, Muslim missionaries spread the message of Allah and provided instruction in the Quran's teachings, although they also permitted continued observance of pre-Islamic traditions. Muslim intellectuals drew freely from the long-established cultural traditions of Persia, India, and Greece, which they became acquainted with during the Umayyad and Abbasid eras.

The Formation of an Islamic Cultural Tradition

Muslim theologians and jurists looked to the Quran and other sources of Islamic doctrine in their efforts to formulate moral guidelines appropriate for their society. The body of civil and criminal law embodied in the *sharia* provided a measure of cultural unity for the vastly different lands of the Islamic world. Islamic law did not by any means erase differences, but it established a common cultural foundation that facilitated dealings between peoples of various Islamic lands and that lent substance to the concept of the *dar al-Islam*.

Promotion of Islamic Values On a more popular level, *ulama, qadis,* and missionaries helped to spread Islamic values throughout the *dar al-Islam. Ulama* and *qadis* held positions at all Islamic courts. By resolving disputes according to Islamic law and ordering public observance of Islamic social and moral standards, they helped to bring the values of the Quran and the sharia into the lives of peoples living far from the birthplace of Islam.

Reverberations of ●●●●●●●●●● ● ●

The Spread of Religious Traditions

As we saw in chapter 10, the postclassical era was marked by the spread of religious traditions—including Islam—well beyond their regions of origin. In the case of Islam, people (including *qadis* and *ulama* who were trained in interpreting *sharia* law), institutions (including *madrasas* and mosques), and the Arabic language as expressed in the Quran provided multiple avenues for the diffusion of Islamic values to areas distant from its birthplace in the Arabian peninsula. Consider the long-term legacies of this common religious foundation—even in the absence of a unified Islamic state—across the *dar al-Islam*. How might this common religious foundation have affected political relationships, cultural developments, or the movement of products and people within the *dar al-Islam* over the long term? How might it have affected relationships between Islamic regions and non-Islamic regions?

Formal educational institutions also helped promote Islamic values. For example, many mosques maintained schools that provided an elementary education and religious instruction. By the tenth century, institutions of higher education known as *madrasas* had begun to appear, and by the twelfth century they had become established in the major cities of the Islamic world. Muslim rulers often supported the madrasas in the interests of recruiting literate and learned students for administrative positions.

Sufis Among the most effective Islamic missionaries were mystics known as Sufis. The term *Sufi* probably came from the patched woolen garments favored by the mystics. Sufis did not deny Islamic doctrine, but they also did not find formal religious teachings to be especially meaningful. Thus, instead of concerning themselves with fine points of doctrine, Sufis worked to deepen their spiritual awareness. Most Sufis led pious and ascetic lives. Some devoted themselves to helping the poor. Many sought a mystical, ecstatic union with Allah, relying on rousing sermons, passionate singing, or spirited dancing to bring them to a state of high emotion. Muslim theologians sometimes mistrusted Sufis, fearing that in their lack of concern for doctrine they would adopt erroneous beliefs. Nevertheless, after the ninth century Sufis became increasingly popular in Muslim societies because of their piety, devotion, and eagerness to minister to the needs of their fellow human beings.

Sufi Missionaries Sufis were especially effective as missionaries because they emphasized devotion to Allah above mastery of doctrine. They sometimes encouraged individuals to revere Allah in their own ways, even if their methods did not have a basis in the Quran. They tolerated the continued observance of pre-Islamic customs, for example, as well as the association of Allah with deities recognized and revered in other faiths. Because of their kindness, holiness, tolerance, and charismatic appeal, Sufis attracted numerous converts, particularly in lands such as Persia and India, where long-established religious faiths such as Zoroastrianism, Christianity, Buddhism, and Hinduism had enjoyed a mass following for centuries.

Hajj The symbol of Islamic cultural unity was the Ka'ba at Mecca, which from an early date attracted pilgrims

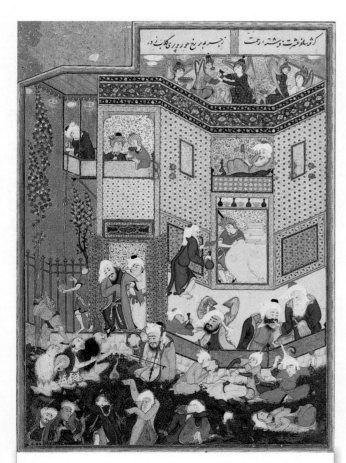

Sufis.
Through song, dance, and ecstatic experiences, sometimes enhanced by wine, Persian Sufis expressed their devotion to Allah, as in this sixteenth-century painting.

madrasas (MAH-drahs-ahs)
Sufis (SOO-fees)

Connecting
the Sources

Sufi mysticism and the appeal of Islam

The problem Although Muslim armies conquered vast territories in Central and Southwest Asia, North Africa, and Iberia in the century after Muhammad's death in 632 C.E., conquest alone cannot explain why so many people in the *dar al-Islam* made sincere and lasting conversions to Islam. Many individuals converted to Islam because of its profound spiritual appeal, made especially popular by Sufi mystics who often served as missionaries. While all Muslims believed that individuals would become close to God in the afterlife, Sufi mystics preached that it was possible to grow close to God while one was still alive if only individuals would surrender themselves, in love, to God. For Sufis, the key to surrendering to and loving God was learning to gain control over one's own ego, which they termed the "greater jihad," or *al-jihad al-akbar* (as opposed to the "lesser jihad," or *al-jihad al-asghar*, of fighting oppressors or injustice). Sufis taught, in short, that the path to God was a path of love, and that this path was open to all who wished to follow.

Below are two excerpts from texts written by exceptionally well-known and influential Sufi mystics: Rabi'a al-'Addawiyya, a woman from Basra (modern Iraq) who lived from about 717–801 C.E., and Abu Hamid al-Ghazali, a man from Khorasan (modern Iran) who lived from 1058–1128 C.E. As you read the documents, think about the reasons why their writings might have appealed to contemporaries and to generations who came after them.

The documents Read the documents below, and consider carefully the questions that follow.

Document 1: *Rabi'a al-'Adawiyya was an early Sufi saint and is the best known woman Sufi mystic in Islamic history. She was sold into slavery as a child, but was reportedly freed later in life because of her religious devotion. She was known for her celibate and ascetic lifestyle and for her passionate devotion to the love of God. Rabi'a herself did not publish any of her poetry or writings, but they were later collected and printed by Faridu d'Din Attar in the thirteenth century. The following is one of the poems attributed to her.*

> *O Lord,*
> *   If tomorrow on Judgment Day*
> *   You send me to Hell,*

> *I will tell such a secret*
> *That Hell will race from me*
> *Until it is a thousand years away.*
>
> *O Lord,*
> *   Whatever share of this world*
> *   You could give to me,*
> *   Give it to Your enemies;*
> *   Whatever share of the next world*
> *   You want to give to me,*
> *   Give it to Your friends.*
> *   You are enough for me.*
>
> *O Lord,*
> *   If I worship You*
> *   From fear of Hell, burn me in Hell.*
>
> *O Lord,*
> *   If I worship You*
> *   From hope of Paradise, bar me from its gates.*
>
> *But if I worship You for Yourself alone*
> *   Then grace me forever the splendor of Your Face.*

Depiction of Rabi'a grinding grain

Document 2: *Abu Hamid al-Ghazali was one of the most important Sufi philosophers and Muslim theologians. As a young man he became a professor at Nizamiyah University in Baghdad, but spiritual transformation caused him to give up the academic life for a life of asceticism, reflection, and writing. He wrote numerous important works seeking to balance the rationalism of Greek philosophy with spiritualism derived from Sufi mysticism. The following selection is taken from his Alchemy of Happiness, originally published in the early twelfth century.*

On the Love of God

O traveller on the way and seeker after the love of God! know that the love of God is a sure and perfect method for the believer to attain the object of his desires. It is a highly exalted station of rest, during the journey of the celestial traveler. It is the consummation of the desires and longings of those who seek divine truth. It is the foundation of the vision of the beauty of the Lord.

The love of God is of the most binding obligation upon every one. It is indeed the spirit of the body, and the light of the eye.

The prophet of God declares that the faith of the believer is not complete, unless he love God and his prophet more than all the world besides. The prophet was once asked, what is faith? He replied, "It is to love God and his prophet more than wife, children and property." And the prophet was continually in the habit of praying, "O my God! I ask for thy love, I ask that I may love whomsoever loves thee, and that I may perform whatsoever thy love makes incumbent upon me."

On the resurrection day all sects will be addressed by the name of the prophet whom each followed, "O people of Moses! O people of Jesus! O people of Mohammed!" even to all the beloved servants of God, and it will be proclaimed to them, "O Friends and beloved of God, come to the blessed union and society of God! Come to Paradise and partake of the grace of your beloved!" When they hear this proclamation, their hearts will leap out of their places, and they will almost lose their reason. Yahya ben Moa'z says, "It is better to have as much love of God, even if only as much as a grain of mustard seed, than seventy years of devotion and obedience without love." Hassan of Basra says, "Whoever knows God, will certainly love him, and whoever knows the world, will shun it."

. . .

O! seeker of divine love, that which renders man favorably inclined to persons of virtuous character, is the fact that God has created man after his own character; as it has come to us in the tradition that, "verily God created man after his own image." Hence whenever man sees or hears of a quality belonging to his own race and kind, as justice, generosity, forgiveness or patience, he will certainly have a sympathy with that quality and exercise love to its possessor. If we hear for instance that in a certain country there is a just sovereign or a just vizier, we heartily love that king or vizier, and we are always praising his excellence and worth, although there is not the least probability of any advantage accruing to us from his justice. Such a sovereign was Nushirvan, who notwithstanding he was an infidel yet as he was just, the heart of every man is drawn towards him. If again we hear of the knowledge, science, clemency or munificence of any persons, as of the Imam Abu Hanifé, of the Imam Shaféi, of Bayézid of Bistan, or of Junéid of Bagdad, the spirit of a man will be attracted towards them on account of those qualities, he will love them, and he will certainly desire to see them and to be with them. If we hear of a generous man, although he may be in a foreign country, and we have no hope of any advantage from him or of any token of his generosity to ourselves, yet still from necessity we will

love him, and whenever his name is mentioned we will invoke blessings upon him and praise him. It is thus with Hatem Tai whose name, though he was an infidel, is upon every tongue, because he was a generous and benevolent man, and all hearts are irresistibly led to love him. . . .

We see then that the love we bear to persons endowed with the virtuous qualities of man, is not bestowed by us for the sake of any fancied advantage from them or any hope of gain, but that on the contrary it is because the spirits of men are created in correspondence with the character of God, and when we see a trace or mark of a quality or affection of a kind like our own, we cannot help being attracted towards it, and must necessarily love it.

Rumi (also: Jalal ad-Din Muhammad Balkhi, Mevlevi or Mawlana (our Lord). Persian Muslim poet and Sufi mystic, founder of the Order of the "Dancing Dervishes."

Questions

- What can these sources definitively tell you about the lives of the people who produced them? What **facts** can be gleaned from these sources?

- In Document 1, what is the main message of the poem? How does Rabi'a's gender complicate our understanding of the role of women in Islam in the century after Muhammad's death?

- In Document 2, why is it important to love God, according to al-Ghazali? How does al-Ghazali's view of loving other people compare with common contemporary visions of Islam as a "religion of the sword"?

- For both documents, how might these exhortations about loving God have appealed to individuals coming into contact with them for the first time?

- Sources such as these can help historians understand the spiritual dimensions of conversion to Islam, especially when read in conjunction with other textual and material evidence.

Source Websites: **Document 1:** al-Adawiyya, Rabi'a, Perfume of the Desert. Translation by Andrew Harvey and Eryk Hanut. Copyright © 1999 by Andrew Harvey and Eryk Hanut. Reprinted with permission from The Theosophical Society in America. **Document 2:** Ghazali, Al. Translation of The Alchemy of Happiness [1873]. "On the Love of God." http://oll.libertyfund.org/?option=com_staticxt&staticfile=show.php%3Ftitle=1844&chapter=141817&layout=html#a_2668237.

from all parts of the Islamic world. Indeed, individuals from far-flung regions made their way to Mecca, visited the holy sites, and learned firsthand the traditions of Islam. Over the centuries these pilgrims helped to spread Islamic beliefs and values to all parts of the Islamic world, and alongside the work of *ulama, qadis,* and Sufi missionaries, their efforts helped to make the *dar al-Islam* not just a name but also a reality.

Islam and the Cultural Traditions of Persia, India, and Greece

As the Islamic community expanded, Muslims of Arab ancestry interacted regularly with peoples from other cultural traditions, especially those of Persia, India, and Greece. In some cases, particularly in lands ruled by the Umayyad and Abbasid dynasties, large numbers of conquered peoples converted to Islam, and they brought elements of their inherited cultural traditions into Islamic society. In other cases, particularly in lands beyond the authority of Islamic rulers, Muslims became acquainted with the literary, artistic, philosophical, and scientific traditions of peoples who chose not to convert.

Persian Influences on Islam Persian traditions quickly found a place in Islamic society, since the culturally rich land fell under Islamic rule at an early date. After the establishment of the Abbasid dynasty and the founding of its capital at Baghdad, Persian administrative techniques were crucial for the organization of the imperial structure through which rulers governed their vast empire. Meanwhile, Persian ideas of kingship—in which kings were wise, benevolent, but nonetheless absolute rulers—profoundly influenced Islamic political thought.

Persian influence was also noticeable in literary works from the Abbasid dynasty. Whereas Arabic served as the language of religion, theology, philosophy, and law, Persian was the principal language of literature, poetry, history, and political reflection. The marvelous collection of stories known as *The Arabian Nights* or *The Thousand and One Nights,* for example, presented popular tales of adventure and romance set in the Abbasid empire and the court of Harun al-Rashid.

Indian Influences on Islam Indian mathematics, science, and medicine also captured the attention of Arab and Persian Muslims who established Islamic states in northern India. Muslims readily adopted what they called

"Hindi" numerals, which European peoples later called "Arabic" numerals, since they learned about them through Arab Muslims. Hindi numerals enabled Muslim scholars to develop an impressive tradition of advanced mathematics, concentrating on algebra (an Arabic word) as well as trigonometry and geometry. From a more practical point of view, Indian numerals vastly simplified bookkeeping for Muslim merchants.

Muslims also found much to appreciate in the scientific and medical thought they encountered in India. With the aid of their powerful and flexible mathematics, Indian scholars were able to carry out precise astronomical calculations, which helped inspire the development of Muslim astronomy. Similarly, Indian medicine appealed to Muslims because of its treatments for specific ailments and its use of antidotes for poisons.

Greek Influences on Islam Muslims also admired the philosophical, scientific, and medical writings of classical Greece. They became especially interested in Plato and Aristotle, whose works they translated and interpreted in commentaries. For example, Ibn Rushd (1126–1198), *qadi* of Seville in the caliphate of Córdoba, followed Aristotle in seeking to articulate a purely rational understanding of the world. Ibn Rushd's work not only helped to shape Islamic philosophy but also found its way to the schools and universities of western Europe, where Christian scholars knew Ibn Rushd as Averroës. During the thirteenth century, his work profoundly influenced the development of scholasticism, the effort of medieval European philosophers to harmonize Christianity with Aristotelian thought. However, after the thirteenth century, Greek philosophy fell out of favor with Muslim philosophers and theologians, who turned instead to teachings from the Quran and Sufi mystics.

Quite apart from philosophy, Greek mathematics, science, and medicine also appealed strongly to Muslims. Greek mathematics did not make use of Indian numerals, but it offered a solid body of powerful reasoning, particularly when dealing with calculations in algebra and geometry. Greek mathematics supported the development of astronomical and geographical scholarship, and studies of anatomy and physiology served as foundations for medical thought. Muslim scholars quickly absorbed these Greek traditions, combined them with influences from India, and used them as points of departure for their own studies. The result was a brilliant flowering of mathematical, scientific, and medical scholarship that provided Muslim societies with powerful tools for understanding the natural world.

Ibn Rushd (IB-uhn RUSHED)

SUMMARY

The prophet Muhammad did not intend to found a new religion. Instead, his intention was to express his faith in Allah and perfect the teachings of earlier Jewish and Christian prophets by announcing a revelation more comprehensive than those Allah had entrusted to his predecessors. His message soon attracted a circle of devout and committed disciples, and by the time of his death most of Arabia had accepted Islam. During the two centuries following the prophet's death, Arab conquerors spread Islam throughout southwest Asia and north Africa and introduced their faith to central Asia, India, the Mediterranean islands, and Iberia. This rapid expansion of Islam encouraged the development of an extensive trade and communications network: merchants, diplomats, and other travelers moved easily throughout the Islamic world exchanging goods and introducing agricultural crops to new lands. Rapid expansion also led to encounters between Islam and long-established religious and cultural traditions, Persian literature and political thought, and classical Greek philosophy and science. Muslim rulers built a society that made a place for those of different faiths, and Muslim thinkers readily adapted earlier traditions to their own needs. As a result of its expansion, its extensive trade and communications networks, and its engagement with other religious and cultural traditions, the *dar al-Islam* became one of the most prosperous and cosmopolitan societies of the postclassical world.

STUDY TERMS

Abbasid dynasty (206)
Abu-Bakr (204)
al-Andalus (209)
Allah (199)
bedouin (200)
caliph (204)
dar al-Islam (200)
Five Pillars of Islam (202)
hadith (201)
hajj (199)
Harun al-Rashid (206)
hijra (202)
Ibn Rushd (214)
Islam (199–200)
jihad (202)
jizya (206)
Ka'ba (201)
madrasas (211)
Mecca (199–202)
Medina (201–202)
Muhammad (200)
Muslim (199)
qadis (206, 210)
Quran (201)
sakk (209)
sharia (202)
Shia (205)
Sufis (211)
Sunni (205)
ulama (206, 210)
Umayyad dynasty (205)
umma (202)

FOR FURTHER READING

Muhammad Manazir Ahsan. *Social Life under the Abbasids.* New York, 1979. Draws on a wide range of sources in discussing dress, food, drink, housing, and daily life during the Abbasid era.

Jonathan P. Berkey. *The Formation of Islam: Religion and Society in the Near East, 600–1800.* Cambridge, 2003. Views the development of Islamic society in the context of relations between Muslims, Jews, and Christians.

John Esposito. *Islam: The Straight Path.* 3rd ed. New York, 2005. The best brief introduction to Islam.

Richard C. Foltz. *Spirituality in the Land of the Noble: How Iran Shaped the World's Religions.* Oxford, 2004. Includes an accessible discussion of Persian influences on the Islamic faith.

Ira M. Lapidus. *A History of Islamic Societies.* Cambridge, 1988. Authoritative survey of Islamic history, concentrating on social and cultural issues.

Ilse Lichtenstadter. *Introduction to Classical Arabic Literature.* New York, 1974. A brief overview, accompanied by an extensive selection of texts in English translation.

M. Lombard. *The Golden Age of Islam.* Princeton, 2004. Concentrates on the social and economic history of the Abbasid period.

Al Qur'an: A Contemporary Translation. Trans. by Ahmed Ali. Princeton, 1984. A sensitive translation of the holy book of Islam.

Francis Robinson, ed. *The Cambridge Illustrated History of the Islamic World.* Cambridge, 1996. An excellent and lavishly illustrated introduction to Islam and the Muslim world.

Michael Wolfe, ed. *One Thousand Roads to Mecca: Ten Centuries of Travelers Writing about the Muslim Pilgrimage.* New York, 1997. Presents selections from twenty-three accounts describing travelers' hajj experiences.

The Resurgence of Empire in East Asia

CHAPTER 12

Panels from the twelfth century Qingming scroll, depicting cosmopolitan life in the city of Kaifeng during the Northern Song dynasty.

EYEWITNESS:
Xuanzang: A Young Monk Hits the Road

Early in the seventh century C.E., the emperor of China issued an order forbidding his subjects to travel beyond Chinese borders into central Asia. In 629, however, a young Buddhist monk slipped past imperial watchtowers under cover of darkness and made his way west. His name was Xuanzang, and his destination was India, homeland of Buddhism. As a young man, Xuanzang had followed his older brother into a monastery, where he became devoted to Buddhism. While studying the Sanskrit language, Xuanzang noticed that Chinese writings on Buddhism contained many teachings that were confusing or even contradictory to those of Indian Buddhist texts. He decided to travel to India, visit the holy sites of Buddhism, and study with the most knowledgeable Buddhist teachers and sages to learn about his faith from the purest sources.

Xuanzang could not have imagined the difficulties he would face. Immediately after his departure from China, his guide abandoned him in the Gobi desert. After losing his water bag and collapsing in the heat, Xuanzang made his way to the oasis town of Turpan on the silk roads. The Buddhist ruler of Turpan provided the devout pilgrim with travel supplies and rich gifts to support his mission. Among the presents were twenty-four letters of introduction to rulers of lands on the way to India (each one attached to a bolt of silk), thirty horses, twenty-five laborers, and five hundred bolts of silk, along with gold, silver, and silk clothes for Xuanzang to use as travel funds. After departing from Turpan, Xuanzang crossed three of the world's highest mountain ranges—the Tian Shan, Hindu Kush, and Pamir ranges—and lost one-third of his party to exposure and starvation in the Tian Shan.

Yet Xuanzang persisted and arrived in India in 630. He lived there for more than twelve years, devoting himself to the study of languages and Buddhist doctrine, especially at Nalanda, the center of advanced Buddhist education in India. He also amassed a huge collection of relics and images as well as some 657 books, all of which he transported back to China to advance the understanding of Buddhism in his native land.

By the time of his return in 645, Xuanzang had logged more than 16,000 kilometers (10,000 miles) on the road. News of the holy monk's efforts had reached the imperial court, and even though Xuanzang had violated the ban on travel, he received a hero's welcome and an audience with the emperor. Until his death in 664, Xuanzang translated Buddhist treatises into Chinese and promoted his faith. His efforts helped to popularize Buddhism and bring about nearly universal adoption of the faith throughout China.

Xuanzang undertook his journey at a propitious time. For more than 350 years after the fall of the Han dynasty, war, invasion, conquest, and foreign rule disrupted Chinese society. Toward the end of the sixth century, however,

Xuanzang (SHWEN-ZAHNG)
Buddhism (BOO-diz'm)
Sanskrit (SAHN-skriht)
Tian Shan (tyahn shahn)

CHRONOLOGY

centralized imperial rule returned to China. The Sui and Tang dynasties restored order and presided over an era of rapid economic growth in China, especially in the areas of agricultural yields and technological innovations. As a result, China stood alongside the Byzantine and Abbasid empires as a political and economic anchor of the postclassical world.

For China the postclassical era was an age of intense interaction with other peoples. Chinese merchants participated in trade networks that linked most regions of the eastern hemisphere. Buddhism spread beyond its homeland of India and attracted a large popular following in China. A resurgent China also made its influence felt throughout east Asia, especially in Korea, Vietnam, and Japan. Although these lands retained their distinctiveness, each drew deep inspiration from China and participated in a larger east Asian society centered on China.

THE RESTORATION OF CENTRALIZED IMPERIAL RULE IN CHINA

For several centuries following the Han dynasty, none of the remaining regional kingdoms was able to assert lasting authority over all of China. In the late sixth century, however, Yang Jian, an ambitious ruler in northern China, embarked on a series of military campaigns that brought all of China once again under centralized imperial rule. Yang Jian's Sui dynasty survived less than thirty years, but the tradition of centralized rule outlived his house. The Tang dynasty replaced the Sui, and the Song succeeded the Tang. The Tang and Song dynasties organized Chinese society so efficiently that China became a center of exceptional agricultural and industrial production, creating an economy so powerful that it affected much of the eastern hemisphere.

The Sui Dynasty

Establishment of the Sui Dynasty Like Qin Shihuangdi some eight centuries earlier, Yang Jian imposed tight political discipline on his own state and then extended his rule to the rest of China. Yang Jian began his rise to power when a Turkish ruler appointed him duke of Sui in northern China. In 580 Yang Jian's patron died, and one year later he claimed both the throne and the Mandate of Heaven for himself. During the next decade Yang Jian sent military expeditions into central Asia and southern China. By 589 the house of Sui ruled all of China.

Like the rulers of the Qin dynasty, the emperors of the Sui dynasty (589–618 C.E.) built a strong, centralized government, but only at great human and financial cost. Indeed, the Sui emperors ordered construction projects, repaired defensive walls, and conducted military campaigns, but did so by levying high taxes and demanding compulsory labor services from their subjects.

The Grand Canal The most elaborate project undertaken during the Sui dynasty was the construction of the Grand Canal, which was one of the world's largest waterworks projects before modern times. The second emperor, Sui Yangdi (reigned 604–618 C.E.), wanted the canal to facilitate trade between northern and southern China, particularly to make the abundant supplies of rice and other food crops from the Yangzi River valley available to residents of northern regions. Since Chinese rivers generally flow from west to east, only an artificial waterway could support such a large volume of bulky trade goods trade between north and south.

The Grand Canal was a series of artificial waterways that ultimately reached from Hangzhou in the south to the imperial capital of Chang'an in the west to a terminus near modern Beijing in the north. Sui Yangdi used canals dug as early as the Zhou dynasty, but he linked them into a network that served much of China. When completed,

Yang Jian (yahng jyahn)
Sui Yangdi (sway yahng-dee)

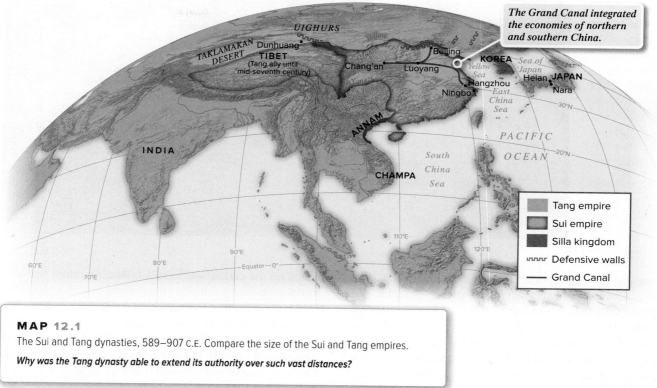

> *The Grand Canal integrated the economies of northern and southern China.*

MAP 12.1

The Sui and Tang dynasties, 589–907 C.E. Compare the size of the Sui and Tang empires.

Why was the Tang dynasty able to extend its authority over such vast distances?

the Grand Canal extended almost 2,000 kilometers (1,240 miles) and reportedly was forty paces wide, with roads running parallel to it on either side.

Though expensive to construct, Sui Yangdi's investment in the Grand Canal paid enormous dividends for the future. It integrated the economies of northern and southern China, thereby establishing an economic foundation for political and cultural unity. Until the arrival of railroads in the twentieth century, the Grand Canal served as the principal conduit for internal trade. Indeed, the canal continues to function even today.

Sui Yangdi's construction projects served China well for a long time, but their dependence on high taxes and forced labor generated hostility toward his rule. The Grand Canal alone required the services of conscripted laborers by the millions. In the late 610s, discontented subjects began to revolt against Sui rule. In 618 a disgruntled minister assassinated the emperor and brought the dynasty to an end.

The Tang Dynasty

Soon after Sui Yangdi's death, a rebel leader seized Chang'an and proclaimed himself emperor of a new dynasty that he named Tang after his hereditary title. The dynasty survived for almost three hundred years (618–907 C.E.), and Tang rulers organized China into a powerful, productive, and prosperous society.

Tang Taizong Much of the Tang success was due to the energy, ability, and policies of the dynasty's second emperor, Tang Taizong (reigned 627–649 C.E.). Taizong was both ambitious and ruthless: in making his way to the imperial throne, he murdered two of his brothers and pushed his father aside. Once on the throne, however, he displayed a high sense of duty and strove conscientiously to provide an effective, stable government. He built a splendid capital at Chang'an, and he saw himself as a Confucian ruler who heeded the interests of his subjects. Contemporaries reported that banditry ended during his reign, that the price of rice remained low, and that taxes levied on peasants amounted to only one-fortieth of the annual harvest—a 2.5 percent tax rate. These reports suggest that China enjoyed an era of unusual stability and prosperity during the reign of Tang Taizong.

Three policies in particular help to explain the success of the early Tang dynasty: maintenance of a well-articulated transportation and communications network, distribution of land according to the principles of the equal-field system, and reliance on a bureaucracy based on merit. All three policies originated in the Sui dynasty, but Tang rulers applied them more systematically and effectively than their predecessors.

Transportation and Communications Apart from the Grand Canal, which served as the principal route for

Grand Canal. Barges make their way through a portion of the Grand Canal near the city of Wuxi in southern China.

long-distance transportation within China, Tang rulers maintained an extensive network of roads. Along the main routes, Tang officials maintained inns, postal stations, and stables. Using couriers traveling by horse, the Tang court could communicate with the most distant cities in the empire in about eight days. Even human runners provided speedy services: relay teams of some 9,600 runners supplied the Tang court at Chang'an with fresh seafood from Ningbo, more than 1,000 kilometers (620 miles) away!

The Equal-Field System The equal-field system governed the allocation of agricultural land. Its purpose was to ensure an equitable distribution of land and to avoid the concentration of landed property that had caused social problems during the Han dynasty. The system allotted land to individuals and their families according to the land's fertility and the recipients' needs. About one-fifth of the land became the hereditary possession of the recipients, and the rest remained available for redistribution when the original recipients' needs and circumstances changed.

For about a century, administrators were able to apply the principles of the equal-field system relatively consistently. By the early eighth century, however, a rapidly rising population brought pressure on the land available for distribution. Meanwhile, influential families found ways to retain land scheduled for redistribution. Furthermore, large parcels of land fell out of the system altogether when Buddhist monasteries acquired them. Nevertheless, during the first half of the Tang dynasty, the system provided a foundation for stability and prosperity in the Chinese countryside.

Bureaucracy of Merit The Tang dynasty also relied heavily on a bureaucracy based on merit. Following the example of the Han dynasty, Sui and Tang rulers recruited government officials from the ranks of candidates who had progressed through the Confucian educational system

based on the classic works of Chinese literature and philosophy. As a result, most officeholders won their posts because of intellectual ability. Members of this talented class were generally loyal to the dynasty, and they worked to preserve and strengthen the state. In fact, the Confucian educational system and the related civil service served Chinese governments so well that with modifications and an occasional interruption, they survived until the collapse of the Qing dynasty in the early twentieth century.

Military Expansion Soon after its foundation, the powerful and dynamic Tang state began to flex its military muscles. In the north, Tang forces brought Manchuria under imperial authority and forced the Silla kingdom in Korea to acknowledge the Tang emperor as overlord. To the south, Tang armies conquered the northern part of Vietnam. To the west, they extended Tang authority almost as far as the Aral Sea and brought a portion of the high plateau of Tibet under Tang control. Territorially, the Tang empire ranks among the largest in Chinese history.

Tang Foreign Relations In an effort to fashion a stable diplomatic order, the Tang emperors revived the Han dynasty's practice of the tribute system. According to Chinese political theory, China was the Middle Kingdom and had the responsibility of bringing order to subordinate lands through a system of tributary relationships. Neighboring lands and peoples would recognize Chinese emperors as their overlords, and envoys from those states would regularly deliver gifts to the court of the Middle Kingdom and perform the kowtow—a ritual prostration during which subordinates knelt before the emperor and touched their foreheads to the ground. In return, tributary states received confirmation of their authority as well as lavish gifts. Because Chinese authorities often had little real influence in these supposedly subordinate lands, there was always something of a fictional quality to the system. Nevertheless, it was extremely important because it institutionalized relations between China and neighboring lands, fostering trade and cultural exchanges as well as diplomatic contacts.

Tang Decline Under able rulers such as Taizong, the Tang dynasty flourished. During the mid–eighth century, however, the careless leadership of an emperor more interested in music and his favorite concubine brought the dynasty to a crisis. In 755 one of the dynasty's foremost military commanders, An Lushan, mounted a rebellion and captured the capital at Chang'an and the secondary capital at Luoyang. His revolt was short-lived: by 763 Tang forces had suppressed An Lushan's army and recovered their capitals. But the rebellion left the dynasty gravely weakened, because Tang commanders had to ask a nomadic Turkish people, the Uighurs, to help them win back their capitals. In return, the Uighurs demanded the right to sack Chang'an and Luoyang after the expulsion of the rebels.

The Tang imperial house never again regained control of affairs. The equal-field system deteriorated, and tax receipts dwindled. Imperial armies were unable to resist invasions of Turkish peoples in the late eighth century. During the ninth century a series of rebellions devastated the Chinese countryside. In an effort to control the rebellions, the Tang emperors granted progressively greater power and authority to regional military commanders, who gradually became the effective rulers of China. In 907 the last Tang emperor abdicated his throne, and the dynasty came to an end.

The Song Dynasty

Following the Tang collapse, warlords ruled China until the Song dynasty reimposed centralized imperial rule in the late tenth century. Though it survived for more than three centuries, the Song dynasty (960–1279 C.E.) never built a very powerful state. Song rulers mistrusted military leaders, and they placed much more emphasis on civil administration, industry, education, and the arts than on military affairs.

Song Taizu The first Song emperor, Song Taizu (reigned 960–976 C.E.), inaugurated this policy. Song Taizu began his career as a junior military officer for a powerful warlord in northern China. He had a reputation for honesty and effectiveness, and in 960 his troops proclaimed him emperor. During the next several years, he and his army subjected the warlords to their authority and consolidated Song control throughout China. He then set about organizing a centralized administration that placed military forces under tight supervision.

Uighurs (WEE-goors)

Song Taizu (sawng tahy-zoo)

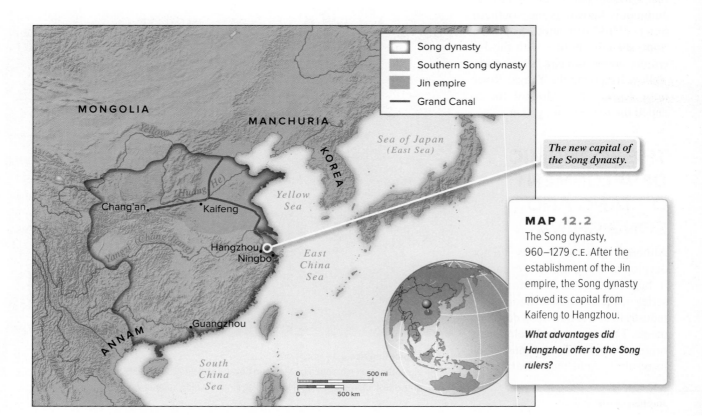

The new capital of the Song dynasty.

MAP 12.2

The Song dynasty, 960–1279 C.E. After the establishment of the Jin empire, the Song dynasty moved its capital from Kaifeng to Hangzhou.

What advantages did Hangzhou offer to the Song rulers?

Song rulers vastly expanded the bureaucracy by creating more opportunities for individuals to seek a Confucian education and take civil service examinations. They accepted many more candidates into the bureaucracy than their Sui and Tang predecessors, and they provided generous salaries for those who qualified for government appointments. They even placed civil bureaucrats in charge of military forces.

Song Weaknesses The Song approach to administration resulted in a more centralized imperial government than earlier Chinese dynasties had enjoyed, but it caused two big problems that eventually caused the dynasty to fall. The first problem was financial: as the number of bureaucrats and the size of their rewards grew, the imperial treasury came under tremendous pressure. That pressure, in turn, aggravated the peasantry, who were expected to shoulder increased taxes.

The second problem was military. Scholar bureaucrats generally had little talent for military affairs, yet they led Song armies in the field and made military decisions. It was no coincidence that nomadic peoples flourished along China's northern border throughout the Song dynasty. In the early twelfth century, the nomadic Jurchen overran northern China, captured the Song capital at Kaifeng, and proclaimed establishment of the Jin empire. Thereafter the Song dynasty moved its capital to the prosperous port city of Hangzhou and survived only in southern China, so that the latter part of the dynasty is commonly known as the Southern Song. This truncated Southern Song shared a border with the Jin empire about midway between the Yellow River and the Yangzi River until 1279, when Mongol forces ended the dynasty altogether.

THE ECONOMIC DEVELOPMENT OF TANG AND SONG CHINA

Although the Song dynasty did not develop a strong military capacity, it benefited from a remarkable series of agricultural, technological, industrial, and commercial developments. This economic development originated in the Tang dynasty, but its results became most clear during the Song, which presided over a land of enormous prosperity. The economic surge of Tang and Song times had implications that went well beyond China, since it stimulated trade and production throughout much of the eastern hemisphere for more than half a millennium, from about 600 to 1300 C.E.

Agricultural Development

Fast-Ripening Rice The foundation of economic development in Tang and Song China was a surge in agricultural production. When Sui and Tang armies ventured into Vietnam, they encountered new strains of fast-ripening rice that enabled cultivators to harvest two crops per year. Transferred to the fertile fields of southern China, fast-ripening rice quickly resulted in an expanded supply of food.

New Agricultural Techniques Chinese cultivators also increased their productivity by adopting improved agricultural techniques. They made increased use of heavy iron plows, and they harnessed oxen (in the north) and water buffaloes (in the south) to help prepare land for cultivation. They enriched the soil with manure and composted organic matter. They also organized extensive irrigation systems. Artificial irrigation made it possible to extend cultivation to new lands, including terraced mountainsides—a development that vastly expanded China's agricultural potential.

Transplanting rice.
An illustration commissioned by the Song government shows peasants how to go about the laborious task of transplanting rice seedlings into a paddy flooded with water.

Jurchen (JUHR-chehn)

Thinking about TRADITIONS

Foreign Influences on China during the Song and Tang Dynasties

During the postclassical period, traders and travelers from a wide variety of Eurasian locations came to China, bringing foreign beliefs and values with them. *Identify some of the ways the Chinese transformed these foreign influences into ideas and practices that fit into long-established traditions.*

Population Growth Increased agricultural production resulted in rapid population growth. After the fall of the Han dynasty, the population of China reached a low point of about 45 million in 600 C.E. By 1000 C.E. it had increased to 60 million. By 1127, when the Jurchen conquered the northern half of the Song state, the Chinese population had passed the 100 million mark, and by 1200 it stood at about 115 million.

Urbanization Increased food supplies encouraged the growth of cities. During the Tang dynasty the imperial capital of Chang'an was the world's most populous city with as many as two million residents. During the Song dynasty, China was the most urbanized land in the world. In the late thirteenth century, Hangzhou, capital of the Southern Song dynasty, had more than one million residents. They supported hundreds of restaurants, taverns, teahouses, brothels, music halls, theaters, clubhouses, gardens, markets, craft shops, and specialty stores dealing in silk, gems, porcelain, lacquerware, and other goods.

Another result of increased food production was the emergence of a commercialized agricultural economy. Because fast-ripening rice yielded bountiful harvests, many cultivators could purchase inexpensive rice and raise vegetables and fruits for sale on the commercial market. Cultivators specialized in crops that grew well in their own regions, and they often exported their harvests to distant regions. By the twelfth century, for example, the wealthy southern province of Fujian imported rice and devoted its land to the production of lychees, oranges, and sugarcane, which fetched high prices in northern markets.

Patriarchal Social Structures Alongside increasing wealth and agricultural productivity, Tang and especially Song China experienced a tightening of patriarchal social structures. During the Song dynasty, for example, the veneration of family ancestors became much more elaborate than before. Indeed, descendants diligently sought the graves of their earliest traceable forefathers and then arranged elaborate graveside rituals in their honor. Whole extended families often traveled great distances to attend annual rituals venerating deceased ancestors—a practice that strengthened the sense of family identity and cohesiveness.

Foot Binding Strengthened patriarchal authority also helps to explain the popularity of foot binding, which spread among privileged classes during the Song era. Foot binding involved the tight wrapping of young girls' feet with strips of cloth, which prevented natural growth and resulted in tiny, malformed, curved feet. Women with bound feet could not walk easily or naturally. Usually they needed canes to walk by themselves, and sometimes they depended on servants to carry them around in litters. Foot binding never became universal in China—it was impractical for peasants or lower-class working women in the cities—but wealthy families often bound the feet of their daughters to enhance their attractiveness, display their high social standing, and gain increased control over the girls' behavior. Like the practice of veiling women in the Islamic world, foot binding placed women of privileged classes under tight supervision of their male guardians, who then managed the women's affairs in the interests of the larger family.

Wu Zhao: The Lady Emperor Ironically, this era of strong patriarchal authority produced a rare female ruler. Wu Zhao (626–706 C.E.), also known as Wu Zetian, was the daughter of a scholar-official. At the age of thirteen, she became a concubine at the court of Tang Taizong, where she attracted notice because of her intelligence, wit, and beauty. After Taizong's death, Wu Zhao became the concubine and later the wife of his successor. In 660 the emperor suffered a debilitating stroke, and Wu Zhao seized the opportunity to direct affairs as administrator of the court. In 690 she went further and claimed the imperial title for herself.

Confucian principles held that political leadership was a man's duty and that women should obey their fathers, husbands, and sons. Thus it was not surprising that factions emerged to oppose Wu Zhao's rule. The lady emperor, however, was resourceful in garnering support. She organized a secret police force to monitor dissident factions, and she ordered brutal punishment for those who stood in her way. She strengthened the civil service system as a way of undercutting aristocratic families that might attempt to displace her. She also generously patronized Buddhists, who returned the favor by composing treatises seeking to legitimize her rule. Although Confucian scholars reviled her, Wu Zhao was an energetic and effective ruler. She quashed rebellions, organized military campaigns, and opened the imperial administration to talented commoners who rose through the civil service system. She held on to her rule until age eighty, when opponents were finally able to force her to abdicate in favor of her son. Yet the lady emperor was unique as a woman who publicly and officially wielded power in a rigidly patriarchal society. Other women exercised influence indirectly or even "ruled from behind a screen," but Wu Zhao was the only woman in Chinese history to claim the imperial title and rule as emperor.

Technological and Industrial Development

Porcelain Abundant supplies of food enabled many people to pursue technological and industrial interests. During the Tang and Song dynasties, Chinese crafts workers generated a remarkable range of technological innovations. During Tang times they discovered techniques for producing high-quality porcelain, which was lighter, thinner, and adaptable to more uses than earlier pottery. Porcelain technology gradually diffused to other societies, yet demand for Chinese porcelain remained high, and the Chinese exported vast quantities of porcelain during the Tang and Song dynasties. Indeed, Chinese porcelain graced the tables of wealthy and refined households in southeast Asia, India, Persia, and the port cities of east Africa. Tang and Song products gained such a reputation that fine porcelain has come to be known generally as *chinaware.*

Metallurgy Tang and Song craftsmen also improved metallurgical technologies, which resulted in a surge of iron and steel production. Chinese craftsmen discovered that they could use coke instead of coal in their furnaces and produce stronger and more useful grades of metal. Between the early ninth and the early twelfth centuries, iron production increased almost tenfold, according to official records. Most of the increased supply of iron and steel went into weaponry and agricultural tools: during the early Song dynasty, imperial armaments manufacturers produced 16.5 million iron arrowheads per year. As in the case of porcelain technology, metallurgical techniques soon diffused to lands beyond China. Indeed, Song military difficulties stemmed partly from the fact that nomadic peoples quickly learned Chinese techniques and fashioned their own iron weapons for use in campaigns against them.

Gunpowder Tang and Song craftsmen also invented entirely new products, tools, and techniques, most notably gunpowder, printing, and naval technologies. During the Tang dynasty, Daoist alchemists seeking elixirs to prolong life soon learned that it was unwise to mix charcoal, saltpeter, sulphur, and arsenic because of the volatility of the resulting compound. Military officials, however, recognized opportunity in the explosive mixture. By the mid–tenth century they were using gunpowder in bamboo "fire lances," a kind of flamethrower, and by the eleventh century they had fashioned primitive bombs.

Chinese naval technology.
A detail from a Song-era painting on silk depicts two sturdy, broadbottomed junks, the workhorses of the Chinese merchant fleet.

The earliest gunpowder weapons had limited military effectiveness. Over time, however, refinements enhanced their capabilities. Knowledge of gunpowder chemistry quickly diffused through Eurasia, and by the late thirteenth century peoples of southwest Asia and Europe were experimenting with metal-barreled cannons.

Printing The precise origins of printing are obscure. It is clear, however, that it became common during the Tang era. The earliest printers employed block-printing techniques: they carved a reverse image of an entire page into a wooden block, inked the block, and then pressed a sheet of paper on top. By the mid–eleventh century, printers had also begun to experiment with reusable, movable type: instead of carving images into blocks, they fashioned dies in the shape of ideographs, arranged them in a frame, inked them, and pressed the frame over paper sheets. Printing made it possible to produce texts quickly, cheaply, and in huge quantities. By the late ninth century, printed copies of Buddhist texts, Confucian works, calendars, agricultural treatises, and popular works were abundant, particularly in southwestern China (modern Sichuan province).

Naval Technology Chinese inventiveness extended also to naval technology. Before Tang times, Chinese mariners did not venture very far from land, relying instead on foreign ships for long-distance maritime trade. During the Tang dynasty, however, Chinese consumers developed a taste for the spices and exotic products of southeast Asian islands, and Chinese mariners increasingly visited those

lands in their own ships. By the time of the Song dynasty, Chinese seafarers sailed ships fastened with iron nails, waterproofed with oils, furnished with watertight bulkheads, driven by canvas and bamboo sails, steered by rudders, and navigated with the aid of the "south-pointing needle"—the magnetic compass. Chinese ships mostly plied the waters between Japan and the Malay peninsula, but some of them called at ports in India, Ceylon, Persia, and east Africa. These long-distance travels helped to diffuse elements of Chinese naval technology, particularly the compass, which soon became the common property of mariners throughout the Indian Ocean basin.

The Emergence of a Market Economy

Increased agricultural production, improved transportation systems, population growth, urbanization, and industrial production combined to stimulate the Chinese economy. China's various regions increasingly specialized in the cultivation of particular food crops or the production of particular manufactured goods. To be sure, the government played an important role in the Chinese economy by regulating the distribution of staple foods and the production of militarily sensitive enterprises such as the iron industry. Nevertheless, millions of cultivators produced fruits and vegetables for sale on the open market, and manufacturers of silk, porcelain, and other goods supplied both domestic and foreign markets. The Chinese economy became more tightly integrated than ever before, and foreign demand for Chinese products fueled rapid economic expansion.

Financial Instruments In fact, trade grew so rapidly during Tang and Song times that China experienced a shortage of the copper coins that served as money for most transactions. To alleviate the shortage, letters of credit came into common use during the early Tang dynasty. Later developments included the use of promissory notes, checks, and even paper money. Indeed, wealthy merchants pioneered the use of printed paper money in the late ninth century. In return for cash deposits from their clients, they issued printed notes that the clients could redeem for merchandise. In a society short of cash, these notes greatly facilitated commercial transactions. Yet they also caused disorder, and sometimes even riots, in the event that merchants were not able to honor their notes.

In the eleventh century, in an effort to forestall such disorder, the Chinese government stepped in and assumed the sole right to issue paper money. The first government-issued paper money appeared in 1024 in Sichuan province, and by the end of the eleventh century it existed throughout imperial China. In spite of continuing problems with paper currency—including counterfeit notes and lapses of

Song era money.
An example of the world's oldest paper money, known as Jiaozi, first printed during the Southern Song dynasty.

What economic conditions during the Southern Song demanded the introduction of paper money?

public confidence in the government's ability to honor its own notes—printed paper money provided a powerful stimulus to the Chinese economy under the Song.

A Cosmopolitan Society Trade and urbanization transformed Tang and Song China into a prosperous, cosmopolitan society. Trade came to China both by land and by sea. Muslim merchants from the Abbasid empire and central Asia—and even subjects of the Byzantine empire—helped to revive the silk roads network and flocked to large Chinese trading centers. Residents of large Chinese cities such as Chang'an and Luoyang became quite accustomed to merchants from foreign lands. Indeed, musicians and dancers from Persia became popular entertainers in the cities of the Tang dynasty. Meanwhile, Arab, Persian, Indian, and Malay mariners arriving by way of the Indian Ocean and South China Sea established sizable merchant communities in the bustling southern Chinese port cities of Guangzhou and Quanzhou.

Guangzhou (gwahng-joh)
Quanzhou (chwahn-joh)

SourcesfromthePast

The Arab Merchant Suleiman on Business Practices in Tang China

The Arab merchant Suleiman made several commercial ventures by ship to India and China during the early ninth century C.E. In 851 an Arab geographer wrote an account of Suleiman's travels, describing India and China for Muslim readers in southwest Asia. His report throws particularly interesting light on the economic conditions and business practices of Tang China.

Young and old Chinese all wear silk clothes in both winter and summer, but silk of the best quality is reserved for the kings. . . . During the winter, the men wear two, three, four, five pairs of pants, and even more, according to their means. This practice has the goal of protecting the lower body from the high humidity of the land, which they fear. During the summer, they wear a single shirt of silk or some similar material. They do not wear turbans. . . .

In China, commercial transactions are carried out with the aid of copper coins. The Chinese royal treasury is identical to that of other kings, but only the king of China has a treasury that uses copper coins as a standard. These copper coins serve as the money of the land. The Chinese have gold, silver, fine pearls, fancy silk textiles, raw silk, and all this in large quantities, but they are considered commodities, and only copper coins serve as money.

Imports into China include ivory, incense, copper ingots, shells of sea turtles, and rhinoceros horn, with which the Chinese make ornaments. . . .

The Chinese conduct commercial transactions and business affairs with equity. When someone lends money to another person, he writes up a note documenting the loan. The borrower writes up another note on which he affixes an imprint of his index finger and middle finger together. Then they put the two notes together, roll them up, and write a formula at the point where one touches the other [so that part of the written formula appears on each note]. Next, they separate the notes and entrust to the lender the one on which the borrower recognizes his debt. If the borrower denies his debt later on, they say to him, "Present the note that the lender gave to you." If the borrower maintains that he has no such note from the lender, and denies that he ever agreed to the note with his fingerprints on it, and if the lender's note has disappeared, they say to him, "Declare in writing that you have not contracted this debt, but if later the lender brings forth proof that you have contracted this debt that you deny, you will receive twenty blows of the cane on the back and you will be ordered to pay a penalty of twenty million copper coins." This sum is equal to about 2,000 dinars [gold coins used in the Abbasid empire]. Twenty blows of the cane brings on death. Thus no one in China dares to make such a declaration for fear of losing at the same time both life and fortune. We have seen no one who has agreed when invited to make such a declaration. The Chinese are thus equitable to each other. No one in China is treated unjustly.

For Further Reflection

■ In what ways might Chinese policies have encouraged business and trade during the Tang dynasty?

Source: Jean Sauvaget, ed. *Relation de la Chine et de l'Inde.* Paris, 1948, pp. 10–11, 15–16, 19–20. (Translated into English by Jerry H. Bentley.)

China and the Hemispheric Economy Indeed, high productivity and trade brought the Tang and Song economy a dynamism that China's borders could not restrain. Chinese consumers developed a taste for exotic goods, which stimulated trade throughout much of the eastern hemisphere. Spices from the islands of southeast Asia made their way to China, along with products as diverse as kingfisher feathers and tortoise shell from Vietnam, pearls and incense from India, and horses and melons from central Asia. In exchange for such exotic items, Chinese sent abroad vast quantities of silk, porcelain, and lacquerware. In central Asia, southeast Asia, India, Persia, and the port cities of east Africa, wealthy merchants and rulers wore Chinese silk and set their tables with Chinese porcelain. China's economic surge during the Tang and Song dynasties thus promoted trade and economic growth throughout much of the eastern hemisphere.

CULTURAL CHANGE IN TANG AND SONG CHINA

Interactions with peoples of other societies encouraged cultural change in postclassical China. The Confucian and Daoist traditions did not disappear, but they made way for a foreign religion—Mahayana Buddhism—and they developed along new lines that reflected the conditions of Tang and Song society.

The Establishment of Buddhism

Foreign Religions in China Buddhist merchants traveling the ancient silk roads visited China as early as the second century B.C.E. During the Han dynasty their faith attracted little interest: Confucianism, Daoism, and cults that honored family ancestors were the most popular cultural alternatives. During the unsettled centuries following the fall of the Han, however, several foreign religions—including Nestorian Christianity, Manichaeism, Zoroastrianism, and Islam—established communities in China. Yet these

Confucianism (kuhn-FYEW-shuhn-iz'm)
Daoism (dow-iz'm)
Manichaeism (mahn-ih-kee-iz'm)

Reverberations of ● ● ● ● ● ● ● ●

The Spread of Religious Traditions

Although Buddhism had spread into China along the Silk Roads by the fourth century C.E., it only began to attract large numbers of Chinese converts during the Tang dynasty. As we have seen, one of the reasons Buddhism became so influential in China was that Buddhist monks sought to accommodate the tenets of Buddhism to Chinese society and culture. As a result, the Buddhism that developed in China during the postclassical period was very much a hybrid. Consider the long-term effects of this amalgamation of traditions for both the development of the Buddhist religion as well as for Chinese society. Given that Buddhism became less and less important in its region of origin (India), did the Chinese expression of Buddhism permanently alter the religion? Additionally, in what ways did the importation of Buddhist ideas—such as the focus on metaphysical themes and logic—influence Chinese culture and politics?

religions of salvation mostly served the needs of foreign merchants trading in China and converts from nomadic societies and did not win a large popular following.

Dunhuang Mahayana Buddhism was different in that it gradually found a popular following in Tang and Song China. Buddhism came to China over the silk roads via the oasis cities of central Asia, and by the fourth century C.E., a sizable Buddhist community had emerged at Dunhuang in western China (modern Gansu province). Between about 600 and 1000 C.E., Buddhists built hundreds of cave temples in the vicinity of Dunhuang and decorated them with murals depicting events in the lives of the Buddha and the boddhisattvas. They also assembled libraries of religious literature and operated scriptoria to produce Buddhist texts. Missions supported by establishments such as those at Dunhuang helped Buddhism to establish a foothold in China.

Buddhism in China Buddhism attracted Chinese interest partly because of its high standards of morality, its intellectual sophistication, and its promise of salvation. Yet practical concerns also help to account for its appeal. Buddhist monastic communities in China accumulated sizable estates donated by wealthy converts, and they commonly stored a portion of their harvests for

Cosmopolitan society.
Foreign music and dance were very popular in the large cities of Tang China. This ceramic model depicts a troupe of musicians from southwest Asia performing on a platform mounted on a camel. Many such models survive from Tang times.

distribution among local residents during hard times. As a result, Buddhist monasteries became important elements in the local economies of Chinese communities.

Buddhism and Daoism In some ways Buddhism posed a challenge to Chinese cultural and social traditions. Buddhist theologians typically placed great emphasis on written texts and used them to explore elaborate investigations into metaphysical themes such as the nature of the soul. Among Chinese intellectuals, however, only the Confucians placed equal emphasis on written texts, and they devoted their energies mostly to practical rather than metaphysical issues. Meanwhile, Daoists had limited interest in written texts of any kind. Buddhist morality also called for individuals to observe an ascetic ideal by following a celibate, monastic lifestyle. In contrast, Chinese morality centered on the family unit and strongly encouraged procreation so that generations of offspring would be available to venerate family ancestors. Some Chinese held that Buddhist monasteries were economically harmful, because they paid no taxes, whereas others scorned Buddhism because of its foreign origins.

Because of these differences and concerns, Buddhist missionaries sought to tailor their message to Chinese audiences. They explained Buddhist concepts in vocabulary borrowed from Chinese cultural traditions, particularly Daoism. They translated the Indian term *dharma* (the basic Buddhist doctrine) as *dao* ("the way" in the Daoist sense of the term), and they translated the Indian term *nirvana* (personal salvation that comes after an individual soul escapes from the cycle of incarnation) as *wuwei* (the Daoist ethic of noncompetition). While encouraging the establishment of monasteries and the observance of celibacy, they also recognized the validity of family life and offered Buddhism as a religion that would benefit the extended Chinese family: one son in the monastery, they taught, would bring salvation for ten generations of his kin.

nirvana (nuhr-VAH-nuh)
wuwei (woo-WAY)

Chan Buddhism The result was a syncretic faith, a Buddhism with Chinese characteristics. One of the more popular schools of Buddhism in China, for example, was the Chan (also known by its Japanese name, Zen). Chan Buddhists had little interest in written texts but, instead, emphasized sudden flashes of insight in their search for spiritual enlightenment. In that respect they resembled Daoists as much as they did Buddhists.

During the Tang and Song dynasties, this syncretic Buddhism became an immensely popular and influential faith in China. Monasteries appeared in all the major cities, and stupas dotted the Chinese landscape. The monk Xuanzang (602–664) was only one of many devout pilgrims who traveled to India to visit holy sites and learn about Buddhism in its homeland. Like Xuanzang, many of those pilgrims returned with copies of treatises that deepened the understanding of Buddhism in China. In the process, they played significant roles in establishing Buddhism as a popular faith in China.

Hostility to Buddhism In spite of its popularity, Buddhism met determined resistance from Daoists and Confucians. Daoists resented the popular following of Buddhism, which resulted in diminished resources available for their own tradition. Confucians despised Buddhists' exaltation of celibacy, and they denounced the faith as an alien superstition.

Persecution During the late Tang dynasty, Daoist and Confucian critics of Buddhism found allies in the imperial court. Beginning in the 840s the Tang emperors ordered the closure of monasteries and the expulsion of Buddhists as well as Zoroastrians, Nestorian Christians, and Manichaeans. Yet Tang rulers did not implement the policy in a thorough way, and foreign faiths were not eradicated. Buddhism in particular enjoyed continued support that enabled it not only to survive but also to influence the development of Confucianism during the Song dynasty.

Neo-Confucianism

The Song emperors did not persecute Buddhists, but they actively supported native Chinese cultural traditions in hopes of limiting the influence of foreign religions. They contributed particularly generously to the Confucian tradition by sponsoring the studies of Confucian scholars and subsidizing the printing and dissemination of Confucian writings.

Confucians and Buddhism Yet the Confucian tradition of the Song dynasty differed from that of earlier times. The earliest Confucians had concentrated resolutely on practical issues of politics and morality, since they were mainly concerned with establishing social order. Confucians of the Song dynasty studied the classic works of their tradition, but they also were inspired by many aspects of Buddhist thought. Indeed, Buddhism both offered a tradition of logical thought and argumentation and dealt with issues not systematically explored by Confucian thinkers, such as the nature of the soul. Because Confucian thought during the Song dynasty reflected the influence of Buddhism as well as original Confucian values, it has come to be known as neo-Confucianism.

Neo-Confucian Influence Neo-Confucianism ranks as an important cultural development for two reasons. First, it illustrates the deep influence of Buddhism in Chinese society. Even though the neo-Confucians rejected Buddhism as a faith, their writings adapted Buddhist themes and reasoning to Confucian interests and values. Second, neo-Confucianism influenced east Asian thought over a very long term. In China, neo-Confucianism enjoyed the status of an officially recognized creed from the Song dynasty until the early twentieth century, and in lands that fell within China's cultural orbit—particularly Korea, Vietnam, and Japan—neo-Confucianism shaped philosophical, political, and moral thought for half a millennium and more.

DEVELOPMENT OF COMPLEX SOCIETIES IN KOREA, VIETNAM, AND JAPAN

Like societies in Byzantium and the *dar al-Islam,* Chinese society influenced the development of neighboring lands during postclassical times. Chinese armies periodically invaded Korea and Vietnam, and Chinese merchants established commercial relations with Japan as well as with Korea and Vietnam. Chinese techniques of government and administration helped shape public life in all three lands, as did Chinese values and cultural traditions. By no means did these lands become absorbed into China: all maintained distinctive identities. Yet they also drew deep inspiration from Chinese examples and built societies that reflected their participation in a larger east Asian society revolving around China.

Korea and Vietnam

During the Tang dynasty, Chinese imperial armies followed in the footsteps of the Qin and Han dynasties by mounting large-scale campaigns of expansion in both Korea and Vietnam. Although the two lands responded differently to Chinese imperial expansion, both borrowed Chinese political and cultural traditions and used them in their own societies.

Chan Buddhism (CHAHN BOO-diz'm)
neo-Confucianism (nee-oh-kuhn-FYEW-shuhn-iz'm)

Thinking about ENCOUNTERS

Chinese Influence in East and Southeast Asia

The postclassical period in China was a time of intense cultural interaction with societies throughout Asia and beyond. *In what ways did this interaction influence the long-term development of other east Asian societies in Korea, Vietnam, and Japan?*

The Silla Dynasty In the seventh century, Tang armies conquered much of Korea before the native Silla dynasty rallied. Both Tang and Silla authorities preferred to avoid a long and costly conflict, so they agreed to a political compromise: Chinese forces withdrew from Korea, and the Silla king recognized the Tang emperor as his overlord.

Thus Korea entered into a tributary relationship with China. Envoys of the Silla kings regularly delivered gifts to Chinese emperors and performed the kowtow, but those concessions brought considerable benefits to the Koreans. In return for their recognition of Chinese supremacy, they received gifts more valuable than the tribute they delivered to China. Moreover, the tributary relationship opened the doors for Korean merchants to trade, and for students to study, in China.

Chinese Influence in Korea Meanwhile, the tributary relationship facilitated the spread of Chinese political and cultural influences to Korea. Korean rulers began to model their court along Chinese lines, and the Silla kings even built a new capital at Kumsong modeled on the Tang capital at Chang'an. Korean scholars went to China to study Chinese thought and literature and took copies of Chinese writings back to Korea. Their efforts helped to build elite Korean interest in the Confucian tradition, and Chinese schools of Buddhism attracted widespread popular interest.

China and Korea differed in many respects. Most notably, perhaps, aristocrats and royal houses dominated Korean society much more than in China. Although the Korean monarchy sponsored Chinese schools and a Confucian examination system, Korea never established a bureaucracy based on merit, and political initiative remained firmly in the hands of the ruling classes. Nevertheless, extensive dealings with its powerful neighbor ensured that Korea reflected the influence of Chinese political and cultural traditions.

China and Vietnam Chinese relations with Vietnam were far more tense than their relations with Korea. When Tang armies ventured into the land that Chinese called Nam Viet, they encountered spirited resistance on the part of the Viet people, who had settled in the region around the Red River. Tang forces soon won control of Viet towns and cities, and they launched efforts to absorb the Viets into Chinese society. The Viets readily adopted Chinese agricultural methods and irrigation systems as well as Chinese schools and administrative techniques. Like their Korean counterparts, Viet elites studied Confucian texts and took examinations based on a Chinese-style education, and Viet traders marketed their wares in China. Vietnamese authorities even entered into tributary relationships with the Chinese court. Yet the Viets resented Chinese efforts to dominate them, and they mounted a series of revolts against Tang authorities. As the Tang dynasty fell during the early tenth century, the Viets won their independence and successfully resisted later Chinese efforts at imperial expansion to the south.

Like Korea, Vietnam differed from China in many ways. Although Buddhism won a large popular following, many Vietnamese retained their indigenous religions in preference to Chinese cultural traditions. Women played a much more prominent role in Vietnamese society and economy than did their Chinese counterparts. Southeast Asian women had dominated local and regional markets for centuries, and they participated actively in business ventures closed to women in the more rigidly patriarchal society of China. Nevertheless, Chinese traditions found a place in the southern land. Indeed, like Korea, Vietnam absorbed political and cultural influence from China and reflected the development of a larger east Asian society centered on China.

Vietnamese dancer.
This Tang dynasty pottery figure is testament to the fact that commercial and tributary relationships introduced southeast Asian performers to China.

Why might sophisticated urban communities in China have appreciated this kind of entertainment?

Early Japan

Chinese armies never invaded Japan, but Chinese traditions deeply influenced early Japanese political and cultural development. The earliest inhabitants of Japan were nomadic peoples from northeast Asia. They migrated to Japan, perhaps across land bridges that formed during an ice age, about two hundred thousand years ago. Their language, material culture, and religion derived from their parent society in northeast Asia. Later migrants, who arrived in several waves from the Korean peninsula, introduced cultivation of rice, bronze and iron metallurgy, and horses into Japan. As the population of the Japanese islands grew and built a settled agricultural society, small states dominated by aristocratic clans emerged. By the middle of the first millennium C.E., several dozen states ruled small regions.

Nara Japan The establishment of the powerful Sui and Tang dynasties in China had repercussions in Japan, where they suggested the value of centralized imperial government. One of the aristocratic clans in Japan insisted on its precedence over the others, although in fact it had never wielded effective authority outside its own territory in central Japan. Nevertheless, inspired by the Tang example, this clan claimed imperial authority and introduced a series of reforms designed to centralize Japanese politics. The imperial house established a court modeled on that of the Tang, instituted a Chinese-style bureaucracy, implemented an equal-field system, provided official support for Confucianism and Buddhism, and in the year 710 moved to a new capital city at Nara (near modern Kyoto) that was a replica of the Tang capital at Chang'an. Never was Chinese influence more prominent in Japan than during the Nara period (710–794 C.E.).

Yet Japan did not lose its distinctive characteristics. While adopting Confucian and Buddhist traditions from China, for example, the Japanese continued to observe the rites of Shinto, their indigenous religion, which revolved around the veneration of ancestors and a host of nature spirits and deities. Japanese society reflected the influence of Chinese traditions but still developed along its own lines.

Heian Japan The experiences of the Heian, Kamakura, and Muromachi periods clearly illustrate the distinctiveness of Japanese society. In 794 the emperor of Japan transferred his court from Nara to a newly constructed capital at nearby Heian (modern Kyoto). During the next four centuries, Heian became the seat of a refined and sophisticated society that drew inspiration from China but also elaborated distinctively Japanese political and cultural traditions.

Under the Heian (794–1185 C.E.), local rulers on the island of Honshu mostly recognized the emperor as Japan's supreme political authority. Unlike their Chinese counterparts, however, Japanese emperors rarely ruled but, rather, served as ceremonial figureheads and symbols of authority.

Shinto (SHIHN-toh)
Heian (HAY-ahn)

Effective power lay in the hands of the Fujiwara family, an aristocratic clan that controlled affairs from behind the throne through its influence over the imperial house and manipulation of its members. Indeed, since the Heian period the Japanese political order has almost continuously featured a split between a publicly recognized imperial authority and a separate agent of effective rule. This pattern helps to account for the remarkable longevity of the Japanese imperial house: because emperors have not ruled, they have not been subject to deposition during times of turmoil.

The cultural development of Heian Japan also reflected both the influence of Chinese traditions and the elaboration of peculiarly Japanese ways. Most literature imitated Chinese models and indeed was written in the Chinese language. Boys and young men who received a formal education in Heian Japan learned Chinese, read the classic works of China, and wrote in the foreign tongue. Officials at court conducted business and kept records in Chinese, and literary figures wrote histories and treatises in the style popular in China. Even Japanese writing reflected Chinese influence, since scholars borrowed many Chinese characters and used them to represent Japanese words. They also adapted some Chinese characters into a Japanese syllabic script, in which symbols represent whole syllables rather than a single sound, as in an alphabetic script.

The Tale of Genji Because Japanese women rarely received a formal Chinese-style education, in Heian times aristocratic women made the most notable contributions to literature in the Japanese language. Of the many literary works that have survived from that era, none reflects Heian court life better than *The Tale of Genji*. Composed by Murasaki Shikibu, a lady-in-waiting at the Heian court who wrote in Japanese syllabic script rather than Chinese characters, this sophisticated work relates the experiences of a fictitious imperial prince named Genji. Living amid gardens and palaces, Genji and his friends devoted themselves to the cultivation of an ultra-refined lifestyle, and they became adept at mixing subtle perfumes, composing splendid verses in fine calligraphic hand, and wooing sophisticated women.

The Tale of Genji also offers a meditation on the passing of time and the sorrows that time brings to sensitive human beings. As Genji and his friends age, they reflect on past joys and relationships no longer recoverable. Their thoughts suffuse *The Tale of Genji* with a melancholy spirit that presents a subtle contrast to the elegant atmosphere of their surroundings at the Heian court. Because of her limited command of Chinese, Lady Murasaki created one of the most remarkable literary works in the Japanese language.

Decline of Heian Japan In the late eleventh century, changes in the countryside brought an end to the Heian court. The equal-field system gradually fell into disuse, and aristocratic clans accumulated most of the islands' lands into vast estates. Two clans in particular—the Taira and the Minamoto—overshadowed the others. During the mid–twelfth century the two engaged in outright war, and in 1185 the Minamoto emerged victorious. Like the Fujiwara family, the Minamoto did not seek to abolish imperial authority in Japan but, rather, claimed to rule the land in the name of the emperor. They installed the clan leader as *shogun*—a military governor who ruled in place of the emperor—and established the seat of their government at Kamakura, near modern Tokyo, while the imperial court remained at Kyoto. For most of the next four centuries, one branch or another of the Minamoto clan dominated political life in Japan.

Medieval Japan

Historians refer to the Kamakura and Muromachi periods as Japan's medieval period—a middle era falling between the age of Chinese influence and court domination of political life in Japan, as represented by the Nara and Heian periods, and the modern age, inaugurated by the Tokugawa dynasty in the sixteenth century, when a centralized government unified and ruled all of Japan. During this middle era, Japanese society and culture took on increasingly distinctive characteristics.

Political Decentralization In the Kamakura (1185–1333 C.E.) and Muromachi (1336–1573 C.E.) periods, Japanese society grew ever more distinctive. Indeed,

shogun (SHOH-gun)

Samurai.
Samurai depart from a palace in Kyoto after capturing it, murdering the guards, seizing an enemy general there, and setting the structure ablaze. The armor and weaponry of the samurai bespeak the militarism of the Kamakura era.

Japan developed a decentralized political order in which provincial lords wielded effective power and authority in local regions where they controlled land and economic affairs. As these lords and their clans vied for power and authority in the countryside, they found little use for the Chinese-style bureaucracy that Nara and Heian rulers had instituted in Japan and still less use for the elaborate protocol and refined conduct that prevailed at the courts. In place of etiquette and courtesy, they valued military talent and discipline. The mounted warrior, the *samurai,* thus came to play the most distinctive role in Japanese political and military affairs.

The Samurai The samurai were professional warriors, specialists in the use of force and the arts of fighting. They served the provincial lords of Japan, who relied on

samurai (SAM-uhr-eye)

the samurai both to enforce their authority in their own territories and to extend their claims to other lands. In return for those police and military services, the lords supported the samurai from the agricultural surplus and labor services of peasants working under their jurisdiction. Freed of obligations to feed, clothe, and house themselves and their families, samurai devoted themselves to hunting, riding, archery, and martial arts.

Thus, although it had taken its original inspiration from the Tang empire in China, the Japanese political order developed along lines different from those of the Middle Kingdom. Yet Japan clearly had a place in the larger east Asian society centered on China. Japan borrowed from China, among other things, Confucian values, Buddhist religion, a system of writing, and the ideal of centralized imperial rule. Though somewhat suppressed during later periods, these elements of Chinese society not only survived in Japan but also decisively influenced Japanese development over the long term.

SUMMARY

The revival of centralized imperial rule in China had profound implications for all of east Asia and indeed for most of the eastern hemisphere. When the Sui and Tang dynasties imposed their authority throughout China, they established a powerful state that guided political affairs throughout east Asia. Tang armies extended Chinese influence to Korea, Vietnam, and central Asia. They did not invade Japan, but the impressive political organization of China prompted the islands' rulers to imitate Tang examples. Moreover, the Sui and Tang dynasties laid a strong political foundation for rapid economic development. Chinese society prospered throughout the postclassical era, partly because of technological and industrial innovation. Tang and Song prosperity touched all of China's neighbors, since it encouraged surging commerce in east Asia. Chinese silk, porcelain, and lacquerware were prized commodities among trading peoples from southeast Asia to east Africa. Chinese inventions such as paper, printing, gunpowder, and the magnetic compass found a place in societies throughout the eastern hemisphere as they diffused across the silk roads and sea-lanes. The postclassical era was an age of religious as well as commercial and technological exchanges: Nestorian Christians, Zoroastrians, Manichaeans, and Muslims all maintained communities in Tang China, and Buddhism became the most popular religious faith in all of east Asia. During the postclassical era, Chinese social organization and economic dynamism helped to sustain interactions between the peoples of the eastern hemisphere on an unprecedented scale.

STUDY TERMS

Buddhism (217)
Chan Buddhism (228)
Confucianism (226)
Daoism (226)
equal-field system (220, 230)
foot binding (223)
Grand Canal (218–219)
Guangzhou (225)
gunpowder (224)
Heian Japan (230)
Jurchen (222)
Kamakura period (230–231)
Mahayana Buddhism (226–227)
Manichaeism (226)
Muromachi period (230–231)
Nam Viet (229)
Nara period (230)
neo-Confucianism (228)
nirvana (227)
paper money (225)
porcelain (224)
Quanzhou (225)
samurai (232)
Sanskrit (217)
Shinto (230)
shogun (230)
Silla dynasty (229)
Song dynasty (221–222)
Song Taizu (221)
Sui dynasty (218)
Sui Yangdi (218)
Tang dynasty (219–221)
Tian Shan (217)
tribute system (220)
Uighurs (221)
wuwei (227)
Xuanzang (217)
Yang Jian (218)

FOR FURTHER READING

Mark Elvin. *The Pattern of the Chinese Past*. Stanford, 1973. A brilliant analysis of Chinese history, concentrating particularly on economic, social, and technological themes.

Robert Finlay. *The Pilgrim Art: The Culture of Porcelain in World History*. Berkeley, 2010. Brilliant study outlining the Chinese invention of porcelain and the product's appeal in the larger world.

Karl Friday. *Samurai, Warfare and the State in Early Medieval Japan*. New York, 2004. A lively analysis with apt comparisons to medieval Europe.

John Kieschnick. *The Impact of Buddhism on Chinese Material Culture*. Princeton, 2003. Fascinating scholarly study exploring the social effects of Buddhism in China.

Dieter Kuhn. *The Age of Confucian Rule: The Song Transformation of China*. Cambridge, Mass., 2009. Emphasizes social and economic developments.

Mark Edward Lewis. *China's Cosmopolitan Empire: The Tang Dynasty*. Cambridge, Mass., 2009. Perhaps the best single volume on Tang China.

Victor Mair, ed. *The Columbia Anthology of Traditional Chinese Literature*. New York, 1994. A comprehensive collection of the classics of Chinese literature, including the superb poetry of the Tang dynasty.

Murasaki Shikibu. *The Tale of Genji*. 2 vols. Trans. by E. Seidensticker. New York, 1976. Fresh and readable translation of Lady Murasaki's classic work.

Roderick Whitfield, Susan Whitfield, and Neville Agnew. *Mogao: Art and History on the Silk Road*. Los Angeles, 2000. Excellent brief discussion of the cave temples and archaeological remains from Dunhuang.

Sally Hovey Wriggins. *The Silk Road Journey with Xuanzang*. Boulder, 2004. A fascinating and well-illustrated account of Xuanzang's journey to India and his influence on the development of Buddhism in China.

India and the Indian Ocean Basin
CHAPTER 13

An oceangoing dhow off the coast of Zanzibar, Indian Ocean. Although this is a modern photograph, the design and sailing technique of dhows have changed little over the centuries.

EYEWITNESS:
Buzurg Sets His Sights on the Seven Seas

Buzurg ibn Shahriyar was a tenth-century shipmaster from Siraf, a prosperous and bustling port city on the Persian Gulf coast. He probably sailed frequently to Arabia and India, and he may have ventured also to Malaya, the islands of southeast Asia, China, and east Africa. Like all sailors, he heard stories about the distant lands that mariners had visited, the different customs they observed, and the adventures that befell them during their travels. About 953 C.E. he compiled 136 such stories in his *Book of the Wonders of India.*

Buzurg's collection included a generous proportion of tall tales. He told of mermaids and sea dragons, of creatures born from human fathers and fish mothers, of serpents that ate cattle and elephants, of birds so large that they crushed houses, and of a talking lizard. Yet alongside the tall tales, many of Buzurg's stories accurately reflected the conditions of his time. One recounted the story of a king from northern India who converted to Islam and requested translations of Islamic law. Others reported on Hindu customs, shipwrecks, encounters with pirates, and slave trading.

Several of Buzurg's stories tempted readers with visions of vast wealth attainable through maritime trade. For example, Buzurg mentioned a Jewish merchant who left Persia penniless and returned from India and China with a shipload of priceless merchandise. Despite their embellishments, his stories faithfully reflected the trade networks that linked the lands surrounding the Indian Ocean in the tenth century. Although Buzurg clearly thought of India as a distinct land with its own customs, he also recognized a larger world of trade and communication that extended from east Africa to southeast Asia and beyond to China.

Just as China served as the principal inspiration of a larger east Asian society in the postclassical era, India influenced the development of a larger cultural zone in south and southeast Asia. Yet China and India played different roles in their respective spheres of influence. In east Asia, China was clearly the dominant power. In south and southeast Asia, however, there emerged no centralized imperial authority like the Tang dynasty in China. Indeed, although several states organized large regional kingdoms, no single state was able to extend its authority to all parts of the Indian subcontinent, much less to the mainland and islands of southeast Asia.

Though politically disunited, during the postclassical era India remained a coherent and distinct society as a result of powerful social and cultural traditions—especially the caste system and the Hindu religion. Beginning in about the eighth century, Islam also began to attract a popular following in India, and after the eleventh century, Islam deeply influenced Indian society alongside the caste system and Hinduism.

Beyond the subcontinent Indian traditions helped to shape a larger cultural zone extending to the mainland and islands of southeast Asia. Throughout most of the region, ruling classes adopted Indian forms of political organization and Indian techniques of statecraft. Indian merchants took their Hindu and Buddhist faiths to southeast Asia, where they attracted sustained interest. Somewhat later, Indian merchants also helped introduce Islam to southeast Asia.

CHRONOLOGY

1st to 6th century	Kingdom of Funan
606–648	Reign of Harsha
670–1025	Kingdom of Srivijaya
711	Conquest of Sind by Umayyad forces
850–1267	Chola kingdom
889–1431	Kingdom of Angkor
1001–1027	Raids on India by Mahmud of Ghazni
11th to 12th century	Life of Ramanuja
12th century	Beginning of the bhakti movement
1206–1526	Sultanate of Delhi
1336–1565	Kingdom of Vijayanagar

While Indian traditions influenced the political and cultural development of southeast Asia, the entire Indian Ocean basin began to move toward economic integration during the postclassical era, as Buzurg ibn Shahriyar's stories suggest. Indeed, innovations in maritime technology, the development of a well-articulated network of sea-lanes, and the building of port cities enabled peoples living around the Indian Ocean to trade and communicate more actively than ever before. As a result, peoples from east Africa to southeast Asia and China increasingly participated in the larger economic, commercial, and cultural life of the Indian Ocean basin.

ISLAMIC AND HINDU KINGDOMS

Like the Han and Roman empires, the Gupta dynasty came under severe pressure from nomadic invaders. From the mid–fourth to the mid–fifth century C.E., Gupta rulers resisted the pressures and preserved order throughout much of the Indian subcontinent. Beginning in 451 C.E., however, White Huns from central Asia invaded India, and by the mid–sixth century the Gupta state had collapsed. Effective political authority quickly devolved to invaders and independent regional power brokers. From the end of the Gupta dynasty until the sixteenth century, when a Turkic-Mongol people known as the Mughals extended their authority to most of the subcontinent, India remained a politically divided land.

The Quest for Centralized Imperial Rule

Northern and southern India followed different political trajectories after the fall of the Gupta empire. In the north, local states contested for power and territory, and politics were turbulent and frequently violent. Nomadic Turkic-speaking peoples from central Asia contributed to this unsettled state of affairs by forcing their way into India. They eventually found niches for themselves in the caste system and became completely absorbed into Indian society. However, until processes of social absorption worked themselves out, the arrival of nomadic peoples caused additional disruption in northern India.

Harsha Even after the collapse of the Gupta dynasty, the ideal of centralized imperial rule did not entirely disappear. During the first half of the seventh century, King Harsha (reigned 606–648 C.E.) temporarily restored unified rule in most of northern India and sought to revive imperial authority. Using a massive military force from his kingdom in the lower Ganges valley, by about 612 Harsha had subdued those who refused to recognize his authority.

Collapse of Harsha's Kingdom Yet even though Harsha was young, energetic, and an able ruler, he was unable to restore permanent centralized rule. Local rulers had established their authority too securely in India's regions for Harsha to overcome them. Ultimately, he fell victim to an assassin and left no heir to maintain his realm. His empire immediately disintegrated, and local rulers once again turned northern India into a contested region as they sought to enlarge their realms at the expense of their neighbors.

The Introduction of Islam to Northern India

The Conquest of Sind Amid nomadic incursions and contests for power, northern India also experienced the arrival of Islam and the establishment of Islamic states. Islam reached India by several routes. One was military: Arab forces entered India as early as the mid–seventh century, although their first expeditions were exploratory ventures rather than campaigns of conquest. In 711, however, a well-organized expedition conquered Sind, the Indus River valley in northwestern India, and incorporated it as a province of the expanding Umayyad empire. At midcentury, along with most of the rest of the *dar al-Islam,* Sind passed into the hands of the Abbasid caliphs. Although political elites eventually took advantage of their distance from the centers of Islamic power to reassert their control over most of Sind, the region remained nominally under the jurisdiction of the caliphs until the collapse of the Abbasid dynasty in 1258.

MAP 13.1

Major states of postclassical India, 600–1600 C.E. Several large rivers and river valleys offered opportunities for inhabitants of northern India.

How did peoples of southern India organize flourishing states and societies in the absence of major rivers?

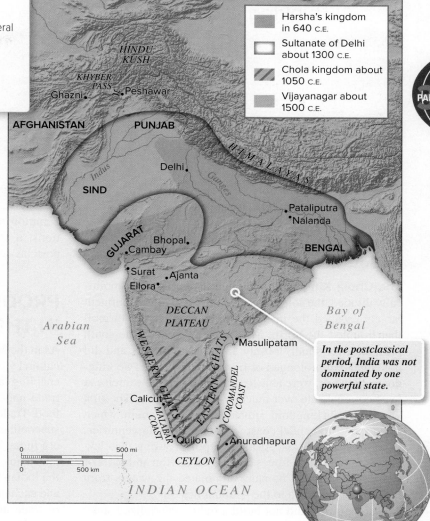

Harsha's kingdom in 640 C.E.

Sultanate of Delhi about 1300 C.E.

Chola kingdom about 1050 C.E.

Vijayanagar about 1500 C.E.

In the postclassical period, India was not dominated by one powerful state.

Merchants and Islam While conquerors brought Islam to Sind, Muslim merchants took their faith to coastal regions in both northern and southern India. Indeed, Muslims dominated trade and transportation networks between India and western lands from the seventh through the fifteenth century. Muslim merchants formed small communities in all the major cities of coastal India, where they played a prominent role in Indian business and commercial life. They frequently married local women, and in many cases they also found places for themselves in Indian society. Thus Islam entered India's port cities in a more gradual but no less effective way than was the case in Sind.

Turkic Migrants and Islam Islam also entered India by a third route: the migrations and invasions of Turkic-speaking peoples from central Asia. During the tenth century, several Turkic groups had become acquainted with Islam through their dealings with the Abbasid caliphate and had converted to the faith. Some of these Muslim Turks moved into Afghanistan, where they established an Islamic state.

Mahmud of Ghazni Mahmud of Ghazni, leader of the Turks in Afghanistan, soon turned his attention to the rich land to the south. Between 1001 and 1027 he mounted seventeen raiding expeditions into India. Taking advantage of infighting between local rulers, he annexed several states in northwestern India and the Punjab. For the most part, however, Mahmud had less interest in conquering India than in plundering the wealth stored in its many temples. Not surprisingly, then, Mahmud's raids did not encourage Indians to turn to Islam.

The Sultanate of Delhi During the late twelfth century, Mahmud's successors mounted a more systematic campaign to conquer northern India and place it under Islamic rule. By the early thirteenth century, they had conquered most of the Hindu kingdoms in northern India and established an Islamic state known as the sultanate of Delhi.

The sultans established their capital at Delhi, a strategic site controlling access from the Punjab to the Ganges valley, and they ruled northern India at least in name for more than three centuries, from 1206 to 1526.

During the fourteenth century the sultans of Delhi commanded an army of three hundred thousand, and their state ranked among the most powerful in the Islamic world. Yet for the most part, the authority of the sultans did not extend far beyond Delhi. They had no permanent bureaucracy or administrative apparatus. Even in their immediate domain, they imposed a thin veneer of Islamic political and military authority on a land populated mostly by Hindus, and they depended on the goodwill of Hindu kings to carry out their policies and advance their interests in local regions. They did not even enjoy comfortable control of their own court: of the thirty-five sultans of Delhi, nineteen were killed by assassins. Nevertheless, the sultans prominently

Mahmud of Ghazni (mah-muhd of gahz-nee)

sponsored Islam and helped to establish a secure place for their faith in the cultural landscape of India.

The Hindu Kingdoms of Southern India

The Chola Kingdom Although it too remained politically divided, the southern part of the Indian subcontinent largely escaped the invasions, chronic war, and turmoil that troubled the north. Most Hindu rulers in the south presided over small, loosely administered states and did not engage in prolonged or frequent conflicts. Two kingdoms, however, were able to expand enough to exercise at least nominal rule over much of southern India. The first was the Chola kingdom, situated in the deep south, which ruled the Coromandel coast for more than four centuries, from 850 to 1267 C.E. At its high point, during the eleventh century, Chola forces conquered Ceylon and parts of southeast Asia, and its navy dominated the waters from the South China Sea to the Arabian Sea.

Chola rulers did not build a tightly centralized state: they allowed considerable autonomy for local and village institutions as long as they maintained order and delivered tax revenues on time. By the twelfth century, however, revolts reduced the size and power of the Chola state, and it reverted to the status of one regional kingdom among many others in southern India.

The Kingdom of Vijayanagar The second state that dominated much of southern India was the kingdom of Vijayanagar, based in the Deccan. The kingdom owed its origin to efforts by the sultans of Delhi to extend their authority to southern India. Officials in Delhi dispatched two brothers, Harihara and Bukka, to represent the sultan and implement court policies in the south. Although they had converted from their native Hinduism to Islam, Harihara and Bukka recognized an opportunity to establish themselves as independent rulers. In 1336 they renounced Islam and proclaimed the establishment of an independent empire of

Vijayanagar (meaning "city of victory"). Indeed, the Hindu kingdom of Vijayanagar was the dominant state in southern India from the mid–fourteenth century until 1565, when it fell to Mughal conquerors from the north.

As in northern India, then, political division and conflict between states in southern India characterized its political history in postclassical times. India did not generate the sort of large-scale, centralized, imperial state that guided the fortunes of postclassical societies in the eastern Mediterranean, southwest Asia, or China. Nevertheless, on the basis of trade, common social structures, and inherited cultural traditions, a coherent and distinctive society flourished in postclassical India.

PRODUCTION AND TRADE IN THE INDIAN OCEAN BASIN

As in the Mediterranean, southwest Asia, and China, agricultural yields increased significantly in postclassical India, enabling large numbers of people to devote themselves to trade and manufacturing rather than the production of food. Trade forged links between the various regions of the subcontinent and fostered economic development in southern India. Trade also created links between India and distant lands, as merchants and manufacturers transformed the Indian Ocean basin into a vast zone of communication and exchange. Yet even though the increasing prominence of trade and industry brought change to Indian society, caste identities and loyalties also remained strong, and the caste system continued to serve as the most powerful organizing feature of Indian society.

Agriculture in the Monsoon World

Monsoons Because of the rhythms of the monsoons, irrigation was essential for the maintenance of a large, densely populated, agricultural society. During the spring and summer, warm, moisture-laden winds from the southwest bring most of India's rainfall. During the autumn and winter, cool and very dry winds blow from the northeast. To achieve their agricultural potential, Indian lands required a good watering by the southern monsoon, supplemented by irrigation during the dry months. Light rain during the spring and summer months or short supplies of water for irrigation commonly led to drought, reduced harvests, and widespread famine.

Irrigation Systems In northern India, large rivers and plentiful surface water provided abundant opportunities to build irrigation systems. Indeed, irrigation had been a fixture of

---

Coromandel (kawr-uh-MAN-dul)
Vijayanagar (vih-juh-yuh-NUH-guhr)

Lodi Gardens.
Lodi Gardens near Delhi is the cemetery of the Lodi sultans, the last dynasty to rule the sultanate of Delhi. Here a tomb reflects the introduction of Islamic architecture into India.

the countryside in northern India since Harappan times. For the most part, however, southern India is an arid land without rivers that can serve as sources for large-scale irrigation. Thus, as southern India became more densely populated, irrigation systems became crucial. Dams, reservoirs, canals, wells, and tunnels appeared in large numbers. Particularly impressive were monumental reservoirs lined with brick or stone that captured the rains of the spring and summer months and held them until the dry season, when canals carried them to thirsty fields. Projects of this size required enormous investments of human energy, both for their original construction and for continuing maintenance, but they led to significant increases in agricultural productivity.

Population Growth As a result of this increased productivity, India's population grew steadily throughout the postclassical era. In 600 C.E., shortly after the fall of the Gupta dynasty, the subcontinent's population stood at about 53 million. By 1000 it had grown 45 percent, to 79 million. Although the rate of growth slowed over the next 500 years, the population of the subcontinent nevertheless reached 105 million by 1500.

Urbanization This demographic surge encouraged the concentration of people in cities. During the fourteenth century, the high point of the sultanate of Delhi, the capital city had a population of about four hundred thousand, which made it second only to Cairo among Muslim cities. Many other cities—particularly ports and trading centers such as Cambay, Surat, Calicut, Quilon, and Masulipatam—had populations well over one hundred thousand.

Trade and the Economic Development of Southern India

Political fragmentation of the subcontinent did not prevent robust trade between the different states and regions of India. As the population grew, opportunities for specialized work became more numerous. Increased trade was a natural result of this process.

Surat (soo-RAHT)
Quilon (kee-yawn)
Masulipatam (mahsu-lih-pah-tahm)

Temple at Ellora.
During the eighth century C.E., workers carved a massive temple out of sheer rock at Ellora in central India. Temple communities like the one that grew up at Ellora controlled enormous resources in postclassical India.

Why did these temple communities control so many resources?

Internal Trade Most regions of the Indian subcontinent were self-sufficient in staple foods such as rice, wheat, barley, and millet. The case was different, however, with metals, salt, and specialized crops that grew well only in certain regions. Iron came mostly from the Ganges River valley near Bengal, copper mostly from the Deccan Plateau, salt mostly from coastal regions, and pepper from southern India. These and other commodities sometimes traveled long distances to consumers in remote parts of the subcontinent.

Southern India and Ceylon benefited especially handsomely from this trade. As invasions and conflicts disrupted northern India, southern regions experienced rapid economic development. The Chola kingdom provided relative stability in the south, and Chola expansion in southeast Asia opened markets for Indian merchants and producers.

Temples and Society The Chola rulers allowed considerable autonomy to their subjects, and the towns and villages of southern India largely organized their own affairs. Public life revolved around Hindu temples, which organized agricultural activities, coordinated work on irrigation systems, and maintained reserves of surplus production for use in times of need. Temples often possessed large tracts of agricultural land, and they sometimes employed hundreds of people. To meet their financial obligations to employees, temple administrators collected a portion of the agricultural yield from lands subject to temple authority.

Administrators were also responsible for keeping order in their communities and delivering tax receipts to the Cholas and other political authorities. In addition, temple authorities served as bankers, made loans, and invested in commercial and business ventures. They also frequently cooperated with the leaders of merchant guilds in seeking commercial opportunities to exploit. Temples thus grew prosperous and became crucial to the economic health of southern India.

Cross-Cultural Trade in the Indian Ocean Basin

Indian prosperity sprang partly from the productivity of Indian society, but it depended also on the vast wealth that circulated in the commercial world of the Indian

SourcesfromthePast

Cosmas Indicopleustes on Trade in Southern India

Cosmas Indicopleustes was a Christian monk from Egypt who lived during the sixth century C.E. and traveled widely throughout north Africa and southwest Asia. On one of his trips, he ventured as far as India and Ceylon, which he described at some length in a work titled The Christian Topography. *Cosmas's account clearly shows that sixth-century India and Ceylon played prominent roles in the larger economy of the Indian Ocean basin.*

Ceylon lies on the other side of the pepper country [southern India]. Around it are numerous small islands all having fresh water and coconut trees. They nearly all have deep water close up to their shores. . . . Ceylon is a great market for the people in those parts. The island also has a church of Persian Christians who have settled there, and a priest who is appointed from Persia, and a deacon and a complete ecclesiastical ritual. But the natives and their kings are heathens. . . .

Since the island of Ceylon is in a central position, it is much frequented by ships from all parts of India and from Persia and Ethiopia, and it likewise sends out many of its own. And from the remotest countries—I mean China and other trading places—it receives silk, aloes, cloves, sandalwood, and other products, and these again are passed on to markets on this side, such as Male [the western coast of southern India], where pepper grows, and to Calliana [a port city near modern Bombay], which exports copper and sesame logs and cloth for making dresses, for it also is a great place of business.

And also to Sind [Gujarat], where musk and castor and spice are procured, and to Persia and the Homerite country [Anatolia], and to Adule [in Ethiopia]. And this island [Ceylon] receives imports from all these markets that we have mentioned and passes them on to the remoter ports, while at the same time exporting its own produce in both directions. . . .

The kings of various places in India keep elephants. . . . They may have six hundred each, or five hundred, some more, some fewer. Now the king of Ceylon gives a good price both for the elephants and for the horses that he has. The elephants he pays for by the cubit [a unit of measurement equivalent to about half a meter or twenty inches]. For the height is measured from the ground, and the price is reckoned at so many gold coins for each cubit—fifty [coins] it may be, or a hundred, or even more. Horses they bring to him from Persia, and he buys them, exempting the importers of them from paying custom duties. The kings of the Indian subcontinent tame their elephants, which are caught wild, and employ them in war.

For Further Reflection

■ Why did Ceylon become such an important location for Indian Ocean trade?

Source: Cosmas Indicopleustes. *The Christian Topography of Cosmas, an Egyptian Monk.* Trans. by J. W. McCrindle. London: Hakluyt Society, 1897, pp. 364–72. (Translation slightly modified.)

Ocean basin. Trade in the Indian Ocean was not new in postclassical times: Indian merchants had already ventured to southeast Asia during the classical era, and they dealt regularly with mariners from the Roman empire who traveled to India in search of pepper. During the postclassical era, however, larger ships and improved commercial organization supported a dramatic surge in the volume and value of trade in the Indian Ocean basin.

As larger, more stable ships came into use, mariners increasingly entrusted their crafts and cargoes to the reasonably predictable monsoons and sailed directly across the Arabian Sea and the Bay of Bengal. In the age of sail, however, it was impossible to make a round trip across the entire Indian Ocean without spending months at distant ports waiting for the winds to change, so merchants usually conducted their trade in stages.

Emporia Because India stood in the middle of the Indian Ocean basin, it was a natural site for emporia and warehouses. Merchants coming from east Africa or Persia exchanged their cargoes at Cambay, Calicut, or Quilon for goods to take back west with the winter monsoon. Mariners

from China or southeast Asia called at Indian ports and traded their cargoes for goods to ship east with the summer monsoon. Indeed, because of their central location, Indian ports became the principal clearinghouses of trade in the Indian Ocean basin, and they became remarkably cosmopolitan centers. Hindus, Buddhists, Muslims, Jews, and others who inhabited the Indian port cities did business with counterparts from all over the eastern hemisphere.

Particularly after the establishment of the Umayyad and Abbasid dynasties in southwest Asia and the Tang and Song dynasties in China, trade in the Indian Ocean surged. Generally, Arabs and Persians dominated the carrying trade between India and points west. During the Song dynasty, Chinese junks also ventured into the western Indian Ocean and called at ports as far away as east Africa. To the east, in the Bay of Bengal and the China seas, Malay and Chinese vessels were most prominent.

Specialized Production As the volume of trade in the Indian Ocean basin increased, lands around the ocean began to engage in specialized production of commodities for the commercial market. Indian artisans, for example, built

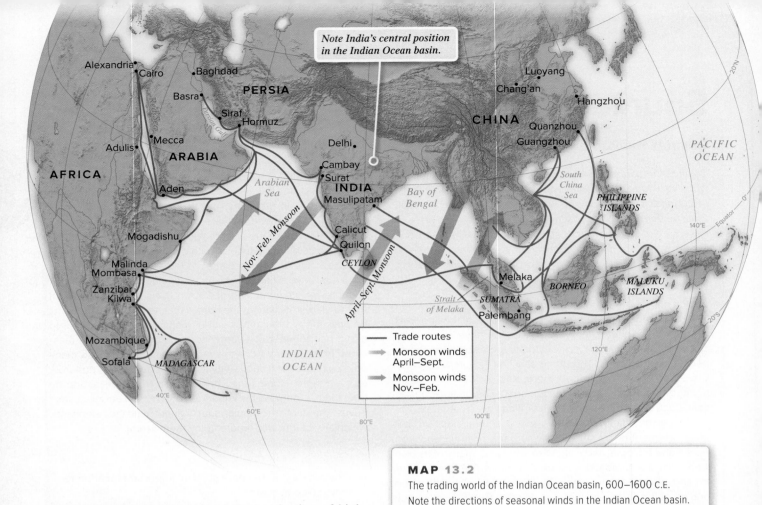

Note India's central position in the Indian Ocean basin.

MAP 13.2

The trading world of the Indian Ocean basin, 600–1600 C.E.
Note the directions of seasonal winds in the Indian Ocean basin.

How would mariners take advantage of these winds to reach their destinations?

thriving local industries around the production of high-quality cotton textiles. These industries influenced the structure of the Indian economy: they created a demand for specific agricultural products, provided a livelihood for thousands of artisans, and enabled consumers to import goods from elsewhere in the Indian Ocean basin.

Other lands concentrated on the production of different manufactured goods and agricultural commodities: China produced silk, porcelain, and lacquerware; southeast Asian lands provided fine spices; incense, horses, and dates came from southwest Asia; and east Africa contributed gold, ivory, and slaves. Thus trade encouraged specialized production and economic development in all lands participating in the trade networks of the Indian Ocean: cross-cultural trade in postclassical times influenced the structure of economies and societies throughout much of the eastern hemisphere.

Caste and Society

The political, economic, and social changes of the postclassical era brought a series of challenges for India's caste system. Migrations, the growing prominence of Islam, economic development, and urbanization all placed pressures on the caste system as it had developed during the Vedic and classical eras. But the caste system has never been a rigid, unchanging structure. Rather, individuals and groups have continuously adjusted it and adapted it to new circumstances.

Adjustments and adaptations of the postclassical era resulted in a caste system that was more complex than in earlier ages and that also extended its geographic reach deeper into southern India than ever before. In the absence of strong central governments, the caste system helped maintain order in local communities by providing guidance on individuals' roles in society and their relationships with others.

Caste and Migration The caste system closely reflected changes in Indian society. It adapted to the arrival of migrants, for example, and helped to integrate them into Indian society. As Turkic peoples or Muslim merchants pursued opportunities in India, they gained recognition as distinct groups under the umbrella of the caste system. They established codes of conduct both for the regulation of behavior within their own groups and for guidance in dealing with members of other castes. Within a few generations their descendants had become absorbed into Indian society.

Caste and Social Change The caste system also accommodated the social changes brought about by trade and economic development. Even before the postclassical era, individuals tended to identify most closely with their *jati* (subcastes), which were usually organized by occupation. In postclassical times, as merchants and manufacturers became increasingly important in the larger economy, they organized powerful workers' guilds to represent their interests. These guilds, however, were largely incorporated into the caste system as distinct *jati*. Thus merchants specializing in particular types of commerce, such as the silk, cotton, or spice trade, established themselves as subcastes, as did artisans working in particular industries, such as the iron, steel, or leather business.

Expansion of the Caste System Besides becoming more complex, the caste system also extended its geographic reach. Caste distinctions first became prominent in northern India following the Aryan migrations. During the postclassical era, the caste system became securely established in southern India as well. Economic development aided this process by encouraging commercial relationships between southern merchants and their caste-conscious counterparts in the north. The emergence of merchant and craft guilds in southern regions strengthened the caste system, since guild members usually organized as a subcaste. Powerful temples also fostered caste distinctions, largely because of the influence of caste-conscious brahmins who supervised temple activities. As a result, by about the eleventh century C.E., caste had become the principal basis of social organization in southern India.

RELIGIOUS DEVELOPMENTS IN SOUTH ASIA

The Indian cultural landscape underwent a thorough transformation during the postclassical era. Jainism and Buddhism lost much of their popular following, although neither belief completely disappeared. In their place, Hindu and Islamic traditions increasingly dominated the cultural and religious life of India after 1000 C.E.

Hinduism and Islam differed profoundly. The Hindu pantheon made places for numerous gods and spirits, for example, whereas Islamic theology stood on the foundation of a firm and uncompromising monotheism. Yet both religions attracted large popular followings throughout the subcontinent, with Hinduism predominating in southern India and Islam finding more popularity in the north than in the south.

The Increasing Popularity of Hinduism

Toward the end of the first millennium C.E., Buddhism flourished in east Asia, central Asia, and parts of southeast Asia but came under great pressure in India. Like Mahayana Buddhism, both Hinduism and Islam promised salvation to devout individuals, and they gradually attracted Buddhists to their own communities. Invasions of India by Turkic peoples also hastened the decline of Buddhism because the invaders looted and destroyed Buddhist stupas and shrines. In 1196 Muslim forces overran the Buddhist schools in the city of Nalanda, torched the libraries, and killed or exiled thousands of monks. Buddhism soon became a minor faith in the land of its birth.

Vishnu and Shiva Hinduism benefited from the decline of Buddhism. One reason for the increasing popularity of Hinduism was the remarkable growth of devotional cults, particularly those dedicated to Vishnu and Shiva, two of

> **Buddhism** (BOO-diz'm)
> **Vishnu** (VIHSH-noo)
> **Shiva** (SHIH-vuh)

Shiva.
Southern Indian artists often portrayed Shiva in bronze sculptures as a four-armed lord of dancers. In this figure from the Chola dynasty, Shiva crushes with his foot a dwarf demon symbolizing ignorance. One hand holds a bell to awaken his devotees, another bears the fire used by Shiva as creator and destroyer of the world, and a third gestures Shiva's benevolence toward his followers.

the most important deities in the Hindu pantheon. Vishnu was the preserver of the world, a god who observed the universe from the heavens and who occasionally entered the world in human form to resist evil or communicate his teachings. In contrast, Shiva was both a god of fertility and a destructive deity: he brought life but also took it away when its season had passed.

Devotional Cults Hindus embraced the new cults warmly because they promised salvation. Devotional cults became especially popular in southern India, where individuals or family groups went to great lengths to honor their chosen deities. Often cults originated when individuals identified Vishnu or Shiva with a local spirit or deity associated with a particular region or a prominent geographic feature. By venerating images of Vishnu or Shiva, offering them food and drink, and meditating on the deities and their qualities, Hindus hoped to achieve a mystic union with the gods that would bring grace and salvation.

Shankara and Ramanuja The significance of Hinduism extended well beyond popular religion: it also influenced philosophy. Just as Buddhism, Christianity, and Islam influenced moral thought and philosophy in other lands, devotional Hinduism guided the efforts of the most prominent philosophers in postclassical India. Brahmin philosophers such as Shankara and Ramanuja took the Upanishads as a point of departure for subtle reasoning and sophisticated metaphysics. Shankara, a southern Indian devotee of Shiva who was active during the early ninth century C.E., took it upon himself to digest all sacred Hindu writings and harmonize their sometimes contradictory teachings into a single, consistent system of thought. In a manner reminiscent of Plato, Shankara held that the physical world was illusion—a figment of the imagination—and that ultimate reality lay beyond the physical senses. Although he was a worshiper of Shiva, Shankara mistrusted emotional services and ceremonies, insisting that only by disciplined logical reasoning could human beings understand the ultimate reality of Brahman, the impersonal world-soul of the Upanishads. Only then could they appreciate the fundamental unity of the world, which Shankara considered a perfectly understandable expression of ultimate reality, even though to human physical senses that same world appears chaotic and incomprehensible.

Ramanuja, a devotee of Vishnu who was active during the eleventh and early twelfth centuries C.E., believed that genuine bliss came from salvation and identification of individuals with their gods. He followed the *Bhagavad Gita* in recommending intense devotion to Vishnu, and he

taught that by placing themselves in the hands of Vishnu, devotees would win the god's grace and live forever in his presence. Thus, in contrast to Shankara's consistent, intellectual system of thought, Ramanuja's philosophy pointed toward a Hindu theology of salvation. Indeed, his thought inspired the development of devotional cults throughout India, and it serves even today as a philosophical foundation for Hindu popular religion.

Islam and Its Appeal

The Islamic faith did not attract much immediate interest among Indians when it arrived in the subcontinent. It won gradual acceptance in merchant communities where foreign Muslim traders took local spouses and found a place in Indian society. Elsewhere, however, circumstances did not favor its adoption, since it often arrived with conquering peoples. Muslim conquerors generally reserved important political and military positions for their Arab, Persian, and Turkic companions. Only rarely did they allow Indians—even those who had converted to Islam—to hold sensitive posts. Because of that policy, conquerors offered little incentive for Indians to convert to Islam.

Conversion to Islam Gradually, however, many Indians converted to Islam. By 1500 C.E. Indian Muslims numbered perhaps twenty-five million—about one-quarter of the subcontinent's population. Some Indians adopted Islam in hopes of improving their positions in society: Hindus of lower castes, for example, hoped to escape discrimination by converting to a faith that recognized the equality of all believers. In fact, Hindus rarely improved their social standing by conversion. Often members of an entire caste or subcaste adopted Islam en masse, and after conversion they continued to play the same social and economic roles that they had before.

Sufis In India as elsewhere, the most effective agents of conversion to Islam were Sufi mystics. Sufis encouraged a personal, emotional, devotional approach to Islam. They did not insist on fine points of doctrine, and they sometimes even permitted their followers to observe rituals or venerate spirits not recognized by the Islamic faith. Because of their piety and sincerity, however, Sufi missionaries attracted individuals searching for a faith that could provide comfort and meaning for their personal lives. Thus, like Hinduism, Indian Islam emphasized piety and devotion. Even though Hinduism and Islam were profoundly different religions, they encouraged the cultivation of similar spiritual values that transcended the social and cultural boundary lines of postclassical India.

The Bhakti Movement In some ways the gap between Hinduism and Islam narrowed in postclassical India because

---

Bhagavad Gita (BUHG-uh-vuhd gee-tah)
Sufis (SOO-fees)

Reverberations of ● ● ● ● ● ● ● ●

The Spread of Religious Traditions

As religious traditions spread from their regions of origin during the postclassical era, the Indian subcontinent became both a region to which Islam spread from central Asia, and also a region that exported its own religion of Hinduism to many parts of southeast Asia. By the tenth century, Indian merchants were also bringing knowledge of Islam to southeast Asia. Consider the long-term effects of the meeting of Islam and Hinduism in India. What were the effects of the popularity of these two religions on Jainism and Buddhism, which had also developed in India? Consider also the long-term effects of the Indianization of southeast Asia through the spread of both Hinduism and Islam. How did Indianization influence social organization, cultural expression, and political life in southeast Asia?

Asian peoples adapted Indian political structures and religions to local needs and interests. Although Indian armed forces rarely ventured into the region, southeast Asian lands reflected the influence of Indian society, as merchants introduced Hinduism, Buddhism, Sanskrit writings, and Indian forms of political organization. Beginning about the twelfth century, Islam also found solid footing in southeast Asia, as Muslim merchants, many of them Indians, established trading communities in the important port cities of the region. Over the next five hundred years, Islam attracted a sizable following and became a permanent feature in much of southeast Asia.

both religions drew on long-established and long-observed cultural traditions. Sufis, for example, often attracted schools of followers in the manner of Indian gurus, spiritual leaders who taught Hindu values to disciples who congregated around them. Even more important was the development of the *bhakti* movement, a cult of love and devotion that ultimately sought to erase the distinction between Hinduism and Islam. The bhakti movement emerged in southern India during the twelfth century, and it originally encouraged a traditional piety and devotion to Hindu values. As the movement spread to the north, bhakti leaders increasingly encountered Muslims and became deeply attracted to certain Islamic values, especially monotheism and the notion of spiritual equality of all believers.

Guru Kabir Eventually, however, the bhakti movement gradually rejected the exclusive features of both Hinduism and Islam. Thus guru Kabir (1440–1518), a blind weaver who was one of the most famous bhakti teachers, went so far as to teach that Shiva, Vishnu, and Allah were all manifestations of a single, universal deity, whom all devout believers could find within their own hearts. The bhakti movement did not succeed in harmonizing Hinduism and Islam. Nevertheless, like the Sufis, bhakti teachers promoted values that helped to build bridges between India's social and cultural communities.

THE INFLUENCE OF INDIAN SOCIETY IN SOUTHEAST ASIA

Just as China stood at the center of a larger east Asian society, India served as the principal source of political and cultural traditions widely observed throughout south and southeast Asia. For a millennium and more, southeast

The States of Southeast Asia

Indian Influence in Southeast Asia Indian merchants visited the islands and mainland of southeast Asia from an early date, perhaps as early as 500 B.C.E. By the early centuries C.E., they had become familiar figures throughout southeast Asia, and their presence brought opportunities for the native ruling elites of the region. In exchange for spices and exotic products, Indian merchants brought textiles, beads, gold, silver, and manufactured metal goods. Southeast Asian rulers used the profits from this trade to consolidate their political control.

Meanwhile, southeast Asian ruling elites became acquainted with Indian political and cultural traditions. Without necessarily giving up their own traditions, they borrowed Indian forms of political organization and accepted Indian religious faiths. On the model of Indian states, for example, they adopted kingship as the principal form of political authority, and they surrounded themselves with courts featuring administrators and rituals similar to those found in India.

Ruling elites also sponsored the introduction of Hinduism or Buddhism—sometimes both—into their courts. They embraced Indian literature such as the *Ramayana* and the *Mahabharata,* which promoted Hindu values, as well as treatises that explained Buddhist views of the world. At the same time, however, they did not show much enthusiasm for the Indian caste system and continued to acknowledge the deities and nature spirits that southeast Asian peoples had venerated for centuries.

Funan The first state known to have incorporated Indian influence into its own traditions was Funan, which dominated the lower reaches of the Mekong River (including

bhakti (BHUK-tee)

Thinking about ENCOUNTERS

Indianization in Southeast Asia

During the postclassical period, Indian societies became critical players in the vast trading networks that crisscrossed the Indian Ocean basin. *Why did these trading relationships encourage other societies, particularly in southeast Asia, to adopt Indian social, religious, and political structures?*

parts of modern Cambodia and Vietnam) between the first and the sixth centuries C.E. Funan grew enormously wealthy because it dominated the Isthmus of Kra, the narrow portion of the Malay peninsula where merchants transported trade goods between China and India. (The short portage enabled them to avoid a long voyage around the Malay peninsula.) The rulers of Funan used the profits from this trade to construct an elaborate irrigation system that supported a highly productive agricultural economy in the Mekong delta.

As trade with India became an increasingly important part of Funan's economy, the ruling classes adopted Indian political, cultural, and religious traditions. They took the Sanskrit term *raja* ("king") for themselves and claimed divine sanction for their rule in the manner of Hindu rulers in India. They established positions for administrators and bureaucrats such as those found at Indian courts and conducted official business in Sanskrit. They introduced Indian ceremonies and rituals and worshiped Vishnu, Shiva, and other Hindu deities. They continued to honor local deities, but they eagerly welcomed Hinduism, which offered additional recognition and divine legitimacy for their rule. At first, Indian cultural and religious traditions were most prominent and most often observed at ruling courts. Over the longer term, however, those traditions extended well beyond ruling elites and won a secure place in southeast Asian society.

Srivijaya During the sixth century C.E., a bitter power struggle weakened Funan internally, and by late century it had passed into oblivion. After the fall of Funan, political leadership in southeast Asia passed to the kingdom of Srivijaya (670–1025 C.E.) based on the island of Sumatra. The kings of Srivijaya built a powerful navy and controlled commerce in southeast Asian waters. They compelled port cities in southeast Asia to recognize their authority, and they financed their navy and bureaucracy from taxes levied on ships passing through the region. They maintained an all-sea trade route between China and India, eliminating the need for the portage of trade goods across the Isthmus of Kra. As the volume of trade with India increased in the postclassical era, the rulers of Srivijaya—like the rulers of Funan—borrowed heavily from Indian cultural traditions. Unlike their counterparts in Funan, however, the rulers of Srivijaya were most attracted to the teachings and practices associated with Buddhism. The Srivijaya kingdom prospered on the fruits of the Indian Ocean trade until the expansive Chola kingdom of southern India eclipsed it in the eleventh century. In the process, Srivijaya played an important role in facilitating cultural exchange in the Indian Ocean world.

Khwaja Khidr.

In India as in other lands, Sufi mystics were the most effective Muslim missionaries. This eighteenth-century painting depicts the Sufi Khwaja Khidr, beloved in Muslim communities throughout northern India as one associated with springtime, fertility, and happiness.

Isthmus of Kra (ihs-muhs of krah)

raja (RAH-juh)

Srivijaya (sree-vih-JUH-yuh)

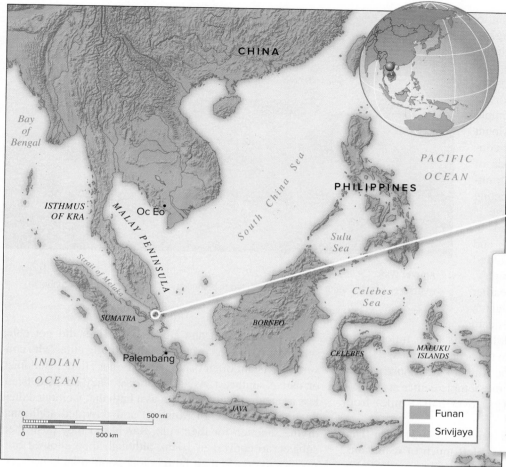

CHINA

Bay
of
Bengal

PACIFIC
OCEAN

PHILIPPINES

ISTHMUS
OF KRA

MALAY PENINSULA

Oc Eo

South China Sea

Sulu
Sea

Strait of Melaka

SUMATRA

Celebes
Sea

BORNEO

CELEBES

MALUKU
ISLANDS

INDIAN
OCEAN

Palembang

JAVA

0   500 mi
0   500 km

Funan

Srivijaya

Most postclassical southeast Asian states grew powerful as a result of their position between China and India.

MAP 13.3

Major states of southeast Asia between about 100 and 1520 C.E. Notice the strategic location of these southeast Asian states on the trade routes between China to the east and India to the west.

How might this have affected the development of states in southeast Asia?

Buddhist temple carving.
Maritime trade flourished in southeast Asia during postclassical times. This ninth-century relief carving from the Buddhist temple at Borobodur in Java depicts a typical southeast Asian ship.

With the decline of Srivijaya, the kingdoms of Angkor (889–1431 C.E.), Singosari (1222–1292 C.E.), and Majapahit (1293–1520 C.E.) dominated affairs in southeast Asia. Whereas Angkor had its base in Cambodia, Singosari and Majapahit were island states based on Java. Angkor made deep commitments to Buddhism; Majapahit was largely a Hindu state. Singosari represented a unique blend of Indian and indigenous traditions. Indeed, at the court of Singosari, religious authorities fashioned a cultural blend of Hindu, Buddhist, and indigenous values. Sculptures at the Singosari court depicted Hindu and Buddhist personalities, for example, but used them to honor local deities and natural spirits rather than Indian deities.

Angkor The magnificent monuments of Angkor testify eloquently to the influence of Indian traditions in southeast Asia. Beginning in the ninth century,

Angkor (AHN-kohr)
Singosari (sihng-oh-sah-ree)
Majapahit (mah-jah-PAH-hit)

the kings of the Khmers began to build a capital city at Angkor Thom. With the aid of brahmin advisors from India, the kings designed the city as a microcosmic reflection of the Hindu world order. At the center, they built a temple representing the Himalayan Mount Meru, which was sometimes conceived of as the sacred abode of Shiva, and surrounded it with numerous smaller temples representing other parts of the Hindu universe.

As the Khmers turned to Buddhism during the twelfth and thirteenth centuries, they added Buddhist temples to the complex, though without removing the earlier structures inspired by Hinduism. The entire complex formed a square with sides of about three kilometers (two miles), surrounded by a moat filled from the nearby Tonle Sap River. During the twelfth century the Khmer kings constructed a smaller but even more elaborate temple center at Angkor Wat, about one kilometer (just over half a mile) from Angkor Thom.

Angkor Wat.
General view of the temple complex dedicated to Vishnu at Angkor Wat in modern Cambodia.

The Khmers abandoned Angkor in 1431 after Thai peoples invaded the capital and left much of it in ruins. Soon the jungle reclaimed both Angkor Thom and Angkor Wat, which remained largely forgotten until French missionaries and explorers rediscovered the sites in the mid–nineteenth century. Today the temple complexes of Angkor stand as vivid reminders of the influence of Indian political, cultural, and religious traditions in southeast Asia.

The Arrival of Islam

Muslim merchants had ventured into southeast Asia by the eighth century, but only during the tenth century did they become prominent in the region. Some came from southern Arabia or Persia, but most were Indians from Gujarat or the port cities of southern India. Thus Indian influence helped to establish Islam as well as Hinduism and Buddhism in southeast Asia.

Conversion to Islam For several centuries Islam maintained a quiet presence in southeast Asia. Small communities of foreign merchants observed their faith in the port cities of the region but attracted little interest on the part of the native inhabitants. Gradually, however, ruling elites, traders, and others who had regular dealings with foreign Muslims became interested in the faith.

Like Hinduism and Buddhism, Islam did not enter southeast Asia as an exclusive faith. Ruling elites who converted to Islam often continued to honor Hindu, Buddhist, or native southeast Asian traditions. They adopted Islam less as an absolute creed than as a faith that facilitated their dealings with foreign Muslims and provided additional divine sanction for their rule. Rarely did they push their subjects to convert to Islam, although they allowed Sufi mystics to preach their faith before popular audiences. As in India, Sufis in southeast Asia appealed to a large public because of their reputation for sincerity and holiness. They allowed converts to retain inherited customs while adapting the message of Islam to local needs and interests.

Melaka During the fifteenth century the spread of Islam gained momentum in southeast Asia, largely because the powerful state of Melaka sponsored the faith throughout the region. Founded during the late fourteenth century by Paramesvara, a rebellious prince from Sumatra, Melaka took advantage of its strategic location in the Strait of Melaka, near modern Singapore, and soon became prominent in the trading world of southeast Asia. By the mid–fifteenth century, Melaka had built a substantial navy that patrolled the waters of southeast Asia and protected the region's sea-lanes. Melakan fleets compelled ships to call at the port, where ruling authorities levied taxes on the value of their cargoes. Thus, like southeast Asian states of earlier centuries, Melaka became a powerful state through the control of maritime trade.

In one respect, though, Melaka differed significantly from the earlier states. Although it began as a Hindu state, Melaka soon became predominantly Islamic. About the mid–fifteenth century the Melakan ruling class converted to Islam. It welcomed theologians, Sufis, and other Islamic authorities to Melaka and sponsored missionary campaigns to spread Islam throughout southeast Asia. By the end of the fifteenth century, mosques had begun to define the urban landscapes of Java, Sumatra, and the Malay peninsula, and Islam had made its first appearance in the spice-bearing islands of Maluku and in the southern islands of the Philippine archipelago.

Thus, within several centuries of its arrival, Islam was a prominent feature in the cultural landscape of southeast Asia. Along with Hinduism and Buddhism, Islam helped link southeast Asian lands to the larger cultural world of India and to the larger commercial world of the Indian Ocean basin.

SUMMARY

With respect to political organization, India differed from postclassical societies in China, southwest Asia, and the eastern Mediterranean basin: it did not experience a return of centralized imperial rule such as that provided by the Tang and Song dynasties, the Umayyad and Abbasid dynasties, and the Byzantine empire. In other respects, however, India's development was similar to that of other postclassical societies. Increased agricultural production fueled population growth and urbanization, while trade encouraged specialized industrial production and rapid economic growth. The vigorous and voluminous commerce of the Indian Ocean basin influenced the structure of economies and societies from east Asia to east Africa. It brought prosperity especially to India, which not only contributed cotton, pepper, sugar, iron, steel, and other products to the larger hemispheric economy but also served as a major clearinghouse of trade. Like contemporary societies, postclassical India experienced cultural change, and Indian traditions deeply influenced the cultural development of other lands. Hinduism and Islam emerged as the two most popular religious faiths within the subcontinent, and Indian merchants helped to establish Hinduism, Buddhism, and Islam in southeast Asian lands. Throughout the postclassical era, India participated fully in the larger hemispheric zone of cross-cultural communication and exchange.

STUDY TERMS

Angkor (247)
Angkor Thom (248)
Angkor Wat (248)
Bhagavad Gita (244)
bhakti movement (244)
Buddhism (243)
caste system (242–243)
Chola kingdom (238)
Coromandel (238)
Funan (245–246)
Gupta dynasty (236)
irrigation systems (238–240)
Isthmus of Kra (246)
jati (243)
King Harsha (236)
Mahmud of Ghazni (237)
Majapahit (247)
Masulipatam (239)
Melaka (248)
Quilon (239)
raja (246)
Ramanuja (244)
Shiva (243)
Singosari (247)
Srivijaya (246)
Sufis (244)
Sultanate of Delhi (237)
Surat (239)
Vijayanagar kingdom (238)
Vishnu (243)

FOR FURTHER READING

Al-Biruni. *Alberuni's India.* 2 vols. Trans. by E. Sachau. London, 1910. English translation of al-Biruni's eleventh-century description of Indian customs, religion, philosophy, geography, and astronomy.

K. N. Chaudhuri. *Asia before Europe: Economy and Civilisation of the Indian Ocean from the Rise of Islam to 1750.* Cambridge, 1990. Controversial and penetrating analysis of economic, social, and cultural structures shaping societies of the Indian Ocean basin.

Ainslie T. Embree and Stephen Hay, eds. *Sources of Indian Tradition.* 2 vols. 2nd ed. New York, 1988. An important collection of primary sources in English translation.

Kenneth R. Hall. *Maritime Trade and State Development in Early Southeast Asia.* Honolulu, 1985. Examines the link between long-distance trade and state building in southeast Asia.

Charles Higham. *The Civilization of Angkor.* London, 2001. Draws usefully on archaeological research in placing Angkor in historical context.

Michel Jacq-Hergoualc'h. *The Malay Peninsula: Crossroads of the Maritime Silk Road (100 B.C.–1300 A.D.).* Leiden, 2002. Scholarly study emphasizing the significance of maritime trade for southeast Asian societies.

Patricia Risso. *Merchants and Faith: Muslim Commerce and Culture in the Indian Ocean.* Boulder, 1995. Surveys the activities of Muslim merchants in the Indian Ocean basin from the seventh to the nineteenth centuries.

Tansen Sen. *Buddhism, Diplomacy, and Trade: The Realignment of Sino-Indian Relations, 600–1400.* Honolulu, 2003. A pathbreaking study exploring trade, diplomacy, and cultural exchanges between postclassical India and China.

Burton Stein. *Vijayanagara.* Cambridge, 1989. A study of the southern Hindu kingdom concentrating on political and economic history.

Romila Thapar. *Early India: From the Origins to A.D. 1300.* Berkeley, 2003. A fresh view by one of the leading scholars of early Indian history.

PART 3 THE POSTCLASSICAL ERA, 500 TO 1000 C.E.

After the collapse of classical societies in Persia, China, India, and the Mediterranean, societies in much of the eastern hemisphere were faced with the monumental tasks of restoring internal order as well as rebuilding networks of contact and exchange that had fallen into disuse. Although the ways societies accomplished these tasks varied, it is nevertheless clear that large portions of Eurasia and North Africa once again came under stable rule between 500 and 1000 C.E. As a consequence, during the postclassical era much of the eastern hemisphere both reintegrated and enhanced the trade networks that had once linked so many of the classical societies.

Religion played an important role in the maintenance of internal order in most postclassical societies, including the Byzantine empire, the Islamic world, and India. Byzantine emperors claimed divine status within the Christian Orthodox church, dramatically enhancing their authority among their subjects. In the Islamic world, the new Muslim faith provided a common language, doctrine, culture, and legal system that served to unite diverse conquered peoples in a common community of believers. In India, the caste system central to Hinduism lent cultural unity to the subcontinent even though it was not ruled by a single power. Because the caste system determined the social role of both groups and individuals, it was a critical factor in maintaining a stable society.

Once they had restored internal order, the postclassical societies reestablished and expanded the trade networks that had once linked the classical societies. This encouraged the exchange of goods, of course, but also encouraged the transfer of technologies and food items that allowed for improved agricultural practices and greater crop productivity—both of which led to population growth. As in the classical era, interaction triggered by trade was also accompanied by cultural interaction. The vast networks of roads and sea-lanes that linked postclassical societies became highways for the exchange of ideas and beliefs as well.

Of these myriad cultural interactions, the spread of religion—including Islam, Buddhism, Hinduism, and Christianity—was perhaps the most obvious and important. In fact, each of these religions spread far beyond their origins in the postclassical era. As a result of Indian Ocean trading networks, Indian merchants brought Hinduism to much of southeast Asia; Islamic traders from both India and Arabia later did the same with their faith. Meanwhile, Buddhists from India and central Asia brought their faith to China, where for a time it enjoyed immense popularity. Finally, Orthodox Christians in Byzantium introduced their faith to the peoples of eastern Europe, who adopted it as their own. As a result of these and other exchanges, the legacies of postclassical societies remain very much with us in the present day.

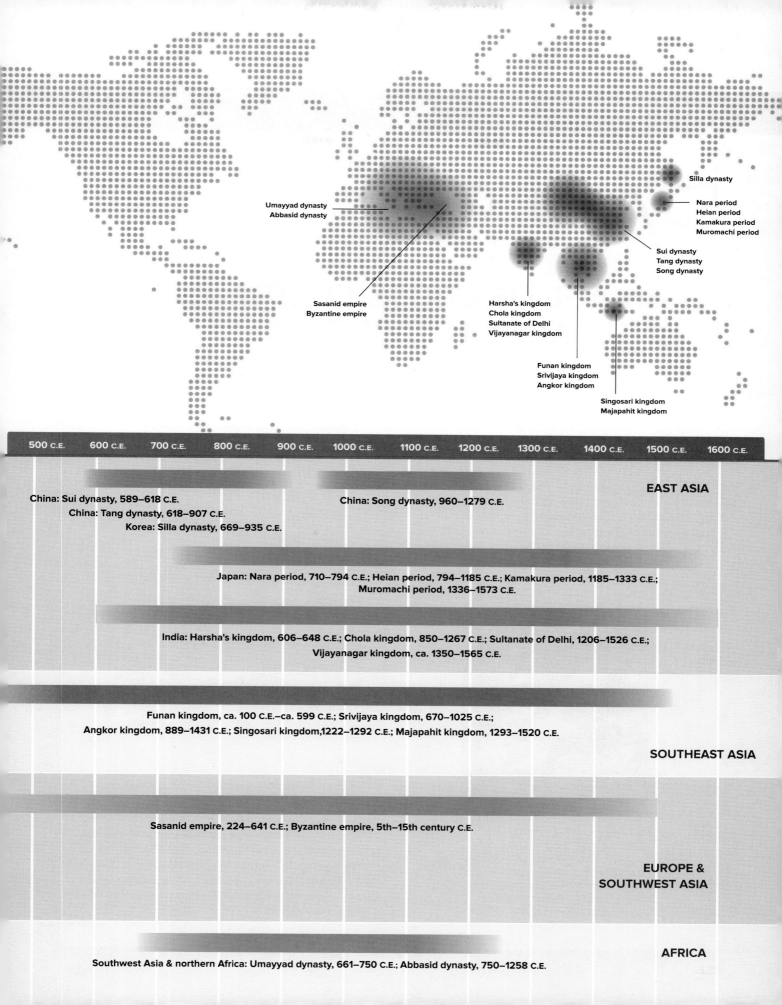

Silla dynasty

Umayyad dynasty
Abbasid dynasty

Nara period
Heian period
Kamakura period
Muromachi period

Sui dynasty
Tang dynasty
Song dynasty

Sasanid empire
Byzantine empire

Harsha's kingdom
Chola kingdom
Sultanate of Delhi
Vijayanagar kingdom

Funan kingdom
Srivijaya kingdom
Angkor kingdom

Singosari kingdom
Majapahit kingdom

500 C.E.	600 C.E.	700 C.E.	800 C.E.	900 C.E.	1000 C.E.	1100 C.E.	1200 C.E.	1300 C.E.	1400 C.E.	1500 C.E.	1600 C.E.

EAST ASIA

China: Sui dynasty, 589–618 C.E.

China: Tang dynasty, 618–907 C.E.

Korea: Silla dynasty, 669–935 C.E.

China: Song dynasty, 960–1279 C.E.

Japan: Nara period, 710–794 C.E.; Heian period, 794–1185 C.E.; Kamakura period, 1185–1333 C.E.;
Muromachi period, 1336–1573 C.E.

India: Harsha's kingdom, 606–648 C.E.; Chola kingdom, 850–1267 C.E.; Sultanate of Delhi, 1206–1526 C.E.;
Vijayanagar kingdom, ca. 1350–1565 C.E.

Funan kingdom, ca. 100 C.E.–ca. 599 C.E.; Srivijaya kingdom, 670–1025 C.E.;
Angkor kingdom, 889–1431 C.E.; Singosari kingdom,1222–1292 C.E.; Majapahit kingdom, 1293–1520 C.E.

SOUTHEAST ASIA

Sasanid empire, 224–641 C.E.; Byzantine empire, 5th–15th century C.E.

**EUROPE &
SOUTHWEST ASIA**

AFRICA

Southwest Asia & northern Africa: Umayyad dynasty, 661–750 C.E.; Abbasid dynasty, 750–1258 C.E.

PART 4

AN AGE OF CROSS-CULTURAL INTERACTION, 1000 TO 1500 C.E.

The half millennium from 1000 to 1500 C.E. differed markedly from earlier eras. During classical and postclassical times, large, regional societies situated in China, India, southwest Asia, and the Mediterranean basin dominated the eastern hemisphere. From 1000 to 1500 C.E., however, nomadic Turkish and Mongol peoples overran settled societies and established vast transregional empires from China to eastern Europe.

A thirteenth-century painting from an illustrated Persian history text depicts Mongol mounted warriors pursuing their fleeing enemies. Note the superb discipline and coordination of the Mongols, who used their superior military skills and organization to regularly defeat armies from a wide range of cultures and states.

Effects of Nomadic Invasions

Nomadic peoples toppled several postclassical states, most notably the Song empire in China and the Abbasid realm in southwest Asia. By building empires that transcended the boundaries of postclassical states, however, nomadic Turks and Mongols laid a political foundation for sharply increased trade and communication between peoples of different societies and cultural regions.

Economic Integration in the Indian Ocean Basin

Increased trade in the Indian Ocean basin also promoted more intense cross-cultural communications. Maritime trade built on the political stability, economic expansion, and demographic growth of the postclassical era. This trade indicated a movement toward economic integration as societies of the Indian Ocean basin concentrated increasingly on cultivating crops or producing goods for export while importing foods or goods that they could not produce very well themselves.

Integration of Peripheral Regions

Demographic growth, economic expansion, and increased trade were not limited to the Indian Ocean basin, China, and southwest Asia in this period. Indeed, the intensification of trade across much of Eurasia also brought relatively isolated areas like sub-Saharan Africa and western Europe into sustained cross-cultural relationships with far distant places. These relationships brought increased prosperity to both regions, which in turn encouraged political centralization and the consolidation of state power.

Centralization in the Americas and Oceania

The indigenous peoples of the Americas and Oceania also built larger and more centralized societies from 1000 to 1500 C.E., with centralized empires appearing in Mesoamerica and Andean South America and agricultural societies emerging in several regions of North America. Although Pacific islanders had limited resources with which to build empires, within their own agricultural and fishing societies they established tightly centralized kingdoms.

A handsome llama fashioned from silver sheet from Inca Peru.

Turmoil in the Eastern Hemisphere

During the fourteenth and fifteenth centuries C.E., much of the eastern hemisphere experienced difficulties not only

A bronze plaque from the kingdom of Benin depicts a local chief flanked by warriors and attendants.

because of warfare arising from the conquests of nomadic peoples but also because of epidemic bubonic plague and global climatic changes that brought cooler temperatures. Together, these problems led to political, social, and economic turmoil throughout much of the eastern hemisphere.

Linking Afro-Eurasia and the Americas

Nevertheless, by the mid–fifteenth century, peoples from China to western Europe were recovering from those difficulties and rebuilding prosperous societies. In their own quest for prosperity, western European peoples unwittingly laid the foundations of a new era in world history. While searching for sea routes to Asian markets, European mariners happened on the continents of North and South America. Their voyages brought the world's various peoples for the first time into permanent and sustained communication, and their interactions triggered a series of consequences that profoundly influenced modern world history. Yet it is important to remember that the European voyages that gave rise to this interdependent and interconnected world occurred precisely because Europeans were seeking to become more involved in the vibrant trade networks that characterized much of the eastern hemisphere in the half-millennium after 1000 C.E.

1. What were some of the positive and negative effects of the nomadic invasions that occurred after 1000 C.E.?

2. What might have been some of the long-term effects of European mariners linking Afro-Eurasia with the Americas?

Nomadic Empires and Eurasian Integration
CHAPTER 14

كورينوا براسفان دوانلد وجلدرا معرفکرد وبادشاه اسلام ازواری ابن اوازی رشنذکه تحفه بجوند من القوم الطالبین وبدان اساره فوقی هرجه نامزد برسن مبارکش طاهرکتب وجون شترعزیز میجهد و صفدلسکر می جهد و برخم سنان کهان ابشازا میانداحت ومکل برلسکرند رافرودامند وشراران کردند و بازسوار رشند و سرصران ترک تاز کردنده وارونت جاست تابسنحکل بود عاقبه الامرصران بشکسند ومتعرف کسته منهم شذند

A thirteenth-century painting from an illustrated Persian history text depicts Mongol mounted warriors pursuing their fleeing enemies. Note the superb discipline and coordination of the Mongols, who used their superior military skills and organization to regularly defeat armies from a wide range of cultures and states.

EYEWITNESS:

The Goldsmith of the Mongolian Steppe

Guillaume Boucher was a goldsmith who lived during the early and middle decades of the thirteenth century. During the 1230s, he left his native Paris and went to Budapest, which was then a part of the kingdom of Hungary. There he was captured by Mongol warriors campaigning in Hungary. The Mongols noticed and appreciated Boucher's talents, and when they left Hungary in 1242, they took him and other skilled captives to their central Asian homeland.

For at least the next fifteen years, Boucher lived at the Mongol capital at Karakorum. Though technically a slave, he enjoyed some prestige. He supervised fifty assistants in a workshop that produced decorative objects of gold and silver for the Mongol court. His most ingenious creation was a spectacular silver fountain in the form of a tree. Four pipes, concealed by the tree's trunk, carried wines and other intoxicating drinks to the top of the tree and then dispensed them into silver bowls from which guests filled their cups. Apart from his famous fountain, Boucher also produced statues in gold and silver, built carriages, designed buildings, and even sewed ritual garments for Roman Catholic priests who conducted services for Christians living at Karakorum.

Boucher was by no means the only European living at the Mongol court. His wife was a woman of French ancestry whom Boucher had met and married in Hungary. The Flemish missionary William of Rubruck visited Karakorum in 1254, and during his sojourn there he encountered men and women from France, Russia, Greece, and England. Other European visitors to the Mongol court found Germans, Slavs, and Hungarians as well as Chinese, Koreans, Turks, Persians, and Armenians, among others. Many thirteenth-century roads led to Karakorum.

Nomadic peoples had made their influence felt throughout much of Eurasia as early as classical times. The Xiongnu confederation dominated central Asia and threatened the Han dynasty in China from the third century B.C.E. to the second century C.E. During the second and third centuries C.E., the Huns and other nomadic peoples from central Asia launched migrations that helped bring down the western Roman empire, and later migrations of the White Huns destroyed the Gupta state in India. Turkish peoples ruled a large central Asian empire from the sixth through the ninth century, and the Uighur Turks even seized the capital cities of the Tang dynasty in the mid–seventh century.

Between the eleventh and fifteenth centuries, nomadic peoples became more prominent than ever before in Eurasian affairs. Turkish peoples migrated to Persia, Anatolia, and India, where they established new states. During the thirteenth and fourteenth centuries, the Mongols established themselves as the most powerful people of the central Asian steppes and then turned on settled societies in China, Persia, Russia, and eastern Europe. By the early fourteenth century, the Mongols had built the largest empire the world has ever seen, stretching from Korea and China in the east to Russia and Hungary in the west.

Most of the Mongol states collapsed during the late fourteenth and fifteenth centuries, but the decline of the Mongols did not signal the end of nomadic peoples' influence on Eurasian affairs. Although a native

---

Karakorum (kahr-uh-KOR-uhm)

CHRONOLOGY

1055	Tughril Beg named sultan
1071	Battle of Manzikert
1206–1227	Reign of Chinggis Khan
1211–1234	Mongol conquest of northern China
1219–1221	Mongol conquest of Persia
1237–1241	Mongol conquest of Russia
1258	Mongol capture of Baghdad
1264–1279	Mongol conquest of southern China
1264–1294	Reign of Khubilai Khan
1279–1368	Yuan dynasty
1295	Conversion of Ilkhan Ghazan to Islam
1336–1405	Life of Tamerlane
1453	Ottoman capture of Constantinople

Chinese dynasty replaced the Mongol state in China, the Mongols continued to threaten its central Asian frontier. Moreover, from the fourteenth through the seventeenth century, Turkish peoples embarked on new campaigns of expansion that eventually brought most of India, much of central Asia, all of Anatolia, and a good portion of eastern Europe under their domination.

The military campaigns of nomadic peoples were sometimes exceedingly destructive. Nomadic warriors demolished cities, slaughtered urban populations, and ravaged surrounding agricultural lands. Yet those same forces also encouraged systematic peaceful interaction between peoples of different societies. Between the eleventh and fifteenth centuries, the imperial campaigns of Turkish and Mongol peoples forged closer links than ever before between Eurasian lands. By fostering cross-cultural communication and exchange on an unprecedented scale, the nomadic empires integrated the lives of peoples throughout much of the eastern hemisphere.

TURKISH MIGRATIONS AND IMPERIAL EXPANSION

Turkish peoples never formed a single, homogeneous group but, rather, organized themselves into clans and tribes that often fought bitterly with one another. All Turkish peoples spoke related languages, and all were nomads or descendants of nomads. From modest beginnings they expanded their influence until they dominated not only the steppes of central Asia but also settled societies in Persia, Anatolia, and India.

Nomadic Economy and Society

Nomadic societies in central Asia developed by adapting to the ecological conditions of arid lands. Central Asia does not receive enough rain to support large-scale agriculture. Oases permit cultivation of limited regions, but for the most part only grasses and shrubs grow on the central Asian steppe lands, and there are no large rivers or other sources of water to support large-scale irrigation systems. Yet grazing animals thrive on grasses and shrubs, and the peoples of central Asia took advantage of this by herding sheep, horses, cattle, goats, and camels.

Nomadic Peoples and Their Animals Nomadic peoples drove their herds and flocks to lands with abundant grass and then moved them along as the animals thinned the vegetation. They carefully followed migratory cycles that took account of the seasons and local climatic conditions and lived mostly off the meat, milk, and hides of their animals. They used animal bones for tools and animal dung as fuel. They made shoes and clothes out of wool from their sheep and skins from their other animals. Their dwellings—large tents called *yurts*—were fashioned with felt made from the wool of their sheep. They even prepared an alcoholic drink from their animals by fermenting mare's milk into a potent concoction known as *kumiss*.

Nomadic and Settled Peoples The aridity of the climate and the nomadic lifestyle limited the development of human societies in central Asia. Intensive agriculture was impossible except in oases, and the need to regularly follow the herds made large-scale craft production impractical. As a result, nomads avidly sought opportunities to trade with settled peoples. Much of that commerce took place on a small scale as nomads sought agricultural products and manufactured goods to satisfy their immediate needs. Often, however, nomads also participated in long-distance trade networks. Because of their mobility and their familiarity with large regions of central Asia, nomadic peoples were ideally suited to organize and lead the caravans that

yurts (yuhrts)

Sources from the Past

William of Rubruck on Gender Relations among the Mongols

From 1253 to 1255, the French Franciscan missionary William of Rubruck traveled extensively in the recently established Mongol empire in hopes of converting the Mongols to Christianity. He was unsuccessful in his principal aim, but he met all the leading Mongol figures of the day, including the Great Khan Möngke. After his return to France, William composed a long account of his journey with descriptions of life on the steppes.

The married women make themselves very fine wagons. . . . One rich [Mongol] or Tartar has easily a hundred or two hundred such wagons with chests. Baatu [a prominent Mongol general and grandson of Chinggis Khan] has twenty-six wives, each of whom has a large dwelling, not counting the other, smaller ones placed behind the large one, which are chambers, as it were, where the maids live: to each of these dwellings belong a good two hundred wagons. . . .

One woman will drive twenty or thirty wagons, since the terrain is level. The ox- or camel-wagons are lashed together in sequence, and the woman will sit at the front driving the ox, which all the rest follow at the same pace. . . .

It is the women's task to drive the wagons, to load the dwellings on them and to unload again, to milk the cows, to make butter and grut [a kind of cheese], and to dress the skins and stitch them together, which they do with a thread made from sinew. They divide the sinew into tiny strands, and then twist them into a single long thread. In addition they stitch shoes, socks and other garments. They never wash clothes, for they claim that this makes God angry and that if they were hung out to dry it would thunder: in fact, they thrash anyone doing laundry and confiscate it. (They are extraordinarily afraid of thunder. In that event they turn out of their dwellings all strangers, and wrap themselves up in black felt, in which they hide until it has passed.) They never wash dishes either, but instead, when the meat is cooked, rinse the bowl in which they are to put it with boiling broth from the cauldron and then pour it back into the cauldron. In addition [the women] make the felt and cover the dwellings.

The men make bows and arrows, manufacture stirrups and bits, fashion saddles, construct the dwellings and wagons, tend the horses and milk the mares, churn the [kumiss] (that is, the mare's milk), produce the skins in which it is stored, and tend and load the camels. Both sexes tend the sheep and goats, and they are milked on some occasions by the men, on others by the women. The skins are dressed with curdled ewe's milk, thickened and salted.

For Further Reflection

■ Why did women play such prominent social and economic roles in nomadic pastoral societies?

Source: William of Rubruck. The Mission of Friar William of Rubruck. Trans. by Peter Jackson. Ed. by Peter Jackson with David Morgan. London: Hakluyt Society, 1990, pp. 74, 90–91. Reprinted by permission of David Higham Associates, Ltd.

---

crossed central Asia and linked settled societies from China to the Mediterranean basin. During the postclassical era and later, Turkish peoples were especially prominent on the caravan routes of central Asia.

Nomadic Society Nomadic society generated two social classes: elites and commoners. Charismatic leaders won recognition as elites and thereby acquired the prestige needed to organize clans and tribes into alliances. Normally, elites did little governing, since clans and tribes looked after their own affairs and resented interference. During times of war, however, elites wielded absolute authority over the forces within their alliances.

This nomadic 'nobility' was a fluid class. Leaders passed elite status along to their heirs, but the heirs could lose their status if they did not continue to provide appropriate leadership for their clans and tribes. Over the course of a few generations, elites could return to the status of commoners. Meanwhile, commoners could win recognition as elites by outstanding conduct, particularly by courageous behavior during war. Then, if they were clever diplomats, they could arrange alliances between clans and tribes and gain enough support to displace established leaders.

Nomadic Religion The earliest religion of the Turkish peoples revolved around shamans—religious specialists who possessed supernatural powers, communicated with the gods and nature spirits, and invoked divine aid on behalf of their communities. Yet many Turkish peoples became attracted to the religious and cultural traditions they encountered when trading with peoples of settled societies, and by the sixth century C.E. many Turks had converted to Buddhism, Nestorian Christianity, or Manichaeism. Partly because of their newly adopted religious traditions and partly because of their prominence in Eurasian trade networks, Turkish peoples also developed a written script.

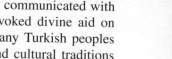

Nestorian (neh-STOHR-eeuhn)
Manichaeism (MAN-ih-kee-ism)

Nomadic life.
A painting from the late fourteenth century by the central Asian artist Mehmed Siyah Qalem suggests the physical hardships of nomadic life. In this scene from a nomadic camp, two men wash clothes (upper left), while another blows on a fire, and a companion tends to a saddle. Bows, arrows, and other weapons are readily available (top right).

Turkish Conversion to Islam   Between the tenth and the fourteenth centuries, most Turkish clans on the steppes of central Asia converted to Islam. Their conversion had great significance. When Turkish peoples began to migrate into settled societies in large numbers, they helped spread Islam to new lands, particularly Anatolia and northern India. The boundaries of the Islamic world thus expanded along with the political and military influence of Turkish peoples.

Military Organization   This expansion took place when nomadic leaders organized vast confederations of peoples under the leadership of a *khan* ("ruler"). In fact, khans rarely ruled directly, instead ruling through the leaders of allied tribes. Yet when organized on a large scale, nomadic peoples wielded enormous military power due mostly to their outstanding cavalry forces. Nomadic warriors had superior equestrian skills. Their arrows flew with deadly accuracy even when launched from the backs of galloping horses. Moreover, units of warriors coordinated their movements to outmaneuver and overwhelm their opponents. Indeed, few armies were able to resist the mobility and discipline of well-organized nomadic warriors. With

such military capabilities, several groups of Turkish nomads began in the tenth century C.E. to seize the wealth of settled societies and build imperial states in the regions surrounding central Asia.

Turkish Empires in Persia, Anatolia, and India

Saljuq Turks and the Abbasid Empire   Turkish peoples entered Persia, Anatolia, and India at different times and for different purposes. They approached Abbasid Persia much as Germanic peoples had earlier approached the Roman empire. From about the mid–eighth to the mid–tenth century, Turkish peoples lived mostly on the borders of the Abbasid realm. By the mid– to late tenth century, large numbers of Saljuq Turks served in Abbasid armies and lived in the Abbasid realm itself. By the mid–eleventh century the Saljuqs overshadowed the Abbasid caliphs so much that in 1055 the caliph recognized the Saljuq leader Tughril Beg as *sultan* ("chieftain"). Tughril first consolidated his hold on the Abbasid capital at Baghdad, then he and his successors extended Turkish rule to Syria, Palestine, and other parts of the realm. For the last two centuries of the Abbasid state, the caliphs served only as figureheads: actual governance lay in the hands of the Turkish sultans.

Abbasid (ah-BAH-sih)
Saljuqs (sahl-JYOOKS)

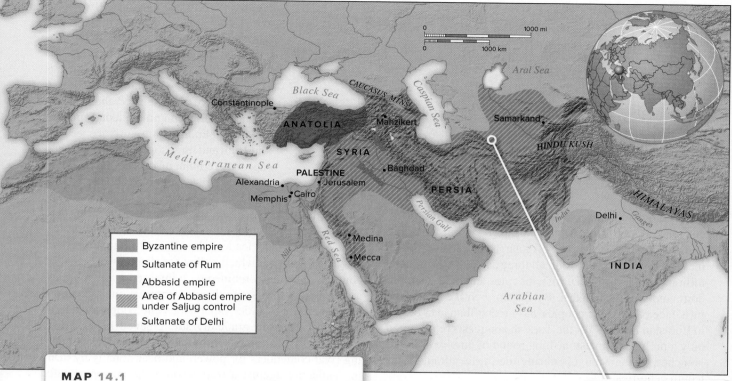

Byzantine empire

Sultanate of Rum

Abbasid empire

Area of Abbasid empire under Saljug control

Sultanate of Delhi

Homeland of Turkish peoples

MAP 14.1

Turkish empires and their neighbors, ca. 1210 C.E. After about 1000 C.E., nomadic Turkish peoples conquered and ruled settled agricultural societies in several regions of Eurasia and north Africa.

How were Turkish peoples able to venture so far from their central Asian homeland?

Saljuq Turks and the Byzantine Empire Some Saljuq Turks began to turn their attention to the rich land of Anatolia, and in the early eleventh century they began migrating there in large numbers. In 1071 Saljuq forces inflicted a devastating defeat on the Byzantine army at Manzikert in eastern Anatolia and took the Byzantine emperor captive. Following that victory Saljuqs and other Turkish groups entered Anatolia almost at will. The peasants of Anatolia, who mostly resented their Byzantine overlords, tended to look on the Saljuqs as liberators rather than as conquerors.

The migrants thoroughly transformed Anatolia. Turkish groups displaced Byzantine authorities and set up their own political and social institutions. They levied taxes on the Byzantine church, restricted its activities, and sometimes confiscated church property. Meanwhile, they welcomed converts to Islam and made political, social, and economic opportunities available to them. By 1453, when Ottoman Turks captured the Byzantine capital at Constantinople, Byzantine and Christian Anatolia had become largely a Turkish and Islamic land.

Ghaznavid Turks and the Sultanate of Delhi While the Saljuqs spearheaded Turkish migrations in Abbasid Persia and Byzantine Anatolia, in the early eleventh century Mahmud of Ghazni led the Turkish Ghaznavids of Afghanistan in raids on lucrative sites in northern India. Although their original goal was plunder, they gradually became more interested in permanent rule. They asserted their authority first over the Punjab and then over Gujarat and Bengal. By the thirteenth century the Turkish sultanate of Delhi claimed authority over all of northern India. Several of the Delhi sultans conceived plans to conquer southern India, but none was able to realize those ambitions. Indeed, the sultans faced constant challenges from Hindu princes in neighboring lands, and they periodically had to defend their northern frontiers from new Turkish or Mongol invaders. They maintained an enormous army with a large elephant corps, but those forces only enabled them to hold on to territories they already had.

Turkish rule had great social and cultural implications in India, as it did in Anatolia. Mahmud of Ghazni was a zealous foe of Buddhism and Hinduism alike, and his forces stripped Buddhist and Hindu establishments of their wealth, destroyed their buildings, and often slaughtered their residents and attendants as well. As Mahmud of Ghazni's forces repressed Buddhism and Hinduism, they encouraged conversion to Islam and enabled their faith to establish a secure presence in northern India.

Thinking about TRADITIONS

The Relationship Between Culture and the Environment

The nomadic peoples of central Asia developed particular social and cultural traditions—such as superior equestrian skills and merit-based leadership—in accordance with the ecological conditions of their arid homelands. *In what ways did these traditions aid nomadic peoples in their various quests for expansion between 1000 and 1500 C.E.?*

Though undertaken by different groups and for different reasons, the Turkish conquests of Persia, Anatolia, and India represented part of a larger expansive movement by nomadic peoples. In all three cases the formidable military prowess of Turkish peoples enabled them to dominate settled societies. By the thirteenth century, the influence of nomadic peoples was greater than ever before in Eurasian history. Yet the Turkish conquests represented only a prelude to an astonishing round of empire building launched by the Mongols during the thirteenth and fourteenth centuries.

THE MONGOL EMPIRES

For most of their history the nomadic Mongols lived on the high steppe lands of eastern central Asia. Like other nomadic peoples, they displayed deep loyalty to kin groups organized into families, clans, and tribes. They frequently allied with Turkish peoples who built empires on the steppes, but they rarely played a leading role in the organization of states before the thirteenth century. Strong loyalties to kinship groups made it difficult for the Mongols to organize a stable society on a large scale. During the early thirteenth century, however, Chinggis Khan (sometimes spelled "Genghis Khan") forged the various Mongol tribes into a powerful alliance that built the largest empire the world has ever seen. Although the vast Mongol realm soon dissolved into a series of smaller empires—most of which disappeared within a century—the Mongols' imperial venture brought the societies of Eurasia into closer contact than ever before.

Chinggis Khan and the Making of the Mongol Empire

The unifier of the Mongols was Temüjin, born about 1167 into a noble family. His father was a prominent warrior who forged an alliance between several Mongol clans and

Chinggis Khan (CHIHN-gihs Kahn)
Temüjin (TEM-oo-chin)
Ulaanbaatar (OOLAHN-bah-tahr)

seemed likely to become a powerful leader. When Temüjin was about ten years old, however, rivals poisoned his father and destroyed the alliance. Abandoned by his father's allies, Temüjin led a precarious existence for some years. He lived in poverty, since rivals seized the family's animals, and several times eluded enemies seeking to eliminate him. A rival once captured him and imprisoned him in a wooden cage, but Temüjin made a daring midnight escape and regained his freedom.

Chinggis Khan's Rise to Power During the late twelfth century, Temüjin made an alliance with a prominent Mongol clan leader. He also mastered the art of steppe diplomacy, which called for displays of personal courage in battle, combined with intense loyalty to allies, a willingness to betray others to improve one's position, and the ability to entice other tribes into cooperative relationships. Temüjin gradually strengthened his position, sometimes by forging useful alliances, often by conquering rival contenders for power, and occasionally by turning suddenly against a troublesome ally. He eventually brought all the Mongol tribes into a single confederation, and in 1206 an assembly of Mongol leaders recognized Temüjin's supremacy by proclaiming him Chinggis Khan ("universal ruler").

Mongol Political Organization Chinggis Khan's policies greatly strengthened the Mongol people. Earlier nomadic state builders had ruled largely through the leaders of allied tribes. But Chinggis Khan mistrusted the Mongols' tribal organization, so he broke up the tribes and forced men of fighting age to join new military units with no tribal affiliations. He chose high military and political officials not on the basis of kinship or tribal status but because of their talents or their loyalty to him. Although he spent most of his life on horseback, Chinggis Khan also established a capital at Karakorum—present-day Har Horin, located about 300 kilometers (186 miles) west of the modern Mongolian capital of Ulaanbaatar—where he built a luxurious palace. As command center of Chinggis Khan's empire, Karakorum symbolized a source of Mongol authority superior to the clan or tribe. Chinggis Khan's policies created a Mongol state that was not only much stronger than any earlier nomadic confederation but also less troubled by conflicts between clans and tribes.

The most important institution of the Mongol state was the army, which magnified the power of the small population. In the thirteenth century the Mongol population stood at about one million people—less than 1 percent of China's numbers. During Chinggis Khan's life, his army numbered only 100,000 to 125,000 Mongols, although

Chinggis Khan.
This painting by a Chinese artist depicts Chinggis Khan at about age sixty. Though most of his conquests were behind him, Chinggis Khan's focus and determination are readily apparent in this portrait.

allied peoples also contributed forces. How was it possible for so few people to conquer the better part of Eurasia?

Mongol Arms Like earlier nomadic armies, Mongol forces relied on outstanding equestrian skills. In addition, their bows were short enough for archers to use while riding, and their arrows could fell enemies at 200 meters (656 feet). Mongol horsemen were among the most mobile forces of the premodern world, sometimes traveling more than 100 kilometers (62 miles) per day to surprise an enemy. Furthermore, the Mongols understood the psychological dimensions of warfare and used them to their advantage. If enemies surrendered without resistance, the Mongols usually spared their lives, and they provided generous treatment for artisans, crafts workers, and those with military skills. In the event of resistance, however, the Mongols ruthlessly slaughtered whole populations, sparing only a few, whom they sometimes drove before their armies as human shields during future conflicts.

Once he had united the Mongols, Chinggis Khan turned his army and his attention to other parts of central Asia, particularly to nearby settled societies. He attacked the various Turkish peoples ruling in Tibet, northern China, Persia, and the central Asian steppes. Those conquests were important because they protected him against

the possibility that other nomadic leaders might challenge his rule. But the Mongol campaigns in China and Persia had especially far-reaching consequences.

The conquest of China was important even in terms of the development of Mongol arms. Indeed, Mongol invaders learned about gunpowder from Chinese military engineers in the early thirteenth century, and soon incorporated gunpowder-based weapons into their arsenal. During the 1250s, as they campaigned in Persia and southwest Asia, the Mongols used catapults and trebuchets to lob gunpowder bombs into cities under siege. Muslim armies soon developed similar weapons in response. These weapons quickly spread to Europe in the mid–thirteenth century, and thus Mongols were critical not only for efficiently using gunpowder weapons in military campaigns, but also for diffusing a technology that forever changed the nature of warfare.

Mongol Conquest of Northern China Chinggis Khan himself extended Mongol rule to northern China, dominated since 1127 C.E. by the nomadic Jurchen people, while the Song dynasty continued to rule in southern China. In 1211 C.E. Mongol raiding parties invaded the Jurchen realm, and by 1215 the Mongols had captured the capital near modern Beijing. This city, under the new name of Khanbaliq ("city of the khan"), also served as the Mongol capital in China. By 1220 the Mongols had largely established control over northern China.

Mongol Conquest of Persia Next, Chinggis Khan led another force to Afghanistan and Persia, ruled at that time by a successor to the Saljuqs known as the Khwarazm shah. The mission was one of revenge, for in 1218 the Khwarazm shah had spurned a diplomatic envoy sent by Chinggis Khan by murdering the whole group. In response, the following year Chinggis Khan took his army west, pursued the Khwarazm shah to an island in the Caspian Sea (where he died), shattered his army, and seized control of his realm.

To ensure that the shah's state would never constitute a challenge to his own empire, Chinggis Khan wreaked destruction on the conquered land. The Mongols ravaged one city after another, demolishing buildings and massacring hundreds of thousands of people. Some cities never recovered. The Mongols also destroyed the delicate *qanat* irrigation systems that sustained agriculture in the arid region, resulting in severely reduced agricultural production. For centuries after the Mongol conquest, Persian chroniclers cursed the invaders and the devastation they visited on the land.

By the time of his death in 1227, Chinggis Khan had laid the foundation of a vast and mighty empire. He had

Jurchen (JUHR-chehn)
Song (SOHNG)
Khanbaliq (Kahn-bah-LEEK)

united the Mongols, established Mongol supremacy in central Asia, and extended Mongol control to northern China in the east and Persia in the west. But Chinggis Khan was a conqueror, not an administrator. He ruled the Mongols themselves through his control over the army, but he did not establish a central government for the lands that he conquered. Instead, he assigned Mongol overlords to supervise local administrators and to extract a generous tribute for the Mongols' own uses. Chinggis Khan's heirs continued his conquests, but they also undertook the task of designing a more permanent administration to guide the fortunes of the Mongol empire.

The Mongol Empires after Chinggis Khan

Chinggis Khan's death touched off a struggle for power among his sons and grandsons. Eventually, his heirs divided Chinggis Khan's vast realm into four regional empires. The great khans ruled China, the wealthiest of Mongol lands. Descendants of Chagatai, one of Chinggis Khan's sons, ruled the khanate of Chagatai in central Asia. Persia fell under the authority of rulers known as the ilkhans, and the khans of the Golden Horde dominated Russia. The great khans were nominally superior to the others, but they were rarely able to enforce their claims to authority. In fact, for as long as the Mongol empires survived, ambition fueled constant tension and occasional conflict among the four khans.

Khubilai Khan The consolidation of Mongol rule in China came during the reign of Khubilai (sometimes spelled Qubilai), one of Chinggis Khan's grandsons. Khubilai was perhaps the most talented of the great conqueror's descendants. He unleashed ruthless attacks against his enemies, but he also took an interest in cultural matters and worked to improve the welfare of his subjects. He actively promoted Buddhism, and he provided support also for Daoists, Muslims, and Christians in his realm. The famous Venetian traveler Marco Polo, who lived almost two decades at Khubilai's court, praised him for his generosity toward the poor and his efforts to build roads. From 1264 until his death in 1294, Khubilai Khan presided over the Mongol empire at its height.

Mongol Conquest of Southern China Khubilai extended Mongol rule to all of China. From his base at Khanbaliq, he relentlessly attacked the Song dynasty in southern China. The Song capital at Hangzhou fell to Mongol forces in 1276, and within three years Khubilai had eliminated resistance throughout China. In 1279 he proclaimed himself emperor and established the Yuan dynasty, which ruled China until its collapse in 1368.

Beyond China, Khubilai had little success as a conqueror. During the 1270s and 1280s, he launched several unsuccessful invasions of Vietnam, Cambodia, and Burma as well as a failed naval expedition against Java involving 500 to 1,000 ships and twenty thousand troops. In 1274 and again in 1281, Khubilai also attempted seaborne invasions of Japan, but on both occasions typhoons thwarted his plans. The storm of 1281 was especially vicious: it destroyed about 4,500 Mongol vessels carrying more than one hundred thousand armed troops—the largest seaborne expedition before World War II.

The Golden Horde As Khubilai consolidated his hold on east Asia, his cousins and brothers tightened Mongol control on lands to the west. Mongols of the group known as the Golden Horde overran Russia between 1237 and 1241 and then mounted exploratory expeditions into Poland, Hungary, and eastern Germany in 1241 and 1242. Mongols of the Golden Horde prized the steppes north of the Black Sea as prime pastureland for their horses, and they used them to maintain a large army. They did not occupy Russia, which they regarded as an unattractive land of forests, but they extracted tribute from the Russian cities and agricultural provinces. The Golden Horde maintained its hegemony in Russia until the mid–fifteenth century, when the princes of Moscow built a powerful Russian state. By the mid–sixteenth century Russian conquerors had extended their control to the steppes, but Mongol khans descended from the Golden Horde continued to rule the Crimea until the late eighteenth century.

The Ilkhanate of Persia While the Golden Horde established its authority in Russia, Khubilai's brother Hülegü toppled the Abbasid empire and established the Mongol ilkhanate in Persia. In 1258 he captured the Abbasid capital of Baghdad after a brief siege. His troops looted the city, executed the caliph, and massacred more than two hundred thousand residents. From Persia, Hülegü's army ventured into Syria, but Muslim forces from Egypt soon expelled them and placed a limit on Mongol expansion to the southwest.

When the Mongols crushed ruling regimes in large settled societies, they discovered that they needed to become governors as well as conquerors. The Mongols had no experience administering complex societies, where successful governance required talents beyond the equestrian and military skills esteemed on the steppes. They had a difficult time adjusting to their role as administrators, and in fact most of their conquests fell out of their hands within a century.

Khubilai (KOO-bih-lie)

Buddhism (BOO-diz'm)

Yuan (yoo-AHN)

Hülegü (Hoo-LAY-goo)

ilkhanate (EEL-kahn-ate)

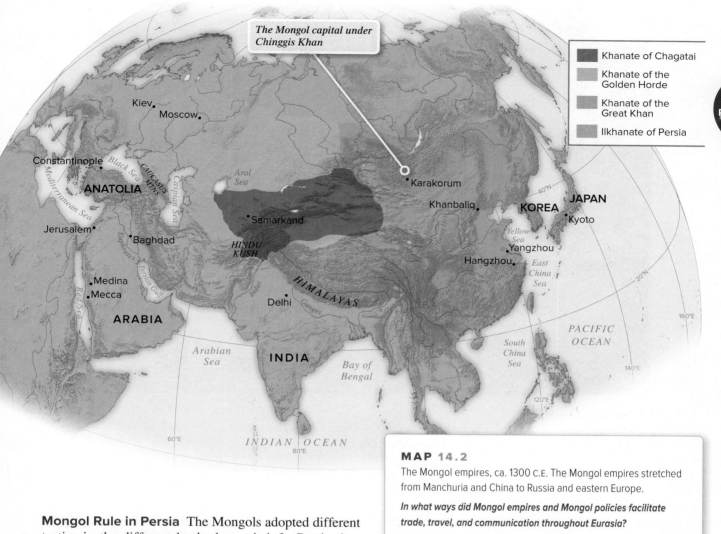

The Mongol capital under Chinggis Khan

Khanate of Chagatai

Khanate of the Golden Horde

Khanate of the Great Khan

Ilkhanate of Persia

PART

Kiev

Moscow

Constantinople

Black Sea

CAUCASUS MTNS

Caspian Sea

ANATOLIA

Mediterranean Sea

Jerusalem

Baghdad

Euphrates

Medina

Mecca

Red Sea

Persian Gulf

ARABIA

Arabian Sea

INDIA

Aral Sea

Samarkand

HINDU KUSH

Indus

Delhi

Ganges

HIMALAYAS

Bay of Bengal

INDIAN OCEAN

60°E

80°E

Karakorum

Khanbaliq

KOREA

JAPAN

Kyoto

Yellow Sea

Yangzhou

Hangzhou

East China Sea

South China Sea

PACIFIC OCEAN

40°N

20°N

160°E

140°E

120°E

MAP 14.2

The Mongol empires, ca. 1300 C.E. The Mongol empires stretched from Manchuria and China to Russia and eastern Europe.

In what ways did Mongol empires and Mongol policies facilitate trade, travel, and communication throughout Eurasia?

Mongol Rule in Persia The Mongols adopted different tactics in the different lands they ruled. In Persia they made important concessions to local interests. Although Mongols and their allies occupied the highest administrative positions, they basically allowed the Persians to run the ilkhanate as long as they delivered tax receipts and maintained order.

Over time, the Mongols even assimilated to Persian cultural traditions. The early Mongol rulers of Persia mostly observed their native shamanism, but they tolerated all religions—including Islam, Nestorian Christianity, Buddhism, and Judaism. Gradually, however, the Mongols gravitated toward Islam. In 1295 Ilkhan Ghazan publicly converted to Islam, and most of the Mongols in Persia followed his example. Ghazan's conversion sparked large-scale massacres of Christians and Jews, and it signaled the absorption of the Mongols into Muslim Persian society.

Mongol Rule in China In China, in contrast, the Mongol overlords stood aloof from their subjects, whom they scorned as mere cultivators. They outlawed intermarriage

between Mongols and Chinese and forbade the Chinese to learn the Mongol language. Some of the victors went so far as to suggest that the Mongols exterminate the Chinese people and convert China itself into pastureland for their horses. In the end, the Mongols decided simply to extract as much revenue as possible from their Chinese subjects. Unlike their counterparts in Persia, the Mongols in China did not make much use of native administrative talent. Instead, they brought foreign administrators—including Arabs, Persians, and even Europeans—into China and placed them in charge.

The Mongols also resisted assimilation to Chinese cultural traditions. They ended the privileges enjoyed by the Confucian scholars, and they dismantled the Confucian educational and examination system, which had produced generations of civil servants for the Chinese

shamanism (SHAH-mah-niz'm)

The siege of Baghdad.
A Persian manuscript illustration depicts Mongol forces camped outside the city walls while residents huddle within.
Note that the Mongols killed about 200,000 residents once the city fell.

bureaucracy. They did not persecute Confucians, but they allowed the Confucian tradition to wither in the absence of official support. Meanwhile, although the Mongols mostly continued to follow their native shamanist cults, they tolerated all cultural and religious traditions in China, including Confucianism, Daoism, Buddhism, and Christianity. Of Khubilai Khan's four wives, his favorite was Chabi, a Nestorian Christian.

The Mongols and Eurasian Integration

In building their vast empire, the Mongols brought tremendous destruction to lands throughout much of the Eurasian landmass. Yet they also sponsored interaction among peoples of different societies and linked Eurasian lands more directly than ever before. Indeed, Mongol rulers positively encouraged travel and communication over long distances. Recognizing the value of regular communications for their vast empire, Chinggis Khan and his successors maintained a courier network that rapidly relayed news, information, and government orders. The network included relay stations with fresh horses and riders so that messages could travel almost nonstop throughout Mongol territories. The Mongols' encouragement of travel and communication facilitated trade, diplomatic travel, missionary efforts, and movements of peoples to new lands.

The Mongols and Trade As a nomadic people dependent on commerce with settled agricultural societies, the Mongols worked to secure trade routes and ensure the safety of merchants passing through their territories. The Mongol khans frequently fought among themselves, but they maintained reasonably good order within their realms and allowed merchants to travel unmolested through their empires. As a result, long-distance travel and trade became much less risky than in earlier times. Merchants increased their commercial investments, and the volume of long-distance trade across central Asia dwarfed that of earlier eras. Lands as distant as China and western Europe became directly linked for the first time because

Daoism (DOW-iz'm)

Thinking about ENCOUNTERS

Pax Mongolica?

In the thirteenth and fourteenth centuries, the Mongols conquered vast portions of the Eurasian landmass, creating the largest empire in history. *Why, despite the extreme violence of Mongol conquest in many areas, did Mongol rule lead to greater cultural interaction among the peoples of Eurasia than ever before?*

India, and western Europe, and in other lands as well. Some diplomatic travelers crossed the entire Eurasian landmass. Several European ambassadors traveled to Mongolia and China to deliver messages from authorities seeking to ally with the Mongols against Muslim states in southwest Asia. Diplomats also traveled west: Rabban Sauma, a Nestorian Christian monk born in Khanbaliq, visited Italy and France as a representative of the Persian ilkhan.

of the ability of individuals to travel across the entire Eurasian landmass.

Diplomatic Missions Like trade, diplomatic communication was essential to the Mongols, and their protection of roads and travelers benefited ambassadors as well as merchants. Throughout the Mongol era the great khans in China, the ilkhans in Persia, and the other khans maintained close communications by means of diplomatic embassies. They also had diplomatic dealings with rulers in Korea, Vietnam,

Missionary Efforts Like the silk roads in earlier times, Eurasian routes during the era of the Mongol empires served as highways for missionaries as well as merchants and diplomats. Sufi missionaries helped popularize Islam among Turkish peoples in central Asia, and Nestorian Christians found new opportunities to win converts when they went to China to serve as administrators for Mongol rulers. Roman Catholic Christians also mounted missionary campaigns in China. (See chapter 18 for further discussion of travel during the Mongol era.)

Resettlement Another Mongol policy that encouraged Eurasian integration was the practice of resettling peoples in new lands. As a nomadic people, the Mongols had limited numbers of skilled artisans and educated individuals, but the more their empire expanded, the more they needed the services of specialized crafts workers and literate administrators. Mongol overlords recruited the talent they needed largely from the ranks of their allies and the peoples they conquered, and they often moved people far from their homelands to sites where they could best make use of their services. Among the most important of the Mongols' allies were the Uighur Turks, who lived mostly in oasis cities along the silk roads. The Uighurs were literate and often highly educated, and they provided not only many of the clerks, secretaries, and administrators who ran the Mongol empires but also units of soldiers who bolstered Mongol garrisons. Arab and Persian Muslims were also prominent among those who administered the Mongols' affairs far from their homelands.

Conquered peoples also supplied the Mongols with talent. When they overcame a city, Mongol forces surveyed the captured population, separated out those with specialized skills, and sent them where there was demand for their services. After the 1230s the Mongols often took censuses of lands they conquered, partly to levy taxes and conscript military forces and partly to locate talented individuals. The Parisian goldsmith Guillaume

Chabi, a Nestorian Christian and the favorite wife of Khubilai Khan, wearing the distinctive headgear reserved for Mongol women of the ruling class.

Uighurs (WEE-goors)

Reverberations ● ● ● ● ● ● ●

The Diffusion of Technologies

Between about 1000 and 1500 C.E., the ever-increasing pace of human interaction in many parts of the world led to a spectacular diffusion of technologies. Technologies include both tools and techniques that humans use to adapt the natural environment to their needs, and thus can range from items like plows and horseshoes to irrigation systems or ideas about which crops to plant. Of course, both the existence of technologies and their diffusion were hardly unique to the period between 1000 and 1500 C.E.—indeed, we have already seen numerous examples of technological diffusion (such as the spread of horse-drawn chariots and iron smelting, among many others) in Parts I–III. But during the period between 1000 and 1500 C.E., increased inter-cultural interactions—especially across and between Eurasia and Africa—led not only to the more rapid diffusion of technologies, but also to the diffusion of particular technologies that would impact the world's history for centuries to come. One of the reasons for the increased pace of interactions across Eurasia and Africa was because of the spread of the *dar-al-Islam* after the eighth century, which we read about in Part III, and especially because of the Muslim merchants who established stable trade routes within and beyond its bounds. Another reason was the huge conquests made by nomadic Turks and Mongols from the eleventh to the thirteenth centuries. In the thirteenth century, Mongol conquests alone provided stable trade routes that connected Eurasia all the way from China to eastern Europe. Each of these developments provided the pathways not only for the introduction of new trade items and spiritual beliefs, but also for the diffusion of technologies from distant regions. Here, we discuss two types of technologies that were widely diffused in this period: technologies of warfare and technologies of transportation.

Technologies of Warfare

In this chapter, we have already seen that Mongols learned about gunpowder from the Chinese during the thirteenth century. Gunpowder, of course, was not new to the Chinese: as we saw in chapter 12, Chinese alchemists discovered the compound during the Han dynasty, and by the eighth century Chinese strategists were using it for military purposes. But when Mongol invaders were introduced to gunpowder, they quickly incorporated its destructive powers into their arsenal of weapons: as early as 1214, for example, Chinggis Khan's armies included an artillery unit. Faced with the power of gunpowder—especially its usefulness in breaking sieges—societies all over Eurasia quickly sought to acquire the technology. Since the Mongols used gunpowder weapons to conquer Persia and other parts of southwest Asia in the mid–thirteenth century, Muslim armies were inspired to quickly incorporate the technology in order to defend themselves. By the mid–thirteenth century gunpowder technology had also reached Europe (chapter 16), and by the early fourteenth century armies across Eurasia possessed cannons. Although early cannons were not particularly accurate, the diffusion of gunpowder technologies permanently altered the nature of warfare. Indeed, over the eight centuries since Mongol armies began to use it, the use of gunpowder technologies has impacted every part of the globe in profound ways.

Technologies of Transportation

The period from around 1000 to 1500 C.E. also witnessed the widespread diffusion of technologies that improved both animal and maritime transportation—technologies that, in turn, allowed for both greater economic integration across long distances as well as greater economic growth. For example, Islamic merchants from north Africa utilized camels to cross the Sahara desert by the late eighth century C.E. (chapter 15). The diffusion of camels across the Sahara led to significant and long-term changes in a variety of sub-Saharan African societies, which included both the introduction of Islam as well as growing wealth resulting from being incorporated into much larger Eurasian markets. In Europe, meanwhile, the diffusion of the horse collar—most likely from both central Asia and north Africa—during the high middle ages helped to fuel European economic growth by allowing horses to pull much heavier loads without choking (chapter 16). The result was that Europeans could use horses for plowing and for transporting heavy loads rather than much slower oxen, which increased the amount of land that could

Boucher was only one among thousands of foreign-born individuals who became permanent residents of the Mongol capital at Karakorum because of their special talents. Like their protection of trade and diplomacy, the Mongols' policy of resettling allies and conquered peoples promoted Eurasian integration by increasing communication and exchange between peoples of different societies.

Decline of the Mongols in Persia and China

Collapse of the Ilkhanate Soon after the long and prosperous reign of Khubilai Khan, the Mongols encountered serious difficulties governing Persia and China. In Persia excessive spending strained the treasury, and overexploitation of the peasantry led to reduced revenues.

Siege of a North African Town, Fourteenth Century.

be plowed as well as the rapidity with which goods could be brought to market. Maritime technologies also diffused widely in this period. For example, the magnetic compass was invented by the Chinese during the Tang or Song dynasties, but by the mid–eleventh century it was being used by mariners throughout the Indian Ocean basin. By the mid–twelfth century, Europeans were also using compasses in the Mediterranean and Atlantic—devices that helped Portuguese mariners find their way into the Indian Ocean in the fifteenth century (chapter 18). In subsequent centuries, European mariners adopted many other maritime technologies from distant cultures—including the astrolabe—which were eventually used to cross the Atlantic to the Americas. Maritime technologies were not only important in Eurasia, however: during the twelfth and thirteenth centuries, voyages using sophisticated maritime techniques between the Hawaiian Islands and Tahiti allowed for the transfer of improved fishhook technologies to Hawaii (chapter 17).

When reading subsequent chapters, consider the effects that the diffusion of technologies have had on societies around the world over the very long term.

When the ilkhan tried to resolve his financial difficulties by ordering the use of paper money in the 1290s, merchants refused to accept paper they regarded as worthless. Commerce ground to a halt until the ilkhan rescinded his order. Meanwhile, factional struggles plagued the Mongol leadership. When the last of the Mongol rulers died without an heir in 1335, the ilkhanate itself simply collapsed. Government in Persia devolved to local levels until late in the fourteenth century, when Turkish peoples reintroduced effective central government.

Decline of the Yuan Dynasty Mongol decline in China was a more complicated affair. As in Persia, it had an economic dimension. The Mongols continued to use the paper money that the Chinese had introduced during the Tang and Song dynasties, but they did not maintain adequate reserves of the bullion that backed up paper notes. The general population soon lost confidence in paper money, and its value plummeted. As in Persia, too, factions and infighting hastened Mongol decline in China. Beginning in the 1320s power struggles, imperial assassinations, and civil war convulsed the Mongol regime in China.

Bubonic Plague Apart from financial difficulties and factional divisions, the Mongol rulers of China also faced an onslaught of epidemic disease. By facilitating trade and communications throughout Eurasia, the Mongols unwittingly expedited the spread of bubonic plague (discussed in chapter 18). During the 1330s plague erupted in southwestern China. From there it spread throughout China and central Asia, and by the late 1340s it had reached southwest Asia and Europe, where it became known as the Black Death. Bubonic plague sometimes killed half or more of an exposed population, particularly during the furious initial years of the epidemic, and it seriously disrupted economies and societies throughout much of Eurasia. In China depopulation and labor shortages that followed on the heels of epidemic plague weakened the Mongol regime.

Because they treated their Chinese subjects as inferiors, the Mongols also faced a rebellious subject population in China. Beginning in the 1340s southern China became a hotbed of peasant rebellion and banditry, which the Mongols could not control. In 1368 rebel forces captured Khanbaliq, and the Mongols departed China en masse and returned to the steppes.

Surviving Mongol Khanates Despite the collapse of the Mongol regimes in Persia and China, Mongol states did not completely disappear. The khanate of Chagatai continued to prevail in central Asia, and Mongols posed a threat to the northwestern borders of China until the eighteenth century. Meanwhile, the khanate of the Golden Horde continued to dominate the Caucasus and the steppe lands north of the Black Sea and Caspian Sea until the mid–sixteenth century, when a resurgent Russian state brought the Golden Horde down. Like Mongols in China, however, Mongols in Russia continued to threaten until the eighteenth century, and Mongols who had settled in the Crimean peninsula retained their identity until Josef Stalin forcibly moved them to other parts of the Soviet Union in the mid–twentieth century.

AFTER THE MONGOLS

By no means did the decline of the Mongols signal the end of nomadic peoples' influence in Eurasia. As Mongol strength waned, Turkish peoples resumed the expansive

MAP 14.3

Tamerlane's empire, ca. 1405 C.E. Notice the similarity between Tamerlane's empire and the ilkhanate of Persia shown on Map 14.2.

To what extent do you think the cities and the administrative infrastructure of the region facilitated Tamerlane's efforts to control his empire?

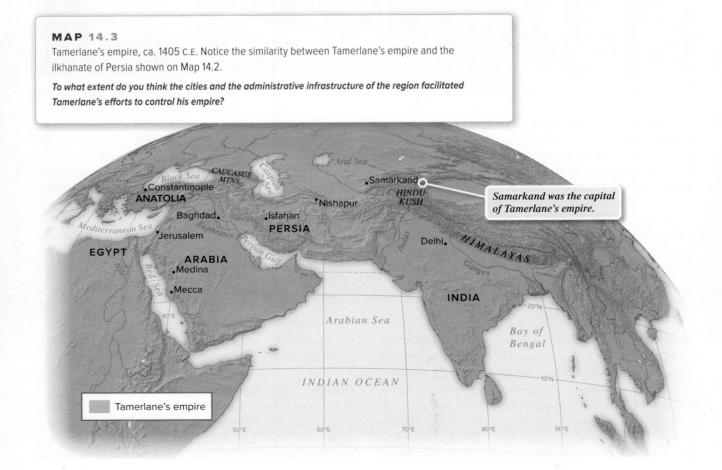

Samarkand was the capital of Tamerlane's empire.

Tamerlane's empire

campaigns that the Mongols had interrupted. During the late fourteenth and early fifteenth centuries, the Turkic-Mongol conqueror Tamerlane built a central Asian empire rivaling that of Chinggis Khan himself. Although Tamerlane's empire foundered soon after his death, it deeply influenced three surviving Turkish Muslim states—the Mughal empire in India, the Safavid empire in Persia, and the Ottoman empire based in Anatolia—and embraced much of southwest Asia, southeastern Europe, and north Africa.

Tamerlane and the Timurids

The Lame Conqueror The rapid collapse of the Mongol states left gaping power vacuums in China and Persia. While the native Ming dynasty filled the vacuum in China, a self-made Turkic-Mongol conqueror named Timur moved on Persia. Because he walked with a limp, contemporaries referred to him as Timur-i lang—"Timur the Lame," an appellation that made its way into English as Tamerlane.

Born about 1336 near Samarkand, Tamerlane took Chinggis Khan as his model. Like Chinggis Khan, Tamerlane came from a family of the minor Mongol and Turkish elites, and had to make his own way to power. Also like Chinggis Khan, he was a charismatic leader and a courageous warrior, and he attracted a band of loyal followers. During the 1360s he eliminated rivals to power, either by persuading them to join him as allies or by defeating their armies on the battlefield, and he won recognition as leader of his own tribe. By 1370 he had extended his authority throughout the khanate of Chagatai and had begun to build a magnificent imperial capital in Samarkand.

For the rest of his life, Tamerlane led his armies on campaigns of conquest. He turned first to the region between Persia and Afghanistan, and he took special care to establish his authority in the rich cities so that he could levy taxes on trade and agricultural production. Next he attacked the Golden Horde in the Caucasus region and Russia, and by the mid-1390s he had severely weakened it. During the last years of the century, he invaded India and subjected Delhi to a ferocious sack. Later Tamerlane campaigned along the Ganges, although he never attempted to incorporate India into his empire. He opened the new century with campaigns in southwest Asia and Anatolia. In 1404 he began preparations for an invasion of China, and he was leading his army east when he fell ill and died in 1405.

Like his model Chinggis Khan, Tamerlane was a conqueror, not a governor. He spent most of his adult life planning and fighting military campaigns. He did not create an imperial administration but, rather, ruled through tribal leaders who were his allies. He appointed overlords in the territories he conquered, but they relied on existing

Tamerlane's tomb.
Spoils from Tamerlane's campaigns and raids enriched the conqueror's capital at Samarkand. They financed, among other buildings, the magnificent tomb where Tamerlane's remains still rest.

bureaucratic structures and simply received taxes and tributes on his behalf.

Tamerlane's Heirs Given its loose organization, it is not surprising that Tamerlane's Timurid empire experienced stresses and strains after the conqueror's death. Tamerlane's sons and grandsons engaged in a long series of bitter conflicts that resulted in the contraction of the Timurid empire and its division into four main regions. For a century after Tamerlane's death, however, they maintained control over the region from Persia to Afghanistan. When the last vestiges of Tamerlane's imperial creation disappeared in the early sixteenth century, the Mughal, Safavid, and Ottoman empires that replaced it all clearly reflected the Turkish, Mongol, and Muslim legacy of the lame conqueror.

The Foundation of the Ottoman Empire

Chapter 24 will discuss the Mughal empire in India and the Safavid empire in Persia, both of which emerged during the early sixteenth century as Tamerlane's empire finally dissolved. The early stages of Ottoman expansion predated Tamerlane, however, and the foundation of the influential

Timur-i lang (tee-MOOR-yee LAHNG)

Ottoman empire throws additional light on the influence of nomadic peoples during the period 1000 to 1500 C.E.

Osman After the Mongol conquest of Persia, large numbers of nomadic Turks migrated from central Asia to the ilkhanate and beyond to the territories in Anatolia that the Saljuq Turks had seized from the Byzantine empire. There they followed charismatic leaders who organized further campaigns of conquest. Among those leaders was Osman, who during the late thirteenth and early fourteenth centuries carved a small state for himself in northwestern Anatolia. In 1299 Osman declared independence from the Saljuq sultan and launched a campaign to build a state at the expense of the Byzantine empire. After every successful operation Osman attracted more and more followers, who came to be known as Osmanlis or Ottomans.

Ottoman Conquests During the 1350s the Ottomans gained a considerable advantage over their Turkish rivals when they established a foothold across the Dardanelles at Gallipoli on the Balkan peninsula. The Ottomans quickly moved to expand the boundaries of their Balkan holdings. By the 1380s they had become by far the most powerful people in the Balkan peninsula, and by the end of the century they were poised to capture Constantinople and take over the Byzantine empire.

Tamerlane temporarily delayed Ottoman expansion in the Byzantine realm. In 1402 his forces crushed the Ottoman army, captured the sultan, and subjected the Ottoman state to the conqueror's authority. After Tamerlane's death, Ottoman leaders had to reestablish their rule in their own realm. Yet by the 1440s the Ottomans had recovered their balance and had begun again to expand in the Byzantine empire.

The Capture of Constantinople The campaign culminated in 1453 when Sultan Mehmed II, known as Mehmed the Conqueror, captured the Byzantine city of Constantinople, thus bringing to an end more than a thousand years of Byzantine rule. After subjecting it to a sack, he made the city his own capital under the Turkish name of Istanbul. With Istanbul as a base, the Ottomans quickly absorbed the remainder of the Byzantine empire. By 1480 they controlled all of Greece and the Balkan region. They continued to expand throughout most of the sixteenth century as well, extending their rule to southwest Asia, southeastern Europe, Egypt, and north Africa. Once again, then, a nomadic people asserted control over a long-settled society and quickly built a vast empire.

Osman (os-MAHN)

SUMMARY

During the half millennium from 1000 to 1500 C.E., nomadic peoples of central Asia played a larger role than ever before in world history. As early as the second millennium B.C.E., they had periodically threatened states from China to the eastern Mediterranean region, and from classical times on they had traded regularly and actively with peoples of settled societies. From 1000 to 1500 their relations with neighboring peoples changed, as they dominated affairs in most of Eurasia through their conquests and their construction of vast transregional empires. Turkish peoples built the most durable of the nomadic empires, but the spectacular conquests of the Mongols most clearly demonstrated the potential of nomadic peoples to project their formidable military power to settled agricultural societies. By establishing connections that spanned the Eurasian landmass, the nomadic empires laid the foundation for increasing communication, exchange, and interaction among peoples of different societies and thereby fostered the integration of the eastern hemisphere. The age of nomadic empires, from 1000 to 1500 C.E., foreshadowed the integrated world of modern times.

STUDY TERMS

Abbasids (258)
Buddhism (262)
Chinggis Khan (260)
Daoism (264)
Ghaznavids (259)
Hülegü (262)
Ilkhan Ghazan (263)
ilkhanate (262)
ilkhans (262)
Jurchen (261)
Karakorum (255)
khan (258)
khanate of Chagatai (262)
Khanbaliq (261)
khans of the Golden Horde (262)
Khubilai Khan (262)
Khwarazm shah (261)
Manichaeism (257)
Mehmed the Conqueror (270)
Mongols (260–269)
Nestorian (257)
Osman (270)
Rabban Sauma (265)
Saljuqs (258)
shamanism (263)
Song (261)
sultan (258)
sultanate of Delhi (259)
Tamerlane (269)
Temüjin (260)
Timur-i lang (269)
Turkish peoples (256–260)
Uighur Turks (265)
Ulaanbaatar (260)
Yuan dynasty (262)
yurts (256)

FOR FURTHER READING

Thomas T. Allsen. *Culture and Conquest in Mongol Eurasia.* Cambridge, 2001. Carefully studies the cultural exchanges sponsored by Mongol rulers, particularly those passing between China and Iran.

Thomas J. Barfield. *The Nomadic Alternative.* Englewood Cliffs, N.J., 1993. A sensitive study of nomadic societies in Africa and Eurasia by a leading anthropologist.

Carter Vaughn Findley. *The Turks in World History.* New York, 2005. A welcome volume that lucidly outlines the history of Turkish peoples and discusses relations between Turks and neighboring peoples.

Charles J. Halperin. *Russia and the Golden Horde: The Mongol Impact on Medieval Russian History.* Bloomington, Ind., 1985. An insightful study of the Golden Horde and its influence on Russian society.

Peter Jackson. *The Mongols and the West, 1221–1410.* London, 2005. Offers a comprehensive review of military, diplomatic, commercial, and cultural relations between Mongol and European societies.

Paul Kahn, ed. *The Secret History of the Mongols: The Origin of Chingis Khan.* Adapted from the translation of F. W. Cleaves. San Francisco, 1984. A translation of the Mongols' history of their own society, adapted for modern readers.

Adam T. Kessler. *Empires beyond the Great Wall: The Heritage of Genghis Khan.* Los Angeles, 1993. Well-illustrated survey of nomadic states in central Asia from the Xiongnu to the Mongols.

Beatrice Forbes Manz. *The Rise and Rule of Tamerlane.* Cambridge, 1989. Scholarly analysis of Tamerlane's career and his empire.

David Morgan. *The Mongols.* Oxford, 1986. Lucid and witty, this remains one of the best short works on the Mongols.

Morris Rossabi. *Khubilai Khan: His Life and Times.* Berkeley, 1988. Excellent scholarly study of the greatest of the great khans.

States and Societies
of Sub-Saharan Africa
CHAPTER 15

The magnificent mosque at Jenne, constructed in the fourteenth century, served as a principal center of Islamic education and scholarship in the Mali empire.

EYEWITNESS:

The Lion Prince of Mali

A remarkable oral tradition preserves the story of the lion prince Sundiata, thirteenth-century founder of the Mali empire in west Africa. Oral traditions include stories, histories, epics, and other accounts transmitted by professional singers and storytellers known in Africa as griots. Until scholars began to collect and publish African oral traditions in the middle of the twentieth century, the story of Sundiata was available only when a griot recited it.

According to the oral tradition, Sundiata's father ruled a small west African kingdom in the northeastern part of what is now the nation of Guinea. Despite his royal parentage, Sundiata had a difficult childhood, because a congenitally defective leg left him partially crippled. When the old king died, his enemies invaded the kingdom and killed the royal offspring, sparing Sundiata because they thought his physical condition would prevent him from posing a threat to their ambitions. But Sundiata overcame his injury, learned to use the bow and arrow, and strengthened himself by hunting in the forest. As Sundiata grew stronger, his enemies began to fear him, and they forced him to seek refuge in a neighboring kingdom. While in exile, Sundiata distinguished himself as a warrior and assembled a powerful cavalry force staffed by loyal followers and allies.

About 1235 Sundiata returned to his homeland and claimed the throne. His cavalry slashed through the countryside and defeated his enemies. Within a few years he had overcome resistance, established the Mali empire, and consolidated his rule throughout the valley of the Niger River. Although he respected traditional religious beliefs and magical powers, Sundiata was a Muslim, and he welcomed Muslim merchants from north Africa into his realm. He built a capital city at Niani, which soon became a thriving commercial center. For two centuries after Sundiata's death about 1260, the lion prince's legacy shaped the lives of west African peoples and linked west Africa with north Africa and the Mediterranean basin.

From the classical era forward, peoples from east Asia to the Mediterranean basin established extensive networks of trade and communication. African peoples living south of the Sahara desert participated in the larger economy of Afro-Eurasia, though not as fully as their counterparts in north Africa. Geographic conditions help to explain why trade and communication networks did not embrace sub-Saharan Africa as readily as they did other regions: the Sahara desert poses a formidable challenge to overland travelers, the African coastlines offer few good natural harbors, and cataracts complicate travel up the continent's major rivers.

Nevertheless, like their Eurasian and north African counterparts, peoples of sub-Saharan Africa organized productive societies, built powerful states, and participated in large-scale networks of communication and exchange. Internal African processes drove much of this development. Between 1000 and 1500 C.E., in the wake of the Bantu and other migrations (discussed in chapter 2), population increases in sub-Saharan Africa led societies there to organize states,

Sundiata (soon-JAH-tuh)
Mali (MAH-lee)
griot (GREE-oh)

CHRONOLOGY

4th century C.E.	Introduction of bananas to Africa
11th to 13th century	Kingdom of Ghana
11th to 15th century	Swahili cities
12th to 15th century	Kingdom of Great Zimbabwe
12th to 16th century	Christian kingdom of Axum
13th to 15th century	Mali empire
1230–1255	Reign of Sundiata
14th to 17th century	Kingdom of Kongo
1312–1337	Reign of Mansa Musa
1324–1325	Mansa Musa's pilgrimage to Mecca

develop centers of economic specialization, and conduct interregional trade. Alongside these internal processes, relations with other peoples of Afro-Eurasia also profoundly influenced the development of African societies. From the early centuries C.E. to 1500 and later as well, trade with lands of the Mediterranean and the Indian Ocean basins encouraged African peoples to produce commodities desired by consumers throughout much of Afro-Eurasia. This trade promoted urban development, the organization of large states and empires, and the introduction of new food crops and new religious beliefs into sub-Saharan Africa.

EFFECTS OF EARLY AFRICAN MIGRATIONS

By 1000 C.E. Bantu-speaking peoples had settled in most parts of Africa south of the equator, and Kushite, Sudanese, Mande, and other peoples had also established communities in lands far from their original homes. For the next several centuries, African peoples built societies on the foundation of small communities that the Bantu and other migrations had generated.

Agriculture and Population Growth

The principal early result of the Bantu and other migrations was to spread agriculture and herding to almost all parts of Africa. As they established agricultural societies, cultivators and herders displaced or absorbed many of the hunting, gathering, and fishing peoples who previously inhabited sub-Saharan Africa. After about 500 B.C.E., most Bantu peoples possessed iron metallurgy, which enabled them to fashion iron tools that facilitated further clearing of lands and extension of agriculture. By the early centuries C.E., cultivation and herding had reached the southernmost parts of Africa. The expansion of agriculture, in turn, resulted in increased agricultural production, rising population, and pressure for continuing migration to new territories.

Bananas The date and mechanism of the introduction of bananas to Africa is a much debated topic, but the arrival of the banana definitely encouraged a fresh migratory surge. First domesticated in southeast Asia, bananas probably entered Africa by way of the Indian Ocean. Between about 300 and 500 C.E., Malay seafarers from the islands

that make up modern Indonesia colonized the island of Madagascar and established banana cultivation there. From Madagascar, bananas easily made the jump to the east African mainland. By 500 C.E. several varieties of bananas had become well established in Africa.

Cultivation of bananas allowed the Bantu to expand into heavily forested regions where yams and millet did not grow well. Indeed, bananas increased the supply of available food, enriched the Bantu diet, and allowed sub-Saharan populations to expand more rapidly than before.

Population Growth The population history of sub-Saharan Africa clearly reflects the significance of iron metallurgy and bananas. In 400 B.C.E., before iron working had deeply influenced the continent's societies, the population of sub-Saharan Africa stood at about 3.5 million. By 800 C.E., after banana cultivation had spread throughout the continent, the sub-Saharan population had climbed to 17 million. And by 1000, when the Bantu migrations had introduced agriculture and iron metallurgy to most regions of sub-Saharan Africa, the population had passed 22 million.

The continuing Bantu migrations, the expansion of Bantu population, and the establishment of new Bantu communities contributed to changes in relationships between Bantu and foraging peoples such as the forest dwellers of central Africa (the people once referred to as pygmies). In the past, the Bantu had often relied on the foragers as guides as they expanded into unfamiliar forest environments. However, as Bantu populations surged, many foragers were displaced by growing numbers of agricultural settlements. As a result, some forest peoples joined the cultivators and effectively integrated into Bantu society, while others retreated deeper into the forest to sustain their small-scale societies.

Political Organization

By 1000 C.E., the Bantu had approached the limits of their expansion. Because agricultural peoples already occupied most of the continent, migrating into new territories and forming new settlements was much more difficult than before. Instead of migrating in search of new lands to cultivate, then, sub-Saharan African peoples developed increasingly complex forms of government that enabled them to organize their existing societies more efficiently.

Kin-Based Societies Most early Bantu societies did not depend on an elaborate hierarchy of officials or a bureaucratic apparatus to administer their affairs. Instead, Bantu peoples governed themselves mostly through family and kinship groups. Usually, Bantu peoples settled in villages with populations averaging about one hundred people. Male heads of families constituted a village's ruling council, which decided public affairs for the entire group. The most prominent of the family heads presided over the village as a chief and represented the settlement when it dealt with neighboring peoples. A group of villages constituted a district, which became the principal focus of loyalties. Usually, there was no chief or larger government for the district. Instead, village chiefs negotiated on matters concerning two or more villages. Meanwhile, within individual villages, family and kinship groups disciplined their own members as necessary.

Chiefdoms This type of organization lends itself particularly well to small-scale communities, but kin-based societies often grew to large proportions. After about 1000 C.E., kin-based societies faced difficult challenges as population growth strained resources. Conflicts between villages and districts became more frequent and more intense. Increased conflict encouraged Bantu communities to organize military forces for both offensive and defensive purposes, and military organization in turn encouraged the development of more formal structures of government.

Many districts fell under the leadership of powerful chiefs, who overrode kinship networks and imposed authority on their territories.

Some of these chiefs conquered their neighbors and consolidated their lands into small kingdoms. These local kingdoms emerged in several regions of sub-Saharan Africa after about 1000 C.E. The kingdoms of Ife and Benin, for example, arose in the forested regions of west Africa. Both realms were city-states in which the court and urban residents controlled the surrounding countryside through family relationships and political alliances. Both Ife and Benin also produced magnificent sculptures that put human faces and figures to the early history of sub-Saharan Africa. Local kingdoms appeared also in southern Africa and central Africa.

Kingdom of Kongo One of the most active areas of political development was the basin of the Congo River (also known as the Zaire River). After about 1000 C.E.

Ife (EE-fehy)
Benin (beh-NEEN)

Benin Plaque.
A bronze plaque from the kingdom of Benin depicts a local chief flanked by warriors and attendants.

population pressures and military challenges encouraged kin-based societies in the Congo region to form small states embracing a few villages each. By 1200 conflict between these small states had resulted in the organization of larger, regional principalities that could better resist political and military pressures. One of the more prosperous of the Congolese states was the kingdom of Kongo, which participated actively in trade networks involving copper, raffia cloth, and nzimbu shells from the Atlantic Ocean. During the fourteenth century the kingdom of Kongo came to embrace much of the modern-day Republic of the Congo and Angola.

The central government of Kongo included the king and officials who oversaw military, judicial, and financial affairs (including a royal currency system based on cowry shells). Beneath the central government were six provinces administered by governors, each of whom supervised several districts administered by subordinate officials. Within the districts, villages ruled by chiefs provided local government. Though not the only kingdom in sub-Saharan Africa, Kongo was perhaps the most tightly centralized of the early Bantu kingdoms. The kingdom of Kongo provided effective organization from the fourteenth until the mid–seventeenth century, when Portuguese slave traders undermined the authority of the kings and the central government.

Kin-based societies did not disappear with the emergence of formal states. In fact, many survived well into the nineteenth century. Yet regional states and large kingdoms became increasingly prominent during the centuries after 1000 C.E. as Bantu and other African peoples responded to population pressures and military challenges facing their societies.

AFRICAN SOCIETY AND CULTURAL DEVELOPMENT

By the eleventh century C.E., Africa was a land of enormous diversity. The peoples of sub-Saharan Africa spoke some eight hundred languages, and the continent supported a wide variety of societies and economies: mobile bands of hunting and gathering peoples, fishing peoples who lived alongside the continent's lakes and coasts, nomadic herders, subsistence farmers who migrated periodically to fresh lands, settled cultivators, and city-based societies that drew their livelihoods from mining, manufacturing, and trade. Although that diversity makes it difficult to speak of African society and cultural development in general terms, certain social forms and cultural patterns appeared widely throughout sub-Saharan Africa.

Social Classes

In kingdoms, empires, and city-states, such as Kongo, Mali, and Kilwa, respectively, African peoples developed complex societies with clearly defined classes: ruling elites, military nobles, administrative officials, religious authorities, merchants, artisans, peasants, and slaves. These societies more or less resembled those found in other settled, agricultural lands of Eurasia organized by powerful states.

In the small states and kin-based societies of sub-Saharan Africa, however, social structures were different. Small states often generated an aristocratic or ruling elite, and they always recognized a class of religious authorities. Yet in general, kinship, sex and gender expectations, and age groupings were the principal considerations that determined social position in such societies.

Kinship Groups   Extended families and clans served as the main foundation of social and economic organization in small-scale agricultural societies. The institution of privately owned property, found in most societies in north Africa and Eurasia, did not exist in sub-Saharan Africa. Instead, communities claimed rights to land and used it in common. The villages of sub-Saharan Africa, where most of the population lived, generally consisted of several extended family groups. Male heads of families jointly governed the village and organized the work of their own groups. They allocated portions of the communal lands for their relatives to cultivate and were responsible for distributing harvests equitably among all members of their groups.

Sex and Gender Relations   Sex and gender relations also influenced the roles and occupations of individuals in society. Workers with special skills were mostly men. Leather tanning, for example, was the work of men who carefully guarded knowledge of their techniques and passed them down to their heirs. Iron working, which was highly prestigious, was also the work of men. Blacksmiths often served as community leaders, and like leather tanners, they passed knowledge of their craft down to their heirs. Men usually undertook the heavy labor of clearing land and preparing it for cultivation, although both men and women participated in the planting and harvesting of crops. Women's roles also included tending to domestic chores and taking primary responsibility for child rearing.

Women's Roles   As in other societies, men largely monopolized public authority. Yet women in sub-Saharan Africa generally had more opportunities open to them than did their counterparts in other lands. Women enjoyed high honor as the sources of life. On at least a few occasions, women made their ways to positions of power, and aristocratic women often influenced public affairs. Women merchants commonly traded at markets, and they participated actively in both local and long-distance trade in Africa. Sometimes women even engaged in combat and organized all-female military units.

The arrival of Islam did not change the status of women in sub-Saharan Africa as dramatically as it did in

PART

Thinking about **TRADITIONS**

Isolation and the Persistence of Traditions in Sub-Saharan Africa

Geographic barriers posed many difficulties for cross-cultural interaction between sub-Saharan African societies and other societies in north Africa and Eurasia. *In what ways did the relative isolation imposed by these barriers contribute to the persistence of distinctly sub-Saharan traditions regarding religion, culture, and community organization in this period?*

Arabia and southwest Asia. South of the Sahara, early converts to Islam came mostly from the ranks of the ruling elites and the merchant classes. Because it did not become a popular faith for several centuries after its introduction, Islam did not deeply influence the customs of most Africans. Even at royal courts where Islam attracted eager converts, Muslims of sub-Saharan Africa simply did not honor the same social codes as their counterparts elsewhere. For the most part, Muslim women in sub-Saharan Africa socialized freely with men outside their immediate families, and they continued to appear and work openly in society. Thus Islam did relatively little to curtail the opportunities available to women or to compromise their status in sub-Saharan Africa.

Age Grades Apart from kinship and expectations based on sex and gender roles, African society also made a place for age groups that included all individuals within a given community born within a few years of one another. Members of age grades performed tasks appropriate for their levels of development, and they often bonded with one another to form tight circles of friends and political allies. Members of an age grade might provide labor for community projects, for example, or take joint responsibility for looking after village elders. They aided members who experienced adversities and helped one another at crucial junctures, such as marriage and the building of a new household. Thus age grades had the effect of establishing social ties that crossed the lines of family and kinship.

Slavery One class of individuals stood apart from the other social groups: slaves. As in other lands, the institution of slavery had had a place in Africa since antiquity. Most slaves were captives of war. Others came from the ranks of debtors, suspected witches, and criminals. Within Africa most slaves probably worked as agricultural laborers, although many also worked as construction laborers, miners, or porters. Slaves were an important form of personal wealth in sub-Saharan Africa. In the absence of private property, sub-Saharans could not become wealthy through the accumulation of landholdings. Instead, the accumulation of slaves enabled individuals or families to display their wealth, to enhance their positions in society, and also to increase their agricultural production. For those reasons, slave trading and slaveholding were prominent features of sub-Saharan African society.

Slave Trading After about the ninth century C.E., the expansion of the trans-Saharan and Indian Ocean trade networks stimulated increased traffic in African slaves. In previous centuries, eastern Europeans had been the main source of slaves in the trading networks of Muslim merchants. Yet the demand for slaves became greater than eastern Europe could supply. As a result, Muslim merchants turned increasingly to sub-Saharan Africa as an alternative source for slaves.

In response to that demand, slave raiding became an increasingly prominent activity within Africa itself. Rulers of large-scale states and empires began to make war on smaller, weaker states and kin-based societies in search of captives. In some years, ten to twenty thousand Africans left their homes as slaves. Although records of the Islamic slave trade are scarce, a lengthy uprising known as the *Zanj* revolt allows a glimpse of the harsh conditions under which many of these slaves toiled. The term *Zanj* referred to black slaves from the Swahili coast, many of whom worked on sugarcane plantations or cleared land for cultivation in southern Mesopotamia by the seventh century C.E. Slave revolts were not uncommon, and about 869 a rebel slave named Ali bin Muhammad organized about fifteen thousand Zanj slaves into a massive force that captured Basra, the most important city of southern Mesopotamia. The rebels then proceeded to establish a state in the region, which was only defeated by the Abbasid rulers fourteen years later.

Though smaller than the Atlantic slave trade of modern times, the Islamic slave trade was a sizable affair: between 750 and 1500 C.E., the number of African slaves transported to foreign lands may have exceeded ten million. The high demand led to the creation of networks within Africa that supplied slaves and served as a foundation for the Atlantic slave trade in later centuries.

African Religion

Peoples of sub-Saharan Africa developed a wide range of languages, societies, and cultural traditions. Religious beliefs and practices in particular took many forms. The continent's peoples referred to their deities by different names, told different stories about them, and honored them with

Zanj (zahn-jee)

different rituals. Yet certain features were common to many religions of sub-Saharan Africa. In combination, these features offer considerable insight into the cultural and religious climate of sub-Saharan Africa in premodern times.

Creator God   Many African peoples had held monotheistic beliefs from the early days of Sudanic agriculture. Although those beliefs were not static over time, many peoples recognized a single divine force as the agent responsible for setting the world in motion and providing it with order. Some peoples believed that this god also sustained the world, intervening indirectly, through spirits, to influence the course of human affairs. Some considered this deity to be all-powerful, others regarded it as all-knowing, and many considered it both omnipotent and omniscient.

Lesser Gods and Spirits   Apart from the superior creator god, Africans recognized many lesser gods and spirits often associated with the elements and with natural features. Unlike the creator god, these lesser deities participated actively in the workings of the world. They could confer or withhold benefits and bring favor or injury to humans. Similarly, most Africans believed that the souls of departed ancestors had the power to intervene in the lives of their descendants: the departed could bring good fortune to descendants who behaved properly and honored their ancestors, and they could also bring misfortune as punishment for evil behavior and neglect of their ancestors' memory. Much of the ritual of African religions focused on honoring deities, spirits, or ancestors' souls to win their favor or regain their goodwill. The rituals included prayers, animal sacrifices, and ceremonies marking important stages of life—such as birth, circumcision, marriage, and death.

Diviners   Like other peoples of the world, Africans recognized classes of religious specialists—individuals who had the power to mediate between humanity and supernatural beings. Often referred to as diviners, they were intelligent people, usually men though sometimes women, who understood clearly the networks of political, social, economic, and psychological relationships within their communities. When afflicted by illness, sterility, crop failure, or some other disaster, individuals or groups consulted diviners to learn the cause of their misfortune. Diviners then consulted oracles, identified the causes of the trouble, and prescribed medicine, rituals, or sacrifices designed to eliminate the problem and bring about a return to normality.

For the most part, African religion concerned itself not with matters of theology but, rather, with the more practical business of explaining, predicting, and controlling the experiences of individuals and groups in the world. Thus African religion strongly emphasized morality and proper behavior as essential to the maintenance of an orderly world. Failure to observe high moral standards would displease deities, spirits, and departed ancestors and ensure that misfortune befell the negligent parties. Because proper moral behavior was so important to their fortunes, family and kinship groups took responsibility for policing their members and disciplining those who fell short of expected standards.

The Arrival of Christianity

Early Christianity in North Africa   Alongside religions that concentrated on the practical matter of maintaining an orderly world, Christianity reached Egypt and north Africa during the first century C.E., soon after the faith's appearance. Alexandria in Egypt became one of the most prominent centers of early Christian thought, and north Africa was the home of St. Augustine, an important leader of the fledgling church.

The Christian Kingdom of Axum   About the middle of the fourth century C.E., Christianity established a foothold in the kingdom of Axum, located in the highlands of modern Ethiopia. The first Axumite converts were probably local merchants who traded with Mediterranean Christians calling at the port of Adulis on the Red Sea. As missionaries visited Ethiopia, the kings of Axum also converted to Christianity. Indeed, the kings of Axum were some of the first royal converts to Christianity, adopting the faith shortly after the Roman emperor Constantine himself. Missionaries later established monasteries, translated the Bible into the Ethiopian

Congolese mask.
Entrancing and enthralling masks like this one from Congo were essential to the proper observance of religious rituals, which often involved communicating with natural or animal spirits. Masks transformed diviners and provided them with powers not accessible to normal humans.

What kinds of feelings might a mask like this have elicited from observers?

Axum (AHK-soom)

Church of St. George.
The church of St. George at Lalibela, Ethiopia, a massive structure in the form of a cross. Workers excavated the surrounding earth and then carved the church itself out of a rock.

language, and worked to popularize Christianity throughout the kingdom.

The fortunes of Christianity in Ethiopia reflected the larger political experience of the region. In the late seventh century C.E., the ruling house of Axum fell into decline, and during the next several centuries the expansion of Islam left an isolated island of Christianity in the Ethiopian highlands. During the twelfth century, however, a new ruling dynasty undertook a centralizing campaign and enthusiastically promoted Christianity as a faith that could provide cultural unity for the land. From the twelfth through the sixteenth century, Christianity enjoyed particular favor in Ethiopia. During the twelfth century, the Ethiopian kings ordered the carving of eleven massive churches out of solid rock—a monumental work of construction that required enormous resources. During the thirteenth century, rulers of Ethiopia's Solomonic dynasty claimed descent from the Israelite kings David and Solomon in an effort to lend additional biblical luster to their authority. The fictional work *Kebra Negast (The Glory of Kings),* which undertook to trace that lineage, has recently become popular among Rastafarians

and devotees of reggae music in Ethiopia, Jamaica, and other lands. Meanwhile, Christianity retained its privileged status in Ethiopia until it fell out of favor following the socialist revolution of 1974.

Ethiopian Christianity During the centuries after the Islamic conquests of Egypt, the Sudan, and northern Africa, Ethiopian Christians had little contact with Christians in other lands. As a result, although Ethiopian Christianity retained basic Christian theology and rituals, it increasingly reflected the interests of its African devotees. Ethiopian Christians believed that a large host of evil spirits populated the world, for example, and carried amulets or charms for protection against these menacing spirits. The twelfth-century carved-rock churches themselves harked back to pre-Christian values, since rock shrines had long been a prominent feature in Ethiopian religion. Not until the sixteenth century, when Portuguese mariners began to visit Ethiopia en route to India, did Ethiopians reestablish

Kebra Nagast (kee-brah NAH-gahst)

Reverberations of ● ● ● ● ● ● ●

The Diffusion of Technologies

Camels had been used for centuries by traders in Arabia and North Africa—thanks especially to the camel saddle invented in about 200 C.E.—before Muslim traders made their way across the Sahara to West Africa in the seventh and eighth centuries. Camels, although living beings, can be considered a technology because their use helped humans adapt the natural environment to their needs, making it possible to reliably and repeatedly traverse the vast Sahara desert. Think about the variety of ways that the diffusion of camels to sub-Saharan Africa—in terms of trade, urban growth, the accumulation of wealth, and the slave trade—affected the region over the very long term.

relations with Christians from other lands. By that time the Portuguese had introduced their Roman Catholic faith to the kingdom of Kongo, and Christianity began to win a place for itself elsewhere in sub-Saharan Africa.

ISLAMIC KINGDOMS AND EMPIRES

After the eighth century C.E., Islam was also introduced to Africa. Islam arrived by two routes: it went to west Africa overland by trans-Saharan camel caravans, and it traveled to coastal east Africa over the sea-lanes of the Indian Ocean in the vessels of merchant mariners. After its introduction, Islam profoundly influenced the political, social, and economic development of sub-Saharan Africa as well as its cultural and religious development. At the same time, Africans in both west and east Africa adapted Islam to their own cultures, giving African Islam distinctly African characteristics.

Trans-Saharan Trade and Islamic States in West Africa

The Sahara desert has never served as an absolute barrier to communication between human societies. Small numbers of nomadic peoples have lived in the desert itself since about 5000 B.C.E. These nomads migrated around the desert and had dealings with other peoples settled on its fringes. In addition, merchants occasionally organized commercial expeditions across the desert even in ancient and classical times.

Camels Yet travel across the Sahara quickened substantially with the arrival of the camel. Camels came to north Africa from Arabia sometime in the first millennium B.C.E.

Ghana (GAH-nuh)
Gao (gou)

and perhaps earlier. During the late centuries B.C.E., a special camel saddle, which took advantage of the animals' distinctive physical structure, also made its way to north Africa. Because a caravan took seventy to ninety days to cross the Sahara and because camels could travel long distances before needing water, they proved to be extremely useful beasts of burden in such an arid region. After about 300 C.E. camels became the preferred transport animals throughout the Sahara.

When Arab conquerors established their Islamic faith in north Africa during the seventh and eighth centuries, they also integrated the region into a rapidly expanding zone of commerce and communication. Soon afterward, Muslims in north Africa began to explore the potential of trade across the Sahara. By the late eighth century, Islamic merchants had trekked across the desert and established commercial relations with societies in sub-Saharan west Africa. There they found a series of long-established trading centers such as Gao, a terminus of caravan routes across the Sahara that offered access to the Niger River valley, which was a flourishing market for copper, ironware, cotton textiles, salt, grains, and carnelian beads.

The Kingdom of Ghana The principal state of west Africa at the time of the Muslims' arrival was the kingdom of Ghana (not related to the modern state of Ghana), situated between the Senegal and Niger rivers in a region straddling the border between the modern states of Mali and Mauritania. Ghana emerged as a kingdom at an uncertain but early date: according to legends preserved by Arab travelers, as many as twenty-two kings ruled in Ghana before Muhammad and his companions embarked on the *hijra*. Ghana probably developed as a state during the fourth or fifth century C.E. when agricultural peoples sought to protect their societies from the raids of camel-riding nomads who increasingly came out of the Sahara. When Muslims arrived in west Africa, the kingdom of Ghana was a regional state much like others that were emerging elsewhere in sub-Saharan Africa.

Gold Trade As trade and traffic across the desert increased, Ghana underwent a dramatic transformation. It became the most important commercial site in west Africa because it was the center for trade in gold, which was in high demand throughout the eastern hemisphere. Muslim merchants flocked to camel caravans traveling across the Sahara to Ghana in search of gold for consumers in the Mediterranean basin and elsewhere in the Islamic world. Ghana itself did not produce gold, but the kings procured nuggets from lands to the south—probably from the region around the

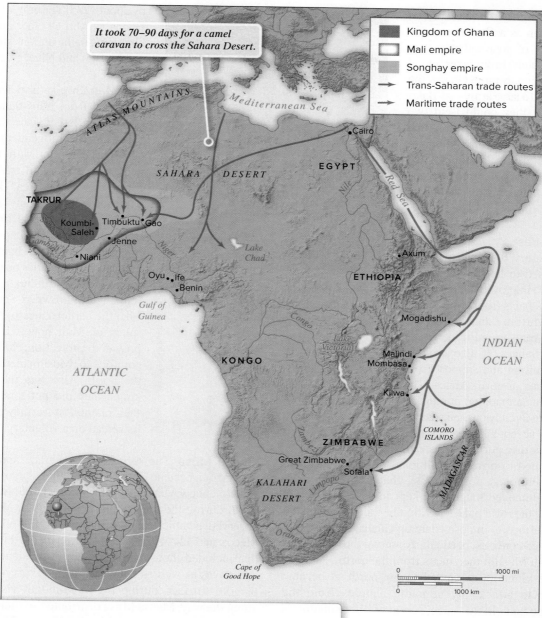

It took 70–90 days for a camel caravan to cross the Sahara Desert.

Legend:
- Kingdom of Ghana
- Mali empire
- Songhay empire
- → Trans-Saharan trade routes
- → Maritime trade routes

MAP 15.1

Kingdoms, empires, and city-states of sub-Saharan Africa, 800–1500 C.E. After the emergence of Islam, trans-Saharan overland routes linked sub-Saharan west Africa with the Mediterranean region, and maritime trade routes linked sub-Saharan east Africa to the Indian Ocean basin.

How critical was the role of trade in the emergence of cities and states in sub-Saharan Africa?

headwaters of the Niger, Gambia, and Senegal rivers, which enjoyed the world's largest supply of gold available at the time. By controlling and taxing trade in the precious metal, the kings both enriched and strengthened their realm. Apart from gold, merchants from Ghana provided ivory and slaves for traders from north Africa. In exchange, they received horses, cloth, small manufactured wares, and salt.

Koumbi-Saleh Integration into trans-Saharan trade networks brought enormous wealth and considerable power to Ghana. The kingdom's capital and principal trading site stood at Koumbi-Saleh, a small town today but a thriving commercial center with a population of some fifteen to twenty thousand people at its peak between the ninth and twelfth centuries. Al-Bakri, a Spanish Muslim traveler of the mid–eleventh century, described Koumbi-Saleh as a flourishing site with buildings of stone and more than a dozen mosques. From taxes levied on trade passing through Ghana, the kings financed a large army—al-Bakri reported that they could field two hundred thousand warriors—that protected the sources of gold, maintained order in the kingdom, kept allied and tributary states in line, and defended Ghana against nomadic incursions from the Sahara.

Islam in West Africa

By about the tenth century, the kings of Ghana had converted to Islam. Their conversion led to improved relations with Muslim merchants from north Africa as well as Muslim nomads from the desert who transported trade goods across the Sahara. It also brought them recognition and support from Muslim states in north Africa. The kings of Ghana made no attempt to impose Islam forcibly on their society, nor did they accept Islam exclusively even for their own purposes. Instead, they continued to observe traditional religious customs: al-Bakri mentioned, for example, that native religious specialists practiced magic and kept idols in the woods surrounding the royal palace at Koumbi-Saleh. Even in the absence of efforts to impose Islam on Ghana, however, the faith attracted converts, particularly among those engaged in trade with Muslim merchants from the north.

As the kingdom expanded to the north, it became vulnerable to attacks by nomadic peoples from the Sahara who sought to seize some of the kingdom's wealth. During the early thirteenth century, raids from the desert weakened the kingdom, and it soon collapsed. Political leadership in west Africa then fell to the powerful Mali empire, which emerged just as the kingdom of Ghana dissolved.

Sundiata

The lion prince Sundiata (reigned 1230–1255) built the Mali empire during the first half of the thirteenth century. Through alliances with local rulers, a reputation for courage in battle, and a large army dominated by cavalry, Sundiata had consolidated his hold on the Mali empire

West African sculpture.
This terra-cotta sculpture from the thirteenth or fourteenth century depicts a helmeted and armored warrior astride a horse with elaborate harness and head protection.

What can this sculpture tell us about the values of the society that produced it?

by about 1235. The empire embraced Ghana as well as other neighboring kingdoms in the regions surrounding the Senegal and Niger rivers.

The Mali Empire and Trade

Mali benefited from trans-Saharan trade on an even larger scale than Ghana had. From the thirteenth until the late fifteenth century, Mali controlled and taxed almost all trade passing through west Africa. Enormous caravans with as many as twenty-five thousand camels linked Mali to north Africa. The capital city of Niani attracted merchants seeking gold, and market cities on the caravan routes such as Timbuktu, Gao, and Jenne grew crowded and wealthy. Like the earlier kings of Ghana, the rulers of Mali honored Islam and provided protection, lodging, and comforts for Muslim merchants from the north. Also like the Ghanaian kings, they did not force Islam on their realm. Rather, they encouraged its spread on a voluntary basis.

Mansa Musa

The significance of trade and Islam for west Africa became clearest during the reign of Sundiata's grand-nephew Mansa Musa, who ruled Mali from 1312 to 1337, during the high point of the empire. Mansa Musa observed Islamic tradition by making his pilgrimage to Mecca in 1324–1325. His party formed a huge caravan that included thousands of soldiers, attendants, subjects, and slaves as well as a hundred camels carrying satchels of gold. In fact, during his three-month visit to Cairo along the way, Mansa Musa distributed so much gold that the metal's value declined by as much as 25 percent on local markets.

Mansa Musa and Islam

Mansa Musa drew great inspiration from his pilgrimage to Mecca, and on returning to Mali he took his religion even more seriously than before. He built mosques, and he sent promising students to study with distinguished Islamic scholars in north Africa. He also established religious schools and brought in Arabian and north African teachers, including four descendants of Muhammad, to make Islam better known in Mali.

Yet within a century of Mansa Musa's reign, Mali was in serious decline: factions crippled the central government, provinces seceded from the empire, and military pressures came both from neighboring kingdoms and from

Timbuktu (tim-buhk-TOO)

Jenne (jehn-neh)

Mansa Musa (MAHN-suh MOO-suh)

Mansa Musa.

Mansa Musa enjoyed a widespread reputation as the wealthiest king in the world. On this map, prepared in 1375 by a cartographer from the Mediterranean island of Majorca, Mansa Musa holds a gold nugget about the size of a grapefruit.

What kinds of objects surround Mansa Musa?

desert nomads. By the late fifteenth century, the Songhay empire had completely overcome Mali. Yet Mansa Musa and other Mali rulers had established a tradition of centralized government that the Songhay realm would continue, and they had ensured that Islam would have a prominent place in west African society over the long term.

Indian Ocean Trade and Islamic States in East Africa

While trans-Saharan caravan traffic linked west Africa to the larger trading world of the eastern hemisphere, merchant mariners sailing the sea-lanes of the Indian Ocean

performed a similar service for Swahili societies in coastal east Africa. *Swahili* is an Arabic term meaning "coasters," referring to those who engaged in trade along the east African coast. Swahili society developed as a result of Bantu migrations to east Africa in the early centuries C.E. These migrants introduced agriculture, cattle herding, and iron metallurgy to the region, and here, as elsewhere in sub-Saharan Africa, they founded complex societies governed by small, local states. As their population increased, Bantu peoples founded settlements on the coasts and offshore islands as well as the interior regions of east Africa. These coast dwellers supplemented their agricultural production with ocean fishing and maritime trade.

The Swahili The Swahili dominated the east African coast from Mogadishu in the north to Kilwa, the Comoro Islands, and Sofala in the south. They spoke a Bantu language, also known as Swahili, supplemented with words and ideas borrowed from Arabic. Swahili peoples

Thinking about **ENCOUNTERS**

Islam in Sub-Saharan Africa

Despite geographical barriers, the period after the eighth century C.E. witnessed increasing cross-cultural interaction between sub-Saharan Africans in west and east Africa with Islamic traders from the north. *How did the introduction of Islam shape sub-Saharan societies and, conversely, how did sub-Saharan societies shape Islam?*

Swahili (swah-HEE-lee)

Kilwa (KILH-wah)

Gerezani Fortress.
Gerezani Fortress on the east African coast at Kilwa, a testament to the wealth and military power of this major Indian Ocean trading city.

developed different dialects, but they communicated readily among themselves because individuals frequently visited other Swahili communities in their ocean-going craft. Indeed, all along the east African coast, Swahili society underwent similar patterns of development with respect to language, religion, architecture, and technology.

In the tenth century, Swahili society attracted increasing attention from Islamic merchants. From the interior regions of east Africa, the Swahili obtained gold, slaves, ivory, and exotic local products, which they traded for pottery, glass, and textiles that Muslim merchants brought from Persia, India, and China.

The Swahili City-States By the eleventh and twelfth centuries, trade had brought important changes to coastal east Africa, just as it had done in west Africa. By controlling and taxing trade within their jurisdictions, local chiefs grew wealthy, strengthened their own authority, and increased the influence of their communities. Gradually, trade concentrated at several coastal and island port cities that enjoyed especially convenient locations: Mogadishu, Lamu, Malindi, Mombasa, Zanzibar, Kilwa, Mozambique, and Sofala. Each of these sites developed into a powerful

city-state governed by a king who supervised trade and organized public life in the region.

The cities themselves underwent an impressive transformation. Whereas most buildings were traditionally made of wood and dried mud, by about the twelfth century Swahili peoples began to construct large coral buildings, and by the fifteenth century the main Swahili towns boasted handsome stone mosques and public buildings. Meanwhile, urban Swahili elites dressed in silk and fine cotton clothes, and they set their tables with porcelain imported from China.

Kilwa Travelers' reports and recent archaeological discoveries have thrown especially clear light on the development of Kilwa, one of the busiest city-states on the east African coast. With a population of about twelve thousand, Kilwa was a thriving city with many stone buildings and mosques. Residents imported cotton and silk textiles as well as perfumes and pearls from India, and archaeologists have unearthed a staggering amount of Chinese porcelain. Merchants of Kilwa imported these products in exchange for gold, slaves, and ivory obtained from interior regions. By the late fifteenth century, Kilwa exported about a ton of gold per year.

Sourcesfrom**thePast**

Ibn Battuta on Muslim Society at Mogadishu

During the fourteenth century the Moroccan jurist Ibn Battuta traveled throughout much of the eastern hemisphere. Twice he visited sub-Saharan Africa: in 1331, when he traveled along the Swahili coast, and in 1351–1352, when he visited the Mali empire. His account of his visit to the Swahili city of Mogadishu offers insight into the mercantile and social customs of the city as well as the hospitality accorded to distinguished visitors.

[Mogadishu] is a town of enormous size. Its inhabitants are merchants possessed of vast resources: they own large numbers of camels, of which they slaughter hundreds every day [for food], and also have quantities of sheep. In this place are manufactured the woven fabrics called after it, which are unequalled and exported from it to Egypt and elsewhere. It is the custom of the people of this town that, when a vessel reaches the anchorage, the sumbuqs, which are small boats, come out to it. In each sumbuq there are a number of young men of the town, each one of whom brings a covered platter containing food and presents it to one of the merchants on the ship saying "This is my guest," and each of the others does the same. The merchant, on disembarking, goes only to the house of his host among the young men, except those of them who have made frequent journeys to the town and have gained some acquaintance with its inhabitants; these lodge where they please. When he takes up residence with his host, the latter sells his goods for him and buys for him; and if anyone buys anything from him at too low a price or sells to him in the absence of his host, that sale is held invalid by them. This practice is a profitable one for them.

When the young men came on board the vessel in which I was, one of them came up to me. My companions said to him, "This man is not a merchant, but a doctor of the law," whereupon he called out to his friends and said to them, "This is the guest of the qadi." There was among them one of the qadi's men, who informed him of this, and he came down to the beach with a number of students and sent one of them to me. I then disembarked with my companions and saluted him and his party. He said to me, "In the name of God, let us

go to salute the Shaikh." "And who is the Shaikh?" I said, and he answered, "The Sultan," for it is their custom to call the sultan "the Shaikh." . . .

When I arrived with the qadi . . . at the sultan's residence, one of the serving-boys came out and saluted the qadi, who said to him, "Take word to the intendant's office and inform the Shaikh that this man has come from the land of al-Hijaz [Arabia]." So he took the message, then returned bringing a plate on which were some leaves of betel and areca nuts, the same to the qadi, and what was left on the plate to my companions and the qadi's students. He brought also a jug of rose-water of Damascus, which he poured over me and over the qadi [i.e., over our hands], and said, "Our master commands that he be lodged in the students' house," this being a building equipped for the entertainment of students of religion. . . .

We stayed there three days, food being brought to us three times a day, following their custom. On the fourth day, which was a Friday, the qadi and students and one of the Shaikh's viziers came to me, bringing a set of robes; these [official] robes of theirs consist of a silk wrapper which one ties round his waist in place of drawers (for they have no acquaintance with these), a tunic of Egyptian linen with an embroidered border, a furred mantle of Jerusalem stuff, and an Egyptian turban with an embroidered edge. They also brought robes for my companions suitable to their position. We went to the congregational mosque and made our prayers behind the maqsura [private box for the sultan]. When the Shaikh came out of the door of the maqsura I saluted him along with the qadi; he said a word of greeting, spoke in their tongue with the qadi, and then said in Arabic, "You are heartily welcome, and you have honored our land and given us pleasure."

For Further Reflection

■ From Ibn Battuta's report, in what ways do you think he is commenting on differences within the *dar-al-Islam,* and in what ways is he noticing connections and continuities?

Source: Gibb, H. A. R., Translator, *The Travels of Ibn Battuta, A.D. 1325–1354,* 4 vols. Cambridge: Hakluyt Society, 1958–1994, 2:374–77. Reprinted by permission of David Higham Associates, Ltd.

Zimbabwe The influence of long-distance trade also had important effects on the interior regions of east Africa. Indeed, trade and the wealth that it brought underwrote the establishment of large and powerful kingdoms in east and central Africa. The best known of these kingdoms was Zimbabwe. The term *zimbabwe* simply refers to the dwelling of a chief. About the early thirteenth century, interior peoples built a magnificent stone complex

known as Great Zimbabwe near Nyanda in the modern state of Zimbabwe. Within stone walls 5 meters (16 feet) thick and 10 meters (32 feet) tall, Great Zimbabwe was a city of stone towers, palaces, and public buildings that served as the capital of a large kingdom. At the time of its greatest extent in the late fifteenth century, up to eighteen

Zimbabwe (zihm-BAHB-way)

thousand people may have lived in the vicinity of Great Zimbabwe, and the kingdom stretched from the outskirts of the Swahili city of Sofala deep into the interior of south-central Africa.

Kings residing at Great Zimbabwe controlled and taxed the trade between the interior and coastal regions. They organized the flow of gold, ivory, slaves, and local products from sources of supply to the coast. Their control over these products enabled them to forge alliances with local leaders and to profit handsomely from commercial transactions. Just as the trans-Saharan trade encouraged the building of states and empires in west Africa, the Indian Ocean trade generated wealth that financed the organization of city-states on the coast and large kingdoms in the interior regions of east and central Africa.

Islam in East Africa In east Africa, as in west Africa, trade brought cultural as well as political changes. Like their counterparts in west Africa, the ruling elites and the wealthy merchants of east Africa converted to the Islamic faith. They did not necessarily give up their religious and cultural traditions but, rather, continued to observe them for purposes of providing cultural leadership in their societies. By adopting Islam, however, they laid a cultural foundation for close cooperation with Muslim merchants. Moreover, Islam served as a fresh source of legitimacy for their rule, since they gained recognition from Islamic states in southwest Asia, and their conversion opened the door to political alliances with Muslim rulers in other lands. Even though the conversion of elite classes did not bring about the immediate spread of Islam throughout their societies, it enabled Islam to establish a presence in east Africa under the sponsorship of influential patrons. The faith eventually attracted interest in larger circles and became one of the principal cultural and religious traditions of east Africa.

SUMMARY

States and societies of sub-Saharan Africa differed considerably from those in other parts of the eastern hemisphere. The foundations of most sub-Saharan societies were the agricultural economy and iron-working skills that Bantu and other peoples spread throughout most of the African continent. As these peoples migrated to new regions and established new communities, they usually based their societies on kin groups rather than the state structures that predominated elsewhere in the eastern hemisphere. When different societies came into conflict with one another, however, they increasingly established formal political authorities to guide their affairs. African peoples organized states of various sizes, some very small and others quite large. When they entered into commercial relationships with Muslim peoples in southwest Asia and north Africa, they also built formidable imperial states in west Africa and bustling city-states in coastal east Africa. These states had far-reaching implications for sub-Saharan societies because they depended on a regular and reliable flow of trade goods—particularly gold, ivory, and slaves—and they encouraged African peoples to organize themselves politically and economically to satisfy the demands of foreign Muslim merchants. Trade also had cultural implications because it facilitated the introduction of Islam, which together with native African traditions profoundly influenced the development of sub-Saharan societies. After the eighth century, ruling elites in both west Africa and coastal east Africa mostly accepted Islam and strengthened its position in their societies by building mosques, consulting Muslim advisors, and supporting Islamic schools. By 1500 C.E. African traditions and Islamic influences had combined to fashion a series of powerful, productive, and distinctive societies in sub-Saharan Africa.

STUDY TERMS

age grades (277)
Axum (278)
bananas (274)
Bantu peoples
    (274–275)
Benin (275)
camels (280–282)
Gao (280)
Ghana (280)
Great Zimbabwe (285)
griot (273)
Ife (275)
Islamic slave trade (277)
Jenne (282)
Kebra Negast (279)
Kilwa (283–284)
kin-based societies
    (275–276)
kingdom of Kongo
    (275–276)
Koumbi-Saleh (281–282)
Mali (273)
Mansa Musa (282)
Sundiata (273)
Swahili (283)
Timbuktu (282)
trans-Saharan trade
    (280–282)
Zanj revolt (277)
Zimbabwe (285)

FOR FURTHER READING

Ibn Battuta. *Ibn Battuta in Black Africa*. Ed. and trans. by Said Hamdun and Noel King. Princeton, 1998. Translations of travel accounts of visits to coastal east Africa and the empire of Mali by a famous fourteenth-century Moroccan traveler.

Christopher Ehret. *The Civilizations of Africa: A History to 1800*. Charlottesville, Va., 2002. An important contribution that views Africa in the context of world history.

J. F. P. Hopkins and N. Levtzion, eds. *Corpus of Early Arabic Sources for West African History*. Princeton, 2000. Translations of numerous important accounts by Muslim merchants and geographers who reported on conditions in west Africa before modern times.

Mark Horton and John Middleton. *The Swahili: The Social Landscape of a Mercantile Society*. Oxford, 2000. Useful survey that draws on both archaeological and written evidence.

Nehemia Levtzion. *Ancient Ghana and Mali*. London, 1973. Concentrates on the political, social, and cultural history of west African kingdoms and empires.

John S. Mbiti. *African Religions and Philosophy*. 2nd ed. London, 1990. A thorough and systematic study of traditional African religions in their cultural context.

Roderick James McIntosh. *The Peoples of the Middle Niger: The Island of Gold*. Oxford, 1998. Fascinating volume emphasizing the environmental context of west African history.

John Middleton. *The World of the Swahili: An African Mercantile Civilization*. New Haven, 1992. Rich scholarly analysis that places modern Swahili society and culture in its historical context.

D. T. Niane, ed. *Sundiata: An Epic of Old Mali*. 2nd ed. Trans. by G. D. Pickett. London, 2006. Translation of the story of Sundiata, founder of the Mali empire, as preserved in African oral tradition.

Jan Vansina. *Paths in the Rainforests: Toward a History of Political Tradition in Equatorial Africa*. Madison, 1990. A brilliant synthesis of early African history by one of the world's foremost historians of Africa.

Christian Western Europe during the Middle Ages
CHAPTER 16

Venice, home of Marco Polo and a legion of merchants, drew enormous prosperity from trade.

EYEWITNESS:

From Venice to China and Back

In 1260 C.E. two brothers, Niccolò and Maffeo Polo, traveled from their native Venice to Constantinople. The Polo brothers were jewel merchants, and while in Constantinople, they decided to pursue opportunities farther east. They went first to trading cities on the Black Sea and the Volga River and then spent three years in the great central Asian trading city of Bokhara. While in Bokhara, they received an invitation to join a diplomatic embassy going to the court of Khubilai Khan. They readily agreed and traveled by caravan to the Mongol court, where the great khan received them and inquired about their land, rulers, and religion.

Khubilai was especially interested in learning more about Roman Catholic Christianity. Thus he asked the Polo brothers to return to Europe and request the pope to send learned theologians who could serve as authoritative sources of information on Christian doctrine. They accepted the mission and returned to Italy in 1269 as envoys of the great khan.

The Polo brothers were not able to satisfy the great khan's desire for expertise in Christian doctrine. The pope designated two missionaries to accompany the Polos, and the party set out in 1271, together with Niccolò's seventeen-year-old son, Marco Polo. Soon, however, the missionaries became alarmed at fighting along the route, and they decided to abandon the embassy and return to Europe. Only the Polos completed the journey, arriving at the Mongol court of Shangdu in 1274. Although they presented Khubilai with presents and letters from the pope rather than the requested missionaries, the great khan received them warmly. In fact, they remained in China in the service of the great khan for the next seventeen years. Their mission gave rise to Marco Polo's celebrated account of his travels, and it signaled the reintegration of Europe into the political and economic affairs of the larger eastern hemisphere.

During the early middle ages—from about 500 to 1000 C.E.—western Europe was a violent and disorderly land. The collapse of the western Roman empire and invasions by migratory peoples wrecked European society and the economy. The Germanic Carolingian empire—ruled most famously by Charlemagne—provided order in much of Europe only for a short time before internal political division and a new series of invasions led to its demise in 843 C.E. As a result of the turmoil and disarray that plagued Europe during the half millennium from 500 to 1000 C.E., western Europeans played little role in the development of a hemispheric economy during the era dominated by the Tang, Song, Abbasid, and Byzantine empires.

However, Europeans did begin to lay the foundations of a more dynamic society in the early middle ages. For example, regional states began to provide a stable political order. New tools and technologies led to increased agricultural production and economic growth. In addition, the western Christian church brought cultural and religious unity to most of Europe. Based on such political, economic, and cultural foundations, Europeans were able to build a vibrant and powerful society from about 1000 to 1300 C.E.—the period known in Europe as the "high middle ages."

Khubilai Khan (KOO-bih-lie Kahn)

CHRONOLOGY

476	Fall of the western Roman empire
480–547	Life of St. Benedict of Nursia
481–511	Reign of Clovis
482–543	Life of St. Scholastica
590–604	Reign of Pope Gregory I
751–843	Carolingian kingdom
768–814	Reign of Charlemagne
800	Coronation of Charlemagne as emperor
843	Dissolution of the Carolingian empire
936–973	Reign of King Otto I of Saxony
962	Coronation of Otto I as Holy Roman Emperor
1066	Norman invasion of England
1096–1099	First crusade
1170–1221	Life of St. Dominic
1182–1226	Life of St. Francis
1187	Recapture of Jerusalem by Saladin
1202–1204	Fourth crusade
1225–1274	Life of St. Thomas Aquinas
1271–1295	Marco Polo's trip to China

Although the idea of empire continued to fascinate European leaders, no one managed to bring all of Europe under their control during the high middle ages. Instead, local rulers organized powerful regional states. Increased agricultural production fueled rapid population growth. Economic expansion led to increased long-distance trade, enriched cities, and helped to create new towns.

Political organization, demographic increase, and economic growth pushed Europeans once again into the larger world. European merchants began to participate directly in the commercial economy of the eastern hemisphere, sometimes traveling as far as China in search of luxury goods. Ambitious military and political leaders expanded the boundaries of Christendom by seizing Muslim-held territories in Spain and the Mediterranean islands. European forces even mounted a series of military crusades that sought to recapture Palestine and the city of Jerusalem from Muslim control. Those efforts clearly demonstrated that Europeans were beginning to play a much larger role in the world than they had for the previous half millennium.

THE QUEST FOR ORDER AND THE ESTABLISHMENT OF REGIONAL STATES

Long after its collapse in the late fifth century C.E. the Roman empire inspired European leaders, who dreamed of a centralized political structure embracing all of Christian Europe. Yet it was not until the late eighth and ninth centuries that a Germanic group, the Franks, temporarily reestablished imperial authority in western Europe. Even then, imperial authority was short-lived and collapsed by the late ninth century. In the late tenth century, a new attempt was made by German princes who formed the Holy Roman Empire, which they viewed as a Christian revival of the earlier Roman empire. In fact, however, the Roman empire returned only in name. All attempts to extend its influence beyond Germany met stiff resistance from the popes and from the princes of other European

lands. Medieval Europe became a political mosaic of independent and competing regional states. Independent monarchies emerged in France and England, and other authorities ruled the various regions of Italy and Spain. These states frequently clashed with one another, and they all faced perennial challenges from within. Yet they organized their own territories efficiently, and they laid the foundations for the emergence of powerful national states in a later era.

The Franks and the Temporary Revival of Empire

Just a few decades after the Germanic general Odovacer deposed the last of the western Roman emperors in 476 C.E., the invaders organized a series of Germanic kingdoms as successor states in place of the Roman empire. However, from the fifth through the eighth centuries, continuing invasions and conflicts among the invaders themselves left western Europe in shambles. A major problem was that none of the Germanic peoples possessed the resources—much

Odovacer (AHD-oh-vah-cer)

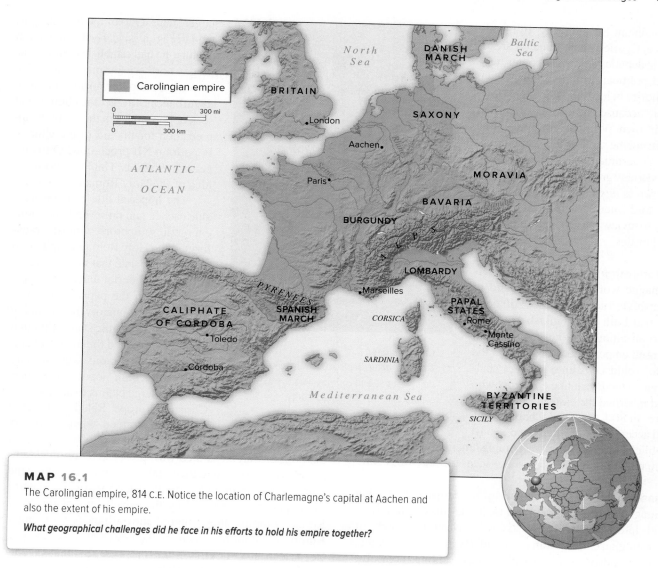

MAP 16.1

The Carolingian empire, 814 C.E. Notice the location of Charlemagne's capital at Aachen and also the extent of his empire.

What geographical challenges did he face in his efforts to hold his empire together?

less the political and social organization—to dominate all the others and establish their hegemony throughout western Europe. Yet by the ninth century, one of these groups—the Franks—not only became the most powerful of the Germanic peoples, but also built an impressive imperial state that temporarily organized about half of the territories formerly embraced by the western Roman empire.

Charlemagne The Franks had won their dominance over other Germanic peoples as a result of strong military leadership as well as the support of the popes in Rome, who appreciated the Franks' conversion to Roman Christianity in the late fifth century. The Frankish realm reached its high point under the rule of the Carolingian family line during the reign of Charlemagne ("Charles the Great"), who ruled from 768 to 814. Charlemagne possessed enormous energy, and the building of the Carolingian empire was in large measure his personal accomplishment. Although barely literate,

Charlemagne was extremely intelligent. He spoke Latin, understood some Greek, and regularly conversed with theologians and other learned men. He also maintained diplomatic relations with the Byzantine empire and the Abbasid caliphate. When Charlemagne inherited the Frankish throne, his realm included most of modern France as well as the lands that now form Belgium, the Netherlands, and southwestern Germany. By the time of his death in 814, Charlemagne had extended his authority to northeast Spain, Bavaria, northern Germany, and Italy as far south as Rome.

Charlemagne's Administration Charlemagne established a court and capital at Aachen (in modern Germany), but he spent most of his reign traveling throughout his realm

Charlemagne (SHAHR-leh-mane)
Carolingian (kah-roe-LIN-gee-uhn)
Aachen (AH-kehn)

to maintain his authority. In his absence, Charlemagne relied on aristocratic deputies, known as counts, who held political, military, and judicial authority in local jurisdictions. However, because the counts often had their own political ambitions that were not the same as those of the central government, Charlemagne instituted a new group of imperial officials known as *missi dominici* ("envoys of the lord ruler"), who traveled annually to review the accounts of all local authorities.

Charlemagne as Emperor Charlemagne worked extremely hard to keep his territories together. Although he had built the Frankish kingdom into an empire, he hesitated to call himself emperor because he knew the title would constitute a direct challenge to the Byzantine emperors who had inherited the eastern Roman empire. In 800, however, Charlemagne did accept the title when Pope Leo III publicly recognized his accomplishments by proclaiming him emperor during religious services on Christmas Day.

Charlemagne.
A bronze statue depicts Charlemagne riding a horse and carrying an orb symbolizing his imperial authority.

Dissolution of the Carolingian Empire Yet Charlemagne's empire did not last long after his death. Indeed, both internal disunity and external invasions brought the Carolingian empire to an early end. By 843 Charlemagne's three grandsons—who fought bitterly among themselves for the title of emperor—decided that they would solve the problem by dividing the empire into three kingdoms. Even had the empire remained unified, however, it was already apparent that local counts in the empire's vast realms were increasingly ignoring the central imperial government in favor of their own interests. Moreover, Muslim invaders from the south, Hungarian Magyar invaders from the east, and Viking invaders from the north all contributed to massive instability in the region and helped to ensure the ultimate dissolution of the empire.

The Holy Roman Empire

Otto I As the Carolingian empire faded during the ninth century, local authorities took responsibility for providing order in their own regions. Gradually, some of them extended their influence beyond their own jurisdictions and built larger states. Otto of Saxony was particularly aggressive. By the mid–tenth century, he had established himself as king in northern Germany, and twice he ventured into Italy to quell political disturbances, protect the church, and seek opportunities in the south. In appreciation for his aid to the church, Pope John XII proclaimed Otto emperor in 962 C.E. Thus was born the idea of the Holy Roman Empire.

The imperial title had considerable cachet, and on several occasions energetic emperors almost transformed the Holy Roman Empire into a hegemonic state that might have reintroduced imperial unity to Europe. Conflict with the papacy, however, prevented the emperors from building a strong and dynamic state. Although the popes crowned the medieval emperors, their relations were usually tense, since both popes and emperors made large claims to authority in Christian Europe. Relations became especially strained when emperors sought to influence the selection of church officials, which the popes regarded as their own prerogative, or when emperors sought to extend their authority into Italy, where the popes had long provided political leadership. Thus when the popes felt threatened by the pretensions of the Holy Roman Empire, they entered into alliances with other European authorities to check the power of the emperors. Because of that, the Holy Roman Empire remained an empire principally in name. Voltaire, the eighteenth-century French writer, once quipped that the Holy Roman Empire was "neither holy, nor Roman, nor an empire." Instead, it was a regional state that ruled Germany and occasionally sought to wield influence in eastern Europe and Italy.

Regional Monarchies in France and England

In the absence of an effective imperial power, regional states emerged throughout medieval Europe. In France and England, princes established regional monarchies on the basis of relationships between lords and their retainers.

Capetian France The French monarchy grew slowly from humble beginnings. When the last of the Carolingians died, in 987 C.E., the lords of France elected a minor noble named Hugh Capet to serve as king. Capet held only a small territory around Paris, and some of his retainers were far more

Capet (KAHP-it)

The Holy Roman Emperors claimed more territory than they could effectively rule.

MAP 16.2

The regional states of medieval Europe, 1000–1300 C.E. Note the large number of states and the different kinds of states that claimed sovereignty in medieval Europe.

How would this variety of states have contributed to instability in Europe?

powerful than he. Over the next three centuries, however, his descendants, known as the Capetian kings, gradually added to their resources, expanded their political influence, and established the right to administer justice throughout the realm. By the early fourteenth century, the Capetian kings had gradually centralized power and authority in France.

The Normans The English monarchy developed quite differently. Its founders were Normans—descendants of Vikings who carved out a state on the peninsula of Normandy in France during the ninth century. Though nominally

subject to Carolingian and later to Capetian rulers, the dukes of Normandy in fact pursued their own interests with little regard for their lords. Within Normandy the dukes built a tightly centralized state in which all authority stemmed from the dukes themselves. The dukes also retained title to all land in Normandy and strictly limited the right of their retainers to grant land to others. In 1066 Duke William of Normandy invaded England, then ruled by descendants of the Angles, the Saxons, and other Germanic peoples. Following a speedy military victory, the duke, now known as William the Conqueror, introduced Norman principles of government and land tenure to England and quickly established a tightly centralized realm.

Both the Capetians and the Normans faced internal challenges from retainers seeking to pursue independent policies or enlarge their powers. Both dynasties also faced external challenges: indeed, they often battled each other, since the Normans periodically sought to expand their possessions

Florence.
The Italian city-state of Florence grew rapidly during the high middle ages. This portrait of the city concentrates on the space enclosed by walls completed in the early fourteenth century.

in France. On the basis of relationships between lords and retainers, however, both the Capetians and the Normans managed to organize regional monarchies that maintained order and provided reasonably effective government.

Regional States in Italy and Iberia

Italian States Regional states emerged also in other lands of medieval Europe, though not on such a large scale as the monarchies of France and England. In Italy, for example, a series of ecclesiastical states, city-states, and principalities competed for power and position. By about the twelfth century, a series of prosperous city-states—including Florence, Bologna, Genoa, Milan, and Venice—dominated not only their own urban districts but also the surrounding hinterlands. Meanwhile, in southern Italy, Norman adventurers invaded territories still claimed by the Byzantine empire and various Muslim states. With papal approval and support, they overcame Byzantine and Muslim authorities, brought southern Italy into the orbit of Roman Catholic Christianity, and laid the foundations for the emergence of the powerful kingdom of Naples.

Christian and Muslim States in Iberia As in Italy, a series of regional states competed for power on the Iberian peninsula. From the eighth to the eleventh century, Muslim conquerors ruled most of the peninsula except for a few small states in northern Spain. Beginning in the mid–eleventh century, though, Christian adventurers from these states began to attack Muslim territories and enlarge their own domains. By the late thirteenth century, the Christian kingdoms of Castile, Aragon, and Portugal controlled most of the Iberian peninsula, leaving only the small kingdom of Granada in Muslim hands.

With its Holy Roman Empire, regional monarchies, ecclesiastical principalities, city-states, and new states founded on conquest, medieval Europe might seem to present a stark contrast to a centralized, reunified land such as China. Moreover, European rulers constantly campaigned to enlarge their holdings at the expense of their neighbors and thus endlessly complicated medieval European politics. Yet the regional states of the middle ages effectively tended to public affairs in limited regions. In doing so, they fashioned alternatives to a centralized empire as a form of political organization.

ECONOMIC GROWTH AND SOCIAL DEVELOPMENT

As regional states provided increasingly effective political organization, regional lords and their vassals took charge of political and military affairs in a system historians have commonly referred to as feudalism. The relative order and stability provided by feudalism eventually encouraged dramatic economic growth and social development in medieval Europe. This economic revival closely resembled the processes that in an earlier era had strengthened China, India, and the Islamic world. Thus, even in the absence of centralized imperial authority, the increased agricultural

Reverberations of

The Diffusion of Technologies

The use of horse collars by Europeans after about the twelfth century allowed horses to pull much heavier loads without choking. This, in turn, meant that horses could be used to pull heavy plows and wagons instead of oxen, and was one of the ways that Europeans increased their agricultural productivity by the thirteenth century. Scholars believe that the diffusion of the horse collar to Europe was a complex phenomenon, with the collar itself diffusing to northern Europe across central Asia, and the breast strap diffusing from north Africa through Islamic Iberia. When thinking about the long-term consequences of the diffusion of technologies, think carefully about the relationship between increased agricultural productivity in Europe (encouraged in part by the adoption of the horse collar) and the ability of Europeans to engage more consistently with regions outside of Europe.

production, urbanization, manufacturing, and trade spurred by feudalism transformed Europe and drew it once again into commercial relationships with distant lands.

Organizing a Decentralized Society

When the short-lived Carolingian empire dissolved, European nobles had little choice but to take responsibility for maintaining order in their own territories. Although most nobles owed nominal allegiance to a higher authority, in reality they acted with growing independence: they collected rents and fees, administered local affairs, mobilized armed forces, and decided legal disputes.

Lords and Retainers To organize their territories the local nobles built military and political relationships with other prominent individuals in their territories. In doing so, they mobilized small private armies by attracting armed retainers into their service with grants of land or money. These grants enabled retainers to devote their energies to the service of their lords rather than the tasks of cultivating food for their families. Retainers became responsible for the organization of local public works projects, the resolution of disputes, and the administration of justice. In exchange, retainers owed loyalty, obedience, and military service to their lords. As a result of these mutual obligations, lords and retainers merged into a hereditary noble class that lived off the surplus agricultural production it extracted from cultivators.

This decentralized political order developed into a complicated network of relationships between lords and retainers. Indeed, a lord with several retainers might himself be a retainer to a higher lord, who in turn might be one of several retainers to an even greater lord in a web of relationships extending from local communities to a king. Although this decentralized political order had the potential

to lead to chaos if retainers decided to pursue their own interests, in several places—including England, Germany, and France—high-ranking lords built powerful states on such foundations.

Serfs, Manors, and the Growth of the Agricultural Economy

Serfs The development of a decentralized political order accompanied fundamental changes in European society. Among the most important of these changes was the creation, during the mid-seventh century, of a new category of peasants called serfs. Serfs were not slaves subject to sale, but neither were they fully free. Instead, landlords allocated serfs a certain portion of land to farm, and in exchange required both labor services as well as a portion of the serfs' harvest. Male serfs typically worked three days a week in the fields of their lords and provided additional labor services during planting and harvesting seasons, while women churned butter, made cheese, brewed beer, spun thread, wove cloth, or sewed clothes for the lords and their families. Because landlords provided them with land to cultivate and sometimes with tools and animals as well, serfs had little opportunity to move to different lands. Indeed, they were able to do so only with the permission of their lord. They even had to pay a fee for the right to marry a serf who worked for a different lord.

Manors During the early middle ages, the institution of serfdom encouraged the development of the manor as the principal form of agricultural organization in western Europe. A manor was a large estate consisting of fields, meadows, forests, domestic animals, and serfs bound to the land. The lord of the manor was a prominent political or military figure who provided government, administration, and justice for the manor. In the absence of thriving cities, manors became largely self-sufficient communities. Lords of the manors maintained mills, bakeries, breweries, and wineries, and serfs produced most of the iron tools, leather goods, domestic utensils, and textiles that the manorial community needed. During the high middle ages, craft skills developed on manors would help fuel an impressive round of economic development in western Europe.

New Crops and Tools Peasant cultivators on manors also cleared forests, drained swamps, and increased the amount of land devoted to agriculture during the middle ages. As they did so, they also experimented with new agricultural techniques and implements. By the high middle ages European cultivators were experimenting with

Manor house.
In this landscape painting from the late fifteenth century, the lord of the manor (in robes) watches his laborers plant grapevines and pick grapes.

new crops and with different cycles of crop rotation to ensure the most abundant harvests without compromising the fertility of the soil. They increased cultivation especially of beans, which not only provided dietary protein but also enriched the land because of their property of fixing nitrogen in the soils where they grow. In addition, European peoples expanded their use of watermills and heavy plows, and introduced new tools like the horseshoe and horse collar—both of which increased the efficiency of agricultural labor. By the thirteenth century, observation and experimentation with new crops and new techniques had vastly increased understanding of agricultural affairs. News of these discoveries circulated widely throughout Europe in books and treatises on household economics and agricultural methods, which in turn led to increased agricultural productivity.

Population Growth Expansion of land under cultivation, improved methods of cultivation, and the use of new tools combined to increase both the quantity and the quality of food supplies. During the centuries from 1000 to 1300, European diets expanded from an almost complete reliance on grains to include meat, dairy products, fish, vegetables, and legumes such as beans and peas. This increase in agricultural productivity supported rapid population growth. In 600 C.E., as the Franks were beginning to gain dominance in western Europe, the European population

stood at about twenty-six million. By 1000, when regional states had ended invasions and restored order, it had edged up to thirty-six million. By 1300, only three hundred years later, the population had reached seventy-nine million. Such rapid demographic growth in turn helped stimulate a vigorous revival of towns and trade in medieval Europe.

The Revival of Towns and Trade

Urbanization With the abundant supplies of food produced on manors during the middle ages, by 1000 C.E. European society was able to support large numbers of urban residents. Attracted by urban opportunities, people from the countryside flocked to established cities and founded new towns at strategically located sites. Cities founded during Roman times, such as Paris, London, and Toledo, became thriving centers of government and business, and new urban centers—such as Venice in northern Italy—also emerged. Northern Italy and Flanders (the northwestern part of modern Belgium) experienced especially strong urbanization. Thus, for the first time since the fall of the western Roman empire, cities began to play a major role in European economic and social development.

Textile Production The growth of towns and cities brought about increasing specialization of labor, which in turn resulted in the dramatic expansion of manufacturing and trade. Manufacturing concentrated especially on the production of wool textiles. The cities of Italy and Flanders in particular became lively centers for the spinning, weaving, and dyeing of wool. Trade in wool products helped to fuel economic development throughout Europe. By the twelfth century the counts of Champagne in northern France sponsored fairs that operated almost year-round and that served as vast marketplaces where merchants from all parts of Europe compared and exchanged goods.

Mediterranean Trade The revival of urban society was most pronounced in Italy, which was geographically well situated to participate in the trade networks of the Mediterranean basin. During the tenth century, for example, the cities of Amalfi and Venice served as ports for merchants engaged in trade with Byzantine and Muslim partners in the eastern Mediterranean. Italian merchants exchanged salt, olive oil, wine, wool fabrics, leather products, and glass

Genoese bankers.
Genoese bankers change money and check the accounts of their clients in this fourteenth-century manuscript illustration.

for luxury goods such as gems, spices, silk, and other goods from India, southeast Asia, and China that Muslim merchants brought to eastern Mediterranean markets.

As trade expanded, Italian merchants established sizable communities in the major ports and commercial centers of the Mediterranean and the Black Sea, and by the mid–thirteenth century some were even beginning to venture as far as central Asia, India, and China in search of commercial opportunities.

The Hanseatic League Although medieval trade was most active in the Mediterranean basin, a lively commerce grew up also in the northern seas. The Baltic Sea and the North Sea were sites of a particularly well-developed trade network known as the Hanseatic League, or more simply as the Hansa—an association of trading cities stretching from Novgorod to London and embracing all the significant commercial centers of northern Europe. The Rhine, the Danube, and other major European rivers linked the Hansa trade network with that of the Mediterranean.

Improved Business Techniques As in postclassical China and the Islamic world, a rapidly increasing volume of trade encouraged the development of credit, banking, and new forms of business organization in Europe. Bankers issued letters of credit to merchants traveling to distant markets, which could then be exchanged for merchandise or cash in the local currency.

Meanwhile, merchants devised new ways of spreading and pooling the risks of commercial investments. They entered into partnerships with other merchants, and they limited the liability of partners to the extent of their individual investments. These arrangements encouraged the formation of commercial partnerships, thus further stimulating the European economy.

Social Change

The Three Estates Medieval social commentators frequently held that European society embraced three estates or classes: "those who pray, those who fight, and those who work." Those who prayed were clergy of the Roman Catholic Church. From lowly parish priests to bishops, cardinals, and popes, the clergy constituted a spiritual estate owing its loyalty to the church rather than to secular rulers. The fighters came from the ranks of nobles. They inherited their positions in society and received an education that concentrated on equestrian skills and military arts. Finally, there were those who worked—the vast majority of the population—who mostly cultivated land as peasants.

The formula dividing society neatly into three classes captures some important truths about medieval Europe. It clearly reflects a society marked by political, social, and economic inequality: although they did not necessarily lead lives of luxury, those who prayed and those who fought enjoyed rights and honors denied to those who worked. Though bound by secular law, for example, clerics were members of an international spiritual society before they were subjects of a lord, and if they became involved in legal difficulties, they normally faced courts of law administered by the church rather than secular rulers. For their part the nobles mostly lived off the surplus production of dependent peasants and serfs.

Chivalry Yet, though expressing some truths, the formula overlooks processes that brought considerable change to medieval European society. Within the ranks of the nobles,

Hanseatic (han-see-AT-ik)

Sources from the Past

Privileges Granted in London to the Hanse of Cologne 1157–1194

The Baltic Sea and the North Sea were centers of a thriving trade network known as the Hansa, an association of trading cities that included all the major commercial centers of Poland, northern Germany, and Scandinavia. The hanse of the German city of Cologne requested Emperor Frederick Barbarossa to make favorable commercial treaties with foreign countries, including with Henry II of England in 1157. The hanse of Cologne then obtained special favors in London, including royal protection of their house and equal privileges with the French in selling wine. By the reign of English King Richard I, the hanse had also obtained freedom from certain tolls throughout England.

Grant of Henry II, 1157. Henry, by the grace of God, King of England, Duke of Normandy and Aquitaine, and Count of Anjou, to his justices, sheriffs, and all officers in England, greetings. I command you to guard, maintain, and protect the men and citizens of Cologne as if they were my own men and my friends; and you are to protect all their wares and merchandise and possessions so that you injure neither them, nor their house in London, nor their merchandise, nor impede their business, nor permit any of these things to be done. For all their things are in my custody and protection. For which reason let them have security and peace on paying their lawful customs; nor shall you exact from them any new customs or duties which they have not been accustomed to pay and which they ought not to pay. And if any one should maliciously transgress this order, see that full justice be done to him without delay.

Grant of Henry II, 1157. Henry, by the grace of God, King of England, Duke of Normandy and Aquitaine, and Count of Anjou, to his sheriffs and bailiffs of London, greetings. I grant that the men of Cologne may sell their wine at the market where French wine is sold, namely, for three denarii the setier. And so I forbid them to be disturbed there or that any one should do them injury or harm.

Grant of Richard I, 1194. Richard, by the grace of God, King of England, Duke of Normandy and Aquitaine, and Count of Anjou, to the archbishops, bishops, earls, barons, justices, sheriffs, and to all officers and bailiffs, and to all his faithful people in England, greeting. Be it known that we have freed our beloved citizens of Cologne and their merchandise from those two solidi which they were accustomed to give for their gild-hall at London, and from all other customs and demands which pertain to us in London and throughout our land of England. We have granted also that they may come and go freely throughout our entire land, and that they may go freely and buy and sell in the fairs of our land, in the city of London, and elsewhere. Therefore we wish and command that the citizens of Cologne shall have the said liberties and free customs throughout all this our realm of England.

For Further Reflection

■ From the agreements above between two English monarchs and the hanse of Cologne, how would you characterize the commercial relationship between European rulers and private trading associations during the medieval period?

Source: J. M. Lappenberg, ed., *Urkundliche Geschichte des Hansischen Stahlhofes zu London* (Hamburg, 1851), Part II, pp. 3–5, reprinted in Roy C. Cave and Herbert H. Coulson, *A Source Book for Medieval Economic History* (Milwaukee: The Bruce Publishing Co., 1936; reprint ed., New York: Biblo & Tannen, 1965), pp. 220–22. Scanned by Jerome S. Arkenberg, Cal. State Fullerton. (Translation slightly modernized.)

---

for example, an emphasis on chivalry and courtly behavior gradually introduced expectations of high ethical standards and refined manners that encouraged warriors to become cultivated leaders of society. Chivalry was an informal but widely recognized code of ethics and behavior considered appropriate for nobles. Church officials originally promoted the chivalric code in an effort to curb fighting within Christendom. By the twelfth century the ritual by which a young man became initiated into the nobility as a knight commonly called for the candidate to place his sword on a church altar and pledge his service to God. Thus, the noble who observed the chivalric code would devote himself to the causes of order, piety, and the Christian faith. Over the long term, then, the code of chivalry helped to soften the manners of the nobility.

Independent Cities The model of the three estates also did not account well for substantial minorities of people, including especially merchants and townspeople. Indeed, by the twelfth century the ranks of workers included not only peasants but also increasing numbers of merchants, artisans, crafts workers, and professionals who filled the growing towns of medieval Europe. Because of their military power, lords could dominate these growing towns and tax their wealth. As towns grew larger, however, urban populations were increasingly able to resist the demands of nobles and guide their own affairs. By the late eleventh century, inhabitants of prosperous towns were demanding that local lords grant them charters of incorporation that exempted them from political regulation and allowed them to manage their own affairs. Sometimes groups of

Fish market.
This painting from 1568 depicts a woman fishmonger working alongside her husband.

Although few routes to public authority were open to women, in the larger towns and cities women worked alongside men as butchers, brewers, bakers, fishmongers, innkeepers, merchants, and occasionally physicians and pharmacists. Women dominated some occupations, particularly those involving textiles and decorative arts, such as sewing, spinning, weaving, and the making of hats, wigs, and fur garments. In addition, most guilds admitted women into their ranks, and some guilds had exclusively female memberships. Despite the persistence of patriarchal social structures, the increasing prominence of women in European society illustrates the significance of towns and cities as agents of social change in medieval Europe.

cities organized leagues to advance their commercial interests, as in the case of the Hansa, or to protect themselves against the encroachments of political authorities.

Guilds The cities of medieval Europe were by no means egalitarian societies. Yet medieval towns and cities also reflected the interests and contributions of the working classes. Merchants and workers in all the arts, crafts, and trades organized guilds that regulated the production and sale of goods within their jurisdictions. By the thirteenth century the guilds had come to control much of the urban economy of medieval Europe. For example, guilds oversaw the teaching of the various trades, established standards of quality for manufactured goods, determined the prices at which members had to sell their products, and regulated the entry of new workers into their groups.

Guilds had social as well as economic significance in that they provided a focus for friendship and mutual support in addition to work. Guild members regularly socialized with one another, and prosperous guilds often built large halls where members held meetings, banquets, and sometimes boisterous drinking parties. Guilds often came to the aid of members and their families by providing financial and moral support for those who fell ill. They also arranged funeral services for their deceased and provided support for survivors. Thus guilds constituted a kind of social infrastructure that made it possible for medieval cities to function.

Urban Women Medieval towns and cities offered fresh opportunities for women as well as for men.

EUROPEAN CHRISTIANITY DURING THE MIDDLE AGES

One of the most important developments of the early middle ages was the conversion of western Europe to Roman Christianity. The Franks, the popes, and the monasteries played important roles in bringing about this conversion. The adoption of Roman Christianity ensured that medieval Europe would inherit crucial cultural elements from classical Roman society, including the Latin language and the institutional Roman church. In addition, Roman Catholic Christianity guided European thought on religious, moral, and ethical matters. Representatives of the Roman church administered the rituals associated with birth, marriage, and death. Most of the art, literature, and music of the middle ages drew inspiration from Christian doctrines and stories. Just as mosques and minarets defined the skylines of Muslim cities, the spires of churches and cathedrals dominated the landscape of medieval Europe, testifying visually to the importance of religion and the pervasive presence of the Roman Catholic church.

Western Christianity also changed in several ways during the late middle ages. As the Roman Catholic church developed an identity distinct from the Eastern Orthodox church, western theologians became reacquainted with the works of Aristotle—mostly unknown to European scholars of the early middle ages—and they produced an impressive synthesis of Aristotelian philosophy and Christian values. Meanwhile, lay classes elaborated a rich tradition of popular religion that represented an effort to express Christianity in meaningful terms.

The Politics of Conversion

Although Christianity was the principal source of religious, moral, and cultural authority in the Mediterranean basin by the time the Roman empire collapsed, western Europeans did not demonstrate a deep commitment to Christianity until the Franks converted to the religion in the late fifth century. By the time of Charlemagne, the Carolingian Franks viewed themselves as protectors of the papacy, and offered the popes both political and military support. Charlemagne also worked to spread Christianity in northern lands through both peaceful and military means. Between 772 and 804, for example, he waged a bitter campaign against the Saxons, a pagan people inhabiting northern Germany. When he finally claimed victory, Charlemagne insisted not only that the Saxons acknowledge him as their political lord, but that they replace their pagan traditions with Christianity. Through campaigns such as this, as well as through diplomacy and the work of missionaries, by the year 1000 C.E. Christianity had won the allegiance of most people throughout western Europe and the Nordic lands.

The Papacy

In addition to the support it received from the Franks, the Roman church increased its authority in Europe through strong papal leadership. When the western Roman empire collapsed, the papacy survived and claimed spiritual authority over all the lands formerly embraced by the empire. Initially, the popes cooperated closely with the Byzantine emperors, who as leaders of the eastern Roman empire seemed to be the natural heirs to Roman authority. Beginning in the late sixth century, however, the popes began increasingly to distinguish the western Christian church based in Rome from the eastern Christian church based in Constantinople. By 1054 C.E., the two churches differed so violently on so many issues that the pope and the patriarch of the eastern church excommunicated each other. After the eleventh century the two branches of Christianity formed distinct identities as the Roman Catholic and Eastern Orthodox churches.

Pope Gregory I The individual most important in providing the Roman church with its sense of identity and direction was Pope Gregory I (590–604 C.E.), also known as Gregory the Great. Most important, Gregory strengthened the pope's control over church doctrine by reasserting papal primacy—the claim that the bishop of Rome was the ultimate authority in the Christian church. Gregory also enhanced the influence of the Roman church in the lives of individuals by emphasizing the sacrament of penance,

which required individuals to confess their sins to their priests and then to atone for their sins by penitential acts prescribed by the priests. In addition, Gregory further strengthened the Roman church by extending its appeal and winning new converts in western Europe through the efforts of missionaries, most of whom were monks. Indeed, Pope Gregory himself was a monk, and he relied heavily on the energies of his fellow monks in seeking converts throughout Europe.

Monasticism

Christian monasticism had its origin in the second century C.E. in Egypt, where devout Christians had formed communes to devote themselves to the pursuit of holiness. When Christianity became legal during the fourth century, the monastic lifestyle became an increasingly popular alternative throughout the Roman empire.

St. Benedict and the Rule During the early days of monasticism, each community developed its own rules, procedures, and priorities. Some communities demanded that their inhabitants follow extremely austere lifestyles that sapped the energy of the monks, whereas others did not establish any clear expectations of their recruits. In response to those haphazard conditions, St. Benedict of Nursia (480–547 C.E.) strengthened the early monastic movement by providing it with discipline and a sense of purpose. In 529 St. Benedict prepared a set of regulations known as Benedict's *Rule* for the monastic community that he had founded at Monte Cassino, near Rome. The *Rule* required monks to take vows to lead communal, celibate lives under the absolute direction of the abbot who supervised the monastery: poverty, chastity, and obedience became the prime virtues for Benedictine monks.

Through the influence of St. Benedict's sister, the nun St. Scholastica (482–543), an adaptation of the *Rule* soon provided guidance for the religious life of women living in convents. Within a century most European monasteries and convents observed the Benedictine *Rule*. Even today most Roman Catholic monasteries observe rules that reflect the influence of the Benedictine tradition.

Monasticism and Society Strengthened by the discipline that the Benedictine *Rule* introduced, monasteries became a dominant feature in the social and cultural life of western Europe throughout the middle ages. Monasteries helped to provide order in the countryside, for example, and to expand agricultural production. Monasteries accumulated large landholdings—as well as authority over serfs working their lands—from the bequests of wealthy individuals, and on those lands they mobilized both monks and serfs to clear forests, drain swamps, and prepare lands for cultivation. Indeed, monasteries organized

St. Scholastica (skuh-LAS-tih-kah)

St. Francis.

St. Francis of Assisi was the son of a wealthy merchant in central Italy, but he abandoned the comforts that he inherited and pledged himself to a life of poverty and preaching. Stories represented in this fresco from the basilica of St. Francis at Assisi report that he preached to the birds and encouraged them to sing in praise of God.

much of the labor that brought about the expansion of agricultural production in early medieval Europe.

Like Buddhist monasteries in Asian lands and charitable religious foundations in Muslim lands, European monasteries provided a variety of social services. They served as inns, places of refuge, orphanages, hospitals, and schools. Some monasteries maintained libraries and scriptoria, where monks copied works of classical literature and philosophy as well as the scriptures and other Christian writings. Almost all works of Latin literature that have come down to the present survive because of copies made by medieval monks. Finally, monasteries served as a source of literate, educated, and talented individuals whose secretarial and administrative services were crucial for the organization of effective government in early medieval Europe.

Dominicans and Franciscans By the twelfth century C.E., however, many Benedictine monasteries had become so successful that the monks residing within them led

comfortable and leisurely lives instead of lives of poverty, chastity, and obedience. In response, some devout Christians responded to this state of affairs by organizing movements designed to champion spiritual over materialistic values. Most prominent of them were St. Dominic (1170–1221) and St. Francis (1182–1226). During the thirteenth century St. Dominic and St. Francis founded orders of mendicants (beggars), known as the Dominican and Franciscan friars, who would have no personal possessions and would have to beg for their food and other needs from audiences to whom they preached. Mendicants were especially active in towns and cities, where they addressed throngs of recently arrived migrants whose numbers were so large that existing urban churches and clergy could not serve them well. The Dominicans and the Franciscans also worked zealously to combat heterodox movements and to persuade heretics to return to the Roman Catholic church.

Because of the various roles they played in the larger society, monasteries and mendicants were particularly effective agents in the spread of Christianity. Monasteries organized life in the countryside and provided social services, while monks and mendicants zealously preached Christianity and tended to the spiritual needs of rural populations. As a result of their efforts, over the decades and centuries monks and mendicants helped to instill Christian values in countless generations of European peasants.

Schools, Universities, and Scholastic Theology

Cathedral Schools By the high middle ages, Europe's increasing wealth and social complexity created a strong demand for educated individuals who could deal with complicated political, legal, and theological issues. In response to such demand, by the eleventh century bishops and archbishops in France and northern Italy organized schools in their cathedrals and invited well-known scholars to serve as master teachers.

By the twelfth century the cathedral schools had established formal curricula. Instruction concentrated on the liberal arts, especially literature and philosophy. Students read the Bible and the writings of the church fathers, as well as classical Latin literature and the few works of Plato and Aristotle that were available in Latin translation. Some cathedral schools also offered advanced instruction in law, medicine, and theology.

Universities About the mid–twelfth century, students and teachers organized academic guilds and persuaded political authorities to grant charters guaranteeing their rights. Student guilds demanded rigorous, high-quality instruction from their teachers, while faculty sought to vest teachers with the right to bestow academic degrees and to control the curriculum in their own institutions.

Nôtre Dame Cathedral.
Architects and laborers sometimes worked more than a century to construct the massive gothic cathedrals of medieval Europe. Built during the twelfth and thirteenth centuries, the magnificent cathedral of Notre Dame in Paris honors the Virgin Mary.

What kinds of feelings might such massive structures have evoked in worshipers?

These guilds had the effect of transforming cathedral schools into universities. By the late thirteenth century, universities had appeared in cities throughout Europe.

Scholasticism: St. Thomas Aquinas The evolution of the university coincided with the rediscovery of the works of Aristotle, which European scholars learned about through increased contacts with Byzantine as well as Muslim philosophers. During the thirteenth century, Latin translations of Aristotle's works spread throughout Europe, and they profoundly influenced almost all branches of thought. The most notable result was the emergence of scholastic theology, which sought to synthesize the beliefs and values of Christianity with the logical rigor of Greek philosophy. The most famous of the scholastic theologians was St. Thomas Aquinas (1225–1274), who spent most of his career teaching at the University of Paris. While holding fervently to his Christian convictions, St. Thomas believed

that Aristotle had understood and explained the workings of the world better than any other thinker. St. Thomas saw no contradiction between Aristotle and Christian revelation. In his view, Aristotle explained the world according to human reason, while Christianity explained it as part of a divine plan. Thus, scholastic theology represented the synthesis of reason and faith. Like the neo-Confucianism of Zhu Xi or the Islamic philosophy of Ibn Rushd, scholastic theology reinterpreted inherited beliefs in light of the most advanced knowledge of the time.

Popular Religion

St. Thomas and the other scholastic theologians addressed a sophisticated, intellectual elite rather than the common people of medieval Europe. The popular masses neither knew nor cared much about Aristotle. For their purposes, Christianity was important primarily as a set of beliefs, ceremonies, and rituals that gave meaning to individual lives and that bound them together into coherent communities.

St. Thomas Aquinas (uh-KWAHY-nuhs)

Sacraments Popular piety generally entailed observance of the sacraments and devotion to the saints recognized by the Roman Catholic church. Sacraments are holy rituals that bring spiritual blessings on the observants. The church recognized seven sacraments, including baptism, matrimony, penance, and the Eucharist. By far the most popular was the Eucharist, during which priests offered a ritual meal commemorating Jesus' last meal with his disciples before his trial and execution by Roman authorities. Because the sacrament kept individuals in good standing with the church, conscientious believers observed it weekly, and the especially devout on a daily basis. Popular beliefs held that the sacrament would protect individuals from sudden death and advance their worldly interests.

Devotion to Saints Popular religion also took the form of devotion to the saints. According to church teachings, saints were human beings who had led such exemplary lives that God held them in special esteem. As a result, they enjoyed special influence with heavenly authorities and were able to intervene on behalf of individuals living in the world. Medieval Europeans frequently invoked the aid of saints, who had reputations for helping living people as well as souls of the dead. Tradition held that certain saints could cure diseases, relieve toothaches, and guide sailors through storms to a port.

The Virgin Mary During the high middle ages, the most popular saint was always the Virgin Mary, mother of Jesus, who personified the Christian ideal of womanhood, love, and sympathy, and who reportedly lavished aid on her devotees. During the twelfth and thirteenth centuries, Europeans dedicated hundreds of churches and cathedrals to the Virgin, among them the splendid cathedral of Notre Dame ("Our Lady") of Paris.

Saints' Relics Medieval Europeans went to great lengths to express their adoration of the Virgin and other saints through veneration of their relics and physical remains, widely believed to retain the powers associated with the holy individuals themselves. Churches assembled vast collections of relics, such as clothes, locks of hair, teeth, and bones of famous saints. Especially esteemed were relics associated with Jesus or the Virgin, such as the crown of thorns that Jesus reportedly wore during his crucifixion or drops of the Virgin's milk miraculously preserved in a vial.

Pilgrimage Some collections of relics became famous well beyond their own regions. Like Muslims making the hajj, pilgrims trekked long distances to honor the saints the relics represented. The making of pilgrimages became so common during the high middle ages that a travel industry emerged to serve the needs of pilgrims. Inns dotted the routes leading to popular churches and shrines, and guides shepherded groups of pilgrims to religious sites and explained their significance. There were even guidebooks that pointed out the major attractions along pilgrims' routes and warned them of difficult terrain and unscrupulous scoundrels who took advantage of visitors.

THE MEDIEVAL EXPANSION OF EUROPE

During the high middle ages, the relationship between western European peoples and their neighbors underwent dramatic change. Powerful states, economic expansion, and demographic growth all strengthened European society, while church officials encouraged the colonization of pagan and Muslim lands as a way to extend the influence of Roman Catholic Christianity. Beginning about the mid–eleventh century, Europeans embarked on expansive ventures on several fronts: Atlantic, Baltic, and Mediterranean. All those ventures signaled clearly that Europeans were beginning to play a much larger role in the affairs of the eastern hemisphere than they had during the early middle ages.

Atlantic and Baltic Colonization

Vinland During the ninth and tenth centuries, seafaring peoples from the Nordic Scandinavian lands began to venture far from Europe to the islands of the North Atlantic Ocean. They occupied Iceland beginning in the late ninth century, and by the end of the tenth century they had discovered Greenland and established a small colony there. About 1000 C.E. Leif Ericsson left the colony at Greenland and

Leif Ericsson (leef ER-ik-suhn)

took an exploratory party south and west, arriving eventually at modern Newfoundland in Canada. Because of the wild grapes growing in the region, Leif called it Vinland. During the years following Leif's voyage, Greenlanders made several efforts to establish permanent colonies in Vinland. Ultimately, however, their efforts failed because they did not have the resources to sustain a settlement over the stormy seas of the North Atlantic Ocean. Nonetheless, the establishment of even a short-lived colony indicated a growing capacity of Europeans to venture into the larger world.

Christianity in Scandinavia While Scandinavians explored the North Atlantic, the Roman Catholic church drew Scandinavia itself into the community of Christian Europe. The kings of Denmark and Norway converted to Christianity in the tenth century. Conversion of their subjects came gradually and with considerable resistance, but royal support for the Roman Catholic church ensured that Christianity would have a place in Danish and Norwegian societies. Between the twelfth and fourteenth centuries, Sweden and Finland followed their neighbors into the Christian faith.

Crusading Orders and Baltic Expansion In the Baltic lands of Prussia, Livonia, and Lithuania, Christian authority arrived in the wake of military conquest. During the era of crusades, zealous Christians formed a series of

MAP 16.3
Medieval expansion of Europe, 1000–1250 C.E. Observe the paths taken by the European crusaders and invaders.

What does the distance of these paths tell you about the military and organizational capabilities, strategies, and aims of Europeans in the high middle ages?

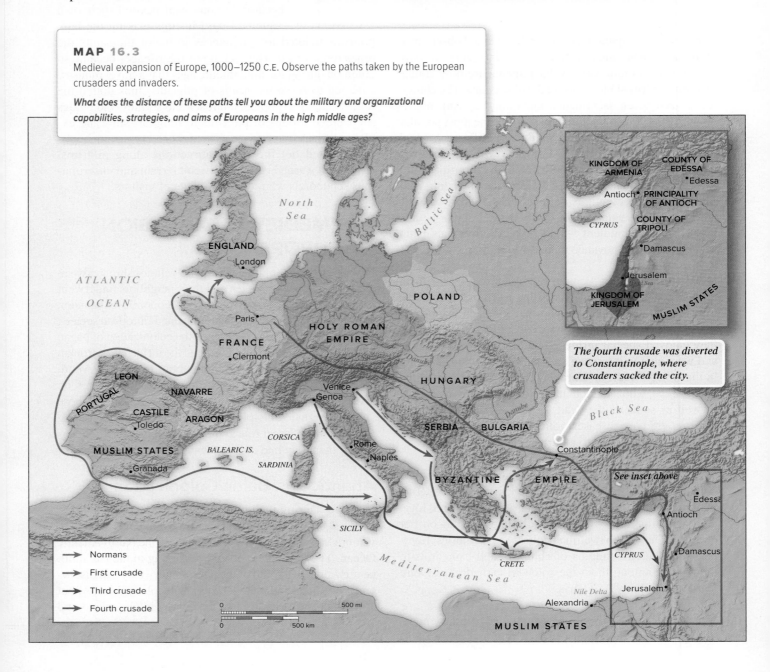

The fourth crusade was diverted to Constantinople, where crusaders sacked the city.

PART 4

Thinking about ENCOUNTERS

The Historical Significance of the Crusades

Military campaigns commonly bring about death and destruction, and the crusades were no exception to the rule. Yet the crusades also prompted important cultural and intellectual exchanges. *What were some of the cultural, intellectual, and economic effects of the Crusades?*

military-religious orders. The most prominent were the Templars, Hospitallers, and Teutonic Knights, who pledged to devote their lives to the struggle against Muslims and pagans. The Teutonic Knights were most active in the Baltic region, where they waged military campaigns against the pagan Slavic peoples during the twelfth and thirteenth centuries. Aided by German missionaries, the Knights founded churches and monasteries in the territories they subdued. By the late thirteenth century, the Roman Catholic church had established its presence throughout the Baltic region, which progressively became absorbed into the larger society of Christian Europe.

The Reconquest of Sicily and Spain

The boundaries of Christian Europe also expanded in the Mediterranean basin. There Europeans came into conflict with Muslims, whose ancestors had conquered the major Mediterranean islands and most of the Iberian peninsula between the eighth and tenth centuries. As their society became stronger, Europeans undertook to reconquer those territories and reintegrate them into Christian society.

The Reconquest of Sicily Most important of the islands was Sicily, which Muslims had conquered in the ninth century. During the eleventh century, Norman warriors returned Sicily to Christian hands after almost twenty years of conflict. Islam did not disappear immediately, but as Muslims either left Sicily or converted to Christianity, Islam gradually disappeared from the island.

The Reconquista of Spain The reconquest of Spain—known as the *reconquista*—took a much longer time than the recapture of Sicily. Following the Muslim invasion and conquest of the early eighth century, the caliphate of Córdoba ruled almost all of the Iberian peninsula. A small Christian state survived in Catalonia in the far northeast, and the kingdom of León resisted Muslim advances in the far northwest. The process of *reconquista* began in the 1060s from these Christian toeholds. By 1150 Christian forces had recaptured Lisbon and established their authority over half of the peninsula. Their successes lured reinforcements from France and England, and in the first half of

the thirteenth century a new round of campaigns brought most of Iberia into Christian hands. Only the kingdom of Granada in the far south of the peninsula remained Muslim. It survived as an outpost of Islam until 1492, when Christian forces mounted a campaign that conquered Granada and completed the *reconquista*.

The political, economic, and demographic strength of Christian Europe helps to explain the reconquests of Sicily and Spain as military ventures. Especially in the case of Spain, however, it is clear that religious concerns also helped to drive the *reconquista*. The popes and other leading clergy of the Roman Catholic church regarded Islam as an affront to Christianity, and they enthusiastically encouraged campaigns against the Muslims. When reconquered territories fell into Christian hands, church officials immediately established bishoprics and asserted Christian authority. They also organized campaigns to convert local populations. As a result of those efforts, the Roman Catholic church began to displace Islam in conquered Spain.

The Crusades

The term *crusade* refers to a holy war. It derives from the Latin word *crux,* meaning "cross," the device on which Roman authorities had executed Jesus. When a pope declared a crusade, warriors would "take up the cross" as a symbol of their faith, sew strips of cloth in the form of a cross on the backs of their garments, and venture forth to fight on behalf of Christianity. The most famous of these crusades were the enormous expeditions that Roman Catholic Christians mounted in an effort to recapture Palestine and the holy city of Jerusalem from Muslim authorities.

Urban II Pope Urban II launched these crusades in 1095. The response to Urban's appeal was immediate and enthusiastic. A zealous preacher named Peter the Hermit traveled throughout France, Germany, and the Low Countries whipping up support among popular audiences. Within a year of Pope Urban's call, the Hermit had organized a ragtag army of poor knights and enthusiastic peasants—including women—and set out for Palestine without training, discipline, weapons, supplies, or plans. Not surprisingly, the campaign was a disaster: many members of Peter's band died, and few made it back to Europe. Yet the campaign indicated the high level of interest that the crusading idea generated among the European public.

The First Crusade Shortly after Peter's ill-fated venture, French and Norman nobles organized a more respectable

reconquista (ray-kohn-KEES-tah)

Brutalities during the Crusades.
The crusades involved brutal conflict and atrocities from all sides. In this twelfth-century manuscript illustration, crusaders lob severed enemy heads at Muslims defending a fortress.

military expedition to the holy land. In late 1096 the crusading armies began the long trek to Palestine. In 1097 and 1098 they captured Edessa, Antioch, and other strategic sites. In 1099 Jerusalem itself fell to the crusaders, who then proceeded to extend their conquests and carve conquered territories into Christian states.

Although the crusaders did not realize it, hindsight shows that their quick victories came largely because of division and disarray in the ranks of their Muslim foes. The crusaders' successes, however, encouraged Turks, Egyptians, and other Muslims to settle their differences, at least temporarily, in the interests of expelling European Christians from the eastern Mediterranean. By the mid–twelfth century the crusader communities had come under tremendous pressure. The crusader state of Edessa fell to Turks in 1144, and during the Third Crusade the Muslim leader Salah al-Din, known to Europeans as Saladin, recaptured Jerusalem in 1187. Crusaders maintained several of their enclaves for another century and even embarked on several more military expeditions, but Saladin's victories sealed the fate of Christian forces in the eastern Mediterranean.

Europeans did not immediately concede Palestine to the Muslims. By the mid–thirteenth century they had launched five major crusades, but none of the later ventures succeeded in reestablishing a Christian presence in Palestine. The fourth crusade (1202–1204) went badly astray. Venetian authorities contracted with military leaders to supply enough ships to transport some thirty thousand crusaders to Palestine. When crusaders could not come up with sufficient funds, Venetians directed them instead to conquer the Italian port city of Zara—a commercial rival of Venice—and then to attack Constantinople, the most important commercial center in the eastern Mediterranean. In fact, the fourth crusade never made it to Palestine. The ignoble venture ended after the crusaders conquered Constantinople, subjected the city to a ruthless sack, and installed a Roman Catholic regime that survived until 1261. The Byzantine empire never fully recovered from this blow, and lumbered along in serious decline until Ottoman Turks toppled it in 1453. Yet even though the later crusades failed in their principal objective, they inspired European dreams of conquest in the eastern Mediterranean until the late sixteenth century.

Consequences of the Crusades   As holy wars intended to reestablish Roman Catholic Christianity in the eastern Mediterranean basin, the crusades were wars of military and political expansion. Yet in the long run, the crusades were much more important for their social, economic, commercial, and cultural consequences. Even as European armies built crusader states in Palestine and Syria, European scholars and missionaries dealt with Muslim philosophers and theologians, and European merchants traded eagerly with their Muslim counterparts. The result was a large-scale exchange of ideas, technologies, and trade goods that profoundly influenced European development. Through their sojourns in Palestine and their regular dealings with Muslims throughout the Mediterranean basin, European Christians became acquainted with the works of Aristotle, Islamic science and astronomy, "Arabic" numerals (which Muslims had borrowed from India), and techniques of paper production (which Muslims had learned from China). They also learned to appreciate new food and agricultural products such as spices, granulated sugar, coffee, and dates as well as trade goods such as silk products, cotton textiles, carpets, and tapestries.

In the early days of the crusades, Europeans had little to exchange for those products other than rough wool textiles, furs, and timber. During the crusading era, however, Italian merchants seeking to meet the rising demand for luxury goods developed new products and marketed them in commercial centers and port cities. Thus Niccolò, Maffeo, and Marco Polo traded in gems and jewelry, and other merchants marketed fine woolen textiles or glassware. By the thirteenth century, large numbers of Italian merchants had begun to travel well beyond Egypt, Palestine, and Syria to avoid Muslim intermediaries and to deal directly with the producers of silks and spices in India, China, and southeast Asia. Thus, although the crusades largely failed as military ventures, they helped encourage the reintegration of western Europe into the larger economy of the eastern hemisphere.

SUMMARY

Like societies in China, India, southwest Asia, and the eastern Mediterranean, western European society experienced massive change from 500 to 1300 C.E. Unlike those societies, however, rulers of medieval Europe were unable to reinstate an imperial form of government for long, and for centuries they did not participate actively in the larger trading world of the eastern hemisphere. Yet western Europeans found ways to maintain relative order and stability by decentralizing political responsibilities and relying on local authorities and regional states for political organization. The development of self-sufficient manors allowed western Europeans to expand agricultural production, which in turn spurred population growth as well as trade. In addition, western Christianity preserved elements of classical Roman society and established a foundation for cultural unity in western Europe. It was on these solid foundations that western Europe underwent thorough political and economic reorganization in the later middle ages. Regional states maintained good order and fostered rapid economic growth. Agricultural improvements brought increased food supplies, which encouraged urbanization, manufacturing, and trade. By the thirteenth century, European peoples traded actively throughout the Mediterranean, Baltic, and North Sea regions, and a few merchants even ventured as far away as China in search of commercial opportunities. The Roman Catholic church prospered, and advanced educational institutions reinforced the influence of Christianity throughout Europe. Christianity even played a role in European political and military expansion, since church officials encouraged crusaders to conquer pagan and Muslim peoples in Baltic and Mediterranean lands. Thus even in the absence of a strong imperial power, by 1300 western European peoples had strengthened their own society and began in various ways to interact regularly with their counterparts in other regions of the eastern hemisphere.

STUDY TERMS

Aachen (291)
Capet (292)
Capetian kings (293)
Carolingian empire (291)
cathedral schools (301)
Charlemagne (291)
chivalry (297)
crusades (304–306)
Eastern Orthodox Church (299–300)
Eucharist (303)
feudalism (294)
Franks (290–291, 299)
guilds (299, 301–302)
Hanseatic League (297)
Holy Roman Empire (290, 292)
Khubilai Khan (289)
Leif Ericsson (303)
manors (295–296)
Normans (293)
Odovacer (290)
Otto of Saxony (292)
Pope Gregory I (300)
Pope Urban II (305)
reconquista (305)
relics (303)
Roman Catholic Church (297–305)
sacraments (303)
scholasticism (302)
serfs (295, 297, 300)
St. Benedict of Nursia (300)
St. Dominic (301)
St. Francis (301)
St. Scholastica (300)
St. Thomas Aquinas (302)
William the Conqueror (293)

FOR FURTHER READING

Thomas Asbridge. *The Crusades*. New York, 2010. A breezy narrative history of the early crusades.

Robert Bartlett. *The Making of Europe: Conquest, Colonization, and Cultural Change, 950–1350*. Princeton, 1993. A well-documented examination of European expansion from a cultural point of view.

Rosalind Brooke and Christopher Brooke. *Popular Religion in the Middle Ages: Western Europe, 1000–1300*. London, 1984. Well-illustrated essays on the faith of the masses.

David Herlihy. *Opera Muliebria: Women and Work in Medieval Europe*. New York, 1990. Examines women's roles both in their own households and in the larger society of medieval Europe.

Benjamin Z. Kedar. *Crusade and Mission: European Approaches toward the Muslims*. Princeton, 1984. Insightful scholarly analysis of European policies toward Muslims during the crusading era.

Michael McCormick. *Origins of the European Economy: Communications and Commerce, A.D. 300–900*. Cambridge, Mass., 2001. A thorough and comprehensive analysis that emphasizes the participation of early medieval Europe in a larger Mediterranean economy.

J. R. S. Phillips. *The Medieval Expansion of Europe*. Oxford, 1988. Excellent survey of European ventures in the larger world during the high and late middle ages.

Daniel Power, ed. *The Central Middle Ages*. Oxford, 2006. Seven leading scholars discuss aspects of medieval European history.

Shulamith Shahar. *The Fourth Estate: A History of Women in the Middle Ages*. Trans. by C. Galai. London, 1983. Well-documented study of women and their status in medieval society.

Christopher Tyerman. *God's War: A New History of the Crusades*. Cambridge, Mass., 2006. A comprehensive review of crusades throughout Europe and the larger Mediterranean basin.

Worlds Apart: The Americas and Oceania

CHAPTER **17**

A handsome llama fashioned from silver from Inca Peru.

EYEWITNESS:

First Impressions of the Aztec Capital

In November 1519 a small Spanish army entered Tenochtitlan, capital city of the Aztec empire. Although they had heard many reports about the wealth of the Aztec empire, nothing prepared them for what they saw. Years after the conquest of the Aztec empire, Bernal Díaz del Castillo, a soldier in the Spanish army, described Tenochtitlan at its high point. The city itself sat in the water of Lake Texcoco, connected to the surrounding land by three broad causeways, and, as in Venice, canals allowed canoes to navigate to all parts of the city. The imperial palace included many large rooms and apartments, and its armory was well stocked with swords, lances, knives, bows, arrows, slings, armor, and shields.

To Bernal Díaz the two most impressive sights were the markets and the temples of Tenochtitlan. The markets astonished him because of their size, the variety of goods they offered, and the order that prevailed there. In the principal market at Tlatelolco, a district of Tenochtitlan, Bernal Díaz found gold and silver jewelry, gems, feathers, embroidery, slaves, cotton, cacao, animal skins, maize, beans, vegetables, fruits, poultry, meat, fish, salt, paper, and tools. It would take more than two days, he said, to walk around the market and investigate all the goods offered for sale. His well-traveled companions-in-arms compared the markets favorably to those of Rome and Constantinople.

The temples also struck Bernal Díaz, though in a different way. Aztec temples were the principal sites of rituals involving human sacrifice. Bernal Díaz described interior rooms of the temple so encrusted with blood that their walls and floors had turned black. Some of the interior rooms held the dismembered limbs of sacrificial victims, and others were resting places for thousands of human skulls and bones.

The contrast between Tenochtitlan's markets and temples challenged Bernal Díaz and his fellow soldiers. In the markets they witnessed peaceful exchange of the kind that took place all over the world. In the temples, however, they saw signs of human sacrifice on a scale rarely matched, if ever, anywhere else in the world. Yet, by the cultural standards of the Aztec empire, both the commercial activity of the marketplaces and the human sacrifice of the temples had a place in the maintenance of the world: trade enabled a complex society to function, and sacrificial rituals pleased the gods and persuaded them to keep the world going.

Although the peoples of Africa, Asia, and Europe interacted regularly before modern times, before 1492 the indigenous peoples of the Americas had only fleeting and random dealings with their contemporaries across the oceans. Yet between 1000 and 1500 C.E. the peoples of North and South America, like their counterparts in the eastern hemisphere, organized large empires with distinctive cultural and religious traditions, and they created elaborate trade networks touching most regions of the Americas.

Tenochtitlan (teh-noch-tee-TLAHN)

Texcoco (TEHS-co-co)

Tlatelolco (tl-tay-LOL-ko)

CHRONOLOGY

The indigenous peoples of Australia and the Pacific islands had irregular and sporadic dealings with peoples outside Oceania. Within Oceania itself, Pacific islanders did maintain links between various island groups by sailing over the open ocean. Yet to a greater extent than their counterparts in the eastern hemisphere, the indigenous peoples of Australia and the Pacific islands built self-sufficient societies that tended to their own needs. Even though they had extremely limited amounts of land and other natural resources to work with, by the thirteenth century C.E. they had established well-organized agricultural societies and chiefly states throughout the Pacific islands.

STATES AND EMPIRES IN MESOAMERICA AND NORTH AMERICA

Mesoamerica entered an era of war and conquest in the eighth century C.E. Great stores of wealth had accumulated in Teotihuacan, the largest early city in Mesoamerica. When Teotihuacan declined, it became a target for less-prosperous but well-organized forces from the countryside and northern Mexico. Attacks on Teotihuacan opened a long era of militarization and empire building in Mesoamerica that lasted until Spanish forces conquered the region in the sixteenth century. Most prominent of the peoples contesting for power in Mesoamerica were the Mexica, the architects of the Aztec empire.

The Toltecs and the Mexica

During the ninth and early tenth centuries, after the collapse of Teotihuacan, several regional states dominated portions of the high central valley of Mexico, the area surrounding Mexico City. Although these successor states and their societies shared the religious and cultural traditions of Teotihuacan, they fought relentlessly among themselves.

Their capital cities all stood on well-defended hill sites, and warriors figured prominently in their works of art.

Toltecs With the emergence of the Toltecs and later the Mexica, much of central Mexico again came under unified rule. The Toltecs began to migrate into the area from the arid land of northwestern Mexico about the eighth century. They settled mostly at Tula, about 50 kilometers (31 miles) northwest of modern Mexico City. There, the Toltecs tapped the waters of the nearby River Tula to irrigate crops of maize, beans, peppers, tomatoes, chiles, and cotton. At its high point, from about 950 to 1150 C.E., Tula supported a population that might have reached sixty thousand people, and another sixty thousand lived in the surrounding region.

The Toltecs also built a compact regional empire with their large and powerful army, and they transformed their capital into a wealthy city with the tribute they exacted from subject peoples. Indeed, the city of Tula became an important center of weaving, pottery, and obsidian work, and residents imported large quantities of jade, turquoise, animal skins, exotic bird feathers, and other luxury goods from elsewhere in Mesoamerica. The Toltecs maintained close relations with societies on the Gulf coast as well as with the Maya of Yucatan. Indeed, Tula shared numerous architectural designs and art motifs with the Maya city of Chichén Itzá some 1,500 kilometers (932 miles) to the east.

Beginning about 1125 C.E. the Toltec empire faced serious difficulties as conflicts between the different ethnic

---

Teotihuacan (teh-o-tee-WAH-kahn)

Mexica (MEHK-si-kah)

Yucatan (yoo-kuh-TAN)

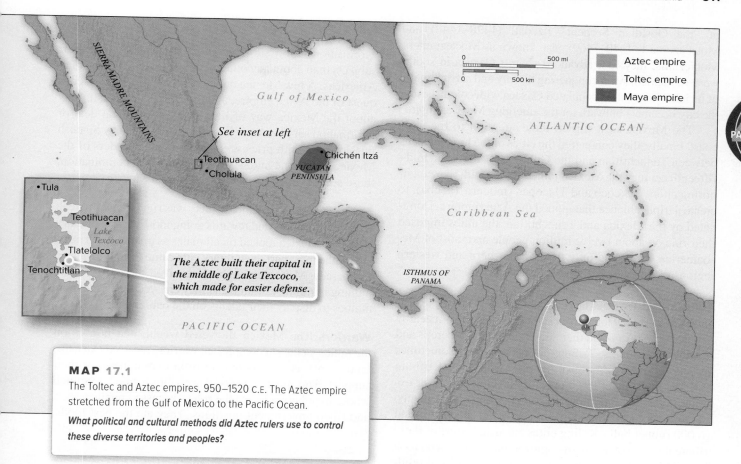

MAP 17.1

The Toltec and Aztec empires, 950–1520 C.E. The Aztec empire stretched from the Gulf of Mexico to the Pacific Ocean.

What political and cultural methods did Aztec rulers use to control these diverse territories and peoples?

Map callout: *The Aztec built their capital in the middle of Lake Texcoco, which made for easier defense.*

groups living at Tula led to civil strife. By the mid–twelfth century large numbers of migrants—mostly nomadic peoples from northwestern Mexico—had entered Tula and settled in the surrounding area. By 1175 the combination of civil conflict and nomadic incursion had destroyed the Toltec state.

The Mexica Among the migrants drawn to central Mexico from northwestern regions was a people who called themselves the Mexica, often referred to as Aztecs because they dominated the alliance that built the Aztec empire in the fifteenth century. (The term *Aztec* derives from *Aztlán*, "the place of the seven legendary caves," which the Mexica remembered as the home of their ancestors.) The Mexica arrived in central Mexico about the middle of the thirteenth century. They had a reputation for making trouble by kidnapping women from nearby communities and seizing land already cultivated by others. On several occasions their neighbors became tired of their disorderly behavior and forced them to move. For a century they migrated around central Mexico, fighting with other peoples and sometimes surviving only by eating fly eggs and snakes.

Tenochtitlan About 1345 the Mexica settled on an island in a marshy region of Lake Texcoco and founded

the city that would become their capital—Tenochtitlan, on top of which Spanish conquerors later built Mexico City. The site offered several advantages. The lake harbored plentiful supplies of fish, frogs, and waterfowl, and it also enabled the Mexica to develop the *chinampa* system of agriculture. The Mexica dredged the fertile muck from the lake's bottom and built it up into small plots of land known as *chinampas*. During the dry season, cultivators tapped water from canals leading from the lake to their plots, and in the temperate climate they grew crops year-round. *Chinampas* were so productive that cultivators were sometimes able to harvest seven crops per year. The lake also served as a natural defense: waters protected Tenochtitlan on all sides, and Mexica warriors patrolled the three causeways that eventually linked their capital to the surrounding mainland.

The Aztec Empire By the early fifteenth century, the Mexica were powerful enough to overcome their immediate neighbors and demand tribute from their new subjects. During the middle decades of the century, the Mexica launched ambitious campaigns of imperial expansion. Under the rule

Itzcóatl (tsee-ko-atl)
Motecuzoma (mo-tec-oo-ZO-ma)

of "the Obsidian Serpent" Itzcóatl (1428–1440) and Motecuzoma I (1440–1469), also known as Moctezuma or Montezuma, they first advanced against Oaxaca in southwestern Mexico. After conquering the city and slaying many of its inhabitants, they populated Oaxaca with colonists, and the city became a bulwark for the emerging Mexica empire.

The Mexica next turned their attention to the Gulf coast. Finally, they conquered the cities of the high plateaus between Tenochtitlan and the Gulf coast. About the mid–fifteenth century the Mexica joined forces with two neighboring cities, Texcoco and Tlacopan (modern Tacuba), to create a triple alliance that guided the Aztec empire. Dominated by the Mexica and Tenochtitlan, the allies imposed their rule on about twelve million people and most of Mesoamerica, excluding only the arid northern and western regions and a few small, independent states.

Tribute and Trade The main objective of the triple alliance was to exact tribute from subject peoples. From nearby peoples the Mexica and their allies received food crops and manufactured items. Tribute obligations were sometimes very oppressive for subject peoples. The annual tribute owed by the state of Tochtepec on the Gulf coast, for example, included 9,600 cloaks, 1,600 women's garments, 200 loads of cacao (the source of cocoa and chocolate), and 16,000 rubber balls. Ruling elites entrusted some of these tribute items to officially recognized merchants, who took them to distant lands and exchanged them for local products including luxury items such as translucent jade, tortoise shells, jaguar skins, parrot feathers, and seashells. The tropical lowlands also supplied vanilla beans and cacao, from which Mexica elites prepared tasty beverages.

Unlike imperial states in the eastern hemisphere, the Aztec empire had no elaborate bureaucracy or administration. The Mexica and their allies simply conquered their subjects and assessed tribute, leaving local governance and the collection of tribute in the hands of the conquered peoples themselves. The allies did not even maintain military garrisons throughout their empire. Nor did they keep a permanent, standing army. Nevertheless, the Mexica in particular had a reputation for military prowess, and fear of reprisal kept most subject peoples in line.

At the high point of the Aztec empire in the early sixteenth century, tribute from some 489 subject territories flowed into Tenochtitlan, which was an enormously wealthy city. The Mexica capital had a population of about two hundred thousand people, and three hundred thousand more lived in nearby towns and suburban areas. The principal market had separate sections for merchants dealing in gold, silver, slaves, cloth, shoes, animal skins, turkeys, dogs, wild game, maize, beans, peppers, cacao, and fruits.

Oaxaca (wah-hah-kah)

Tlacopan (Tee-laaa-co-pawn)

Mexica Society

More information survives about the Mexica and their subjects than about any other people of the pre-Columbian Americas. A few Mexica books survived the Spanish conquest of the Aztec empire, and they offer direct testimony about the Mexica way of life. Moreover, a great deal of information survives from interviews conducted by Spanish missionaries with priests, elders, and other leaders of the Mexica during the mid–sixteenth century. In combination, these sources shed considerable light on Mexica society.

Social Structure Mexica society was rigidly hierarchical, with public honors and rewards going mostly to the military elite. The Mexica looked on all males as potential warriors, but for the most part the military elite came from the Mexica aristocracy. Men of noble birth received the most intense training in military affairs, and they enjoyed the best opportunities to display their talents on the battlefield.

Warriors The Mexica showered wealth and honors on the military elite. Accomplished warriors received extensive land grants as well as tribute from commoners for their support. The most successful warriors formed a council whose members selected the ruler, discussed public issues, and filled government positions. They ate the best foods,

Mexica tribute list.
A Spanish copy of a Mexica list records tribute owed by six northwestern towns to the ruler Motecuzoma II. Every two years the towns delivered, among other items, women's skirts and blouses, men's shirts, warriors' armor and shields, an eagle, and various quantities of maize, beans, and other foods.

and they consumed most of the luxury items that came into Mexica society by way of trade or tribute. Even dress reflected social status in Mexica society. Sumptuary laws required commoners to wear coarse, burlaplike garments made of henequen but permitted aristocrats to drape themselves in cotton. Successful warriors also enjoyed the right to don brightly colored capes and adorn themselves with lip plugs and eagle feathers.

Mexica Women Women played almost no public role in a society so dominated by military values, but they wielded influence within their families and enjoyed honor as mothers of warriors. Mexica women did not inherit property or hold official positions, and the law subjected them to the strict authority of their fathers and husbands. However, women were prominent in the marketplaces, as well as in crafts involving embroidery and needlework.

With the exception of a few who dedicated themselves to the service of a temple, all Mexica women married. Mexica values taught that their principal function was to bear children, and society recognized the bearing of children as equal to a warrior's capture of enemies in battle. Indeed, women who died in childbirth won the same fame as warriors who died valiantly on the battlefield.

Priests Alongside the military aristocracy, a priestly class also ranked among the Mexica elite. Priests received a special education in calendrical and ritual lore, and they presided over religious ceremonies that the Mexica viewed as crucial to the continuation of the world. Priests read omens and explained the forces that drove the world, thereby wielding considerable influence as advisors to Mexica rulers. On a few occasions, priests even became supreme rulers of the Aztec empire: the ill-fated Motecuzoma II (reigned 1502–1520), ruler of the Aztec empire when Spanish invaders appeared in 1519, was a priest of the most popular Mexica cult.

Cultivators and Slaves The bulk of the Mexica population consisted of commoners who lived in hamlets cultivating lands allocated to their families by community groups known as *calpulli*. Originally, *calpulli* members claimed descent from common ancestors, but over time ancestry became less important than the fact that groups of families lived together in communities, organized their own affairs, and allocated community property to individual families. In addition to cultivating plots assigned by their *calpulli*, Mexica commoners also worked on the lands of aristocrats or warriors and contributed labor services to public works projects. Cultivators delivered periodic tribute payments to state agents, who distributed a portion of what they collected to the elite classes and stored the remainder in state granaries and warehouses. In addition to these cultivators of common birth, Mexica society included slaves, who usually worked as domestic servants. Most

slaves were not foreigners, but Mexica who entered slavery because of financial distress or criminal behavior.

Artisans and Merchants Skilled artisans, particularly those who worked with gold, silver, and other items destined for consumption by the elite, enjoyed considerable prestige in Mexica society. Merchants specializing in long-distance trade occupied an important but somewhat more tenuous position in Mexica society. Indeed, although these merchants supplied important luxuries to the elite as well as political and military intelligence about the lands they visited, they often fell under suspicion as greedy profiteers.

Mexica Religion

When they migrated to central Mexico, the Mexica already spoke the Nahuatl language, which had been the prevalent tongue in the region since the time of the Toltecs. The Mexica soon adopted other cultural and religious traditions, some of which dated from the time of the Olmecs, shared by all the peoples of Mesoamerica. Most Mesoamerican peoples played a ball game in formal courts, for example, and maintained a complicated calendar based on a solar year of 365 days and a ritual year of 260 days. The Mexica enthusiastically adopted the ball game, and they also kept a sophisticated calendar.

Mexica Gods The Mexica also absorbed the religious beliefs common to Mesoamerica. Two of their principal gods—Tezcatlipoca, "the Smoking Mirror," and Quetzalcoatl, "the Feathered Serpent"—had figured in Mesoamerican pantheons at least since the time of Teotihuacan. Tezcatlipoca was a powerful figure, the giver and taker of life and the patron deity of warriors, whereas Quetzalcoatl supported arts, crafts, and agriculture. Like their predecessors, the Mexica believed that their gods had set the world in motion through acts of individual sacrifice. By letting their blood flow, the gods had given the earth the moisture it needed to bear maize and other crops. To win the favor of the gods and ensure the continuation of the world, the Mexica also engaged in sacrificial blood-letting. Mexica priests regularly performed acts of self-sacrifice, piercing their earlobes or penises with cactus spines in honor of the primeval acts of their gods.

Ritual Bloodletting Mexica priests also presided over the sacrificial killing of human victims. From at least the time of the Olmecs, Mesoamerican peoples had regarded the ritual sacrifice of human beings as essential to the

calpulli (kal-po-lee)
Nahuatl (na-watl)
Tezcatlipoca (tehs-cah-tlee-poh-cah)
Quetzalcoatl (keh-tzahl-koh-AHTL)

SourcesfromthePast

Mexica Expectations of Boys and Girls

Bernardino de Sahagún was a Franciscan missionary who worked to convert the native peoples of Mesoamerica to Christianity in the mid-sixteenth century. He interviewed Mexica elders and assembled a vast amount of information about their society before the arrival of Europeans. His records include the speeches made by midwives as they delivered infants to aristocratic families. The speeches indicate clearly the roles men and women were expected to play in Mexica society.

[To a newborn boy the midwife said:] "Heed, hearken: thy home is not here, for thou art an eagle, thou art an ocelot; thou art a roseate spoonbill, thou art a troupial. Thou art the serpent, the bird of the lord of the near, of the nigh. Here is only the place of thy nest. Thou hast only been hatched here; thou hast only come, arrived. Thou art only come forth on earth here. Here dost thou bud, blossom, germinate. Here thou becomest the chip, the fragment [of thy mother]. Here are only the cradle, thy cradle blanket, the resting place of thy head: only thy place of arrival. Thou belongest out there; out there thou hast been consecrated. Thou hast been sent into warfare. War is thy desert, thy task. Thou shalt give drink, nourishment, food to the sun, the lord of the earth. Thy real home, thy property, thy lot is the home of the sun there in the heavens. . . . Perhaps thou wilt receive the gift, perhaps thou wilt merit death [in battle] by the obsidian knife, the flowered death by the obsidian knife. . . ."

And if it were a female, the midwife said to her when she cut her umbilical cord: "My beloved maiden, my beloved

noblewoman, thou has endured fatigue! Our lord, the lord of the near, of the nigh, hath sent thee. Thou hast come to arrive at a place of weariness, a place of anguish, a place of fatigue where there is cold, there is wind. . . . Thou wilt be in the heart of the home, thou wilt go nowhere, thou wilt nowhere become a wanderer, thou becomest the banked fire, the hearth stones. Here our lord planteth thee, burieth thee. And thou wilt become fatigued, thou wilt become tired; thou art to provide water, to grind maize, to drudge; thou art to sweat by the ashes, by the hearth."

Then the midwife buried the umbilical cord of the noblewoman by the hearth. It was said that by this she signified that the little woman would nowhere wander. Her dwelling place was only within the house; her home was only within the house; it was not necessary for her to go anywhere. And it meant that her very duty was drink, food. She was to prepare drink, to prepare food, to grind, to spin, to weave.

For Further Reflection

■ How did gender roles and expectations of Mexica society compare with those of other settled, agricultural societies, such as China, India, the Islamic world, sub-Saharan Africa, and Europe?

Source: de Sahagún, Bernardino. *Florentine Codex: General History of the Things of New Spain,* 13 vols. Trans. by Charles E. Dibble and Arthur J. O. Anderson. Copyright © 1950 by University of Utah Press. Used with permission.

---

world's survival. The Mexica, however, placed much more emphasis on human sacrifice than their predecessors had. To a large extent the Mexica enthusiasm for human sacrifice followed from their devotion to the god Huitzilopochtli as the patron deity of Mexica warriors. Military successes in the fourteenth century, when the Mexica subjected neighboring peoples to their rule, increasingly persuaded them of Huitzilopochtli's favor. As Mexica military successes mounted, the priests of Huitzilopochtli's cult demanded sacrificial victims to keep the war god appeased.

Some of the victims were Mexica criminals, and others came as tribute from neighboring peoples or from the ranks of warriors captured on the battlefield. In all cases the Mexica viewed human sacrifice not as a gruesome form of entertainment but, rather, as a ritual essential to the world's survival. They believed that the blood of sacrificial victims sustained the sun and secured a continuing supply of moisture for the earth, thus ensuring that human

communities would be able to cultivate their crops and perpetuate their societies.

Peoples and Societies of North America

Beyond Mexico the peoples of North America developed a rich variety of political, social, and cultural traditions. Many North American peoples depended on hunting, fishing, and foraging. In the arctic and subarctic regions, for example, diets included whale, seal, and walrus supplemented by land mammals such as moose and caribou. Peoples in coastal regions consumed fish, and in interior regions they hunted large animals such as bison and deer. Throughout the continent nuts, berries, roots, and grasses supplemented the meat provided by hunters and fishers. Like their counterparts elsewhere, hunting, fishing, and foraging peoples of North America built societies on a relatively small scale, since food resources in the wild would not support dense populations.

Huitzilopochtli (we-tsee-loh-POCK-tlee)

Mexica sacrificial bloodletting.
In this manuscript illustration an aide stretches a victim over a sacrificial altar while a priest opens his chest, removes the still-beating heart, and offers it to Huitzilopochtli. At the bottom of the structure, attendants remove the body of an earlier victim.

Mound-Building Peoples The most impressive structures of the woodlands were the enormous earthen mounds that dotted the countryside throughout the eastern half of North America. Woodlands peoples used these mounds as stages for ceremonies and rituals, as platforms for dwellings, and occasionally as burial sites. Although modern development has destroyed most of these mounds, several surviving examples demonstrate that they sometimes reached gigantic proportions.

Cahokia The largest surviving structure is a mound at Cahokia near East St. Louis, Illinois. More than 30 meters (100 feet) high, 300 meters (1,000 feet) long, and 200 meters (650 feet) wide, it was the third-largest structure in the western hemisphere before the arrival of Europeans. Only the temple of the sun in Teotihuacan and the temple of Quetzalcóatl in Cholula were larger. When the Cahokia society was at its height, from approximately 900 to 1250 C.E., more than one hundred smaller mounds stood within a few kilometers of the highest and most massive mound. Scholars have estimated that during the twelfth century, fifteen thousand to thirty-eight thousand people lived in the vicinity of the Cahokia mounds.

Trade Because peoples north of Mexico had no writing, information about their societies comes almost exclusively from archaeological discoveries. Burial sites reveal that mound-building peoples recognized social classes, since they bestowed grave goods of differing quality and quantities

Pueblo (PWEB-loh)
Navajo (NAH-vah-ho)
Iroquois (EER-uh-kwah)
Cahokia (kuh-HOH-kee-uh)

Pueblo and Navajo Societies In several regions of North America, agricultural economies enabled peoples to maintain settled societies with large populations. In what is now the American southwest, for example, Pueblo and Navajo peoples tapped river waters to irrigate crops of maize, which constituted as much as 80 percent of their diets. Although the hot and dry environment periodically brought drought and famine, by about 700 C.E. the Pueblo and the Navajo had begun to construct permanent stone and adobe buildings. Archaeologists have discovered about 125 sites where agricultural peoples built village communities.

Iroquois Peoples Large-scale agricultural societies also emerged in the woodlands east of the Mississippi River. Woodlands peoples began to cultivate maize and beans during the early centuries C.E., and after about 800 these cultivated foods made up the bulk of their diets. By 1000 the Owasco people had established a distinct society in what is now upstate New York, and by about 1400 the five Iroquois nations (Mohawk, Oneida, Onondaga, Cayuga, and Seneca) had emerged from Owasco society. Women were in charge of Iroquois villages and longhouses, in which several related families lived together, and supervised cultivation of fields surrounding their settlements. Men took responsibility for affairs beyond the village—hunting, fishing, and war.

Thinking about **TRADITIONS**

The Mexica and Mesoamerican Bloodletting Rituals

The Mexica practiced bloodletting rituals much like those observed in Maya, Teotihuacan, Toltec, and other earlier Mesoamerican societies. Yet the Mexica shed human blood much more copiously than their predecessors. *Why might the Mexica have emphasized this particular cultural tradition so much more strongly than earlier Mesoamerican peoples?*

The Great Serpent Mound.
Originally constructed about 1000 C.E., this mound sits atop a ridge in modern Ohio. The serpent's coiled tail is visible at the left, while its open mouth holds an egg on the right.

Why would the builders of this mound have adopted an aerial perspective?

experiences of early South American societies have been reconstructed largely on the basis of archaeological evidence and information recorded by Spanish conquerors. As in Mesoamerica, cities and secular government in South America began to overshadow ceremonial centers and priestly regimes during the centuries from 1000 to 1500 C.E. Toward the end of the period, like the Mexica in Mesoamerica, the Incas built a powerful state, extended their authority over a vast region, and established the largest empire South America had ever seen.

The Coming of the Incas

After the disappearance of the Chavín and Moche societies, a series of autonomous regional states organized public affairs in Andean South America. The states frequently clashed, but rarely did one of them gain a long-term advantage over the others. For the most part they controlled areas either in the mountainous highlands or in the valleys and coastal plains.

Chucuito In the highlands, people depended on the cultivation of potatoes and the herding of llamas and alpacas—camel-like beasts that were the only large domesticated animals anywhere in the Americas before the sixteenth century. After the twelfth century the kingdom of Chucuito dominated the highland region on the border between modern Peru and Bolivia. There, inhabitants built elaborately terraced fields where cultivators harvested potatoes of many different colors, sizes, and tastes.

Chimu Inhabitants of the coastal lowlands depended not on potatoes but on maize and sweet potatoes, which were grown with the aid of irrigation networks that tapped the rivers and streams flowing from the Andes mountains. Some lowland societies, such as the kingdom of Chimu, grew large and powerful in the half millennium before the emergence of the Incas in the mid–fifteenth century. Indeed, Chimu's capital city, Chanchan, had a population that exceeded fifty thousand and may have approached one hundred thousand.

For several centuries, regional states such as Chucuito and Chimu maintained order in Andean South America. Yet within a period of about thirty years, they and other regional states fell under the domination of the dynamic and expansive society of the Incas. The word *Inca* originally was the title of the rulers of a small kingdom in the valley

on their departed kin. Archaeologists have shown, too, that trade linked widely separated regions and peoples of North America. An elaborate network of rivers—notably the Mississippi, Missouri, Ohio, and Tennessee rivers—facilitated travel and trade by canoe in the eastern half of North America. Throughout the eastern woodlands, archaeologists have turned up stones with sharp cutting edges from the Rocky Mountains, copper from the Great Lakes region, seashells from Florida, minerals from the upper reaches of the Mississippi River, and mica from the southern Appalachian mountains. Indeed, the community at Cahokia probably owed its size and prominence to its location at the hub of North American trade networks. Situated near the confluence of the Mississippi, Missouri, and Ohio rivers, Cahokia was most likely the center of trade and communication networks linking the eastern woodlands of North America with the lower Mississippi valley and lands bordering the Gulf of Mexico.

STATES AND EMPIRES IN SOUTH AMERICA

Like the peoples north of Mexico, South American peoples had no tradition of writing before the arrival of Spanish invaders in the early sixteenth century. As a result, the

Chucuito (CHEW-keeto)
Chanchan (CHAHN-chahn)

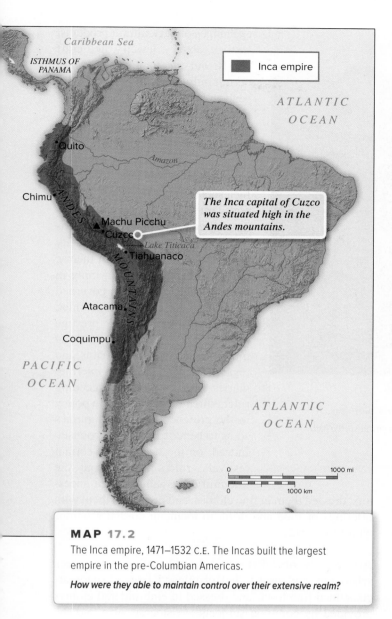

The Inca capital of Cuzco was situated high in the Andes mountains.

MAP 17.2

The Inca empire, 1471–1532 C.E. The Incas built the largest empire in the pre-Columbian Americas.

How were they able to maintain control over their extensive realm?

By the late fifteenth century, the Incas had built a huge empire stretching more than 4,000 kilometers (2,500 miles) from modern Quito to Santiago. It embraced almost all of modern Peru, most of Ecuador, much of Bolivia, and parts of Chile and Argentina. Only the tropical rain forests of the Amazon and other river valleys set a limit to Inca expansion to the east, and the Pacific Ocean defined its western boundary. With a population of about 11.5 million, the Inca empire easily ranked as the largest state ever built in South America.

The Incas ruled as a military and administrative elite. They led armies composed mostly of conquered peoples, and they staffed the bureaucracy that managed the empire's political affairs. But the Incas themselves were not numerous enough to overwhelm their subjects. Thus, they sought to encourage obedience among subject peoples by taking hostages from their ruling classes and forcing them to live at the Inca capital. Also, when conquered peoples became restive or uncooperative, the Incas sent loyal subjects to colonize the area and to establish military garrisons. When conquered peoples rebelled, Inca armies resettled them in distant parts of the empire.

Quipu and Inca Administration Administration of the Inca empire rested with a large class of bureaucrats. In the absence of writing, bureaucrats relied on a mnemonic aid known as *quipu* to keep track of their responsibilities. Quipu consisted of an array of small cords of various colors and lengths, all suspended from one large, thick cord. Experts tied a series of knots in the small cords, which sometimes numbered a hundred or more, to help them remember certain kinds of information. Most quipu recorded statistical information having to do with population, state property, taxes, and labor services that communities owed to the central government. Occasionally, though, quipu also helped experts to remember historical information having to do with the establishment of the Inca empire, the Inca rulers, and their deeds. Although much more unwieldy and less flexible than writing, quipu enabled Inca bureaucrats to keep track of information well enough to run an orderly empire.

Cuzco The Inca capital at Cuzco served as the administrative, religious, and ceremonial center of the empire. At its high point in the late fifteenth century, Cuzco's population may have reached three hundred thousand. Most prominent of the residents were the Inca rulers and high nobility, the high priests of the various religious cults, and the hostages of conquered peoples who lived with their families under the watchful eyes of Inca guardians. Cuzco had many handsome buildings of red stone, and the most important temples and palaces sported gold facings.

of Cuzco, but in modern usage the term refers more broadly to those who spoke the Incas' Quechua language, or even to all subjects of the Inca empire.

The Inca Empire After a long period of migration in the highlands, the Incas settled in the highland region around Lake Titicaca about the mid–thirteenth century. At first they lived as one among many peoples inhabiting the region. About 1438, however, the Inca ruler Pachacuti (reigned 1438–1471) launched a series of military campaigns that vastly expanded the Incas' authority. Pachacuti first extended Inca control over the southern and northern highlands and then turned his forces on the coastal kingdom of Chimu. Though well defended, Chimu had to submit to the Incas when Pachacuti gained control of the waters that supplied Chimu's irrigation system.

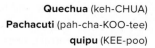

Quechua (keh-CHUA)
Pachacuti (pah-cha-KOO-tee)
quipu (KEE-poo)

Inca city.
Machu Picchu, an Inca settlement built beginning in 1430, was 8,000 feet above sea level.

What kinds of technology would the Inca have needed to construct a stone city at such a high altitude?

Inca Roads A magnificent and extensive road system enabled the central government at Cuzco to communicate with all parts of the far-flung Inca empire and to dispatch large military forces rapidly to distant trouble spots. Two roads linked the Inca realm from north to south—one through the mountains, the other along the coast. Scholars have estimated the combined length of these roads at 16,000 kilometers (9,944 miles). A corps of official runners carried messages along the roads so that news and information could travel between Cuzco and the most distant parts of the empire within a few days. When the Inca rulers desired a meal of fresh fish, they dispatched runners from Cuzco to the coast more than 320 kilometers (200 miles) away and had their catch within two days. Like roads in empires in other parts of the world, the Incas' roads favored their efforts at centralization.

Inca Society and Religion

Trade Despite these splendid roads, Inca society did not generate large classes of merchants and skilled artisans. On the local level the Incas and their subjects bartered agricultural produce and handcrafted goods among themselves. Long-distance trade, however, fell under the supervision of the central government. Administrators organized

exchanges of agricultural products, textiles, pottery, jewelry, and craft goods, but the Inca state did not permit individuals to become independent merchants. In the absence of a market economy, then, there was no opportunity for a large class of professional, skilled artisans to emerge.

Ruling Elites The main classes in Inca society were the rulers, aristocrats, priests, and peasant cultivators of common birth. The Incas considered their chief ruler a deity descended from the sun. In theory, this god-king owned everything in the Inca realm, which he governed as an absolute and infallible ruler. Inca rulers retained their prestige even after death. Their descendants mummified the royal remains and regarded departed kings as intermediaries with the gods. Succeeding rulers often deliberated state policy in the presence of royal mummies so as to benefit from their counsel. Indeed, on the occasion of certain festivals, rulers brought out the mummified remains of their ancestors, dressed them in fine clothes, and presented them with offerings of food and drink to maintain cordial relations with former rulers.

Aristocrats and Priests Like the ruling elites, Inca aristocrats and priests led privileged lives. Aristocrats consumed fine foods and dressed in embroidered clothes provided by common subjects. Aristocrats also had the right to wear large ear spools that distended their lobes so much that Spanish conquerors referred to them as "big ears." Priests often came from royal and aristocratic families. They led celibate and ascetic lives, but they deeply influenced Inca society because of their education and their responsibility for overseeing religious rituals. The major temples supported hundreds of priests, along with attendants and virgin women devoted to divine service who prepared ceremonial meals and wove fine ritual garments for the priestly staff.

Peasants The cultivators were mostly peasants of common birth who lived in communities known as *ayllu,* similar to the Mexica's *calpulli,* which were the basic units of rural society. Ranging in size from small villages to larger towns, each *ayllu* consisted of several families who lived together, sharing land, tools, animals, crops, and work. Instead of

Inca veneration of the dead.
Descendants prepare a ritual meal for a mummified Inca ruler (depicted in the background).

also showed special favor to the god Viracocha, creator of the world, humankind, and all else in the universe. The cult of the sun, however, outshone all the others. In Cuzco alone some four thousand priests, attendants, and virgin devotees served Inti, whose temple attracted pilgrims from all parts of the Inca empire. Priests of all cults honored their deities with sacrifices, which in Inca society usually took the form of agricultural produce or animals such as llamas and guinea pigs rather than humans.

Moral Thought Alongside sacrifices and ritual ceremonies, Inca religion had a strong moral dimension. The Incas taught a concept of sin as a violation of the established social or natural order, and they believed in a life beyond death during which individuals would receive rewards or punishments based on the quality of their earthly lives. Sin, they believed, would bring divine disaster both for individuals and for their larger communities. The Incas also observed rituals of confession and penance by which priests absolved individuals of their sins and returned them to the good graces of the gods.

THE SOCIETIES OF OCEANIA

Inhabitants of Oceania did not interact with peoples of different societies as frequently or systematically as did their counterparts in the eastern hemisphere, but they built and maintained flourishing societies. The aboriginal peoples of Australia ventured over vast stretches of their continent and created networks of trade and exchange between hunting and gathering societies. Meanwhile, throughout the Pacific Ocean, islanders built complex agricultural societies. By the time European mariners sailed into the Pacific Ocean in the sixteenth century, the larger island groups had sizable populations, hierarchical social orders, and hereditary chiefly rulers. In the central and western Pacific, mariners sailed regularly between island groups and established elaborate trade networks. Islanders living toward the eastern and western edges of the Pacific Ocean also had occasional dealings with American and Asian peoples, sometimes with significant consequences for the Pacific island societies.

The Nomadic Foragers of Australia

Although the aboriginal peoples of Australia learned how to expertly exploit the resources of the continent, they did not turn to agriculture as did their neighbors to the north in New Guinea. The inhabitants of New Guinea began to herd swine and cultivate root crops about 5000 B.C.E., and the inhabitants of islands in the Torres Strait (which separates Australia from New Guinea) took up gardening soon

paying taxes or tribute, peasants also worked on state lands administered by aristocrats. Much of the production from these state lands went to support the ruling, aristocratic, and priestly classes. The rest went into state storehouses for public relief in times of famine and for the support of widows, orphans, and others unable to cultivate land for themselves. Apart from agricultural work, peasants also owed compulsory labor services to the Inca state. Men provided the heavy labor required for the construction, maintenance, and repair of roads, buildings, and irrigation systems. Women delivered tribute in the form of textiles, pottery, and jewelry. With the aid of quipu, Inca bureaucrats kept track of the labor service and tribute owed by local communities.

Inca Gods: Inti and Viracocha Members of the Inca ruling class venerated the sun as a god and as their major deity, whom they called Inti. They also recognized the moon, the stars, the planets, the rain, and other natural forces as divine. Some Incas, including the energetic ruler Pachacuti,

Inti (ihn-tee)
Viracocha (veer-rah-coh-chah)

thereafter. In contrast, the aboriginal peoples of northern Australia maintained nomadic, foraging societies until European peoples migrated to Australia in large numbers during the nineteenth and twentieth centuries.

Trade As a result of their mobile and nomadic way of life, aboriginal Australians frequently interacted with peoples of neighboring societies. Even though as nomads they did not accumulate large quantities of material goods, groups regularly exchanged surplus food and small items when they met. Eventually, this sort of small-scale exchange enabled trade goods to spread throughout most of Australia. Baler and oyster pearl shells were among the most popular trade items. Archaeologists have turned up many of these shells fashioned into jewelry more than 1,600 kilometers (1,000 miles) from the waters where the oysters bred. Peoples on the north coast also engaged in a limited amount of trade with mariners from New Guinea and the islands of southeast Asia. Australian spears and pearly shells went north in exchange for items such as iron axes, which were much coveted by aboriginal peoples who had no tradition of metallurgy.

Cultural and Religious Traditions In spite of seasonal migrations, frequent encounters with peoples from other aboriginal societies, and trade, the cultural traditions of Australian peoples did not diffuse much beyond the regions inhabited by individual societies. Aboriginal peoples paid close attention to the prominent geographic features of the lands around them. Often they conducted religious observances designed to ensure continuing supplies of animals, plant life, and water. Given the intense concern of aboriginal peoples with their immediate environments, their cultural and religious traditions focused on local matters and did not appeal to peoples from other regions.

The Development of Pacific Island Societies

By the early centuries C.E., human migrants had established agricultural societies in almost all the island groups of the Pacific Ocean. About the middle of the first millennium C.E., they ventured to the large islands

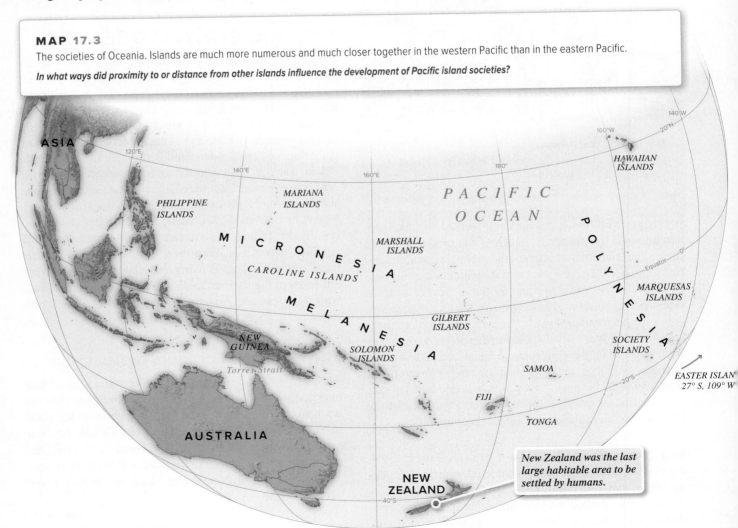

MAP 17.3

The societies of Oceania. Islands are much more numerous and much closer together in the western Pacific than in the eastern Pacific.

In what ways did proximity to or distance from other islands influence the development of Pacific island societies?

New Zealand was the last large habitable area to be settled by humans.

Reverberations of

The Diffusion of Technologies

Although the Polynesian islands were remote from other land masses and from one another, between 1000 and 1500 C.E. Polynesian peoples nevertheless managed to diffuse technologies even to islands thousands of miles away. In the twelfth and thirteenth centuries, Tahitians who sailed to the Hawaiian islands introduced new ways of organizing society, new linguistic terms, and new technologies for constructing fish hooks—all of which were adopted by Hawaiian peoples. Given the importance of fish in the Hawaiian diet, how might new technologies for catching fish have impacted Hawaiian health and population over the long term? In the context of Polynesian societies, consider whether or not the diffusion of technologies that improved fishing techniques could be seen as being as important as the spread of gunpowder technologies or as the horse collar in Eurasia.

of New Zealand—the last large, habitable region of the earth to receive members of the human species. After 1000 C.E. Polynesians inhabiting the larger Pacific islands grew especially numerous, and their surging population prompted remarkable social and political development.

Trade between Island Groups In the central and western regions of the Pacific, where several clusters of islands are relatively close to one another, mariners linked island societies. Regional trade networks facilitated exchanges of useful goods such as axes and pottery, exotic items such as shells and decorative ornaments, and sometimes even foodstuffs. Regional trade within individual island groups served social and political as well as economic functions, since it helped ruling elites establish and maintain harmonious relations with one another. In some cases, trade crossed longer distances and linked different island groups. Inhabitants of the Tonga, Samoa, and Fiji islands traded mats and canoes, for example, and also intermarried, thus creating political and social relationships.

Long-Distance Voyaging Elsewhere in Polynesia, vast stretches of deep blue water made it much more complicated to travel between different island groups and societies. As a result, regular trade networks did not emerge in the eastern Pacific Ocean. Nevertheless, mariners undertook lengthy voyages on an intermittent basis, sometimes with momentous results. After the original settlement of Easter Island about 300 C.E., for example, Polynesian mariners probably ventured to the western coast of South America, where they learned about the cultivation of sweet potatoes. Between about 400 and 700 C.E., mariners spread sweet potatoes throughout Polynesia and beyond. The new crop quickly became a prominent source of food in all the islands it

reached. Thus long-distance voyages were responsible for the dissemination of sweet potatoes to remote islands situated thousands of kilometers from the nearest inhabited lands.

Another case of long-distance voyaging prompted social changes in the Hawaiian Islands. For centuries after the voyages that brought the original settlers to the islands in the early centuries C.E., there was little travel or communication between Hawai'i and other Polynesian societies. During the twelfth and thirteenth centuries, however, a series of two-way voyages linked Hawai'i with Tahiti and the Marquesas Islands. Memories of those voyages survive in oral traditions that relate the introduction into Hawai'i of new chiefly and priestly lines from Tahiti. Evidence for the voyages comes also from Hawaiian adoption of fishhook styles from Tahiti and words from the Tahitian language.

Population Growth While undertaking regular or intermittent voyages over long distances, islanders throughout the Pacific Ocean also built productive agricultural and fishing societies. They cultivated taro, yams, sweet potatoes, bananas, breadfruit, and coconuts, and they kept domesticated pigs and dogs. They also fed on abundant supplies of fish. After about the fourteenth century, as their population increased, the inhabitants of Hawai'i built ingenious fishponds that allowed small fry to swim from the ocean through narrow gates into rock-enclosed spaces but prevented larger fish from escaping. Fishponds thus enabled Hawaiians to harvest large quantities of mature fish with relative ease. The establishment of agricultural and fishing societies led to rapid population growth in all the larger Pacific island groups. In Hawai'i, the most heavily populated of the Polynesian island groups, the human population may have exceeded five hundred thousand when European mariners arrived in the late eighteenth century.

Dense populations sometimes led to environmental degradation and social strife on small islands with limited resources. Easter Island in particular was the site of dramatic problems arising from overpopulation. Polynesian migrants originally settled Easter Island in the early centuries C.E., and during the era from about 1100 to 1500, their descendants numbered about ten thousand. This population placed tremendous pressure on the island's resources. By 1500, islanders fought one another ferociously for those resources, engaging in brutal massacres of their enemies and the desecration of their bodies. As their society disintegrated, they sometimes resorted to cannibalism for lack of sufficient food.

Polynesian oceangoing vessels.
A late-eighteenth-century sketch of priests traveling across Kealakekua Bay in Hawaiʻi wearing helmets made from gourds and foliage. Note the construction of the canoes. Using oceangoing vessels such as these, Polynesian peoples discovered and populated all the inhabitable islands of the vast Pacific Ocean.

Nan Madol In other lands, dense populations promoted social organization on a scale never before seen in Oceania. On Pohnpei in the Caroline Islands, for example, the Sandeleur dynasty built a powerful state and organized construction of a massive stone palace and administrative center at Nan Madol. Built mostly during the period from 1200 to 1600, the complex included ninety-three artificial islets protected by seawalls and breakwaters on three sides.

Development of Social Classes Indeed, beginning about the thirteenth century, expanding populations prompted residents of many Pacific islands to develop increasingly complex social and political structures. Especially on the larger islands, workers became more specialized: some concentrated on cultivating certain crops while others devoted their efforts to fishing or crafts production. Distinct classes emerged as well. The islands of Tonga, Tahiti, and Hawaiʻi had especially stratified societies with sharp distinctions between various classes of high chiefs, lesser chiefs, and commoners. Hawaiian society also recognized distinct classes of priests and skilled artisans as well as common classes.

The Formation of Chiefly States In addition to distinct social classes, island societies generated strong political leadership. Ruling chiefs generally oversaw public affairs in portions of an island, in an entire island, or occasionally in several islands situated close to one another. In Tonga and Hawaiʻi,

Thinking about **ENCOUNTERS**

The Effects of Long-Distance Trade in the Americas and Oceania

Within limited regions, societies in the Americas and Oceania established trade networks, tributary relations, or imperial authority over neighboring peoples. In addition, some societies supported networks of long-distance trade. *What are some examples in which long-distance trade altered or shaped societies in either the Americas or Oceania?*

Nan Madol.
A massive wall constructed of basalt rock protects a burial site at Nan Madol in Pohnpei.

high chiefs frequently launched campaigns to bring additional islands under their control and create large centralized states. Rarely, however, were these militant chiefs able to overcome geographic and logistic difficulties and realize their expansionist ambitions before the nineteenth century.

Nevertheless, high chiefs guided the affairs of complex societies throughout Polynesia. They allocated lands to families, mobilized labor for construction projects, and organized men into military forces. They commanded enormous respect within their societies. In Hawai'i, for example, the classes of high chiefs known as *ali'i nui* intermarried, ate the best fish and other foods that were *kapu* ("taboo") to

commoners, and had the right to wear magnificent cloaks adorned with thousands of bright red and yellow bird feathers. Indeed, a *kapu* forbade commoners to approach or even cast a shadow on the *ali'i nui*.

Polynesian Religion High chiefs often claimed that their power descended directly from the gods. They also worked closely with priests, who served as intermediaries between human communities and the gods. Gods of war and agriculture were common throughout the Pacific islands, but individual islands and island groups recognized deities particular to their own regions and interests. The most distinctive architecture of early Pacific societies was the ceremonial precinct and temple structure known as *marae* (or *heiau* in Hawaiian). *Marae* often had several terraced floors, with a rock or coral wall designating the boundaries of the sacred space. In Tonga and Samoa, temples made of timber and thatched roofs served as places of worship, sacrifice, and communication between priests and the gods, whereas in eastern Polynesia religious ceremonies took place on platforms in open-air courtyards.

Pacific island societies did not enjoy access to the range of technologies developed by continental peoples until after the sixteenth century. Yet Pacific islanders cleverly exploited their environments, established productive agricultural economies, built elaborate, well-organized societies, and reached out when possible to engage in trade with their neighbors. Their achievements testify anew to the human impulses toward densely populated communities and interaction with other societies.

SUMMARY

The original inhabitants of the Americas and Oceania lived in societies that were considerably smaller than those of the eastern hemisphere. Unlike their counterparts in the eastern hemisphere, they did not possess metallurgical technologies or transportation technologies based on wheeled vehicles and domesticated animals. Nevertheless, long before they entered into sustained interaction with European and other peoples, they built complex societies and developed sophisticated cultural and religious traditions. Indigenous peoples established foraging, fishing, and agricultural societies throughout the Americas, and they fashioned tools from wood, stone, and bone that enabled them to produce enough food to support sizable communities. In Mesoamerica and Andean South America, they also built imperial states that organized public affairs on a large scale.

The original inhabitants of Australia and the Pacific islands built societies on a smaller scale than did the peoples of the Americas, but they too devised effective means of exploiting the natural environment and organizing flourishing communities. Australia was a continent of foraging nomadic peoples, whereas the Pacific islands supported densely populated agricultural societies. Although they had limited communication with peoples of the Americas or the eastern hemisphere, the peoples of Oceania traded and interacted regularly with their neighbors, and inhabitants of the Pacific islands sometimes undertook lengthy voyages to trade with distant island groups.

STUDY TERMS

aboriginal peoples (319)
ali'i nui (323)
ayllu (318)
Aztec (311–313)
Cahokia (315)
calpulli (313)
Chanchan (316)
Chimu (316–317)
chinampa system (311)
Chucuito (316)
Cuzco (317)
Huitzilopochtli (314)
Inca (316–317)
Inti (319)
Iroquois (315)
Itzcóatl (311)
kapu (323)
marae (323)
Mexica (310)
Motecuzoma (311)
Nahuatl (313)
Nan Madol (322)
Navajo (315)
Oaxaca (312)
Pachacuti (317)
Polynesians (321)
Pueblo (315)
Quechua (317)
Quetzalcoatl (313)
quipu (317)
Tenochtitlan (309)
Teotihuacan (310)
Texcoco (309)
Tezcatlipoca (313)
Tlacopan (312)
Tlatelolco (309)
Toltecs (310)
Viracocha (319)
Yucatan (310)

FOR FURTHER READING

Peter Bellwood. *The Polynesians: Prehistory of an Island People.* Rev. ed. London, 1987. Well-illustrated popular account emphasizing the origins and early development of Polynesian societies.

Inga Clendinnen. *Aztecs: An Interpretation.* Cambridge, 1991. A brilliant recreation of the Mexica world, concentrating on cultural and social themes.

George A. Collier, Renato I. Rosaldo, and John D. Wirth, eds. *The Inca and Aztec States, 1400–1800: Anthropology and History.* New York, 1982. Seventeen well-focused essays represent approaches that scholars have taken to the Inca and Aztec empires.

Ross Hassig. *Aztec Warfare: Imperial Expansion and Political Control.* Norman, Okla., 1988. A solid scholarly study of Mexica military affairs and their role in the building of the Aztec empire.

Peter Hiscock. *Archaeology of Ancient Australia.* London, 2008. Comprehensive overview of the current state of archaeological investigation into aboriginal culture and history.

John Hyslop. *The Inka Road System.* New York, 1984. A careful archaeological study.

Patrick V. Kirch. *On the Road of the Winds: An Archaeological History of the Pacific Islands before European Contact.* Berkeley, 2000. A valuable synthesis of recent scholarship by the foremost contemporary archaeologist of the Pacific islands.

David Lewis. *We, the Navigators: The Ancient Art of Landfinding in the Pacific.* Honolulu, 1973. Fascinating reconstruction of traditional methods of noninstrumental navigation used by Pacific Islanders.

Charles C. Mann. *1491: New Revelations of the Americas before Columbus.* New York, 2006. Summarizes a great deal of archaeological research on the pre-Columbian Americas.

Michael E. Moseley. *The Incas and Their Ancestors: The Archaeology of Peru.* Rev. ed. London, 2001. A comprehensive survey of Andean history through the era of the Incas.

Cross-Cultural Interactions
CHAPTER 18

Persian Manuscript
Illumination Depicting
Giraffe with Keeper.

EYEWITNESS:
On the Road with Ibn Battuta

One of the great world travelers of all time was the Moroccan legal scholar Ibn Battuta. Born in 1304 at Tangier, Ibn Battuta followed family tradition and studied Islamic law. In 1325 he left Morocco to make a pilgrimage to Mecca. He traveled by caravan across north Africa and through Egypt, Palestine, and Syria, arriving at Mecca in 1326. After completing his hajj, Ibn Battuta spent a year visiting Mesopotamia and Persia, then traveled by ship through the Red Sea and down the east African coast as far south as Kilwa. By 1330 he had returned to Mecca, but then soon set off for India when he learned that the sultan of Delhi offered handsome rewards to foreign legal scholars. In 1333 he arrived in Delhi after following a long and circuitous land route that took him through Egypt, Syria, Anatolia, Constantinople, the Black Sea, and the great trading cities of central Asia, Bokhara and Samarkand.

For the next eight years, Ibn Battuta remained in India, serving mostly as a *qadi* (judge) in the government of the sultan of Delhi. In 1341 Ibn Battuta began his travels again, this time making his way around southern India, Ceylon, and the Maldive Islands before continuing to China about 1345. He visited the bustling southern Chinese port cities of Quanzhou and Guangzhou, where he found large communities of Muslim merchants, before returning to Morocco in 1349 by way of southern India, the Persian Gulf, Syria, Egypt, and Mecca.

Still, Ibn Battuta's travels were not complete. In 1350 he made a short trip to the kingdom of Granada in southern Spain, and in 1353 he joined a camel caravan across the Sahara desert to visit the Mali empire, returning to Morocco in 1355. During his travels Ibn Battuta visited the equivalent of forty-four modern countries and logged more than 117,000 kilometers (73,000 miles). His account of his adventures stands with Marco Polo's book among the classic works of travel literature.

Between 1000 and 1500 C.E., the peoples of the eastern hemisphere traveled, traded, communicated, and interacted more regularly and intensively than ever before. The large empires of the Mongols and other nomadic peoples provided a political foundation for that cross-cultural interaction. When they conquered and pacified vast regions, nomadic peoples provided safe roads for merchants, diplomats, missionaries, and other travelers. Quite apart from the nomadic empires, improvements in maritime technology led to increased traffic in the sea-lanes of the Indian Ocean and the South China Sea. As a result, long-distance travel became much more common than in earlier eras.

Merchants and travelers exchanged more than trade goods. They diffused technologies and spread religious faiths. They also exchanged diseases that caused deadly epidemics. During the middle decades of the fourteenth century, bubonic plague traveled the trade routes and spread through most of Eurasia. During its initial, furious onslaught, bubonic plague caused death and destruction on a huge scale and interrupted long-distance trade networks.

Ibn Battuta (ih-bun BAH-too-tah)

qadi (KAH-dee)

CHRONOLOGY

1253–1324	Life of Marco Polo
1287–1288	Rabban Sauma's embassy to Europe
1304–1369	Life of Ibn Battuta
1304–1374	Life of Francesco Petrarca
1330s	First outbreaks of bubonic plague in China
1347	Arrival of bubonic plague in the Mediterranean basin
1368–1644	Ming dynasty
1405–1433	Zheng He's expeditions in the Indian Ocean
1466–1536	Life of Desiderius Erasmus of Rotterdam
1488	Bartolomeu Dias's voyage around Africa
1492	Christopher Columbus's first voyage to the western hemisphere
1497–1498	Vasco da Gama's voyage to India

By the early fifteenth century, however, societies had begun to recover from the plague. Chinese and western European peoples in particular had restabilized their societies and begun to renew cross-cultural contacts. In Europe, this effort had profound consequences for modern world history. As they sought entry to the markets of Asia, European mariners sailed to the western hemisphere and the Pacific Ocean. Their voyages brought the peoples of the eastern hemisphere, the western hemisphere, and Oceania into permanent and sustained interaction with one another. Thus between 1000 and 1500, cross-cultural interactions pointed toward global interdependence, a principal characteristic of modern world history.

LONG-DISTANCE TRADE AND TRAVEL

Travelers embarked on long-distance journeys for a variety of reasons. Three of the more important motives for long-distance travel between 1000 and 1500 C.E. were trade, diplomacy, and missionary activity. The cross-cultural interactions that resulted helped spread technological innovations throughout the eastern hemisphere.

Patterns of Long-Distance Trade

Merchants engaged in long-distance trade relied on two principal networks of trade routes. Luxury goods of high value relative to their weight, such as silk textiles and precious stones, often traveled overland on the silk roads. Bulkier commodities, such as steel, stone, and building materials, traveled the sea-lanes of the Indian Ocean, because it would have been unprofitable to transport them overland. The silk roads linked all of the Eurasian landmass, and trans-Saharan caravan routes drew west Africa into the larger economy of the eastern hemisphere. The sea-lanes of the Indian Ocean served ports in southeast Asia, India, Arabia, and east Africa while also offering access via the South China Sea to ports in China, Japan, Korea, and the islands of southeast Asia. Thus, in combination, land and sea routes touched almost every corner of the eastern hemisphere.

Trading Cities As the volume of trade increased, the major trading cities and ports grew rapidly, attracting buyers, sellers, brokers, and bankers from parts near and far. When a trading or port city enjoyed a strategic location, maintained good order, and resisted the temptation to levy excessive customs fees, it had the potential to become a major emporium. A case in point is Melaka (in modern Malaysia). Founded in the 1390s, within a few decades Melaka became the principal clearinghouse of trade in the eastern Indian Ocean. The city's authorities policed the strategic Strait of Melaka and maintained a safe market that welcomed all merchants and levied reasonable fees on goods exchanged there. By the end of the fifteenth century, Melaka had a population of some fifty thousand people, and, according to one report, more than eighty languages could be heard in the city's streets.

Although the early period of Mongol conquest in the first half of the thirteenth century caused economic decline, especially in China and southwest Asia, eventually Mongol rule proved to be a boon for overland trade. Under Mongol rule, merchants traveling the silk roads faced less risk of banditry or political turbulence than in previous times. Meanwhile, strong economies in China, India, and western Europe fueled demand for foreign commodities.

Marco Polo The best-known long-distance traveler of Mongol times was the Venetian Marco Polo (1253–1324), who, with his father and his uncle, traveled and traded throughout Mongol lands in the late thirteenth century. When Marco Polo returned to Europe in 1295, stories of

---

Melaka (may-LAH-kah)

Sourcesfromthe**Past**

Ibn Battuta on Customs in the Mali Empire

Long-distance travelers often encountered unfamiliar customs in foreign societies. The Moroccan traveler Ibn Battuta approved heartily when staying with hosts who honored the values of his own Muslim society, but he had little tolerance for those who did not. Here he describes what he witnessed at the sultan's court in the Mali empire.

The Blacks are the most respectful of people to their king and abase themselves most before him. They swear by him, saying Mansa Sulaiman ki [the law of Mansa Sulaiman, the Mali sultan]. If he summons one of them at his session in the cupola . . . the man summoned removes his robe and puts on a shabby one, takes off his turban, puts on a dirty skull-cap and goes in with his robe and his trousers lifted half way to his knees. He comes forward humbly and abjectly, and strikes the ground hard with his elbows. He stands as if he were prostrating himself in prayer, and hears what the Sultan says like this. If one of them speaks to the Sultan and he answers him, he takes his robe off his back, and throws dust on his head and back like someone making his ablutions with water. I was astonished that they did not blind themselves.

When the Sultan makes a speech in his audience those present take off their turbans from their heads and listen in silence. Sometimes one of them stands before him, recounts what he has done for his service, and says: "On such and such a day I did such and such, and I killed so and so on such and such a day." Those who know vouch for the truth of that and he does it in this way. One of them draws the string of his bow, then lets it go as he would do if he were shooting. If the Sultan says to him: "You are right" or thanks him, he takes off his robe and pours dust on himself. That is good manners among them. . . .

Among their good practices are their avoidance of injustice; there is no people more averse to it, and their Sultan does not allow anyone to practice it in any measure; [other good practices include] the universal security in their country, for neither the traveller nor the resident there has to fear thieves or bandits . . . their punctiliousness in praying, their perseverance in joining the congregation, and in compelling their children to do so; if a man does not come early to the mosque he will not find a place to pray because of the dense crowd; it is customary for each man to send his servant with his prayer-mat to spread it out in a place reserved for him until he goes to the mosque himself. . . . They dress in clean white clothes on Fridays; if one of them has only a threadbare shirt he washes it and cleans it and wears it for prayer on Friday. They pay great attention to memorizing the Holy Qur'an. . . .

Among their bad practices are that the women servants, slave-girls and young daughters appear naked before people, exposing their genitals. I used to see many like this in [the fasting month of] Ramadan, for it is customary for the fararis [commanders] to break the fast in the Sultan's palace, where their food is brought to them by twenty or more slave-girls, who are naked. Women who come before the Sultan are naked and unveiled, and so are his daughters. On the night of the twenty-seventh of Ramadan I have seen about a hundred naked slave-girls come out of his palace with food; with them were two daughters of the Sultan with full breasts and they too had no veil. They put dust and ashes on their heads as a matter of good manners. [Another bad practice:] Many of them eat carrion, dogs and donkeys.

For Further Reflection

■ Discuss the various ways in which Islamic influences and established local customs came together in the Mali empire.

Source: Gibb, H. A. R., trans. *The Travels of Ibn Battuta, A.D. 1325–1354,* 4 vols. London: Hakluyt Society, 1958–94, 4:960, 965–66. Reprinted by permission of David Higham Associates, Ltd

his adventures were compiled by a third party and circulated widely throughout Europe. In spite of occasional exaggerations and tall tales, Marco's stories about the textiles, spices, gems, and other goods he observed during his travels deeply influenced European readers eager to participate in the lucrative trade networks of Eurasia. Indeed, in the wake of the Polos came hundreds of others, whose travels helped to increase European participation in the larger economy of the eastern hemisphere.

Political and Diplomatic Travel

Marco Polo came from a family of merchants, and merchants were among the most avid readers of his stories.

Yet his experiences also throw light on long-distance travel undertaken for political and diplomatic purposes. Khubilai Khan and the other Mongol rulers of China did not entirely trust their Chinese subjects and regularly appointed foreigners to administrative posts. Indeed, while in China Marco reported that Khubilai appointed him governor of the large trading city of Yangzhou, and that he represented Khubilai Khan's interests on diplomatic missions.

Mongol-Christian Diplomacy The emergence of elaborate trading networks and the establishment of vast imperial states created great demand for political and diplomatic representation during the centuries after

1000 C.E. The thirteenth century was a time of especially active diplomacy involving distant parties. During the 1240s and 1250s, for example, Pope Innocent IV dispatched a series of envoys who invited the Mongol khans to convert to Christianity and join Europeans in an alliance against the Muslims in control of Jerusalem. The khans declined the invitation, proposing in reply that the pope and European Christians submit to Mongol rule or face destruction.

Rabban Sauma Although the early round of Mongol-European diplomacy offered little promise of cooperation, the Mongols later initiated another effort. In 1287 the Mongol ilkhan of Persia planned to invade the Muslim-held lands of southwest Asia and capture Jerusalem. In hopes of attracting support for the project, he dispatched Rabban Sauma, a Nestorian Christian priest of Turkish ancestry, as an envoy to the pope and European political leaders. Although his efforts did not succeed in garnering European support for Mongol plans, such diplomatic activity illustrates the complexity of political affairs in the eastern hemisphere and the need for diplomatic consultation over long distances.

The expansion of Islamic influence in the eastern hemisphere encouraged a different kind of politically motivated travel. Legal scholars and judges played a crucial role in Islamic societies, since the *sharia* prescribed religious observances and social relationships based on the Quran. Conversions to Islam and the establishment of Islamic states in India, southeast Asia, and sub-Saharan Africa created a demand for Muslims educated in Islamic law. After about the eleventh century, educated Muslims from southwest Asia and north Africa regularly traveled to recently converted lands to help instill Islamic values.

Ibn Battuta Best known of the Muslim travelers was Ibn Battuta (1304–1369). Islamic rulers governed most of the lands Ibn Battuta visited, but very few Muslims educated in the law were available in those lands. With his legal credentials Ibn Battuta had little difficulty finding government positions. As *qadi* and advisor to the sultan of Delhi, he supervised the affairs of a wealthy mosque and heard cases at law, which he strictly enforced according to Islamic standards of justice. On one occasion Ibn Battuta sentenced a man to receive eighty lashes because he had drunk wine eight years earlier. Ibn Battuta also served as *qadi* in both east and west Africa, where he consulted with Muslim rulers and offered advice about government, women's dress, and proper relationships between the sexes. Like many other legal scholars whose stories went unrecorded, Ibn Battuta provided guidance in the ways of Islam in societies recently converted to the faith.

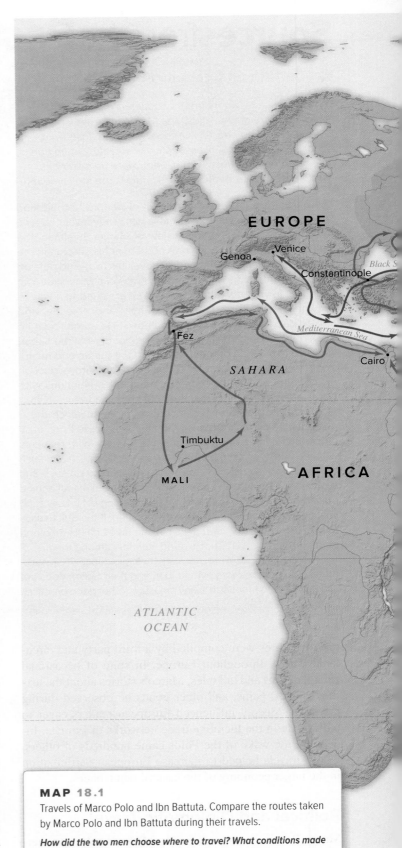

MAP 18.1

Travels of Marco Polo and Ibn Battuta. Compare the routes taken by Marco Polo and Ibn Battuta during their travels.

How did the two men choose where to travel? What conditions made it possible for them to travel so far from their homes?

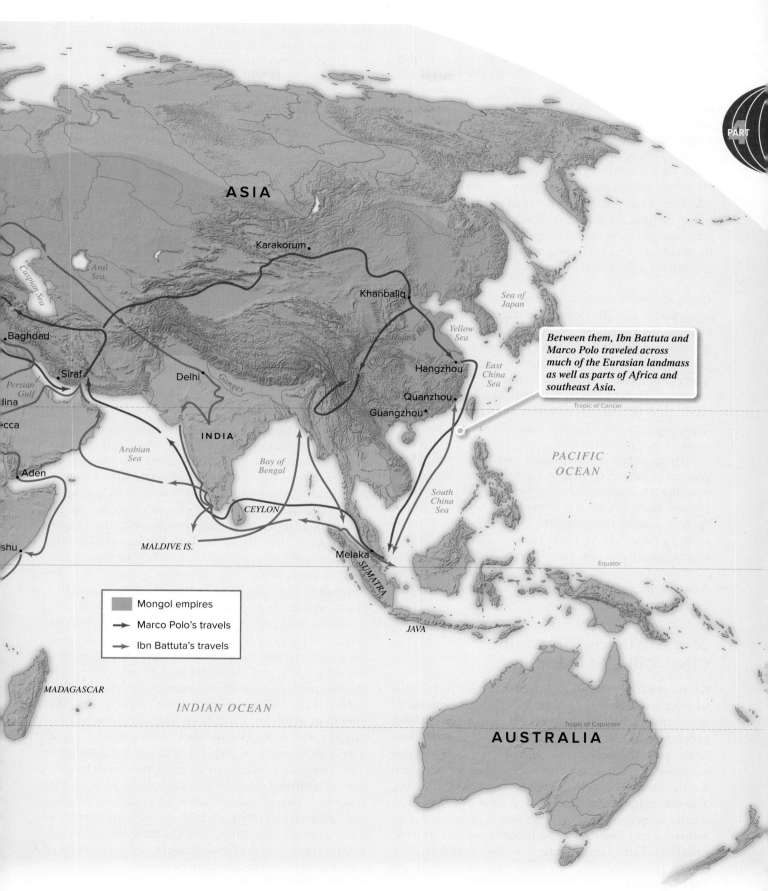

PART

ASIA

Caspian Sea

Aral Sea

Karakorum

Khanbaliq

Sea of Japan

Baghdad

Huang He

Yellow Sea

Siraf

Delhi

Ganges

Hangzhou

East China Sea

Between them, Ibn Battuta and Marco Polo traveled across much of the Eurasian landmass as well as parts of Africa and southeast Asia.

Persian Gulf

dina

Quanzhou

Tropic of Cancer

cca

Guangzhou

INDIA

Arabian Sea

Bay of Bengal

PACIFIC OCEAN

Aden

South China Sea

CEYLON

shu

MALDIVE IS.

Melaka

Equator

SUMATRA

Mongol empires

Marco Polo's travels

Ibn Battuta's travels

JAVA

MADAGASCAR

INDIAN OCEAN

Tropic of Capricorn

AUSTRALIA

Missionary Campaigns

Sufi Missionaries Islamic values spread not only through the efforts of legal scholars but also through the missionary activities of Sufi mystics. As in the early days of Islam, Sufis in the period from 1000 to 1500 ventured to recently conquered or converted lands and sought to win a popular following for the faith in India, southeast Asia, and sub-Saharan Africa. Sufis did not insist on a strict, doctrinally correct understanding of Islam but, rather, emphasized piety and devotion to Allah. They even tolerated continuing reverence of traditional deities. By taking a flexible approach to their missions, the Sufis spread Islamic values without facing the resistance that unyielding and doctrinaire campaigns might have provoked.

Christian Missionaries Meanwhile, Roman Catholic missionaries also traveled long distances in the interests of spreading Christianity. Missionaries accompanied the crusaders and other forces to all the lands where Europeans extended their influence after the year 1000. In lands where European conquerors maintained a long-term presence—such as the Baltic lands, the Balkan region, Sicily, and Spain—missionaries attracted converts in large numbers, and Roman Catholic Christianity became securely established.

The most ambitious missions sought to convert Mongols and Chinese to Roman Catholic Christianity. Yet even though Roman Catholic authorities in Europe dispatched many priests and missionaries to China during the early fourteenth century, they ultimately won few converts. In part, east Asia was just too distant for the resources available to the Roman Catholic church. Moreover, Christianity seemed to have little appeal to east Asian peoples, who already possessed sophisticated religious and cultural traditions.

Long-Distance Travel and Cross-Cultural Exchanges

Cultural Exchanges Long-distance travel of all kinds, whether for commercial, political, diplomatic, or missionary purposes, encouraged cultural exchanges between peoples of different societies. Songs, stories, religious ideas, philosophical views, and scientific knowledge all passed readily among travelers who ventured into the larger world during the era from 1000 to 1500 C.E. The troubadours of western Europe, for example, drew on the poetry, music, and love songs of Muslim performers when developing the literature of courtly love. Similarly, European scientists avidly consulted their Muslim and Jewish counterparts in Sicily and Spain to learn about their understanding of the natural world.

Large numbers of travelers also facilitated agricultural and technological diffusion during the period from 1000 to 1500. The magnetic compass, for example, invented in China during the Tang or Song dynasty, spread throughout the Indian Ocean basin during the eleventh century, and by the mid–twelfth century European mariners used compasses in the Mediterranean and the Atlantic Ocean. The compass was a boon to maritime trade, because it allowed mariners to sail over long stretches of deep water with confidence in their ability to find their destinations and return home safely.

Spread of Crops Long-distance journeys enabled Muslim travelers to introduce new food and commercial crops—such as citrus fruits and Asian rice—to sub-Saharan Africa, which enriched west African diets after the eleventh century. Muslims also introduced cotton to west Africa, and by 1100, cotton fabrics had become popular with the ruling elites and wealthy merchants of the west African kingdoms. Cotton grew well in the savannas, and by 1500 it was the principal textile produced in sub-Saharan Africa.

Sugarcane Muslims were also instrumental in the continuing diffusion of sugarcane. Muslim merchants and other travelers had begun large-scale cultivation of sugarcane in southwest Asia and north Africa during the Abbasid caliphate. After the twelfth century, Muslims facilitated the westward spread of sugarcane by acquainting European crusaders with crystallized sugar refined from cane. Up to that time Europeans had little access to refined sugar, and they relied on honey and fruits as sweeteners. They immediately appreciated the convenience of refined sugar. Italian entrepreneurs began to organize sugarcane plantations on Mediterranean islands such as Sicily, Cyprus, Crete, and Rhodes, and investors began to seek suitable locations throughout the Mediterranean basin. The cultivation of sugarcane had deep social and economic implications. Like their Muslim predecessors, European sugar producers often staffed their plantations with slave laborers, and the growth of plantations fueled an increasing demand for Muslim war captives and black Africans who could supply labor services. Beginning in the sixteenth century, Europeans sought to recreate this model when they established large sugarcane plantations in the Americas. Indeed, the diffusion of sugarcane is only one important example of how the increased pace of trade, cultural interaction, and conquest in the period 1000–1500 allowed ideas, technologies, and material goods to spread throughout the eastern hemisphere on an unprecedented scale.

Sufis (SOO-fees)

Cultural exchanges: The game of Chess

An illustration from a manuscript of 1282 depicts a Christian (left) playing chess with a Muslim (right). Chess was one of the many cultural elements that passed from Muslim to Christian societies during the crusading era.

CRISIS AND RECOVERY

As Eurasian peoples traveled, traded, and interacted over long distances, they also unwittingly spread disease pathogens. When diseases broke out among previously unexposed populations, they often caused widespread epidemics that severely disrupted whole societies. During the fourteenth century, bubonic plague erupted in epidemics that ravaged societies throughout most of Asia, Europe, and north Africa. Epidemic plague struck intermittently until the seventeenth century, but by the fifteenth century Chinese and western European societies in particular had begun to recover from its effects.

Bubonic Plague

The Little Ice Age About 1300 C.E. a process of global climatic change caused temperatures to decline significantly throughout the world. For more than five hundred years, the earth experienced a "little ice age," when temperatures were much cooler than in the era 1000–1300 C.E. Markedly cooler temperatures meant shorter growing seasons, which caused agricultural production to decline in many lands. Across much of Eurasia, the cooler temperatures of the little ice age made it much more difficult to produce enough food for subsistence. That, in turn, led to famine and sometimes even starvation. In some northerly lands, such as Greenland, agriculture ceased to be a practical possibility.

Origins of Epidemic Bubonic Plague As they struggled to cope with the cooling climate, peoples in much of the eastern hemisphere suddenly encountered a new challenge in the form of devastating epidemic disease. Bubonic plague spread from the Yunnan region of southwestern China, where it probably had been endemic for centuries. The plague bacillus infects rodents such as rats, squirrels, and prairie dogs, and fleas transmit the pathogen from one rodent to another. If rodent populations decline, fleas seek other hosts and sometimes spread the disease to human victims. In the early fourteenth century, Mongol military campaigns helped spread plague from Yunnan to China's interior, and by the 1350s it had spread to widely scattered regions of China. In some afflicted areas contemporaries reported that plague carried away two-thirds of the population.

Spread of Plague During the 1340s Mongols, merchants, and other travelers helped spread the disease along trade routes west of China. By 1346 it had reached the Black Sea ports of Caffa and Tana. In 1347 Italian merchants fled plague-infected Black Sea ports and unwittingly spread the disease throughout the Mediterranean basin. By 1348, following the trade routes, plague had sparked epidemics in most of western Europe.

Wherever it appeared, bubonic plague—which Europeans referred to as the "Black Death"—struck with frightful effects. Victims developed inflamed lymph nodes, particularly in the neck, armpit, and groin areas, and most died within a few days after the onset of symptoms. Internal hemorrhaging often discolored the inflammations to a black or purple hue. These swellings were

Connecting
the Sources

Individual experiences of the bubonic plague

The problem
The rapid spread of bubonic plague from China to most of Eurasia in the fourteenth century was a disaster that had profound and lasting effects on historical developments in China, central and southwest Asia, north Africa, and Europe, from massive population decline to economic disruption to social and political unrest. Although historians and scientists continue to dispute exact mortality rates, it is clear that the plague killed many millions of people, reducing populations wherever it struck by at least 25 percent, and sometimes much more. When exploring the history of disasters like the plague, it can be easy to forget that each individual who lived through the event—or died from it—had his or her own story, feelings, and family. In world history, while it is important to understand the "big picture," it is also important to remember that the "big picture" is always composed of millions of individual stories. These individual stories remind us that experiencing terrible events was not easier for individuals just because many suffered similar fates, or because they occurred a long time ago.

The following documents are only two examples—one from Italy and the other from Syria—of how individuals experienced the plague as it tore through Europe and southwest Asia in 1348.

The documents
Read the documents below, and consider carefully the questions that follow.

Document 1: *Francesco Petrarca (1304–1374) was an Italian scholar and early humanist who lived through the plague that* struck Italy in 1348. Scholars believe he wrote the following letter, known as the Metrica, to himself in about 1348.

> *O what has come over me? Where are the violent fates pushing me back to? I see passing by, in headlong flight, time which makes the world a fleeting place. I observe about me dying throngs of both young and old, and nowhere is there a refuge. No haven beckons in any part of the globe, nor can any hope of longed for salvation be seen. Wherever I turn my frightened eyes, their gaze is troubled by continual funerals: the churches groan encumbered with biers, and, without last respects, the corpses of the noble and the commoner lie in confusion alongside each other. The last hour of life comes to mind, and, obliged to recollect my misfortunes, I recall the flocks of dear ones who have departed, and the conversations of friends, the sweet faces which suddenly vanished, and the hallowed ground now insufficient for repeated burials. This is what the people of Italy bemoan, weakened by so many deaths; this is what France laments, exhausted and stripped of inhabitants; the same goes for other peoples, under whatever skies they reside. Either it is the wrath of God, for certainly I would think that our misdeeds deserve it, or it is just the harsh assault of the stars in their perpetually changing conjunctions. . . . Dense shadows have covered me with fear. For whosoever thinks they can recall death and look upon the moment of their passing with fearless face is either mistaken or mad, or, if he is fully aware, then he is very courageous.*

Document 2: *Ibn al-Wardi (c. 1290–1349) was a Muslim writer who lived and worked in Aleppo (modern Syria). He wrote the*

called buboes, which gave rise to the term *bubonic plague.* Bubonic plague typically killed 60 to 70 percent of its human victims. In some small villages and towns, disease wiped out the entire population. Plague also returned to claim new victims. In Europe plague erupted intermittently from the 1340s until the late 1600s.

Some parts of the eastern hemisphere did not suffer directly from plague epidemics. The long, cold winters of Scandinavia, for example, discouraged the proliferation of plague-bearing rodents and fleas. For reasons unknown, India also seems to have avoided the worst effects of the plague. In fact, Indian population grew from 91 million in the year 1300 to 97 million a century later. Epidemics also largely bypassed sub-Saharan Africa.

Population Decline In lands hard hit by plague, however, it took a century and more to begin recovery from the demographic consequences of the disease. In 1300 China's population, already reduced by conflicts with the Mongols, stood at eighty-five million. In 1400, after about seventy years of epidemic plague, China's population amounted to only seventy-five million. A century later demographic recovery was under way, and China's population rebounded to one hundred million. European society

following *Essay on the Report of the Pestilence* after the plague struck his region in the spring of 1348. The next year, in March 1349, al-Wardi himself died of the plague.

The Bubonic Plague in Europe. 1411 illustration of plague-infected people, taken from the Toggenburg Bible.

This plague is for the Muslims a martyrdom and a reward, and for the disbelievers a punishment and a rebuke. . . . I take refuge in God from the yoke of the plague. Its high explosion has burst into all countries and was an examiner of astonishing things. Its sudden attacks perplex the people. The plague chases the screaming without pity and does not accept a treasure for ransom. Its engine is far-reaching. The plague enters into the house and swears it will not leave except with all of its inhabitants. . . . Among the benefits of this . . . is the removal of one's hopes and the improvement of his earthly works. It awakens men from their indifference for the provisioning of their final journey. . . . Come then, seek the aid of God Almighty for raising the plague, for He is the best helper. Oh God, we call You better than anyone did before. We call You to raise from us the pestilence and plague. . . . We plead with You, by the most honored of the advocates, Muhammad, the Prophet of mercy, that You take away from us this distress. Protect us from the evil and the torture and preserve us.

Questions

- What can these sources definitively tell you about the lives of the people who produced them? What **facts** can be gleaned from these sources?
- In Document 1, what is Petrarca's state of mind? How does he describe the effects of the plague on himself and his loved ones? Do you think his reaction to the plague would have been shared by others in Italy, or might others have reacted differently?
- In Document 2, what is the cause of the plague, according to al-Wardi? How does he describe the effects of the plague on those around him? What kinds of advantages does he argue that the plague has brought?
- For both documents, how do each of the men view God's role in the plague? What are the similarities between the two excerpts? What are the differences? Finally, do you think their experience of the plague is representative, given that both were highly educated men? Why or why not? How useful are individual stories in interpreting and understanding world historical events?

Source Citations: **Document 1:** Francesco Petrarca: Ad Seipsum (To Himself) (Epistola Metrica I, 14: lines 1–55). Translated version by Jonathan Usher, Italian Studies Department's Virtual Humanities Lab at Brown University. Used with permission. **Document 2:** John Aberth, *The First Horseman: Disease in Human History* (Upper Saddle River, N.J.: Pearson Prentice Hall, 2007), pp. 42–43.

also reeled from the effects of bubonic plague. From seventy-nine million in 1300, European population dropped by almost 25 percent to sixty million in 1400. As in China, demographic recovery in Europe was under way in 1500, when European population climbed to eighty-one million. Islamic societies in southwest Asia, Egypt, and north Africa also suffered devastating population losses, and demographic recovery took much longer there than in China and Europe. In Egypt, human population probably did not reach preplague levels until the nineteenth century.

Social and Economic Effects Because of its heavy demographic toll, bubonic plague disrupted societies and economies throughout Eurasia and north Africa. Such high death rates caused huge labor shortages, which in turn generated social unrest. In western Europe, for example, urban workers demanded higher wages, and many left their homes in search of better conditions. Political authorities responded by freezing wages and forbidding workers to leave their homes. Peasants in the countryside also sought to improve their circumstances by moving to regions where landlords offered better terms. Landlords responded to this challenge by restricting the freedom of peasants to move. As a result of sharply conflicting interests, disgruntled workers and peasants mounted a series of rebellions that rocked both the towns and the countryside of western Europe and were extinguished only after considerable social disruption and loss of life.

By the seventeenth century the plague had lost much of its ferocity. Epidemics occurred more sporadically, and they did not seriously diminish human populations. Since the 1940s antibiotic drugs have brought the disease largely under control among human populations, although it survives in rodent communities throughout much of the world.

Ming jar.
Ming artisans won worldwide fame for their blue-and-white porcelain, which inspired the founders of the Delft porcelain factory in the Netherlands. This covered jar dates from the early fifteenth century.

Recovery in China: The Ming Dynasty

By the mid–fourteenth century the Mongol's Yuan dynasty was experiencing very difficult times. Financial mismanagement led to serious economic difficulties, and political conflicts led to factional fighting among the Mongols themselves. In 1368, with bubonic plague raging, the Yuan dynasty collapsed, and the Mongols departed China en masse, leaving China in a state of both demographic and political turmoil. However, an increasing birthrate soon helped to replenish human numbers, and political recovery accompanied the demographic rebound.

Hongwu   When the Yuan dynasty fell, the governance of China returned to Chinese hands. The new emperor came from a family so poor that he spent much of his youth as a beggar. Because of his size and strength, he came to the notice of military commanders, and he made his way through the ranks to lead the rebellious forces that toppled the Yuan dynasty. In 1368 he became Emperor Hongwu, and he proclaimed the establishment of the Ming ("brilliant") dynasty, which lasted until 1644.

Ming Centralization   Hongwu immediately set about eliminating all traces of Mongol rule and establishing a government on the model of traditional Chinese dynasties. Although Hongwu had little interest in scholarly matters, he reestablished the Confucian educational and civil service systems to ensure a supply of talented officials and bureaucrats. At the same time, he moved to centralize his authority. In 1380, when he suspected his chief minister of involvement in a treasonous plot, Hongwu executed the minister and his allies and then abolished the minister's position altogether. From that time forward the Ming emperors ruled directly, without the aid of chief ministers.

Mandarins and Eunuchs   The Ming emperors insisted on absolute obedience to the policies and initiatives of the central government. They relied heavily on the mandarins, a special class of officials sent out as emissaries of the central government to ensure local compliance with imperial policy. The Ming emperors also relied more heavily on eunuchs than had any of their predecessors. Eunuchs had long been considered reliable because they could not generate families and build power bases that might challenge ruling houses. Yet Ming emperors intent on centralization placed even more importance on the service of eunuchs, because they expected that servants whose fortunes depended exclusively on the emperors' favor would work especially diligently to advance the emperors' interests.

The tightly centralized administration instituted by the early Ming emperors lasted more than five hundred years. Although the dynasty fell in 1644 to Manchu invaders, who

Yuan (yoo-AHN)

Hongwu (hawng-woo)

eunuchs (YOO-nihks)

Thinking about **ENCOUNTERS**

Long-Distance Travel and Cross-Cultural Exchanges

With the aid of long-distance travelers, many cultural traditions, technologies, and biological species spread widely through the eastern hemisphere: Islam, Christianity, gunpowder, the compass, sugarcane, bubonic plague, and others as well. *Which do you consider the most important short- and long-term effects of long-distance travel in the period 1200 to 1500 C.E.?*

founded the Qing dynasty, the Manchus retained the administrative framework of the Ming state, which largely survived until the collapse of the Qing dynasty in 1911.

Economic Recovery While building a centralized administration, the Ming emperors also worked toward economic recovery. The new rulers conscripted laborers to rebuild irrigation systems that had fallen into disrepair, and agricultural production surged as a result. At the same time, they promoted the manufacture of porcelain, lacquerware, and fine silk and cotton textiles. They did not actively promote trade with other lands, but private Chinese merchants conducted a thriving business marketing Chinese products in ports and trading cities from Japan to the islands of southeast Asia. Meanwhile, domestic trade surged within China, reflecting increasing productivity and prosperity.

Cultural Revival Alongside political and economic recovery, the Ming dynasty sponsored a kind of cultural revival in China. Emperor Hongwu tried to eradicate all signs of the recent nomadic occupation by discouraging the use of Mongol names and the wearing of Mongol dress. Ming emperors actively promoted Chinese cultural traditions, particularly the Confucian and neo-Confucian schools. Hongwu's successor, Yongle, even organized the preparation of a vast encyclopedia that compiled all significant works of Chinese history, philosophy, and literature. This *Yongle Encyclopedia* ran to almost twenty-three thousand manuscript rolls, each equivalent to a medium-size book, and was a clear signal of Ming interest in supporting native Chinese cultural traditions.

Recovery in Western Europe: State Building

Demographic recovery strengthened states in western Europe as it did in China. In Europe, however, political authority rested with a series of regional states rather than a centralized empire. By the late fifteenth century, states in Italy, Spain, France, and England had devised techniques of government that vastly enhanced their power.

During the later middle ages (1300–1500), internal problems as well as bubonic plague complicated European political affairs. The Holy Roman Empire survived in name, but effective authority lay with the German princes and the Italian city-states rather than the emperor. In Spain descendants of Muslim conquerors held the kingdom of Granada in the southern portion of the Iberian peninsula. Meanwhile, the kings of France and England sparred constantly over lands claimed by both.

Taxes and Armies By the late fifteenth century, however, regional states in western Europe had greatly strengthened their societies. The state-building efforts of the later middle ages involved two especially important elements. The first was the development of fresh sources of finance, usually through new taxes levied directly on citizens and subjects. The second was the maintenance of large standing armies, which, particularly since the Hundred Years War, were often composed of mercenary forces and equipped with gunpowder weapons, supported by state funds.

Italian States The state-building process began in Italy, where profits from industrial production and trade enriched the major cities. Beginning in the thirteenth century, the principal Italian states—the city-states of Milan, Venice, and Florence, the papal state based in Rome, and the kingdom of Naples—began to finance their needs for military forces and larger bureaucracies by levying direct taxes and issuing long-term bonds that they repaid from treasury receipts. With fresh sources of finance, the principal Italian states strengthened their authority within their boundaries as well as in their surrounding areas.

France and England During the fourteenth and fifteenth centuries, Italian administrative methods made their way beyond the Alps. Partly because of the enormous expenses they incurred during the Hundred Years War (1337–1453), the kings of France and England began to levy direct taxes and assemble powerful armies. Rulers in both lands asserted the authority of the central government over the nobility. In France, King Louis XI (reigned 1461–1483) accomplished this by maintaining a permanent army of about fifteen thousand well-armed troops. Because the expense of maintaining such forces was beyond the means of the nobility, Louis and his successors enjoyed a decisive edge over ambitious subordinates seeking to challenge royal authority.

Spain The process of state building was most dramatic in Spain, where the marriage in 1469 of Fernando of Aragon and Isabel of Castile united the two wealthiest Iberian realms. Receipts from the sales tax, the primary source of royal income, supported a powerful standing army. Under Fernando and Isabel, popularly known as the Catholic Kings, Christian forces completed the *reconquista* by conquering the kingdom of Granada and absorbing it into their state. The Catholic Kings also projected their authority beyond Iberia. When a French army threatened the kingdom of Naples in 1494, they seized southern Italy, and by 1559 Spanish forces had established their hegemony throughout most of the Italian peninsula.

Qing (ching)

Yongle (YAWNG-leh)

Fernando of Aragon (fer-NAWN-doh of ah-ruh-GAWN)

Isabel of Castile (IHZ-uh-bel of ka-steel)

reconquista (ray-kohn-KEES-tah)

Competition between European states intensified as they tightened their authority in their territories. This competition led to frequent small-scale wars between European states, and it encouraged the rapid development of military and naval technology. As states sought technological advantages over their neighbors, they encouraged the refinement and improvement of weapons, ships, and sails. When one state acquired powerful weapons—such as ships equipped with cannons—neighboring states sought to outdo their rivals with more advanced devices. Thus technological innovations vastly strengthened European armies just as they began to venture again into the larger world.

Recovery in Western Europe: The Renaissance

Demographic recovery and state-building efforts in western Europe coincided with a remarkable cultural flowering known as the Renaissance. The French word *renaissance* means "rebirth," and it refers here to a period of artistic and intellectual creativity from the fourteenth to the sixteenth century in western Europe, which reflected increasing European participation in the affairs of the eastern hemisphere. Painters, sculptors, and architects of the Renaissance era drew inspiration from classical Greek and Roman artists rather than from their medieval predecessors. In their efforts to revive classical aesthetic standards, they transformed European art. Meanwhile, Renaissance scholars known as humanists looked to classical rather than medieval literary models, and they sought to update medieval moral thought and adapt it to the needs of a bustling urban society.

Italian Renaissance Art Just as they pioneered new techniques of statecraft, the Italian city-states also pioneered Renaissance innovations in art and architecture. In search of realistic depictions, Italian artists studied the human form and represented the emotions of their subjects. Italian painters such as Leonardo da Vinci (1452–1519) relied on the technique of linear perspective to represent the three dimensions of real life on two-dimensional surfaces. Sculptors such as Donatello (1386–1466) and Michelangelo Buonarotti (1475–1564) sought to depict their subjects in natural poses that reflected the actual workings of human muscles rather than the awkward and rigid postures of earlier sculptures.

Renaissance (ren-uh-SAHNS)

Leonardo da Vinci
(lee-uh-NAHR-doh duh VIHN-chee)

Michelangelo Buonarotti (mik-uhl-AN-juh-loh baw-nahr-RAW-tee)

Desiderius Erasmus (des-i-DEER-ee-uhs ih-raz-muhs)

The Cathedral of Florence.
Brunelleschi's magnificent dome on the cathedral of Florence dominates the city's skyline even today.

Why was such a dome considered revolutionary during the Renaissance?

Renaissance Architecture Renaissance architects designed buildings in the simple, elegant style preferred by their classical Greek and Roman predecessors. Their most impressive achievement was the construction of domed buildings—awesome structures that enclosed large spaces but kept them open and airy under massive domes. Roman architects had built domes, but their technology and engineering did not survive the collapse of the Roman empire. In the early fifteenth century, however, the Florentine architect Filippo Brunelleschi (1377–1446) reinvented equipment and designs for a large dome. During the 1420s and 1430s, he oversaw the construction of a magnificent dome on the cathedral of Florence, which residents took as a symbol of the city's wealth and leadership in artistic and cultural affairs.

The Humanists Like Renaissance artists and architects, scholars and literary figures known as humanists drew inspiration from classical models. The term *humanist* referred to scholars interested in the humanities—literature, history, and moral philosophy. They had nothing to do with the secular and often antireligious interests of movements that go under the name of humanism today: on the contrary, Renaissance humanists were deeply committed to Christianity. Several humanists worked diligently to prepare accurate texts and translations of the New Testament and other important Christian writings. Most notable of them was Desiderius Erasmus of Rotterdam (1466–1536), who in 1516 published the first edition of the Greek New Testament along with a revised Latin translation and copious annotations. Other humanists drew inspiration from the intense spirituality and high

Thinking about TRADITIONS

Comparative Cultural Revivals

Ming China and Renaissance Europe both experienced cultural revival in the fifteenth century. *To what extent did their respective classical traditions influence cultural developments in the two lands?*

moral standards of early Christianity and promoted those values in their society.

Humanists scorned the dense and often convoluted writing style of the scholastic theologians. Instead, they preferred the elegant and polished language of classical Greek and Roman authors and the early church fathers, whose works they considered more engaging and more persuasive than those of medieval philosophers and theologians. Thus humanists such as the Florentine Francesco Petrarca, known in English as Petrarch (1304–1374), traveled throughout Europe searching for manuscripts of classical works. In the monastic libraries of Italy, Switzerland, and southern France, they found hundreds of Latin writings that medieval scholars had overlooked. During the fifteenth century, Italian humanists became acquainted with Byzantine scholars and enlarged the body of classical Greek as well as Latin works available to scholars.

Humanist Moral Thought Classical Greek and Latin values encouraged the humanists to reconsider medieval ethical teachings. Medieval moral philosophers had taught that the most honorable calling was that of monks and nuns who withdrew from the world and dedicated their lives to prayer and contemplation, but the humanists drew inspiration from classical authors such as Cicero, who demonstrated that it was possible to lead a morally virtuous life while participating actively in the affairs of the world. Renaissance humanists argued that it was perfectly honorable for Christians to enter into marriage, business relationships, and public affairs, and they offered a spirited defense for those who rejected the cloister in favor of an active life in society. Humanist moral thought thus represented an effort to reconcile Christian values and ethics with the increasingly urban and commercial society of Renaissance Europe.

Renaissance Europe and the Larger World Quite apart from the conscious effort to draw inspiration from classical antiquity, Renaissance art and thought also reflected increasing European participation in the affairs of the eastern hemisphere. As merchants linked Europe to the larger hemispheric economy, European peoples

---

Francesco Petrarca (frahn-CHES-kaw PEE-trahrk-a)

St. Mark in Alexandria.
A painting by Venetian artists Gentile and Giovanni Bellini reflects Renaissance interests in the Muslim world. The painting depicts St. Mark (standing in the pulpit, left) preaching in Alexandria, Egypt. The audience includes Egyptians, Berbers, Turks, Persians, Ethiopians, and Mongols.

experienced increased prosperity, which enabled them to invest resources in artistic production and support for scholarship. Renaissance painters filled their canvases with images of silk garments, ceramic vessels, lacquered wood, spice jars, foreign peoples, and exotic animals that had recently come to European attention. Princes and wealthy patrons commissioned hundreds of these paintings, which brought a cosmopolitan look to their palaces, residences, and places of business.

This enchantment with the larger world extended also into the realm of ideas. The Italian humanist Giovanni Pico della Mirandola (1463–1494) perhaps best reflected the enthusiasm of Renaissance scholars to comprehend the world beyond western Europe. In his exuberant *Oration on the Dignity of Man* (1486), Pico made a spirited effort to harmonize the divergent teachings of Plato, Aristotle, Judaism, Christianity, and Islam, not to mention Zoroastrianism and various occult and mystical traditions. His ambitious endeavor was ultimately unsuccessful: Pico had limited information about several of the traditions he sought to reconcile, and he sometimes offered superficial interpretations of doctrines that he imperfectly understood. Nevertheless, his *Oration* gave eloquent voice to the burning desire of many European scholars to understand the larger world. It is not surprising that just as Pico and other Renaissance humanists were undertaking that effort, European mariners were organizing expeditions to explore the lands and seas beyond Christendom.

EXPLORATION AND COLONIZATION

As peoples of the eastern hemisphere recovered from demographic collapse and restored order to their societies, they also sought to revive the networks of long-distance trade and communication that epidemic plague had disrupted. Most active in that effort were China and western Europe—the two societies that recovered most rapidly from the disasters of the fourteenth century. During the early Ming dynasty, Chinese ports accommodated foreign

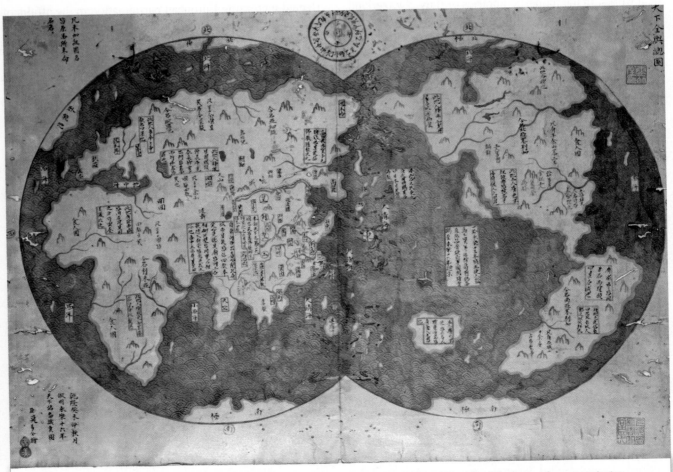

World map is believed by some to have been compiled by Zheng He. Zheng He (1371–1435), or Cheng Ho, China's most famous navigator.

Reverberations of ● ● ● ● ● ● ● ● ●

The Diffusion of Technologies

When European mariners set out to spread Christianity and explore commercial possibilities in the Atlantic and Indian Ocean basins, they employed a combination of technologies that had been diffused over the centuries from east and southwest Asia. One particularly effective combination was the use of technologies of transportation such as the compass (and later the astrolabe) along with technologies of warfare—especially cannons mounted on the sides of their ships. These diffused technologies allowed Europeans the ability to travel effectively by sea, and to compel—using deadly force—vessels from other regions to comply with their desire to dominate trade. While Europeans were not able to dominate maritime trade completely, consider how important their use and adaptation of a variety of diffused technologies to suit their own goals were in their ability to explore the world's oceans between the fifteenth and the eighteenth centuries.

traders, and mariners mounted a series of enormous naval expeditions that visited almost all parts of the Indian Ocean basin. Meanwhile, by the end of the fifteenth century, Europeans not only had established sea-lanes to India but also had made several return voyages to the American continents, thus inaugurating a process that brought all the world's peoples into permanent and sustained interaction.

The Chinese Reconnaissance of the Indian Ocean Basin

Having ousted the Mongols, the early Ming emperors were not eager to have large numbers of foreigners residing in China. Yet the emperors permitted foreign merchants to trade in the closely supervised ports of Quanzhou and Guangzhou, where they obtained Chinese silk, porcelain, and manufactured goods in exchange for pearls, gems, spices, and cotton fabrics. The early Ming emperors also refurbished the large Chinese navy built during the Song dynasty, and they allowed Chinese merchants to participate in overseas trading ventures in Japan and southeast Asia.

Zheng He's Expeditions Moreover, for almost thirty years, the Ming government sponsored a series of seven unprecedented naval expeditions designed to establish a Chinese presence in the Indian Ocean basin. Emperor Yongle organized the expeditions for two main purposes: to impose imperial control over foreign trade with China and to impress foreign peoples with the power and might of the Ming dynasty. Indeed, he might well have hoped to extend the tributary system, by which Chinese dynasties traditionally recognized foreign peoples, to lands in the Indian Ocean basin.

The expeditions took place between 1405 and 1433. Leading them was the eunuch admiral Zheng He, a Muslim from Yunnan in southwestern China who became a trusted advisor of Yongle. Zheng He embarked on each voyage with an awesome fleet of vessels complemented by armed forces large enough to overcome resistance at any port where the expedition called. On the first voyage, for example, Zheng He's fleet consisted of 317 ships accompanied by almost twenty-eight thousand armed troops. Many of these vessels were mammoth, nine-masted ships with four decks capable of accommodating five hundred or more passengers. Measuring up to 124 meters (408 feet) long and 51 meters (166 feet) wide, these ships were by far the largest marine craft the world had ever seen.

On the first three voyages, Zheng He took his fleet to southeast Asia, India, and Ceylon. The fourth expedition went to the Persian Gulf and Arabia, and later expeditions ventured down the east African coast, calling at ports as far south as Malindi in modern Kenya. Throughout his travels, Zheng He liberally dispensed gifts of Chinese silk, porcelain, and other goods. In return he received rich and unusual presents, including African zebras and giraffes.

Chinese Naval Power Zheng He generally sought to attain his goals through diplomacy, and for the most part he had little need to engage in hostilities. But a contemporary reported that Zheng He did not shrink from violence when he considered it necessary to impress foreign peoples with China's military might. He ruthlessly suppressed pirates who had long plagued Chinese and southeast Asian waters. He also intervened in a civil disturbance to establish his authority in Ceylon, and he made displays of military force when local officials threatened his fleet in Arabia and east Africa. The seven expeditions established a Chinese presence and reputation in the Indian Ocean basin. Returning from his fourth voyage, Zheng He brought envoys from thirty states who traveled to China and paid their respects at the Ming court.

End of the Voyages Yet suddenly, in the mid-1430s, the Ming emperors decided to end the expeditions. Confucian ministers, who mistrusted Zheng He and the eunuchs who supported the voyages, argued that resources committed to the expensive expeditions should go to better uses. Moreover, during the 1420s and 1430s the Mongols mounted a

Zheng He (jung ha)

new military threat from the northwest, and land forces urgently needed financial support.

Thus in 1433, after Zheng He's seventh voyage, the expeditions ended. Chinese merchants continued to trade in Japan and southeast Asia, but imperial officials destroyed most of the nautical charts that Zheng He had carefully prepared. The decommissioned ships sat in harbors until they rotted away, and Chinese craftsmen forgot the technology of building such large vessels. Yet Zheng He's voyages demonstrated clearly that China could exercise military, political, and economic influence throughout the Indian Ocean basin.

European Exploration in the Atlantic and Indian Oceans

As Chinese fleets reconnoitered the Indian Ocean, European mariners were preparing to enter both the Atlantic and the Indian Ocean basins. Unlike Zheng He and his companions, however, Europeans ventured onto the seas not for diplomatic reasons but to expand the boundaries of Roman Catholic Christianity and to profit from commercial opportunities. In the process, they made extensive use of technologies—particularly the magnetic compass and gunpowder—that had been diffused to Europe in the midtwelfth and mid-thirteenth centuries, respectively.

Portuguese Exploration The experience of Portugal illustrates that mixture of motives. During the fifteenth century Prince Henrique of Portugal, often called Prince Henry the Navigator, embarked on an ambitious campaign to spread Christianity and increase Portuguese influence on the seas. In 1415 he watched as Portuguese forces seized the Moroccan city of Ceuta, which guarded the Strait of Gibraltar from the south. He regarded his victory both as a blow against Islam and as a strategic move enabling Christian vessels to move freely between the Mediterranean and the Atlantic.

Colonization of the Atlantic Islands Following the capture of Ceuta, Henrique encouraged Portuguese mariners

Ceuta (SYOO-tuh)

to venture into the Atlantic. During their voyages they discovered the Madeiras and Azores Islands, all uninhabited, which they soon colonized. Later discoveries included the Cape Verde Islands, Fernando Po, São Tomé, and Principe off the west African coast. Because these Atlantic islands enjoyed fertile soils and a Mediterranean climate, Portuguese entrepreneurs soon began to cultivate sugarcane there, often in collaboration with Italian investors. Italians had financed sugar plantations in the Mediterranean islands since the twelfth century, and their commercial networks provided a ready means to distribute sugar to Europeans, who were rapidly developing a taste for sweets.

Slave Trade During the middle decades of the fifteenth century, a series of Portuguese fleets also explored the

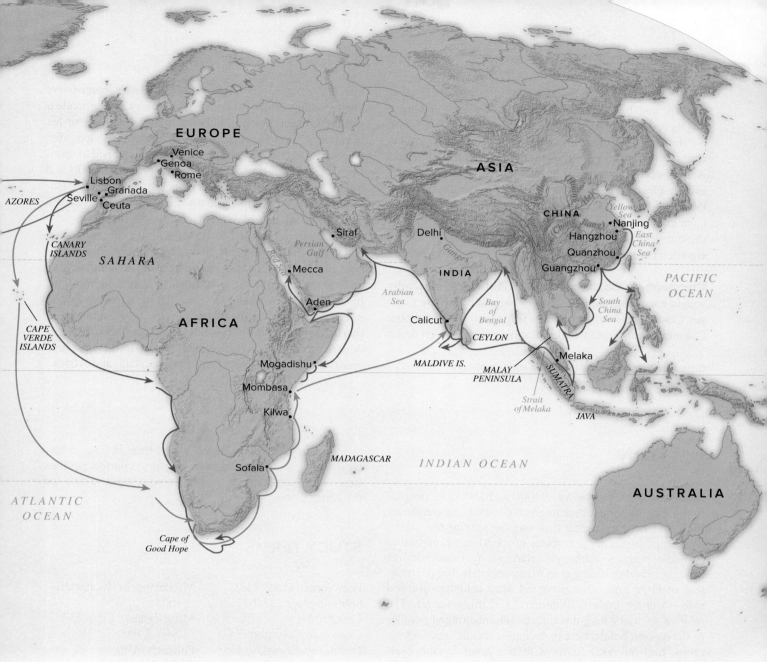

west African coast. Originally, the Portuguese traded guns, textiles, and other manufactured items for African gold and slaves. Soon, Portuguese traders changed the nature of the African slave trade by dramatically increasing its volume and by sending slaves to new destinations. In the mid–fifteenth century the Portuguese dispatched thousands of slaves annually to recently founded plantations in the Atlantic islands, where the slaves worked as laborers. The use of African slaves to perform heavy labor on commercial plantations soon became common practice, and it fueled the development of a huge, Atlantic-wide trade that, by the end of the nineteenth century, delivered as many as twelve million enslaved Africans to destinations in North America, South America, and the Caribbean region.

Indian Ocean Trade While some Portuguese mariners traded profitably in west Africa, others sought to eliminate the role of Muslim and Italian intermediaries in the Asian silk and spice trades by finding a sea-lane from Europe around Africa and into the Indian Ocean. By 1488 Bartolomeu Dias had sailed around the Cape of Good Hope and entered the Indian Ocean. In 1497 Vasco da Gama departed Portugal with the intention of sailing to India. After rounding the Cape of Good Hope, he cruised up the east African coast and found a Muslim pilot who showed him how to take advantage of the seasonal monsoon winds to

Bartolomeu Dias (bahr-tol-oh-mew DEE-uhs)
Vasco da Gama (VAS-koh duh GAM-uh)

sail across the Arabian Sea to India. In 1498 he arrived at Calicut, and by 1499 he had returned to Lisbon with a hugely profitable cargo of pepper and spices.

For most of the following century, Portuguese merchants and mariners dominated trade between Europe and Asia. Indeed, they attempted to control all shipping in the Indian Ocean by overpowering the vessels of Arabs, Persians, Indians, and southeast Asians. They did not have enough ships to oversee all trade in the region, but the entry of Portuguese mariners into the Indian Ocean signaled the beginning of European imperialism in Asia.

Christopher Columbus While Portuguese seafarers sought a sea route around Africa to India, the Genoese mariner Cristoforo Colombo, known in English as Christopher Columbus, conceived the idea of sailing west to reach Asian

Cristoforo Colombo (crihs-toh-for-oh kuh-LUHM-boh)

markets. Because geographers in the eastern hemisphere knew nothing of the Americas, Columbus's notion made a certain amount of sense, although many doubted that his plan could lead to profitable trade because of the long distances involved. After the king of Portugal declined to sponsor an expedition to test Columbus's plan, Fernando and Isabel of Spain agreed to underwrite a voyage. In 1492 Columbus set sail. Later that year his fleet of three ships reached land at San Salvador (Watling Island) in the Bahamas.

Columbus returned to Spain without the gold, silk, and spices that he had expected to find, but he persistently held that he had reached islands near the Asian mainland and the markets of China and Japan. Yet although Columbus himself never acknowledged that his expeditions had not reached Asia, by the end of the fifteenth century other mariners who came to explore the Caribbean and the American continents realized that the western hemisphere constituted a world apart from Europe, Asia, and Africa.

SUMMARY

In the five centuries between 1000 and 1500 C.E., peoples in the eastern hemisphere interacted with more frequency than ever before. In part this was because of the stability created by the large empires of the Mongols and other nomadic peoples. Although conquest by these empires brought initial destruction to many societies, the pacification of large areas that occurred after conquest allowed safe travel for traders, diplomats, and missionaries. The relative safety of long-distance travel encouraged peoples of the eastern hemisphere to exchange technologies, ideas, crops, and religious faiths with one another with ever-increasing frequency. Yet just as we saw at the end of the classical period, one of the unintended consequences of increased cross-cultural interaction was the spread of epidemic disease to distant regions. Indeed, in the fourteenth century bubonic plague tore through much of Eurasia, leaving death and destruction in its wake and severely weakening cross-cultural ties. However, by the early fifteenth century societies had begun to recover from the plague, and China and Europe in particular began to renew cross-cultural contacts. Although both Chinese and European efforts at renewing these contacts had momentous consequences, the ocean voyages of Europeans in this period fundamentally shaped modern world history when they accidentally made contact with peoples from

the western hemisphere. For the first time in human history, cross-cultural interactions began to connect peoples from both hemispheres, with enormous significance for the entire globe.

STUDY TERMS

Bartolomeu Dias (343)
bubonic plague (336)
Ceuta (342)
Cristoforo Columbo (344)
Desiderius Erasmus (338)
eunuchs (336)
Fernando of Aragon (337)
Filippo Brunelleschi (338)
Francesco Petrarca (339)
gunpowder (337, 342)
Hongwu (336)
Ibn Battuta (327, 329–330)
Isabel of Castile (337)
Khubilai Khan (329)
Leonardo da Vinci (338)
mandarins (336)
Marco Polo (328)
Melaka (328)

Michelangelo Buonarotti (338)
Ming dynasty (336–337, 340–341)
Petrarch (339)
Prince Henry the Navigator (342)
qadi (327)
Qing (337)
reconquista (337)
Renaissance (338)
Sufis (332)
sugarcane (332, 342)
Vasco da Gama (343)
Yongle (337)
Yuan (336)
Zheng He (341)

FOR FURTHER READING

Janet L. Abu-Lughod. *Before European Hegemony: The World System*, A.D. *1250–1350*. New York, 1989. An important study of long-distance trade networks during the Mongol era.

Jerry H. Bentley. *Old World Encounters: Cross-Cultural Contacts and Exchanges in Pre-Modern Times*. New York, 1993. Studies cultural and religious exchanges in the eastern hemisphere before 1500 C.E.

Timothy Brook. *The Confusions of Pleasure: Commerce and Culture in Ming China*. Berkeley, 1998. The best introduction to Ming China, with emphasis on social and cultural history.

Jerry Brotton. *The Renaissance Bazaar: From the Silk Road to Michelangelo*. Oxford, 2002. A provocative and well-illustrated study arguing that encounters in the larger world deeply influenced Renaissance cultural development in Europe.

K. N. Chaudhuri. *Asia before Europe: Economy and Civilisation of the Indian Ocean from the Rise of Islam to 1750*. Cambridge, 1990. Controversial and penetrating analysis of economic, social, and cultural structures shaping societies of the Indian Ocean basin.

Ross E. Dunn. *The Adventures of Ibn Battuta: A Muslim Traveler of the 14th Century*. Berkeley, 1986. Fascinating reconstruction of Ibn Battuta's travels and experiences.

Brian Fagan. *The Little Ice Age: How Climate Made History, 1300–1850*. New York, 2000. Popular account of the little ice age, with emphasis on its effects in Europe and North America.

Robert S. Gottfried. *The Black Death: Natural and Human Disaster in Medieval Europe*. New York, 1983. The best general study of bubonic plague and its effects in Europe.

John Larner. *Marco Polo and the Discovery of the World*. New Haven, 1999. Excellent study of Marco Polo and his significance, based on a thorough review of both textual evidence and recent scholarship.

Louise L. Levathes. *When China Ruled the Seas: The Treasure Fleet of the Dragon Throne, 1405–1433*. New York, 1994. Excellent popular account of Zheng He's voyages.

PART 4 AN AGE OF CROSS-CULTURAL INTERACTION, 1000 TO 1500 C.E.

Although the postclassical societies of the eastern hemisphere had restored order and stability to the region by 1000 C.E., invasions and conquest by nomadic peoples caused most postclassical societies to collapse between the eleventh and the fourteenth centuries. These nomadic invaders included the Mongols, who conquered so much of Eurasia in the thirteenth and fourteenth centuries that they built the largest empire the world has ever seen.

Mongol conquest initially resulted in monumental human and physical destruction. However, once conquest was complete, Mongol overlords facilitated accelerated communication within their vast imperial domains. Thus, from China to eastern Europe, traders, diplomats, missionaries, travelers, and pilgrims moved overland with greater ease than ever before, and encouraged ever-stronger networks of communication and exchange.

The Indian Ocean basin also grew far more integrated in the centuries between 1000 and 1500 C.E. Indeed, by 1500 the Indian Ocean served as a highway linking peoples from China to east Africa. As with the overland routes of the Mongol empire, this Indian Ocean highway encouraged the diffusion of scientific and intellectual knowledge, technologies like gunpowder and the compass, and food crops such as cotton and sugarcane—all of which profoundly influenced the development of societies throughout the eastern hemisphere.

Yet as at the end of the classical period, increased overland and seaborne interaction in the eastern hemisphere also led to the diffusion of disease pathogens. In the fourteenth century, the bubonic plague spread rapidly from China across most of Eurasia, leaving millions dead in its wake. Such massive fatalities severely disrupted networks of communication and trade. However, by the end of the fifteenth century these networks had recovered once again. Indeed, they recovered so well that western Europeans—who had long been on the margins of Eurasian trade networks—sought eagerly to find alternate routes to the lucrative markets of east and southeast Asia. In one attempt to reach these markets by sailing west rather than east, Europeans instead stumbled on the Americas.

As European mariners ventured across the Atlantic and into the Americas, they unwittingly inaugurated a new era in world history, because they initiated a long-term process that brought all regions and peoples of the earth into permanent and sustained interaction for the first time in human history. Indeed, the formation and reconfiguration of global networks of power, communication, and exchange that followed from the initial contact between the two hemispheres rank among the most prominent themes of modern world history.

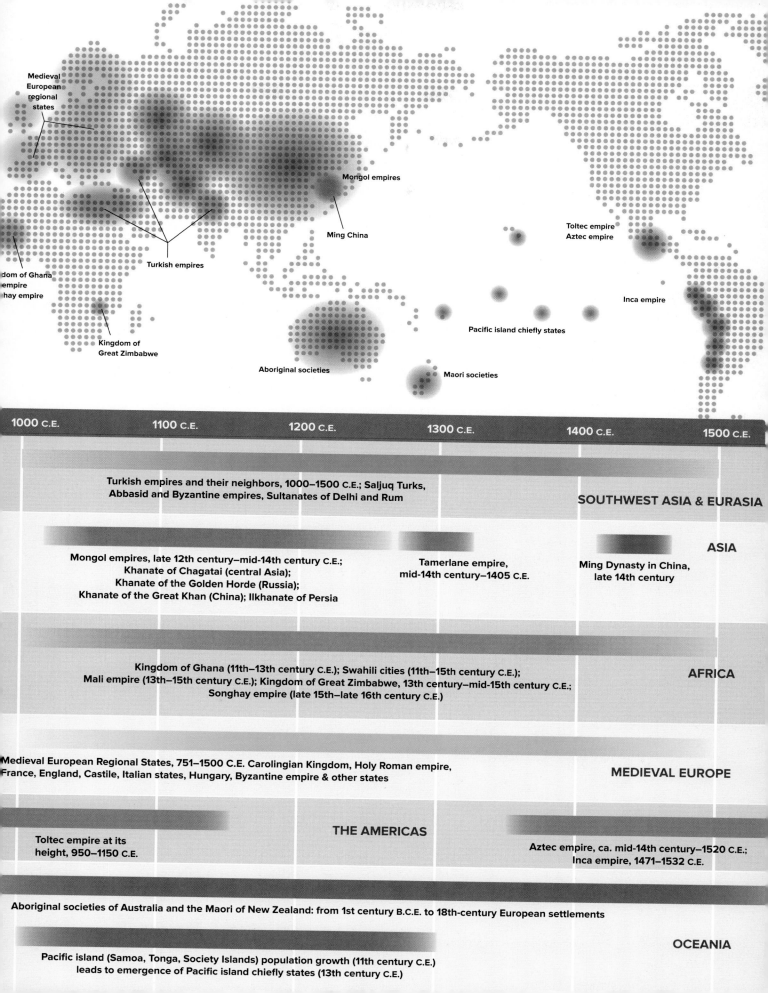

Medieval
European
regional
states

Mongol empires

Ming China

Toltec empire
Aztec empire

Turkish empires

...dom of Ghana
...empire
...hay empire

Inca empire

Kingdom of
Great Zimbabwe

Pacific island chiefly states

Aboriginal societies

Maori societies

1000 C.E.	1100 C.E.	1200 C.E.	1300 C.E.	1400 C.E.	1500 C.E.

Turkish empires and their neighbors, 1000–1500 C.E.; Saljuq Turks, Abbasid and Byzantine empires, Sultanates of Delhi and Rum

SOUTHWEST ASIA & EURASIA

ASIA

Mongol empires, late 12th century–mid-14th century C.E.; Khanate of Chagatai (central Asia); Khanate of the Golden Horde (Russia); Khanate of the Great Khan (China); Ilkhanate of Persia

Tamerlane empire, mid-14th century–1405 C.E.

Ming Dynasty in China, late 14th century

AFRICA

Kingdom of Ghana (11th–13th century C.E.); Swahili cities (11th–15th century C.E.); Mali empire (13th–15th century C.E.); Kingdom of Great Zimbabwe, 13th century–mid-15th century C.E.; Songhay empire (late 15th–late 16th century C.E.)

MEDIEVAL EUROPE

Medieval European Regional States, 751–1500 C.E. Carolingian Kingdom, Holy Roman empire, France, England, Castile, Italian states, Hungary, Byzantine empire & other states

THE AMERICAS

Toltec empire at its height, 950–1150 C.E.

Aztec empire, ca. mid-14th century–1520 C.E.; Inca empire, 1471–1532 C.E.

Aboriginal societies of Australia and the Maori of New Zealand: from 1st century B.C.E. to 18th-century European settlements

OCEANIA

Pacific island (Samoa, Tonga, Society Islands) population growth (11th century C.E.) leads to emergence of Pacific island chiefly states (13th century C.E.)

glossary&pronunciationkey

Abbasid (ah-BAH-sihd) Cosmopolitan Arabic dynasty (750–1258) that replaced the Umayyads; founded by Abu al-Abbas and reached its peak under Harun al-Rashid.

Abdül Hamid II Reigned 1876–1909 C.E. Sultan of the Ottoman Empire whose despotic style of rule led to the creation of many opposition groups and to his deposition by dissidents in 1909.

Abolitionism Antislavery movement.

Absolutism Political philosophy that stressed the divine right theory of kingship: the French king Louis XIV was the classic example.

Abu Bakr (ah-BOO BAHK-uhr) First caliph after the death of Muhammad.

Achaemenid empire (ah-KEE-muh-nid) First great Persian empire (558–330 B.C.E.), which began under Cyrus and reached its peak under Darius.

Adam Smith 1723–1790. Scottish philosopher and founder of modern political economy, and a key figure in the Scottish Enlightenment. Best known for *An Inquiry into the Nature and Causes of the Wealth of Nations,* published in 1776.

Adwa 1896 Battle in which the Ethiopians badly defeated would-be Italian conquerors.

Aegean Sea Sea located between the mainlands of modern Greece and Turkey.

Aeschylus (ES-kuh-luhs) Greek tragedian, author of the *Oresteia.*

Afonso d'Albuquerque 1453–1515 C.E. Commander of the Portuguese forces in the Indian Ocean in the early 16th century. He was responsible for seizing Hormuz, Goa, and Malacca, which allowed the Portuguese to control Indian Ocean trade.

African National Congress South African political party formed in 1912 that provided consistent opposition to the apartheid state, and eventually became the majority party at the end of the apartheid era in 1994.

Age grades Bantu institution in which individuals of roughly the same age carried out communal tasks appropriate for that age.

Ahimsa (uh-HIM-suh) Jain term for the principle of nonviolence to other living things or their souls.

Ahura Mazda (uh-HOORE-uh MAHZ-duh) Main god of Zoroastrianism who represented truth and goodness and was perceived to be in an eternal struggle with the malign spirit Angra Mainyu.

Akbar Mughal emperor from 1556–1605. Known for his tolerance for religion, and thought to be one of the greatest Mughal emperors.

Al-Andalus (al-ANN-duh-luhs) Islamic Spain.

al-Qaeda Meaning "the base", a global militant Islamic organization founded by Osama bin Laden in 1988 or 1989.

Alexander of Macedon King of the ancient Greek kingdom of Macedon from 336–323 BCE. He was responsible for creating one of the largest ancient empires, stretching from Greece to Egypt and northern India.

Aliʻi nui Hawaiian class of high chiefs.

Allah (AH-lah) God of the monotheistic religion of Islam.

Amon-Re (AH-muhn RAY) Egyptian god, combination of the sun god Re and the air god Amon.

Anastasio Somoza Garcia 1896–1956. Brutal leader of the U.S.-trained Guarda Nacional in Nicaragua who became president and dictator in 1934.

Ancien Régime Meaning "old order," and refers to the period prior to the French Revolution in 1789.

Angkor (AHN-kohr) Southeast Asian Khmer kingdom (889–1432) that was centered on the temple cities of Angkor Thom and Angkor Wat.

Anti-Semitism Term coined in the late nineteenth century that was associated with a prejudice against Jews and the political, social, and economic actions taken against them.

Antigonid empire The smallest of the three states that split from Alexander the Great's massive empire in 275 B.C.E. The Antigonid empire occupied Greece and Macedon.

Antonianism African syncretic religion, founded by Dona Beatriz, that taught that Jesus Christ was a black African man and that heaven was for Africans.

Ao One of the six Shang dynasty (1766–1122 B.C.E.) capitals near the modern city of Zheng-zhou.

Apartheid (ah-PAHR-teyed) South African system of "separateness" that was implemented in 1948 and that maintained the black majority in a position of political, social, and economic subordination.

Appeasement British and French policy in the 1930s that tried to maintain peace in Europe in the face of German aggression by making concessions.

Arianism Early Christian heresy that centered on teaching of Arius (250–336 C.E.) and contained the belief that Jesus was a mortal human being and not coeternal with God; Arianism was the focus of Council of Nicaea.

Armenian Massacres Campaign of extermination undertaken by the Ottomans against two million Armenians living in Ottoman territory during World War I.

Artha Hindu concept for the pursuit of economic well-being and honest prosperity.

Arthashastra (AR-thah-sha-strah) Ancient Indian political treatise from the time of Chandragupta Maurya; its authorship was traditionally ascribed to Kautalya, and it stressed that war was inevitable.

Aryans (AIR-ee-anns) Indo-European migrants who settled in India after 1500 B.C.E.; their union with indigenous Dravidians formed the basis of Hinduism.

Ashoka Third monarch of the Indian Mauryan dynasty–also known as Ashoka the Great–who ruled most of the Indian subcontinent from 269–232 BCE.

Association of Southeast Asian Nations (ASEAN.) Regional organization established in 1967 by Thailand, Malaysia, Singapore, Indonesia, and the Philippines; the organization was designed to promote economic progress and political stability; it later became a free-trade zone.

Assyrians (uh-SEAR-ee-uhns) Southwest Asian people who built an empire that reached its height during the eighth and seventh centuries B.C.E.; it was known for a powerful army and a well-structured state.

Astrolabe Navigational instrument for determining latitude.

Ataturk 1881–1938 C.E. Meaning "Father of the Turks," his real name was Mustafa Kemal. He was a Turkish army officer, reformer, and the first president of the modern Republic of Turkey after the Ottoman defeat in World War I.

Aten Monotheistic god of Egyptian pharaoh Akhenaten (r. 1353–1335 B.C.E.) and a very early example of monotheism.

Attica The region surrounding the ancient city of Athens.

Audiencias Spanish courts in Latin America.

Augusto César Sandino 1893–1934. Nationalist and liberal general of Nicaragua who fundamentally opposed U.S. intervention. He was murdered in 1934 by Anastacio Somoza Garcia's forces.

Aurangzeb Sixth Mughal emperor who reigned from 1658–1707 CE. Under his reign the empire stretched to its largest extent, covering most of the Indian subcontinent.

Auschwitz Camp established by the Nazi regime in occupied Poland, which functioned both as a concentration camp and an extermination camp. Approximately one million Jews were killed there.

Australopithecus (ah-strah-loh-PITH-uhkuhs) "Southern ape," oldest known ancestor of humans; it lived from around four million down to around one million years ago, and it could walk on hind legs, freeing up hands for use of simple tools.

Austronesians People who as early as 2000 B.C.E. began to explore and settle islands of the Pacific Ocean basin.

Avesta Book that contains the holy writings of Zoroastrianism.

Axum African kingdom centered in Ethiopia that became an early and lasting center of Coptic Christianity.

Aztec empire Central American empire constructed by the Mexica and expanded greatly during the fifteenth century during the reigns of Itzcoatl and Motecuzoma I.

Babur Central Asian conqueror who founded the Mughal dynasty in northern India. Reigned 1519–1530 CE.

Balfour Declaration British declaration from 1917 that supported the creation of a Jewish homeland in Palestine.

Ban Zhao 45–115 C.E. Renowned female historian and scholar of the Han dynasty, and author of the Book of Han.

Bantu (BAN-too) African peoples who originally lived in the area of present day Nigeria; around 2000 B.C.E. they began a centuries-long migration that took them to most of sub-Saharan Africa; the Bantu were very influential, especially linguistically.

Barack Obama 1961–. 44th president of the United States, who served from 2009–2017. Obama was the first U.S. president of African heritage.

Baron de Montesquieu 1689–1755 C.E. French political philosopher who advocated the separation of legislative, executive, and judicial government powers.

Battle of Gaugamela October 1, 331 B.C.E. The final meeting between Alexander of Macedon and King Darius III of Persia, in which Alexander was victorious.

Bedouins (BEHD-oh-ihnz) Nomadic Arabic tribespeople.

Benefice Grant from a lord to a vassal, usually consisting of land, which supported the vassal and signified the relationship between the two.

Benito Juarez Mexican lawyer of Zapotec Indian origin who served as president of Mexico for five terms, the first beginning in 1858 and the last ending in 1872.

Benito Mussolini Italian politician and leader of the National Fascist Party, who ruled the country from 1922 until his removal from the post in 1943.

Berlin Conference Meeting organized by German chancellor Otto von Bismarck in 1884–1885 that provided the justification for European colonization of Africa.

Bezant Byzantine gold coin that served as the standard currency of the Mediterranean basin from the sixth through the twelfth century.

Bhagavad Gita (BUH-guh-vahd GEE-tuh) "Song of the Lord," an Indian short poetic work drawn from the lengthy *Mahabharata* that was finished around 400 C.E. and that expressed basic Hindu concepts such as karma and dharma.

Bhakti (BAHK-tee) Indian movement that attempted to transcend the differences between Hinduism and Islam.

Black Hand Pre–World War I secret Serbian society; one of its members, Gavrilo Princip, assassinated Austrian archduke Francis Ferdinand and provided the spark for the outbreak of the Great War.

Blitzkrieg German style of rapid attack through the use of armor and air power that was used in Poland, Norway, Denmark, Belgium, the Netherlands, and France in 1939–1940.

Bodh Gaya Town southwest of Pataliputra in which Gautama (Buddha) received enlightenment while sitting under a bo tree.

Bodhisattvas (BOH-dih-SAT-vuhs) Buddhist concept regarding individuals who had reached enlightenment but who stayed in this world to help people.

Bogomils Bulgarian group active in the 10th and 11th centuries that believed in rejecting the material world and extreme ascetisicm.

Bolshevik (BOHL-shih-vehk) Russian communist party headed by Lenin.

Book of Songs The oldest existing collection of Chinese poetry, dating from the 11th to the 7th centuries B.C.E.

Bourgeoisie Middle class in modern industrial society.

Boxer Rebellion Uprising by a secret Chinese society called the Society of the Righteous and Harmonious Fists that lasted from 1900–1901.

Brahmins (BRAH-minz) Hindu caste of priests.

Brezhnev Doctrine Policy developed by Leonid Brezhnev (1906–1982) that claimed for the Soviet Union the right to invade any socialist country faced with internal or external enemies; the doctrine was best expressed in Soviet invasion of Czechoslovakia.

BRICs Acronym for the fast-growing and developing economies of Brazil, Russia, India, and China.

Buddha (BOO-duh) The "enlightened one," the term applied to Siddhartha Gautama after his discoveries that would form the foundation of Buddhism.

Buddhism (BOO-diz'm) Religion, based on Four Noble Truths, associated with Siddhartha Gautama (563–483 B.C.E.), or the Buddha; its adherents desired to eliminate all distracting passion and reach nirvana.

Bunraku (boon-RAH-koo) Japanese puppet theater.

Byzantine Empire (BIHZ-ann-teen) Long-lasting empire centered at Constantinople; it grew out of the end of the Roman empire, carried the legacy of Roman greatness, and was the only classical society to survive into the early modern age; it reached its early peak during the reign of Justinian (483–565).

Caesaropapism Concept relating to the mixing of political and religious authority, as with the Roman emperors, that was central to the church-versus-state controversy in medieval Europe.

Cahokia (kuh-HOH-kee-uh) Large structure in modern Illinois that was constructed by the mound-building peoples; it was the third largest structure in the Americas before the arrival of the Europeans.

Caliph (KAL-ihf) "Deputy," Islamic leader after the death of Muhammad.

Camillo di Cavour 1810–1861 C.E. Prime Minister to King Vittorio Emmanuel II of Piedmont and Sardinia, and key figure in bringing about the unification of Italy.

Capetian (cah-PEE-shuhn) Early French dynasty that started with Hugh Capet.

Capitalism An economic system with origins in early modern Europe in which private parties make their goods and services available on a free market.

Capitulation Highly unfavorable trading agreements that the Ottoman Turks signed with the Europeans in the nineteenth century that symbolized the decline of the Ottomans.

Carolingians Germanic dynasty that was named after its most famous member, Charlemagne.

Carthage Northern African kingdom, main rival to early Roman expansion, that was defeated by Rome in the Punic Wars.

Çatal Hüyük Important Neolithic settlement in Anatolia (7250–6150 B.C.E.).

Cathars Medieval heretics, also known as the Albigensians, who considered the material world evil; their followers renounced wealth and marriage and promoted an ascetic existence.

Catholic Reformation Sixteenth-century Catholic attempt to cure internal ills and confront Protestantism; it was inspired by the reforms of the Council of Trent and the actions of the Jesuits.

Caudillos (KAW-dee-ohs) Latin American term for nineteenth-century local military leaders.

Central Powers World War I term for the alliance of Germany, Austria-Hungary, and the Ottoman empire.

Chagatai One of Chinggis Khan's sons, whose descendants ruled central Asia through the Chagatai khanate.

Chan Buddhism (CHAHN BOO-diz'm) Influential branch of Buddhism in China, with an emphasis on intuition and sudden flashes of insight instead of textual study.

Chanchan (chahn-chahn) Capital of the pre-Incan, South American Chimu society that supported a large population of fifty thousand.

Charlemagne King of the Franks, who ruled most of Western Europe in the late 8th and early 9th centuries C.E.

Charles V Reigned 1519–1556. Emperor who inherited the Hapsburg family's Austrian territories as well as the Kingdom of Spain. When he became emperor in 1519, his empire stretched from Austria to Peru.

Chavín cult Mysterious but very popular South American religion (1000–300 B.C.E.).

Chimu Pre-Incan South American society that fell to Incas in the fifteenth century.

Chinampas Agricultural gardens used by Mexica (Aztecs) in which fertile muck from lake bottoms was dredged and built up into small plots.

Chinggis Khan (1206–1227 CE) Founder of the Mongol Empire and conqueror of most of Eurasia.

Chivalry European medieval code of conduct for knights based on loyalty and honor.

Chola Southern Indian Hindu kingdom (850–1267), a tightly centralized state that dominated sea trade.

Christopher Columbus (1451–1506) Italian explorer and colonizer who made four trans-Atlantic voyages from Europe to the Americas beginning in 1492.

Chu Autonomous state in the central Yangzi region of China during the Zhou dynasty (1122–256 B.C.E.).

Chucuito Pre-Incan South American society that rose in the twelfth century and fell to the Incas in the fifteenth century.

City-state Urban areas that controlled surrounding agricultural regions and that were often loosely connected in a broader political structure with other city-states.

Civil Code Civil law code promulgated by Napoleon Bonaparte in 1804.

Civil Service Examinations A battery of grueling tests given at the district, provincial, and metropolitan levels that determined entry into the Chinese civil service during the Ming and Qing dynasties.

Cixi 1835–1908 C.E. Former imperial concubine who established herself as effective ruler of the Qing dynasty in the fifty years prior to the end of Qing rule in 1908. She was hated by millions for her lavish spending, corruption, and resistance to reform.

Cohong Specially licensed Chinese firms that were under strict government regulation.

Collectivization Process beginning in the late 1920s by which Stalin forced the Russian peasants off their own land and onto huge collective farms run by the state; millions died in the process.

COMECON The Council for Mutual Economic Assistance, which offered increased trade within the Soviet Union and eastern Europe; it was the Soviet alternative to the United States' Marshall Plan.

Comfort Women Mainly Korean, Taiwanese, and Manchurian women who were forced into service by the Japanese army to serve as prostitutes to the Japanese troops during World War II.

Communalism A term, usually associated with India, that placed an emphasis on religious rather than national identity.

Communism Philosophy and movement that began in middle of the nineteenth century with the work of Karl Marx; it has the same general goals as socialism, but it includes the belief that violent revolution is necessary to destroy the bourgeois world and institute a new world run by and for the proletariat.

Confucianism (kuhn-FYOO-shuhn-iz'm) Philosophy, based on the teachings of the Chinese philosopher Kong Fuzi (551–479 B.C.E.), or Confucius, that emphasizes order, the role of the gentleman, obligation to society, and reciprocity.

Congress of Vienna Gathering of European diplomats in Vienna, Austria, from October 1814 to June 1815. The representatives of the "great powers" that defeated Napoleon—Britain, Austria, Prussia, and Russia—dominated the proceedings, which aimed to restore the prerevolutionary political and social order.

Conquistadores (kohn-KEE-stah-dohrayz) Spanish adventurers such as Cortés and Pizarro who conquered Central and South America in the sixteenth century.

Constitutionalism Movement in England in the seventeenth century that placed power in Parliament's hands as part of a constitutional monarchy and that increasingly limited the power of the monarch; the movement was highlighted by the English Civil War and the Glorious Revolution.

Containment Concept associated with the United States and specifically with the Truman Doctrine during the cold war that revolved around the notion that the United States would contain the spread of communism.

Corporation A concept that reached mature form in 1860s in England and France; it involved private business owned by thousands of individual and institutional investors who financed the business through the purchase of stocks.

Corpus iuris civilis (KOR-puhs yoor-uhs sih-VEE-lihs) *Body of the Civil Law,* the Byzantine emperor Justinian's attempt to codify all Roman law.

Council of Trent 1545–1563. Assembly of high Roman Catholic church officials which met over a period years to institute reforms in order to increase morality and improve the preparation of priests.

Crimean War 1853–1856 C.E. War fought on the Crimean peninsula between Russia on one side and Great Britain, France, the Ottoman Empire, and Sardinia on the other.

Criollos (kree-OH-lohs) Creoles, people born in the Americas of Spanish or Portuguese ancestry.

Cross staff Device that sailors used to determine latitude by measuring the angle of the sun or the pole star above the horizon.

Crystal Palace Glass and iron structure that housed an exhibition in London in 1851 to display industrial products.

Cuneiform Written language of the Sumerians, probably the first written script in the world.

Cult of Dionysis devotees of the god of wine in ancient Greece. By the 5th century B.C.E. the cult had gone from wild, emotional displays to reserved, thoughtful tributes.

Daimyo (DEYEM-yoh) Powerful territorial lords in early modern Japan.

Dao Key element in Chinese philosophy that means the "way of nature" or the "way of the cosmos."

Daodejing (DOW-DAY-JIHNG) Book that is the fundamental work of Daoism.

Daoism (DOW-i'zm) Chinese philosophy with origins in the Zhou dynasty; it is associated with legendary philosopher Laozi, and it called for a policy of noncompetition.

Dar al-Islam The "house of Islam," a term for the Islamic world.

Dasas Ancient Aryan Indian term for enemies or subject peoples.

Declaration of Independence Drafted by Thomas Jefferson in 1776; the document expressed the ideas of John Locke and the Enlightenment, represented the idealism of the American rebels, and influenced other revolutions.

Declaration of the Rights of Man and the Citizen Document from the French Revolution (1789) that was influenced by the American Declaration of Independence and in turn influenced other revolutionary movements.

Decolonization Process by which former colonies achieved their independence, as with the newly emerging African nations in the 1950s and 1960s.

Deer Park of Sarnath Park near the city of Benares where the Buddha publicly announced his doctrine in the year 528 B.C.E.

Deism (DEE-iz'm) An Enlightenment view that accepted the existence of a god but denied the supernatural aspects of Christianity; in deism, the universe was an orderly realm maintained by rational and natural laws.

Descamisados "Shirtless ones," Argentine poor who supported Juan and Eva Perón.

Détente A reduction in cold war tension between the United States and the Soviet Union from 1969 to 1975.

Devshirme Ottoman requirement that the Christians in the Balkans provide young boys to be slaves of the sultan.

Dharma (DAHR-muh) Hindu concept of obedience to religious and moral laws and order; also, the basic doctrine of Buddhism.

Dhimmi (dihm-mee) Islamic concept of a protected people that was symbolic of Islamic toleration during the Mughal and Ottoman empires.

Dhow Indian, Persian, and Arab ships, one hundred to four hundred tons, that sailed and traded throughout the Indian Ocean basin.

Diaspora People who have settled far from their original homeland but who still share some measure of ethnic identity.

Dionysus Greek god of wine, also known as Bacchus; Greek plays were performed in his honor.

Dominicans An order of mendicants founded by St. Dominic (1170–1221 C.E.) whose purpose was to live in poverty and serve the religious needs of their communities.

Domingo Faustino Sarmiento 1811–1888 C.E. Argentine intellectual, writer, and activist who became the 7th president of Argentina.

Dravidians a family of languages spoken in southern India and Sri Lanka, or the peoples who speak them. Some scholars believe Dravidians were the original inhabitants of India prior to Aryan settlement, though this is controversial.

Dreadnoughts A class of British battleships whose heavy armaments made all other battleships obsolete overnight.

Duma Russian parliament, established after the Revolution of 1905.

Dunhuang Oasis in modern western China that became a site of Buddhist missionary activity by the 4th century C.E.

Durham Report Report issued in 1839 by the British Earl of Durham and recent governor-general of Canada, which advocated significant self-government for a united Canada.

Dutch learning European knowledge that reached Tokugawa Japan.

East India Company British joint-stock company that grew to be a state within a state in India; it possessed its own armed forces.

Economic Nationalism Economic policies pursued by many governments affected by the Great Depression in which the nation tries to become economically self-sufficient by imposing high tariffs on foreign goods. The policy served to exacerbate the damaging effects of the Depression around the world.

Eight-legged essay Eight-part essays that an aspiring Chinese civil servant had to compose, mainly based on a knowledge of Confucius and the Zhou classics.

Eleanor of Aquitaine 1122–1204 C.E. Aristocratic woman from the city of Poitiers, modern France, who supported poets and entertainers known as troubadours.

Eleusinian Mysteries Cult in ancient Greece that encouraged initiates to observe high moral standards.

Emancipation Manifesto Manifesto proclaimed by the Russian Tsar Alexander II in 1861 that abolished the institution of serfdom and freed 23 million serfs.

Encomienda (ehn-KOH-mee-ehn-dah) System that gave the Spanish settlers (*encomenderos*) the right to compel the indigenous peoples of the Americas to work in the mines or fields.

Engenho Brazilian sugar mill; the term also came to symbolize the entire complex world relating to the production of sugar.

English Civil War 1642–1649. A series of armed conflicts between the English crown and the English Parliament over political and religious differences.

Enlightenment Eighteenth-century philosophical movement that began in France; its emphasis was on the preeminence of reason rather than faith or tradition; it spread concepts from the Scientific Revolution.

Epicureans (ehp-ih-kyoo-REE-uhns) Hellenistic philosophers who taught that pleasure—as in quiet satisfaction—was the greatest good.

Equal-field system Chinese system during the Tang dynasty in which the goal was to ensure an equitable distribution of land.

Essenes Jewish sect that looked for the arrival of a savior; they were similar in some of their core beliefs to the early Christians.

Estates General Prior to 1789, the French legislative assembly that consisted of three classes (or Estates) of men: the clergy, the aristocracy, and the commoners.

Etruscans (ih-TRUHS-kuhns) Northern Italian society that initially dominated the Romans; the Etruscans helped convey Greek concepts to the expanding Romans.

Eugenics A late 19th and early 20th century movement that sought to improve the gene pool of the human race by encouraging those deemed fit to have more children, and by discouraging those deemed unfit from reproducing. The movement was deeply tied to racism, and was eventually adopted by the German Nazi regime to justify the extermination of 'undesirable' populations.

Eunuchs (YOO-nihks) Castrated males, originally in charge of the harem, who grew to play major roles in government; eunuchs were common in China and other societies.

European Community (EC) Organization of European states established in 1957; it was originally called the European Economic Community and was renamed the EC in 1967; it promoted economic growth and integration as the basis for a politically united Europe.

European Union Established by the Maastricht Treaty in 1993, a supranational organization for even greater European economic and political integration.

Fascism Political ideology and mass movement that was prominent in many parts of Europe between 1919 and 1945; it sought to regenerate the social, political, and cultural life of societies, especially in contrast to liberal democracy and socialism; fascism began with Mussolini in Italy, and it reached its peak with Hitler in Germany.

Ferdinand Magellan (1480–1521) Portuguese explorer who organized the expedition that completed the first circumnavigation of the Earth.

Five Pillars The foundation of Islam: (1) profession of faith, (2) prayer, (3) fasting during Ramadan, (4) almsgiving, and (5) pilgrimage, or hajj.

Five-year plans First implemented by Stalin in the Soviet Union in 1928; five-year plans were a staple of communist regimes in which every aspect of production was determined in advance for a five-year period; five-year plans were opposite of the free market concept.

Four Noble Truths The foundation of Buddhist thought: (1) life is pain, (2) pain is caused by desire, (3) elimination of desire will bring an end to pain, (4) living a life based on the Noble Eightfold Path will eliminate desire.

Franciscans An order of mendicants founded by St. Francis (1182–1226 C.E.) whose purpose was to live in poverty and serve the religious needs of their communities.

Frederick Barbarossa 1152–1190 C.E. Medieval emperor with lands in modern southern Germany who tried and failed to conquer Lombardy in modern Italy.

Front de Libération Nationale (FLN) The Algerian organization that fought a bloody guerrilla war for freedom against France.

Fu Hao Favorite consort of King Wu Ding of the Shang dynasty (13th century B.C.E.), whose richly appointed tomb remained intact until the modern era.

Fukuzawa Yukichi 1835–1901. Prominent Japanese who traveled around Europe and North America after the Meiji Restoration to evaluate foreign administrative systems and constitutions.

Fulani (foo-LAH-nee) Sub-Saharan African people who, beginning in the seventeenth century, waged a series of wars designed to impose their own strict interpretation of Islam.

Gandhara Kingdom in modern Pakistan and Afghanistan established by the Persian emperor Darius in about 520 B.C.E.

Gathas (GATH-uhs) Zoroastrian hymns believed to be compositions by Zarathustra.

Gauchos (GOW-chohz) Argentine cowboys, highly romanticized figures.

Gaul Name of the region of modern France during the ancient Greek and Roman period.

General Agreement on Tariffs and Trade (GATT) Free-trade agreement first signed in 1947; by 1994 it had grown to 123 members and formed the World Trade Organization (WTO).

Ghana (GAH-nuh) Kingdom in west Africa during the fifth through the thirteenth century whose rulers eventually converted to Islam; its power and wealth was based on dominating trans-Saharan trade.

Ghazi (GAH-zee) Islamic religious warrior.

Ghaznavids Turkish tribe under Mahmud of Ghazni who moved into northern India in the eleventh century and began a period of greater Islamic influence in India.

Gilgamesh Legendary king of the Mesopotamian city-state of Uruk (ca. 3000 B.C.E.), subject of the *Epic of Gilgamesh,* world's oldest complete epic literary masterpiece.

Glasnost (GLAHS-nohst) Russian term meaning "openness" introduced by Mikhail Gorbachev in 1985 to describe the process of opening Soviet society to dissidents and public criticism.

Globalization The breaking down of traditional boundaries in the face of increasingly global financial and cultural trends.

Global warming The emission of greenhouse gases, which prevents solar heat from escaping the earth's atmosphere and leads to the gradual heating of the earth's environment.

Glorious Revolution 1688–1689. The events that led to the replacement of the Catholic English King James II by his Protestant daughter Mary II and her Dutch husband William of Orange.

Golden Horde Mongol tribe that controlled Russia from the thirteenth to the fifteenth century.

Gracchi Brothers Tiberius and Gaius, brothers in the Roman Republic who worked to limit the amount of land individuals could hold in order to alleviate social conflict during the 2nd century B.C.E.

Greater East Asia Co-Prosperity Sphere Japanese plan for consolidating east and southeast Asia under their control during World War II.

Great Game Nineteenth-century competition between Great Britain and Russia for the control of central Asia.

Great Zimbabwe Large sub-Saharan African kingdom in the fifteenth century.

Greek Fire Devastating incendiary weapon used mainly at sea by Byzantine forces in the 7th and 8th centuries C.E.

Greenpeace An environmental organization founded in 1970 and dedicated to the preservation of earth's natural resources.

Griots Professional singers, historians, and story-tellers in sub-Saharan Africa.

Guomindang (GWOH-mihn-dahng) Chinese nationalist party founded by Sun Yat-sen (1866–1925) and later led by Jiang Jieshi; it has been centered in Taiwan since the end of the Chinese civil war.

Gupta (GOOP-tah) Indian dynasty (320–550 C.E.) that briefly reunited India after the collapse of the earlier Mauryan dynasty.

Guru Kabir 1440–1518 C.E. A blind weaver who became the most important teacher in the bhakti movement, which sought to harmonize Hinduism and Islam.

Hacienda (HAH-see-ehn-dah) Large Latin American estates.

Hagia Sophia (HAH-yah SOH-fee-uh) Massive Christian church constructed by the Byzantine emperor Justinian and later converted into a mosque.

Hajj (HAHJ) Pilgrimage to Mecca.

Hammurabi's Code (hahm-uh-RAH-beez) Sophisticated law code associated with the Babylonian king Hammurabi (r. 1792–1750 B.C.E.).

Hangzhou Capital of the Southern Song dynasty in the late 13th century.

Hannibal Barca Carthaginian general who devastated the Italian peninsula during the Second Punic War, 218–201 B.C.E.

Hanseatic League A commercial confederation of guilds and market towns that dominated trade in coastal Northern Europe from the 13th to the 17th centuries.

Harappan (hah-RAP-puhn) Early brilliant Indian society centered in Harappa and Mohenjo-daro.

Harijans "Children of God," Gandhi's term for the Untouchables.

Hebrews Semitic-speaking nomadic tribe influential for monotheistic belief in Yahweh.

Heian (HAY-ahn) Japanese period (794–1185), a brilliant cultural era notable for the world's first novel, Murasaki Shikibu's *The Tale of Genji.*

Hellenistic Era Phase in Greek history (328–146 B.C.E.), from the conquest of Greece by Philip of Macedon until Greece's fall to the Romans; this era was a more cosmopolitan age facilitated by the conquests of Alexander the Great.

Helots Servants to the Spartan state, who were neither chattel slaves nor free.

Hieroglyphics (heye-ruh-GLIPH-iks) Ancient Egyptian written language.

Hijra Muhammad's migration from Mecca to Medina in 622, which is the beginning point of the Islamic calendar and is considered to mark the beginning of the Islamic faith.

Hinayana (HEE-nah-yah-nuh) Branch of Buddhism known as the "lesser vehicle," also known as Theravada Buddhism; its beliefs include strict, individual path to enlightenment, and it is popular in south and southeast Asia.

Hinduism Main religion of India, a combination of Dravidian and Aryan concepts; Hinduism's goal is to reach spiritual purity and union with the great world spirit; its important concepts include dharma, karma, and samsara.

Holocaust German attempt in World War II to exterminate the Jews of Europe.

Home front Term made popular in World War I and World War II for the civilian "front" that was symbolic of the greater demands of total war.

Homer Supposed author of the ancient Greek epic poems the *Iliad* and the *Odyssey.*

Hominid (HAWM-ih-nihd) A creature belonging to the family Hominidae, which includes human and humanlike species.

Homo erectus (HOH-MOH ee-REHK-tuhs) "Upright-walking human," which existed from one million to two hundred thousand years ago; *Homo erectus* used cleavers and hand axes and learned how to control fire.

Homo sapiens (HOH-MOH SAY-pee-uhns) "Consciously thinking human," which first appeared around two hundred fifty thousand years ago and used sophisticated tools.

Huitzilopochtli (wee-tsee-loh-pockt-lee) Sun god and patron deity of the Aztecs.

Hundred Days of Reform Chinese reforms of 1898 led by Kang Youwei and Liang Qichao in their desire to turn China into a modern industrial power.

Hundred Years' War 1337–1453 C.E. Series of intermittent wars between France and England over the control of modern France.

Hyksos (HICK-sohs) Invaders who seized the Nile delta and helped bring an end to the Egyptian Middle Kingdom.

Iconoclasts (eye-KAHN-oh-klasts) Supporters of the movement, begun by the Byzantine Emperor Leo III (r. 717–741), to destroy religious icons because their veneration was considered sinful.

Ilkhanate (EEL-kahn-ate) Mongol state that ruled Persia after abolition of the Abbasid empire in the thirteenth century.

IMF International Monetary Fund. An international organization founded in 1945 to promote the stabilization of world currencies.

Imperialism Term associated with the expansion of European powers and their conquest and colonization of African and Asian societies, mainly from the sixteenth through the nineteenth century.

Inca empire Powerful South American empire that would reach its peak in the fifteenth century during the reigns of Pachacuti Inca and Topa Inca.

Indentured labor Labor source for plantations; wealthy planters would pay the laboring poor to sell a portion of their working lives, usually seven years, in exchange for passage.

India Act 1935 British Act that transferred to India the institutions of a self-governing state.

Indian Partition Period immediately following Indian and Pakistani independence in 1947, in which millions of Muslims sought to move to Pakistan from India, and millions of Hindus sought to move from Pakistan to India. It was marked by brutal sectarian violence, and the deaths of between one half million and a million people.

Indian Rebellion of 1857 Ultimately unsuccessful rebellion in North and Central India by a large portion of the Bengal Army and the civil population against British rule.

Indo-Europeans Tribal groups from southern Russia who, over a period of millennia, embarked on a series of migrations from India through western Europe; their greatest legacy was the broad distribution of Indo-European languages throughout Eurasia.

Indra Early Indian god associated with the Aryans; Indra was the king of the gods and was associated with warfare and thunderbolts.

Intifada Palestinian mass movement against Israeli rule in the Gaza Strip and other occupied territories.

Investiture (ihn-VEHST-tih-tyoor) One aspect of the medieval European church-versus-state controversy, the granting of church offices by a lay leader.

Iroquois (EAR-uh-kwoi) Eastern American Indian confederation made up of the Mohawk, Oneida, Onondaga, Cayuga, and Seneca tribes.

Isfahan Capital city of the Safavid Empire (modern Iran), founded by Shah Abbas in the early 17th century.

Islam Monotheistic religion announced by the prophet Muhammad (570–632); influenced by Judaism and Christianity, Muhammad was considered the final prophet because the earlier religions had not seen the entire picture; the Quran is the holy book of Islam.

Ismail Reigned 1501–1524. Founder of the Safavid dynasty in modern Iran.

Jainism (JEYEN-iz'm) Indian religion associated with the teacher Vardhamana Mahavira (ca. 540–468 B.C.E.) in which every physical object possessed a soul; Jains believe in complete nonviolence to all living beings.

Jati Indian word for a Hindu subcaste.

Java An island in modern Indonesia, and formerly home to the capital of the Dutch East Indies at the city of Batavia (modern Jakarta), founded 1619.

Jenne-jeno Settlement in the middle Niger River region in Africa that flourished from the 4th to the 8th centuries C.E. Known for iron production.

Jews a member of the people and cultural community whose traditional religion is Judaism and who trace their origins through the ancient Hebrew people of Israel to Abraham.

Jizya (JIHZ-yuh) Tax in Islamic empires that was imposed on non-Muslims.

John of Montecorvino 1247–1328 C.E. Franciscan missionary who traveled to China in 1291 in order to win converts to Christianity.

Joint-stock companies Early forerunner of the modern corporation; individuals who invested in a trading or exploring venture could make huge profits while limiting their risk.

Ka'ba (KAH-buh) Main shrine in Mecca, goal of Muslims embarking on the hajj.

Kabuki (kah-BOO-kee) Japanese theater in which actors were free to improvise and embellish the words.

Kama Hindu concept of the enjoyment of physical and sexual pleasure.

Kamikaze (KAH-mih-kah-zee) A Japanese term meaning "divine wind" that is related to the storms that destroyed Mongol invasion fleets; the term is symbolic of Japanese isolation and was later taken by suicide pilots in World War II.

Kanun (KAH-noon) Laws issued by the Ottoman Süleyman the Magnificent, also known as Süleyman Kanuni, "the Lawgiver."

Kapu Hawaiian concept of something being taboo.

Karma (KAHR-mah) Hindu concept that the sum of good and bad in a person's life will determine his or her status in the next life.

Khoikhoi South African people referred to pejoratively as the Hottentots by Europeans.

Khwarazm Shah Ruler of Afghanistan and Persia in 1218, when Chinggis Khan sought to trade with his realm. After Khwarazm shah murdered Chinggis Khan's envoys, Chinggis' forces devastated Persia in 1219.

King Kashta Circa 750 B.C.E. Kushite king who Egyptianized Nubia and conquered Upper Egypt.

Knossos City on the island of Crete that flourished during the Minoan period during the 3rd millennium B.C.E.

Kong Fuzi 551–479 C.E. Original name of Confucius, Chinese philosopher and teacher of ethics.

Kongo Central African state that began trading with the Portuguese around 1500; although their kings, such as King Affonso I (r. 1506–1543), converted to Christianity, they nevertheless suffered from the slave trade.

Koumbi-Saleh Important trading city along the trans-Saharan trade route from the eleventh to the thirteenth century.

Krishna One of the incarnations of the Hindu god Vishnu, who appears in the Bhagavad-Gita as the teacher of Arjuna.

Kshatriyas (KSHAHT-ree-uhs) Hindu caste of warriors and aristocrats.

Kulaks Land-owning Russian peasants who benefited under Lenin's New Economic Policy and suffered under Stalin's forced collectivization.

Kumiss An alcoholic drink of the nomadic groups of Central Asia made of fermented mare's milk.

Kush Nubian African kingdom that conquered and controlled Egypt from 750 to 664 B.C.E.

Lamaist Buddhism (LAH-muh-ihst BOOdiz'm) Branch of Buddhism that was similar to shamanism in its acceptance of magic and supernatural powers.

La Reforma Political reform movement of Mexican president Benito Juárez (1806–1872) that called for limiting the power of the military and the Catholic church in Mexican society.

Latifundia (LAT-ih-FOON-dee-uh) Huge state-run and slave-worked farms in ancient Rome.

Lawbook of Manu Circa 500 B.C.E. Book of verses in the Hindu canon that spells out the norms of religious, domestic, and social life in ancient India.

Lázaro Cárdenas 1895–1970. President of Mexico who nationalized the oil industry in 1938.

League of Nations Forerunner of the United Nations, the dream of American president Woodrow Wilson, although its potential was severely limited by the refusal of the United States to join.

Lebensraum (LAY-behnz-rowm) German term meaning "living space"; the term is associated with Hitler and his goal of carving out territory in the east for an expanding Germany.

Lech, Walesa (WAH-lehn-sah, LEHK) Leader of the Polish Solidarity movement.

Legalism Chinese philosophy from the Zhou dynasty that called for harsh suppression of the common people.

Levée en masse (leh-VAY on MASS) A term signifying universal conscription during the radical phase of the French revolution.

Lex talionis (lehks tah-lee-oh-nihs) "Law of retaliation," laws in which offenders suffered punishments similar to their crimes; the most famous example is Hammurabi's Laws.

Li (LEE) Confucian concept, a sense of propriety.

Li Bai 701–761 C.E. One of the most popular poets of the Tang era, famous for his commentary on Chinese social life.

Lin Zexu 1785–1850 C.E. Chinese scholar and official appointed by the Qing government to destroy the illegal opium trade conducted by the British and other European and American traders.

Linear A Minoan written script.

Linear B Early Mycenaean written script, adapted from the Minoan Linear A.

Little Ice Age Period beginning in about 1300 C.E. when global temperatures declined for about 500 years.

Louis Riel 1844–1885 C.E. Leader of metis and indigenous people who organized the unsuccessful Northwest Rebellion against Canadian settlement in 1885. Riel was executed by Canadian authorities.

Louis the Pious 814–840 C.E. Only surviving son of Charlemagne, who held his father's empire together until his sons split it up after his death in 843.

Louis XVI French king from 1774 until his deposition in 1792, who was executed in 1793 during the French Revolution.

Luddites Early-nineteenth-century artisans who were opposed to new machinery and industrialization.

Machismo (mah-CHEEZ-moh) Latin American social ethic that honored male strength, courage, aggressiveness, assertiveness, and cunning.

Madrasas (MAH-drahs-uhs) Islamic institutions of higher education that originated in the tenth century.

Magi Member of a priestly caste in ancient Persia.

Magyars (MAH-jahrs) Hungarian invaders who raided towns in Germany, Italy, and France in the ninth and tenth centuries.

Mahabharata (mah-hah-BAH-rah-tah) Massive ancient Indian epic that was developed orally for centuries; it tells of an epic civil war between two family branches.

Mahayana (mah-huh-YAH-nah) The "greater vehicle," a more metaphysical and more popular northern branch of Buddhism.

Majapahit (MAH-ja-PAHT) Southeast Asian kingdom (1293–1520) centered on the island of Java.

Mali (MAH-lee) West African kingdom founded in the thirteenth century by Sundiata; it reached its peak during the reign of Mansa Musa.

Manchus Manchurians who conquered China, putting an end to the Ming dynasty and founding the Qing dynasty (1644–1911).

Mandate of Heaven Chinese belief that the emperors ruled through the mandate, or approval, of heaven contingent on their ability to look after the welfare of the population.

Mandate system System that developed in the wake of World War I when the former colonies ended up mandates under European control, a thinly veiled attempt at continuing imperialism.

Manichaeism (man-ih-KEE-iz'm) Religion founded by the prophet Mani in the third century C.E., a syncretic version of Zoroastrian, Christian, and Buddhist elements.

Manila City in modern Phillipines, and formerly capital of the Spanish colony of the Philippines, founded in 1565.

Manor Large estates of the nobles during the European middle ages, home for the majority of the peasants.

Mao Zedong Leader of the Chinese Communist Party from the 1930s and founder of the People's Republic of China from 1949 until his death in 1976.

Maori (mow-ree) Indigenous people of New Zealand.

Marae Polynesian temple structure.

Marathon Battlefield scene of the Athenian victory over the Persians in 490 B.C.E.

Marco Polo 1254–1324 C.E. Italian merchant whose account of his travels to China and other lands became legendary.

Maroons Runaway African slaves.

Marshall Plan U.S. plan, officially called the European Recovery Program, that offered financial and other economic aid to all European states that had suffered from World War II, including Soviet bloc states.

Martin Luther 1483–1546. German monk and Catholic priest who became a critical figure in what became known as the Protestant Reformation after challenging the corruption of the church in his *Ninety-Five Theses,* published 1517.

Mauryan empire Indian dynasty (321–185 B.C.E.) founded by Chandragupta Maurya and reaching its peak under Ashoka.

Maya (Mye-uh) Brilliant Central American society (300–1100) known for math, astronomy, and a sophisticated written language.

Maya ball game Game in which Maya peoples used a hard rubber ball to propel through a ring without using their hands. Often used for ritual and ceremonial purposes.

May Fourth Movement Chinese movement that began 4 May 1919 with a desire to eliminate imperialist influences and promote national unity.

Mecca City in modern Saudi Arabia that was the birthplace of Mohammed and remains the holiest Muslim pilgrimage site.

Medes (meeds) Indo-European branch that settled in northern Persia and eventually fell to another branch, the Persians, in the sixth century B.C.E.

Meiji Restoration (MAY-jee) Restoration of imperial rule under Emperor Meiji in 1868 by a coalition led by Fukuzawa Yukichi and Ito Hirobumi; the restoration enacted western reforms to strengthen Japan.

Melaka (may-LAH-kah) Southeast Asian kingdom that was predominantly Islamic.

Mesopotamia Term meaning "between the rivers," in this case the Tigris and Euphrates; Sumer and Akkad are two of the earliest societies.

Mestizo (mehs-TEE-zoh) Latin American term for children of Spanish and native parentage.

Métis (may-TEE) Canadian term for individuals of mixed European and indigenous ancestry.

Millet An autonomous, self-governing community in the Ottoman empire.

Ming Chinese dynasty (1368–1644) founded by Hongwu and known for its cultural brilliance.

Minoan (mih-NOH-uhn) Society located on the island of Crete (ca. 2000–1100 B.C.E.) that influenced the early Mycenaeans.

Missi dominici (mihs-see doh-mee-neechee) "Envoys of the lord ruler," the noble and church emissaries sent out by Charlemagne.

Mithraism (MITH-rah-iz'm) Mystery religion based on worship of the sun god Mithras; it became popular among the Romans because of its promise of salvation.

Mochica (moh-CHEE-kuh) Pre-Incan South American society (300–700) known for their brilliant ceramics.

Modu 210–174 B.C.E. Highly successful leader of the Xiongnu peoples of the Central Asian steppes.

Mohenjo-daro Set of ancient cities in modern southeast Pakistan, near the Indus river, that flourished in the third millennium B.C.E.

Moksha Hindu concept of the salvation of the soul.

Monotheism (MAW-noh-thee-iz'm) Belief in only one god, a rare concept in the ancient world.

Monroe Doctrine American doctrine issued in 1823 during the presidency of James Monroe that warned Europeans to keep their hands off Latin America and that expressed growing American imperialistic views regarding Latin America.

Mughals (MOO-guhls) Islamic dynasty that ruled India from the sixteenth through the eighteenth century; the construction of the Taj Mahal is representative of their splendor; with the exception of the enlightened reign of Akbar, the increasing conflict between Hindus and Muslims was another of their legacies.

Muhammad (muh-HAH-mehd) Prophet of Islam (570–632).

Muhammad Ali Reigned 1805–1848. Egyptian general who built a powerful army on the European model and became the effective ruler of Egypt in spite of its official status as an Ottoman territory.

Mujahideen Meaning "Islamic warriors," a group who fought against Soviet intervention in Afghanistan in 1979. They were supplied and trained by United States CIA operatives, which helped lead to a Soviet withdrawal in 1989.

Munich Conference 1938 meeting between Germany, Great Britain, Italy, and France in which attendees agreed to German expansion in Czechoslovakia. The conference is considered part of the policy of appeasement that led Adolf Hitler to believe he had a free hand in Europe.

Muslim A follower of Islam.

Mycenaean (meye-seh-NEE-uhn) Early Greek society on the Peloponnese (1600–1100 B.C.E.) that was influenced by the Minoans; the Mycenaeans' conflict with Troy is immortalized in Homer's *Odyssey.*

Nara era Japanese period (710–794), centered on the city of Nara, that was the highest point of Chinese influence.

National Policy Nineteenth-century Canadian policy designed to attract migrants, protect industries through tariffs, and build national transportation systems.

NATO The North Atlantic Treaty Organization, which was established by the United States in 1949 as a regional military alliance against Soviet expansionism.

Ndongo (n'DAWN-goh) Angolan kingdom that reached its peak during the reign of Queen Nzinga (r. 1623–1663).

Neandertal (nee-ANN-duhr-tawl) Early humans (100,000 to 35,000 years ago) who were prevalent during the Paleolithic period.

Negritude (NEH-grih-tood) "Blackness," a term coined by early African nationalists as a means of celebrating the heritage of black peoples around the world.

Nelson Mandela 1918–2013 C.E. South African revolutionary and politician who consistently fought against the apartheid state until its demise in 1994. He became the first black president of South Africa, and served from 1994–1999.

Neo-Confucianism (nee-oh-kuhn-FYOO-shuhn-iz'm) Philosophy that attempted to merge certain basic elements of Confucian and Buddhist thought; most important of the early Neo-Confucianists was the Chinese thinker Zhu Xi (1130–1200).

Neolithic New Stone Age (10,000–4000 B.C.E.), which was marked by the discovery and mastery of agriculture.

Nestorian (neh-STOHR-ee-uhn) Early branch of Christianity, named after the fifth-century Greek theologian Nestorius, that emphasized the human nature of Jesus Christ.

New Economic Policy (NEP) Plan implemented by Lenin that called for minor free-market reforms.

Nicholas II Reigned 1894–1917. Russian Tsar who was first deposed and then executed, along with his family, in the Russian Revolution.

Nirvana (nuhr-VAH-nuh) Buddhist concept of a state of spiritual perfection and enlightenment in which distracting passions are eliminated.

Noble Eightfold Path Final truth of the Buddhist Four Noble Truths that called for leading a life of balance and constant contemplation.

Nonaligned Movement Movement in which leaders of former colonial states sought to assert their independence from either Soviet or U.S. domination. The initial meeting was held in 1955 in Bandung, Indonesia.

North American Free Trade Agreement (NAFTA) Regional accord established in 1993 between the United States, Canada, and Mexico; it formed world's second largest free-trade zone.

Nubia (NOO-bee-uh) Area south of Egypt; the kingdom of Kush in Nubia invaded and dominated Egypt from 750 to 664 B.C.E.

Nubians a member of one of the group of peoples that formed a powerful empire between Egypt and Ethiopia from the 6th to the 14th centuries.

Oceania Term referring to the Pacific Ocean basin and its lands.

Odovacer Germanic general who deposed Romulus Augustus in 476 C.E., thus bringing about the end of the western Roman Empire.

Olmecs Early Mesoamerican society (1200–100 B.C.E.) that centered on sites at San Lorenzo, La Venta, and Tres Zapotes and that influenced later Maya.

Olympe de Gouges 1748–1793 C.E. French feminist who authored the *Declaration of the Rights of Woman and the Female Citizen* at the start of the French Revolution in 1789, which advocated for equal rights for women. De Gouges was later executed by the Jacobins during the Terror.

Oracle bones Chinese Shang dynasty (1766–1122 B.C.E.) means of foretelling the future.

Organization of African Unity (OAU) An organization started in 1963 by thirty-two newly independent African states and designed to prevent conflict that would lead to intervention by former colonial powers.

Organization of Petroleum Exporting Countries (OPEC) An organization begun in 1960 by oil-producing states originally for purely economic reasons but that later had more political influence.

Osiris Ancient Egyptian god that represented the forces of nature.

Ottoman empire Powerful Turkish empire that lasted from the conquest of Constantinople (Istanbul) in 1453 until 1918 and reached its peak during the reign of Süleyman the Magnificent (r. 1520–1566).

Paleolithic Old Stone Age, a long period of human development before the development of agriculture.

Palestinian Liberation Organization (PLO) Organization created in 1964 under the leadership of Yasser Arafat to champion Palestinian rights.

Paris Peace Accords Agreement reached in 1973 that marked the end of the United States' role in the Vietnam War.

Parsis (pahr-SEES) Indian Zoroastrians.

Parthians Persian dynasty (247 B.C.E.–224 C.E.) that reached its peak under Mithradates I.

Paterfamilias (PAH-tur fuh-MEE-lee-ahs) Roman term for the "father of the family," a theoretical implication that gave the male head of the family almost unlimited authority.

Patriarch (PAY-tree-ahrk) Leader of the Greek Orthodox church, which in 1054 officially split with the Pope and the Roman Catholic church.

Patricians Roman aristocrats and wealthy classes.

Paul of Tarsus Christian apostle who sought converts in the 1st century Roman Empire and was executed for being a threat to peace and stability.

Pax Romana (pahks roh-MAH-nah) "Roman Peace," a term that relates to the period of political stability, cultural brilliance, and economic prosperity beginning with unification under Augustus and lasting through the first two centuries C.E.

Peninsulares (pehn-IHN-soo-LAH-rayz) Latin American officials from Spain or Portugal.

Perestroika (PAYR-eh-stroy-kuh) "Restructuring," a Russian term associated with Gorbachev's effort to reorganize the Soviet state.

Period of the Warring States Last centuries of the Zhou dynasty (403–221 B.C.E.) when wars divided the region until the establishment of the Qin dynasty ended the disunity.

Peter the Great Reigned 1682–1725. Russian tsar of the Romanov family who sought to remake Russia on the modern of the western European states.

Pharaohs (FARE-ohs) Egyptian kings considered to be gods on earth.

Philip of Macedon King of Macedon who reigned from 359–336 B.C.E. Responsible for bringing all of Greece under his control in 338 B.C.E.

Pico Giovanni Pico della Mirandola, 1463–1494 C.E. Italian humanist who sought to harmonize the various religions and philosophies of the world.

Plebians (plih-BEE-uhns) Roman common people.

Pogrom Yiddish word meaning "devastation," referring to an organized massacre of a particular ethnic group–especially Jews in Eastern Europe.

Polis (POH-lihs) Greek term for the city-state.

Popol Vuh (paw-pawl vuh) Mayan creation epic.

Prague Spring Period in 1968 in which the communist leader of Czechoslovakia, Alexander Dubcek, launched a reform movement aimed at softening Soviet-style rule. The movement was crushed when Russian forces invaded.

Prehistory The period before the invention of writing.

Proletariat Urban working class in a modern industrial society.

Protestant Reformation Sixteenth-century European movement during which Luther, Calvin, Zwingli, and others broke away from the Catholic church.

Protoindustrialization Also called the "putting-out system," in which entrepreneurs delivered raw materials to families in the countryside, who would then spin and weave the materials into garments. The entrepreneurs would then pick up the garments, pay the families, and sell them on the market.

Ptolemaic (TAWL-oh-may-ihk) Term used to signify both the Egyptian kingdom founded by Alexander the Great's general Ptolemy and the thought of the philosopher Ptolemy of Alexandria (second century C.E.), who used mathematical formulas in an attempt to prove Aristotle's geocentric theory of the universe.

Punt Land that traded with the ancient kingdoms of Egypt, whose exact whereabouts are unknown but may be in or near modern Eritrea.

Putting-out system Method of getting around guild control by delivering unfinished materials to rural households for completion.

Qadi Islamic judge.

Qanat (kah-NAHT) Persian underground canal.

Qi (chee) Chinese concept of the basic material that makes up the body and the universe.

Qin (chihn) Chinese dynasty (221–207 B.C.E.) that was founded by Qin Shihuangdi and was marked by the first unification of China and the early construction of defensive walls.

Qing (chihng) Chinese dynasty (1644–1911) that reached its peak during the reigns of Kangxi and Qianlong.

Qizilbash (gih-ZIHL-bahsh) Term meaning "red heads," Turkish tribes that were important allies of Shah Ismail in the formation of the Safavid empire.

Quetzalcoatl (keht-zahl-koh-AHT'l) Aztec god, the "feathered serpent," who was borrowed originally from the Toltecs; Quetzalcoatl was believed to have been defeated by another god and exiled, and he promised to return.

Quinto (KEEN-toh) The one-fifth of Mexican and Peruvian silver production that was reserved for the Spanish monarchy.

Quipu (KEE-poo) Incan mnemonic aid comprised of different-colored strings and knots that served to record events in the absence of a written text.

Quran (koo-RAHN) Islamic holy book that is believed to contain the divine revelations of Allah as presented to Muhammad.

Ram Mohan Roy 1772–1833 C.E. Bengali intellectual who sought to harmonize aspects of European society with those of Indian society with the goal of reforming India along progressive lines.

Ramayana (rah-mah-yah-nah) Ancient Indian masterpiece about the hero Rama that symbolized the victory of *dharma* (order) over *adharma* (chaos).

Rape of Nanjing Japanese conquest and destruction of the Chinese city of Nanjing in the 1930s.

Re Sun god in ancient Egypt, and the chief deity among Egyptian gods.

Realpolitik (ray-AHL-poh-lih-teek) The Prussian Otto von Bismarck's "politics of reality," the belief that only the willingness to use force would actually bring about change.

Reconquista (ray-kohn-KEE-stah) Crusade, ending in 1492, to drive the Islamic forces out of Spain.

Reconstruction System implemented in the American South (1867–1877) that was designed to bring the Confederate states back into the union and also extend civil rights to freed slaves.

Relics physical remains of saints or religious figures assembled by churches for veneration.

Rhapta Port that emerged as a principal commercial center in East Africa in the centuries around the turn of the millennium.

Roman Empire An empire that succeeded the Roman Republic during the reign of Augustus, which dates from 27 B.C.E. to 395 C.E.

Roman Republic Period of Roman society from 509 B.C.E. to 27 B.C.E. characterized by republican form of government.

Romanov (ROH-mah-nahv) Russian dynasty (1610–1917) founded by Mikhail Romanov and ending with Nicholas II.

Ronald Reagan 1911–2004. 40th president of the United States, who served from 1981–1989. Reagan was noted for his anti-communism.

Rubaiyat (ROO-bee-aht) "Quatrains," famous poetry of Omar Khayyam that was later translated by Edward Fitzgerald.

Safavid (SAH-fah-vihd) Later Persian empire (1501–1722) that was founded by Shah Ismail and that became a center for Shiism; the empire reached its peak under Shah Abbas the Great and was centered on the capital of Isfahan.

Sakk Letters of credit that were common in the medieval Islamic banking world.

Saladin 1137–1193 C.E. Muslim leader and crusader who recaptured Jerusalem from the Christians in 1187.

Saljuqs (sahl-JYOOKS) Turkish tribe that gained control over the Abbasid empire and fought with the Byzantine empire.

Samsara (sahm-SAH-ruh) Hindu term for the concept of transmigration, that is, the soul passing into a new incarnation.

Samurai (SAM-uhr-eye) A Japanese warrior.

Sappho Poetess who wrote around 600 B.C.E., known for writing about physical attraction between women.

Sasanids (suh-SAH-nids) Later powerful Persian dynasty (224–651) that would reach its peak under Shapur I and later fall to Arabic expansion.

Sati (SUH-TEE) Also known as *suttee,* Indian practice of a widow throwing herself on the funeral pyre of her husband.

Satrapies System of provincial government in the Persian Empire, in which administration is divided into provinces, each of which was called a satrapy.

Satraps (SAY-traps) Persian administrators, usually members of the royal family, who governed a satrapy.

Satyagraha (SAH-tyah-GRAH-hah) "Truth and firmness," a term associated with Gandhi's policy of passive resistance.

Schism Mutual excommunication of the Roman Pope and Byzantine Patriarch in 1054 over ritual, doctrinal, and political differences between the two Christian churches.

Scholasticism Medieval attempt of thinkers such as St. Thomas Aquinas to merge the beliefs of Christianity with the logical rigor of Greek philosophy.

Scientific racism Nineteenth-century attempt to justify racism by scientific means; an example would be Gobineau's *Essay on the Inequality of the Human Races.*

Scramble for Africa Period between about 1875 and 1900 in which European powers sought to colonize as much of the African continent as possible.

Seleucids (sih-LOO-sihds) Persian empire (323–83 B.C.E.) founded by Seleucus after the death of Alexander the Great.

Self-determination Belief popular in World War I and after that every people should have the right to determine their own political destiny; the belief was often cited but ignored by the Great Powers.

Self-Strengthening Movement Chinese attempt (1860–1895) to blend Chinese cultural traditions with European industrial technology.

Semitic (suh-miht-ihk) A term that relates to the Semites, ancient nomadic herders who spoke Semitic languages; examples of Semites were the Akkadians, Hebrews, Aramaics, and Phoenicians, who often interacted with the more settled societies of Mesopotamia and Egypt.

Sepoys Indian troops who served the British.

Serfs Peasants who, though not chattel slaves, were tied to the land and who owed obligation to the lords on whose land they worked.

Sericulture The cultivation of silkworms for the production of silk.

Shamanism (SHAH-mah-niz'm) Belief in shamans or religious specialists who possessed supernatural powers and who communicated with the gods and the spirits of nature.

Shang Yang 390–338 B.C.E. Minister to the Duke of Qin state in Western China, and important developer of the political philosophy of Legalism.

Shari'a (shah-REE-ah) The Islamic holy law, drawn up by theologians from the Quran and accounts of Muhammad's life.

Shia (SHEE-ah) Islamic minority in opposition to the Sunni majority; their belief is that leadership should reside in the line descended from Ali.

Shintoism (SHIHN-toh-iz'm) Indigenous Japanese religion that emphasizes purity, clan loyalty, and the divinity of the emperor.

Shiva (SHEE-vuh) Hindu god associated with both fertility and destruction.

Shogun (SHOH-gun) Japanese military leader who ruled in place of the emperor.

Shudras (SHOO-druhs) Hindu caste of landless peasants and serfs.

Siberia Region to the east of Russia in northeastern Europe, which was conquered by the Russians between 1581 and 1639.

Siddhartha Gautama (sih-DHAR-tuh GOW-tau-mah) Indian *kshatriya* who achieved enlightenment and became known as the Buddha, the founder of Buddhism.

Sikhs (SIHKS) Adherents of an Indian syncretic faith that contains elements of Hinduism and Islam.

Silk roads An extensive network of trade routes that linked much of Eurasia with North Africa during the Classical Period.

Sinicization Process by which non-Han Chinese people come under the cultural or political domination of Han Chinese.

Sino-Japanese War War between China and Japan from 1897–1901, over the status of Korea. The Chinese were badly defeated.

Social Darwinism Nineteenth-century philosophy, championed by thinkers such as Herbert Spencer, that attempted to apply Darwinian "survival of the fittest" to the social and political realm; adherents saw the elimination of weaker nations as part of a natural process and used the philosophy to justify war.

Socialism Political and economic theory of social organization based on the collective ownership of the means of production; its origins were in the early nineteenth century, and it differs from communism by a desire for slow or moderate change compared with the communist call for revolution.

Solidarity Polish trade union and nationalist movement in the 1980s that was headed by Lech Walesa.

Solon Aristocrat in Athens in the 6th century B.C.E. who forged a compromise between wealthy aristocrats and discontented common and landless classes who threatened rebellion.

Song (SOHNG) Chinese dynasty (960–1279) that was marked by an increasingly urbanized and cosmopolitan society.

Soviets Russian elected councils that originated as strike committees during the 1905 St. Petersburg disorders; they represented a form of local selfgovernment that went on to become the primary unit of government in the Union of Soviet Socialist Republics. The term was also used during the cold war to designate the Soviet Union.

Spanish Inquisition Institution organized in 1478 by Fernando and Isabel of Spain to detect heresy and the secret practice of Judaism or Islam.

Srivijaya (sree-VIH-juh-yuh) Southeast Asian kingdom (670–1025), based on the island of Sumatra, that used a powerful navy to dominate trade.

St. Basil 329–379 C.E. Byzantine Christian reformer who prepared regulations for monasteries emphasizing poverty, charity, and chastity.

St. Ignatius Loyola 1491–1556 C.E. A Basque nobleman and soldier who later devoted his life to religion and founded the missionary Society of Jesus (the Jesuits).

Stateless societies Term relating to societies such as those of sub-Saharan Africa after the Bantu migrations that featured decentralized rule through family and kinship groups instead of strongly centralized hierarchies.

Stoics (STOH-ihks) Hellenistic philosophers who encouraged their followers to lead active, virtuous lives and to aid others.

Strabo (STRAH-boh) Greek geographer (first century C.E.).

Strategic Arms Limitations Talk (SALT) Agreement in 1972 between the United States and the Soviet Union.

Stupas (STOO-pahs) Buddhist shrines.

Sufis (SOO-fees) Islamic mystics who placed more emphasis on emotion and devotion than on strict adherence to rules.

Sui (SWAY) Chinese dynasty (589–618) that constructed the Grand Canal, reunified China, and allowed for the splendor of the Tang dynasty that followed.

Süleyman (SOO-lee-mahn) Ottoman Turkish ruler Süleyman the Magnificent (r. 1520–1566), who was the most powerful and wealthy ruler of the sixteenth century.

Sultan Selim III Reigned 1789–1807. Ottoman sultan whose efforts at reform threatened his elite fighting corps (the Jannissaries), who revolted and locked him up.

Sumerians (soo-MEHR-ee-uhns) Earliest Mesopotamian society.

Sun Yat-sen (1866–1925) Chinese Revolutionary and first provisional president of the Republic of China following the 1911 Chinese Revolution.

Sundiata (soon-JAH-tuh) Founder of the Mali empire (r. 1230–1255), also the inspiration for the *Sundiata,* an African literary and mythological work.

Sunni (SOON-nee) "Traditionalists," the most popular branch of Islam; Sunnis believe in the legitimacy of the early caliphs, compared with the Shiite belief that only a descendant of Ali can lead.

Suu Kyi, Aung San (SOO KEY, AWNG SAHN) Opposition leader (1945–) in Myanmar; she was elected leader in 1990 but she was not allowed to come to power; she was a Nobel Peace Prize recipient in 1991. She was finally released from house arrest in November 2010.

Swahili (swah-HEE-lee) East African citystate society that dominated the coast from Mogadishu to Kilwa and was active in trade. Also a Bantu language of East Africa, or a member of a group who speaks this language.

Sykes-Picot Treaty Secret 1917 treaty between the British and French, with the agreement of Russia, to divide the modern Middle East between them after the end of World War I.

Taino (TEYE-noh) A Caribbean tribe who were the first indigenous peoples from the Americas to come into contact with Christopher Columbus.

Taiping rebellion (TEYE-pihng) Rebellion (1850–1864) in Qing China led by Hong Xiuquan, during which twenty to thirty million were killed; the rebellion was symbolic of the decline of China during the nineteenth century.

Tale of Genji Japanese literary work written during the Heian Period (794–1185 C.E.) by the aristocratic woman Murasaki Shikibu.

Taliban Strict Islamic organization that ruled Afghanistan from 1996 to 2002.

Tang Taizong (TAHNG TEYE-zohng) Chinese emperor (r. 627–649) of the Tang dynasty (618–907).

Tanzimat "Reorganization" era (1839–1876), an attempt to reorganize the Ottoman empire on Enlightenment and constitutional forms.

Temüjin (TEM-oo-chin) Mongol conqueror (ca. 1167–1227) who later took the name Chinggis Khan, "universal ruler."

Tenochtitlan (the-NOCH-tee-tlahn) Capital of the Aztec empire, later Mexico City.

Teotihuacan (tay-uh-tee-wah-KAHN) Central American society (200 B.C.E.–750 C.E.); its Pyramid of the Sun was the largest structure in Mesoamerica.

Terra Australis Incognita Meaning "unknown southern land," it refers to land that European explorers had speculated must exist in the world's southern hemisphere from the 2nd to the 18th centuries.

Terra Nullius Concept meaning "land belonging to no one" used frequently by colonial powers who sought to justify the conquest of nomadic lands.

Teutonic Knights Crusading European order that was active in the Baltic region.

Third Rome Concept that a new power would rise up to carry the legacy of Roman greatness after the decline of the Second Rome, Constantinople; Moscow was referred to as the Third Rome during the fifteenth century.

Three Estates The three classes of European society, composed of the clergy (the first estate), the aristocrats (the second estate), and the common people (the third estate).

Three Principles of the People Philosophy of Chinese Guomindang leader Sun Yat-sen (1866–1925) that emphasized nationalism, democracy, and people's livelihood.

Thucydides Athenian historian who wrote a history of the Peloponnesian war in the 5th century B.C.E.

Tian (TEE-ehn) Chinese term for heaven.

Tikal (tee-KAHL) Maya political center from the fourth through the ninth century.

Timur-i lang (tee-MOOR-yee LAHNG) "Timur the Lame," known in English as Tamerlane (ca. 1336–1405), who conquered an empire ranging from the Black Sea to Samarkand.

Tokugawa (TOH-koo-GAH-wah) Last shogunate in Japanese history (1600–1867); it was founded by Tokugawa Ieyasu who was notable for unifying Japan.

Tokugawa Bakufu Feudal style of government that ruled Japan under the direction of shoguns from 1603 until the Meiji Restoration in 1868.

Toltecs Central American society (950–1150) that was centered on the city of Tula.

Trail of Tears Forced relocation of the Cherokee from the eastern woodlands to Oklahoma (1837–1838); it was symbolic of U.S. expansion and destruction of indigenous Indian societies.

Treaty of Nanjing 1842 Treaty forced on China by Great Britain after Britain's victory in the first Opium War, which forcibly opened China to western trade and settlement.

Treaty of Versailles 1919 treaty between the victorious Entente powers and defeated Germany at the end of World War I, which laid the blame for the war on Germany and exacted harsh reparations.

Treaty of Waitangi Treaty between British government and indigenous Maori peoples of New Zealand in 1840 that was interpreted differently by both sides and thus created substantial Maori opposition to British settlement.

Triangular trade Trade between Europe, Africa, and the Americas that featured finished products from Europe, slaves from Africa, and American products bound for Europe.

Tribunes Officials elected by plebians (commoners) in the Roman Republic to represent their interests in the Roman government.

Triple Alliance Pre–World War I alliance of Germany, Austria-Hungary, and Italy.

Triple Entente (ahn-TAHNT) Pre–World War I alliance of England, France, and Russia.

Troubadors A class of traveling poets and entertainers enthusiastically patronized by Medieval aristocratic women in modern southern France and northern Italy.

Truman Doctrine U.S. policy instituted in 1947 by President Harry Truman in which the United States would follow an interventionist foreign policy to contain communism.

Tsar (ZAHR) Old Russian term for king that is derived from the term *caesar*.

Tula Original region of the Toltec people, located to the northwest of modern Mexico City.

Twelve Tables Rome's first set of laws, established in 449 B.C.E.

Twelver Shiism (SHEE'i'zm) Branch of Islam that stressed that there were twelve perfect religious leaders after Muhammad and that the twelfth went into hiding and would return someday; Shah Ismail spread this variety through the Safavid empire.

Uighurs (WEE-goors) Turkish tribe.

Ukiyo Japanese word for the "floating worlds," a Buddhist term for the insignificance of the world that came to represent the urban centers in Tokugawa Japan.

Ulaanbaatar (OO-lahn-bah-tahr) Mongolian city.

Ulama Islamic officials, scholars who shaped public policy in accordance with the Quran and the *sharia*.

Umayyad (oo-MEYE-ahd) Arabic dynasty (661–750), with its capital at Damascus, that was marked by a tremendous period of expansion to Spain in the west and India in the east.

Umma (UM-mah) Islamic term for the "community of the faithful."

United Nations (UN) Successor to the League of Nations, an association of sovereign nations that attempts to find solutions to global problems.

Upanishads (oo-PAHN-ee-shahds) Indian reflections and dialogues (800–400 B.C.E.) that reflected basic Hindu concepts.

Urdu (OOR-doo) A language that is predominant in Pakistan.

Uruk (OO-rook) Ancient Mesopotamian city from the fourth millennium B.C.E. that was allegedly the home of the fabled Gilgamesh.

Utopian Socialism Movement that emerged around 1830 to establish ideal communities that would provide the foundation for an equitable society.

Vaishyas (VEYES-yuhs) Hindu caste of cultivators, artisans, and merchants.

Vaqueros (vah-KEHR-ohs) Latin American cowboys, similar to the Argentine gaucho.

Varna (VAHR-nuh) Hindu word for caste.

Varuna (vuh-ROO-nuh) Early Aryan god who watched over the behavior of mortals and preserved the cosmic order.

Vedas (VAY-duhs) "Wisdom," early collections of prayers and hymns that provide information about the Indo-European Aryans who migrated into India around 1500 B.C.E.; *Rig Veda* is the most important collection.

Velvet revolution A term that describes the nonviolent transfer of power in Czechoslovakia during the collapse of Soviet rule.

Venta, La (VEHN-tuh, lah) Early Olmec center (800–400 B.C.E.).

Venus figurines Small Paleolithic statues of women with exaggerated sexual features.

Vernacular (ver-NA-kyoo-lar) The language of the people; Martin Luther translated the Bible from the Latin of the Catholic church into the vernacular German.

Versailles (vehr-SEYE) Palace of French King Louis XIV.

Viet Minh North Vietnamese nationalist communists under Ho Chi Minh.

Vietnamization President Richard Nixon's strategy of turning the Vietnam War over to the South Vietnamese.

Vijayanagar (vee-juh-yah-NAH-gahr) Southern Indian kingdom (1336–1565) that later fell to the Mughals.

Vikings A group that raided the British Isles from their home at Vik in southern Norway.

Vishnu (VIHSH-noo) Hindu god, preserver of the world, who was often incarnated as Krishna.

Vo Nguyen Giap 1912–2013. Vietnamese general who served as Ho Chi Minh's right-hand man and is credited with the strategy behind the Vietnamese victory at the battle of Dien Bien Phu.

Volksgeist (FOHLKS-geyest) "People's spirit," a term that was coined by the German philosopher Herder; a nation's volksgeist would not come to maturity unless people studied their own unique culture and traditions.

Volta do mar (VOHL-tah doh MAHR) "Return through the sea," a fifteenth century Portuguese sea route that took advantage of the prevailing winds and currents.

Voltaire (vohl-TAIR) 1712–1778 C.E. French Enlightenment writer and philosopher famous for his wit and criticism of the Catholic church. His real name was Francois-Marie Arouet.

Voudou (voo-doo) Syncretic religion practiced by African slaves in Haiti.

Waldensians Twelfth-century religious reformers who criticized the Roman Catholic church and who proposed that the laity had the right to preach and administer sacraments; they were declared heretics.

Wanli (wahn-LEE) Chinese Ming emperor (r. 1572–1620) whose refusal to meet with officials hurried the decline of the Ming dynasty.

War chariots An ancient horse-drawn two-wheeled vehicle used in war.

War Communism The Bolshevik policy of nationalizing industry and seizing private land during the civil war.

Warsaw Pact Warsaw Treaty Organization, a military alliance formed by Soviet bloc nations in 1955 in response to rearmament of West Germany and its inclusion in NATO.

W. E. B. DuBois 1868–1963. African American activist and intellectual who championed the movement of American blacks back to Africa.

White Huns A nomadic people from Central Asia who occupied Bactria (modern Afghanistan) in the 4th century C.E. and eventually crossed the Hindu Kush mountains into India.

Wind wheels Prevailing wind patterns in the Atlantic and Pacific Oceans north and south of the equator; their discovery made sailing much safer and quicker.

Witch Hunts Period in the 16th and 17th centuries in which about 110,000 people (mainly women) were tried as witches in western Europe.

Witte, Sergei (VIHT-tee, SAYR-gay) Late-nineteenth-century Russian minister of finance who pushed for industrialization.

Woodrow Wilson 1856–1924. President of the United States during World War I and author of the "Fourteen Points," one of which envisioned the establishment of the League of Nations.

World Health Organization (WHO) United Nations organization designed to deal with global health issues.

World Trade Organization (WTO) An organization that was established in 1995 with more than 120 nations and whose goal is to loosen barriers to free trade.

Wu Zhao 626–706 C.E. Concubine of Emperor Tang Taizong, who seized imperial power for herself in 690 after Taizong became debilitated.

Wuwei (woo-WAY) Daoist concept of a disengagement from the affairs of the world.

Xia (shyah) Early Chinese dynasty (2200–1766 B.C.E.).

Xianyang (SHYAHN-YAHNG) Capital city of the Qin empire.

Xiao (SHAYOH) Confucian concept of respect for one's parents and ancestors.

Xinjiang (shin-jyahng) Western Chinese province.

Xuanzang (SHWEN-ZAHNG) Seventh-century Chinese monk who made a famous trip to India to collect Buddhist texts.

Yahweh (YAH-way) God of the monotheistic religion of Judaism that influenced later Christianity and Islam.

Yangshao (YAHNG-show) Early Chinese society (2500–2200 B.C.E.).

Yangzi (YAHNG-zuh) River in central China.

Yin One of the six Shang dynasty (1766–1122 B.C.E.) capitals near the modern city of Anyang.

Yongle (YAWNG-leh) Chinese Ming emperor (r. 1403–1424) who pushed for foreign exploration and promoted cultural achievements such as the *Yongle Encyclopedia.*

Young Turks Nineteenth-century Turkish reformers who pushed for changes within the Ottoman empire, such as universal suffrage and freedom of religion.

Yu (yoo) Legendary founder of the Xia dynasty (ca. 2200 B.C.E.).

Yuan (yoo-AHN) Chinese dynasty (1279–1368) that was founded by the Mongol ruler Khubilai Khan.

Yucatan (yoo-kuh-TAN) Peninsula in Central America, home of the Maya.

Yurts (yuhrts) Tents used by nomadic Turkish and Mongol tribes.

Zaibatsu (zeye-BAHT-soo) Japanese term for "wealthy cliques," which are similar to American trusts and cartels but usually organized around one family.

Zambos (ZAHM-bohs) Latin American term for individuals born of indigenous and African parents.

Zamudio, Adela (ZAH-moo-dee-oh, ah-DEH-lah) Nineteenth-century Bolivian poet, author of "To Be Born a Man."

Zarathustra (zar-uh-THOO-struh) Persian prophet (ca. sixth century B.C.E.) who founded Zoroastrianism.

Zemstvos (ZEHMST-voh) District assemblies elected by Russians in the nineteenth century.

Zen Buddhism Japanese version of Chinese Chan Buddhism, with an emphasis on intuition and sudden flashes of insight instead of textual study.

Zheng He (1371–1433) Admiral in China's Ming Dynasty who carried out seven extensive oceanic voyages in the early 15th century.

Zhou (JOH) Chinese dynasty (1122–256 B.C.E.) that was the foundation of Chinese thought formed during this period: Confucianism, Daoism, Zhou Classics.

Zhu Xi (ZHOO-SHEE) Neo-Confucian Chinese philosopher (1130–1200).

Ziggurats (ZIG-uh-rahts) Mesopotamian temples.

Zimbabwe (zihm-BAHB-way) Former colony of Southern Rhodesia that gained independence in 1980.

Zionism National movement for the return of Jewish people to the historic land of Israel, founded in the 1890s by Theodor Herzl.

Zoroastrianism (zohr-oh-ASS-tree-ahn-iz'm) Persian religion based on the teaching of the sixth-century-B.C.E. prophet Zarathustra; its emphasis on the duality of good and evil and on the role of individuals in determining their own fate would influence later religions.

photo credits

Index

Aachen (Germany), 291, 291 (*map*)
Abbas the Great, shah of Safavid empire (reigned 1588–1629), 449, 450, 453, 456, 458, 459
Abbasid dynasty, 204 (*map*), 206–7, 236–37, 258, 259 (*map*), 450
Abdül Hamid II, Ottoman sultan (reigned 1876–1909), 541
aboriginal peoples, 75–76, 319
abortion, 671
Abraham (Hebrew patriarch), 18, 202
absolute monarchies, 379, 380–82
absolutism, 381–82
Abu al-Abbas (722–754), 206
Abu Bakr (573–634), 204
academic guilds, 301
Achaemenid empire (558–330 B.C.E.), 84, 84 (*illus.*), 86–90, 87 (*map*), 96–97, 139, 183
Actium, battle of (31 B.C.E.), 150
al-'Addawiyya, Rabi'a (717–801 C.E.), 212–13 (*source document*)
Adulis (Ethiopia), 278
Aegean Sea, 87, 140, 182
Aeschylus (fifth century B.C.E.), 147
Afghanistan: in Kushan empire, 122; Islamic State of, 237, 652, 668; Soviet Union in, 651–52, 668; U.S. in, 652, 668–69; war in Iraq and, 668–670; refugees from, 672. *See also* Bactria
Afghan-Soviet war (1979–1988), 668
Afonso I (Nzinga Mbemba), king of Kongo (reigned 1506–1542), 413–14
Africa: agriculture in, 7, 27, 28–29, 605; climatic change in, 28–29; African cultivators, 42–43; rice and, 42; slavery in, 144, 418; maritime trade and, 281 (*map*); Christianity in, 412, 413–14, 416; social change in early modern, 416–17; French exploration in, 532, 532 (*illus.*); imperialism in, 533, 543–47, 546 (*map*); scramble for, 543–44; gold and, 546; British colonies in, 564, 604, 648–49; WWI in, 572, 603–4; Great Depression and, 603, 605; colonization and, 604–5; nationalism in, 605–6, 648–49; infrastructure in, 605; independence in, 648; HIV/AIDS in, 667. *See also* central Africa; east Africa; north Africa; south Africa; sub-Saharan Africa; west Africa; *specific countries, regions, and peoples*

African Americans, 425–26, 482, 526, 526 (*illus.*)
African diaspora, 424–27
African National Congress (ANC), 649
Afrikaners, 545–47
age of access, 663–64
age of anxiety, 581–594
age of independence, 513–14, 530
age sets and age grades, 42, 277
agriculture: in complex societies, 2, 5; in Mesopotamia, 5–6, 14–15; in Africa, 7, 27, 28–29, 605; in Mesoamerica, 7, 63, 65–68, 71; population growth and, 7, 8, 46–47, 49, 52, 72, 76, 115, 179, 274–75, 321; in South America, 7, 64, 72–73; in southwest Asia, 7; spread of, 7, 42; sub-Saharan Africa and, 7, 28, 41, 42–43, 274–75; astronomy, mathematics and, 17; calendar and, 17; in Egypt, 27, 28, 29–30, 30 (*illus.*); in Nile River valley, 27, 29–30; in Nubia, 27, 29–30; climate and, 35; in Indus River valley, 45–46, 48; in India, 45–47, 119, 122, 123, 133, 238–240; in China, 52, 56, 59–61, 60 (*illus.*), 102, 106, 111, 115, 218, 220, 222–23, 437; terraces, 60, 60 (*illus.*), 67, 222; in North America, 64, 315; Mochica, 73; in Oceania, 75–77; in New Guinea, 76; Lapita peoples, 77; in Persia, 86, 89, 93–94; in Roman empire, 148, 152–53; in Greece, 152–53; in Palestine, 153; in Syria, 153; in Byzantine empire, 187; in Islamic empires, 207–8, 456–57; equal-field system, 220; medieval Europe and, 294–96, 296 (*illus.*); *chinampa* system of, 311; cash crops, 405, 424; in Japan, 442; of India, 538; during Great Depression, 585; collectivization of, 590, 644. *See also* Columbian exchange; cultivators; food crops; irrigation; plantations; *specific countries and products*
Aguinaldo, Emilio, 549
ahimsa (nonviolence), 127, 128, 599
Ahura Mazda (god), 96 (*illus.*), 96–97, 97 (*source document*)
AIDS. *See* HIV/AIDS
air pollution, 666, 666 (*illus.*)
airplanes, 567
Akbar, Mughal emperor (reigned 1556–1605), 454–55, 455 (*illus.*), 458, 459–460

Akhenaten, Pharaoh (reigned 1353–1335 B.C.E.), 40
Akkad (Mesopotamia), 10
Akkadian language, 8
Alaric, king of Visigoths (c. 410), 171
Alaska, U.S. purchase of, 548
Albania, 567, 615
d'Albuquerque, Afonso (sixteenth century), 359–361
Aleppo (Spain), 458
Alexander II, Russian tsar (reigned 1855–1881), 507 (*illus.*), 508
Alexander of Macedon (Alexander the Great 356–323 B.C.E.): death of, 90, 142; in Egypt, 90, 142; in Persia, 90, 97, 142; tetradrachm with head of, 90, 90 (*illus.*); reign of, 95, 160; in India, 120, 142; heirs of, 122; empire of, 139, 142 (*map*); conquests of, 141–42; warrior carving, 141, 141 (*illus.*)
Alexandra, empress of Russia, 588
Alexandria (Egypt), 143, 160, 278
Alexandrian Library (Egypt), 143
Alexandrian Museum (Egypt), 143
alfalfa, 91
Algeria, 544, 648
Ali (Muhammad's cousin and son-in-law, fourth caliph 656–661 C.E.), 205, 205 (*illus.*), 452–53
Ali bin Muhammad (slave, c. 869), 277
ali'i nui (chiefs), 323
All Quiet on the Western Front (Remarque), 582
Allah (God), 199, 200–202, 203 (*source document*)
Allied powers, 614, 619–621. *See also* World War II
Allies and Associated Powers (Triple Entente), 561, 562, 564. *See also* World War I
Almagest (Ptolemy), 388
alphabets: Phoenician, 19–20, 21 (*illus.*), 144; Greek, 20, 21 (*illus.*), 39; Roman, 20; Cyrillic, 193
Amalfi (Italy), 296
Amenhotep IV, Pharaoh (reigned 1353–1335 B.C.E.), 40
American Express Train (Palmer), 524, 524 (*illus.*)
American revolution (1775–1781), 469, 471–73, 472 (*map*), 490, 514
Americanization, 662, 663 (*source document*)
Americas: migrations to, 7, 63–64, 72, 501, 522–23, 528; societies of, 15; hunting and gathering societies in,

64–65, 72; encounters in, 64, 75; centralization in, 253; indigenous peoples of, 309, 324, 396, 400, 409, 515–16; long-distance trade in, 322; European exploration in, 342, 349, 464; diseases in, 366 (*illus.*), 366–68; food crops of, 384, 417, 437, 456–57; Iberia in, 397–98, 401–2; colonization in, 397–406, 399 (*map*); multicultural societies in, 401–2; religion in, 406. *See also* Canada; Latin America; North America; South America; *specific peoples*
Amon (god), 31, 40
Amon-Re (god), 40
An Lushan (eighth century), 221
Analects (Confucius), 102, 104 (*source document*), 112–13 (*source document*), 436
Anatolia, 539
Anatolia (Turkey): Hittites in, 11, 22–23; Ionian Greeks in, 89–90, 140–41; Mycenaeans in, 138; Christianity in, 164; Byzantine empire and, 182, 186, 192; Turkish empires in, 259; population of, 457
ANC. *See* African National Congress
ancestors, 57, 223, 230
ancien régime, 473, 474, 485
al-Andalus, 209–10. *See also* Spain
Andean cultures. *See* South America
Anderson, Jourdan (nineteenth century), 528 (*source document*)
Andes mountains, 72, 74
Angkor kingdom (889–1431 C.E.), 247, 248
Angkor Thom, 248
Angkor Wat, 248, 248 (*illus.*)
Angles peoples, 172, 172 (*map*)
Anglicans, 375
Angola, 413, 415, 427, 648
Angra Mainyu (god), 96, 97 (*source document*)
animals: domestication of, 7, 8, 21, 65; extinction of, 64, 665; sacrifices, 128, 154, 319; gladiators and wild, 150; nomadic peoples and, 256; Columbian exchange and, 366–67, 368; global trade impacts on, 369. *See also specific animals*
Anschluss (union), 616
Anthony, Saint, 416